Organizing Subsystem

Input
A portion of the organization's: 1. People 2. Money 3. Raw materials 4. Machines

Process (Organizing Process)
1. Reflecting on plans and objectives 2. Establishing major tasks 3. Dividing major tasks into subtasks 4. Allocating resources and directives for subtasks 5. Evaluating results of organizing strategy

Output
Organization

Principles of Modern Management

Principles of Modern Management
Functions and Systems

Second Edition

Samuel C. Certo
Indiana State University

wcb
Wm. C. Brown Company Publishers
Dubuque, Iowa

wcb
group

wcb
group
Wm. C. Brown *Chairman of the Board*
Mark C. Falb *Executive Vice-President*

wcb
Wm. C. Brown Company Publishers
College Division

wcb
Wm. C. Brown Company Publishers, College Division

Lawrence E. Cremer *President*
David Wm. Smith *Vice-President, Marketing*
E. F. Jogerst *Vice-President, Cost Analyst*
David A. Corona *Assistant Vice-President,*
Production Development and Design
Book Team
James L. Romig *Executive Editor*
Marcia H. Stout *Marketing Manager*
William A. Moss *Production Editorial Manager*
Marilyn A. Phelps *Manager of Design*
Mary M. Heller *Visual Research Manager*

Cover photo by Dave Plank/Deborah Wolfe, LTD

Copyright © 1980, 1983 by Wm. C. Brown Company Publishers

Library of Congress Catalog Card Number: 82–71358

ISBN 0–697–08084–6

Second Printing, 1983

Printed in the United States of America

2–08084–02

To Mimi, Trevis, Matthew, and Sarah
—those for whom I attempt to manage

A Note to Students from the Authors

This book contains a wealth of management wisdom which has been offered and accumulated by several generations of both scholars and practicing managers. I sincerely hope that it proves valuable to you today as a source for learning about management and also tomorrow as a reference book for meeting professional challenges.

Abbreviated Table of Contents*

*For a listing of the other management topics which are integrated within chapters (such as production management and international management), please refer to the expanded table of contents or the subject index located at the back of the text.

Statement of Integration

The basic sectional and chapter divisions of this second edition have remained as they were in the first edition. The several new and timely topics, however, that have been added and integrated and thoroughly developed within this framework include: production and operations management, international management, strategy formulation and implementation, minorities in the workforce, and the contingency approach to management. For more details on how these topics are developed, they should be looked up in the subject index at the back of the book.

Contents

Section 1
Introduction to Management

Section 2 Planning

Section 4
Influencing

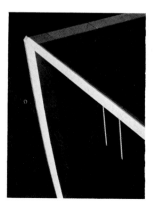

Section 6
Managing in the Future

Preface

My personal philosophy concerning the character of a high-quality text has crystalized over the past several years. I feel that for any text to be worthwhile it must meet the criteria of not only containing appropriate theoretical material but also of facilitating both student learning and the instructional processes. This second edition of *Principles of Modern Management* has been designed to effectively meet both of these criteria.

As with the first edition, the purpose of this edition is to prepare students to be managers. To accomplish this purpose, the management theory included in this text has been selected as a result of close constant contact with colleagues, students, managers, accrediting agencies such as the American Assembly of Collegiate Schools of Business (AACSB), and societies of practicing managers such as the American Management Association (AMA).

Organization

Overall, management theory presented in this text is divided into six main sections: "Introduction to Management," "Planning," "Organizing," "Influencing," "Controlling," and "Managing in the Future."

Section 1, "Introduction to Management," lays the groundwork necessary to study management. Chapter 1, "Defining Management," explains the meaning of the term *management* as it is used in the text, while chapter 2, "Approaches to Managing," presents several fundamental but different ways that managers perceive their jobs. The last chapter in this section, "Organizational Objectives," discusses the nature of goals that organizations can adopt, and also explains the relationship between these goals and the management process.

Section 2, "Planning," elaborates on planning activities as a primary management function. Chapter 4, the first chapter in this section, presents the basics of planning, while chapter 5, "Making Decisions," discusses the decision-making process as a component of the planning process. Chapter 6, "Plans and Planning Tools," discusses various managerial plans and the related planning tools available to help formulate them. The last chapter in this section discusses implementing the planning process, that is, putting the planning process into action.

Section 3, "Organizing," discusses organizing activities as a major management function. Chapter 8 presents the fundamentals of organizing, and chapter 9 elaborates on how to organize various worker activities appropriately. Chapter 10, "Providing Appropriate Human Resources for the Organization," discusses obtaining people who will make desirable contributions to organizational objectives. The last chapter in this section focuses on the implications of changing an organization.

Section 4, "Influencing," discusses how managers should deal with people. The four chapters in this section discuss the fundamentals of influencing and communication, leadership, motivation, and managing groups, respectively.

Section 5, "Controlling," analyzes the performance of control activities as another basic management function. Chapter 16, "Principles of Controlling," presents the basics of controlling, while chapter 17, "Control Tools," contains a number of useful aids managers can use to enhance the success of their controlling efforts. Chapter 18, "Information," defines information and also elaborates on the role information plays in the controlling process.

The last section of this text is entitled "Managing in the Future." The two chapters in this section discuss, respectively, the responsibilities that future managers will have to society and the skills that people of the future must possess to be successful as managers.

Special Features

The emphasis on both management functions and management systems in the presentation of management theory in the first edition has been enthusiastically received by instructors and students alike. Therefore for this edition, rather than changing this basic format, I simply chose to improve upon the timeliness and usefulness of this approach by integrating a number of carefully chosen topics within this functions-systems framework. These newly added topics include production and operations management, international management, the contingency approach to management, strategy formulation and implementation, decision trees, and minorities in the workforce. In addition to these newly integrated topics, all chapters in this new edition have been updated where necessary to incorporate important and current management thinking.

Aids to the Reader

Several features of this text were designed to make the study of management more effective and more enjoyable. A list of these features and an explanation of each follow.

Chapter Outlines   The opening pages of each chapter contain a chapter outline that previews the textual material that follows and helps the reader keep the information in perspective while it is being read.

Learning Objectives   The opening pages of each chapter also contain a set of learning objectives that are intended as guidelines on how to study the chapter.

Introductory Cases with "Flashes" Back to the Case   The opening of each chapter contains a case study that introduces readers to management problems related to chapter content. Detailed "Back to the Case" sections appear throughout each chapter and apply specific areas of management theory discussed in the chapter to the introductory case.

Cartoons   A limited number of cartoons was carefully selected to illustrate chapter content in an everyday way.

Marginal Notes   Each chapter contains marginal notes and key words that can be helpful in the initial reading of the chapter and also for review.

Figures   Figures or line drawings are used extensively and thoroughly explained to clarify and emphasize theoretical concepts.

Exhibits   All chapters contain a short reading that is intended to link the management theory presented in that chapter with a similar situation in an actual company. Exhibits in this edition have been updated to emphasize today's usefulness of management concepts discussed.*

Chapter Summaries   Each chapter contains a summary that helps to organize content and to indicate topics of the greatest importance.

---

*All real-life materials in this text were chosen because of their special relevance to management concepts discussed in the chapter. However, because changes take place so rapidly in the real world of business and government, certain facts and figures contained in these materials may be somewhat outdated.

Discussion Questions   The concluding pages of each chapter contain a set of discussion questions that test understanding of the chapter material and can serve as vehicles for study and for class discussion.

Concluding Cases   The concluding pages of each chapter contain at least one "real life" case that further applies chapter content to related management situations. End-of-chapter cases are new to this edition. They are wide in their scope of subjects covered, including news accounts from the field of business, government, sports, and the like.*

Glossary   Major management terms and their definitions are at the end of the text and appear in boldface type along with the textual pages on which discussion of the terms appears.

Photographs and Drawings   Photographs and drawings that depict various management situations are used throughout this text to help bridge the gap between management theory and authentic situations.

Supplementary Material

A number of ingredients have been developed to complement the use of *Principles of Modern Management*. Although the text itself was designed to offer a desirable amount of material for a high-quality course in principles of management, special supplements are available to further enrich the learning situation in which the text is used. These supplements and a discussion of each follow.

Workbook of Study Activities   This is a sourcebook of various learning activities and is to be used in conjunction with the text.** The second edition of this workbook contains several new and modified exercises and sections that correspond to the revised text, of course. Workbook elements that correspond to those in each text chapter include:

> *An extended chapter summary*   Extended summaries are helpful for quick review of textual material.
> *Learning assessment activities*   For each chapter of the text, the workbook contains a series of twenty objective questions that test understanding of chapter content. Correct answers and the numbers of text pages on which answers are explained are furnished for all questions.
> *Experiential exercises, activities, projects, cases*   A number of diverse in-class and out-of-class learning activities that further illustrate the content of each text chapter are provided.

> A suggested sequence for using the text and the workbook jointly is shown in figure P.1

Book of Readings   This revised reader contains over thirty articles specifically chosen to broaden the scope of management theory discussed in the revised text.*** A substantial number of very recent articles has been included in this edition to ensure that students are furnished information that is timely as well as of high quality.

---

*All real-life materials in this text were chosen because of their special relevance to management concepts discussed in the chapter. However, because changes take place so rapidly in the real world of business and government, certain facts and figures contained in these materials may be somewhat outdated.

**Certo, Samuel C., and Graf, Lee A. *Experiencing Modern Management: A Workbook of Study Activities*. Dubuque, Iowa: Wm. C. Brown Company Publishers, second edition, 1983.

***Samuel C. Certo, Daniel C. Brenenstuhl, and Kenneth E. Newgren, *Fundamental Readings in Modern Management: Functions and Systems* (Dubuque, Iowa: William C. Brown Company Publishers, second edition 1983).

Figure P.1 Suggested sequence for using the text and student workbook jointly.

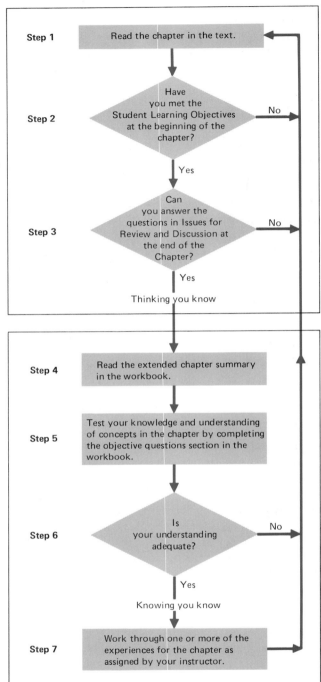

Principles of
Modern Management:
Functions and Systems

Experiencing
Modern Management:
A Workbook of
Student Activities

Instructional Aids

In addition to the supplements just described, several other ingredients of the *Principles of Modern Management* learning package have also been designed to enhance the learning environment in which this text is used. These ingredients attempt to do this by offering various optional aids to the management instructor. These aids include the following.

Lecture Enrichment Kit   This unique and innovative kit contains an array of materials and a looseleaf notebook that instructors can use to organize lectures to best suit the needs of their students. These materials include (a) lecture outlines; (b) brief in-class exercises; (c) two-color and black-and-white transparencies depicting material in the text as well as material outside the text; (d) real-life examples of main points of management theory, and (e) theoretical extension of management concepts discussed in the text. Material from the instructor's manual can also be put into this notebook. In addition, the flexibility of this kit allows instructors to include their own information in lecture planning.

Instructor's Manual   For each chapter in the text, the instructor's manual includes (a) notes on the introductory case; (b) notes on the concluding case; and (c) solutions to end-of-chapter discussion questions. For each workbook chapter there are sections discussing (a) purposes of each learning experience contained in that chapter; (b) suggestions on how these experiences can be used; and (c) sample learning experience results. A matrix that lists each exercise and suggests use with individuals, small groups, large groups, and combinations of groups is provided. This material can also be inserted in the lecture enrichment kit notebook. Supplemental films and listening tapes are also listed.

Test Manual   Testing instruments for the text are (a) a test bank of cases; (b) discussion question test bank; (c) matching-test bank; (d) fill-in-the-blank test bank; (e) true/false test bank; and (f) multiple-choice test bank. (A significant portion of these items have been statistically validated.) All questions have been evaluated by the Board of Reviewers.

Computerized Test Service   Using the test manual as a source, instructors can call or write in specifications for their tests and receive a customized test master.

Planning Guide   This fold-out matrix provides an overview of the entire *Principles of Modern Management* Learning Package and illustrates how the various elements create an integrated, comprehensive learning tool.

Transparencies   Approximately eighty transparencies are available to instructors. These transparencies cover the illustrations as well as the theoretical extensions and practical issues from the Lecture Enrichment Kit.

Goal

My primary goal in developing the *Principles of Modern Management* learning package—this text and its supportive materials—is to help students acquire high-quality knowledge about management. As an educator, attempting to reach this goal has been both challenging and personally rewarding. I will certainly be indebted to you—both students and instructors—if, after you have used this text, and perhaps some of its supportive materials, you will tell me how I may better reach this goal in my third edition of *Principles of Modern Management*.

Samuel C. Certo

Acknowledgments

I am very proud of the quality of the *Principles of Modern Management* learning package—this text and its related ancillaries. To be perfectly honest, however, this learning package, as with all major publications, has evolved over a period of several years and is due largely to the efforts of a number of people. I am extremely pleased at this time to be able to recognize those individuals who have made significant contributions to this project.

Professor Lee A. Graf, Illinois State University, deserves special recognition for the quality end-of-chapter cases that he contributed to the text. These cases are all based on current "real company" issues and create a very distinctive pedagogic tool that instructors can use to enhance student learning.

In addition, several other colleagues have made valuable contributions through numerous activities such as reviewing manuscripts at various stages of completion and assisting in the development of various ancillary instructional materials. These individuals are:

Reviewers

Dan Baugher
Pace University

Chester H. Bigger
Auburn University at Montgomery

Arnold J. Bornfriend
Worcester State College

N. E. (Ted) Brown
Mount Royal College,
Alberta, Calgary, Canada

Thomas W. Faranda
Inver Hills Community College
& University of Minnesota

Russel M. Fischer
Marshall University

James B. Genseal
Joliet Jr. College

Stanley D. Guzell
Youngstown State University

James P. Kuttner
University of North Dakota

Steven W. Lamb
Indiana State University

Rick A. Lester
University of Alabama, Huntsville

Miller C. Lovett
University of Massachusetts, Boston

Harriette S. McCaul
Moorehead State University

Victor G. Panico
California State University, Fresno

Alan Patrick
Towson State University

Elizabeth R. Redstone
Cuyahoga Community College

William J. Richardson
University of Texas, Austin

Bruce C. Sherony
Northern Michigan University

Edgar Ray Smith
University of Tennessee

Robert A. Snyder
Northern Kentucky University

Patricia Sutton
Marshall University

Frank Tomassi
Johnson and Wales College

Test Question Suppliers and Evaluators

Chester H. Bigger
Auburn University, Montgomery

Karen Dill Bowerman
California State University, Fresno

Mark A. Friend
Fairmont State College

Michael E. Gordon
University of Tennessee, Knoxville

Stanlee G. Kissel
Somerset County College

Steven W. Lamb
Indiana State University

Rick A. Lester
University of Alabama, Huntsville

Norbert F. Lindskog
The Loop College, City Colleges of Chicago

Rebecca Montgomery
University of Southern Mississippi

Roy N. Moore
University of Southern Mississippi

Bruce C. Sherony
Northern Michigan University

Charles H. Wetmore
California State University, Fresno

Edward L. Goebel, my dean, and Robert P. Steinbaugh, my chairperson, also contributed to this project. Their support and assistance were invaluable. Without such administrators, projects like the *Principles of Modern Management* learning package never get beyond the idea stage.

I deeply appreciate the personal and professional encouragement that I received from Daniel C. Brenenstuhl, Arizona State University; Lee A. Graf, Illinois State University; Steven W. Lamb, Indiana State University; Kenneth E. Newgren, Florida State University; and Alden J. Smith, Indiana State University. Also, the inspiration that Keith Davis has afforded me to make this text and its ancillaries the best possible should not go unmentioned. Getting to know and work with Keith over the past few years has been very satisfying and enlightening.

The people who provided me with clerical assistance during this project were extremely professional. Marilyn Meads, Janet Brown, and Terri Cooper deserve a special thanks for their outstanding performance.

The staff at Wm. C. Brown Company Publishers was very helpful during this project. Roger Ross, business editor, and Kathleen L. Loy, associate developmental editor, afforded me guidance and direction on numerous occasions. I would like to thank them and the rest of the WCB staff for being patient yet confident.

In closing, I would like to thank my family for its understanding during both the "highs" and "lows" of this project. Sincere interest shown by the Rushes—William, Mary, Bill, Jr., Mindy, and Meredith helped to keep me going. Of course, a very special thanks to my parents Samuel C. Certo, Sr., and Annette Certo. Their contribution to this project defies written description.

Principles of Modern Management

Section 1 consists of three chapters that serve to introduce the topic of management. Chapter 1 defines management as the process of reaching organizational goals by working with and through people and other resources. Management is presented as a task important not only to society as a whole but also to individuals who hold management positions. The management task itself is shown to involve planning, organizing, influencing, and controlling, and to be aimed solely at accomplishing organizational objectives. In essence, managers must strive to be both effective and efficient through the judicious exercise of human, technical, and conceptual skills. Important insights related to production and operations management as well as international management are outlined. The point is also made in this chapter that management principles are universal, or applicable to all types of businesses and organizations.

Chapter 2 further introduces the topic of management by discussing various approaches that managers should emphasize while managing: the classical approach, the behavioral approach, the management science approach, the contingency approach, and the system approach. The classical approach advocates that managers manage by emphasizing the "one best way" to do a job, as well as by analyzing the management task as a whole. The behavioral approach supports the idea that managers manage by emphasizing an analysis of the people within an organization. The management science approach suggests that managers manage by emphasizing the use of mathematical models and other quantitative aids. The contingency approach recommends that management action must be based upon the specific situation facing a manager. And the main theme of the system approach is that managers manage by viewing and reacting to an organization as a set of interrelated parts that function as a whole to achieve objectives.

This text's approach to the principles of management emphasizes the organization as a system that managers should assess and react to from a contingency or situation viewpoint, basing their observations upon an integration of information from the behavioral, classical, and management science approaches. This integration of information will become clearer after reading the five remaining sections of the text: (1) planning, (2) organizing, (3) influencing, (4) controlling, and (5) managing in the future.

Chapter 3, "Organizational Objectives," concludes the introduction to the topic of management by discussing the relationship between management and organizational objectives. Organizational objectives are presented as the targets toward which a management system is directed and as being derived from organizational purpose. Since both organizational and individual objectives exist within organizations, it becomes the task of managers to encourage individuals to pursue organizational objectives even if the objectives are inconsistent with individual goals.

Chapter 3 recommends that an organization's formal objectives should reflect environmental trends that could influence the operation of the organization. It also is recommended that organizational objectives be clear, simple, precise, and operational, and that they be based upon the thoughts of managers as well as on the opinions of other organization members. Management by objectives (MBO) is presented as a tool that managers can adopt to guide an organization, mainly by using organizational objectives.

Section 1
Introduction to Management

Student Learning Objectives

From studying this chapter I will attempt to acquire:

1. An understanding of the importance of management to society and individuals
2. An understanding of the role of management
3. An ability to define management in several different ways
4. An ability to list and define the basic functions of management
5. An understanding of production and operations management
6. Working definitions of managerial effectiveness and managerial efficiency
7. An understanding of basic management skills and their relative importance to managers
8. An understanding of the universality of management and international management

Chapter Outline

Defining Management

Introductory Case 1
Understanding Management

Mike Williams was a full-time employee of Shillito's, a large department store in downtown Cincinnati. As a salesperson in the men's furnishings department, his primary responsibility was selling men's clothing. There were times, however, when he was assigned to the departmental stockroom to store new merchandise received from suppliers. In total, the men's furnishings department consisted of ten part-time salespeople and seven full-time salespeople.

Williams was twenty-one years old and had just graduated from the University of Cincinnati as a journalism major, but he had not been hired as a management trainee. All such trainee positions had been filled before Williams applied for a job, but he was offered a sales position open at the time in the men's furnishings department. Williams decided to accept the sales position because he respected the people he met while interviewing at Shillito's and thought that it would be beneficial to his career to be in an environment where he could see how marketing concepts were applied. Williams eventually developed into a conscientious worker and took his job assignments very seriously.

It was December 10 and Williams had now been with Shillito's over a year. This day began as any normal working day. Williams parked his car in the store garage, walked to the store cashier to check out the daily money allotment that he used to make change for his customers, and walked to his department to deposit his money in a cash register drawer. Since a few minutes remained before the store was to open, Williams straightened out the merchandise in his sales area to make sure his customers could easily find what they wanted. The bell sounded, indicating to employees that it was 9:30 A.M. and that customers were now entering the store. Williams began waiting on his customers.

What happened to Williams at 11:30 A.M. on December 10 he would never forget. The departmental sales supervisor informed him that the departmental manager, Jim McGee, wanted to see him as soon as possible. Williams immediately started walking towards McGee's office and nervously began wondering why McGee wanted to see him.

When Williams arrived, McGee greeted him and asked him to be seated. McGee could see that Williams was somewhat nervous and tried to put him at ease. Williams's nervousness immediately turned into excitement as McGee told him that his work over the past year was of very high quality. In fact, McGee was so pleased that he offered Williams the position of assistant departmental manager. McGee's current assistant departmental manager was resigning in three weeks.

Despite Williams's quick acceptance, McGee said that he didn't want a decision immediately and gave Williams two weeks to think about the offer. He suggested that during the two weeks Williams find out as much as possible about the management function before making a final decision.

Williams left McGee's office proud of his past performance and determined to discover some of the basic characteristics of management that would help him to make an intelligent decision. The more Williams thought, the more he appreciated McGee's suggestion. Williams realized that he didn't actually know what management was all about. Although he knew that he liked selling, he needed some time to decide if he really wanted to be a manager. After acquiring some understanding of management, Williams felt sure he could intelligently decide whether or not to accept McGee's offer.

Discussion Issues

1. If you were Mike Williams, how would you start gathering information about management?
2. Do you think you would like to be a manager? Why?
3. List and describe five activities that you think managers perform.

What's Ahead

The information in this chapter is designed to help an individual such as Mike Williams understand the basics of management. Management is defined through (1) a discussion of the importance of management both to society and to individuals, (2) a thorough description of the management task, and (3) a discussion of the universality of management.

Managers influence all phases of our modern organizations. Plant managers run manufacturing operations that produce our clothes, food, and automobiles. Sales managers maintain a sales force that markets goods. Personnel managers provide organizations with a competent and productive work force. A quick look at the "jobs available" section in the classified advertisements of any major newspaper, with their descriptions of many different types of management activities, will confirm this importance of management (see figure 1.1).

The Importance of Management

Our society simply could not exist as we know it today or improve its present status without a steady stream of managers to guide its organizations. Peter Drucker makes this same point in stating that effective management is quickly becoming the main resource of developed countries and the most needed resource of developing ones.[1] In short, our country desperately needs good managers.

Importance to Society

In addition to being important to our society as a whole, management is vital to many individuals simply because they can earn their living by being managers. Government statistics show that management positions have held a steady 9 to 10 percent of a sometimes quickly growing work force since 1950.[2] These managers typically come from varying backgrounds and have diversified educational specialities. Many individuals who originally trained to be accountants, teachers, financiers, or even writers eventually make their livelihood from being some type of manager. In the short run, the demand for managers may vary somewhat from year to year.[3] In the long run, however, managerial positions can yield high salaries, status, interesting work, personal growth, and intense feelings of accomplishment. Today's economy holds many returns for competent managers. As the cartoon on the next page implies, however, all jobs have aspects that some people would rate undesirable.

Importance to Individuals

The preceding information furnishes Mike Williams, the prospective manager in the introductory case, with insights concerning the significance of the decision he is about to make. Management positions are usually important not only to society as a whole but also to the individuals holding these positions. In general, managers make some societal contributions to creating the standard of living we all enjoy and thereby obtaining corresponding rewards for making these contributions. Williams's management position initially will be fairly low at Shillito's, but as he moves up within the organization, the societal contributions he makes and the corresponding rewards he receives probably will become quite substantial.

Back to the Case

Figure 1.1 The variety of management positions available.

SR. MANAGEMENT DEVELOPMENT SPECIALIST

We are a major metropolitan service employer of over 5,000 employees seeking a person to join our management development staff. Prospective candidates will be degreed with 5 to 8 years experience in the design, implementation, and evaluation of developmental programs for first line and mid-level management personnel. Additionally, candidates must demonstrate exceptional oral and written communications ability and be skilled in performance analysis, programmed instruction, and the design and the implementation of reinforcement systems.

If you meet these qualifications, please send your resume, including salary history and requirements to:

BOX RS-653
An Equal Opportunity Employer

BRANCH MGR—$18,000. Perceptive pro with track record in adm & lending has high visibility with respected firm.
Box PH-165

AVIATION FBO MANAGER NEEDED

Southeast Florida operation catering to corporate aviation. No maintenance or aircraft sales — just fuel and the best service. Must be experienced. Salary plus benefits commensurate with qualifications. Submit complete resume to: **Box LJO-688**

DIVISION CREDIT MANAGER

Major mgf. corporation seeks an experienced, shirt-sleeve credit manager to handle the credit and collection function of its midwest division (Chicago area). Interpersonal skills are important, as is the ability to communicate effectively with senior management. Send resume with current compensation to: **Box NM-43**

Accounting Manager

Growth opportunity. Michigan Ave. location. Acctg. degree, capable of supervision. Responsibilities include G/L, financial statements, inventory control, knowledge of systems design for computer applications. Send resume, incl. salary history to: **Box RJM-999**
An Equal Opportunity Employer

FINANCIAL MANAGER

CPA/MBA (U of C) with record of success in mngmnt positions. Employed, now seeking greater opportunity. High degree of professionalism, exp. in dealing w/financial inst., strong communication & analytical skills, stability under stress, high energy level, results oriented. Age 34, 11 yrs exper. incl. major public acctng, currently 5 years as Financial VP of field leader. Impressive references.
Box LML-666

MARKET MANAGER

Major lighting manufacturer seeks market manager for decorative outdoor lighting. Position entails establishing and implementing marketing, sales, and new product development programs including coordination of technical publications and related R & D projects. Must locate at Denver headquarters. Send resume to **Box WM-214**
No agencies please.

GENERAL MANAGER

Small industrial service company, privately owned, located in Springfield, Missouri, needs aggressive, skilled person to make company grow in profits and sales. Minimum B.S. in Business, experienced in all facets of small business operations. Must understand profit. Excellent opportunity and rewards. Salary and fringes commensurate with experience and performance.
Box LEM-116

FOUNDRY SALES MANAGER

Aggressive gray iron foundry located in the Midwest, specializing in 13,000 tons of complex castings yearly with a weight range of 2 to 400 pounds, is seeking experienced dynamic sales manager with sound sales background in our industry. Salary commensurate with experience and excellent benefit package.
Box MO-948

PERSONNEL MANAGER

Publicly owned, national manufacturer with 12 plants, 700 employees, seeks first corporate personnel director. We want someone to administer programs in:

- Position and rate evaluations
- Employee safety engineering
- Employee training
- Employee communications
- Employee benefits
- Federal compliance

Qualifications: minimum of 3–5 years personnel experience in mfg. company, ability to tactfully deal on shirt-sleeve basis with employees at all levels from all walks of life, free to travel. Position reports to Vice President, Operations. Full range of company benefits, salary $16,000 to $20,000. Reply in complete confidence to:

Box JK-236

DOONESBURY by Garry Trudeau

DOONESBURY: Copyright, 1973, G.B. Trudeau/Distributed by Universal Press Syndicate.

Besides understanding the significance of being a manager and its related potential benefits, prospective managers should know what the management task entails. The following sections introduce the basics of the management task through discussions of the role of management and management's definition.

The Role of Management

Essentially, the role of managers is to guide organizations toward goal accomplishment. All organizations exist for some purpose or objective, and managers have the responsibility for combining and using organizational resources to ensure that the organizations achieve their purposes. Management moves organizations toward these purposes or goals by assigning activities that organization members perform. If these activities are designed effectively, the production of each individual worker represents a contribution to the attainment of organizational goals. Management strives to encourage individual activity that will lead to reaching organizational goals and to discourage individual activity that hinders organizational goal accomplishment. "There is no idea more important to managing than goals. Management has no meaning apart from its goals."[4] Management must keep organizational goals clearly in mind at all times.

What Management Entails:
1. Reaching goals

Defining Management

To minimize confusion, students of management should be aware that the term *management* can be and often is used in several different ways.[5] For instance, it can simply refer to the process that managers follow to accomplish organizational goals. The term can also be used, however, to refer to a body of knowledge. In this context, management is a cumulative body of information that furnishes insights on how to manage. Management also can be the term used to pinpoint those individuals who guide and direct organizations. It is also commonly used to designate a career devoted to the task of guiding and directing organizations. An understanding of these various uses and related definitions of management should help students and practitioners eliminate miscommunication during management-related discussions.

2. Several meanings

As used most commonly in this text, **management** is defined as the process of reaching organizational goals by working with and through people and other organizational resources. A comparison of this definition with definitions of management offered by several different contemporary management thinkers (see figure 1.2)[6] shows that there is some agreement that management has the following three main characteristics: (1) management is a process or series of continuing and related activities; (2) management involves and concentrates on reaching organizational goals; and (3) management reaches these goals by working with and through people and other organizational resources. A discussion of each of these characteristics follows.

3. Our meaning

The Management Process: Management Functions

The preceding sections in this chapter outline the basic role of managers and broadly define management. This section elaborates on the definition of management by listing and describing the four basic **management functions** or activities that make up the management process. These functions are planning, organizing, influencing, and controlling.

Management Functions:

1. Planning involves choosing tasks that must be performed to attain organizational goals, outlining how the tasks must be performed, and indicating when the tasks should be performed. Planning activity focuses on attaining goals. Managers, through their plans, outline exactly what

1. Planning

Figure 1.2 Contemporary definitions of management.

Management —
1. Is the process by which a cooperative group directs actions of others toward common goals. (Massie and Douglas)
2. Involves the coordination of human and material resources toward objective accomplishment. (Kast and Rosenzweig)
3. Is the coordination of all resources through the processes of planning, organizing, directing, and controlling in order to attain stated objectives. (Sisk)
4. Is establishing an effective environment for people operating in formal organizational groups. (Koontz and O'Donnell)
5. Entails activities undertaken by one or more persons in order to coordinate the activities of others in the pursuit of ends which cannot be achieved by any one person. (Donnelly, Gibson, and Ivancevich)

organizations must do to be successful. They are concerned with organizational success in the near future or short run as well as success in the more distant future or long run.

2. Organizing

2. Organizing can be thought of as assigning the tasks developed during planning to various individuals and/or groups within the organization. Organizing creates a mechanism to put plans into action. People within the organization are given work assignments that contribute to goal attainment. Tasks are organized so that the output of individuals contributes to the success of departments, which contributes to the success of divisions, which in turn contributes to the overall success of organizations.

3. Influencing

3. Influencing* is another of the basic functions within the management process. This function is also commonly referred to as motivating, leading, directing, or actuating and is primarily concerned with people within organizations. Influencing can be defined as the process of guiding the activities of organization members in appropriate directions. Appropriate direction, as used in this definition, is any direction that helps the organization move toward goal attainment. The ultimate purpose of influencing is to increase productivity. Human-oriented work situations usually generate higher levels of production over the long run than work situations that people find distasteful.

4. Controlling

4. Controlling is the management function for which managers: (a) gather information that measures recent performance within the organization; (b) compare present performance to pre-established performance standards; and (c) from this comparison, determine if the organization should be modified to meet pre-established standards. Controlling is an ongoing process. Managers continually gather information, make their comparisons, and then try to find new ways of improving production through organizational modification.

---

*Although the term *motivating* is used to signify this people-oriented management function more commonly than *influencing* in early management literature, the term *influencing* is used consistently in this text because it is a broader term and allows more flexibility when discussing people-oriented issues. Later in this text, motivating is discussed as a major part of influencing.

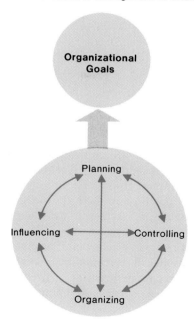

Management Process and Goal Attainment

The four functions of management have been discussed individually. In reality, however, managers quickly discover that planning, organizing, influencing, and controlling are integrally related and cannot be separated. Figure 1.3 illustrates this interrelationship among the four functions and also that managers use these activities solely for the purpose of reaching organizational goals. Basically, these functions are interrelated because the performance of one depends upon the performance of the others. To illustrate, organizing is based on well-thought-out plans developed during the planning process, while influencing systems must be tailored to reflect both these plans and the organization design used to implement the plans. The fourth function, controlling, proposes possible modifications to existing plans, organization structure, and/or the motivation system to develop a more successful effort.

The information in this section has been only a brief introduction to the four management functions. Later sections of this text are devoted primarily to developing these functions in much more detail.

Management and Production

In order to reach goals, all managers face the challenge of planning, organizing, influencing, and controlling to produce some type of product. Naturally, these products vary significantly from organization to organization. For example, it is the purpose of managers in automobile factories to produce cars, of managers in hospitals to produce healthy people, and of managers in universities to produce educated individuals.

Production is simply defined as the transformation of organizational resources into products. As used in this definition, organizational resources are all assets available to a manager to generate products; transformation is the set of steps necessary to change organizational resources into products; and products are various commodities aimed at meeting human needs. Figure 1.4 summarizes what constitutes organizational resources, transformation, and products and the relationships among them.

Figure 1.4 Production variables and relationships among them.

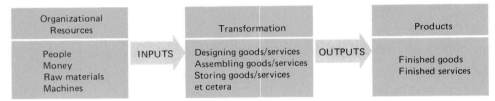

From this discussion it is easy to see the importance of management being continually aware of the status and use of organizational resources. These resources are of four basic types: (1) human resources, (2) monetary resources, (3) raw materials resources, and (4) capital resources. Human resources are the people who work for an organization. The skills they possess and their knowledge of the work system are invaluable to managers. Monetary resources are amounts of money managers use to purchase goods and services for the organization. Raw materials are ingredients acquired to be used directly in the manufacturing of products. For example, rubber is a raw material that a company like B. F. Goodrich would purchase with its monetary resources and use directly in the manufacturing of tires. Lastly, capital resources are the machines an organization uses during the manufacturing process. Modern machines or equipment can be a major factor in maintaining desired production levels, while worn-out or antiquated machinery can make it impossible for an organization to keep pace with competitors.

Operations Management

Managing Production

The process of managing production in organizations is commonly called "operations management." According to Chase and Aquilano, **operations management** is the performance of the managerial activities entailed in selecting, designing, operating, controlling, and updating productive systems.[7] Figure 1.5 presents these activities, gives descriptions of each, and categorizes them as being either periodic or continual. The distinction between periodic activities and continual activities is based upon the relative frequency of the occurrence of each; periodic activities are performed from time to time and continual activities are essentially never ending. Although this list of activities is not meant to be exhaustive, the performance of them in the relative frequencies implied in figure 1.5 will increase the probability of efforts in operations management being successful.

Continual vs. Periodic

Managerial Performance

General standards exist that can be used to describe the quality of managerial performance regardless of the type of organization being managed. These standards relate to the concepts of managerial effectiveness and managerial efficiency. The following sections discuss these concepts in more detail.

Managerial Effectiveness

Managerial Effectiveness Continuum

As managers use their resources they must strive to be both effective and efficient. **Managerial effectiveness** is defined in terms of resource utilization in relation to organizational goal attainment. If organizations are using their resources to attain their goals, the managers are effective. In reality, there are degrees of managerial effectiveness. The closer organizations come to achieving their goals, the more effective the managers are said to be. Figure 1.6 shows managerial effectiveness as a continuum ranging from "ineffective" to "effective." Depending on how close organizations come to achieving their goals, managers' effectiveness may fall anywhere on the managerial effectiveness continuum.

Figure 1.5 Major activities performed to manage production.

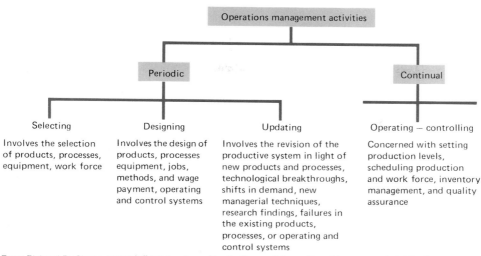

From Richard B. Chase and Nicholas Aquilano, *Production and Operations Management: A Life Cycle Approach*, 3rd ed., 1981, p. 5. Copyright © by Richard D. Irwin, Inc. Reprinted by permission of Richard D. Irwin, Inc.

Figure 1.6 A continuum for managerial effectiveness.

Managerial Efficiency

Managerial efficiency is defined in terms of the proportion of total organization resources that contribute to productivity during the manufacturing process. The higher this proportion, the more efficient the manager. The more resources wasted or unused during the production process, the more unefficient the manager. As with management effectiveness, management efficiency is best described as being on a continuum ranging from inefficient to efficient. *Inefficient* assumes that a very small proportion of total resources contributes to productivity during the manufacturing process while *efficient* assumes that a very large proportion contributes. Figure 1.7 presents the continuum of managerial efficiency.

Managerial Efficiency Continuum

As figure 1.8 shows, the concepts of managerial effectiveness and efficiency are obviously related. Managers could be relatively ineffective, their organizations making very little progress toward goal attainment, primarily because of major inefficiencies or poor utilization of resources during the production process. On the other hand, managers could be somewhat effective despite their inefficiency. Perhaps demand is so high for their finished goods that managers can get an extremely high price per unit sold and thus absorb inefficiency costs.

Relationship between Effectiveness and Efficiency

For example, some oil companies in Saudi Arabia could probably absorb many managerial inefficiencies simply because of the high price at which oil sells. Management in this situation has a chance to be somewhat effective despite its inefficiency. Thus, managers can be effective without being efficient and vice versa. To maximize organizational success, however, managers must be both effective and efficient.

Figure 1.7 A continuum for managerial efficiency.

Inefficient Management   Efficient Management

(No resources contribute   (All resources contribute
to production)   to production)

Figure 1.8 Various combinations of managerial effectiveness and managerial efficiency.

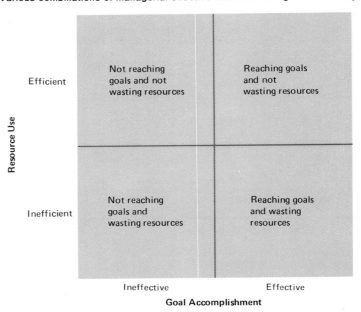

Efficient · Not reaching goals and not wasting resources · Reaching goals and not wasting resources

Inefficient · Not reaching goals and wasting resources · Reaching goals and wasting resources

Resource Use

Ineffective   Effective

Goal Accomplishment

Back to the Case

Mike Williams now has specific information on what management is and what managers do. If Williams becomes a manager, he will have to acquire a clear understanding of departmental objectives and help McGee to guide the department toward obtaining these objectives. This guidance, of course, will involve not only working with other departmental members but also all other departmental resources.

Williams will also have to manage his department primarily by planning, organizing, influencing, and controlling. In other words, he will need to outline how jobs must be performed to reach departmental objectives, assign these jobs to appropriate departmental workers, encourage these workers to perform their jobs, and make changes when needed to enhance the attainment of departmental objectives. Also, as Williams performs these four functions he will need to remember that they are interrelated and must blend together appropriately if he is to be a successful manager.

To manage successfully, Williams will have to view his department as producing a special type of product. In essence, Mike should see his department as a collection of organizational resources that is transformed into men's furnishings products made available for customer purchase. Primary resources made available to Williams in a retailing organization will probably include human resources (workers), monetary resources (money to pay salaries, buy inventory, etc.) and capital resources (cash registers, etc.). In addition, it will be important to Williams's long-running success that he continually try to improve this production process in his department.

Williams's wise use of the resources available to his department will be imperative. In using these resources, Williams should strive to be both effective and efficient, or to reach departmental goals without wasting department resources.

Figure 1.9 Relative importance of management skills to various levels of management.

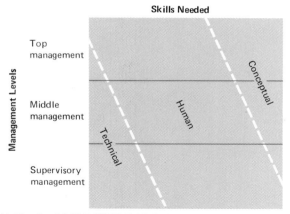

Paul Hersey, Kenneth H. Blanchard, MANAGEMENT OF ORGANIZATIONAL BEHAVIOR: Utilizing Human Resources, 3rd ed., © 1977, p. 7. Reprinted by permission of Prentice-Hall, Inc., Englewood Cliffs, New Jersey.

Management Skills

No discussion of organizational resources would be complete without mentioning management skills, perhaps the primary determinant of how effective and efficient managers will be. According to an article by Robert L. Katz, managerial success depends primarily on performance rather than personality traits.[8] Katz also states that managers' ability to perform is a result of the managerial skills they possess. If managers have necessary management skills, they will probably perform well and be relatively successful. On the other hand, if managers do not have necessary management skills, they will probably perform poorly and be relatively unsuccessful.

Katz indicates that three types of primary skills are important for successful management performance. Managers must have technical skills, conceptual skills, and human skills. Technical skills involve using specialized knowledge and expertise in executing work-related techniques and procedures. Examples of technical skills include engineering, computer programming, and accounting. **Technical skills** are mostly related to working with "things"—processes or physical objects. **Human skills** are those that build cooperation within the team being led. Human skills involve working with attitudes, communication, individuals and groups, and individual interests; in short, working with people. **Conceptual skills** involve the ability to see the organization as a whole. Managers with conceptual skills are better able to understand how various functions of the organization complement one another, the relationship of the organization to its environment, and how changes in one part of the organization affect the rest of the organization.

Basically, as one moves from lower management to upper management, conceptual skills become more important and technical skills become less important (see figure 1.9). The supportive rationale is that as managers advance in an organization, their tasks become less involved with the actual production activity or technical areas and they become more concerned with guiding the organization as a whole. Human skills, however, are extremely important to managers at top, middle,[9] and lower or supervisory levels.[10] The common denominator of all management levels is people.

Exhibit 1 gives an actual example from the business world in its account of how W. Thomas Beebe and David C. Garrett, Jr. used their interpersonal skills to maintain a sense of teamwork at Delta Airlines.

Three Primary Skills:

1. Technical
2. Human

3. Conceptual

Importance of Management Skills

Exhibit 1

(Photo: Courtesy of Delta Airlines)

ATLANTA—In February 1979, James Burnett's paycheck came up $38 short. Delta Airlines hadn't paid him enough overtime for the day he came in at 2 a.m. to repair an L-1011 engine.

When his supervisor wouldn't help, the 41-year-old mechanic wrote Delta's president, David C. Garrett Jr. He complained that "the pay problem we have experienced is bad and it has caused a lot of good men to go sour on the company." Three days later, Mr. Burnett got his money and an apology from top management. Delta even changed its pay policy, increasing overtime pay for mechanics called in outside normal working hours.

Such reaction from top executives to the little problems of Delta's 36,500 employees isn't an isolated incident. It's part of a sophisticated personnel policy to maintain what Delta calls its best asset: an unusually productive and loyal work force. The strategy, which includes virtual open-door access for all employees to top management, has kept Delta largely nonunion and made it a consistent money-maker in an industry plagued with labor-management strife.

Carefully Institutionalized

At the heart of Delta's philosophy is a concept it calls "the Delta family feeling." More than a slogan, it's an attitude that was nurtured by the airline's founder, the late C. E. Woolman, and then carefully institutionalized by W. Thomas Beebe, Delta's current chairman. "It's just a feeling of caring within the company," says Mr. Beebe.

The approach has its drawbacks. Because few people quit, it's tough to move up in seniority. A Dallas baggage handler on the night shift complains: "We figured we'd be 103 years old before we got day shift." And some employees say that because there isn't a clear-cut promotion system, they have to buddy up to supervisors to get ahead.

"Pay a Little Penalty"

Nevertheless, it's difficult to find workers with serious complaints. Delta promotes from within, pays better than most airlines and rarely lays off workers. When other airlines cut employment during the 1973 oil embargo, Mr. Beebe told senior management: "Now the time has come for the stockholders to pay a little penalty for keeping the team together."

Delta makes sure employees embrace the family concept by carefully screening job applicants. Stewardesses, for instance, are culled from thousands of applicants, interviewed twice and then sent to Delta's psychologist, Dr. Sidney Janus. "I try to determine their sense of cooperativeness or sense of teamwork," he says. At Delta, "you don't just join a company, you join an objective."

Delta holds yearly employee meetings with top management and lets workers make what would normally be considered management decisions. A committee of flight attendants chooses uniforms for Delta's 6,000 stewards and stewardesses. "That's important. You have to live in them," says flight attendant Pam Webb. Mechanics even choose their immediate supervisors.

But Delta can be tough. Recently it fired a flight attendant trainee because she complained about having to train between 10 p.m. and 12 a.m. on a Saturday night before an 8 a.m. company exam. "She had a little attitude problem," says Mary Ruth Rouse, supervisor of flight attendant training. "We had visions of her refusing to go out on flights."

And Delta can be downright prudish. In May it fired flight attendant Linda Lehner for exposing her derriere in Playboy magazine. "We attempt to hire young ladies for these jobs, and we expect them to act like that," says Mr. Garrett, Delta's president. On duty, stewardesses can't even wear open-toed shoes.

For years union organizers have tried without success to organize Delta workers. "They have a relationship with their employees that's most difficult to break into," says Frank O'Connell of the Transport Workers of America. The last union vote at Delta occurred in 1955. There hasn't been a strike since 1947. Only pilots and flight dispatchers—about 1% of the work force—are organized.

A Free Trip

"If we ever become unionized it will be because we've made mistakes," says Mr. Beebe. But the company didn't make mistakes with Arnie Rich. The Northeast Airlines mechanic worried about losing his union protection when Delta merged with Northeast in 1972. Delta flew him and his wife to Atlanta so he could talk to Delta employees. "I walked out into the hangar at three in the morning and talked to people," he says. "I asked has anyone been fired? What do you get fired for? Everybody was just happy."

Without union work rules, Delta is free to switch employees to different jobs as needed. During the 1973 fuel crunch, for instance, Delta reassigned 700 pilots and flight attendants to jobs loading bags and taking reservations. The company believes cross training helps employees understand how their jobs fit with overall company goals.

Help from Colleagues

Delta will go to great lengths to get an employee's side of the story. "Three years ago, the marketing manager in Fort Worth, Texas, was in serious trouble," says C. P. Knecht, former vice-president, marketing programs. "He kept reporting expenses we couldn't find. Everybody said we should fire him."

The Fort Worth man said medicine he was taking for a blood disease causes his memory to lapse. Mr. Knecht thought he was lying. But he flew to Forth Worth to meet with the man's doctor who verified the story. Delta transferred the man to a less demanding job.

Such understanding seems to give employees a family-like esprit de corps. Mr. Burnett, the mechanic, lost a week of work last January when his 16 year old daughter died in a car accident. Forty other mechanics each worked an hour on his time card so he wouldn't lose any pay.

During peak periods, pilots and gate agents help load bags to speed up departures. Robert Oppentander, senior vice-president, finance, says this is one reason Delta continually leads the industry in service and profits. Since 1974, according to the Civil Aeronautics Board, Delta has had the fewest complaints per passenger boarded of any major airline. And Delta's 1979 net income of $103.4 million accounted for more than a fourth of the entire industry's profit last year.

"At Christmas you see top management come and pitch in," says Scotty McCarthy, 31, who started as a baggage handler 10 years ago. "I've gone over to Eastern at peak times and seen mountains of bags, and I've seen one guy trying to handle all this. Does anyone come over to help him? No, ma'am."

Mr. Beebe says Delta holds firm on its policy of promoting from within. "We've got hundreds of college degree graduates working on the ramp knowing they will be promoted if their work merits it," he says. But we don't have any stars," such as Eastern's top man, Frank Borman. "Usually, it turns out to be an ego trip which is bad for the company. We want people who will enjoy and want to be working for the team."

International Management

Across National Borders

In discussing fundamentals of management, this section has focused on management functions, goal attainment, production, operations management, and managerial performance. In addition, however, some understanding of international management is generally thought to be necessary in order to have a thorough and contemporary understanding of the fundamentals of management.[11] **International management** is defined simply as performing management activities across national borders. The following material elaborates on international management by discussing (1) multinational corporations and (2) international versus domestic management.

The Multinational Corporation

Operations in Other Countries

The term *multinational corporation (MNC),* has been defined in several different ways in conversation and textbooks alike.[12] An MNC is defined in this text as a company that has significant operations in more than one country. Raymond Vernon gives further insight into the MNC by indicating that an MNC carries out its activities on an international scale that disregards national boundaries and on the basis of a common strategy from a corporation center.[13]

Sample MNC's

A list of MNC's in this country would certainly include such companies as Ford, General Motors, Mobil Oil, Firestone Tire, and Massey-Ferguson. Ford, General Motors, Mobil Oil, and Firestone each have over 2,500 employees in South Africa alone.[14] An executive of Massey-Ferguson has described its international involvement as the combining of French-made transmissions, British-made engines, Mexican-made axles, and United States-made sheet metal parts to produce in Detroit a tractor for sale in Canada.[15]

Degrees of Multinationalization

In addition to whether or not a particular company is an MNC, the degree to which a company is multinationalized should also be considered. Neil H. Jacoby implies that there are six stages a company goes through to reach the highest degree of multinationalization.[16] Figure 1.10 presents each of these stages and indicates the degree of multinationalization each represents. As you can see in this figure, multinationalization ranges from a slightly multinationalized organization that simply exports products to a highly multinationalized organization that has some of its owners in other countries.

Organizational Size and International Operations

What is the relationship between the size of an organization and its participation in international operations? In general, the larger the organization, the greater the likelihood that it participates in international operations of some sort. Supporting this generalization is the fact that companies like General Electric, Lockheed, and DuPont have annually accumulated over $1 billion from sales of exports. However, exceptions to this generalization also exist. For example, BRK Electronics, a small firm in Aurora, Illinois, has won a substantial share of the world's sales of smoke detectors. By setting up local distributors in Italy, France, and England, BRK export sales climbed from $124,000 in 1973 to $4 million in 1978.[17]

International vs. Domestic Management

Differences in the Management Situation

International management differs from domestic or uninational management because it involves operating—

1. within different national sovereignties;
2. under widely disparate economic conditions;
3. with peoples living within different value systems and institutions;
4. in places experiencing the industrial revolution at different times;
5. often over greater geographical distance; and
6. in national markets varying greatly in population and area.[18]

Figure 1.10 Six stages of multinationalization.

Stage I	Stage II	Stage III	Stage IV	Stage V	Stage VI
Exports its products to foreign countries	Establishes sales organizations abroad	Licenses use of its patents and know-how to foreign firms that make and sell its products	Establishes foreign manufacturing facilities	Multinationalizes management from top to bottom	Multinationalizes ownership of corporate stock

A Complex Situation

Figure 1.11 shows some of the more important implications for management generated by these six variables and the relationships among them. Keep in mind that not all relationships among these variables appear in this figure. To illustrate how to interpret figure 1.11, refer first to the Different National Sovereignties variable. You will see that according to the chart different national sovereignties generate different legal, monetary, and political systems. In turn, each legal system implies a unique set of relevant rights and obligations in relation to property, taxation, antitrust or control of monopoly, corporate law, and contract law. These in turn require the firm to acquire new skills within the organization to assess these international legal considerations. The skills are new in the sense of being different from that required in a purely domestic setting.

International Management and This Text

The significant trend that already exists in the United States and other countries toward developing business relationships in and with other countries is expected to accelerate even more in the future.[19] Additional insights into how to manage within the complicated international situation will be mentioned periodically throughout this text.

The Universality of Management

Management principles are **universal,** or applicable to all types of organizations (business organizations, churches, sororities, athletic teams, hospitals, etc.) and organizational levels. Naturally, managers' jobs are somewhat different in each of these organizations because each organization requires the use of specialized knowledge, exists in unique working and political environments, and uses different technology. However, job similarities also exist because of the common basic management activities necessary in all organizations: planning, organizing, influencing, and controlling.

Henri Fayol stated that all managers should possess certain characteristics, such as positive physical qualities, mental qualities, and special knowledge related to the specific operation.[20] B. C. Forbes, also describing manager characteristics, emphasized the importance of certain more personal qualities in successful managers. He inferred that enthusiasm, earnestness of purpose, confidence, and faith in their worthwhileness are primary characteristics of successful managers. Forbes describes Henry Ford as follows:

> At the base and birth of every great business organization was an enthusiast, a man consumed with earnestness of purpose, with confidence in his powers, with faith in the worthwhileness of his endeavors. The original Henry Ford was the quintessence of enthusiasm. In the days of his difficulties, disappointments, and discouragements, when he was wrestling with his balky motor engine—and wrestling likewise with poverty—only his inexhaustible enthusiasm saved him from defeat.[21]

Fayol and Forbes can describe these desirable characteristics of successful managers only because of the universality concept: the basic ingredients of the successful management situation are applicable to organizations of all types.

Figure 1.11 Management implications based on six variables in international system and relationships among them.

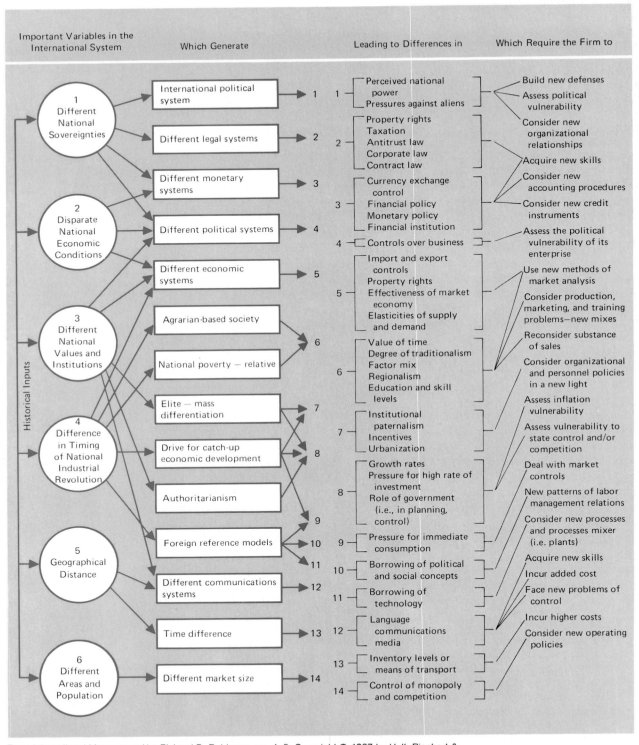

From *International Management* by Richard D. Robinson, pp. 4–5. Copyright © 1967 by Holt, Rinehart & Winston, Inc. Reprinted by permission of Holt, Rinehart & Winston.

To be successful as a manager, Mike Williams must possess technical skills, human skills, and conceptual skills. Since if Williams becomes a manager, it will be a relatively low-level management position, human skills, technical skills, and conceptual skills would probably be ranked 1, 2, and 3 respectively in terms of their order of importance to him. Of course, as Williams moves up the management hierarchy, this ranking of importance will change.

Mike Williams may eventually become involved with some phase(s) of international management at Shillito's. For example, as he moves toward top management he could become involved in plans to locate a new store in Canada. If this expansion were to materialize, Mike and others on his management team will have to determine specifics regarding the complex difference between U.S. and Canadian business environments and plan to manage accordingly.

If Williams decides to become a manager, the management experience he will acquire will be valuable if he moves to other management levels of Shillito's or to other companies in the retailing business or to other industries. If Williams accepts this position, he can help to ensure his success by being enthusiastic, earnest, confident, and secure in his worthwhileness.

In the final analysis, Williams can probably best determine whether or not he likes to manage by accepting McGee's offer.

The following points are stressed within this chapter:

Summary

1. Management is a function important to society in general and also to the livelihood and existence of many individuals.

2. Managers' basic role is combining and using organizational resources to ensure that organizations achieve their goals. Managers do this mainly through the interrelated activities of planning, organizing, influencing, and controlling.

3. Management is a universal discipline and can be defined as the process of reaching organizational goals by working with and through people and other resources. Production is the transformation of organizational resources into products, and operations management is the process of managing production. Managers must strive to be both effective and efficient in their use of organizational resources within the production process.

4. In general, management skills are the primary determiners of managerial performance. Three fundamental types of management skills are technical skills, conceptual skills, and human skills. The relative importance of each of these three types of skills to managers varies, depending upon whether the manager in question is a lower-level manager, a middle-level manager, or an upper-level manager.

5. Understanding issues involved in international management is becoming more important for modern managers. The conduct of business across national borders and the existence of multinational corporations are becoming much more commonplace.

Issues for Review and Discussion

1. What is the main point illustrated in the case at the beginning of the chapter?
2. How important is the management function to society?
3. How important is the management function to individuals?
4. What is the basic role of managers?
5. How is management defined in this text? What main themes are contained in this definition?
6. List and define each of the four functions of management.
7. Outline the relationship between the four management functions.
8. What is production?
9. What are the major activities involved in managing production?
10. Explain the term *operations management.*
11. List and define the basic organizational resources managers have at their disposal.
12. What is the relationship between organizational resources and production?
13. Draw and explain the continuum of managerial effectiveness.
14. Draw and explain the continuum of managerial efficiency.
15. Are management effectiveness and management efficiency related concepts? If so, how?
16. According to Katz's article, what are the three primary types of skills important to management success? Define each of these types of skills.
17. Describe the relative importance of each of these three types of skills to managers.
18. Discuss the relevance of Beebe and Garrett's actions at Delta.
19. What is international management?
20. Describe the stages of multinationalization.
21. Contrast international and domestic management.
22. What is meant by "the universality of management"?

Sources of Additional Information

Alpander, Guvenc G. "Training First-Line Supervisors to Criticize Constructively." *Personnel Journal,* March 1980, pp. 216–21.

Cheit, E. F., ed. *The Business Establishment.* New York: John Wiley & Sons, 1964.

Cole, A. H. *Business Enterprise and Its Setting.* Cambridge, Mass.: Harvard University Press, 1959.

Drucker, P. *Management: Tasks, Responsibilities, Practices.* New York: Harper & Row Publishers, 1974.

Elliott, Clifford, and Yoo, Jang H. "Innovations in the Japanese Distributive System: Are the Barriers to Entry Being Lifted?" *Akron Business and Economic Review,* Spring 1980, pp. 28–33.

Hayes, James L. "Making a Professional Manager." *Management Review* 69 (November 1980): 2–3.

Koontz, H. *Toward a Unified Theory of Management.* New York: McGraw-Hill, 1964.

Moore, D. G. "What Makes a Top Executive." *Personnel* 37 (1960): 8–19.

Ozawa, Terutomo. "Japan's Industrial Groups." *MSU Business Topics,* Autumn 1980, pp. 33–41.

Ready, R. K. *The Administrator's Job.* New York: McGraw-Hill, 1969.

Roethlisberger, F. J. "The Foreman: Master and Victim of Double Talk." In *Man in Organization.* Cambridge, Mass.: Belknap Press, 1968.

Sayles, L. R. *Managerial Behavior.* New York: McGraw-Hill, 1964.

Thomas, W. C. "Generalist Versus Specialist: Careers in a Municipal Bureaucracy." *Public Administration Review* 21 (1961): 8–15.

Veiga, John F. "Do Managers on the Move Get Anywhere?" *Harvard Business Review,* March/April 1981, pp. 20–22, 26–30, 34–38.

1. Peter F. Drucker, "Management's New Role," *Harvard Business Review,* November–December 1969, p. 54.

2. *Statistical Abstract of the United States,* 93d ed. (Washington, D.C.: U.S. Bureau of the Census, 1972), p. 230.

3. "Who Are the Unemployed?" *U.S. News and World Report,* 16 November 1970, p. 54.

4. Robert Albanese, *Management: Toward Accountability for Performance* (Homewood, Ill.: Richard D. Irwin, 1975), p. 49.

5. For a more detailed description of each of these definitions of management, see Dalton E. McFarland, *Management: Principles and Practice,* 4th ed. (New York: Macmillan, 1974), pp. 6–10.

6. Joseph L. Massie and John Douglas, *Managing: A Contemporary Introduction* (Englewood Cliffs, N.J.: Prentice-Hall, 1973), p. 24. Fremont E. Kast and James E. Rosenzweig, *Organization and Management: A Systems Approach,* 2d ed. (New York: McGraw-Hill, 1974), p. 6. Henry L. Sisk, *Management and Organization,* 2d ed. (Cincinnati: South-Western Publishing Co., 1974), p. 13. Harold Koontz and Cyril O'Donnell, *Principles of Management: An Analysis of Managerial Functions,* 5th ed. (New York: McGraw-Hill, 1972), p. 42. James H. Donnelly, Jr., James L. Gibson, and John M. Ivancevich, *Fundamentals of Management: Functions, Behavior, Models* (Homewood, Ill.: Business Publications, 1975), p. 4.

7. Richard B. Chase and Nicholas J. Aquilano, *Production and Operations Management: A Life Cycle Approach* (Homewood: Richard D. Irwin, 1981), p. 4.

8. Robert L. Katz, "Skills of an Effective Administrator," *Harvard Business Review,* January-February, 1955, pp. 33–41.

9. W. Earl Sasser, Jr. and Frank S. Leonard, "Let First-Level Supervisors Do Their Job," *Harvard Business Review,* March/April 1980, pp. 113–21.

10. Peter D. Couch, "Learning to Be a Middle Manager," *Business Horizons,* February 1979, pp. 33–41.

11. American Assembly of Collegiate Schools of Business, "Accreditation Council Policies, Procedures, and Standards," 1980–1981, St. Louis, Mo.

12. J. Behrman, *Some Patterns in the Rise of the Multinational Enterprise* (Chapel Hill: University of North Carolina Press, 1969).

13. U.S. Department of Commerce, "The Multinational Corporation: Studies on U.S. Foreign Investment," vol. 1 (Washington, D.C.: U.S. Government Printing Office).

14. "South Africa's Foot-dragging Vexes U.S. Companies," *Business Week,* 20 October 1980, p. 56.

15. Robert W. Stevens, "Scanning the Multinational Firm," *Business Horizons* 14 (June 1971): 53.

16. Neil H. Jacoby, "The Multinational Corporation," *The Center Magazine* 3, no. 1 (May 1970) pp. 37–55.

17. Grover Starling, *The Changing Environment of Business* (Boston: Kent Publishing Company, 1980), p. 140.

18. This section is based primarily on Richard D. Robinson, *International Management* (New York: Holt, Rinehart & Winston, 1967), p. 3–5.

19. Raymond Vernon and Louis T. Wells, Jr., *Manager in the International Economy* (Englewood Cliffs: Prentice-Hall, Inc., 1981), p. 4.

20. Henri Fayol, *General and Industrial Management* (London: Sir Isaac Pitman & Sons, 1949).

21. B. C. Forbes, *Forbes,* 15 March 1976, p. 128.

Concluding Case 1
Continental, the "Giant Killer" of the Telecommunications Industry

(Photo: Continental Telephone)

Continental Telephone, a small independent telephone company based in Atlanta, is viewed by its competitors as one of the most aggressively managed firms in the telecommunications field. Orville Wright, president of MCI Communications Corporation, has said that Continental has done more than GTE, United Telecommunication, and other large telecommunication companies to prepare itself for competition in this constantly changing field. Continental's progressive preparation can be attributed to the managerial ability of Charles Wohlstetter, founder and chairman, who at age seventy continues to run the company aggressively.

Wohlstetter is guiding the company to new competitive markets with a carefully planned acquisition strategy. The company, a large collection of rural telephone exchanges, is becoming a sophisticated supplier of data and voice communications services. Recently, Continental has made several acquisitions and joint-venture investments that the company should find useful in becoming a major supplier of data and voice communication equipment to the business community.

The acquisition of American Satellite Corporation (AmSat), a joint venture with Fairchild Industries, Inc., places Continental in a strong position in satellite transmission. Continental has also added Executone Corporation, a private branch exchange marketing company. Executone enables Continental to develop a business in intelligent terminals and digital telephone switches that will eventually become the basis for an automated office.

These and other investments are providing the foundation for a long-distance data communications network to handle voice and data that management at Continental feels will allow it eventually to surpass even AT&T. Presently, a Continental customer has to call across the country using Bell lines. However, this is changing as the FCC has permitted the company to bypass the national telephone switching network. According to one Continental official, they will be able to develop a better and cheaper way to deliver long-distance telephone service through

AmSat. This official claims that at present Continental can set up a satellite-receiving station for 10 percent less than it costs AT&T to lay similar ground cables.

During the 1960s, Wohlstetter single-handedly developed Continental from his personal involvement in a faltering Alaskan telephone exchange to a collection of 1,800 rural telephone exchanges throughout thirty-seven states. Now he has elicited the aid of successful top management to assist the company in the development of the communications market and to succeed him when he retires. Two key executives, James Napier and Robert La Blanc, have been selected by Wohlstetter to aid him in the running of Continental. La Blanc, an engineer by training and a former marketing manager at AT&T, is viewed by outsiders as Wohlstetter's wisest acquisition. Napier (Continental's president) has been described by his colleagues and competitors as "the supreme telephone operating man." In addition, he is an extremely knowledgeable and progressive man. On the other hand, La Blanc (Continental's vice-chairman) is felt to be the visionary with the understanding of competitive telecommunication markets to implement Wohlstetter's long-range plans.

This case is adapted from "Continental Telephone: Taking on the Giants in Telecommunications," *Business Week*, 9 February 1981, pp. 50–53.

Discussion Issues

1. How might the term *management* be used in reference to Continental?
2. Identify the important management skills that Wohlstetter, La Blanc, and Napier appear to possess. How might these skills aid in the continued success of the company?
3. Which one of the four basic management functions do you think contributed the most to the previous success of Continental?
4. Which of the basic management functions will contribute to the future success of the company?

Student Learning Objectives

From studying this chapter I will attempt to acquire:

1. An understanding of the classical approach to managing
2. An appreciation for the work of Frederick W. Taylor, Frank and Lillian Gilbreth, Henry L. Gantt, and Henri Fayol
3. An understanding of the behavioral approach to managing
4. An understanding of the studies at the Hawthorne Works of the Western Electric Company
5. An understanding of the management science approach to managing
6. An understanding of how the management science approach has evolved
7. An understanding of the system approach to managing
8. An understanding of how triangular management and the contingency approach to management are related

Chapter Outline

Approaches to Managing

Introductory Case 2
Analyzing Fastburger

Trevis Randolph is owner and manager of a Fastburger hamburger stand in downtown Columbus, Ohio. His primary competitors are McDonald's, Burger King, and Burger Chef, all located within three blocks of Fastburger. This concentration of fast-food hamburger stands exists because of the large number of people who work and shop within walking distance of the area. Lunch hours always have the potential of producing more people than any two of these four restaurants can service. Typically, these customers desire extremely good service because they want to continue their shopping as soon as possible or get back to work within an hour.

Although Fastburger has been in operation only one year, three signs of failure are already apparent. First and of foremost importance in the short run, expenses are high and profits are low. The outflow of money for operating expenses during the past year was twice as much as the inflow from sales. To complicate matters, Randolph has just learned from his meat supplier that the cost of hamburger patties will be increasing in the near future. The extremely high turnover rate among the Fastburger employees is a second sign of failure. Only three of the original twenty-five employees have remained with Randolph during the entire first year of operation. The recruiting and training of new employees recently has been taking more and more of Randolph's time. Randolph knows that Fastburger's high turnover is caused by competitors "stealing" his employees. In effect, Fastburger has become the training grounds for employees of McDonald's, Burger King, and Burger Chef. A third sign of failure is that Fastburger has failed to develop a consistent clientele over the year. Randolph has noticed that very few customers come to Fastburger regularly. Each new business day brings several new faces.

Randolph thinks that he has enough money saved to support Fastburger for one more year. If conditions don't change during that year, however, Fastburger will go bankrupt. Randolph must improve the position of his company quickly.

Discussion Issues

1. What problem areas should Trevis Randolph consider while analyzing his company?
2. What actions do you think Randolph may have to take as a result of his analysis?
3. Do you think that an organization like Fastburger can be saved? Why or why not?

What's Ahead

A manager like Trevis Randolph should know that there are several approaches to analyzing management situations and trying to solve organizational problems such as the ones at Fastburger. This chapter explains five approaches to managing: (1) the classical approach, (2) the behavioral approach, (3) the management science approach, (4) the contingency approach, and (5) the system approach. The system approach is emphasized in this text.

Chapter 1 focused primarily on defining management. This chapter presents various approaches to analyzing and reacting to the management situation. Each approach recommends a basically different method of analysis and a different type of management action as a result of this analysis.

Over the years, disagreement on exactly how many different approaches to management exist and what each approach entails has been common. In an attempt to organize and condense the various approaches, Donnelly, Gibson, and Ivancevich[1] combined the ideas of Koontz and O'Donnell,[2] and Massie and Haynes[3] and offered these three: (1) the classical approach, (2) the behavioral approach, and (3) the management science approach. They stated that their objective was to simplify a discussion of the field of management without sacrificing significant information.

The following sections build on the work of Donnelly, Gibson, and Ivancevich and present the classical approach, the behavioral approach, the management science approach, and the contingency approach as four of the five primary approaches to analyzing the management task. The fifth approach, the system approach, is presented as a more recent trend in management thinking and is the approach emphasized in this text.

The **classical approach to management** is the result of the first significant concentrated effort to develop a body of management thought. Management writers who participated in this effort are considered the pioneers of management study. Many of their thoughts were subjective opinions based on direct management experience as well as the thoughts and opinions of other managers. The classical approach to management stresses efficiency and recommends that managers continually strive to increase organizational efficiency to increase production.

For discussion purposes, the classical approach to management breaks into two distinct areas. The first area, lower-level management analysis, consists primarily of the work of Frederick W. Taylor, Frank and Lillian Gilbreth, and Henry L. Gantt. These individuals mainly studied the jobs of workers at lower levels of the organization. The second category, a comprehensive analysis of management, concentrates more on studying the management function as a whole. The primary contributor to this category is Henri Fayol. Figure 2.1 illustrates the division of the classical approach into these two areas and lists the major contributors to each.

Lower-Level Management Analysis

Lower-level management analysis concentrates on the "one best way" to perform a task, that is, how can a task situation be structured to get the highest production from workers. Efficiency is a major concern. The process of finding this "one best way" has

(margin notes)
Five Approaches to Management

The Classical Approach

Emphasis on Efficiency

Lower-Level Management Analysis

Comprehensive Analysis of Management

"One Best Way"

Frederick W. Taylor (Photo: Historical Pictures Service, Inc.)

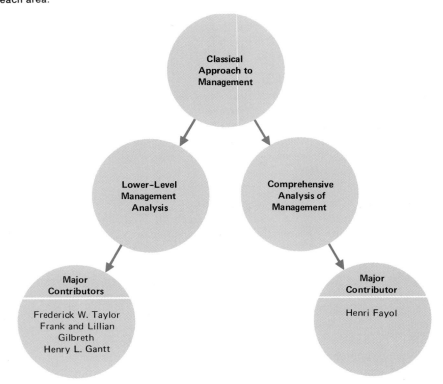

become known as the scientific method of management or, simply, **scientific management.** Although the techniques of scientific managers could conceivably be applied to all management levels, their research, research applications, and illustrations relate mostly to lower-level managers. Frederick W. Taylor, Frank and Lillian Gilbreth, and Henry L. Gantt were the major contributors to this area, and their work is summarized in the following sections.

Frederick W. Taylor (1856-1915)

Father of Scientific Management

Because of the significance of his contributions, Frederick W. Taylor is commonly called the "father of scientific management." His primary goal was to increase worker efficiency by scientifically designing jobs. His basic premise was that there was "one best way" to do a job and that that "way" should be discovered and put into operation.

Perhaps the best illustration of Taylor's scientific method and his management philosophy lies in a description of how he modified the job of several employees whose sole responsibility was shoveling materials at the Bethlehem Steel Company.[4] During the modification process, Taylor made the assumption that any worker's job could be reduced to a science. To construct the "science of shoveling," he obtained answers— through observation and experimentation—to the following questions:

1. Will a first-class worker do more work per day with a shovelful of five pounds, ten pounds, fifteen, twenty, thirty, or forty pounds?
2. What kinds of shovels work best with which materials?
3. How quickly can a shovel be pushed into a pile of materials and pulled out properly loaded?
4. How much time is required to swing a shovel backwards and throw the load a given horizontal distance accompanied by a given height?

Figure 2.2 Primary variables considered in analyzing motions.

Variables of the Worker	Variables of the Surroundings, Equipment, and Tools	Variables of the Motion
1. Anatomy	1. Appliances	1. Acceleration
2. Brawn	2. Clothes	2. Automaticity
3. Contentment	3. Colors	3. Combination with other motions and sequence
4. Creed	4. Entertainment, music, reading, etc.	4. Cost
5. Earning power	5. Heating, cooling, ventilating	5. Direction
6. Experience	6. Lighting	6. Effectiveness
7. Fatigue	7. Quality of material	7. Foot-pounds of work accomplished
8. Habits	8. Reward and punishment	8. Inertia and momentum overcome
9. Health	9. Size of unit moved	9. Length
10. Mode of living	10. Special fatigue-eliminating devices	10. Necessity
11. Nutrition	11. Surroundings	11. Path
12. Size	12. Tools	12. "Play for position"
13. Skill	13. Union rules	13. Speed
14. Temperament	14. Weight of unit moved	
15. Training		

As Taylor began formulating answers to these types of questions, he developed insights on how to increase the total amount of materials shoveled per day. He increased worker efficiency by matching shovel size with such factors as men, materials, and height and distance materials were to be thrown. After the third year that Taylor's shoveling efficiency plan was in operation, records at Bethlehem Steel indicated that the total number of shovelers needed was reduced from about 600 to 140, the average number of tons shoveled per worker per day rose from sixteen to fifty-nine, the average earnings per worker per day rose from $1.15 to $1.88, and the average cost of handling a ton of 2,240 pounds dropped from $0.072 to $0.033—an obviously impressive application of "scientific management" to the task of shoveling.

Frank Gilbreth (1868–1924), Lillian Gilbreth (1878–1972)

The Gilbreths were also significant contributors to the scientific method. By definition, therefore, they ascribed to finding and using the "one best way" to perform a job. The primary investigative tool in their research was **motion study,** which consisted of reducing each job to the most basic movements possible. This motion analysis was then used to establish job preformance standards and eliminate unnecessary or wasted movement.

Reducing Job to Basic Movements

During a motion analysis, the Gilbreths considered the work environment, the motion itself, and behavioral variables concerning the workers. Figure 2.2 lists the primary factors that fall into each of these groups. The analysis of each of these variables in a task situation was obviously a long, involved, and tedious process.

The earlier years of Frank Gilbreth's life were spent as an apprentice bricklayer. This experience showed Gilbreth that bricklayers were either productive or unproductive, primarily depending upon which motions they used to lay brick. Gilbreth, after studying bricklaying motions, surmised that bricklayers could increase their output significantly by concentrating on performing some motions and eliminating the performance of other motions.

Figure 2.3 shows a portion of the results of one of Gilbreth's bricklaying motion studies. For each bricklaying activity, Gilbreth indicated whether or not it should be omitted for the sake of efficiency and why. He reduced the twelve motions per brick listed under "The Wrong Way" to the two motions per brick listed under "The Right Way." Gilbreth's bricklaying motion study resulted in reducing the number of motions necessary to lay a brick by approximately 70 percent and tripling bricklaying production.

Frank and Lillian Gilbreth (Photo: The Bettmann Archive, Inc.)

Figure 2.3 Partial results for one of Gilbreth's bricklaying motion studies.

Operation No.	The Wrong Way Motions Per Brick $\frac{1}{4}\frac{1}{2}\frac{3}{4}\frac{4}{4}$	The Right Way Motions Per Brick $\frac{1}{4}\frac{1}{2}\frac{3}{4}\frac{4}{4}$	Pick and Dip Method. The Exterior Four Inches (Laying to the Line).
1	Step for mortar	Omit	On the scaffold the inside edge of mortar box should be plumb with inside edge of stock platform. On floor the inside edge of mortar box should be twenty-one in. from wall. Mortar boxes never over four ft. apart.
2	Reach for mortar	$\frac{4}{4}$	Do not bend any more than absolutely necessary to reach mortar with a straight arm.
3	Work up mortar	Omit	Provide mortar of right consistency. Examine sand screen and keep in repair so that no pebbles can get through. Keep tender on scaffold to temper up and keep mortar worked up right.
4	Step for brick	Omit	If tubs are kept four ft. apart, no stepping for brick will be necessary on scaffold. On floor keep brick in a pile not nearer than one ft. nor more than four ft. six ins. from wall.
5	Reach for brick	Included in 2	Brick must be reached for at the same time that the mortar is reached for, and picked up at exactly the same time the mortar is picked up. If it is not picked up at the same time, allowance must be made for operation.
6	Pick up right brick	Omit	Train the leader of the tenders to vary the kind of brick used as much as possible to suit the conditions; that is, to bring the best brick when the men are working on the line.
7	Mortar, box to wall	$\frac{4}{4}$	Carry stock from the staging to the wall in the straightest possible line and with an even speed, without pause or hitch. It is important to move the stock with an even speed and not by quick jerks.
8	Brick, pile to wall	Included in 7	Brick must be carried from pile to wall at exactly same time as the mortar is carried to the wall, without pause or jerk.
9	Deposit mortar on wall	Included in 7	If a pause is made, this space must be filled out. If no pause is made, it is included in No. 7.
10	Spreading mortar	Omit	The mortar must be thrown so as to require no additional spreading and so that the mortar runs up on the end of the previous brick laid, or else the next two spaces must be filled out.
11	Cutting off mortar	Omit	If the mortar is thrown from the trowel properly, no spreading and no cutting is necessary.
12	Disposing of mortar	Omit	If mortar is not cut off, this space is not filled out. If mortar is cut off, keep it on trowel and carry back on trowel to box, or else butter on end of brick. Do not throw it on mortar box.

By permission of Hive Publishing Company.

Henry L. Gantt (Photo: Historical Pictures Service, Inc.)

Role of Scientific Management

Henry L. Gantt (1861–1919)

A third major contributor to the area of scientific mangement was Henry L. Gantt. He, like Taylor and the Gilbreths, was interested in increasing worker efficiency. His interest in scientific management may have resulted from his working with Taylor both at Midvale and Bethlehem Steel. Gantt attributed unsatisfactory or ineffective tasks and piece rates primarily to the fact that they were set on what had been done in the past or on somebody's *opinion* of what could be done. According to Gantt, *exact scientific knowledge* of what could be done should be substituted for opinion. He considered this the role of scientific management.

Gantt's management philosophy is described by his statement that "the essential differences between the best system of today and those of the past are the manner in which tasks are 'scheduled' and the manner in which their performance is rewarded."[5] Following his own rationale, Gantt tried to improve systems or organizations through task scheduling innovation, and bonus or compensation innovation.

Scheduling Innovation

The Gantt chart, the primary scheduling tool he developed, is still used in many organizations today. Basically, this chart provides managers with an easily understood summary of what work was scheduled for specific time periods, how much of this work was completed and by whom. The Gantt chart is covered in much more detail in the planning section of this text.

Gantt Chart

Reward Innovation: The Bonus

Gantt seemed more aware of the human side of production than either Taylor or the Gilbreths. Gantt wrote that "the taskmaster (manager) of the past was practically a slave driver, whose principal function was to force workmen to do that which they had no desire to do, or interest in doing. The task setter of today under any reputable system of management is not a driver. When he asks the workmen to perform tasks, he makes it to their interest to accomplish them, and is careful not to ask what is impossible or unreasonable."[6]

People Emphasis

Taylor had developed a system that allowed for all workers to be paid at the same rate. Gantt, however, in an effort to encourage people to higher levels of production, developed a system wherein workers could earn a bonus in addition to the piece rate if they went beyond their production quota for the day. Gantt felt strongly that worker compensation needed to correspond not only to production through the piece-rate system but also to overproduction through the bonus system.

Piece Rate Plus Bonus

Trevis Randolph, the owner/manager of Fastburger in the introductory case, could gain many valuable insights on how to turn Fastburger around from the information presented in this last section. A classical management approach would mean that by stressing organizational efficiency—by looking for the "one best way" to perform jobs at Fastburger—Randolph could increase his production. In this regard, Randolph should be asking himself if the tools provided for Fastburger employees are of appropriate size and shape. As a simplified example, are the knives used to apply mustard or mayonnaise of appropriate size to require only one swipe or is more than one swipe necessary to adequately cover the hamburger bun?

Randolph might also want to determine how a motion study could eliminate unnecessary or wasted human movement at Fastburger. As examples, are such products as hamburgers, french fries, and drinks located for easy insertion into customer bags or must an employee walk several steps in the process? Would

certain Fastburger employees be more efficient over an entire working day if they sat rather than stood while working?

Randolph should also seriously consider efficient scheduling and bonuses as two important areas of management activity at Fastburger. For example, he should make sure that the appropriate number of people with the appropriate skills are scheduled to work during peak hours and that fewer people work during slow hours. Unnecessary people working during slow hours usually results in labor costs with very little return. Proper scheduling will cut costs.

Just because people are properly scheduled and show up for work, however, does not necessarily mean that they will be productive. Randolph might want to consider offering his employees bonuses if they produce beyond some production goal. If the production goals seem unreasonable or are impossible to attain, however, workers will probably begin to resent both Randolph and his company, and could become more nonproductive than ever.

Back to the Case

Comprehensive Analysis of Management

Comprehensive analysis of management, the second area of the classical approach, concentrates on studying the management function as a whole. Whereas scientific managers approach the study of management primarily in terms of job design, comprehensive managers are concerned with the entire range of managerial performance.

Among the well-known contributors to the comprehensive view were Chester Barnard,[7] Alvin Brown,[8] Henry S. Dennison,[9] Luther Gulick and Lyndall Urwick,[10] J. D. Mooney and A. C. Reiley,[11] and Oliver Sheldon.[12] Perhaps the most notable of all contributors to the comprehensive view of management is Henri Fayol. His book *General and Industrial Management* presents a management philosophy that many modern managers still look to for advice and guidance.[13]

Henri Fayol (1841–1925)

Fayol, a Frenchman, began his work career as a mining engineer and was concerned mainly with overcoming the fire hazards of coal mining. Later in his career his interests shifted first to geological issues involved in coal mining and then to the study of the management function. Over thirty years of practical experience gave Fayol the information base from which would come his theory of administration. This theory was actually the beginning of many of our modern-day thoughts concerning the management task.

Elements of Management

Because of his writings on the elements of management and the general principles of management, Fayol is usually regarded as the pioneer of administrative theory. The elements of management he outlined—planning, organizing, command, coordination, and control—are still considered worthwhile divisions under which to study, analyze, and put into action the management process. The similarities between Fayol's elements of management and the functions of management outlined in chapter 1 (planning, organizing, influencing, controlling) are apparent.

General Principles of Management

The general principles of management suggested by Fayol in 1916 are still considered by most managers to be important to the success of modern organizations. These principles follow in the order developed by Fayol and are accompanied by corresponding definitional themes:[14]

1. *Division of work*   Work should be divided among individuals and groups to ensure that effort and attention are focused on special portions of the task. Fayol presents work specialization as the best way to use the human resources of the organization.

2. *Authority*   The concepts of authority and responsibility are closely related. Authority is defined by Fayol as the right to give orders and the power to exact obedience. Responsibility involves being accountable and, therefore, is naturally associated with authority. When one assumes authority, one also assumes responsibility.

3. *Discipline*   A successful organization requires the common effort of workers. Penalties, however, only should be applied judiciously to encourage this common effort.

4. *Unity of command*   Workers should receive orders from only one manager.[15]

5. *Unity of direction*   The entire organization should be moving toward a common objective, in a common direction.

6. *Subordination of individual interests to the general interests*   The interests of one person should not have priority over the interests of the organization as a whole.

7. *Remuneration*   Many variables, such as cost of living, supply of qualified personnel, general business conditions, and success of the business, should be considered in determining the rate of pay a worker will receive.

8. *Centralization*   Fayol defined centralization as lowering the importance of the subordinate role. Decentralization is increasing the same importance. The degree to which centralization or decentralization should be adopted depends on the specific organization in which the manager is working.

9. *Scalar chain*   Managers in hierarchies are actually part of a chainlike authority scale. Each manager, from the first-line supervisor to the president, possesses certain amounts of authority. The president possesses the most authority; the first-line supervisor possesses the least authority. The existence of this chain implies that lower-level managers should always keep upper-level managers informed of their work activities. The existence of and adherence to this scalar chain are necessary if organizations are to be successful.

10. *Order*   For the sake of efficiency and to keep coordination problems to a minimum, all materials and people that are related to a specific kind of work should be assigned to the same general location in the organization.

11. *Equity*   All employees should be treated as equally as possible.

12. *Stability of tenure of personnel*   Retaining productive employees should always be a high priority of the manager. Recruitment and selection costs, as well as increased reject rates, are usually associated with hiring new workers.

13. *Initiative*   Management should take steps to encourage worker initiative. Initiative can be defined as new or additional work activity undertaken through self-direction.

14. *Esprit de corps*   Management should encourage harmony and general good feelings among employees.

Fayol's general principles of management cover a broad range of topics. Organizational efficiency, the handling of people, and appropriate management action seem to be the three general themes stressed. With the writings of Fayol, the study of management as a broad comprehensive activity began to receive the attention it deserved.

Limitations of the Classical Approach

Individual contributors to the classical approach were probably encouraged to write about their experiences largely because of the success they enjoyed. Structuring work to be more efficient and defining the manager's role more precisely yielded significant improvement in productivity, which individuals such as Taylor and Fayol were quick to document.

The human variable of the organization, however, may not be adequately empha- **Inadequate Emphasis** sized in the classical approach. People working today probably are not as influenced **on People** by the bonuses the classical approach advocates as they were in the nineteenth century. It is generally agreed that the critical interpersonal areas, such as conflict, communication, leadership, and motivation, were not emphasized enough in the classical approach.

The **behavioral approach to management** emphasizes striving to increase production **The Behavioral** through an understanding of people. If managers understand their people and adapt **Approach** their organizations to them, organizational success usually will follow.

The behavioral approach is usually described as beginning with a series of studies conducted between 1924 and 1932. These studies investigated the behavior and attitudes of workers at the Hawthorne (Chicago) Works of the Western Electric Company.[16] Accounts of these studies are usually divided into phases: the Relay Assembly Test Room Experiments and the Bank Wiring Observation Room Experiment.

The Relay Assembly Test Room Experiments

These experiments originally had a scientific management orientation.[17] The purpose of the investigation was to determine the relationship between intensity of lighting and efficiency of workers as measured by worker output. Two groups of female employees were used as subjects. The light intensity for one group was varied, while the light intensity of the other group was held constant. Through this research method, the experimenters hoped to isolate the effect of changes in lighting on worker productivity. The experimenters believed that if productivity was studied long enough under various working conditions, those working conditions that maximized production would be found. Detailed records concerning weather conditions, temperature, rest periods, work hours, and humidity were kept to help determine the "one best" set of working conditions.

The results of the experiments were a surprise to the researchers. No matter what condition employees were exposed to, production increased. A consistent relationship between productivity and working conditions seemed nonexistent. An extensive interviewing campaign was begun to determine why the subjects continued to increase production. The following are the main reasons, as formulated from the interviews:

1. The subjects found working in the test room enjoyable.
2. The new supervisory relationship during the experiment allowed subjects to work freely without fear.
3. Subjects realized they were taking part in an important and interesting study.
4. The subjects themselves seemed to become friendly as a group.

The conclusion of the experimenters was that human factors within organizations could significantly influence production. More research was needed to evaluate the potential impact of this human component in organizations.

The Bank Wiring Observation Room Experiment

The purpose of the Bank Wiring Observation Room Experiment was to make a more detailed analysis of the social relationships in a work group.[18] More specifically, the study focused on the effect of group piecework incentives on a group of men who assembled terminal banks for use in telephone exchanges. The group piecework incentive system dictated that the harder a group worked as a whole, the more pay each member of that group received.

The experimenters believed that the study would find that members of the work group would pressure one another to work harder so that each member of the group would receive more pay. To the surprise of the researchers, the opposite occurred. The work group pressured the faster workers to slow down their work rate. In essence, people whose work rate would have increased individual salaries were pressured by the group rather than those people whose work rate would have decreased individual salaries. Evidently people were more interested in preserving the work group than in making more money.

The researchers concluded that social groups in organizations can effectively exert enough pressure to influence individuals to disregard monetary incentives.

When taken together, the series of studies conducted at the Hawthorne plant gave management thinkers a new direction for research. The human variable in the organization needed much more analysis since it obviously could either increase or decrease production drastically. Managers recognized that they must understand this influence to maximize its positive effects and minimize its negative effects. This attempt to understand people is still a major force of today's organizational research. More current behavioral findings and their implications for management are presented in much greater detail in later sections of this text.

Back to the Case

The preceding material on comprehensive analysis of management implies that Trevis Randolph might be able to improve Fastburger by evaluating and improving the entire range of his own behavior. In this regard, for example, Randolph should make sure that Fastburger employees receive orders from only one source and that everyone at Fastburger is working together to accomplish company objectives. Discipline should be handed out judiciously, and to minimize coordination problems at Fastburger, all people and materials should be assigned locations where related work takes place.

The preceding material on the behavioral approach to management suggests that to turn Fastburger around, Randolph should consider the people at Fastburger and evaluate the impact that their feelings and personal relationships have on the company. Randolph also should encourage his employees to be more productive by trying to make their work more enjoyable, allowing them to work more freely and without fear, and creating opportunities for them to become more friendly with one another. In essence, Randolph should strive to understand his people thoroughly and to adapt himself and Fastburger to suit their unique characteristics.

Churchman, Ackoff, and Arnoff define the management science or operations research (OR) approach as (1) an application of the scientific method to problems arising in the operation of a system, and (2) the solving of these problems by solving mathematical equations representing the system.[19] The **management science approach** suggests that managers can best improve their organizations by using the scientific method and mathematical techniques to solve operational problems.

The Management Science Approach

Using Scientific Method and Mathematical Models

The Beginning of the Management Science Approach

The management science or operations research (OR) approach can be traced back to World War II. During this era, leading scientists were asked to help solve complex operational problems that existed in the military.[20] The scientists were organized into teams that eventually became known as operations research or OR groups. As an example of a problem that these groups encountered: one OR group was asked to determine which gunsights would best stop German attacks on the British mainland.

These OR groups typically included physicists or other "hard scientists" who used the problem-solving method with which they had the most experience: the scientific method. The **scientific method** dictated that scientists:

What is the Scientific Method?

1. Systematically *observe* the system whose behavior must be explained to solve the problem
2. Use these specific observations to *construct* a generalized framework (a model) that is consistent with the specific observations and from which consequences of changing the system can be predicted
3. Use the model to *deduce* how the system will behave under conditions that have not been observed but could be observed if the changes were made

4. Finally, *test* the model by performing an experiment on the actual system to see if the effects of changes predicted using the model actually occur when the changes are made[21]

The OR groups became very successful in using the scientific method to solve their operational problems.

Management Science Today

After World War II the world again became interested in manufacturing and selling products. The success of the OR groups had been so obvious in the military that managers were anxious to try management science techniques in an industrial environment. After all, managers also had complicated operational problems.

By 1955, the management science approach to solving industrial problems had proven to be very effective. Many people found this approach valuable and saw great promise in refining and sophisticating its techniques and analytical tools. Managers and universities alike anxiously began these refinement and sophistication attempts.

By 1965, the management science approach was being used in many companies and applied to many diverse management problems, such as production scheduling, finding a location for a new plant, and product packaging.[22]

Management Science Applied to Many Areas

Characteristics of Management Science Applications

Four primary characteristics usually are present in situations in which management science techniques are applied.[23] First, some management problems are so complicated that managers need help in analyzing a large number of variables. Management science techniques increase the effectiveness of these managers' decision making. Second, a management science application generally uses economic implications as guidelines for making a particular decision. Perhaps this is because management science techniques are best suited for analyzing more quantifiable factors, such as sales, expenses, and units of production. Third, the use of mathematical models to investigate the decision situation is typical in management science applications. Models are constructed to represent reality and then used to determine how the real-world situation might be improved. The fourth characteristic of a management science application is the use of a computer. The great complexity of managerial problems and the sophisticated mathematical analysis required of problem-related information are two factors that make the computer very valuable to the management science analyst.

Today, managers are using such management science tools as inventory control models, network models, and probability models as aids in the decision-making process. Future sections of this text outline some of these models in more detail and illustrate their applications to management decision making. Because the evolution of management science thought is still in process, the arrival of more and more sophisticated analytical techniques can be expected as time passes.

The Contingency Approach

Management Action Depends on the Situation

The next approach to management to be covered in this chapter is called the "contingency approach." In simple terms, the **contingency approach to management** emphasizes the viewpoint that what managers do in practice depends on, or is contingent upon, a given set of circumstances—a situation.[24] In essence, this approach emphasizes "if-then" relationships. "If" this situational variable exists, "then" this is the action a manager should probably take. As an example, if a manager has a group of inexperienced subordinates, then the contingency approach would recommend that she lead in a different fashion than if she had an experienced group.

In general, the contingency approach attempts to outline the conditions or situations in which various management methods have the best chance of being successful.[25] This approach is based on the premise that although there is probably no one best way

Solving Management Problems

to solve a management problem in all organizations, there probably is one best way to solve any given management problem in any one organization. Perhaps the main challenges of using the contingency approach are (1) perceiving organizational situations as they actually exist; (2) choosing management tactics best suited to those situations; and (3) competently implementing those tactics.

Although the notion of a contingency approach to management is not new, [26] the use of the term itself is relatively new. In addition, the contingency approach to management has become a very popular discussion topic for contemporary management writers. The general concensus of these writings seems to indicate that if managers are to apply management concepts, principles, and techniques successfully, they must consider the realities of the specific organizational circumstances they face.[27]

Application Must Fit Situations

The System Approach

The system approach to management is based upon general system theory. Ludwig von Bertalanffy, a scientist who worked mainly in the areas of physics and biology, is recognized as the founder of general system theory.[28] The main premise of general system theory is that to understand fully the operation of an entity, it must be viewed as a system. A **system** is defined as a number of interdependent parts functioning as a whole for some purpose. For example, according to general system theory, to fully understand the operations of the human body, one must understand the workings of its interdependent parts (ears, eyes, brain, etc.). General system theory integrates the knowledge of various specialized fields so that the system as a whole can be better understood.[29]

Founder of General System Theory

Interdependent Parts Functioning As a Whole

Types of Systems

According to von Bertalanffy, there are two basic types of systems: closed systems and open systems. **Closed systems** are not influenced by and do not interact with their environments. They are mostly mechanical and have necessary predetermined motions or activities that must be performed regardless of their environment. A clock is an example of a closed system. Regardless of its environment, a clock's wheels, gears, and so forth, must function in a predetermined way if the clock as a whole is to exist and serve its purpose. The second type of system, the **open system**, is constantly interacting with its environment. A plant is an example of an open system. Constant interaction with the environment influences its state of existence and its future. In fact, the environment determines whether or not the plant will live.

No Interaction with Environment

Interaction with Environment

Systems and "Wholeness"

The concept of "wholeness" is very important in general system analysis. The system must be viewed as a whole and modified only through changes in the parts of the system. A thorough knowledge of interrelationships between the parts and how each part functions must be present before modifications of the parts can be made for the overall benefit of the system. L. Thomas Hopkins has outlined six guidelines that emphasize the importance of system "wholeness" to be remembered during system analysis:[30]

Wholeness Guidelines in System Analysis

1. The whole should be the main focus of analysis, with the parts receiving secondary attention.
2. Integration is the key variable in wholeness analysis. Integration is defined as the interrelatedness of the many parts within the whole.
3. Possible modifications in each part should be weighed in relation to possible effects on every other part.
4. Each part has some role to perform in order that the whole can accomplish its purpose.
5. The nature of the part and its function is determined by its position in the whole.

Figure 2.4 The open management system.

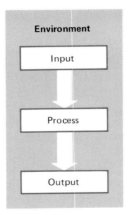

6. All analysis starts with the existence of the whole. The parts and their interrelationships should then evolve to best suit the purpose of the whole.

Since the system approach to management is based upon general system theory, analysis of the management situation as a system is stressed. The following sections present the parts of the management system and recommend information that can be used to analyze the system.

The Management System

As with all systems, the **management system** is composed of a number of parts that function on an interdependent basis to achieve a purpose. The main parts of the management system are organizational input, organizational process, and organizational output. As discussed in chapter 1, these parts consist of organizational resources, the production process, and finished goods, respectively. The parts represent a combination that exists to achieve organizational objectives, whatever they may be.

The management system is an open system, one that interacts with its environment (see figure 2.4). Environmental factors with which the management system interacts include the government, customers, and competitors. Each of these represents a potential environmental influence that could significantly change the future of a management system.

Environmental impact on management cannot be overemphasized. As an example, the United States federal government, through its Occupational Safety and Health Act (OSHA) of 1970, is still encouraging management to take costly steps to safeguard workers. Many managers are frustrated because they feel the safeguards are not only too expensive but also unnecessary. In exhibit 2, Duke Kimbrell, president of the North Carolina Textile Manufacturers Association, indicates that added expense caused by a recent court decision regarding the safety of textile workers may cause many textile manufacturers to go out of business.

Information for Management System Analysis

As noted earlier, to better understand a system, general system theory allows for the use of information from many specialized disciplines. This certainly holds true for the management system just presented. Information from any discipline can increase the

Figure 2.5 Triangular management model.

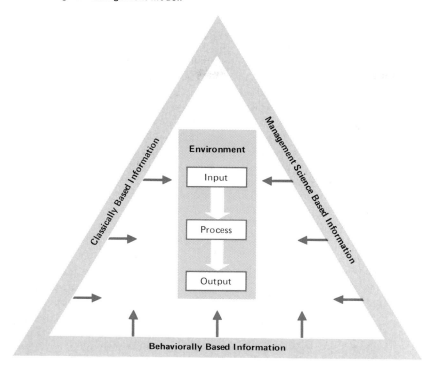

understanding of management system operations and thereby enhance the success of the system. A broad, sweeping statement such as this, however, presents a problem. Where do managers go to get this information?

The information used to discuss the management system in the remainder of this text comes from three primary sources: (1) the classical approach to management, (2) the behavioral approach to management, and (3) the management science approach to management. Using these three sources of information to analyze the management system is referred to as **triangular management.** Figure 2.5 presents the triangular management model. The three sources of information in the triangular management model are not meant to represent all the information that can be used to analyze the management system. Rather, they are the three bodies of management-related information that would probably be most useful to managers analyzing the management system.

Three Sources of
Information

A synthesis of classically based information, behaviorally based information, and management science-based information is critical to the effective management of the management system. This information is integrated and presented in this text in the five remaining major sections. These five sections discuss management systems and (1) planning (chapters 4–7), (2) organizing (chapters 8–11), (3) influencing (chapters 12–15), (4) controlling (chapters 16–18), and (5) managing in the future (chapters 19–20). In addition, some information in these sections will be presented from a contingency viewpoint where appropriate in order to give added emphasis to the practical application of management principles.

This Text Combines
Approaches

Exhibit 2

(Photo © 1980 *The Charlotte Observer*)

Government and labor-union studies estimate that at least 20 percent of America's textile-mill workers get it from inhaling microscopic particles of leaves and stems when bales of raw cotton fiber are processed at the mills. Eventually, it causes chronic coughing, shortness of breath and sometimes even death. Byssinosis—an emphysemalike affliction commonly known as brown-lung disease—was one of the recognized health hazards that inspired the Occupational Safety and Health Act, the 1970 law that allows the Labor Department to set standards to protect workers from toxic substances. Last week, in a ruling with broad implications for United States regulatory policy, the Supreme Court came down squarely on the side of the workers.

In a 5-to-3 decision, the Court ruled that the 1970 act does not require government regulators to consider the costs to industry of complying with standards on toxic substances. The ruling brought cheers from labor groups and squawks of protest from textile manufacturers. In the White House it caused considerable confusion. Ronald Reagan, swept to power partly on the strength of his promise to reduce the regulatory burden on business, had planned to use cost-benefit analysis of Federal standards as one of his chief tools, easing restrictions if the cost of compliance seemed to outweigh the benefits they achieved. The brown-lung ruling appears to mount a serious challenge to that approach.

Too Strict: The case before the Court was a suit filed by the American Textile Manufacturers Institute and twelve major textile companies against the Occupational Safety and Health Administration. According to the plaintiffs, OSHA's standard requiring mills to reduce cotton-dust levels to no more than 200 micrograms per cubic meter of air was simply too strict. Installing the air-filtration systems needed to meet it, the plaintiffs said, would impose unreasonable costs on manufacturers and might drive small companies out of business. Industry lawyers argued that the 1970 law required OSHA to make sure that the benefits of health regulations bore a reasonable relationship to the cost of compliance. The standard did not meet that test, they complained.

The Reagan Administration had asked the High Court not to rule on the case on the ground that its own newly appointed regulators are reviewing existing standards. The Justices flatly rejected that request—and the textile manufacturers' arguments. As the Court saw it, the crucial issue was the language of the 1970 act. It states that the Secretary of Labor "shall set the standard which most adequately assures, to the extent feasible . . . that no employee will suffer material impairment of health or functional capacity."

The majority decided that the critical phrase was "to the extent feasible." Writing for his colleagues, Justice William J. Brennan cited dictionary definitions of "feasible" and concluded that it means "capable of being done." That, he wrote, was the only limit Congress had placed on standard-setters. "Congress itself defined the basic relationship between costs and benefits, by placing the 'benefit' of worker health above all other considerations save those making attainment of this 'benefit' unachievable," wrote Brennan.

Textile workers were jubilant. "It's the best thing that's happened since they invented zippers," said Paul Kline, 60, a byssinosis victim who is now vice president of the Brown Lung Association of South Carolina. But manufacturers called it a "disappointment." Duke Kimbrell, president of the North Carolina Textile Manufacturers Association, warned that companies that make coarse cotton products, such as canvas and corduroy, will have to shut down or convert to synthetic fibers, and that big firms that can afford the added expenses will pass them along in the form of higher consumer prices. Industry analysts agree. But they question another industry contention—that the regulations will drive companies abroad. The main result, says Jay Meltzer of Goldman, Sachs & Co., will be to "hasten the move toward synthetics."

The Reagan Administration's cost cutters tried to put the best face possible on the ruling. James C. Miller, director of regulatory affairs for the Office of Management and Budget, stressed that it "does not cover any agency but OSHA, and it does not cover all of the OSHA act." Cost-benefit analysis on other fronts, he suggested, probably would be unaffected. He hinted that since the Supreme Court based its decision on the language of the 1970 law, the Administration might press for legislative changes. "Maybe the Congressional mandate needs to be changed," Miller said.

Revisionism: But OSHA's "excesses" are a favorite target of deregulators, and the Supreme Court ruling could turn out to be an important symbolic defeat for the Administration. This week the agency's tarnished image will get further burnishing. The Council on Economic Priorities, a liberal research group, is releasing a report on "Occupational Safety and Health in the Chemical Industry" that suggests that OSHA has done much good, despite industry foot-dragging. According to the CEP, illness and injury rates among chemical workers have dropped 23 percent over the last eight years—at an annual cost to industry of only $140 per worker.

Whatever impact the ruling has on Reagan's efforts to deregulate, there is one lesson in the brown-lung controversy that is worth remembering. The same pieces of equipment that reduce worker exposure to cotton dust— air-filtration systems and remote-control bale openers— have improved both the productivity of manufacturing plants and the quality of the products they turn out. Students of cost-benefit analysis would do well to take into account the fact that in some industries efforts to protect the health of workers also can serve the private purpose.
MERRILL SHEILS with DIANE CAMPER in Washington, PEGGY CLAUSEN in New York and bureau reports

Back to the Case

Trevis Randolph might want to consider using the management science approach to solve his operational problems. According to the scientific method, Randolph first should spend some time observing what takes place at Fastburger. Second, he should use these observations to develop a firm understanding of how Fastburger operates as a whole. Next, Randolph should apply his understanding of Fastburger's operations to predict how various changes might help or hinder the company as a whole. Before implementing possible changes, Randolph should test them on a small scale to see if they will actually affect Fastburger as desired.

Randolph might also want to consider applying the system approach to Fastburger's problems. He then would want to view Fastburger as a system, or a number of interdependent parts that function as a whole to reach Fastburger objectives. Fastburger also should be seen as an open system, or a system that exists in and is influenced by its environment. Major factors within the environment include Fastburger's customers and competitors, and the government.

Randolph has three primary sources of information available to help him to analyze and react to Fastburger as a system. Basically, these sources represent information from the classical, behavioral, and management science approaches to management. In essence, this combination of management approaches will probably be of more help to Randolph in managing Fastburger than any one of these approaches alone. This combination of approaches is called triangular management. Naturally, what Randolph finally decides to do should depend upon his own unique organizational situation— the contingency approach.

Summary

The following points are stressed within this chapter:

1. Five approaches to analyzing and reacting to the management situation are the classical approach, the behavioral approach, the management science approach, the contingency approach, and the system approach. The classical approach advocates management through efficiency and organization. The behavioral approach suggests that an understanding of people is the most important component of a management situation. The management science approach, a much more quantitative technique, emphasizes the use of mathematical models to solve complex operational problems. The contingency approach emphasizes that any action managers take depend on the situations those managers face.

2. Management is discussed in the remainder of this text, using the system approach. The system approach advocates viewing the management situation as a management system composed of a number of interdependent parts. These parts relate to inputs, process, and outputs. The management system is an open system, one that interacts with and is influenced by its environment.

3. For a management system to operate successfully, it must be viewed as a whole and evaluated against an integration of classically based information, behaviorally based information, and management science-based information. Using these three main sources of information to analyze the management system is called triangular management. Naturally, contingency-based information should also be used to increase the probability that the management system will be successful.

1. List the five approaches to managing.
2. Define the classical approach to managing.
3. Compare and contrast the contributions to the classical approach made by Frederick W. Taylor, Frank and Lillian Gilbreth, and Henry L. Gantt.
4. How does Henri Fayol's contribution to the classical approach differ from those of Taylor, the Gilbreths, and Gantt?
5. What is scientific management?
6. Describe motion study as used by the Gilbreths.
7. Describe Gantt's innovation in the area of worker bonuses.
8. List and define Fayol's general principles of management.
9. What is the primary limitation to the classical approach to managing?
10. Define the behavioral approach to managing.
11. What is the significance of the studies at the Hawthorne Electric Plant?
12. What is the management science approach to managing?
13. What are the steps in the scientific method of problem solving?
14. List and explain three characteristics of situations in which management science applications are usually made.
15. Define the contingency approach to management.
16. What is a system?
17. What is the difference between a closed system and an open system?
18. Explain the relationship between system analysis and "wholeness."
19. What are the parts of the management system?
20. What is triangular management?

Sources of Additional Information

Abernathy, William J.; Clark, Kim B.; and Kantrow, Alan M. "The New Industrial Competition." *Harvard Business Review,* September/October 1981, pp. 68–81.

Berle, A. A. Jr., and Means, G. C. *The Modern Corporation and Private Property.* New York: Macmillan, 1932.

Boddewyn, J. "Frederick Winslow Taylor Revisited." *Academy of Management Journal* 4 (1961): 100–107

Braddick, Bill, and Boyle, Denis. "Business Success in a Changing World." *Personnel Management* 13, no. 6 (June 1981): 37–39, 48.

Brech, E. F. L. *Organization.* London: Longmans, Green, 1957.

Carey, A. "The Hawthorne Studies: A Radical Criticism." *American Sociological Review* 32 (1967): 403–16.

Church, A. H., and Alford, L. P. "The Principles of Management." *American Machinist* 36 (1912): 857–61.

Davis, R. C. *Industrial Organization and Management.* 2d ed. New York: Harper & Row Publishers, 1940.

Davis, R. C. *The Fundamentals of Top Management.* New York: Harper & Row Publishers, 1951.

Davis, R. C. "A Philosophy of Management." *Academy of Management Journal* 1 (1958): 37–40.

Dennison, H. D. *Organization Engineering.* New York: McGraw-Hill, 1931.

Franklin, William H., Jr. "What Japanese Managers Know That American Managers Don't." *Administrative Management* 42, no. 9 (September 1981): 36–39, 51–54, 56.

Gilbreth, F. B. *Motion Study.* New York: D. Van Nostrand Co., 1911.

Gilbreth, L. M. *The Psychology of Management.* New York: Sturgis and Walton Co., 1914.

Holden, P. E.; Fish, L. S.; and Smith, H. L. *Top-Management Organization and Control.* New York: McGraw-Hill, 1941.

Hoxie, R. F. *Scientific Management and Labor.* New York: Appleton-Century-Crofts, 1915.

Kakar, S. *Frederick Taylor: A Study in Personality and Innovation.* Cambridge, Mass.: The M.I.T. Press, 1970.

Martindell, J. *The Scientific Appraisal of Management.* New York: Harper & Row Publishers, 1950.

Merrill, H. F., ed. *Classics in Management.* New York: American Management Association, 1960.

Metcalf, H. C., and Urwick, L., eds. *Dynamic Administration: The Collected Papers of Mary Parker Follett.* New York: Harper & Row Publishers, 1942.

Ouchi, William. "Going from A to Z: Thirteen Steps to a Theory Z Organization." *Management Review* 70, no. 5 (May 1981): 8–16.

Rogers, David. "Managing in the Public and Private Sectors: Similarities and Differences." *Management Review* 70, no. 5 (May 1981): 48–49.

Notes

1. James H. Donnelly, Jr., James L. Gibson, and John M. Ivancevich, *Fundamentals of Management: Functions, Behavior, Models* (Homewood, Ill.: Business Publications, 1975), p. 12.

2. Harold Koontz and Cyril O'Donnell, *Management: A Systems and Contingency Analysis of Managerial Functions* (New York: McGraw-Hill, 1976), p. 57.

3. W. Warren Haynes and Joseph L. Massie, *Management*, 2d ed. (Englewood Cliffs, N.J.: Prentice-Hall, 1969), pp. 4–13.

4. Frederick W. Taylor, *The Principles of Scientific Management* (New York: Harper & Row Publishers, 1947), pp. 66–71.

5. Henry L. Gantt, *Industrial Leadership* (New Haven, Conn.: Yale University Press, 1916), p. 57.

6. Gantt, *Industrial Leadership*, p. 85.

7. Chester I. Barnard, *Organization and Management* (Cambridge, Mass.: Harvard University Press, 1952).

8. Alvin Brown, *Organization of Industry* (Englewood Cliffs, N.J.: Prentice-Hall, 1947).

9. Henry S. Dennison, *Organization Engineering* (New York: McGraw-Hill, 1931).

10. L. Gulick and L. Urwick, eds., *Papers on the Science of Administration* (New York: Institute of Public Administration, 1937).

11. J. D. Mooney and A. C. Reiley, *Onward Industry!* (New York: Harper & Brothers, 1931). With some modifications, appeared as *The Principles of Organization* (New York: Harper & Brothers, 1939).

12. Oliver Sheldon, *The Philosophy of Management* (London: Sir Isaac Pitman and Sons, 1923).

13. Henri Fayol, *General and Industrial Management* (London: Sir Isaac Pitman and Sons, 1949).

14. Fayol, *General and Industrial Management*, pp. 19–42.

15. For a provacative discussion of the principle of unity of command, see James I. Mashburn and Bobby C. Vaught, "Two Heads Are Better Than One: The Case for Dual Leadership," *Management Review*, December 1980, pp. 53–56

16. For detailed summaries of these studies, see *Industrial Worker* 2 vols. (Cambridge, Mass.: Harvard University Press, 1938); and F. J. Roethlisberger and W. J. Dickson, *Management and the Worker* (Cambridge, Mass.: Harvard University Press, 1939).

17. For additional information, see George C. Homans, *Fatigue of Workers: Its Relation to Industrial Production* (New York: Committee on Work in Industry, National Research Council, Reinhold Publishing, 1941).

18. Homans, *Fatigue of Workers*.

19. C. West Churchman, Russell L. Ackoff, and E. Leonard Arnoff, *Introduction to Operations Research* (New York: John Wiley & Sons, 1957), p. 18.

20. F. S. Hillier and G. J. Lieberman, *Introduction to Operations Research* (San Francisco: Holden-Day, 1967), pp. 3–4.

21. James R. Emshoff, *Analysis of Behavioral Systems* (New York: Macmillan, 1971), p. 10.

22. C. C. Shumacher and B. E. Smith, "A Sample Survey of Industrial Operations Research Activities II," *Operations Research* 13 (1965): 1023–27.

23. Discussion concerning these factors is adapted from James H. Donnelly, James L. Gibson, and John M. Ivancevich, *Fundamentals of Management: Functions, Behavior, Models* (Homewood, Ill.: Business Publications, 1975), pp. 302–3.

24. Harold Koontz, "The Management Theory Jungle Revisited," *Academy of Management Review* 5, no. 2 (1980): 175–87.

25. Fred Luthans, *Introduction to Management: A Contingency Approach* (New York City: McGraw-Hill, 1976), p. 31.

26. Dennis J. Moberg and James L. Koch, "A Critical Appraisal of Integrated Treatments of Contingency Findings," *Academy of Management Journal* 18 (March 1975): 122.

27. J. W. Lorsch, "Organization Design: A Situational Perspective," *Organizational Dynamics* 6, no. 2 (1977): 2–4.

28. For a more detailed development of von Bertalanffy's ideas, see "General System Theory: A New Approach to Unity of Science," *Human Biology*, December 1951, pp. 302–61.

29. Ludwig von Bertalanffy, *Problems of Life* (New York: John Wiley & Sons, 1952).

30. Thomas Hopkins, *Integration: Its Meaning and Application* (New York: Appleton-Century-Crofts, 1937), pp. 36–49.

Concluding Case 2
American Express: Boosting Productivity

Ruth C. Finley (Photo: Courtesy Ruth C. Finley)

During the last few years American Express (AmEx) has been faced with heavy competition from bank cards such as MasterCard and VISA. These bank cards are not as expensive as AmEx for cardholders or merchants to use. Furthermore, merchants receive same-day reimbursement from the banks, a service yet to be offered by AmEx. With this increased competition, it is critical that the corporation be run as efficiently as possible to encourage customers to use AmEx cards. Slow customer service in replacing lost cards and in issuing new cards has had a detrimental effect on AmEx. For each day a customer is without a card the company loses approximately $2.70 in charge volume. Furthermore, once the customer starts using a competitor's card he or she may continue to do so even after the new card is received.

In 1978, AmEx began a productivity-improvement program. Ruth C. Finley, regional vice-president for commercial sales, developed the program. Finley's program was designed to speed up and improve customer service. Operations were broken down into discrete elements. Each element was measured in terms of time required to complete the element; performance standards were set; and methods were established to meet the standards. The program was based on examining the end products of customer service as if they were as tangible as a new car. Finley felt that customers were concerned with time accuracy, and the responsiveness of the company. The original pilot program centered on breaking down all service operations into these three factors. First, task forces were developed to identify and measure the elements, and then they developed ways to improve them.

One task force found that it was taking an average of thirty-five days to process applications for personal charge cards. The task force investigated patterns of customer inquiries and discovered that customers became impatient if they had not received an answer within three weeks. The result: the task force set a standard of two weeks to issue a card. Once the standard was set, the task force studied the processing of the applications from the mail room to the card-issuing staff to see how the standard could be met. Since the task forces included local managers from varying departments, specific process improvements were well coordinated. One regional director noted that the task-force system breaks down the barriers between departments. Finley felt it was important to include local managers in the task force so that no one thought the project was a "headquarters-directed witchhunt."

The original productivity-improvement program has produced some dramatic results nationwide. The processing of responses to cardholder inquiries has been speeded up to ten days instead of sixteen days. In addition, response to financial inquiries from merchants has been reduced from fourteen to four days. Replacement of lost or stolen cards has been reduced from fourteen or more days to as little as two days. These improvements, among others, have led to increased customer satisfaction. Not only have the customers benefited but so has AmEx as the speedup replacement of lost cards and the quicker issuance of new ones has resulted in $2.4 million in additional revenue and $1.4 million in additional profits.

By taking the productivity-improvement program nationwide other unexpected results have occurred. For instance, increased communication among regional centers has evolved. A task force was set up in Phoenix to investigate telephone inquiries. They found that by having a specially trained unit to handle incoming calls that required more research and a unit to handle routine calls, the average time for phone calls could be reduced by 23 percent. This procedure was shared with the other two regional centers located in Fort Lauderdale, Florida, and New York. According to Randy Williams, regional director for customer service in Phoenix, under normal conditions this procedure would have remained Phoenix's secret.

Finley intends to continue training and education in the program so that it is accepted throughout the organization. For instance, in Phoenix, new employees at all levels are indoctrinated into the functions of each department so that they understand their own department's impact on the customer's perception of service. The program tends to be viewed by some managers as a ''Big Brother'' approach to management. However, Finley maintains it is meant purely to spot possible backlogs or trouble areas. It is hoped that future training and education will dissolve this view.

This case is adapted from ''Boosting Productivity at American Express.'' *Business Week*, 5 October 1981, pp. 62–64.

Discussion Issues

1. What management approach is American Express's productivity-improvement program most like and why?
2. How might the Gilbreths perform a motion study of the processing of applications for personal charge cards? Set up the possible variables.
3. How might the behavioral approach be used to improve productivity in the processing of applications?
4. How might the productivity improvement be addressed from a systems perspective?
5. Explain the processing of applications at American Express from a systems perspective (use inputs, processes, and outputs as a framework for your explanation).

Student Learning Objectives

From studying this chapter I will attempt to acquire:

1. An understanding of organizational objectives
2. An appreciation for the importance of organizational objectives
3. An ability to tell the difference between organizational objectives and individual objectives
4. A knowledge of the areas in which managers should set organizational objectives
5. An understanding of the development of organizational objectives
6. Some facility in writing good objectives
7. An awareness of how managers use organizational objectives and help others to attain the objectives
8. An appreciation for the potential of a management by objectives (MBO) program

Chapter Outline

Organizational Objectives

Introductory Case 3
Getting an Organization on Track

It's 9 A.M. and four people are seated around an executive conference table in a leased downtown Chicago office. Each individual had recently resigned from a major industrial concern to become an employee and equal owner of a new company named Management and Organization Development Consultants (MODC). MODC will sell management consulting services to companies experiencing financial difficulties.

These four people, the founders of MODC, are the company's only employees at the moment, but they all are extremely talented, eager to make this new company a success, and well aware of the challenges they face. The group agreed beforehand which position each person initially would hold. The people and their positions are Daniel C. Murray, president; Marilyn L. Smite, vice-president for finance, Kenneth M. Neville, vice-president for marketing; and James N. Jacobs, vice-president for personnel. The interrelationships of these individuals is shown in figure A.

The purpose of the meeting this morning is to get MODC off the ground. President Murray officially opens the meeting by asking the vice-presidents to propose the business activities they would like to pursue in their respective areas:

MURRAY: Why don't we start with the finance area? Marilyn, what activity do you propose to get your area off the ground?
SMITE: Well, probably the first thing I would like to do is apply to borrow approximately $100,000 for working capital during the first year of our operation. We'll need money to pay salaries for new people, buy typewriters, and so forth. I think that's where I should begin.
MURRAY: O.K. Ken, what's your reaction to the marketing area?
NEVILLE: Dan, I've been thinking quite a bit about this. I would like to initiate a direct mail campaign to advertise our services as soon as possible. Over the year I'll probably need around $55,000 to keep our advertising at the level where I think it should be.
MURRAY: Wow! I didn't think we'd need that much money for advertising during our first year. Let's move to the personnel area. Jim, what are your proposed activities?
JACOBS: In my opinion we'll need twelve new people within the next three months and twenty more six months thereafter. These people will include sales representatives, management consultants, secretaries, and a full-time lawyer to advise MODC.
MURRAY: O.K. Let's go back and discuss each of these proposed activities. . . .

Case figure 3.1 Management and organization development consultants organization chart to date.

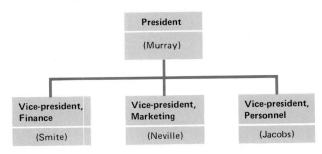

Discussion Issues

1. What role do you think the objectives of an organization should play in a meeting such as the one described?
2. Compare the proposed activities of the MODC vice-presidents. Do they seem compatible? Why?
3. Would you have conducted this meeting differently than Murray did? If so, how? If not, why?

What's Ahead

Dan Murray, president of MODC, would find the material in this chapter very useful. Organizational objectives are extremely important guidelines that managers such as Murray should use to get an organization on the right track and to keep it there. This chapter discusses (1) the general nature of organizational objectives, (2) different types of organizational objectives, (3) various areas in which organizational objectives should be set, (4) how managers actually work with organizational objectives, and (5) management by objectives (MBO).

Definition of Organizational Objectives

Organizational objectives are the targets toward which the open management system is directed. Organizational input, process, and output, as discussed in chapter 2, all exist to reach organizational objectives (see figure 3.1). If properly developed, organizational objectives reflect the purpose of the organization; that is, they flow naturally from organizational purpose. If an organization is accomplishing its objectives, it is simultaneously accomplishing its purpose and thereby justifying its reason for existence.

Organizations exist for various purposes and thus have various types of organizational objectives. A hospital, for example, may have the primary purpose of providing high quality medical assistance to the community. Therefore its primary objective focuses on furnishing this assistance. The primary purpose of a business organization, on the other hand, is to make a profit. The primary objective of the business organization, therefore, concentrates on making that profit. To illustrate, the primary organizational objective of the Lincoln Electric Company is profit oriented and has been stated as follows:

> The goal of the organization must be this—to make a better and better product to be sold at a lower and lower price. Profit cannot be the goal. Profit must be a by-product. This is a state of mind and a philosophy. Actually, an organization doing this job as it can be done will make large profits which must be properly divided between user, worker, and stockholder. This takes ability and character.[1]

John F. Mee has suggested that organizational objectives for businesses can be summarized with the following comments:

1. Profit is the motivating force for managers.
2. Service to customers by the provision of desired economic values (goods and services) justifies the existence of the business.
3. Social responsibilities do exist for managers in accordance with ethical and moral codes established by the society in which the industry resides.[2]

Objectives Flow from Organizational Purpose

Figure 3.1 Existence of open management system to reach organizational objectives.

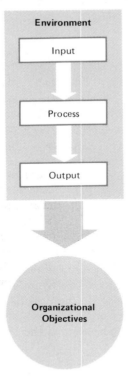

Objectives Are
Guidelines for:

Importance of Organizational Objectives

Marshall E. Dimock stresses that "fixing your objective is like identifying the North Star—you sight your compass on it and then use it as the means of getting back on track when you tend to stray."[3] Organizational objectives give managers and all other organization members important guidelines for action in such areas as decision making, organizational efficiency, organizational consistency, and performance evaluation. How organizational objectives function as guidelines in each of these areas is discussed in the paragraphs that follow.

Guide for Decision Making

1. Decision making

A significant portion of managerial responsibility involves making decisions that inevitably influence the everyday operation and existence of the organization and organization members. Once managers have a clear understanding of organizational objectives, they know the direction in which the organization must move. It then becomes their responsibility to make decisions that move the organization toward the achievement of organizational objectives. Exhibit 3 contains a profile of John Tillotson, who runs a small business as a publisher of three magazines. Within this profile, it is easy to see how Tillotson has made numerous organizational decisions using the objective of profit as a guideline.

Guide for Organizational Efficiency

2. Increasing efficiency

Since inefficiency results in a costly waste of human effort and resources, managers should strive to increase organizational efficiency whenever possible. Efficiency is defined in terms of the total amount of human effort and resources an organization uses to move itself toward attainment of organizational goals. Therefore, before organi-

Figure 3.2 Eight types of organizational objectives and related rankings by upper-level managers.

Type of Objective	Percent Rating as Highly Important	Percent Indicating Significant for Corporate Success
Organizational efficiency	81	71
High productivity	80	70
Profit maximization	72	70
Organizational growth	60	72
Industrial leadership	58	64
Organizational stability	58	54
Employee welfare	65	20
Social welfare	16	8

From G. W. England, "Organizational Goals and Expected Behavior of American Managers," *Academy of Management Journal* 10 (1967): 108. Used with permission.

zational efficiency can improve, managers must have a clear understanding of organizational goals. Only then will they be able to use the limited resources at their disposal as efficiently as possible.

Guide for Organizational Consistency

Most organization members often need work-related directives. If organizational objectives are used as the basis for these directives, the objectives serve as a guide to consistently encourage such things as productive activity, quality decision making, and effective planning results.

3. Establishing consistency

Guide for Performance Evaluation

Periodically, the performance of all organization members is evaluated to assess individual productivity and to determine what might be done to increase productivity.

4. Making performance evaluations useful

Organizational goals are the guidelines or criteria that should be used as the basis for these evaluations. Those individuals who contribute most to obtaining organizational goals should be considered the most productive. Specific recommendations on increasing productivity should be comprised of suggestions on what individuals can do to better help the organization move toward goal attainment.

Back to the Case

The discussion of organizational objectives in this last section offers Dan Murray, the president of MODC, useful insights on how to get his company off the ground. As the introductory case ended, the four founders of MODC were discussing the type of finance, marketing, and personnel activities that should be undertaken during the first year of operation. Dan Murray should now realize that such decisions cannot be made intelligently until MODC's purpose and its objectives are clearly outlined. He and his managers should set objectives in the profit area as well as in the service and social responsibility areas. Establishment of organizational objectives at MODC will help its managers to guide the company appropriately, to make better decisions, to assess the level of company efficiency, to be consistent, and to evaluate the performance of MODC employees.

Organizational objectives can be separated into two categories: organizational objectives and individual objectives. Recognizing the two categories of objectives and reacting to each type appropriately is a challenge that all modern managers face.

Types of Objectives in Organizations

Exhibit 3

John Tillotson Uses Profit Objective as Guideline for Making Decisions

(Photo: Modern Handcraft, Inc.)

John Tillotson publishes three little-known but profitable magazines: The Workbasket, Flower and Garden, and Workbench. He made his fortune doing things differently than most publishers. The success of his Kansas City company, Modern Handcraft Inc., suggests that small-business owners shouldn't necessarily rush to copy bigger rivals.

"To make a living with these types of magazines," says David Z. Orlow, a New York marketing consultant specializing in periodicals, "you have to be a really good manager. You have to run a tight ship."

The 58-year-old Mr. Tillotson does that. He has avoided mistakes much bigger publishers have made promoting similar magazines. Notes Mr. Orlow about Mr. Tillotson: "There have been all kinds of bankruptcies in gardening publications. He's one of the survivors."

Profiting in special-interest magazines that appeal to people who garden or knit, crochet and sew and to the do-it-yourself carpenter and home handyman is no mean trick. "Big publishers," says an industry specialist, "enter the field thinking they can spend more on promotion and get more readers to attract more advertising. Then they don't get it. There is no more littered road in publishing."

Mr. Tillotson's tight operation is apparent from the mastheads of his magazines. Two list only three editorial employees. Another masthead lists more, but several, he says, are part-timers. Many magazines employ scores of writers and editors. Mr. Tillotson relies heavily on outside contributors, paying them $300 to $1,000 an article.

Most magazines depend heavily on advertising. But Modern Handcraft publications get as much as 75% of their revenue from subscriptions. The three magazines had combined revenue of $14.3 million last year. While most publishers use outside companies to maintain subscriber records, the Tillotson magazines do it themselves with an efficient computer system using an optical scanner that can "read" typewritten words.

In their battle for readers and advertisers, big magazines such as Time and Newsweek spend heavily for circulation. Advertisers buy space in these publications based on the number of readers the magazines deliver. A drop in circulation could be interpreted as a loss in popularity.

"Newsweek has to replace thousands of subscribers every week just to stay even," says Charles I. Tannen, an editor at Folio, a publication for magazine management. The average subscriber fails to renew after staying with a magazine 4.3 years, Mr. Tannen says. So big-circulation magazines must promote extensively to keep up.

But circulation at the Tillotson magazines has been allowed to drop at times without great harm. In fact, it can be better strategy to absorb a circulation decline, Mr. Tillotson says, than to spend more money trying to prevent a slide.

Promotion decisions, nevertheless, are a crucial aspect of the business. Direct mail sent third-class is the main promotional tool. Responses to previous mailings indicate how many pieces of mail must be sent to produce a certain number of new readers. Mr. Tillotson explains the process: "We look at the subscription expirations coming in the next 24 months, calculate what the renewals will be (based on past renewal rates) and then figure how much promotion is needed to maintain the same circulation."

If the cost seems too high, circulation is allowed to drop. Between 1978 and 1980, Flower and Garden's circulation shrank to 500,000, a decline of 100,000 subscribers.

Responses to direct mail can be affected by many factors. Mr. Tillotson has found, for example, that people tend to ignore promotional mail in times of crisis. When Americans were held hostage in Iran, he says, mail responses were off.

Appeals go to subscribers when they don't renew. "We keep mailing to them until the cost exceeds our cost of signing up a new subscriber," Mr. Tillotson says. That can mean as many as eight mailings to those whose subscriptions have lapsed. However, higher postal rates have forced the company to cut the number of renewal mailings in recent years, he says.

Modern handcraft doesn't solicit pay-later subscriptions. "Every collection letter means an additional expense," Mr. Tillotson says. A subscription to The Workbasket is only $4, he notes, and the cost of a few dunning letters to a subscriber can eat up 10% of the subscription price.

Postal rates have become a significant cost for all publishers. But the new rates penalize smaller publications, Mr. Tillotson says, because to qualify for the lowest piece rate, six pieces of mail must be sent to the same postal zone. His magazines don't have six or more subscribers in many zones. The company's average mail rate is 23.6 cents a pound. An average issue weighs two ounces to 2½ ounces, he says. So postage runs three cents to 3.7 cents a copy. "One cent on a million copies is $10,000," he says to emphasize the effect of a seemingly small rate increase.

Mr. Tillotson closely oversees operations by doing everything except printing the magazines. That is done more economically outside. He went to computerized record keeping and learned programming before the change so he could hold his own with computer specialists. "I'd heard data processors were empire builders," he says.

Anyone with such aspirations would be in the wrong place at Modern Handcraft. Mr. Tillotson has halved his work force to 100 people since the first computer system was installed 18 years ago.

From Sanford L. Jacobs, "Specialty-Magazine Publisher Succeeding with a Difference," *The Wall Street Journal,* 14 September 1981, p. 29. Reprinted by permission of Wall Street Journal. Copyright Dow Jones and Company, Inc., 1981. All rights reserved.

Organizational Objectives

Two Categories of
Objectives in Organizations

Organizational objectives are the formal targets of the organization and are set to help the organization accomplish its purpose. They concern such areas as organizational efficiency, high productivity, and profit maximization. G. W. England conducted a study in which 1,072 upper-level managers were asked to rate eight different types of corporate objectives according to the objectives' (1) importance and (2) significance for company success. The results are presented in figure 3.2. Organizational efficiency, high productivity, and profit maximization were ranked one, two, and three respectively in terms of both importance and significance for company success. The eight types of objectives shown in figure 3.2 certainly do not reflect the only areas in which organizational objectives are made, but they probably do indicate the most common ones.

Individual Objectives

Individual objectives also exist within organizations. **Individual objectives** are the personal goals each organization member would like to reach as a result of his or her activity within the organization. These objectives might include high salary, personal growth and development, peer recognition, and societal recognition. Each individual within an organization has personal reasons for working now and for working or not working in the future.

Compatibility of
Organizational and
Individual Objectives

A management problem arises when organizational objectives and individual objectives are not compatible.[4] For example, a professor may have an individual goal of working at a university primarily to gain peer recognition. Perhaps she pursues this recognition primarily by channeling most of her effort and energies into research. This professor's individual objective could make a significant contribution to the attainment of organizational objectives if she happened to be at a university whose organizational objectives emphasize conducting research. On the other hand, her individual objective might contribute little or nothing to organizational goal attainment if she was employed at a primarily teaching-oriented university. Rather than improving her general teaching ability and the quality of her courses, as the university goals would suggest, she would be secluded in the library writing research-related articles.

One alternative managers have in situations of this type is to structure the organization so that individuals have the opportunity to accomplish individual objectives while contributing to organizational goal attainment. For example, the teaching-oriented university referred to in the previous paragraph could take steps to ensure that good teachers received peer recognition, such as an "excellence in teaching" award. In this way, professors could strive for their personal peer-recognition goal while also contributing to the university's organizational objective of good teaching.

Integration of Objectives

An objective or goal integration model can assist managers trying to understand and solve problems related to conflict between organizational and personal objectives. Jon Barrett's model, presented in figure 3.3, depicts a situation in which the goals or objectives in area C are the only individual goals (area A) compatible with organizational objectives (area B). Area C represents the extent of **goal integration.**

Overcoming Incompatibility
of Objectives

Managers should keep two things in mind about the individual depicted in the figure 3.3 model: (1) this individual will tend to work for goals in area C without much managerial encouragement because the attainment of these goals will result in some type of reward the individual considers valuable; and (2) this individual will usually not work for goals outside area A without some significant type of management encouragement because the attainment of these goals holds little promise of reward the individual considers valuable. Barrett suggests that "significant types of management encouragement" could be (1) modifications to existing pay schedules, (2) considerate treatment from superiors, and (3) additional opportunities to engage in informal social relationships with peers.

Introduction to Management

Figure 3.3 Goal integration model.

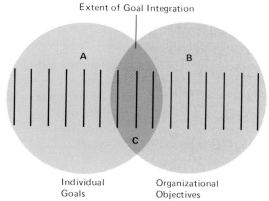

Extent of Goal Integration

A   B

C

Individual   Organizational
Goals   Objectives

From Jon H. Barrett, *Individual Goals and Organizational Objectives: A Study of Integration Mechanisms*, p. 5. Copyright © 1970 by the Institute for Social Research, The University of Michigan. Used with permission.

Back to the Case

After reading about the different types of objectives that generally exist in an organization, a manager like Dan Murray should easily see that working with objectives is no easy matter. Murray must identify organizational objectives and individual objectives that exist at MODC and then determine the extent of goal integration between them. He may have to encourage MODC employees to work towards achieving organizational objectives outside the area of integration by modifying pay schedules, treating his employees very considerately, and providing opportunities for employees to engage in informal social relationships with their peers.

Areas for Organizational Objectives

Peter F. Drucker, one of the most influential management writers of modern times, indicates that the very survival of a management system may be endangered if managers emphasize only a profit objective. This single-objective emphasis encourages managers to take action that will make money today with little regard for how a profit will be made tomorrow.[5]

In practice, managers should strive to develop and attain a variety of objectives in all management system areas where activity is critical to the operation and success of the system. The eight key areas in which Drucker advises managers to set management system objectives are:

1. *Market standing*   Managers should set objectives indicating where they would like to be in relation to their competitors.
2. *Innovation*   Managers should set objectives outlining their commitment to the development of new methods of operation.
3. *Productivity*   Managers should set objectives outlining target levels of production.
4. *Physical and financial resources*   Managers should set objectives with regard to use, acquisition, and maintenance of capital and monetary resources.
5. *Profitability*   Managers should set objectives that specify the profit the company would like to generate.
6. *Manager performance and development*   Managers should set objectives that specify rates and levels of managerial productivity and growth.

7. *Worker performance and attitude*   Managers should set objectives that specify rates and levels of worker productivity and attitudes.
8. *Public responsibility*   Managers should set objectives that indicate the company's responsibilities to its customers and society and to what extent the company intends to live up to those responsibilities.

Objectives and Controversy

According to Drucker, since the first five goal areas relate to tangible, impersonal characteristics of organizational operation, most managers would not dispute the designation of these as key areas. Designation of the last three as key areas could arouse some managerial opposition, however, since these areas are more personal and subjective. Regardless of potential opposition, an organization should have objectives in all eight areas to maximize its probability of success.

Working with Organizational Objectives

One Year or Less
One to Five Years
Five to Seven Years

What Is the Principle of the Objective?

Appropriate objectives are fundamental to the success of any organization. Theodore Levitt states that some leading industries may be on the verge of facing the same financial disaster as the railroads because of objectives inappropriate for their organizations.[6] Any manager, therefore, should approach the development, use, and modification of organizational objectives with utmost seriousness. In general, an organization should have (1) **short-run objectives** (targets to be achieved within one year or less), (2) **intermediate-run objectives** (targets to be achieved within from one to five years), and (3) **long-run objectives** (targets to be achieved within from five to seven years).

The necessity of predetermining appropriate organizational objectives has led to the development of what is called the principle of the objective. The **principle of the objective** is that before managers initiate any action, organizational objectives should be clearly determined, understood, and stated.[7]

Establishing Organizational Objectives

Three Steps in Establishing Objectives

The three main steps that managers must take to develop a set of working organizational objectives are: (1) determine the existence of any environmental trends that could significantly influence the operation of the organization; (2) develop a set of objectives for the organization as a whole; and (3) develop a hierarchy of organizational objectives. These three steps are interrelated and usually require input from several people at different levels and operational sections of the organization. Each step is further developed in the paragraphs that follow.

Analyzing Trends

How to Analyze the Environment

The first step in setting organizational objectives is to list major trends that have existed in the organizational environment over the past five years and determine if these trends have had a noticeable impact on organizational success. Conceivably, the trends could include such factors as marketing innovations of competitors; governmental controls; and social trends, such as the women's liberation movement. Management should then decide which present trends and which new trends are likely to affect organizational success over the next five years. This decision will determine what kinds of objectives are set at various levels of the organization.

Developing Objectives for the Organization as a Whole

After analyzing environmental trends, management should develop objectives that reflect this analysis for the organization as a whole. For example, the analysis may show that a major competitor has been continually improving its products over the past five years and, as a result, is gaining an increasingly larger share of the market. In reaction to this trend, management should set a product improvement objective in an effort to

Figure 3.4 Calculations for return on investment.

$$\text{Return on Investment} = \frac{\text{Total dollar amount earned}}{\text{Total dollar amount invested to keep organization operating}}$$

$$\text{Return on Investment} = \frac{\$50,000 \text{ (Earnings)}}{\$500,000 \text{ (Investment)}} = .10 = 10\% \text{ (Rate of return)}$$

keep up with competitors. This product improvement objective, then, directly results from identification of a trend within the organizational environment and also from the organizational purpose of profit.

The following paragraphs illustrate how management might set financial objectives, product-market mix objectives, and functional objectives for the organization as a whole:

Establishing Financial Objectives

In some organizations, government regulations guide management's setting of financial objectives. Managers of public utility organizations, for example, have definite guidelines specifying what types of financial objectives they are allowed to set. In organizations free from governmental constraints, the setting of financial objectives is influenced mainly by (1) return on investment and (2) financial comparison of an organization with its competitors.

Return on investment is the amount of money an organization earns in relation to the amount of money invested to keep the organization in operation.[8] Figure 3.4 shows how to use earnings of $50,000 and an investment of $500,000 to calculate a return on investment. If the calculated return on investment is too low, managers can set an overall objective to modify the organization's rate of return.

Information on organizational competition is available through published indexes, such as Dun and Bradstreet's "Ratios for Selected Industries." These ratios reflect industry averages for key financial areas. Comparing company figures with these industrial averages should tell management in which areas new financial objectives probably should be set or ways in which existing objectives should be modified.

Establishing Product-Market Mix Objectives

Product-market mix objectives outline which products—and the relative number or mix of these products—the organization will attempt to sell. Granger suggests the following five steps to formulate product-market mix objectives:[9]

1. Examination of key trends in the business environments of the product-market areas.
2. Examination of growth trends (both market and volume) and profit trends (for the industry and for the company) in the individual product mix areas.
3. Separation of product-market areas into those that are going to pull ahead and those that are going to drag. For promising areas these questions need to be asked: How can these areas be made to flourish? Should additional injections of capital, marketing effort, technology, management talent, or the like be used? For the less promising areas these questions are pertinent: Why is the product lagging? How can this be corrected? If it cannot be corrected, should the product be milked for whatever can be regained or should it be withdrawn from the market?
4. Consideration of the need or desirability of adding new products or market areas to the mix. In this regard, management should ask these questions: Is there a profit gap to be filled? Based on the criteria of profit opportunity,

Example of Overall Objectives:

1. Financial objectives

2. Product-market mix objectives

compatibility, and feasibility of entry, what are possible new areas of interest in order of priority? What sort of programs (acquisitions or internal development) does the company need to develop the desired level of business in these areas?

5. Derivation of an optimum yet realistic product-market mix profile based on the conclusions reached in steps 1–4. This profile embodies the product-market mix objectives, which should be consistent with the organization's financial objectives. Interaction while setting these two kinds of objectives is advisable.

Establishing Functional Objectives

3. Functional Objectives

All organizations have certain key functional areas, such as marketing, accounting, and personnel. Functional objectives that are consistent with the financial and product-market mix objectives should be developed for these areas. People in the organization should perform their functions in a way that helps the organization attain its other objectives.[10]

Back to the Case

The preceding information implies that MODC will be in serious trouble if it has only profit objectives. Management should also develop objectives in such areas as market standing, innovation, productivity, physical and financial resources, management performance and development, worker performance and attitude, and public responsibility. These objectives should generally be set for the short run, intermediate run, and long run.

Before developing any objectives, however, management should pinpoint any environmental trends that could influence MODC operations. Objectives that reflect the environmental trends could then be set for MODC as a whole. Such objectives normally would include financial and product-market mix objectives.

Developing a Hierarchy of Objectives

In practice, an organizational objective must be broken down into subobjectives so that individuals in different levels and sections of the organization know what they must do to help reach the overall organizational objective.[11] An organizational objective is attained only after the subobjectives have been reached.

Overall Organizational Objective and Assigned Subobjectives

The overall organizational objective and the subobjectives assigned to the various people or units of the organization are referred to as a **hierarchy of objectives.** Figure 3.5 presents a sample hierarchy of objectives for a middle-sized company.

Conflicting Subobjectives

Suboptimization exists when subobjectives are conflicting or not directly aimed at accomplishing the overall organizational objective. Figure 3.5 shows that suboptimization could exist within this company between the first subobjective for the finance and accounting department and the second subobjective for the supervisors. Suboptimization would result if supervisors needed new equipment to maintain production and the finance and accounting department couldn't approve the loan without company borrowing surpassing 50 percent of company assets. In this situation, established subobjectives would be aimed in different directions. A manager would have to choose which subobjective would best contribute to obtaining overall objectives and should therefore take precedence.

Figure 3.6 illustrates suboptimization. Managers can attempt to minimize suboptimization by (1) developing a thorough understanding of how various parts of the organization relate to one another and (2) making sure that subobjectives properly reflect these relationships.

Figure 3.5 Hierarchy of objectives for a medium-sized organization.

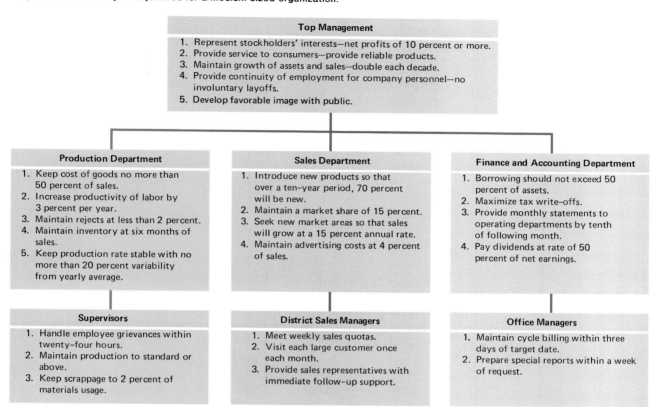

Top Management

1. Represent stockholders' interests—net profits of 10 percent or more.
2. Provide service to consumers—provide reliable products.
3. Maintain growth of assets and sales—double each decade.
4. Provide continuity of employment for company personnel—no involuntary layoffs.
5. Develop favorable image with public.

Production Department

1. Keep cost of goods no more than 50 percent of sales.
2. Increase productivity of labor by 3 percent per year.
3. Maintain rejects at less than 2 percent.
4. Maintain inventory at six months of sales.
5. Keep production rate stable with no more than 20 percent variability from yearly average.

Sales Department

1. Introduce new products so that over a ten-year period, 70 percent will be new.
2. Maintain a market share of 15 percent.
3. Seek new market areas so that sales will grow at a 15 percent annual rate.
4. Maintain advertising costs at 4 percent of sales.

Finance and Accounting Department

1. Borrowing should not exceed 50 percent of assets.
2. Maximize tax write-offs.
3. Provide monthly statements to operating departments by tenth of following month.
4. Pay dividends at rate of 50 percent of net earnings.

Supervisors

1. Handle employee grievances within twenty-four hours.
2. Maintain production to standard or above.
3. Keep scrappage to 2 percent of materials usage.

District Sales Managers

1. Meet weekly sales quotas.
2. Visit each large customer once each month.
3. Provide sales representatives with immediate follow-up support.

Office Managers

1. Maintain cycle billing within three days of target date.
2. Prepare special reports within a week of request.

Joseph L. Massie, John Douglas, MANAGING, © 1973, p. 221. Reprinted by permission of Prentice-Hall, Inc., Englewood Cliffs, New Jersey.

Figure 3.6 Suboptimization.

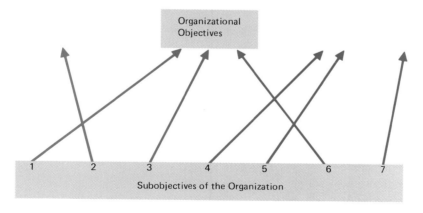

Organizational Objectives

1 2 3 4 5 6 7

Subobjectives of the Organization

Guidelines for Establishing Quality Objectives

As with all humanly developed commodities, the quality of goal statements can vary drastically. Managers can increase the quality of their objectives, however, by following some general guidelines:

1. *Managers should allow the people responsible for attaining the objectives to have a voice in setting them*   Often, the people responsible for attaining the objectives know their job situation better than the managers do and can help to make the objectives more realistic. Work-related problems that these people face should be thoroughly considered when trying to develop meaningful objectives.

2. *Managers should state objectives as specifically as possible*   Precise statements will minimize confusion and misunderstanding and ensure that the employees have explicit directions for what they should do.

3. *Managers should relate objectives to specific actions whenever necessary*   In this way employees will not have to infer what they should do to accomplish their goals.

4. *Managers should pinpoint expected results*   Employees should know exactly how managers will determine whether or not an objective has been reached.

Making Objectives Effective

5. *Managers should set goals high enough that employees will have to strive to meet them, but not so high that employees give up trying to meet them*   Managers want employees to work hard, but not to be frustrated.

6. *Managers should specify when goals are expected to be achieved*   Employees must know the time frame for accomplishing their objectives. They then can be somewhat flexible and pace themselves accordingly.

7. *Managers should set objectives only in relation to other organizational objectives*   In this way conflicting objectives or suboptimization can be kept to a minimum.

8. *Managers should state objectives clearly and simply*   The written or spoken word should not get in the way of communicating a goal to organization members.

Guidelines for Making Objectives Operational

Objectives must be stated in operational terms. That is, if an organization has **operational objectives,** managers should be able to tell if the objectives are being attained by comparing the actual results with goal statements.

For example, assume that a physical education instructor has set the following set of objectives for the students enrolled in the class:

1. Each student will strive to develop a sense of balance.
2. Each student will attempt to become flexible.
3. Each student will try to become agile.
4. Each student will try to become strong.
5. Each student will work on becoming powerful.
6. Each student will strive to become durable.

These objectives are not operational because the activities or operations a student must perform to attain them are not specified. Additional information, however, can easily make the objectives operational. For example, the fifth physical education objective could be replaced with: Each student will strive to develop the power to do

Figure 3.7 Nonoperational objectives vs. operational objectives.

Nonoperational Objectives	Operational Objectives
1. Improve product quality.	1. Reduce quality rejects to 2 percent.
2. Improve communications.	2. Hold weekly staff meetings and initiate a newsletter to improve communications.
3. Improve social responsibility.	3. Hire fifty hard-core unemployed each year.
4. Issue monthly accounting reports on a more timely basis.	4. Issue monthly accounting reports so they are received three days following the close of the accounting period.

From *Management: Concepts and Situations* by Howard M. Carlisle. © 1976, Science Research Associates, Inc. Adapted by permission.

After objectives have been set for MODC as a whole, management should develop a hierarchy of objectives for the organization. The development of the hierarchy would entail breaking down MODC's overall objectives into subobjectives so that all individuals within the company know what they must do to help MODC reach its overall objectives. In establishing this hierarchy of objectives, however, MODC management must be careful not to suboptimize or establish subobjectives that conflict with one another.

MODC management should set objectives that are clear, consistent, challenging, and specific. Perhaps most important of all, MODC objectives should be operational. Also, allowing workers to participate in establishing MODC objectives will help to ensure that the objectives are realistic and that MODC employees will be committed to reaching them.

Back to the Case

---

standing-broad jumps the distance of his or her height plus one foot. Figure 3.7 shows four basically nonoperational objectives and how each can be modified to be made operational.

Obtaining Objectives

Attainment of organizational objectives is the obvious goal of all conscientious managers. Managers quickly discover, however, that moving the organization toward goal attainment requires taking appropriate means or actions within the organization to reach the desired end. This process is called means-ends analysis.

Basically, **means-ends analysis** entails "(1) starting with the general goal to be achieved; (2) discovering a set of means, very generally specified, for accomplishing this goal; and (3) taking each of these means, in turn, as a new subgoal and discovering a more detailed means for achieving it."[12] Figure 3.8 shows a possible relationship between means and ends in an organizational setting.

What Is Means-ends Analysis?

Effective managers are aware of the importance of not only setting organizational objectives, but clearly outlining the means by which these objectives can be attained. They know that means-ends analysis is important for guiding their own activities as well as for those of their subordinates. The better everyone within the organization understands the means by which goals are to be attained, the greater the probability that the goals actually will be reached.

Figure 3.8 Relationship between means and ends.

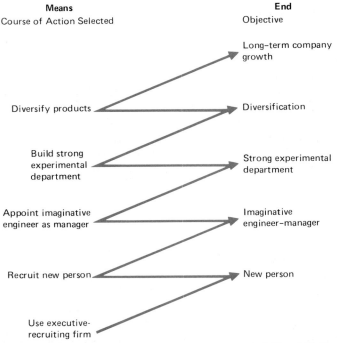

Newman, Summer, Warren, THE PROCESS OF MANAGEMENT, 2nd ed., © 1967, p. 383. Reprinted by permission of Prentice-Hall, Inc., Englewood Cliffs, New Jersey.

How to Use Objectives

As stated previously, organizaional objectives flow naturally from organizational purpose and reflect the organization's environment. Managers must have a firm understanding of the influences that mold organizational objectives because as these influences change, the objectives themselves must change. Objectives are not unchangeable directives. In fact, a significant managerial responsibility is to help the organization to change objectives when a change is necessary.

Management by Objectives (MBO)

Some managers believe that organizational objectives are such an important and fundamental part of management that they use a management approach based exclusively on organizational objectives. This management approach, called **management by objectives (MBO),** has been popularized mainly through the writings of Peter Drucker, [13, 14] and basically has three main characteristics:

1. All individuals within an organization are assigned a specialized set of objectives that they try to reach during a normal operating period. These objectives are mutually set and agreed upon by individuals and their managers.
2. Performance reviews are conducted periodically to determine how close individuals are to attaining their objectives.
3. Rewards are given to individuals on the basis of how close they come to reaching their goals.[15]

Factors Necessary for a Successful MBO Program

Certain key factors are necessary for an MBO program to be successful.[16] First, appropriate goals must be set by top managers of the organization. All individual MBO goals are based on these overall objectives. If overall objectives are inappropriate, individual MBO objectives also will be inappropriate, and the related individual work activity will be nonproductive. Second, managers and subordinates together must develop and agree on each individual's goals. Both managers and subordinates must feel that the individual objectives are just and appropriate if each party is to use them seriously as a guide for action. Third, employee performance should be conscientiously evaluated against established objectives. This evaluation will help to determine if the objectives are fair and if appropriate means are being used to attain them. Fourth, management must follow through on the employee performance evaluations and reward employees accordingly.[17] All organization members must realize that the MBO effort is a serious one and that employees, therefore, should seriously perform their designated roles.

MBO Programs: Advantages and Disadvantages

The rise in popularity of MBO programs in organizations has been obvious. Many managers seem to be willing and eager to manage by objectives. Experienced MBO managers say that there are two advantages to this management approach. First, MBO programs continually emphasize what should be done in an organization to achieve organizational goals. Second, the MBO process secures employee commitment to attaining organizational goals. Because managers and subordinates have developed objectives together, both parties are more interested in working together to reach those goals.

Managers also admit that MBO programs have disadvantages.[18] One disadvantage is that because organization members develop objectives together, they actually have less time in which to do their work. MBO programs also seem to generate a large volume of paperwork. Elaborate written goals, careful communication of goals, and detailed performance evaluations naturally increase the volume of paperwork in an organization.

Most managers seem to think, however, that MBO's advantages outweigh its disadvantages and that, overall, MBO programs are beneficial.

MODC management should not only make sure that an appropriate set of organizational objectives has been developed but also that the means by which these objectives can be attained are clearly outlined for MODC employees. MODC management should also remember that as the environment and other conditions change, MODC objectives should change accordingly.

After carefully analyzing the MODC situation, management may decide to initiate an MBO program in the company. If so, each MODC employee should develop with his or her manager a set of mutually agreed upon objectives. Performance reviews should give employees feedback on their progress in achieving these goals, and rewards should be given to those employees who make the most progress.

Back to the Case

Summary

The following points are stressed within this chapter:

1. Organizational objectives are the targets toward which the organization is directed and they flow naturally from the purpose of the organization. Organizational objectives are important in that they indicate what action should or should not be taken.

2. Managers should (1) know that both organizational and personal objectives exist in organizations and try to maximize consistency between them; (2) set objectives in critical areas that reflect present and/or future trends in the environment; and (3) establish a hierarchy of objectives to give direction to the various segments and levels within an organization.

3. Managers should make organizational objectives operational and pinpoint the means through which the objectives can be reached. Such objectives should not be considered rigid targets, but should should be reviewed periodically and modified whenever necessary to better serve the purpose of the organization.

4. Management by objectives (MBO) is a management approach based exclusively on organizational objectives. MBO primarily involves: (1) organization members and their managers generating a set of mutually agreed upon organizational objectives for individual organization members; (2) managers evaluating organization members on how close they come to reaching their goals; and (3) managers rewarding organization members based on this evaluation.

Issues for Review and Discussion

1. What are organizational objectives and how do they relate to organizational purpose?
2. Explain why objectives are important to an organization.
3. List four areas in which organizational objectives can act as important guidelines for performance.
4. Explain the difference between organizational objectives and individual objectives.
5. What is meant by goal integration?
6. List and define eight key areas in which organizational objectives should be set.
7. How do environmental trends affect the process of establishing organizational objectives?
8. How does return on investment relate to setting financial objectives?
9. Define product-market mix objectives. What process should a manager go through to establish them?
10. What are functional objectives?
11. What is a hierarchy of objectives?
12. Explain the purpose of a hierarchy of objectives.
13. How does suboptimization relate to a hierarchy of objectives?
14. List eight guidelines a manager should follow to establish quality organizational objectives.
15. How does a manager make objectives operational?
16. Explain the concept of means-ends analysis.
17. Should a manager ever modify or change existing organizational ojectives? If no, why? If yes, when?
18. Define MBO and describe its main characteristics.
19. List and describe the factors necessary for an MBO program to be successful.
20. Discuss the advantages and disadvantages of MBO.

Chacko, Thomas I.; Stone, Thomas H.; and Brief, Arthur P. "Participation in Goal-Setting Programs: An Attributional Analysis." *Academy of Management Review* 4, no. 3, (July1979): 433–38.

Cyert, Richard M., and March, James G. *A Behavioral Theory of the Firm.* Englewood Cliffs, N.J.: Prentice-Hall, 1963.

Dowst, Somerby (C.P.M.). "Classify Your Objectives." *Purchasing* 25 (April 1979): 38.

Drucker, Peter. *Managing for Results.* New York: Harper & Row Publishers, 1964.

Etzioni, Amitai. *Modern Organizations.* Englewood Cliffs, N.J.: Prentice-Hall, 1964.

Flippo, Edwin B. *Management: A Behavioral Approach.* Boston: Allyn & Bacon, 1966.

Frisbie, Gilbert, and Mabert, Vincent A. "Crystal Ball vs. System: The Forecasting Dilemma." *Business Horizons* 24 (September/October 1981): 72–76.

Godiwalla, Yezdi M.; Meinhart, Wayne A.; and Warde, William A. "General Management and Corporate Strategy." *Managerial Planning* 30, no. 2 (September/October 1981): 17–23, 19.

Hughes, Charles L. *Goal Setting.* New York: American Management Association, 1965.

Koontz, Harold, and O'Donnell, Cyril. *Principles of Management.* 3d ed. New York: McGraw-Hill, 1964.

McFarland, Dalton E. *Management: Principles and Practices.* New York: Macmillan, 1964.

Miller, D. W., and Starr, M. K. *Executive Decisions and Operations Research.* Englewood Cliffs, N.J.: Prentice-Hall, 1960.

Newman, William H. *Administrative Action.* Englewood Cliffs, N.J.: Prentice-Hall, 1963.

Odiorne, George S. *Management by Objectives.* Belmont, Calif.: Pitman Publishing Corporation, 1965.

Odiorne, George S. *Management Decision by Objectives.* Englewood Cliffs, N.J.: Prentice-Hall, 1969.

Scanlan, Burt K. "Maintaining Organizational Effectiveness—A Prescription for Good Health." *Personnel Journal* 59 (May 1980): 381, 422.

Schleh, Edward C. *Management by Results.* New York: McGraw-Hill, 1969.

Wikstrom, Walter S. *Managing by—and with—Objectives.* New York: National Industrial Conference Board, 1968.

Sources of Additional Information

1. James F. Lincoln, "Intelligent Selfishness and Manufacturing," Bulletin 434 (New York: Lincoln Electric Company).

2. John F. Mee, "Management Philosophy for Professional Executives," *Business Horizons,* December 1956, p. 7.

3. Marshall E. Dimock, *The Executive in Action* (New York: Harper & Brothers, 1945), p. 54.

4. Thomas J. Murray, "The Unseen Corporate 'War'," *Dun's Review,* June 1980, pp. 110–14.

5. Peter F. Drucker, *The Practice of Management* (New York: Harper & Row, 1954), pp. 62–65, 126–29

6. Theodore Levitt, "Marketing Myopia," *Harvard Business Review,* July-August 1960, p. 45.

7. Mee, "Management Philosophy for Professional Executives," p. 7.

8. Joseph G. Louderback and George E. Manners, Jr., "Integrating ROI and CVP," *Management Accounting,* April 1981, pp. 33–39.

9. Adapted, by permission of the publisher, from "How to Set Company Objectives," by Charles H. Granger, *Management Review,* July 1970. © 1970 by American Management Association, Inc. All rights reserved.

10. Granger, "How to Set Company Objectives," p. 7.

11. Charles H. Granger, "The Hierarchy of Objectives," *Harvard Business Review,* May-June 1964, pp. 63–74.

12. James G. March and Herbert A Simon, *Organizations* (New York: John Wiley & Sons, 1958), p. 191.

13. Drucker, *The Practice of Management.*

14. Peter Drucker, Harold Smiddy, and Ronald G. Greenwood, "Management by Objectives," *The Academy of Management Review* 6, no. 2 (April 1981): 225

15. For a more detailed analysis of these characteristics, see Henry L. Tosi, John R. Rizzo, and Stephen J. Carroll, "Setting Goals in Management by Objectives," *California Management Review,* Summer 1970, pp. 70–78.

16. For characteristics that usually make an MBO program unsuccessful, see Dale D. McConkey, "Twenty Ways to Kill Management by Objectives," *Management Review,* October 1972, pp. 4–13.

17. William H. Franklin, Jr., "Create an Atmosphere of Positive Expectations," *Administrative Management,* April 1980, pp. 32–34.

18. Charles H. Ford, "Manage by Decisions, Not By Objectives," *Business Horizons,* February 1980, pp. 7–18.

Notes

Concluding Case 3
South Africa's Barlow Rand

(Photo: Mitchell Osborne, The Image Bank)

Major corporations in South Africa are faced with a dichotomous situation. On the one hand, the companies have tremendous opportunities to utilize the many natural resources of South Africa. Yet, they are unable to reap the rewards from these resources due to frequent strikes and shortage of skilled workers, which, in many instances, are a result of South Africa's discriminatory racial laws and customs. Specifically, these problems are quite detrimental to labor-intensive companies. One such company, Barlow Rand Ltd. (South Africa's largest industrial conglomerate) has redesigned its corporate strategy to combat the situation.

The company is primarily concerned with achieving a secure labor force, which is quite difficult to attain due to the apartheid policies of the country. South Africa's overall economy grew 8 percent in 1980. However, the country contains one million unskilled, unemployed blacks. For those blacks who are employed, companies must receive government permission, on an individual basis, to promote an unskilled worker to a skilled-apprentice position. Presently there are approximately 100,000 vacancies in skilled jobs. In addition, at professional levels in 1981, it is expected there will be three openings for each engineering graduate. To add to the problem, a series of illegal strikes by blacks occurred in 1980.

Recognizing the potential impact that these problems can have on the long-term success of the company, Barlow Rand Ltd. has adopted a "head-on" confrontation approach. One immediately observable adjustment is that top executives are spending a tremendous amount of time planning and implementing new labor programs. A. M. Rosholt wants to change the company's strategy from growth by acquisition to internal growth. He, therefore, feels that labor relations are too important for personnel specialists to handle; for labor relations to be successful, Rosholt insists on top management involvement. A productive labor force is crucial for organizational survival.

During the past fifty-three years, Barlow Rand has risen from a family-owned trading company to a large conglomerate. In 1927 the company began selling Caterpillar farm and construction equipment. It made its debut in the mining business in 1971 by acquiring Rand Mines Ltd., which mines coal and 10 percent of South Africa's gold, and in 1980 acquired a controlling interest in C. G. Smith and Company, the nation's largest sugar producer and manufacturer of chemicals and flooring. Many other acquisitions and investments have provided the company with sales of $4.6 billion and profits of $456.8 million in 1980.

The company's growth through acquisition may be coming to a halt. According to Rosholt, the company has acquired just about everything that is available in South Africa. In addition, foreign acquisitions are highly unlikely as the country's foreign-exchange controls make it extremely expensive to export capital. The company is left with the strategy of internal growth, with labor being its potentially greatest problem. And a problem it is, as the company forecasters predict that Barlow Rand may have a 30 percent shortage of skilled labor within the next three years. For a company that employs 191,000 people, 75 percent of which are black and 10 percent Asian, the problem will be difficult to correct. For two years the company has been haggling with government officials to gain permission to elevate blacks to skilled apprentice status. The results of the two-year negotiations have been slight as the company was allowed to raise only eight blacks to skilled-apprentice positions.

In addition to government negotiations, Rosholt has implemented several programs to gain the favor of skeptical black union leaders. First, the company is recognizing black unions regardless of union size or whether they are registered with the government. Secondly, the company intends to raise black wages to base wage and salary increases on job performances rather than race. Finally, Barlow Rand has established forty-five literacy centers to aid in the transition of the blacks from unskilled to skilled jobs.

Rosholt has also made it clear to his divisional managers that he expects the new labor policies to be precisely implemented. He has required each division to make an annual labor-relations report directly to him and has asked divisions to evaluate each other's plans. Recently Rosholt conducted two of these evaluative meetings demonstrating his keen interest in the improvement of labor relations.

The benefits of the new policies have been demonstrated recently. Several South African companies such as Ford, Goodyear, Toyota, and others were confronted with a series of wildcat strikes; Barlow Rand remained unscathed.

This case is based upon "Barlow Rand: Seeking a Stable Labor Force," *Business Week*, 9 February 1981, p. 90, 92.

Discussion Issues

1. What appear to be the primary organizational objectives of Barlow Rand Ltd.? Which do you feel is probably weighted more heavily at this time?
2. What do you suppose the objectives of the black laborers might be after examining the policies the company is implementing?
3. Can Barrett's Goal Integration Model be used to explain the situation facing many of South Africa's labor intensive firms? Explain.
4. Is Barlow Rand Ltd. using the management by objectives approach? Explain your answer.

Planning is one of the four major management functions that must be performed for organizations to have long-run success. The material in this section flows smoothly from section 1. Section 1 introduced the topic of management and ended with a discussion of organizational objectives. According to generally accepted management theory, once managers have developed organizational objectives they are ready to start planning.

Chapter 4, "Fundamentals of Planning," defines planning as the process of determining how an organization will get where it wants to go. Thus, the fundamental purpose of planning is to accomplish organizational objectives. Strategic and tactical planning as well as the steps of the planning process are discussed. Strategy and strategy management are discussed as part of strategic planning. In addition, three primary approaches to planning—the high probability approach, the maximizing approach, and the adaptive approach—are presented. A combination of these three approaches is suggested as the most useful approach in most management situations.

The planning process inevitably involves making decisions. Chapter 5, "Making Decisions," defines a decision as a choice made between two or more alternatives. Various types of decisions and a format for determining who is responsible for making those decisions are discussed. Also covered in this chapter are the six elements of the decision situation: (1) the state of nature, (2) the decision maker, (3) goals to be served, (4) relevant alternatives, (5) ordering of alternatives, and (6) a choice of alternatives. Combinations of these elements are shown to make up the five steps of the decision-making process. Decision-making conditions—complete certainty, complete uncertainty, and risk—also are discussed in chapter 5. In addition, the analytical tools that can help managers make decisions that minimize risk—probability theory and decision trees—are explained and illustrated.

Chapter 6 explains various plans that should be made within an organization and the tools available to make the plans. A plan is defined as specific action proposed to help an organization achieve its objectives. Critical dimensions of plans that managers should scrutinize during plan development are also discussed in this chapter. These dimensions are the degree to which the plan is used over and over again (re-petitiveness dimension); the amount of time the plan covers (time dimension); the portion of the organization the plan covers (scope dimension); and the level of the organization the plan addresses (level dimension). Based primarily upon the repetitiveness dimension, plans are categorized into standing plans (those used over and over again) and single-use plans (those used only a few times). A discussion of why plans fail and an explanation of plant facilities planning and human resources planning follow.

Chapter 6 also covers forecasting and scheduling. The specific, usable forecasting techniques presented are the jury of executive opinion method, the sales force estimation method, and the time series analysis method. Guidelines for choosing a particular forecasting method and information on the use of the product life cycle during the forecasting period are also explained. In discussing scheduling, Gantt charts and PERT (program evaluation and review techniques) are covered in detail.

The central theme of chapter 7, "Implementing the Planning Process," is that plans are only as good as the process the manager implements to develop them. Implementation based on a subsystem approach is recommended. A discussion on planning and the chief executive follows in which it is noted that the chief executive of the organization is not always the primary organizational planner. Instead, an appointed planner whose primary responsibility is organizational planning may work closely with the chief executive.

Organizational planners are presented as individuals who should have the following qualifications: (1) they should have some experience in the organization for which they are planning; (2) they should be able to see the organization as a whole; (3) they should be able to detect and react to important environmental trends; and (4) they should get along well with others. Their main duties are described as evaluating the present planning process, assessing planning needs, projecting planning benefits, designing the planning subsystem, and developing a work timetable. It is recommended that planners ensure planning process success by persuading top management to clearly demonstrate its support of the planning process, by designing an appropriate planning subsystem, by maintaining an implementation-focused planning orientation, and by obtaining input from the right people.

Section 2
Planning

Student Learning Objectives

From studying this chapter I will attempt to acquire:

1. A definition of planning and an understanding of its purposes
2. A knowledge of the advantages and potential disadvantages of planning
3. An understanding of the types of planning and how they should be used
4. An understanding of how planning relates to various levels of management
5. Insights on how the major steps of the planning process are related
6. Definitions for the three approaches to planning
7. A personal philosophy concerning which approach to planning should be used

Chapter Outline

Fundamentals of Planning

Introductory Case 4
Planning for Planning

In a way, the line managers of the company were relieved when they realized that they themselves were responsible for planning. They certainly did not want any outsider or staff person to tell them what they were going to do.

On the other hand, planning was entirely new to them and they had a difficult time deciding where to start, just what to do, and when to do it. All of them seemed to go off in different directions, as the company president remarked in a staff meeting. It appeared that the cost of independence was too high. They needed help.

"Do we need to organize to plan, and if so, how do we relate organizational structure to corporate growth?" asked the president.

"I think we ought to relate organizational planning to the present. Let the future take care of itself," said the controller.

"You can't really do that either, if our plans are going to run for over a year," observed the director of marketing.

"It is important not to overlook the need for procedures and standard forms if we are going to plan," said the director of administration.

"Before we get through, I'll bet our company plan will cost us thousands of dollars," the controller thought out loud.

"The more I think of it, the more I'm sure we need some kind of organizational structure. I'm willing to plan, but somebody has to show me when and how and about what," said the director of manufacturing.

"Perhaps the best thing for us to do," the president replied, "is to develop a plan to plan for this corporation's next fiscal year."

From ESSENTIALS OF MANAGEMENT by Harold Koontz. Copyright © 1978 by McGraw-Hill Book Company. Used with permission of Mc-Graw-Hill Book Co.

Discussion Issues

1. Evaluate the controller's statement that the future of the organization should take care of itself.
2. What is meant by "planning for planning"?
3. What factors should be considered in the president's plan for planning?

Planning

What's Ahead

The introductory case makes the obvious point that managers must know how to plan. The material in this chapter describes the fundamentals of planning as managers should understand them. Specifically, this chapter (1) outlines the general characteristics of planning; (2) discusses various types of planning; (3) lists and explains the steps in the planning process; and (4) presents various approaches to planning.

Defining Planning

In essence, **planning** is the process of determining how the organization can get where it wants to go. Chapter 3 emphasized the importance of organizational objectives and explained how to develop them. Planning is the process of determining exactly what the organization will do to accomplish its objectives. In more formal terms, planning has been defined as "the systematic development of action programs aimed at reaching agreed business objectives by the process of analyzing, evaluating, and selecting among the opportunities which are foreseen."[1]

Purposes of Planning

Over the years, management writers have presented several different purposes of planning. For example, C. W. Roney indicates that organizational planning has two purposes: protective and affirmative. The protective purpose of planning is to minimize risk by reducing the uncertainties surrounding business conditions and clarifying the consequences of related management action. The affirmative purpose of planning is to increase the degree of organizational success.[2] Still another purpose of planning is to establish a coordinated effort within the organization. An absence of planning is usually accompanied by an absence of coordination and, therefore, usually contributes to organizational inefficiency.

The fundamental purpose of planning, however, is to help the organization reach its objectives. As stated by Koontz and O'Donnell, the primary purpose of planning is to "facilitate the accomplishment of enterprise and objectives."[3] All other purposes of planning are simply spin-offs of this fundamental purpose.

Planning: Advantages and Potential Disadvantages

A vigorous planning program has many advantages. One advantage to planning is that it helps managers to be future oriented. They are forced to look beyond their normal everyday problems to project what may face them in the future. Managers who look only at the present and neglect the future seem headed toward certain failure. Decision coordination is a second advantage of a sound planning program. A decision should not be made today without some idea of how it will affect a decision that will have to be made tomorrow. The planning function assists managers in their efforts to coordinate their decisions. A third advantage to planning is that it emphasizes organizational objectives. Since organizational objectives are the starting points for planning, managers are constantly reminded of exactly what their organization is trying to accomplish.

General Characteristics of Planning

How Will Organization Get Where It Wants to Go?

Protective Purpose
Affirmative Purpose
Coordination Purpose

Fundamental Purpose

Emphasizes Future
Coordinates Decisions
Emphasizes Objectives

CROCK by Rechin, Parker and Wilder, © Field Enterprises, Inc., 1976, Courtesy Field Newspaper Syndicate.

There is some evidence that, as a group, most managers feel that planning is extremely advantageous to the organization. In a study by Steiglitz, 280 managers were asked to assess the relative importance of such functions as public relations, organizational meetings, organizational planning, and organizational control. Over 65 percent of these managers ranked planning as the most important function.[4] Exhibit 4 contains the ideas of Jack Mitchell, a top manager at Scientific Data Systems, concerning the advantages of planning.

Potential Disadvantages

If the planning function is not well executed within the organization, however, planning may have several disadvantages. For example, an overemphasized planning program could take too much managerial time. Managers must strike an appropriate balance between time spent on planning and time spent on their other functions of organizing, influencing, and controlling. If they don't, some activities that are extremely important to the success of the organization may be neglected. Usually, the disadvantages of planning result from the planning function being used incorrectly.[5] Overall, planning's advantages generally outweigh its disadvantages.

Profits and Planning

In previous sections of this chapter, a case has been built for the importance of planning and the advantages of managers using some type of planning process. Perhaps the most convincing information supporting effective managerial planning is the typical relationship that exists between managerial planning and organizational profits. A study conducted by D. W. Karger analyzed a group of organizations from 1960 to 1970. Figure 4.1 shows that Karger found (1) a trend within this group toward increasing the use of formal planning programs rather than informal planning programs and (2) an accompanying trend of higher and higher pretax profits.[6]

Primacy of Planning

Foundation Function

Planning is the primary management function—the function that precedes and is the foundation for the organizing, influencing, and controlling functions of managers. Only after managers have developed their plans can they determine how they want to structure their organization, place their people, and establish organizational controls. As discussed in chapter 1, planning, organizing, influencing, and controlling are interrelated. Planning is the foundation function and the first function to be performed. Organizing, influencing, and controlling are interrelated and based upon the results of planning. Figure 4.2 shows this relationship.

Figure 4.1 Trend toward increased formal planning programs and higher pretax profits.

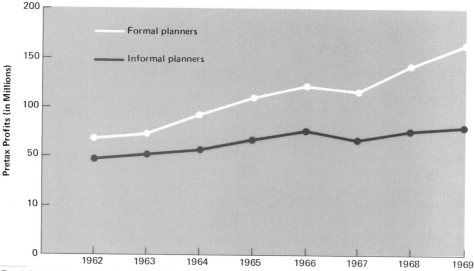

Reprinted with permission from *Long-Range Planning*, vol. 6, D. W. Karger, "Integrated Formal Long-Range Planning and How to Do It," Copyright 1973, Pergamon Press, Ltd.

Figure 4.2 Planning as the foundation for organizing, influencing, and controlling.

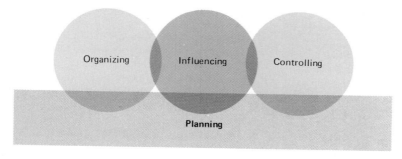

Back to the Case

Managers such as the ones in the introductory case should realize from reading this section that planning is the process of determining what the management system should do to reach its objectives and that, in fact, the primary purpose of planning is to assist the organization in reaching its objectives. Despite their apparent lack of knowledge about the planning function, the managers in the case are on the right track. They should seriously continue their pursuit of planning activities because of the many related benefits. One particularly notable advantage is probable increased profits. The planning process, however, if used inappropriately, also has potential disadvantages. Planning is the primary management function and these managers should not begin to organize, influence, or control until the planning process has been completed. Planning is the foundation management function upon which all other functions within their organization should be based.

Exhibit 4

Planning Advantages at Scientific Data Systems

Eighteen years ago, Jack Mitchell was one of the founders of Scientific Data Systems (SDS), one of the most successful computer companies of the 1960s. He retired a millionaire at 42 after Xerox Corp. bought SDS, which then had sales of more than $100 million. Last year, at age 55, he and several colleagues from SDS started all over again with a company named, once again, Scientific Data Systems. They produce small business computers Mitchell designed during his early retirement.

Many small company executives seem to think a comprehensive business plan is wasteful and unnecessary, something only the big companies do. For me, with this company, it's absolutely essential. It's a road map we use, a modus operandi, and if we're successful it will be in part because of the business plan.

Many small companies probably think they don't have sufficient information and data to formulate a plan. But that isn't the point. Preparing a plan forces you to understand what you want to do and how and when you can do it.

I developed our business plan from extensive research on production, marketing, and operations. It's for three years out and, with more than 50 pages, is four times bigger than the one we had at the old company. I wanted every detail. Running a business is difficult enough without not knowing what you're doing. On production, for instance, before we started I took a complete parts list for making a computer and determined the total cost of producing a unit, including labor. I came within $100 of the actual per unit cost. Knowing that was critical to our plans for marketing and operations.

It was a terrible job writing the plan, absolutely painful. I had the whole thing in my mind and thought I would rip it off in two days. But even with the original SDS experience and with a product already developed, I didn't realize how little I really knew. It took three weeks of steady, hard work to complete the plan.

You keep asking yourself, How am I going to build the product? Who will buy it? What's the competition? Will I be able to compete with them? How will I sell it? What financing is needed now, a year, two years from now? What will the cash flow be for those periods? It took time and pain but the answers came. Then we knew we had both a product and a company.

There's a secondary advantage to having a complete plan. It can make it easier to obtain financing. If the plan makes sense, the chances are better for obtaining the financing, whether starting up or ongoing.

Once you've got a plan it has to be kept current by continually researching the competition and your product, making changes if necessary but keeping ahead of day-to-day operations. The projections of performance and operations a year or two out are milestones to aim for. You always know where you are, and if you don't make it to the next milestone, at least you can find out why from the plan.

Our business plan also is essential to me personally for charting my own future. I've learned you take a beating running a small company, and I can't say I really enjoy it. What I do is design and build computers, and I'd like to get out of the financial side and the daily operations. But I'm a penny pincher, and I'm being cautious about increasing the executive staff until we have the level of cash flow the business plan says would warrant the addition of people. Now that the minus signs are beginning to be replaced by pluses behind the cash flow, I check the document with even greater interest.

Reprinted with permission of *INC.* magazine, June 1979.

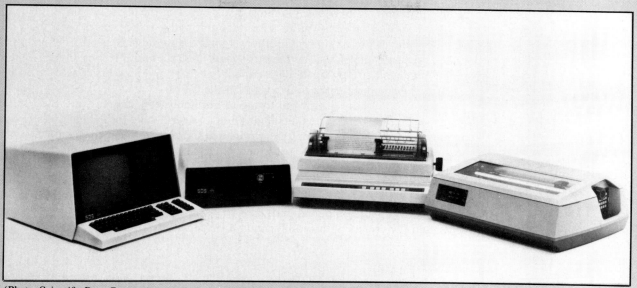

(Photo: Scientific Data Systems)

Types of Planning

In general, most planning activities can be divided into two types: tactical planning and strategic planning. An explanation and comparison of each of these types and an outline of how they should be used follows.

Strategic Planning

Long-range Planning

Strategic planning is long-range planning that focuses on the organization as a whole. Managers consider the organization as a total unit and ask themselves what must be done in the long run to attain organizational goals. Long range is usually defined as a period of time extending about three to five years into the future. Hence, in long-range planning managers are trying to determine what their organization should do to be successful at some point three to five years in the future.

Managers may have a problem trying to decide exactly how far into the future they should extend their strategic planning. As a general rule, they should follow the **commitment principle.** The commitment principle states that managers should commit funds for planning only if they can anticipate, in the foreseeable future, a return on planning expenses as a result of the long-range planning analysis. Realistically, planning costs are an investment and, therefore, should not be incurred unless a reasonable return on that investment is anticipated. The following sections elaborate further upon strategic planning by (1) defining strategy; (2) outlining the strategy management process; and (3) discussing how to formulate strategy.

What Is the Commitment Principle?

Defining Strategy

Purpose of Objectives Strategy

Strategy is defined as a broad and general plan developed to reach long-range organizational objectives. Actually, strategy is the end result of strategic planning. Every organization should have a strategy of some sort.[7] In order for a strategy to be worthwhile, however, it must be consistent with organizational objectives, which, in turn, must be consistent with organizational purpose. Figure 4.3 illustrates this relationship between organizational objectives and strategy by presenting sample organizational objectives and strategies for three well-known business organizations.

Strategy Management

Strategy management is defined as the process of ensuring that an organization possesses and benefits from the use of an appropriate organizational strategy. As used within this definition, an appropriate strategy is a strategy best suited to the needs of an organization at a particular time.

Appropriate Strategy

The process of strategy management is generally thought to consist of four sequential and continuing steps: (a) strategy formulation; (b) strategy implementation; (c) strategy results measurement; and (d) strategy evaluation. The relationships and definitions of each of these steps is presented in figure 4.4.

Four Steps in Strategy Management

Perhaps the most important lesson to be learned from figure 4.4 is that the actual making of a strategy is only one of four important steps in strategy management. In order for an organization to get maximum benefit from a strategy, it must be implemented or put into action; constantly watched to see what effect the strategy is having on the organization; and evaluated or examined to see if it is having the effect management desires. If the effect is desirable perhaps the strategy could remain as is, with strategy-results measurement and strategy evaluation continuing to determine if change will be necessary in the future. If the effect of a strategy is undesirable, however, management would probably start the entire strategy management process over again by formulating a different strategy.

All Steps Are Important

Figure 4:3 Examples of organizational objectives and related strategies for three organizations in different business areas.

Company Name	Type of Business	Sample Organization Objective(s)	Strategy to Accomplish Sample Objective(s)
(a)	Automobile manufacturer	1. Regain market share recently lost to General Motors 2. Regain quality reputation that was damaged due to Pinto gas tank explosions	1. Resize and down size present models 2. Continue to produce subcompacts, intermediates, standards, and luxuries 3. Emphasize use of programmed combustion engines instead of diesel engines
(b)	Fast food	Increase productivity	1. Increase people efficiency 2. Increase machine efficiency
(c)	Transportation	1. Continue company growth 2. Continue company profits	1. Modernize the Illinois Central Railroad 2. Develop valuable real estate holdings 3. Complete an appropriate railroad merger

(a) and (b). Based upon E. Meadows, "How Three Companies Increased Their Productivity," *Fortune* 101 (March 10, 1980): 92–101. (c) From William B. Johnson, "The Transformation of a Railroad," *Long-Range Planning* 9 (December 1976): 18–23.

How to Formulate Strategy

Although formulating strategy is only one of four steps in the strategy management process, it has probably received more attention in the management literature than any of the other steps. This section discusses some of the major insights on formulating strategy that this literature presents. More specifically, this section focuses on (1) questions to ask to formulate strategy and (2) product portfolio analysis.

Focus on Strategy Formulation

Questions to Ask to Formulate Strategy[8]

A synthesis of the ideas of several contemporary management writers seems to suggest that formulating appropriate organizational strategy is a process of answering four basic questions. These questions are as follows:

Answering Questions Results in Strategy

What are the purpose(s) and objective(s) of the organization? The answer to this question tells where the organization wants to go. As stated earlier, appropriate strategy reflects organizational purpose and objectives. By answering this question during strategy formulation, managers are likely to remember this important point and thereby minimize inconsistencies among purposes, objectives, and strategies.

Where Does The Organization Want to Go?

Where is the organization presently going? The answer to this question can tell a manager if an organization is achieving organizational goals and, if so, whether or not the level of such progress is satisfactory. Whereas the first question focused on where the organization wants to go, this one focuses on where the organization is actually going.

Is The Organization Making Progress?

Figure 4.4 The process of strategy management.

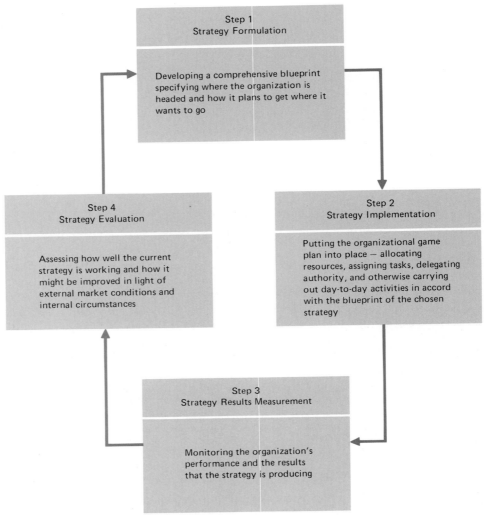

From *Strategy and Policy: Concepts and Cases,* rev. ed., by Arthur A. Thompson, Jr., and A. J. Strickland, III, p. 24. Copyright © 1981 by Business Publications, Inc. Used with permission of Business Publications, Inc.

**Problems
Opportunities
Strengths
Weaknesses**

In what kind of environment does the organization now exist? Both internal and external environments, factors both inside and outside the organization, are covered in this question. Its answer can help managers pinpoint organizational strengths, weaknesses, problems, and opportunities that exist. Naturally, appropriate strategy will reflect such factors. For example, assume that a poorly trained middle-management team and a sudden influx of competitors in a market are factors that exist respectively in the internal and external environments of an organization. Any strategy formulated, if it is to be appropriate, should probably deal with these factors.

**How Does The Organization
Get Where It Wants to Go?**

What can be done to better achieve organizational objectives in the future? The answer to this question actually results in the strategy of the organization. This question should only be answered, however, after the manager has had adequate opportunity to reflect on the answers to the previous three questions. In other words, a manager can develop appropriate organizational strategy only if he or she has a clear understanding of where the organization wants to go, where the organization is going, and the environment in which the organization exists.

Figure 4.5 Model used to make product portfolio analysis.

Market share

	High	Low
Market growth High	Star products	Sweepstakes products
Market growth Low	Cash cow products	Dog products

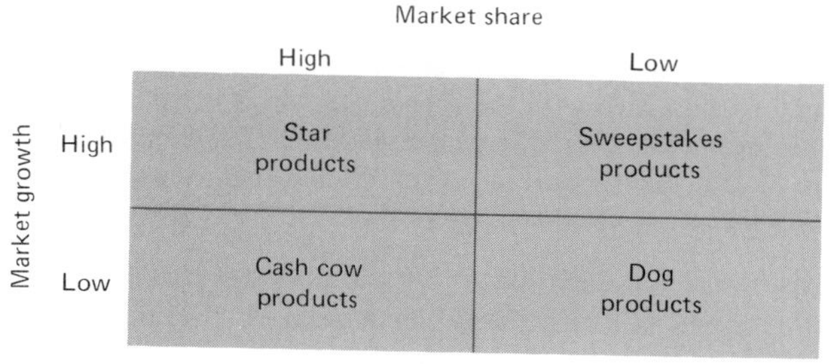

From Gilbers D. Harrell and Richard O. Kiefer, Multinational Strategic Market Portfolios,'' *Michigan State University Business Topics*, Winter 1981, p. 6. Used with permission.

Product Portfolio Analysis

As you probably suspect, organizational strategy can, and generally does, focus on many different organizational areas.[9] Some of these major areas are marketing, finance, production, research and development, personnel, and public relations.[10] Fortunately, to complement answers to strategy-related questions such as those discussed in the previous section, several different and useful tools have been developed to assist managers in actually developing their strategies. One such tool that is gaining wide acceptance in recent times is called "product portfolio analysis." **Product portfolio analysis** is the development of product-related strategy that is based primarily on market share of products and growth of the markets in which products are selling.[11]

The model used to make a product portfolio analysis is shown in figure 4.5. Basically, this model shows various possible combinations of market share and market growth that products can possess and the name each product is called, depending upon which combination it possesses. Products that capture a high share of a market that has only slight growth are called "cash cow products." For these products, a company should probably adopt the simple strategy of maintaining its product investment in order to "milk" as much cash out of the market as possible. Products that capture a high share of a rapidly growing market are called "star products." Normally, an appropriate strategy for star products is to invest in greater production and product improvement in order to capture a greater share of the market as it grows. "Sweepstakes products" capture a low share of a rapid growth market. Here, the strategy of increasing production in order to gain a significant payoff might be appropriate. Lastly, "dog products" have low market share of a slowly growing market. Management may wish to consider discontinuing the production of these products in order to concentrate more on products in other categories.

Companies like General Electric, Westinghouse, and Shell Oil have used product portfolio analysis in their strategy management processes. There are, however, some possible pitfalls managers should avoid in using this technique. For example, the product portfolio analysis model does not consider such factors as (1) various types of risk associated with product development; (2) threats that inflation and other economic conditions can create in the future; and (3) social, political, and ecological pressures.[12] Managers must remember to weigh such factors carefully when designing organizational strategy that is based upon this model.

Tactical Planning

Tactical planning is short-range planning that emphasizes current operations of various parts of the organization. Short range is defined as a period of time extending only about one year or less into the future. Managers use tactical planning to outline what the various parts of the organization must do for the organization to be successful at some point one year or less into the future.[13]

Market Share

Market Growth

Strategies for Specific Products

Potential Pitfalls

Short-range Planning

Coordinating Strategic and Tactical Planning

Russell L. Ackoff makes the following statement about strategic vs. tactical planning:

> In general, strategic planning is concerned with the longest period worth considering; tactical planning is concerned with the shortest period worth considering. Both types of planning are necessary. They complement each other. They are like the head and tail of a coin. We can look at them separately, even discuss them separately, but we cannot separate them in fact.[14]

In other words, managers need both tactical and strategic planning programs, but these programs must be highly related to be successful. Tactical planning should focus on what to do in the short run to help the organization achieve the long-run objectives determined by strategic planning.

Planning and Levels of Management

Time Spent Planning

Top management of an organization has the primary responsibility for seeing that the planning function is carried out. Although all levels of management typically are involved in the planning process, upper-level managers usually spend more time planning than lower-level managers. Lower-level managers are highly involved with the everyday operations of the organization and, therefore, normally have less time to contribute to planning than top management. Middle-level managers usually spend more time planning than lower-level managers, but less time than upper-level managers. Figure 4.6 shows the increase in planning time spent as managers move from lower-level to upper-level management positions. In small as well as in large organizations, deciding on the amount and nature of work that managers should personally handle is extremely important.[15]

Scope of Planning

The type of planning managers do also changes as managers move up in the organization. Typically, lower-level managers plan for the short run; middle-level managers plan for a somewhat longer run; and upper-level managers plan for an even longer run. Lower-level managers' expertise with everyday operations makes them the best planners for what can be done in the short run to reach organizational objectives. Upper-level managers usually have the best understanding of the organizational situation as a whole and are therefore better equipped to plan for the long run. Figure 4.7 shows that as managers move from lower to upper management, they spend more time on long-range planning and less time on short-range planning.

Back to the Case

From this discussion on the types of planning, the managers in the introductory case should realize that a successful planning program should include both strategic (long-range) planning and tactical (short-range) planning. Basically, this strategic planning will involve the process of strategy management: (1) strategy formulation; (2) strategy implementation; (3) strategy results measurement; and (4) strategy evaluation. To actually design a strategy, the managers in the introductory case can answer certain key questions with information generated using product portfolio analysis. As a general rule, they should invest funds for strategic planning only to the extent that they can realistically anticipate, in the foreseeable future, a return on long-range planning expenses. These managers also must make sure that tactical planning reflects strategic planning and that planning activities are shared with managers at various levels of the organization. The amount of time they spend planning and the type of planning (strategic or tactical) each of them does will depend on their managerial level within the organization.

Figure 4.6 Increase in planning time as manager moves from lower-level to upper-level management positions.

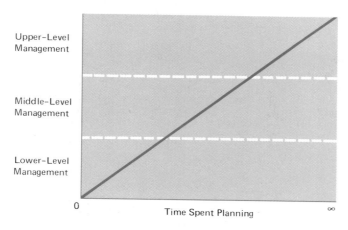

Figure 4.7 Movement of planning activities from a short-range to a long-range emphasis as manager moves from a lower-level to an upper-level management position.

	Today	One Week Ahead	One Month Ahead	Three to Six Months Ahead	One Year Ahead	Two Years Ahead	Three to Four Years Ahead	Five to Ten Years Ahead
President	1%	2%	5%	17%	15%	25%	30%	5%
Vice-president	2%	4%	10%	29%	20%	20%	13%	2%
Works Manager	4%	8%	15%	38%	20%	10%	5%	
Superintendent	6%	10%	20%	43%	10%	9%	2%	
Department Manager	10%	10%	25%	39%	10%	5%	1%	
Section Supervisor	15%	20%	25%	37%	3%			
Group Supervisor	38%	40%	15%	5%	2%			

Reprinted with the special permission of DUN'S REVIEW, April 1957, Copyright 1957, Dun & Bradstreet Publications Corporation.

The planning process contains six major steps: (1) stating organizational objectives, (2) listing alternative ways of reaching organizational objectives, (3) developing premises upon which each alternative is based, (4) choosing best alternative for reaching objectives, (5) developing plans to pursue chosen alternative, and (6) putting plans into action. Figure 4.8 shows how these steps relate to one another.

Steps in the Planning Process

Figure 4.8 Elements of the planning process.

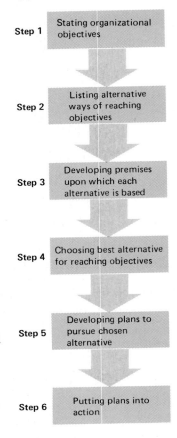

Step 1 — Stating organizational objectives

Step 2 — Listing alternative ways of reaching objectives

Step 3 — Developing premises upon which each alternative is based

Step 4 — Choosing best alternative for reaching objectives

Step 5 — Developing plans to pursue chosen alternative

Step 6 — Putting plans into action

Stating Organizational Objectives

A clear statement of organizational objectives is necessary for planning to begin, since planning focuses on how the management system will reach those objectives.[16] Chapter 3 discusses how the objectives themselves are developed.

Listing Alternative Ways of Reaching Objectives

Once organizational objectives have been clearly stated, managers should list as many available alternatives as possible for reaching those objectives.

Developing Premises upon Which Each Alternative Is Based

Assumptions

To a large extent, the feasibility of using any one alternative to reach organizational objectives is determined by the **premises,** or assumptions, upon which the alternative is based. For example, two alternatives managers could generate to reach the organizational objective of increasing profit might be: (1) increase the sale of products presently being produced, or (2) produce and sell a completely new product. Alternative 1 would be based on the premise or assumption that the organization would get a larger share of an existing market. Alternative 2 would be based on the premise that a new product for this organization would capture a significant portion of a new market. Managers should list all of the premises for each alternative.

Figure 4.9 Three approaches to planning.

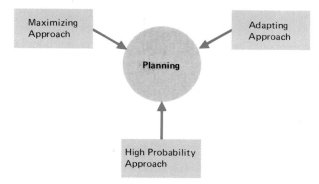

From the information in this section the managers in the introductory case should be able to derive a "plan for planning." Their planning group should complete the six major steps of the planning process.

Following these steps will assure the managers of a generally accepted strategy upon which to base their planning activities and thereby increase the probability that their planning will be effective.

Back to the Case

Choosing the Best Alternative for Reaching Objectives

An evaluation of alternatives must include an evaluation of the premises upon which the alternatives are based. Managers will usually find that the premises upon which some alternatives are based are unreasonable and therefore exclude those alternatives from further consideration. This elimination process helps managers to determine which alternative would be best to accomplish organizational objectives. The decision making required for this step is discussed more fully in chapter 5.

Developing Plans to Pursue Chosen Alternative

After an alternative has been chosen, managers begin actually to develop their plans. Strategic (long-range) and tactical (short-range) plans now are formulated.[17] More information relating to the development of plans is presented in chapter 6.

Putting Plans into Action

Once plans have been developed, they are ready to be put into action. The plans should furnish the organization with both long-range and short-range direction for activity. Implementing plans and the planning process is the main focus of chapter 7.

Three basic approaches or philosophies to performing the planning function are usually discussed by management planners: (1) the high probability approach, (2) the maximizing approach, and (3) the adapting approach.[18] Figure 4.9 presents each of these approaches as a basically different way of planning. More information on each of these approaches follows.

Approaches to Planning

The High Probability Approach

The **high probability** approach to planning is based on the philosophy that there should be a high probability that the organization will be *somewhat* successful. Emphasis is not on being as successful as possible but on reaching some acceptable level of success.

Planners using this approach take action aimed directly at ensuring this acceptable level of success. For example, they carefully analyze organizational objectives to make sure they are feasible. The management system will have a difficult time reaching its target level of desired success if organizational objectives are unrealistic. Even a moderate level of success could be impossible to attain if organizational objectives are unreasonable. Another action taken by high probability planners is to verify that organizational objectives are measurable. The planners must be sure that the target level of success can be measured, and they must know exactly how it will be measured. High probability planners always seek a feasible and practical way of obtaining desired success. This way may not be the best possible way, but it probably will have the highest probability of reaching the target level of success.

Obviously, the high probability approach to planning has both advantages and disadvantages. Among its advantages is that this approach usually generates an extremely feasible plan. Planners focus only on finding a practical way of attaining the desired success level. A disadvantage of the high probability approach is that it usually does not encourage creative plans. Planners seldom deviate significantly from the past because the high probability approach, by definition, is an extremely conservative way of reaching the desired level of success.

The Maximizing Approach

The **maximizing approach** is based on the philosophy that the organization should be as successful as possible. From this viewpoint, planners are not content with the acceptable level of success characteristic of the high probability approach, but emphasize maximizing success instead.

Planners using the maximizing approach make constant use of quantitative techniques, the most used of which is probably the mathematical model. A mathematical model is a mathematical representation of an actual system. Planners build a mathematical model of the system for which they are planning and then base their plans on how that model reacts to induced changes. Through the use of these models and other mathematical techniques, maximizing approach planners try to:

(a) minimize the resources required to obtain a specific level of performance,
(b) maximize the performance that can be attained with resources that are (or are expected to be) available, or (c) obtain the best balance of costs (resources consumed) and benefits (performance).[19]

The maximizing approach to planning, like the high probability approach, has advantages and disadvantages. An advantage is that this approach continually emphasizes reaching the full profit potential of an organization and uses sophisticated quantitative techniques to develop plans. In terms of disadvantages, the maximizing approach generally treats components of organizations as completely quantifiable and predictable, even though, realistically, some aspects of organizations, such as human behavior, are not.

The Adapting Approach

The **adapting approach** emphasizes that effective planning concentrates on helping the organization to change or adapt to internal and/or external variables. This approach is based on the philosophy that an inability to adapt is the major obstacle to organizational success. Planners who use this approach (1) see organizational change as inevitable; (2) concentrate on anticipating future changes; and (3) determine, through organizational analysis, how to best modify the organization as the time for change approaches.

Figure 4.10 Combination approach to planning.

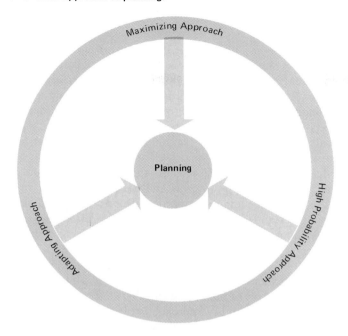

The adapting approach has the advantage of focusing on both the internal and external environments of the organization to predict organizational changes. Regardless of the planning approach used, this environmental analysis is necessary if an organization is to remain viable. Possible disadvantages of the adapting approach include a lesser emphasis on organizational objectives than either the high probability or the maximizing approaches and the possibility that organizational analysis and resulting changes become an end in themselves rather than a means to success.

Which Approach to Use

The planning approach most managers should use is probably some mixture or combination of the high probability, maximizing, and adapting approaches. Essentially, each approach should be used systematically to deal with various related factors within the organization. This **combination approach** emphasizes the advantages and deemphasizes the disadvantages of each of the other approaches. Figure 4.10 illustrates this combination approach to planning.

As an example, the manager of a Ford automobile dealership who has the organizational objective of increasing new car sales by 12 percent over the next year has decided to formulate his total planning program using the combination approach. This manager knows from market research that new car sales for his Galaxie 500 model are already reaching a significant portion of potential customers in his market area. He also knows that approximately the same number of new Galaxies have been purchased in each of the past five years. From this information the manager reasonably concludes that an acceptable level of success for Galaxie sales for the next year would be to approximate the level of past sales in each of the last five years.

To achieve this acceptable level of success, the manager could use the high probability approach to planning. Given the condition of the market, he should move toward developing a feasible plan that approximates what the organization did last year. Creative planning would have minimal returns in the situation because the market

Emphasis on Advantages, Deemphasis on Disadvantages of Planning Approaches

already is somewhat saturated with the Ford Galaxie. Since the manager knows that Galaxie sales will probably not contribute to his organizational objective of increasing sales 12 percent, the best he realistically can hope for in relation to Galaxie sales is to maintain past performance.

This dealership, however, also sells the Ford Mustang. Market research indicates that this car is very pleasing to consumers and that its sales potential is still very high. As a result, the manager's planning for this product realistically should reflect the maximizing approach. Since the Mustang is a desirable product and has a high potential market, conditions are appropriate for attempting to maximize sales through a rigorous combination of advertising and sales training. Basically, the manager can strive to increase overall sales 12 percent by planning in such a way that he sells as many Mustangs as possible.

This Ford dealership manager also senses that the present trend toward buying foreign compact cars will continue to grow and become extremely significant within the next five to ten years. The adaption approach to planning could help the manager to determine how his organization could be modified to compete with this changing consumer demand as it grows more significant. Perhaps plans to emphasize better service in the future or to stress national loyalty in his advertising will be the resultant modifications.

Overall, the Ford dealership manager has developed a planning program aimed at the organizational objective of increasing sales by 12 percent. The program itself is a combination of the high probability approach to planning, the maximizing approach to planning, and the adapting approach to planning. One of these approaches, by itself, probably would not have been successful in helping the manager to develop a realistic plan for reaching his organizational objective.

Back to the Case

As the managers in the introductory case begin their planning process, they will have to decide what approach to planning they want to use. Do they want to plan for some acceptable level of success or do they want to try to be as successful as possible? Or, do they want to plan for adaption and assume that success will follow? As with most managers, they will probably decide that over the long run a combination of these three approaches will be best for the organization.

The following points are stressed within this chapter:

1. Planning is the process of determining how the organization can get where it wants to go. The primary purpose of planning, therefore, is to facilitate the accomplishment of organizational objectives. All other purposes are spin-offs of this primary purpose.

2. The advantages an organization gains by planning are numerous. Potential disadvantages are also a factor but are usually the result of the planning process being used incorrectly. The fact that effective planning has been credited with increasing profits should emphasize to managers the importance of the planning process.

3. Planning is the primary management function—the function that precedes and is the foundation for the organizing, influencing, and controlling functions of managers.

4. In general, there are two types of planning: strategic (long-range) planning and tactical (short-range) planning. Both types must be highly related for a planning program to be successful.

5. As managers move from lower-level to upper-level management positions, they can expect to spend more time planning. They will also find that the emphasis of their planning activities will change from tactical planning to strategic planning.

6. Basically, the planning process contains six major steps: (1) stating organizational objectives, (2) listing alternative ways of reaching objectives, (3) developing premises upon which each alternative is based, (4) choosing the best alternative for reaching objectives, (5) developing plans to pursue chosen alternative, and (6) putting plans into action.

7. Three approaches to planning are the high probability approach, the maximizing approach, and the adapting approach. The high probability approach emphasizes planning for some acceptable level of success, while the maximizing approach stresses planning to obtain as much success as possible. The adapting approach concentrates on success through planning for change. The most advisable approach to planning, however, is a combination of these three that reflects the current organization situation.

Issues for Review and Discussion

1. What is planning?
2. What is the main purpose of planning?
3. List and explain the advantages of planning.
4. Why are the disadvantages of planning called *potential* disadvantages?
5. What is the relationship between profits and planning?
6. What is the significance of exhibit 4?
7. Explain the phrase *primacy of planning.*
8. List and define the two types of planning.
9. What is strategy?
10. Describe the strategy management process.
11. How can a manager use product portfolio analysis?
12. How should managers attempt to coordinate strategic and tactical planning?
13. How does the amount of time managers spend planning change as they move from lower-level to upper-level management positions?
14. What kinds of planning activities do managers perform as they move from lower-level to upper level management positions?
15. List the six steps in the planning process.
16. Outline the relationships between these six steps.
17. Explain the high probability approach to planning.
18. Explain the maximizing approach to planning.
19. Explain the adapting approach to planning.
20. Explain the combination approach to planning.

Sources of Additional Information

Aguilar, F. J. *Scanning the Business Environment.* New York: Macmillan, 1967.

Ansoff, H. I. *Corporate Strategy.* New York: McGraw-Hill, 1965.

Belohlav, James. "Long Range Planning: Some Common Misconceptions." *Managerial Planning* 30, no. 2 (September/October 1981): 41–43.

Belohlav, James A., and Waggener, Herman A. "Keeping the 'Strategic' in Your Strategic Planning." *Managerial Planning,* March/April 1980, pp. 23–25.

Branch, M. C. *Planning: Aspects and Applcations.* New York: Macmillan, 1966.

Emery, J. C. *Organizational Planning and Control Systems.* New York: Macmillan, 1971.

Ewing, D. W., ed. *Long-Range Planning for Management.* New York: Harper & Row Publishers, 1964.

Gluck, Frederick W.; Kaufman, Stephen P.; and Walleck, A. Steven. "Strategic Management for Competitive Advantage." *Harvard Business Review,* July/August 1980, pp. 154–61.

Hall, William K. "Survival Strategies in a Hostile Environment." *Harvard Business Review,* September/October 1980, pp. 75–85.

Henry, H. W. *Long-Range Planning Practices in 45 Industrial Companies.* Englewood Cliffs, N.J.: Prentice-Hall, 1967.

LeBreton, P. P., and Henning, D. A. *Planning Theory.* Englewood Cliffs, N.J.: Prentice-Hall, 1961.

Naor, Jacob. "How to Make Strategic Planning Work for Small Business." *S.A.M. Advanced Management Journal,* Winter 1980, pp. 35–39.

Steiner, G. A. *Managerial Long-Range Planning.* New York: McGraw-Hill, 1963.

Thompson, S. *How Companies Plan.* New York: American Management Association, 1962.

1. Harry Jones, *Preparing Company Plans: A Workbook for Effective Corporate Planning* (New York: John Wiley & Sons, 1974), p. 3.

2. C. W. Roney, "The Two Purposes of Business Planning," *Managerial Planning,* November-December 1976, pp. 1–6.

3. Harold Koontz and Cyril O'Donnell, *Management: A Systems and Contingency Analysis of Management Functions* (New York: McGraw-Hill, 1976), p. 130.

4. H. Stieglitz, *The Chief Executive and His Job,* Personnel Policy Study no. 214 (New York: National Industrial Conference Board, 1969).

5. For a discussion on several of these disadvantages, see George R. Terry, *Principles of Management* (Homewood, Ill.: Richard D. Irwin, 1972), pp. 198–200.

6. D. W. Karger, "Integrated Formal Long-Range Planning and How to Do It," *Long-Range Planning* 6, no. 4 (1973): 31–34.

7. George Sawyer, "Elements of Strategy," *Management Planning,* May/June 1981, pp. 3–59.

8. Discussion in this section is based primarily upon Thomas H. Naylor and Kristin Neva, "Design of a Strategic Planning Process," *Managerial Planning,* January/February, 1980, pp. 2–7; Donald W. Mitchell, "Pursuing Strategic Potential," *Managerial Planning,* May/June, 1980, pp. 6–10; Benton E. Gup, "Begin Strategic Planning by Asking Three Questions," *Managerial Planning,* November/December, 1979, pp. 28–31, 35; L. V. Gerstner, Jr., "Can Strategic Planning Pay Off?" *Business Horizons* 15 (1972): 5–16.

9. Lawrence R. Jauch and Richard N. Osborn, "Toward An Integrated Theory of Strategy," *Academy of Management Review* 6, no. 3 (July 1981): 491–98.

10. Yezdi M. Godiwalla, Wayne A. Meinhart, and William D. Warde, "How CEO's Form Corporate Strategy," *Management World,* May 1981, pp. 28–29, 44.

11. Bruce D. Henderson, *Henderson on Corporate Strategy* (Cambridge, Mass: ABT Books, 1979).

12. Harold W. Fox, "The Frontiers of Strategic Planning: Intuition or Formal Models?" *Management Review,* April 1981, pp. 8–14.

13. For a detailed discussion of basic differences between strategic and tactical planning, see George A. Steiner, *Top Management Planning* (Toronto: Collier-Macmillan, 1969), pp. 37–39.

14. Russell L. Ackoff, *A Concept of Corporate Planning* (New York: John Wiley & Sons, 1970), p. 4.

15. G. E. Tibbits, "Small Business Management: A Normative Approach," *MSU Business Topics,* Autumn 1979, pp. 5–12.

16. George C. Sawyer, "The Hazards of Goal Conflict in Strategic Planning," *Managerial Planning,* May/June 1980, pp. 11–13, 27.

17. For more detailed information on how strategic planning takes place, see Richard F. Vancil and Peter Lorange, "Strategic Planning in Diversified Companies," *Harvard Business Review,* January–February 1975, pp. 81–90; and William R. King and David I. Cleland, "A New Method for Strategic Systems Planning," *Business Horizons,* August 1975, pp. 55–64.

18. These three approaches are based on a discussion of the three philosophies of planning. See Russell L. Ackoff, *A Concept of Planning* (New York: Wiley-Interscience, 1970), pp. 6–20.

19. Ibid, p. 12–13.

Concluding Case 4
RCA's Planning Problems

Thornton F. Bradshaw (Photo: © 1982 John Neubauer)

Edgar H. Griffiths (Photo: Allen Green)

Edgar H. Griffiths was recently removed from his position as chairman of the board and chief executive of RCA Corporation. In his place, the board appointed Thorton F. Bradshaw, former president of Atlantic Richfield Company and an individual with an excellent administrative reputation. It was reported that Griffiths was ousted by the board due to a performance marked by bitter public dismissals and cold internal fighting that blocked long-range planning. The board was hopeful that with the appointment of Bradshaw the climate would be cleared.

Bradshaw is faced with several problems in his new position. Long-range plans for each of the company's businesses must be developed. In addition, RCA is counting on Bradshaw to foster stable leadership while changing the social atmosphere of the company from one that encourages intense politicking to one that rewards performance. Bradshaw himself sees an improved social atmosphere as his most significant challenge.

When Griffiths took the position of chief executive and chairman in 1976, the board looked to him for long-range plans for all of RCA's operations. However, he responded with emphasis on short-term profits. According to one source, long-range planning at RCA meant, "What are we going to do after lunch?" This planning approach proved unsuccessful as 1980 profits dropped from those of 1977. In addition, the board was plagued with a series of dismissals and resignations, all due, it appeared, to Griffiths' management style.

The board made several attempts to remedy these concerns, but were met with passive resistance from Griffiths. For example, to temper Griffiths's emphasis on short-term planning, the board sought a president with a long-term approach to planning, but Griffiths delayed appointing anyone to the position. In 1980, the board insisted that Griffiths hire Maurice R. Valente, which he did. Six months later Valente was fired because, according to Griffiths, "his performance did not meet the expectations of the board." Griffiths's sudden and widely publicized dismissal of Jane Cahill Pfeiffer, chairman of RCA's National Broadcasting Company, further demonstrated Griffiths's inability to find a successor, handle public relations, and control information about internal affairs.

Much of the board's dissatisfaction with Griffiths was related to his management style. Instability in the president's office during the 1970s (Robert Sarnoff was ousted and later, Anthony L. Conrad resigned), stimulated corporate managers to choose sides in order to survive. Politicking ran rampant. According to one individual, "Griffiths fanned those flames as much as anyone. His style was to exalt someone as a hero one day and denounce him as a goat the next." Griffiths failed to inform the board on some critical issues and would pressure the board into doing things his way. If the board hesitated, Griffiths would lose his temper until the board yielded to his view.

The company's earnings also demonstrated that problems existed. RCA's earnings in 1980 were behind those of 1979, primarily due to higher interest costs, higher research and development expenses, and start-up costs related to the SelectaVision videodisc program. RCA's earnings per common share dropped to $3.19 (10.6%), slightly above the $3.11 reported in 1977, the beginning of Griffiths's reign.

Bradshaw intends to improve RCA's climate. He feels that politics have pulled the company apart and he would like to bring into effect a "meritocracy" to improve the atmosphere. Bradshaw believes that meritocracy begins with openness with people in the company and with the press.

Bradshaw brings tremendous credentials to the position. While president of ARCO, he and the chairman, Robert O. Anderson, developed an extremely profitable integrated oil company out of a mediocre refinery. He gained the reputation of being an excellent administrator, comfortable in discussions of technology, controllership, and corporate governance.

According to Bradshaw, the future success of RCA is embedded in the ability to anticipate and utilize the technological revolution in communications. He sees RCA's present position enabling it to dominate the revolution due to its tremendous technological base. Not only does RCA have a good foothold in the consumer electronics business but also in the developing telecommunications market. With proper long-term planning, Bradshaw may be able to bring RCA out of an economic slump.

This case is adapted from "Why Griffiths is Out as RCA's Chairman," *Business Week*, February 2, 1981, pp. 72–73.

Discussion Issues

1. Why do you think Griffiths's planning emphasis led to his replacement as chairman of the board for RCA? Explain.
2. What were some of the results that materialized from Griffiths's short-term planning perspective?
3. Do you think RCA's board had a strategic plan to follow? Explain.
4. What approach to planning do you suspect will provide the focus for Bradshaw's actions? Explain.

Student Learning Objectives

From studying this chapter I will attempt to acquire:

1. A fundamental understanding of the term *decision*
2. An understanding of each element of the decision situation
3. An ability to use the decision-making process
4. An appreciation for the various situations in which decisions are made
5. An ability to use probability theory and decision trees as decision-making tools

Chapter Outline

Exhibit 5: Nolan Bushnell Decides about Pizza Time Theatre

Making Decisions

Introductory Case 5
Deciding What to Do

The Winslow Hardware Company is a medium-sized hardware store in a suburb twenty miles from downtown Cleveland. The suburb itself has mostly middle-income residents and a population of nearly 35,000. It is worth noting, however, that the population over the past three years has decreased slightly.

Mr. Winslow, owner and manager of the hardware store, has just finished compiling an analysis of what has happened to the store's net sales and profits in each of the last six years. Much to his disappointment, net sales and profits have decreased over the last three years. The actual figures per year are shown below:

Year	Net Sales	Net Profit
1974	$570,680	$57,337
1975	590,890	58,690
1976	620,400	60,400
1977	600,338	60,000
1978	580,000	50,009
1979	570,905	57,900

The Winslow Hardware Company, like most hardware stores, handles numerous diversified products. In an attempt to reverse the decreasing net sales and profit trends, Winslow has been considering the following alternatives: (1) expanding his product line to include tool rentals and lawn treatment products, (2) reducing the number of salespeople he has in the store, and (3) reducing product prices to significantly increase sales volume and, thus, net profits. Although Mr. Winslow feels that each of these alternatives is feasible, he has not decided yet which alternative(s) to implement.

Discussion Issues

1. List three additional alternatives that Winslow could consider to reverse the decreasing sales and net profit trends.
2. What information would Winslow need to evaluate the three alternatives listed in the case?
3. If you were Winslow, what criteria would you use to decide which alternative should be implemented at the Winslow Hardware Company?

What's Ahead

In the introductory case, Mr. Winslow, the owner and manager of the Winslow Hardware Company, must make a decision about the future of his company. The purpose of this chapter is to assist individuals such as Mr. Winslow by discussing: (1) the fundamentals of decisions, (2) the elements of the decision situation, (3) the decision-making process, (4) various decision-making conditions, and (5) decision-making tools. These topics are all of critical importance to managers and other individuals who make decisions.

Definition of a Decision

A **decision** is a choice made between two or more available alternatives. "Choosing the best alternative for reaching an objective," the fourth step of the planning process as presented in chapter 4, is, strictly speaking, making a decision. Although decision making is covered in the planning section of this text, managers also must make decisions when performing the other three managerial functions: organizing, controlling, and influencing.

Everyone is faced with decision situations each day. Perhaps a decision situation simply involves choosing among studying, swimming, or golfing when considering alternative ways of spending the day. It does not matter, however, which alternative is chosen; only that a choice is actually made.[1] Exhibit 5 traces the events involved as Nolan Bushnell decides to go into business for himself rather than working for Warner Communications. Obviously, Bushnell's decision was very financially rewarding.

Practicing managers must make numerous decisions every day.[2] Not all of these decisions are equal in significance to the organization. Some affect a large number of organization members, cost much money to carry out, and/or have a long-run effect on the organization. Others are fairly insignificant and affect only a small number of organization members, cost very little to carry out, and have only a short-run effect on the organization.

Choice between Alternatives

Significant and Insignificant Decisions

"I'm going back to plain white shirts! I can't make co-ordinate decisions this early in the morning!"

From the *Wall Street Journal* and Dave Gerard.

Exhibit 5

Nolan Bushnell Decides about Pizza Time Theatre Inc.

Bushnell and Chuck E. Cheese (Photo: John McDermott)

Venture capitalists routinely come across way-out investment proposals. But few have sounded wackier, yet paid off more handsomely, than Pizza Theatre Inc. of Sunnyvale, Calif. The company operates a rapidly growing, 50-restaurant chain of fast-food pizza parlors in which food is almost the least of the attractions.

The real action is in the roomfuls of coin-operated electronic games designed to divert, amuse and swallow the quarters of customers waiting for their pizzas to cook. Even more entertainment is provided, free of charge, by troupes of singing, talking, joke-telling robots dressed up to resemble Muppet-like characters.

Pizza Time Theatre Inc. is the creation of Nolan Bushnell, 38, a micro-electronics expert. In 1972 Bushnell founded the successful Atari electronic games company with a $500 initial investment. Four years later, he sold out to Warner Communications, ending up with $15 million in cash and debentures, and took the post of chairman of his company, which became a new Warner subsidiary. Since then, Atari has broadened from electronic games to personal computers. Bushnell had been working on the Pizza Time concept at Atari; but before the first of the computerized robots, a wisecracking rat named Chuck E. Cheese, emerged from the lab, the company had been bought by Warner Communications.

Though Warner's management permitted Bushnell to open an initial Pizza Time Theater restaurant in San Jose in 1977, the parent company never saw much future in the idea. In 1978 Bushnell resigned his chairmanship, put up $500,000 to buy back the Pizza Time concept from his old employer, and went into business for himself.

By the fall of 1979, Bushnell had plowed $1.8 million more of his personal wealth into Pizza Time Theater Inc. and had opened four more outlets on the West Coast. But to expand further he needed more money. Bushnell therefore turned to venture capitalists for backing. Says Wallace Davis, 63, whose venture capital firm, Mayfield Fund, invested $750,000 in the company: "I'm not a game player or a big pizza eater. But I was impressed observing the customers at Pizza Time restaurants. People really seemed to enjoy themselves there." Another attraction for investors was Bushnell's good business record at Atari.

In January 1980 several venture capitalists put up $2.5 million in return for 669,333 shares of Pizza Time stock at $3.75 per share. Ten months later, investors bought an additional 572,941 shares at $5.25. In April of this year, a syndicate of securities underwriters sold 1.17 million shares to the general public at $15 per share, or nearly triple what the venture capitalists had paid less than six months earlier. And the stock has climbed higher still. Last week Pizza Time Theater was selling for $23.25 per share, or more than six times what the stock was worth 18 months earlier, when the first venturesome capitalists bought a slice of the Pizza Time action.

From TIME, 10 August 1981, p. 47. Copyright 1981 Time, Inc. All rights reserved. Reprinted by permission from TIME.

Figure 5.1 Traditional and modern ways of handling programmed and nonprogrammed decisions.

Types of Decisions	Decision-Making Techniques	
	Traditional	*Modern*

Programmed:
Routine, repetitive decisions
Organization develops specific
   processes for handling them
	1. Habit
	2. Clerical routine:
	   Standard operating
	     procedures
	3. Organization structure:
	   Common expectations
	   A system of subgoals
	   Well-defined
	     informational channels
		1. Operations research:
		   Mathematical analysis
		   Models
		   Computer simulation
		2. Electronic data
		   processing

Nonprogrammed:
One-shot, ill-structured,
   novel, policy decisions
Handled by general problem-
   solving processes
	1. Judgment, intuition,
	   and creativity
	2. Rules of thumb
	3. Selection and training
	   of executives
		Heuristic problem-solving
		   techniques applied to:
		(a) training human
		     decision makers
		(b) constructing heuristic
		     computer programs

From Herbert A. Simon, *The Shape of Automation* (New York: Harper and Row, 1965), p. 62. Used with permission.

Although managers must make both relatively significant and insignificant decisions, they should scrutinize the significant decisions very carefully. Significant decisions can have a major impact not only on the management system itself but also on the career of the manager.

Types of Decisions

Decisions are categorized by how much time managers must spend in making them, what proportion of the organization must be involved in making them, and the organizational functions on which they focus.[3] Probably the most generally accepted method of categorizing decisions, however, is based on computer technology language and divides decisions into two basic types: programmed and nonprogrammed.[4]

Routine and Repetitive

According to Herbert A. Simon, **programmed decisions** are routine and repetitive, and the organization typically develops specific ways to handle them. A programmed decision might involve determining how products will be arranged on the shelves of a grocery store. This is a routine and repetitive problem for the organization, and standard arrangement decisions typically are made according to established management guidelines.

One-shot Occurrences

Nonprogrammed decisions, on the other hand, typically are one-shot occurrences and are usually less structured than programmed decisions. A nonprogrammed decision might involve whether or not a grocery store should carry an additional type of bread. This decision would be more of a "one-shot" occurrence and certainly would not be clear-cut. The manager must consider whether the new bread will stabilize bread sales by competing with existing bread carried in the store or increase bread sales by offering a choice of bread to the customer who has never before bought bread in the store. These types of issues must be dealt with before management can finally decide whether or not to offer the new bread in the store. Figure 5.1 shows traditional and modern ways of handling programmed and nonprogrammed decisions.

Programmed and nonprogrammed decisions should be thought of as being at opposite ends of a programming continuum, as shown in figure 5.2. The continuum also indicates that some decisions may not clearly be either programmed or nonprogrammed, but some combination of the two.

Figure 5.2 Continuum of extent of decision programming.

Figure 5.3 Level of managers responsible for making decisions as decision scope increases from *A* to *B* to *C*.

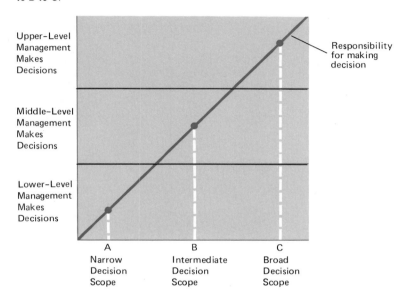

The Responsibility for Making Organizational Decisions

Many different kinds of decisions must be made within an organization—such as how to manufacture a product, how to maintain machines, how to insure product quality, and how to establish advantageous relationships with customers. With varied decisions of this sort, some type of rationale must be developed that stipulates who within the organization has the responsibility for making which decisions.

One such rationale is based primarily on two factors: (1) the scope of the decision to be made and (2) levels of management. The **scope of the decision** refers to the proportion of the total management system that the decision will affect. The greater this proportion, the broader the scope of the decision is said to be. *Levels of management* simply refers to lower-level management, middle-level management, and upper-level management. The rationale for designating who makes which decisions is this: the broader the scope of a decision, the higher the level of the manager responsible for making that decision. Figure 5.3 illustrates this rationale.

What Is the Scope of a Decision?

Level of Management

Examples from the business world of this decision-making rationale are easily obtained. One such example is the manner in which E. I. DuPont de Nemours and Company handle decisions related to the research and development function.[5] As you can see from figure 5.4, this organization has relatively narrow scope research and development decisions, such as "when to test market," made by lower-level managers, and relatively broad scope research and development decisions, such as "authorizing full-scale plant construction," made by upper-level managers.

Even though a manager may have the responsibility for making a particular decision, he or she does not necessarily have to make that decision without the assistance

Help in Making Decisions

Figure 5.4 How scope of decision affects management-level-making decision at E. I. DuPont de Nemours and Company.

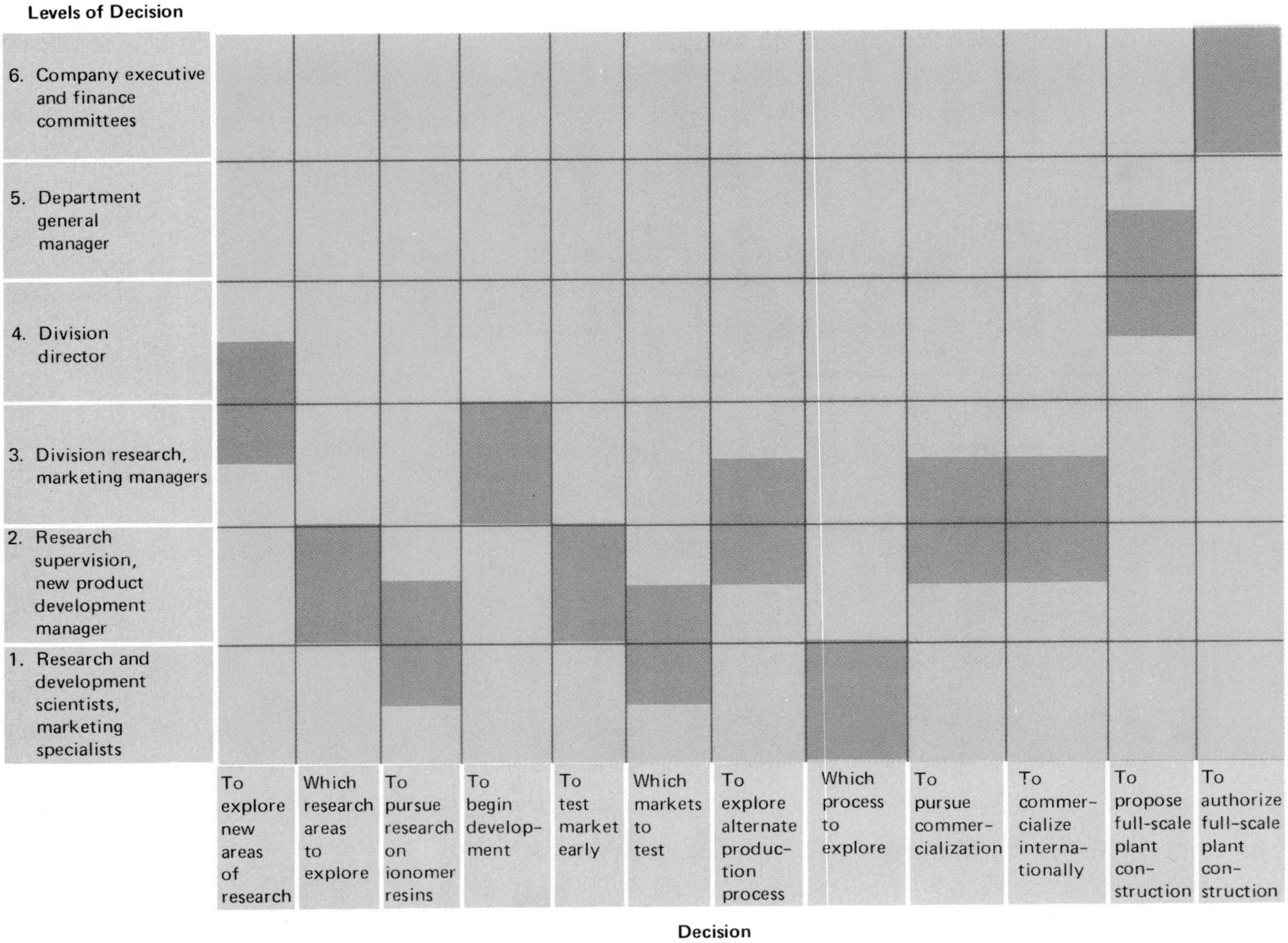

Levels of Decision

Levels of Decision	To explore new areas of research	Which research areas to explore	To pursue research on ionomer resins	To begin develop-ment	To test market early	Which markets to test	To explore alternate produc-tion process	Which process to explore	To pursue commer-cialization	To commer-cialize interna-tionally	To propose full-scale plant con-struction	To authorize full-scale plant con-struction
6. Company executive and finance committees												■
5. Department general manager											■	
4. Division director	■											
3. Division research, marketing managers	■		■				■		■	■		
2. Research supervision, new product development manager		■		■	■	■		■				
1. Research and development scientists, marketing specialists		■		■		■						

Decision

of other organization members. The manager can ask the advice of other managers and/or subordinates in making a decision. In fact, some managers advise having groups make certain decisions.

Everyone Agrees

Consensus is one method managers can use in getting a group to arrive at a particular decision.[6] Consensus is agreement on a decision by all individuals involved in making the decision. It usually occurs after lengthy deliberation and discussion by members of the decision group, who may be either all managers, or a mixture of managers and subordinates.

Decisions through Consensus

Decisions through consensus have both advantages and disadvantages. Among the advantages are the points that managers can focus "several heads" on making a decision and that individuals in the decision group are more likely to be committed to implementing a decision if they helped to make it. The main disadvantage to decisions through consensus is that discussions relating to the decisions tend to be quite lengthy and, therefore, very costly.

Figure 5.5 Environmental factors that can influence managerial decision making.

Internal Environment	External Environment

1. Organizational personnel component
  a. Educational and technological background and skills
  b. Previous technological and managerial skill
  c. Individual member's involvement and commitment to attaining system's goals
  d. Interpersonal behavior styles
  e. Availability of human resources for utilization within the system
2. Organizational functional and staff units component
  a. Technological characteristics of organizational units
  b. Interdependence of organizational units in carrying out their objectives
  c. Intraunit conflict among organizational functional and staff units
  d. Interunit conflict among organizational functional and staff units
3. Organizational level component
  a. Organizational objectives and goals
  b. Integrative process integrating individuals and groups into contributing maximally to attaining organizational goals
  c. Nature of the organization's product service
	4. Customer component
	  a. Distributors of product or service
	  b. Actual users of product or service
	5. Suppliers component
	  a. New materials suppliers
	  b. Equipment suppliers
	  c. Product parts suppliers
	  d. Labor supply
	6. Competitor component
	  a. Competitors for suppliers
	  b. Competitors for customers
	7. Sociopolitical component
	  a. Government regulatory control over the industry
	  b. Public political attitude towards industry and its particular product
	  c. Relationship with trade unions with jurisdiction in the organization
	8. Technological component
	  a. Meeting new technological requirements of own industry and related industries in production of product or service
	  b. Improving and developing new products by implementing new technological advances in the industry

Reprinted from "Characteristics of Organizational Environments and Perceived Environmental Uncertainty" by Robert B. Duncan, published in *Administrative Science Quarterly* 17, no. 3 (Sept. 1972): 315, by permission of the *Administrative Science Quarterly*.

Back to the Case

Because he has a number of alternatives from which to choose, Mr. Winslow is faced with a formal decision situation. In addition, Mr. Winslow should scrutinize this decision very carefully because of its significance to the organization and to himself. The decision itself is highly nonprogrammed and, therefore, will probably be characterized by judgment rather than simple quantitative data. As the highest-level store manager, Winslow should be responsible for making this relatively large-scope decision. This does not mean, however, that Winslow must make the decision by himself. He can ask for the advice of other organization members and perhaps even appoint a group of employees to arrive at a consensus on which alternative should be implemented.

Elements of the Decision Situation

Wilson and Alexis have indicated that there are six basic parts or elements of the decision situation.[7] These parts and their respective definitions are presented in the sections that follow.

State of Nature

This element refers to those aspects of the decision maker's environment that can affect his or her choice. Robert B. Duncan conducted a study in which he attempted to identify environmental characteristics that influenced decision makers. He grouped the characteristics into two categories: the internal environment and the external environment (see figure 5.5).[8]

Decision Environment

The Decision Makers

Decision makers are the individuals or groups who actually make the choice between alternatives. According to Dale, decision makers can have four different orientations: the receptive orientation, the exploitation orientation, the hoarding orientation, and the marketing orientation.

The Receptive Orientation

Decision makers who have a receptive orientation feel that the source of all good is outside themselves, and therefore they rely heavily on suggestions from other organization members. Basically, they like others to make their decisions for them.

The Exploitation Orientation

Decision makers with an exploitation orientation also believe that good is outside themselves, and they are willing to take ethical or unethical steps to steal ideas necessary to make good decisions. They build their organization on the ideas of others and typically extend little or no credit for the ideas to anyone but themselves.

The Hoarding Orientation

The hoarding orientation is characterized by decision makers who preserve the status quo as much as possible. They accept little outside help, isolate themselves from others, and are extremely self-reliant. These decision makers emphasize maintaining their present existence.

The Marketing Orientation

Marketing-oriented decision makers consider themselves commodities that are only as valuable as the decisions they make. They try to make decisions that will enhance their value and are therefore conscious of what others think of their decisions.[9]

The ideal decision-making orientation, however, is one that emphasizes trying to realize the potential of the organization as well as of the decision maker. These decision makers try to use all of their talents and are influenced mainly by reason and sound judgment. Ideal decision makers do not possess the qualities of the four undesirable decision-making orientations just described.

Goals to Be Served

The third main element of the decision situation is the goals that decision makers seek to attain. In the case of managers, these goals should most often be organizational objectives. (Chapter 3 contains specifics about organizational objectives.)

Relevant Alternatives

The decision situation is usually comprised of at least two relevant alternatives. **A relevant alternative** is one that is considered feasible for implementation and also for solving an existing problem. If an alternative clearly cannot be implemented or will not solve an existing problem, it is an irrelevant alternative. Irrelevant alternatives should be excluded from the decision-making situation.

Weak Approaches to Decision Making

Ideal Approach to Decision Making

Objectives

Feasible Alternatives

Figure 5.6 Model of the decision-making process.

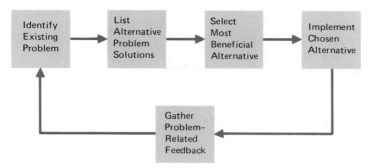

Ordering of Alternatives

The decision situation must have a process or mechanism that ranks alternatives from most desirable to least desirable. The process can be subjective, objective, or some combination of the two. Past experience of the decision maker is an example of a subjective process, and the rate of output per machine is an example of an objective process.

Ranking Alternatives

Choice of Alternatives

The last element of the decision situation is an actual choice between available alternatives. This choice establishes the fact that a decision is made. Typically, managers choose the alternative that maximizes long-run return for the organization.

Making the Decision

In making his decision, Winslow should be aware of all elements in the decision situation. His analysis should include both the internal and the external environments of the hardware company, and his final decision should be based on realizing the store's potential as well as his own. Reason and sound judgement should characterize his orientation as decision maker. Winslow should keep organizational objectives in mind as well as a listing of relevant alternatives that could be used to eliminate his problems. He then should place the list of relevant alternatives in some order of desirability and choose which alternative to implement.

Back to the Case

A decision is choosing one alternative from a set of available alternatives. The **decision-making process** is defined as the steps the decision maker takes to actually choose this alternative. Evaluation of a decision should be at least partially based on the process used to make the decision.[10]

A model of the decision-making process is presented in figure 5.6. In order of occurrence, the steps this model suggests to make decisions are: (1) identifying an existing problem, (2) listing possible alternatives to solve this problem, (3) selecting the most beneficial of these alternatives to solve the problem, (4) putting the selected alternative into action, and (5) gathering feedback to find out if the implemented alternative is alleviating the identified problem. The following paragraphs elaborate upon each of these steps and explain their interrelationships.

The Decision-Making Process

Steps in Making Decisions

Identifying an Existing Problem

Decision making is essentially a problem-solving process that involves eliminating barriers to organizational goal attainment. Naturally, the first step in this elimination process is identifying exactly what these problems or barriers are. Only after the barriers have been discovered and adequately identified can management take steps to

Decisions Involve Problems

Figure 5.7 Additional factors that limit a manager's number of acceptable alternatives.

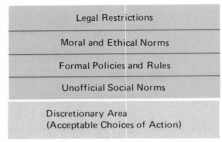

| Legal Restrictions |
| Moral and Ethical Norms |
| Formal Policies and Rules |
| Unofficial Social Norms |
| Discretionary Area (Acceptable Choices of Action) |

eliminate them. Chester Barnard has stated that organizational problems will be brought to the attention of managers mainly through (1) orders issued by managers' supervisors, (2) situations relayed to managers by their subordinates, and/or (3) the normal activity of the managers themselves.[11]

Listing Alternative Problem Solutions

Ways to Solve Decision Problems

Once a problem has been identified, the various alternative problem solutions should be listed. Very few organizational problems have only one solution, and, therefore, managers should not have the attitude that a problem can only be solved in one way. Instead, they must develop the frame of mind that influences them to search out the many alternative solutions that exist for most organizational problems.

Before searching for alternative solutions, managers must be aware of the limits on the types of alternatives they can use. Tannenbaum, Weschler, and Massarik list the following five factors as limitations on the number of problem-solving alternatives available to a manager: (1) authority factors, (2) biological factors, (3) physical factors, (4) technological factors, and (5) economic factors.[12] What these authors are saying is that certain alternatives may not be feasible for the following reasons: (1) a manager's superior has told the manager that the alternative is feasible; (2) human factors within the organization are inappropriate to implement the alternatives; (3) physical facilities of the organization are inappropriate for certain alternatives to be seriously considered; (4) the level of organizational technology is inadequate for certain alternatives; or (5) certain alternatives are too costly for the organization.

Discretionary Area

Figure 5.7 presents additional factors that can limit managers' decision alternatives. This figure uses the term *discretionary area* to designate feasible alternatives available to managers. Factors that limit this discretionary area are legal restrictions, moral and ethical norms, formal policies and rules, and unofficial social norms.[13]

Selecting the Most Beneficial Alternative

Decision makers can select the most beneficial solution only after they have evaluated each alternative very carefully. This evaluation should consist of three steps. First, decision makers should list, as accurately as possible, the potential effects of each alternative as if the alternative had already been chosen and implemented. Second, decision makers should assign a probability factor to each of these potential effects. This would indicate how probable the occurrence of the effect would be if the alternative was implemented. Third, keeping organizational goals in mind, decision makers should compare each alternative's expected effects and their respective probabilities. The alternative that seems to be most advantageous to the organization should be chosen for implementation.

Making the Right Choice

Planning

Implementing the Chosen Alternative

The next step is to actually put the chosen alternative into action. Decisions must be supported by appropriate action if they are to have a chance of being successful.

Gathering Problem-Related Feedback

Evaluating Decision Action

Even after the chosen alternative has been implemented, the task of decision makers is not complete. They must gather feedback to determine the effect of the implemented alternative on the identified problem. If the identified problem is not being solved as a result of the implemented alternative, managers should continue to search out and implement some other alternative that will reduce the impact of the existing problem. On the other hand, if the problem is solved as a result of the implemented alternative, managers can turn their attention to solving other organizational problems.

Assumptions of the Decision-Making Process

This model of the decision-making process is based on three primary assumptions.[14] First, the model assumes that humans are economic beings with the objective of maximizing satisfaction or return. Second, the model is based on the assumption that within the decision-making situation all alternative solutions as well as the possible consequences of each alternative are known to the managers. The last assumption is that decision makers have some priority system that allows them to rank the desirability of each alternative. If each of these assumptions is met in the decision-making situation, decision makers will probably make the best possible decision for the organization. In reality, one or more of these assumptions are usually not met, and related decisions are, therefore, usually something less than the best possible for the organization.

Back to the Case

Mr. Winslow should try to identify the problem that is causing both sales and profit to decline. Once he identifies this problem, he should list possible problem solutions. He may discover after identifying the problem that the alternatives he's already considered are inappropriate. After listing feasible alternatives, Mr. Winslow should evaluate the alternatives, select one to implement, and then implement it. Gathering problem-related feedback is extremely important for Winslow once the alternative has been implemented. This feedback will indicate whether or not the problem has been solved and if additional managerial action is necessary.

Decision-Making Conditions

Predictability and the Future

In most instances it is usually impossible for decision makers to be sure of exactly what the future consequences of an implemented alternative will actually be. The word *future* is the key in discussing decision-making conditions. For all practical purposes, because organizations and their environments are constantly changing, future consequences of implemented decisions are not perfectly predictable.

In general, there are three different conditions under which decisions are made. Each of these conditions is based on the degree to which the future outcome of a decision alternative is predictable. These conditions are (1) the complete certainty condition, (2) the complete uncertainty condition, and (3) the risk condition.[15] Figure 5.8 shows these three conditions on a continuum of predictability of organizational environment with complete certainty at one end and complete uncertainty at the other.

Complete Certainty Condition

Results of Alternative Are Known

The **complete certainty condition** exists when decision makers know exactly what the results of an implemented alternative will be. In this instance managers have complete knowledge about a decision. Since all they have to do is list outcomes for alternatives and then pick the outcome with the highest payoff for the organization, they probably

Figure 5.8 Continuum of decision-making conditions.

Complete Certainty Condition	Risk Condition			Complete Uncertainty Condition
	(Low risk)	(Intermediate risk)	(High risk)	

will find it easy to make sound decisions. For example, the outcome of an investment alternative based on buying government bonds is, for all practical purposes, completely predictable due to established government interest rates. Deciding to implement this alternative essentially would be making a decision in a complete certainty situation. Unfortunately, most organizational decisions are made outside of the complete certainty situation.

Complete Uncertainty Condition

Results of Alternative Are Unknown

The **complete uncertainty condition** exists when decision makers have absolutely no idea what the results of an implemented alternative will be. The complete uncertainty condition would exist, for example, if there was no historical data on which to base a decision. Not knowing what happened in the past makes it difficult to predict what will happen in the future. In this situation, decision makers usually find that sound decisions are merely a matter of chance. An example of a decision made in a complete uncertainty situation would be choosing to pull the candy machine lever labeled "Surprise of the Day" rather than choosing to pull a lever that will deliver a candy bar that looks delicious. It is fortunate that few organizational decisions are made in the complete uncertainty situation.

Risk Condition

The primary characteristic of the **risk condition** is that decision makers have only enough information about the outcome of each alternative to estimate how probable the outcome will be if the alternative is implemented. Obviously, the risk condition is somewhere between the complete certainty situation and the complete uncertainty situation. For example, the manager who hires two extra salespeople to increase annual organizational sales is deciding in a risk situation. He or she may feel that the probability is high that these two new salespeople will increase total sales, but it is impossible to know for sure. Some risk is associated with this decision.

Results of Alternative Are Somewhat Known

In reality *degrees* of risk can be associated with decisions made in the risk situation. The lower the quality of information related to the outcome of an alternative, the closer the situation is to the complete uncertainty situation and the higher the risk associated with choosing the alternative. Most decisions made in organizations normally have some amount of risk associated with them.

Positive Outcomes from Foreign Investment

As a classic example of decision making under the risk condition, consider the manager who is attempting to decide whether or not to invest in foreign operations. Normally, managers who make such a decision to invest do so because they feel that an investment alternative of this sort will generally have outcomes such as (1) reducing or eliminating high transportation costs; (2) participating in the rapid expansion of a market abroad; (3) obtaining foreign technical, design, and marketing skills; and (4) earning higher profits.[16]

Risk and Foreign Investment

There is, however, some risk associated with the decision to invest in foreign operations. For example, political complications between the investing company and various factions within the host country—the country in which the investment is made—could prohibit the desired outcomes from materializing. Figure 5.9 presents various

Figure 5.9 Political risk in investing in a foreign country.

Sources of Political Risk	Groups through Which Political Risk can be Generated	Political Risk Effects: Types of Influence on International Business Operations
Competing political philosophies (nationalism, socialism, communism)	Government in power and its operating agencies	Confiscation: loss of assets without compensation
Social unrest and disorder	Nonparliamentary opposition groups (e.g., anarchist or guerrilla movement working from within or outside of country)	Expropriation with compensation: loss of freedom to operate
Vested interests of local business groups		Operational restrictions: market shares, product characteristics, employment policies, locally shared ownership, and so forth
Recent and impending political independence	Nonorganized common interest groups: students, workers, peasants, minorities, and so forth	Loss of transfer freedom: financial (for example, dividends, interest payments), goods, personnel, or ownership rights
Armed conflicts and internal rebellions for political power	Foreign governments or inter-governmental agencies such as the EEC	Breaches or unilateral revisions in contracts and agreements
New international alliances	Foreign governments willing to enter into armed conflict or to support internal rebellion	Discrimination such as taxes, compulsory subcontracting
		Damage to property or personnel from riots, insurrections, revolutions, and wars

From *International, Business and Multinational Enterprise*, rev. ed., by Stefan H. Robock, Kenneth Simmons, and Jack Zwick, p. 291. Copyright © by Richard D. Irwin, Inc. Used with permission of Richard D. Irwin, Inc.

possible sources of the political risk, several groups within the host country that might generate the risk, and possible effects of the risk on the investing organization.

The likelihood of desirable outcomes of foreign investments actually materializing will probably always be somewhat uncertain and will vary from country to country. Nevertheless, managers faced with this decision of making foreign investments must assess this likelihood as accurately as possible. Obviously, a poor decision to invest in another country can cause serious financial problems for the investing company. Figure 5.10 describes some of the services managers subscribe to that weigh political, economic, and social factors by which the company can assess various risk levels associated with investing in different foreign countries.

Assessing Likelihood

From reading this section, Mr. Winslow can see that his decision-making condition is somewhere between complete certainty and complete uncertainty about the outcome of his alternatives. Therefore, the decision for his store is being made under the risk condition. Mr. Winslow will have to determine how probable the outcomes for each of his alternatives actually are.

Back to the Case

Although some writers indicate that more subjective tools such as extrasensory perception (ESP)[17] can be important to decision making, most managers tend to emphasize more objective decision-making tools, such as linear programming, queuing or waiting-line methods, and game theory.[18] Perhaps the two most widely used of these more objective decision-making tools, however, are probability theory and decision trees. The following paragraphs explain probability theory and decision trees and illustrate how the two can be used to help managers make better decisions.

Decision-Making Tools

Aids in Decision Making

Figure 5.10 How some managers assess risk of doing business abroad.

CAN A COMPUTER TELL THE RATIO OF RISK?

To help them cope with the uncertainties of doing business abroad, many companies subscribe to services that publish country-risk indexes, somewhat like Moody's bond or Value Line stock ratings. Though there is some debate about the usefulness of numerically rating countries for risk, the client lists of the three organizations read like the FORTUNE 500.

A company considering expanding into Indonesia, for example, might well consult all three of that country's ratings. It could look at the BERI (for Business Environment Risk Index) rating, which ranks countries on a scale of 1 to 100. Indonesia scores a 45.5, a low enough rating to be marked a "high risk." A similar index put out by Business International (BI), an advisory service for multinationals, gives Indonesia a slightly more respectable 58. Finally, the World Political Risk Forecasts (WPRF) service of Frost & Sullivan, a business research organization, expresses its own rather dim view of Indonesia in its January, 1980, forecast: a company doing business there stands a 31 percent chance of a major business loss owing to political developments in the next eighteen months and a 45 percent chance of loss within five years. A better bet for investment would be nearby Singapore — BERI score 74.9, BI rating 79, and WPRF loss probability of only 19 percent in the next five years.

Executives appreciate these rating services because they are relatively cheap ($500 a year for BERI, $1,500 for WPRF), and they boil down the complex forecast to simple numbers. Says Frederick Haner, the University of Delaware business professor who compiles the BERI rating, "Executives treat these numbers as though they came from God directly." In fact, they are derived from weighting and averaging the evaluations of economic, political, and social factors in foreign countries made by panels of "experts." BI's information comes from its employees around the world; WPRF and BERI don't identify their panelists beyond describing them as experts from business, government, and academia.

The most frequent criticism of this indexing is that, although it is based on largely subjective evaluations, the figures imply a mathematical precision that really isn't there. One risk analyst for a major United States corporation calls indexing "a substitute for thought." But the purveyors of risk ratings — and many of their clients — claim indexing is a useful tool, though obviously not the only one, for assessing risk. In any case, the troubled world of international business has made risk rating a growth industry. — **GRANT F. WINTHROP**

From Grant F. Winthrop, *Fortune*, 24 March 1980, p. 95. © 1980 Time Inc. All rights reserved.

Probability Theory

Decision-making Tool for Risk Situations

EV = I × P

Probability theory is a decision-making tool used in risk situations or situations wherein decision makers are not completely sure of the outcome of an implemented alternative. Probability refers to the likelihood that an event or outcome will actually occur and allows decision makers to calculate an expected value for each alternative. The **expected value (EV)** for an alternative is the income (I) it would produce multiplied by its probability of making that income (P). In formula form, $EV = I \times P$. Decision makers should follow the general rule of choosing and implementing the alternative with the highest expected value.

An example will make the relationship between probability, income, and expected value more clear. A manager is trying to decide where to open a store that specializes in renting surfboards. He is considering three possible location alternatives (A, B, and C), all of which seem very feasible. For the first year of operation, the manager has projected that under ideal conditions he would earn $90,000 in Location A, $75,000 in Location B, and $60,000 in Location C. After studying historical weather patterns, however, the manager has determined that there is only a 20 percent chance or a .2 probability of ideal conditions during the first year of operation in Location A. Locations B and C have a .4 and a .8 probability respectively for ideal conditions during the first year. Expected values for each of these locations are as follows: Location A— $18,000; Location B—$30,000; Location C—$48,000. Figure 5.11 shows the situation this decision maker is faced with.

According to this probability analysis, the manager should open a store in Location C, the alternative with the highest expected value.

Figure 5.11 Expected values for locating surfboard rental store in each of three possible locations.

Alternative (Locations)	Potential Income	Probability of Income	Expected Value of Alternatives
A	$90,000	.2	$18,000
B	75,000	.4	30,000
C	60,000	.8	48,000
	I	X	P	=	EV

Decision Trees

More Complicated Decisions

Graphic Decision-making Tool

In the previous section, probability theory was applied to a relatively simple decision situation. Some decisions, however, are more complicated and involve a series of steps. These steps are interdependent; that is, each step is influenced by the step that precedes it. **A decision tree** is a graphic decision-making tool typically used to evaluate decisions containing a series of steps.[19]

Decision Trees and Production

John F. Magee[20] has developed a classic illustration that outlines how decision trees can be applied to a production decision. In his illustration, the Stygian Chemical Company must decide whether to build a small or a large plant to manufacture a new product with an expected life of ten years.

Decision Trees Outline Decision Situations

The basics of a decision tree that outlines the situation facing Stygian is presented in Figure 5.12. This figure clearly shows that management must decide (Decision Point #1) whether to build a small plant or a large one. If the choice is to build a large plant, the company could face product demands of high or low average demand, or high initial and then low demand. If, on the other hand, the choice is to build a small plant, the company could face either initially high or initially low product demand. If the small plant is built, however, and high product demand exists during an initial two-year period, management could then choose whether or not to expand its plant (Decision Point #2). Whether the decision is made to expand the plant or not to expand, management could then face either high or low product demand.

Now that various possible alternatives related to this decision have been outlined, the financial consequence of each different course of action must be compared before a final choice can be made. To adequately compare these consequences, management must: (1) study estimates of investment amounts necessary for building a large plant, for building a small plant, and for expanding a small plant; (2) weigh probabilities of facing different product demand levels for various decision alternatives; and (3) consider projected income yields per decision alternative.

Analysis of the expected values and net expected gain for each decision alternative will help management to decide on an appropriate choice. Net expected gain is defined in this situation as the expected value of an alternative minus investment cost. In Magee's example in figure 5.12, building a large plant yields the highest net expected gain. As a result, Stygian management should decide to build the large plant.

Figure 5.12 A basic decision tree illustrating the decision facing Stygian management.

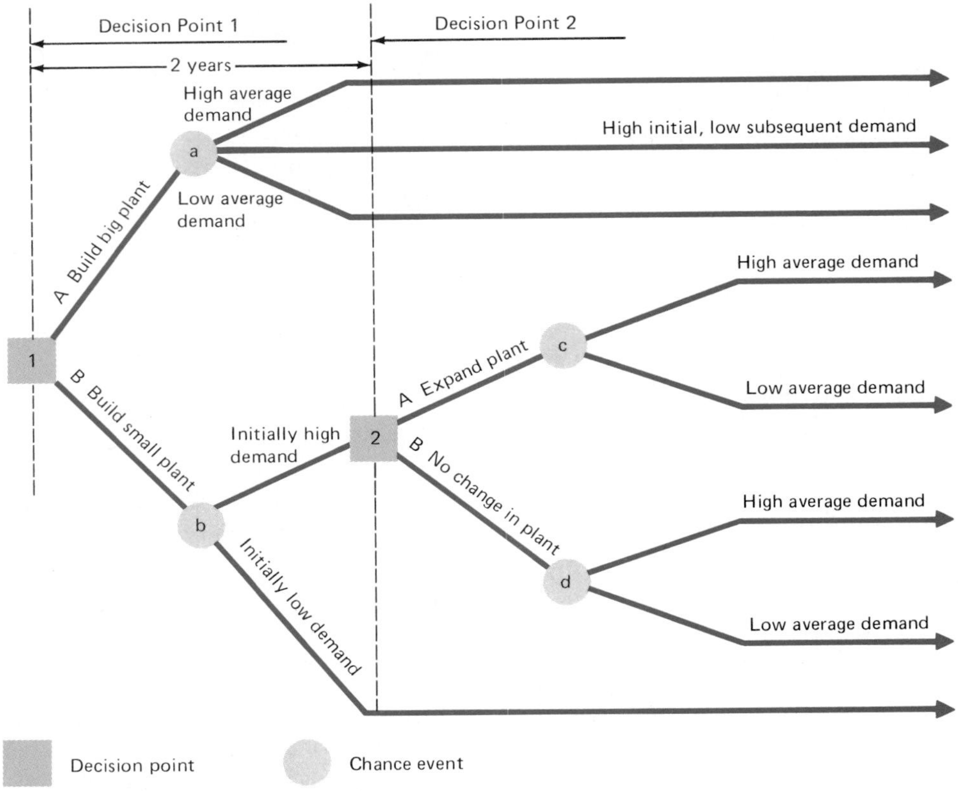

Decision point ▢   Chance event ⬤

Back to the Case

Mr. Winslow has two tools available to help him make his decision. First, he can use probability theory to obtain an expected value for each alternative and then choose the alternative with the highest expected value. Second, he may determine that rather than a relatively simple choice between his three alternatives, he must really decide between a series of steps related to each of these alternatives. In this case he can use a decision tree to assist him in picturing and evaluating each of the three series. Winslow must remember, however, that business judgment is an essential adjunct to the effective use of any decision-making tool. The purpose of the tool is to improve the quality of the judgment, not to replace it.[21] In the end Winslow will choose the alternative most advantageous for the organization.

Summary

The following points are stressed within this chapter:

1. A decision is a choice made between two or more available alternatives. Practicing managers quickly realize that they must make many decisions, some very significant and some fairly insignificant. Decisions managers make can be described as programmed, nonprogrammed, or somewhere between the two.

2. In terms of responsibility for making organizational decisions, as the scope of a decision increases, the higher the level of manager who should make that decision. Although a manager may be responsible for making a particular decision, he or she can ask others to help in the decision process and perhaps have a group make a decision through consensus.

3. Decision-making situations include elements concerning the state of nature, the decision makers, the goals to be served, relevant alternatives, an ordering of alternatives, and a choice of alternatives. The decision-making process incorporates these elements by identifying a problem, listing possible alternatives to solve this problem, selecting the most beneficial of these alternatives, putting the chosen alternative into action, and gathering feedback related to the implemented alternative.

4. Three possible conditions under which decisions are made are complete certainty, complete uncertainty, and risk.

5. Probability theory and decision trees are two decision-making tools that can be used to assess the risk associated with organizational decisions. These tools will not make decisions for managers, but they will help managers to make better decisions through risk analysis.

---

1. What is a decision?
2. Describe the difference between a significant decision and an insignificant decision. Which would you rather make? Why?
3. List three programmed and three nonprogrammed decisions that the manager of a nightclub would probably have to make.
4. Explain the rationale for determining which managers in the organization are responsible for making which decisions.
5. What is the consensus method of making decisions? When would you use it?
6. List and define the six basic elements of the decision-making situation.
7. How does the receptive orientation for decision making differ from the ideal orientation for decision making?
8. List as many undesirable traits of a decision maker as possible. (They are implied within the explanations of the exploitation, hoarding, and marketing orientations to decision making.)

9. What is a relevant alternative? An irrelevant alternative?
10. Draw and describe in words the decision-making process presented in this chapter.
11. What is meant by the term *discretionary area*?
12. List the assumptions on which the decision-making process presented in this chapter is based.
13. Explain the difference between the complete certainty and complete uncertainty decision-making situation.
14. What is the risk-decision-making situation?
15. Are there degrees of risk associated with various decisions? Why?
16. How do decision makers use probability theory? Be sure to discuss expected value in your answer.
17. What is a decision tree?
18. Under what conditions are decision trees usually used as decision-making tools?

Sources of Additional Information

Alexis, M., and Wilson, C. Z. *Organizational Decision-Making.* Englewood Cliffs, N.J.: Prentice-Hall, 1967.

Benshael, Jane G. "Making the Right Decision." *International Management* 34 (April 1979): 30–31.

Cohen, Herb. "How You Can Get What You Want By Negotiation." *Nation's Business* 69, no. 5 (May 1981): 87–90.

Duncan, Jack W. *Decision Making and Social Issues.* Hinsdale, Ill.: Dryden Press, 1973.

Fox, Harold W. "The Frontiers of Strategic Planning: Intuition or Formal Models?" *Management Review* 70, no. 4 (April 1981): 8–14.

Harrison, E. Frank. *The Managerial Decision-Making Process.* Boston: Houghton Mifflin, 1975.

Kassouf, Sheen. *Normative Decision Making.* Englewood Cliffs, N.J.: Prentice-Hall, 1970.

Kast, F. E., and Rosenzweig, J. E. *Organization and Management: A Systems Approach.* New York: McGraw-Hill, 1970.

Kepner, Charles, and Tregoe, Benjamin. *The Rational Manager.* New York: McGraw-Hill, 1965.

March, James, and Simon, Herbert. *Organizations.* New York: John Wiley & Sons, 1958.

Miller, D. W., and Starr, M. K. *Executive Decision and Operations Research.* 2d ed. Englewood Cliffs, N.J.: Prentice-Hall, 1969.

Raiffa, Howard. *Decision Analysis: Introductory Lectures on Choices under Uncertainty.* Reading, Mass.: Addison-Wesley, 1968.

Schlaifer, Robert. *Probability and Statistics for Business Decisions.* New York: McGraw-Hill, 1959.

Shull, Fremont; Delbecq, Andre; and Cummings, L. L. *Organizational Decision Making.* New York: McGraw-Hill, 1970.

Simon, Herbert. *Administrative Behavior.* New York: Macmillan, 1961.

Simon, Herbert. *Administrative Behavior.* 3d ed. New York: Free Press, 1976.

Stephenson, Blair Y., and Franklin, Stephen G. "Better Decision-Making for a 'Real-World' Environment." *Administrative Management* 42, no. 7 (July 1981): 24–26, 36, 38.

Wind, Yoram, and Mahajan, Vijay. "Designing Product and Business Portfolios." *Harvard Business Review,* January/February 1981, pp. 155–65.

Notes

1. Jack W. Duncan, *Decision Making and Social Issues* (Hinsdale, Ill.: Dryden Press, 1973), p. 1.

2. S. M. Perrone, "Understanding the Decision Process," *Administrative Management,* May 1968, pp. 88–92.

3. Mervin Kohn, *Dynamic Managing: Principles, Process, Practice* (Menlo Park, Calif.: Cummings Publishing Company, 1977), pp. 58–62.

4. Herbert A. Simon, *The New Science of Management Decision* (New York: Harper & Row, 1960), pp. 5–8.

5. *The D of Research and Development* (Wilmington, Del.: E. I. DuPont de Nemours and Company, 1966), pp. 28–29.

6. Jack J. Holder, Jr., "Decision Making by Consensus," *Business Horizons,* April 1972, pp. 47–54.

7. Charles Wilson and Marcus Alexis, "Basic Frameworks for Decision," *Academy of Management Journal* 5, no. 2 (August 1962): 151–64.

8. Robert B. Duncan, "Characteristics of Organizational Environments and Perceived Environmental Uncertainty," *Administrative Science Quarterly* 17, no. 3 (September 1972): 313–27.

9. See Ernest Dale, *Management: Theory and Practice* (New York: McGraw-Hill, 1973), pp. 548–49. This section of Dale's test is based on Erich Fromm, *Man for Himself* (New York: Holt, Rinehart & Winston, 1947), pp. 62–117.

10. Douglas R. Emery and Francis D. Tuggle, "On the Evaluation of Decisions," *MSU Business Topics,* Spring 1976, pp. 40–48.

11. Chester I. Barnard, *The Function of the Executive* (Cambridge, Mass.: Harvard University Press, 1938).

12. For further elaboration on these factors, see Robert Tannenbaum, Irving R. Weschler, and Fred Massarik, *Leadership and Organization: A Behavioral Science Approach* (New York: McGraw-Hill, 1961), pp. 277–78.

13. For more discussion of these factors, see F. A. Shull, Jr., A. L. Delbecq, and L. L. Cummings, *Organizational Decision Making* (New York: McGraw-Hill, 1970).

14. These assumptions are adapted from James G. March and Herbert A. Simon, *Organizations* (New York: John Wiley & Sons, 1958), pp. 137–38.

15. F. E. Kast and J. E. Rosenzweig, *Organization and Management: A Systems Approach* (New York: McGraw-Hill, 1970), p. 385.

16. National Foreign Trade Council, 1971 Survey, cited in Frederick D. Sturdivant, *Business and Society: A Managerial Approach* (Homewood, Ill.: Richard D. Irwin, 1977), p. 425.

17. John Mihalasky, "ESP in Decision Making," *Management Review,* April 1975, pp. 32–37.

18. The scope of this text does not permit elaboration on these three decision-making tools. However, for an excellent discussion on how these tools are used in decision making, see Richard M. Hodgetts, *Management: Theory, Process and Practice* (Philadelphia: W. B. Saunders, 1975), pp. 254–66.

19. William A. Spurr and Charles P. Bonini, *Statistical Analysis for Business Decisions* (Homewood, Ill.: Richard D. Irwin, 1967), pp. 202–17.

20. P. G. Moore, "Technique Vs. Judgment in Decision Making," *Organizational Dynamics* 2 (1973–74): 69–79.

21. Charles H. Lang, "Decision Making," *Manage,* August 1959.

Concluding Case 5
Sears's "Scattershot" Approach to Decision Making

Edward A. Brennan (Photo: Richard Faverty, *Business Week*)

Sears has become the highest-operating-cost mass merchandiser today, with general and administrative expenses amounting to 29 percent of sales, compared with 23 percent for J. C. Penney Company and 19 percent for K-Mart Corporation. One competitor estimates that Sears would have to decrease costs by $100 million a year to be competitive with others such as K-Mart. He further suggests that with Sears's unwieldly cost structure, Sears needs a 50 percent markup to make a profit in products, while competitors need only a 35 percent markup.

Sears's merchandising profit margin dropped dramatically from 3.1 percent in 1976 to 2.2 percent in 1979. Once the 1980 figures are compiled, it is expected to drop further. Merchandising profits have also declined from $439 million in 1976 to $367 million in 1979. During the first three quarters of 1980, earnings dropped 80 percent. In addition, credit and operations lost $8.1 million during that period. Presently, Sears's stock is at a twenty-year low.

In an attempt to recover financially, the managers of retailing operations have made some significant changes, such as centralized purchasing stations, early retirement incentives, and store modernization. Recently, Edward R. Telling, Sears's chairman and merchandise executive, has demonstrated a willingness to develop new retail growth areas. For instance, Sears is opening five freestanding-business-machine stores that will eventually serve business and consumers. However, Sears has also made a series of erratic, unrelated moves that appear to be based on a trial-and-error approach to management decision making.

For example, in an attempt to appeal to more affluent people, the company began stocking expensive, high-fashion merchandise, ignoring their own image of the provider of merchandise for America's heartland. The affluent demonstrated little interest in these goods, and its traditional customers reacted negatively to the higher prices. In addition, Sears took a "get-tough" policy with the company's suppliers by informing them that Sears would no longer carry products that were slow sellers in the stores. Suppliers, in turn, found new customers and expanded their branded-product lines. One former buyer says that Sears has, historically, romanced their vendors, but now, due to the existing get-tough policy, suppliers are running to non-Sears businesses. (Consequently, Sears ends up with products that are the same as everyone else's. Why should a consumer purchase a Sears's product when it could have a branded item?) In 1977, Sears engaged in a successful price war with K-Mart. Sales rose by 16 percent; however price cuts had obliterated profits as earnings fell by 10 percent for Sears.

(Photo: Richard Faverty, *Business Week*)

(Photo: Richard Faverty, *Business Week*)

Most of these ill-conceived decisions were made within an increasingly unruly management structure. Sears gave its field people virtual autonomy in promotional pricing, store size, and product selection, while it continually expanded its corporate management staff to organize its many activities. During the early days of continual growth, this practice was sound. However, in the 1970s, Sears continued to add executives, increase its overhead, and add an increasingly complex corporate structure of unruly dimension.

In 1976, Sears increased its national merchandising groups from five to nine groups. These groups control buying, market development, promotion, and pricing. Sears also created the position of senior vice-president, field. This position was formed to coordinate the five territorial management teams that run the tremendous network of stores and catalog houses owned by Sears. Furthermore, a national retail sales staff was developed to act as a liaison between the corporate office and the field.

Louis W. Stern (a marketing professor at Northwestern University) contends that "Sears's management structures on top of management structures" have hindered timely decisions and good execution of ideas as well as have led to a tremendous cost. Now Sears is faced with the enormous task of reducing costs through the elimination of unneeded corporate managers, recovering its traditional customers, and regaining the confidence of departed suppliers. Edward A. Brennan, the new chairman of the merchandise group, is faced with developing ways to solve these problems. The overall strategy he proposes is to standardize Sears stores. Brennan suggests that Sears must approach the business as though it were a single store. He contends that there must be consistency from store to store. He says, "If there is a right way to do something, then that right way should be used in New York, Los Angeles, and Miami."

This case is adapted from "How Sears Became a High-Cost Operator," *Business Week,* February 16, 1981, pp. 52–57.

Discussion Issues

1. Categorize, by type, the decisions Sears faced. Did Sears executives use the modern or the more traditional approach to make these decisions? Explain.
2. What element of the decision situation is most responsible for Sears's ill-conceived decisions? Support your answer.
3. Listed below are four yardsticks against which alternatives should be evaluated to determine which alternative is best. Which of these does it appear Sears's management overlooked in the process of selecting courses of action? Explain.

   Yardsticks Against Which You May Rate
Alternative Solutions

   Risk-risk—Compare the expected gain if your decision is the "right" one with the expected loss if your decision is the "wrong" one.

   Economy of effort—Answer the question, Which alternative will give the best result with the least disruptive effect on the organization? (How much change in people, methods, and processes will each alternative require?)

   Timing—"Is the organization ready for a major change?" People make decisions work; if your people reject your decision, the results could be disastrous for everyone (especially you).

   Acceptability—"Will higher management readily buy this solution?" "Can you 'sell' executives on your solution?"[21]
4. Assume you are a member of top management at Sears. List and discuss what you feel are viable solutions to the financial problems facing Sears.

Student Learning Objectives

From studying this chapter I will attempt to acquire:

1. A complete definition of a plan
2. An understanding of various types of plans
3. Insights on why plans fail
4. A knowledge of various planning areas within an organization
5. A definition of forecasting
6. An ability to see the advantages and disadvantages of various methods of sales forecasting
7. A definition of scheduling
8. An ability to use Gantt charts and PERT

Chapter Outline

Plans and Planning Tools

Introductory Case 6
A Planning Incident

Jane and Paul were partners in a small machine shop that did jobbing or contract work predominantly for machine tool manufacturers. Due to a transportation strike, the shop was virtually shut down for a few days. The partners came in every day, of course, and one morning Jane mentioned that it had been months since both of them had sat down to discuss their business in general terms. The daily routine had kept them so busy that there hardly had been time to say good morning.

Paul agreed and suggested that they get at it right then and there. During the next two hours they discussed everything from how old their machines were to putting in new vending machines for coffee and sandwiches. What seemed to concern the partners most, however, was that most of their equipment was quite old, dating back to World War II days in many instances. This situation made matching the competition's quality and speed of output difficult.

Finally, Jane leaned back in her chair. "Paul, we've got to get our costs down. We can't do it overnight, but we can make that one of our major goals over the next few years. If we don't, we're just going to lose out on the bidding on new contracts."

Paul nodded his assent. "You're right, and there's something else too. For a long time we've been preaching quality to our people, but it's really difficult for them with the equipment they've got to work with. We could lower costs and emphasize quality successfully if we could get some modern machinery in here. From what I've learned in the trade journals, with new machine tools we could drop our costs 10 to 20 percent over the next five years."

Excerpt from pp. 153–154 in ORGANIZATIONAL MANAGEMENT: SYSTEMS AND PROCESS by Earl F. Lundgren. Copyright © 1974 by Earl F. Lundgren. Reprinted by permission of Harper & Row, Publishers, Inc.

Discussion Issues

1. Given Jane and Paul's situation, list the kinds of plans they probably need.
2. Write some sample plans that could be developed given the planning needs you listed in number 1.
3. What kind of information would Jane and Paul need to actually develop the plans you have written?

What's Ahead

Chapter 5 focused on the decision-making phase or the evaluation-of-alternatives phase of the planning process. This chapter continues the discussion of the planning process by emphasizing what managers do after choosing the best alternative to acomplish organizational objectives. They begin to formulate specific plans based on this alternative.

Jane and Paul, the partners in the introductory case, need to formulate plans for their organization, and the material in this chapter is meant to assist them. Fundamental facts about plans and tools managers can use to develop plans are presented. To this end, the remainder of this chapter is divided into two main sections: "Plans" and "Planning Tools."

Plans

The first half of this chapter covers the fundamental facts about plans, by (1) defining what a plan is, (2) outlining the dimensions of a plan, (3) listing various types of plans, (4) discussing why plans fail, and (5) explaining two major organizational areas in which planning usually takes place.

Plan: A Definition

Recommended Action

A **plan** is a specific action proposed to help the organization achieve its objectives. According to Sisk, "planning, the process of evaluating all relevant information and the assessment of probable future developments, results in the statement of a recommended course of action—a plan."[1] Regardless of how important experience-related intuition may be to managers, successful management action and strategy typically is based on reason. Rational managers are extremely important to the development of an organizational plan.[2]

Dimensions of Plan

Kast and Rosenzweig have indicated that a plan has four major dimensions: (1) repetitiveness, (2) time, (3) scope, and (4) level.[3] Each dimension is an independent characteristic of a plan and should be considered during plan development.[4]

Repetitiveness

Is Plan Used Again and Again?

The **repetitiveness dimension** describes the extent to which a plan is used time after time. Some plans are specially designed for one certain situation that is relatively short run in nature. Plans of this sort are essentially nonrepetitive. On the other hand, some plans are designed to be used time after time and are designed for situations that exist continually over the long run. These plans are basically repetitive in nature.

Time

Length of Time Plan Covers

The **time dimension** of a plan is the length of the time period the plan covers. In chapter 4, strategic planning was defined as long run in nature, and tactical planning was defined as short run. It follows, then, that strategic plans cover relatively long periods of time, while tactical plans cover relatively short periods of time.

"Things must be going badly—he keeps referring to it as my plan."
From the *Wall Street Journal.*

Scope

Is Plan for Entire Organization?

The **scope dimension** describes the portion of the total management system at which the plan is aimed. Some plans are designed to cover the entire open management system: the organizational environment, organizational inputs, organizational process, and organizational outputs. A plan for the management system as a whole can be referred to as a master plan. Some plans, however, are developed to cover only a portion of the management system. An example would be a plan developed to cover the recruitment of new workers, a portion of the organizational input segment of the management system. The greater the portion of the management system that a plan covers, the broader the scope of the plan is said to be.

Level

Which Level of Organization Is Plan for?

The **level dimension** of a plan indicates the level of the organization at which the plan is aimed. Top-level plans are those designed for the top-management level of the organization, while middle-level and lower-level plans are designed for middle-level and lower-level management respectively. Because of the very nature of the management system, however, plans for any level of the organization have some effect on all other levels. All parts of the management system are interdependent, and no single part can be affected without some effect on all other parts.

Figure 6.1 illustrates the level dimension and the other previously described dimensions of an organizational plan. In essence, this figure stresses that when managers develop a plan, they should consider the degree to which the plan will be used over and over again, the period of time the plan will cover, the parts of the management system on which the plan focuses, and the organizational level at which the plan is aimed.

Back to the Case

Jane and Paul, the partners in the introductory case, could learn from the first section of this chapter many valuable facts about how to develop plans for their organization. First, they should understand that plans are recommendations for future action and therefore should be action oriented. They should also consider how often their plans will be used, the length of time the plans will cover, at what proportion of the organization the plans are aimed, and the level of the organization on which the plans focus.

Figure 6.1 Four major dimensions to consider when developing a plan.

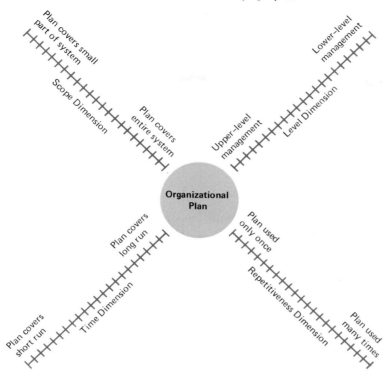

Types of Plans

Using primarily the repetitiveness dimension as a guide, organizational plans usually are divided into two types: standing plans and single-use plans. **Standing plans** are used over and over again because they focus on organizational situations that occur repeatedly, while **single-use plans** are used only once or several times because they focus on dealing with relatively unique situations within the organization. Figure 6.2 illustrates that standing plans can be subdivided into policies, procedures, and rules, and that single-use plans can be subdivided into programs and budgets.[5]

Repetitive Situations vs. Unique Situations

Standing Plans

Policies

A **policy** is a standing plan that furnishes *broad* guidelines for channeling management thinking in specified directions. As a result of this "channeled thinking," management is guided toward taking action consistent with reaching organizational objectives. A policy is essentially a general expression of management intent on what action should be taken to achieve organizational objectives. For example, an organizational policy relating to personnel might be worded as follows: "Our organization will strive to recruit only the most talented employees." This policy statement is very broad and only gives managers a general idea of what to do in the area of personnel employment. The

Broad Guidelines for Action

Figure 6.2 Standing plans and single-use plans.

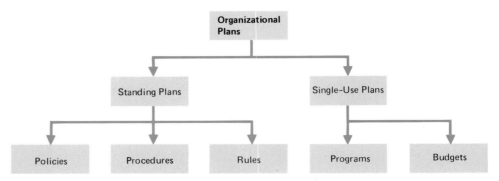

policy is intended to display the extreme importance management has attached to hiring competent employees and to guiding action accordingly. Other organizational areas in which policy statements are usually written are listed in figure 6.3.

Procedures

Series of Actions

A **procedure** is a standing plan that outlines a series of related actions that must be taken to accomplish a particular task. In general, procedures outline more specific action than do policies. Organizations usually have many different sets of procedures that cover various tasks to be accomplished. The sample procedure in figure 6.4 lists the series of steps recruiters take to interview prospective personnel at Indiana State University.

Rules

Mandatory Activities

A **rule** is a standing plan that designates specific required action. In essence, a rule indicates what an organization member should or should not do. A rule precisely outlines desired action and, therefore, allows no room for interpretation. An example of a rule would be that all students must be seated in silence immediately after the bell rings, signaling the beginning of class. The concept of rules may be more clear after thinking about the purpose and nature of rules in such games as Scrabble and Monopoly.

Although policies, procedures, and rules are all standing plans, they are all defined differently and have different purposes within the organization. Policies provide general guidelines for action to channel the thinking of managers. Procedures, on the other hand, outline more specific actions to be taken by managers and present sequential steps that should be performed to accomplish a task. Rules pinpoint more specific action than either policies or procedures, and allow no room for interpretation. The specific actions outlined by rules are mandatory. As figure 6.5 illustrates, for the standing plans of an organization to be effective, policies, procedures, and rules must be consistent and mutually supportive.

Single-Use Plans

Programs

Programs Aid
Success Indirectly

A **program** is a single-use plan designed to carry out a special project within an organization. The project itself typically is not intended to be in existence over the entire life of the organization. However, the program exists to achieve some purpose that, if accomplished, will contribute to the long-run success of the organization.

Figure 6.3 Organizational areas in which policy statements usually are written.

I. General Management

A. *Divisions and functional staffs*
   1. Authority and responsibilities of divisions concerning pricing, capital authorization, interdivisional transfers, product areas, and authority retained in central headquarters
   2. Functional staff relationships at headquarters and authority in divisions

B. *Growth*
   1. Sales rate
   2. Profit rate
   3. Acquisitions

C. *Planning*
   1. Budgets
   2. Company basic lines of business
   3. Comprehensive planning
   4. Organization

D. *Policy authority and statements*

E. *Miscellaneous*
   1. Acceptance of gifts or services by employees
   2. Answering correspondence
   3. Computer procurement
   4. Disaster control
   5. Employment of consultants
   6. Gifts and gratuities to government and company personnel
   7. Internal auditor reports
   8. Political activities of managers
   9. Records management

II. Marketing

A. *Products and services sold*
   1. Types
   2. Inventory of parts
   3. Licensing
   4. Modification
   5. Quality
   6. Warranty

B. *Customers*
   1. Contract clearance
   2. Export sales
   3. Interdivisional transfers
   4. Market areas
   5. Market channels
   6. Relations with customers, including dealers and distributors
   7. Service for customers
   8. Size of customers

C. *Pricing*
   1. Authority to price
   2. Compliance with antitrust laws
   3. Discounting
   4. Resale price maintenance
   5. Timing of price change

D. *Sales promotion*
   1. Advertising media
   2. Product publicity

III. Production

A. *Assignments of products to divisions*

B. *Contracting*

C. *Manufacturing methods*

D. *Production control*

E. *Production planning*

F. *Quality control*

G. *Safety*

H. *Shipping*

I. *Size of production runs*

J. *Stabilization of production*

K. *Tooling*

IV. Procurement

A. *Make-or-buy decisions*

B. *Minimum procurement quantities*

C. *Purchasing channels*

D. *Relations with suppliers*

E. *Types of vendors*

V. Research

A. *Allocating funds*

B. *Basic research*

C. *Evaluating results*

D. *Inventions*

E. *Patents*

F. *Research areas*

G. *Research records*

H. *Trademarks*

VI. Finance

A. *Audit*

B. *Budget*
   1. Developing
   2. Controlling

C. *Credit*
   1. Customers
   2. Employees

D. *Dividend policy*
   1. Size relative to profit
   2. Stabilizing

E. *Expenditures*
   1. Authority to spend company money
   2. Contributions and donations

F. *Protecting capital*
   1. Insurance
   2. Reserves

G. *Structure*
   1. Debt rations
   2. Long-term financing
   3. Short-term financing

VII. Facilities

A. *Decision-making process for expenditure*

B. *Location*

C. *Maintenance*

D. *Replacement*

VIII. Personnel

A. *Collective bargaining and union relations*

B. *Communications systems*

C. *Employment and recruiting*

D. *Equal opportunities*

E. *Hours of work*

F. *Incentives and bonuses*

G. *Pensions*

H. *Selection*

I. *Services*
   1. Food service
   2. Health and safety
   3. Insurance
   4. Recreational and educational activities
   5. Retirement
   6. Sick leave
   7. Transportation and parking

J. *Training and education*

K. *Wages and salaries*

L. *Working conditions*

IX. Public Relations

A. *Community*

B. *Conflict of interests*

C. *Contributions*

D. *Determining contents of communications*

E. *Extent of function*

F. *Role of executives*

G. *Selecting media for communications*

X. Legal

A. *Clearance of contracts*

B. *Compliance with law*

C. *Patents for employee inventors*

D. *Protection of proprietory rights*

E. *Reservation of rights and interests*

F. *Real property leases*

Figure 6.4 Procedure for interviewing prospective personnel at Indiana State University.

1. Any candidate brought to campus for an interview should be a best prospect of at least three qualified persons whose credentials have been examined. Personnel supply in an academic field may reduce the number of possible candidates.

2. Before an invitation is extended to a candidate who must travel a distance greater than five hundred miles to reach Terre Haute, the department chairperson should:
   a. ascertain the existence of the vacancy or authorization by a call to the assistant vice-president for academic affairs.
   b. forward to the dean and assistant vice-president credentials which should include, if possible, parts d, e, f, and g, Item 6, below.

3. Any administrative person who is scheduled to interview a candidate should be forwarded credentials for the candidate prior to the interview.

4. Interviews with administrative personnel should be scheduled as follows:
   A candidate whose probable academic rank will be instructor or assistant professor should talk with the dean prior to the assistant vice-president. A candidate whose academic rank should probably be associate professor, in addition to the dean and assistant vice-president, should be scheduled for an interview with the vice-president for academic affairs. In addition to the above, a candidate for appointment as professor or department chairperson should also be scheduled for a meeting with the president.

5. Although courtesy to the candidate may demand that the interview schedule be maintained, the vice-president, at his or her discretion or in agreement with the suggestion by the chairperson, dean, or assistant vice-president, may cancel the interview for the candidate with the president.

6. A recommendation for appointment should contain the following:
   a. a letter from the department chairperson (or dean) setting forth the recommendation and proposing the academic rank and salary.
   b. a statement from the dean if the recommendation letter is prepared by the department chairperson.
   c. the completed university resume form. This can be completed by the candidate when on campus or returned to the chairperson by mail later, but must be included.
   d. vitae information.
   e. placement papers.
   f. official transcripts (especially important if placement papers are not current or prepared by a university bureau).
   g. as many as three letters of recommendation, one or two of these reflecting the candidate's current assignment. These letters are necessary if the placement materials have not been updated to contain current recommendations.
   h. a written report on any telephone conversations concerning the candidate made by the department chairperson.

7. Because of the difficulty in arranging interviews on Saturday, campus visits should occur during the week.

8. Whenever possible, accommodations at the Hulman Center should be limited to one overnight. The university cannot accept any charge for hotel accommodations other than at the Hulman Center. "Hotel accommodations" are defined to be lodging only, and not food, telephone, or other personal services.

9. Travel can be reimbursed in one of the following ways:
   a. a candidate traveling in-state will have mileage paid, at the rate of eight cents per mile. The official Indiana map is used to compute mileage rather than a speedometer reading.
   b. a candidate traveling from out-of-state can claim the cost of air fare (tourist class) or train fare (coach class).
   c. a candidate who may choose to drive from out-of-state cannot be paid a mileage cost. Instead, air-fare and train-fare amounts are determined and the lesser of the two is paid as an automobile mileage reimbursement.

From *Indiana State University Handbook* 1969, Revised in 1970 and in 1972, Terre Haute, Indiana.

Figure 6.5 A successful standing-plan program with mutually supportive policies, procedures, and rules.

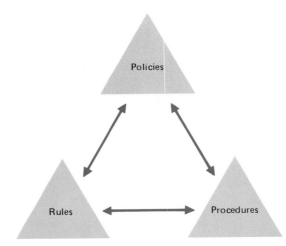

A common example of a program is the management development program found in many organizations. This program exists to raise managers' skill level in one or more of the skills mentioned in chapter 1: technical skills, conceptual skills, or interpersonal skills. Increasing the skill level of these managers, however, is not an end in itself. The purpose of the program is to produce competent managers who are equipped to help the organization be successful over the long run. Once managerial skills have been raised to a desired level, the management development program can be deemphasized.

Budgets

A **budget** is a single-use financial plan that covers a specified length of time. A firm's budget is a plan detailing how funds will be spent on labor, raw materials, capital goods, and so on, as well as how the funds for these expenditures will be obtained.[6] Although budgets are planning devices, they are also strategies for organizational control and are covered in more detail in the section of this text on control.

Financial Plan

Why Plans Fail

A very useful bit of information for any prospective manager would be an explanation of why organizational plans fail. If managers know why plans fail, they can take steps to eliminate the factors that cause failure and thereby increase the probability that their plans will be successful. A study by K. A. Ringbakk indicates that plans fail when:

1. Corporate planning is not integrated into the total management system.
2. There is a lack of understanding of the different steps of the planning process.
3. Management at different levels in the organization has not properly engaged in or contributed to planning activities.
4. Responsibility for planning is wrongly vested solely in the planning department.
5. Management expects that plans developed will be realized with little effort.
6. In starting formal planning, too much is attempted at once.
7. Management fails to operate by the plan.
8. Financial projections are confused with planning.
9. Inadequate inputs are used in planning.
10. Management fails to see the overall planning process.[7]

Mistakes in Developing Plans

Planning Areas: Input Planning

As discussed earlier, organizational inputs, process, outputs, and environment are major factors in determining how successful a management system will be. Naturally, a comprehensive organizational plan should focus on each of these factors. The following two sections cover planning in two areas normally associated with the input factor: plant facilities planning and manpower planning. Planning in areas such as these is normally called input planning, the development of proposed action that will furnish sufficient and appropriate organizational resources for reaching established organizational objectives.

What Is Input Planning?

Plant Facilities Planning

Plant facilities planning involves developing the type of plant facility an organization needs to reach its objectives. The following two sections discuss site selection and layout patterns as two important aspects of plant facilities planning.

Is a Plant Adequate?

Figure 6.6 Major areas of consideration when selecting a plant site and sample exploratory questions.

Major Areas for Consideration in Site Selection	Sample Question to Begin Exploring Major Areas
Profit	
Market location	Where are our customers in relation to the site?
Competition	What competitive situation exists at the site?
Operating costs	
Suppliers	Are materials available near the site at reasonable cost?
Utilities	What are utility rates at the site? Are they sufficiently available?
Wages	What wage rates are paid in comparable organizations near the site?
Taxes	What are tax rates on income, sales, property, etc. for the site?
Investment costs	
Land/development	How expensive is land and construction at the site?
Others	
Transportation	Are airlines, railroads, highways, etc. available to the site?
Laws	What laws exist related to zoning, pollution, etc. that influence operations if the site is chosen?
Labor	Does an adequate labor supply exist around the site?
Unionization	What degree of unionization exists in the site area?
Living conditions	Are housing, schools, etc. appropriate around the site?
Community relations	Is the community supportive of the organization moving into the area?

Adapted from E. S. Groo, "Choosing Foreign Locations: One Company's Experience," *Columbia Journal of World Business*, September/October 1977, p. 77. Used with permission.

Site Selection

One major consideration in developing the type of plant facility an organization needs to reach its objectives is site selection. **Site selection** is the determination of where a plant facility should be located. Figure 6.6 contains a listing of several major areas to be considered when selecting a plant site and sample questions that can be asked to begin exploring these areas. Exhibit 6 is an account of how the Pacific Gas and Electric Company located a nuclear power plant just two-and-one half miles from a major earthquake fault and not much farther from several others. This choice of location has caused such public criticism that there is a good chance that the plant will never open. The company could lose as much as $2 billion.

As implied in the case of the Pacific Gas and Electric Company, the specifics of a site-selection process will vary from organization to organization. Normally, the specifics of the process will also depend upon whether a site is being selected in a home country or a foreign country. If in a foreign country, management will probably find that foreign governments take different lengths of time to approve site purchases and that political pressures slowing down or preventing purchase of a site may vary drastically from country to country.

Site Selection

Selecting a Site in Another Country

Figure 6.7 Results of weighing seven site variables for six countries.

Criteria	Maximum Value Assigned	Sites					
		Japan	Chile	Jamaica	Australia	Mexico	France
Living conditions	100	70	40	45	50	60	60
Accessibility	75	55	35	20	60	70	70
Industrialization	60	40	50	55	35	35	30
Labor availability	35	30	10	10	30	35	35
Economics	35	15	15	15	15	25	25
Community capability and attitude	30	25	20	10	15	25	15
Effect on company reputation	35	25	20	10	15	25	15
Total	370	260	190	165	220	275	250

Adapted from E. S. Groo, "Choosing Foreign Locations: One Company's Experience," *Columbia Journal of World Business,* September/October 1977, p. 77. Used with permission.

Many organizations use a weighting process to compare site differences among foreign countries. Basically, this weighting process involves (1) deciding on a set of variables that are critical to obtaining an appropriate site, (2) assigning each of these variables a weight or rank of relative importance, and (3) ranking alternative sites, depending upon how they reflect these different variables.

How the Weighting Process Works

As an example, figure 6.7 shows the results of such a weighting process for seven different site variables and six different countries. In this figure, "living conditions" is worth 100 points and is the most important variable, while "effect on company reputation" is worth 35 points and is the least important variable. Also in figure 6.7, various countries are given a number of points for each variable, depending upon the importance of the variable and how it exists within the country. Our illustration shows that, given the established set of weighted criteria, Japan, Mexico, and France received more points and therefore are more desirable sites than Chile, Jamaica, or Australia.

Illustrating the Weighting Process

Layout Patterns

In addition to selecting a plant site, choosing an appropriate layout pattern can also be a major consideration in plant facilities planning. A **layout pattern** is defined as the overall arrangement of machines, equipment, materials handling, aisles, service areas, storage areas, and work stations within a production facility. The primary objective of layout is to optimize the arrangement of these variables to provide the maximum total contribution to productivity.[8]

Maximizing Contribution to Productivity

It is generally agreed that there are three basic layout patterns: (1) process layout, (2) product layout, and (3) fixed-position layout. **Process layout** is a layout pattern based primarily on grouping together similar types of equipment. The layout in hospitals and department stores are examples of process layout. **Product layout** is a layout pattern mostly based on the progressive steps by which the product is made. The automobile assembly line and the manufacturing of furniture are examples of the use of product layout. Lastly, the **fixed-position layout** is a layout pattern that, because of the weight or bulk of the product being manufactured, has workers, tools, and materials rotating around a stationary product. Ships and airplanes are usually manufactured under the fixed-position layout.

Similar Equipment Progressive Steps Stationary Product

Exhibit 6

Pacific Gas and Electric Locates Near Major Earthquake Fault

California's Diablo Canyon plant: An embattled atomic-power industry braces for a major confrontation

(Photo: Wide World Photos)

In the dry brown hills outside San Luis Obispo on the California coast, the forces are massing for the nation's next major showdown on nuclear power. On one side is the anti-nuclear Abalone Alliance, which is planning a huge protest complete with blockaded roads and amphibious landing teams. On the other are thousands of police officers and sheriffs' deputies from as far away as Oakland, 200 miles to the north. At the center of the dispute is the 2,190-megawatt Diablo Canyon nuclear power plant—perhaps the most controversial atomic facility in America's troubled nuclear-power industry.

Sometime in the next few weeks the Nuclear Regulatory Commission will grant a license to Diablo Canyon, and employees of Pacific Gas & Electric Co., owner and operator of the plant, will start loading fuel, which has been on the site for five years, for low-level tests. But the Abalone Alliance, backed by hundreds of demonstrators from other anti-nuclear and environmental groups across the country, hopes to make the plant's start-up as difficult as possible by blockading it from all contact by land with the outside world.

Earthquake: The planned protest is merely the latest in a series of demonstrations and legal maneuvers that delayed licensing and helped swell the cost of the plant from an original estimate of $350 million to more than $2 billion. And even though its opponents have failed to stop the project, they are just as adamant as ever. One big reason: the Diablo Canyon plant lies just 2½ miles from a major active earthquake fault—and not much farther away from several others (map). Although Pacific Gas & Electric has fortified the plant to withstand a quake measuring 7.5 on the Richter scale and the NRC has declared it safe, its opponents are not convinced. The site, they argue, is simply too dangerous. "The NRC has decided that people in this area are expendable," says John Gofman, an emeritus professor from the University of

California at Berkeley. "The best-laid plans of mice and men have gone wrong so often that if you have your head screwed on, you don't build a plant there."

The looming confrontation at Diablo Canyon is only one of the problems plaguing the U.S. nuclear industry. Even before the accident at Three Mile Island in 1979, orders for new reactors were slumping as utilities realized that demand for new electric power was leveling off after years of steady growth. The TMI incident made matters considerably worse. Immediately after it, the NRC put Diablo Canyon and five other nuclear plants on hold for operating licenses and designed new rules to make nuclear-plant design and operation safer.

Over the past two years utilities across the country have had to retrofit existing nuclear plants, retrain workers and revise operating procedures to bring facilities into compliance with the new regulations—an exercise that cost millions of dollars. Industry officials got a slight boost from the election of President Reagan, a firm supporter of nuclear power: this year nuclear's share of total power generation is expected to increase slightly for the first time since 1979. But according to the NRC, eight proposed nuclear plants have been canceled during this fiscal year. And on Wall Street the industry is considered moribund, for the time being at least. "I think the view is that Reagan will help in terms of getting licenses and construction permits and maybe shorten the whole [construction] cycle somewhat," says Robert McCloy, an analyst at Kidder, Peabody & Co. "But in terms of new nuclear orders, it's going to take a lot more than the government saying it is pro-nuclear."

Figure 6.8 Three basic layout patterns.

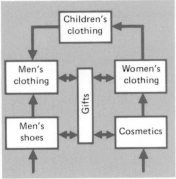

Process Layout in a Department Store

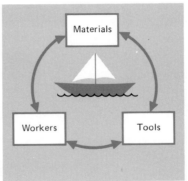

Fixed Position Layout in Building a Ship

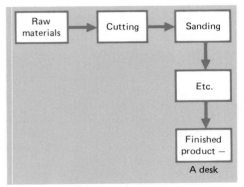

Product Layout in Furniture Manufacturing

Figure 6.8 illustrates each of these basic layout patterns. As implied by this figure, appropriate plant layout reflects the process required to develop the goods or services that the organization produces. It should also be mentioned that an appropriate layout for any one plant may be some combination of these three basic layout patterns.

Manpower Planning

Human resources are another area with which input planners usually are concerned. Organizational objectives cannot be attained without appropriate manpower or personnel. Future needs for manpower are mainly influenced by employee turnover, the nature of the present workforce, and the rate of growth of the organization.[9]

Is Manpower Adequate?

Personnel planners should try to answer questions such as: (1) What types of people does the organization need to reach its objectives? (2) How many of each type are needed? (3) What steps for the recruitment and selection of these people should the organization take? (4) Can present employees be further trained to fill future needed positions? (5) At what rate are employees lost to other organizations? These are not the only questions personnel planners should ask, but they are representative.

What Is Manpower Planning?

Figure 6.9 shows the manpower planning process as developed by Bruce Coleman. According to this model, **manpower planning** involves reflecting on organizational objectives to determine overall manpower needs, comparing these needs to the existing manpower inventory to determine net manpower needs, and, finally, seeking appropriate organization members to meet the net manpower needs.

Back to the Case

Jane and Paul should probably develop both standing plans and single-use plans for their business. Standing plans include policies, procedures, and rules and should be developed for situations that occur repeatedly. Single-use plans include programs and budgets, and should be developed to help manage more nonrepetitive situations. Jane and Paul should become thoroughly aware of the reasons why plans fail and take steps to avoid these pitfalls.

The information in the preceding section should also indicate to Jane and Paul that they probably should concern themselves with plant facilities planning and manpower

planning. Plant facilities planning entails developing the type of plant facility their company will need to reach its objectives. Since Jane and Paul already have an operating plant, plant site location as a part of plant facilities planning will probably not be too important to them. Layout patterning as a part of plant facilities planning, however, will probably be very interesting to them; and analyzing and improving upon their present plant layout could be of great benefit to them. Manpower planning involves obtaining and/or developing the personnel the organization will need to reach its objectives.

Figure 6.9 The manpower planning process.

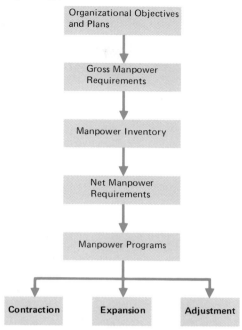

Planning tools are techniques managers can use to help develop plans. The remainder of this chapter discusses forecasting and scheduling, two of the most important of these tools.

Planning Tools
Techniques for Developing Plans

Forecasting

Forecasting is the process of predicting future environmental happenings that will influence the operation of the organization. Although sophisticated forecasting techniques are relatively modern, the concept of forecasting can be traced at least as far back in the management literature as Fayol.[10] The importance of forecasting lies in its ability to help managers better understand the future makeup of the organizational environment, which, in turn, helps them to formulate more effective plans.

Predicting the Future

William C. House, in describing the Insect Control Services Company, has developed an excellent illustration of how forecasting works. Figure 6.10 lists the primary factors that Insect Control Services attempts to measure in developing its forecast. In general, Insect Control Services forecasts by attempting to:

1. Establish the relationships between industry sales and national economic and social indicators
2. Determine the impact of government restrictions concerning the use of chemical pesticides upon the growth of chemical, biological, and electromagnetic energy pest control markets
3. Evaluate sales growth potential, profitability, resources required, and risks involved in each of its market areas (commercial, industrial, institutional, governmental, and residential)
4. Evaluate the potential for expansion of marketing efforts in geographical areas of the United States as well as in foreign countries
5. Determine the likelihood of technological breakthroughs that would make existing product lines obsolete[11]

Gross National Product — Measure of total dollars available for industrial, commercial, institutional, and residential purchases of insect control units.

Personal Consumption Expenditures — Measure of dollars available for consumer purchases of:

1. *Services* — affect potential contract insect control services.
2. *Durables* — affect market potential for residential units.
3. *Nondurables* — affect sales of food, drugs, and other products that influence expansion of industrial and commercial users of insect control equipment.

Governmental Purchases of Goods, Services — Measure of spending for hospitals, government food services, other institutions that purchase insect control equipment.

Gross Private Domestic Investment in New Plant and Equipment — A measure of business expansion which indicates the size and nature of market potential for industrial and commercial purchases of insect control units in new or expanded existing establishments.

Industrial Production for Selected Industries — Measure of expansion of industrial output for industries that are users, potential users of insect control units, or materials suppliers for insect control services. Such expansion (or contraction) of output will likely affect:

1. Industrial and commercial purchases of insect control units.
2. Availability of materials used to manufacture insect control units.

Employment and Unemployment Levels — Indicates availability or scarcity of human resources available to augment Insect Control Services human resources pool.

Consumer, Wholesale Prices — Measure of ability, willingness of homeowners to purchase residential units and of the availability and cost of raw materials and component parts.

Corporate Profits — Indicates how trends in prices, unit labor costs, and productivity affect corporate profits. Size of total corporate profits indicates profit margins in present and potential markets and funds available for expansion.

Business Borrowings, Interest Rates — Measures of the availability and cost of borrowed funds needed to finance working capital needs and plant and equipment expansion.

Adapted, with permission, from *Managerial Planning*, January/February 1977, published by the Planning Executives Institute, Oxford, Ohio 45056.

In addition to the more general process of organizational forecasting illustrated by Insect Control Services are specialized types of forecasting, such as economic forecasting, technological forecasting, social trends forecasting, and sales forecasting.

The Importance of Sales Forecasting

Although a complete organizational forecasting process can and usually should include all of the types of forecasting mentioned in the preceding paragraph, sales forecasting is typically cited as the "key" organizational forecast. A sales forecast is a prediction of how high or how low sales will be over the period of time under consideration. It is the "key" forecast because it serves as the fundamental guideline for planning within the organization. Once the sales forecast has been completed, managers can decide if more salespeople should be hired; if more money for plant expansion must be borrowed; or if layoffs are upcoming and cutbacks in certain areas are necessary. The following section outlines various methods of sales forecasting.

Methods of Sales Forecasting

Jury of Executive Opinion Method

Executives Predict Sales

The **jury of executive opinion method** of sales forecasting is very straightforward. A group of managers within the organization assembles to discuss their opinions on what will happen to sales in the future. Since these discussion sessions usually revolve around the hunches or experienced guesses of each of the managers, the resulting forecast is usually a blending of expressed opinions.

A more recently developed forecasting method similar to the jury of executive opinion method is called the delphi method.[12] This method also gathers, evaluates, and summarizes expert opinions as the basis for a forecast.[13] The basic delphi method employs the following steps:

Step 1 Various experts are asked to answer independently, in writing, a series of questions about the future of sales or whatever other area is being forecasted.

Step 2 A summary of all answers is then prepared. No expert knows how any other expert answered the questions.

Step 3 Copies of the summary are given to the individual experts with the request that they modify their original answers if they think they should.

Step 4 Another summary is made of these modifications and copies again are distributed to the experts. This time, however, expert opinions that deviate significantly from the norm must be justified in writing.

Step 5 A third summary is made of the opinions and justifications, and copies are distributed to the experts. Justification for all answers is now required in writing.

Step 6 The forecast is generated from all of the opinions and justifications that arise from step 5.

Sales Force Estimation Method

The **sales force estimation method** solicits the opinions of company salespeople instead of company managers. Salespeople interact with customers and can use this interaction as a basis for predicting future sales. As with the jury of executive opinion method, the resulting forecast generally is a compromise of the views of the salespeople as a group.

Time Series Analysis Method

The **time series analysis method** predicts future sales by analyzing the historical relationship between sales and time. Information showing the relationship between sales and time is typically presented on a graph, as in figure 6.11. This presentation clearly displays past trends, which can be used to predict future sales.

Results of the time series method analysis shown in figure 6.11 would be considered desirable by most managers. However, since in the long run products generally go through what is called a product life cycle, the results are probably overly optimistic. A **product life cycle** is the five stages through which most new products and services will pass. These five stages are introduction, growth, maturity, saturation, decline, and obsolescence.

Figure 6.12 shows how these five stages are related to product sales over a period of time. In the introduction stage, a product is brand new and sales are just beginning to build. In the growth stage, because the product has been in the marketplace for some time and is now becoming more accepted, product sales are continuing to climb. During the maturity stage, competitors have entered the market and while sales are still climbing, they normally climb at a slower rate than in the growth stage. After the maturity stage comes the saturation stage. At this time nearly everyone who wants the product already has it. Sales during the saturation stage are typically due to replacing a worn-out product or to population growth. The last product life cycle stage, decline and obsolescence, finds the product being replaced by a competing product.

Managers may be able to keep products out of the decline and obsolescence stage through high-quality product improvements. On the other hand, a product such as a scissors may never reach this last stage due to the lack of competing products.

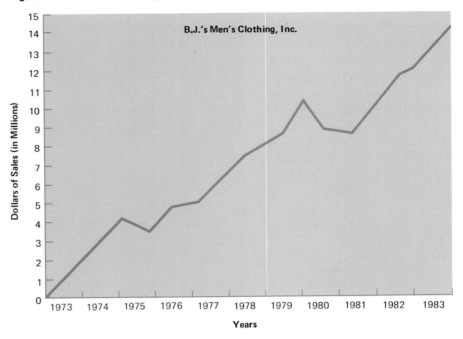

Figure 6.11 Time-series analysis method.

Evaluating Sales Forecasting Methods

Advantages and
Disadvantages

The sales forecasting methods just described are not the only ones available to managers. Other methods include the statistical correlation method and the computer simulation method.[14] The methods discussed, however, do provide a basic foundation for understanding sales forecasting. In practice, managers find that each sales forecasting method has both advantages and disadvantages, as shown in figure 6.13. Before deciding to use a particular sales forecasting method, managers must carefully weigh the advantages and disadvantages as they relate to the managers' particular organization. Managers may decide to use a combination of these methods rather than just one method. Whatever method a manager finally adopts, the framework should be logical, fit the needs of the organization, and be capable of adaptation to changes in the environment.[15]

Back to the Case

From reading this last section Jane and Paul would know that one of the planning tools available to them is forecasting. Forecasting is predicting future environmental events that will influence the operation of the organization. Although various specific types of forecasting available to Jane and Paul include economic forecasting, technological forecasting, and social trends forecasting, their "key" forecast will be the sales forecast. Methods of sales forecasting

available to Jane and Paul include the jury of executive opinion method, the sales force estimation method, and the time series analysis method evaluated against the life cycle of specific products. Before adopting a specific sales-forecasting method, Jane and Paul should weigh the relative advantages and disadvantages of each method, given their management situation. Once they have completed their sales forecast, detailed planning within the organization can begin.

Figure 6.12 Stages of the product life cycle.

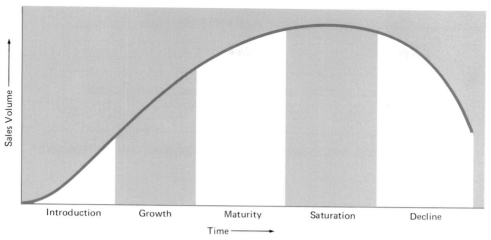

Material in this figure adapted from *Sales Forecasting* (New York: The Conference Board, Inc., 1978), pp. 11–12, 31–44, 47–80.

Figure 6.13 Advantages and disadvantages of three methods of sales forecasting.

Sales Forecasting Method	Advantages	Disadvantages
Jury of executive opinion	1. Can provide forecasts easily and quickly 2. May not require the preparation of elaborate statistics 3. Pools a variety of specialized viewpoints for experience and judgment 4. May be the only feasible means of forecasting, especially in the absence of adequate data	1. Is inferior to a more factual basis of forecasting since it is based so heavily on opinion. 2. Requires costly executive time 3. Is not necessarily more accurate because opinion is averaged 4. Disperses responsibility for accurate forecasting 5. Presents difficulties in making breakdowns by products, time intervals, or markets for operating purposes.
Sales force estimation	1. Uses specialized knowledge of people closest to the market 2. Places responsibility for the forecast in the hands of those who must produce the results 3. Gives sales force greater confidence in quotas developed from forecasts 4. Tends to give results greater stability because of the magnitude of the sample 5. Lends itself to the easy development of product, territory, customer, or sales representatives breakdowns	1. Sales representatives of some firms may be poor estimators, being either more optimistic or more pessimistic than conditions warrant 2. If estimates are used as a basis for setting quotas, sales representatives are inclined to understate the demand to make the goal easier to achieve 3. Sales representatives are often unaware of the broad economic patterns shaping future sales and are thus incapable of forecasting trends for extended periods 4. Since sales forecasting is a subsidiary function of the sales force, sufficient time may not be made available for it 5. Requires an extensive expenditure of time by executives and sales force 6. Elaborate schemes are sometimes necessary to keep estimates realistic and free from bias
Time series analysis	1. Forces the forecaster to consider the underlying trend, cycle, and seasonal elements in the sales series 2. Takes into account the particular repetitive or continuing patterns exhibited by the sales in the past 3. Provides a systematic means of making quantitative projections	1. Assumes the continuation of historical patterns of change in sales components without considering outside influences that may affect sales in the forecast period 2. Is often unsatisfactory for short-term forecasting, since, for example, the pinpointing of cyclical turning points by mechanical projections is seldom possible 3. May be difficult to apply in cases where erratic, irregular forces disrupt or hide the regularity of component patterns within a sales series 4. Requires technical skill, experience and judgment

From Philip Kotler, *Marketing Management, Analysis, Planning, and Control,* 1967, p. 291. Reprinted by permission of Prentice-Hall, Inc., Englewood Cliffs, New Jersey.

Figure 6.14 Completed Gantt chart.

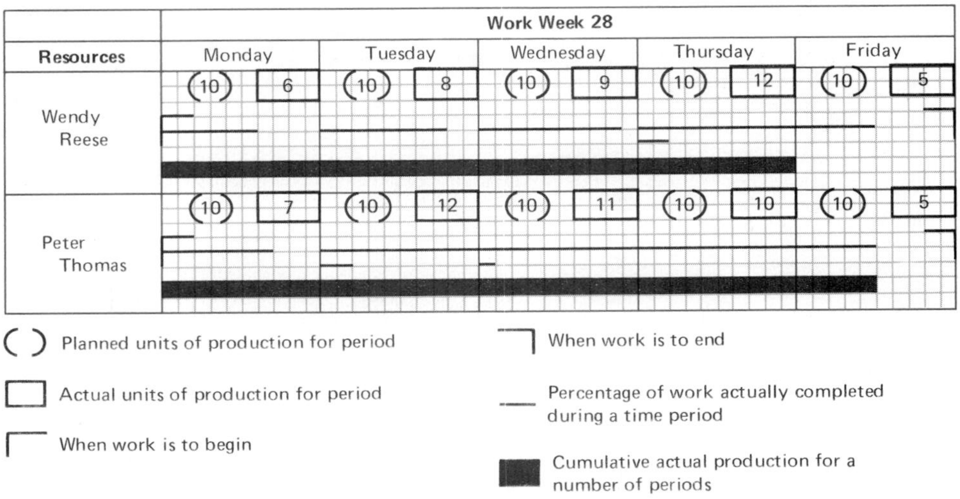

	Work Week 28				
Resources	Monday	Tuesday	Wednesday	Thursday	Friday
Wendy Reese	(10) 6	(10) 8	(10) 9	(10) 12	(10) 5
Peter Thomas	(10) 7	(10) 12	(10) 11	(10) 10	(10) 5

( )　Planned units of production for period

☐　Actual units of production for period

⌐　When work is to begin

¬　When work is to end

—　Percentage of work actually completed during a time period

■　Cumulative actual production for a number of periods

Scheduling

Lists of Activities

Basically, **scheduling** is the process of formulating detailed listings of activities that must be accomplished to attain an objective. This detailed listing is an integral part of an organizational plan. Gantt charts and network analysis are two scheduling techniques discussed in the paragraphs that follow.

Gantt Charts

Scheduling Device

As the name implies, the **Gantt chart** is a scheduling device developed by Henry L. Gantt. This chart is essentially a bar graph with time on the horizontal axis and the resource to be scheduled on the vertical axis. Possible resources to be scheduled include management system inputs, such as human resources and machines.

Figure 6.14 shows a completed Gantt chart for a work period entitled "Work Week 28." The resources scheduled over the five work days on this chart are human resources: Wendy Reese and Peter Thomas. During this work week both Reese and Thomas were scheduled to produce ten units a day for five days. Actual units produced, according to the Gantt chart, however, show a deviation from this planned production. There were days when each of these individuals produced more than ten units, as well as days when each produced fewer than ten units. Cumulative production on the chart shows that Reese produced forty units and Thomas produced forty-five units over the five days.

Uses of the Gantt Chart

Although Gantt charts may seem quite simple at first glance, they can have many valuable uses for managers. First, managers can use the chart as a summary overview of how organizational resources are being used. From this summary, managers can detect such facts as which resources are consistently contributing to productivity. Second, managers can use the Gantt chart to help coordinate organizational resources. The Gantt chart can show which resources are not being used during specific periods and, therefore, can be scheduled to work on other production efforts. Third, Gantt chart records can be used to establish realistic worker output standards. For example, if workers are completing scheduled work too quickly, output standards may need to be raised so that workers are scheduled for more work per time period.

Program Evaluation and Review Technique (PERT)

The main weakness of the Gantt chart is that it does not contain any information about the interrelationship of tasks to be performed. All tasks to be performed are listed on the chart, but there is no way of telling if one task must be performed before another can be completed. The Program Evaluation and Review Technique (PERT), a technique which evolved partially from the Gantt chart, is a scheduling tool designed to emphasize the interrelationship of tasks.

Interdependence of Tasks

Defining PERT

PERT is a network of project activities showing both estimates of time necessary to complete each activity within the project and the sequential relationship between activities that must be followed to complete the project. PERT was developed in 1958 for use in designing the Polaris submarine weapon system.[16] The individuals involved in managing this project felt that Gantt charts and other existing scheduling tools were of little use because of the complicated nature of the Polaris project and the interdependence of its tasks.[17]

Network of Project Activities

The PERT network contains two primary elements: activities and events. **Activities** are specified sets of behavior within a project, while **events** are the completions of major project tasks. Within the PERT network each event is assigned corresponding activities that must be performed before the event can materialize.[18]

What Are Activities and Events?

A sample PERT network designed for the building of a house is presented in figure 6.15. In this figure, events are symbolized by circles and activities are symbolized by arrows. To illustrate, figure 6.15 indicates that after the event "Foundation Complete" (represented by a circle) has materialized, certain activities (represented by an arrow) must be performed before the event of "Frame Complete" (represented by another circle) can materialize.

Two other features of the network in figure 6.15 also should be emphasized. First, the left-to-right presentation of events shows how events interrelate or the sequence in which they should be performed. Second, the numbers in parentheses above each arrow indicate the units of time necessary to complete each activity. These two features should help managers to ensure that only necessary work is being done on a project and that no project activities are taking too long.

Critical Path

Close attention should be paid to the critical path of a PERT network. The **critical path** is the sequence of events and activities requiring the longest period of time to complete. This path is called the critical path because a delay in the time necessary to complete this sequence results in a delay for the completion of the entire project. The critical path in figure 6.15 is indicated by thick arrows, while all other paths are indicated by thin arrows. Managers try to control a project by keeping it within the time designated by the critical path.

Sequence Requiring Longest Period of Time

Steps in Designing a PERT Network

When designing a PERT network, managers should follow four primary steps:

Step 1 Managers should list (a) all activities/events that must be accomplished for a project and (b) the sequence in which these activities/events should be performed.

Step 2 Managers should determine how much time will be needed to complete each activity/event.

Step 3 Managers should design a PERT network that reflects all of the information contained in steps 1 and 2.

Step 4 Managers should identify the critical path.

Figure 6.15 PERT network designed for building a house.

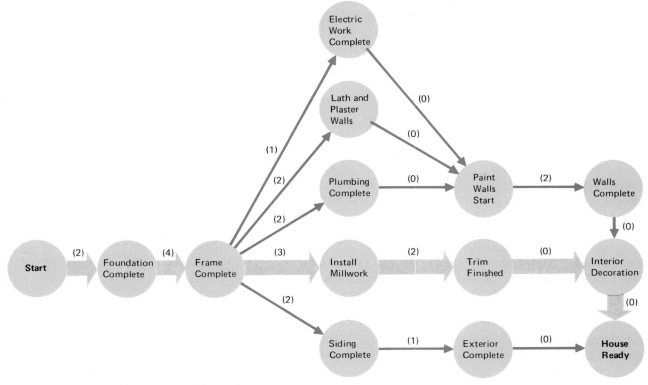

Reprinted by permission of the Sperry Rand Corporation.

Back to the Case

Scheduling is the other planning tool available to Jane and Paul. Scheduling involves the detailed listing of activities that must be accomplished to reach an objective. Two scheduling techniques that Jane and Paul might want to consider using are Gantt charts and PERT. Essentially, Gantt charts are bar graphs with time on the horizontal axis and the resource to be scheduled on the vertical axis. In developing their Gantt charts, Jane and Paul should remember that these charts also can provide information for such management activities as conducting worker-performance evaluations, coordinating resources, and setting production standards. Jane and Paul also should keep in mind that relationships between tasks are not represented in Gantt charts.

PERT, however, is a scheduling technique that would show Jane and Paul the relationships between tasks. Managers who use a PERT network have a flowchart showing activities, events, and approximate amounts of time necessary to complete each activity. Jane and Paul should pay particular attention to the critical path on the PERT network. This path represents the sequence of activities and events requiring the longest amount of time to complete. The total time required to follow the critical path to project completion should be Jane and Paul's target time for finishing the project.

The following points are stressed within this chapter:

Summary

1. A plan is a specific action proposed to help the organization attain its objectives.
2. The fundamental dimensions of plans are repetitiveness, time, scope, and level. Using primarily the repetitiveness dimension as a guide, organizational plans can be divided into two types: standing plans and single-use plans. Standing plans can be subdivided into policies, procedures, and rules; and single-use plans can be subdivided into programs and budgets.
3. One of the primary input planning areas is plant facilities planning, or developing a plant appropriate for organizational objectives. Selecting a site and layout pattern that are appropriate for a particular plant are two main tasks involved in plant facilities planning. Another important input planning area is manpower planning, or developing and/or obtaining manpower necessary to accomplish organizational objectives.
4. Forecasting is a planning tool, and is the process of predicting future environmental happenings important to the existence of the organization. Although various types of forecasts exist, the sales forecast is usually called the "key" forecast because it is a guide for planning within the organization. Various methods of sales forecasting include the jury of executive opinion method, the sales force estimation method, and the time series analysis method. The product life cycle can tell managers if time series information might be overly optimistic.
5. Scheduling is also a planning tool, and is the detailed listing of activities that must be performed to reach organizational objectives. Gantt charts and PERT analysis are two principal scheduling tools. The Gantt chart is basically a bar graph with time on the horizontal axis and the resource to be scheduled on the vertical axis. A PERT network is comprised basically of activities and events.

Issues for Review and Discussion

1. What is a plan?
2. List and describe the basic dimensions of a plan.
3. Is there a difference between standing plans and single-use plans? If so, what is the difference?
4. Compare and contrast policies, procedures, and rules.
5. What are the two main types of single-use plans?
6. Why do organizations have programs?
7. Of what use is a budget to managers?
8. Summarize the ten factors that cause plans to fail.
9. What is input planning?
10. Evaluate the importance of plant facilities planning to the organization.
11. What major factors should be involved in site selection?
12. Define layout patterns.
13. List and describe three basic layout patterns.
14. Describe the manpower planning process.
15. What is a planning tool?
16. Describe the measurements usually employed in forecasting. Why are these taken?
17. Draw and explain the product life cycle.
18. Discuss the advantages and disadvantages of three methods of sales forecasting.
19. Elaborate on the statement that "all managers should spend some time scheduling."
20. What is a Gantt chart? Draw a simple chart to assist you in your explanation.
21. How can information related to the Gantt chart be used by managers?
22. How is PERT a scheduling tool?
23. How is the critical path related to PERT?
24. List the steps necessary to design a PERT network.

Sources of Additional Information

Aguilar, Francis. *Scanning the Business Environment.* New York: Macmillan, 1967.

Allen, Louis A. "Managerial Planning: Back to Basics." *Management Review,* April 1981, pp. 15–20.

Anderholm III, Fred; Gaertner, James; and Milani, Ken. "The Utilization of PERT in the Preparation of Marketing Budgets." *Managerial Planning* 30, no. 1 (July/August 1981): 18–23.

Ansoff, H. Igor, et al. *Acquisition Behavior of U.S. Manufacturing Firms, 1946–65.* Nashville: Vanderbilt University Press, 1971.

Anthony, Robert. *Planning and Control Systems: A Framework for Analysis.* Cambridge, Mass.: Harvard University Press, 1966.

Baker, B. N., and Eris, R. L. *An Introduction to PERT-CPM.* Homewood, Ill.: Richard D. Irwin, 1964.

Baumol, William. *Business Behavior, Value, and Growth.* New York: Harcourt, Brace & World, 1966.

Glueck, William. *Business Policy: Strategy Formation and Management Action.* 2d ed. New York: McGraw-Hill, 1976.

Goetz, Billy E. *Management Planning and Control.* New York: McGraw-Hill, 1949.

Koontz, Harold, and O'Donnell, Cyril. *Principles of Management.* 4th ed. New York: McGraw-Hill, 1960.

Levin, R. I., and Kirkpatrick, C. A. *Planning and Control with PERT/CPM.* New York: McGraw-Hill, 1966.

Martino, R. L. *Finding the Critical Path.* New York: American Management Association, 1964.

McHale, John. *The Future of the Future.* New York: George Braziller, 1969.

Naylor, Thomas H. "Strategic Planning Models." *Managerial Planning* 30, no. 1 (July/August, 1981): 3–11.

Tagiuri, Renato. "Planning: Desirable and Undesirable." *Human Resource Management,* Spring 1980, pp. 11–14.

Thompson, James. *Organizations in Action.* New York: McGraw-Hill, 1967.

Thompson, Stewart. *How Companies Plan.* New York: American Management Association, 1962.

Webb, Stan G. "Productivity Through Practical Planning." *Administrative Management* 42, no. 8 (August 1981): 47–50.

Notes

1. Henry L. Sisk, *Management and Organization* (Cincinnati: South-Western Publishing Company, 1973), p. 101.

2. Stewart Thompson, "What Planning Involves," American Management Association Research Study no. 54, 1962.

3. Fremont E. Kast and James E. Rosenzweig, *Organization and Management: A Systems Approach* (New York: McGraw-Hill, 1970), pp. 443–49.

4. For discussion on expanding this list of four characteristics to thirteen, see P. LeBreton and D. A. Henning, *Planning Theory* (Englewood Cliffs, N.J.: Prentice-Hall, 1961), pp. 320–44. These authors list the dimensions of a plan as (1) complexity, (2) significance, (3) comprehensiveness, (4) time, (5) specificity, (6) completeness, (7) flexibility, (8) frequency, (9) formality, (10) confidential nature, (11) authorization, (12) ease of implementation, and (13) ease of control.

5. For further discussion on each type of plan, see Herbert G. Hicks and C. Ray Gullett, *The Management of Organizations* (New York: McGraw-Hill, 1976), pp. 271–78.

6. J. Fred Weston and Eugene F. Brigham, *Essentials of Managerial Finance* (New York: Holt, Rinehart & Winston, 1971), p. 107.

7. Kjell A. Ringbakk, "Why Planning Fails," *European Business,* July 1970.

8. Richard J. Hopeman, *Production: Concepts, Analysis, Control* (Columbus: Bobbs-Merrill, 1975), pp. 137–39.

9. Dale S. Beach, *Personnel: The Management of People at Work* (New York: Macmillan, 1975), p. 220.

10. Henri Fayol, *General and Industrial Management* (New York: Pitman Publishing, 1949).

11. William C. House, "Environmental Analysis: Key to More Effective Dynamic Planning," *Managerial Planning,* January/February 1977, pp. 25–29.

12. Olfa Hemler, "The Uses of Delphi Techniques in Problems of Educational Innovatings," no. 3499, RAND Corporation, December 1966.

13. A. R. Fusfeld and R. N. Foster, "The Delphi Technique: Survey and Comment," *Business Horizons* 14 (1971): 63–74.

14. For elaboration on these methods, see George A. Steiner, *Top Management Planning* (London: Collier-Macmillan Ltd., 1969), pp. 223–27.

15. Gilbert Frisbie and Vincent A. Mabert, "Crystal Ball vs. System: The Forecasting Dilemma," *Business Horizons* 24, no. 5 (September/October 1981): 72–76.

16. Willard Fazar, "The Origin of PERT," *The Controller,* December 1962.

17. Harold L. Wattel, *Network Scheduling and Control Systems CAP/PERT* (Hempstead, N.J.: Hofstra University, 1964).

18. R. J. Schonberger, "Custom-Tailored PERT/CPM Systems," *Business Horizons* 15 (1972): 64–66.

Concluding Case 6
Planning at Coors

Peter and Jeffrey Coors (Photo: Brian Payne)

In recent years, the brewing industry has experienced a monumental shakeup. While the Miller Brewing Company and Anheuser-Busch, Inc. have recently increased their market share through a combination of aggressive marketing and substantial plant investments, fifty-three other independent brewers have disappeared from the brewing scene. As Miller Brewing was blanketing the airways with advertising aimed mainly at upsetting Busch's number-one position in the market, Coors was slipping from fourth to fifth in the market, with its income declining by 21 million dollars over a two-year period. Using hyperaggressive marketing techniques, Miller was successful in pushing its way from seventh to second place in national sales as companies such as Coors, not Busch, were being hurt the most.

For many years Coors had prided itself on being strictly a quality-oriented beer producer. It concentrated on uniformity in one brand, which was brewed using an un-usual process that avoids pasteurization. A longtime belief of the Coors family has been that heat causes deterioration in beer. Because of its quality image, company executives believed that it could maintain sales in the states surrounding Colorado with little promotion. But with the advent of the Miller-Busch marketing battles and a nationwide boycott by Coors's striking brewery workers, it became evident that a change was needed.

As a result of recent efforts to improve its position, Chairman William K. Coors has announced that "the great Miller blitz has been blunted." Coors has rebounded to the higher levels of profits of the past, with a volume of sales also significantly higher than they were a few years ago. This increase in profits and volume of sales corresponded to Miller's big push. Substantial credit for this Coors comeback has been given to a new generation of Coors family members who have implemented a number of modern management ideas. Jeffrey Coors, who headed the development of Coors Light, and Peter H. Coors, senior vice-president for sales and marketing, seem well equipped to ensure a good future for the Coors Brewing Company.

Two encouraging signs, from a management viewpoint, are that Coors is now testing its first super-premium beer and it has completed its first formal strategic plan for corporate growth. This plan includes the eventual invasion of eastern markets and a more than doubling of total brewing capacity to 35 million barrels a year. In essence, Coors will spend one billion dollars over the next decade for this expansion and in the near future hopes to pass both the Pabst Brewing Company and the Joseph Schlitz Brewing Company to become the country's third largest brewer.

This case is based upon "Adolph Coors: Brewing Up Plans for An Invasion of the East Coast," *Business Week,* September 28, 1980, pp. 120 and 124.

Discussion Issues

1. Pinpoint several different parts of the Coors operation that will probably be affected by the planning presently taking place. Be sure to mention how the parts would be affected.
2. Develop a sample policy, procedure, and rule that seem consistent with Coors's planning effort. Discuss each sample with respect to its repetitiveness, time, scope, and level.
3. Do you think that the development of a sales forecast would be part of planning activities on Coors's drawing board? Why? If so, discuss the method(s) that might be used to perform this forecasting and explain why you would use the method(s).
4. Discuss how PERT and critical path analysis could be used as part of the planning process at Coors.

Student Learning Objectives

From studying this chapter I will attempt to acquire:

1. An understanding of the planning subsystem
2. A knowledge of when the chief executive can also be the primary planner in an organization
3. An appreciation for the qualifications and duties of the planner
4. A base for evaluating the performance of the planner
5. A framework for developing a plan for planning
6. General guidelines for getting the most return from the planning process

Chapter Outline

Implementing the Planning Process

Introductory Case 7
The Planning Executive

The Bluestone Dairy Company began fifty years ago by selling only homogenized milk. Over the past ten years, however, the product line has been expanded to include margarine, butter, cream, ice cream, and skim milk. The company obviously has been doing very well. Although Bluestone is still under one roof, profits have increased steadily and the number of employees has gone from twelve to one hundred in its fifty years of business.

To date, the president of the Bluestone Dairy Company is also the chief planning executive. He gathers and analyzes all information necessary to make planning decisions, decides which plans should be implemented, and then supervises the implementation of the plans. The president seems convinced that a major factor in Bluestone's success over the years is the traditional control that he has held on planning. He supports the idea that the chief executive of Bluestone should also be its chief planning officer.

The president, however, has recently received a memo from a department manager hired two years ago that is forcing him to reevaluate the Bluestone planning process. This particular department manager has a reputation for being extremely competent, and all other Bluestone managers listen very closely to him. The memo reads in part: "I would like to recommend that Bluestone takes steps to implement a new planning process. This process, as proposed, would consist of the following steps:

1. The president will determine, and circulate throughout the company, Bluestone's tentative objectives for the coming year.
2. On the basis of these objectives, each department manager at Bluestone will prepare a plan indicating how his or her department can contribute to organizational success. Thoughts and ideas of the department manager's subordinates will be considered in formulating these plans.
3. A newly created director of planning will be appointed to develop a comprehensive plan that integrates these departmental plans. This new director will then advise Bluestone's president concerning the plans the organization should adopt for the next year."

Discussion Issues

1. If you were president of Bluestone, how would you answer the memo?
2. What are the advantages and disadvantages of both the present and the proposed planning processes?
3. Which factors within the organization tend to support the implementation of the proposed planning process? Which tend to support retaining the present planning process?

What's Ahead

The introductory case finds the president of the Bluestone Dairy Company faced with deciding how the planning process should be implemented within his organization. The material in this chapter recommends that this implementation decision only should be made after a thorough consideration of (1) the planning subsystem, (2) planning and the chief executive, (3) the planner, (4) a plan for planning, and (5) maximizing the effectiveness of the planning process.

Once managers understand the fundamentals of planning, they can take steps to implement the planning process in their organization. This implementation is the key to a successful planning process. Even though managers might be experts on facts related to planning and the planning process, if they cannot transform this understanding into appropriate action, they are not able to generate useful organizational plans.

One way of approaching this implementation is to view planning activities as an organizational subsystem. A **subsystem** is a system created as part of the process of the overall management system. Figure 7.1 illustrates this relationship between the overall management system and a subsystem. Subsystems help managers to better organize the overall system and to enhance its success.

Figure 7.2 presents the ingredients of the planning subsystem. The purpose of this subsystem is to increase the effectiveness of the overall management system through more effective planning. This subsystem helps managers to better identify planning activities within the overall system and, therefore, to better guide and direct these activities.

Obviously, only a portion of organizational resources are used as input in the planning subsystem. This input is allocated to the planning subsystem and transformed into output by following the steps of the planning process.

Examples of how planning subsystems are organized in the industrial world are the more informal planning subsystem at the Quaker Oats Company and the more formal planning subsystem at the Sun Oil Company.[1]

Quaker Oats Company

At Quaker Oats speculations about the future are conducted, for the most part, on an informal basis. To help anticipate particular social changes in the future, communication lines have been opened with various groups believed to be the harbingers of change. To spearhead this activity, a "noncommittee" has been organized whose members represent a diversity of orientations. They listen to what is going on—monitor social changes—and thus augment the company's understanding of social change.

Sun Oil Company

Several groups within Sun Oil Company are engaged in formal business planning and forecasting. Operational planning with a five-year horizon is done annually. The planning activity with the longest time horizon exists within the Sun Oil Company of Pennsylvania, the corporation's refining, transportation, and marketing arm. A centralized strategic planning group, reporting to the vice-president of development and planning, is responsible for assisting top management in setting the company's long-term objec-

---

The Planning Subsystem

What Is a Subsystem?

The Purpose of Subsystems

The Quaker Oats Planning Subsystem

The Sun Oil Planning Subsystem

Figure 7.1 Relationship between overall management system and a subsystem.

Overall Management System

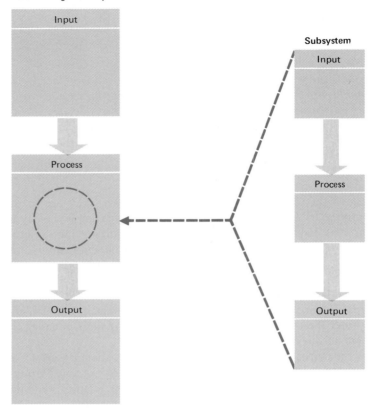

tives, developing strategic plans to achieve these objectives, and identifying likely consumer needs and market developments of the future that might indicate business areas for diversification. Current efforts are focused on discussing a series of strategic issues with the executive committee, a planning process designed to generate a restatement of long-term objectives.

Back to the Case

The president of the Bluestone Dairy Company could see after reading this section that organizational planning should be viewed as a subsystem of his overall management system. The resources he allocates as input for this subsystem will be transformed into organizational plans through the subsystem process. Any planning alternatives he may be considering should be compared on the basis of costs of subsystem input and process as well as the expected benefits of subsystem output.

Planning and the Chief Executive

The Chief Executive Has Many Roles

Henry Mintzberg has pointed out that top managers or chief executives of organizations have many different roles to perform.[2] As organizational figureheads, they must represent their organizations in a variety of social, legal, and ceremonial matters. As leaders, they must ensure that organization members are properly guided in relation to organizational goals. As liaisons, they must establish themselves as links between their organizations and factors outside their organizations. As monitors, they must

Figure 7.2 Planning subsystem.

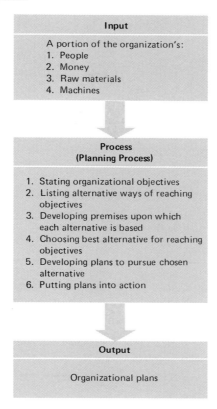

Input
A portion of the organization's:
1. People
2. Money
3. Raw materials
4. Machines

Process (Planning Process)
1. Stating organizational objectives
2. Listing alternative ways of reaching objectives
3. Developing premises upon which each alternative is based
4. Choosing best alternative for reaching objectives
5. Developing plans to pursue chosen alternative
6. Putting plans into action

Output
Organizational plans

assess organizational progress. As disturbance handlers, they must settle disputes between organization members. And as resource allocators, they must determine where resources will be placed to benefit their organizations best.

In addition to these many and varied roles, chief executives are responsible for organizational planning. The final responsibility for organizational planning clearly rests with top management. As the scope of planning broadens to include a larger portion of the management system, it becomes increasingly important for chief executives to become more involved in the planning process.

As planners, chief executives seek answers to the following broad questions:

1. In what direction should the organization be going?
2. In what direction is the organization going now?
3. Should something be done to change this direction?
4. Is the organization continuing in an appropriate direction?[3]

Keeping informed about social, political, and scientific trends is of utmost importance in helping chief executives to answer these questions.

Given both the importance of top management participation in organizational planning and the importance of top management performing other time-consuming roles, more and more top managers obtain planning assistance by establishing a position for an organization planner.[4] Just as managers can ask others for help and advice in making decisions, they can involve others in formulating organizational plans.

Chief executives of most substantial organizations need help to plan.[5] The remainder of this chapter, therefore, assumes that the organization planner is an individual who is not the chief executive of the organization. The planner is presented as a manager responsible for giving assistance to the chief executive on organizational

The Chief Executive Also Is Responsible for Planning

Planning Assistance

Beetle Bailey by Mort Walker

planning issues. If by chance the planner and the chief executive are the same person in a particular organization, the following discussion relating to the planner can be modified slightly to relate also to the chief executive.

Back to the Case

As planner, the president of Bluestone is responsible for performing such time-consuming functions as keeping abreast of internal and external trends that could affect Bluestone's future. Because the allotment of time necessary to perform the planning function is so large and because the president of Bluestone has many activities to perform within the organization in addition to organization planning, he may want to consider appointing a director of planning who could assist him in performing planning activities.

The Planner

Perhaps the most important input in the planning subsystem is the planner. This individual combines all other input and influences subsystem process so that effective organizational plans become subsystem output. The planner is responsible not only for the plans that are developed but also for advising management about what action should be taken in relation to those plans.

Regardless of who actually does the planning or the organization in which the planning is being done, the qualifications, duties, and evaluation of the planner are very important considerations in increasing the effectiveness of the planning subsystem.

Qualifications of Planners

Experience

First, the individual who performs the planning activities for an organization should be a person with considerable practical experience within that organization. Preferably, the planner should have been an executive in one or more of the organization's major departments. This experience should help the planner to develop plans that are practical and tailor-made for the organization.

See Organization As a Whole

Second, the planner should be able to replace any narrow view of the organization (probably acquired while holding other organizational positions) with an understanding of the organization as a whole. The planner must know how all parts of the organization function and interrelate. In other words, she or he must possess an abundance of the conceptual skills mentioned in chapter 1.

Figure 7.3 Narrowing in the planning process.

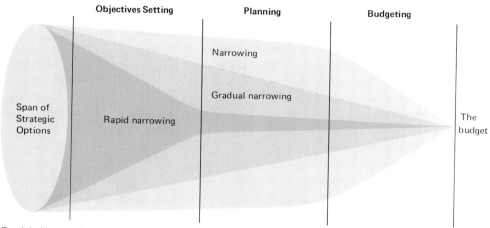

Third, the planner should have some knowledge of and interest in the social, political, technical, and economic trends that could affect the future of the organization. The planner must have some skill in defining these trends and the expertise to determine how the organization should react to them to maximize success. This particular qualification cannot be overemphasized.

Detect and React to Trends

The fourth and last qualification is that the planner should be able to work well with others. He or she inevitably will work closely with several key members of the organization, and should possess personal characteristics that will be helpful in collaborating and advising effectively. The ability to communicate clearly, both orally and in writing, is one of the most important of these characteristics.[6]

Get Along with Others

Duties of Planners

An individual who has the primary responsibility for corporate planning has at least three general duties to perform: (1) overseeing the planning process, (2) evaluating developed plans, and (3) solving planning problems.[7] Each of these duties is discussed in the following sections.

Overseeing the Planning Process

First, and perhaps foremost, the planner must see that planning gets done. To this end, the planner establishes rules, guidelines, and planning objectives that apply to the planner and others involved in the planning process. In essence, the planner must develop a plan for planning.

A conceptualization of the planning process presented by Lorange and Vancil furnishes a planner with a broad guideline to use in developing a plan for planning.[8] This conceptualization stresses that the planning process is essentially a continued narrowing of strategic options. In other words, the planning process is aimed at narrowing broad strategic options down to specific action that the organization should take to accomplish its objectives. Figure 7.3 presents a specific plan—a budget—that is the result of the "narrowing" of strategic options, objectives, the planning process, and the budgeting process.

The Process Must "Narrow"

Figure 7.4 Relationships among symptoms, problems, and opportunities that face the planner.

Systems Problem Solving

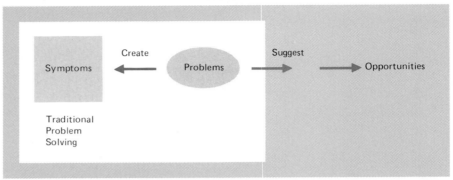

Narrowing Rates

Figure 7.3 also illustrates that a planning process can narrow at three different rates: slow narrowing, gradual narrowing, and rapid narrowing. Exactly how fast narrowing should take place depends upon the situation and the organization. Obviously, narrowing must keep pace with established planning objectives, but not proceed so quickly that creativity and thoroughness are excluded from the planning process. In general, the more gradual the narrowing of the planning process, the more time planning will take and the more expensive it will be. A plan for planning should involve some consideration of this narrowing process and the rate at which it should proceed.

Evaluating Developed Plans

The second general duty of the planner is to evaluate plans that have been developed. After the narrowing process has been completed, the planner must decide if (1) plans are sufficiently challenging for the organization; (2) plans are complete; and (3) plans are consistent with organizational objectives. If the developed plans do not fulfill these three requirements, they should be modified appropriately.

Should Plans Be Modified?

Solving Planning Problems

The planner also has the duty to gather information that will help solve planning problems. Sometimes, the planner may find it necessary to conduct special studies within the organization to obtain this information. The planner then can recommend what the organization should do in the future to deal with these problems and forecast how the organization might benefit from related opportunities.

Information

Problems

Symptoms

Opportunities

As an example, a planner may observe that production objectives set by the organization are not being met. This is a symptom of a planning problem. The problem causing these symptoms might be that objectives are unrealistically high or that plans developed to achieve production objectives are inappropriate. The planner must gather information pertinent to the problem and suggest to management how the organization can solve its problem and become more successful. King and Cleland have presented the relationship among problems, symptoms, and opportunities in figure 7.4.

Specific Duties

The three duties of a planner just discussed—overseeing the planning process, evaluating developed plans, and solving planning problems—are general comments on the activities the planner must perform. Figure 7.5 lists probable specific responsibilities of an organization planner at a large manufacturing company. As this list of responsibilities implies, the main focus of the planner's activities is to advise management

Figure 7.5 Responsibilities of an organization planner.

The planner has the responsibility to —

1. Provide information to assist management in formulating long- and short-range goals and plans of the company. Also assist in the updating of these goals plus general monitoring of attainment.
2. Coordinate activities and prepare special studies centering on acquisition, disposals, joint endeavors, manufacturing rights, and patents.
3. Serve as resource for determining the acquisition, disposal, and movement of physical properties.
4. Encourage the stimulation of ideas from management toward broadening company operations; extract these ideas and follow up on possibilities.
5. Develop, recommend, and obtain management approval of plans, procedures, and policies to be followed in implementing diversification program.
6. Perform basic research on diversification, using such sources as the American Management Association, National Industrial Conference Board, Research Institute of America, and others.
7. Perform internal and external economic studies to secure necessary information for overall planning.
8. Utilize staff service personnel plus line and committee persons in accumulating and evaluating data.
9. Analyze the company's physical properties and personnel capabilities to determine production spans.
10. In conjunction with staff services, periodically survey performance capabilities of sales, engineering, manufacturing, and service components of the company.
11. Conduct an initial survey of the manufacturing organization's physical properties (facilities, equipment, and tools) and keep information current.
12. Investigate and determine possibilities of other significant use for our basic products.
13. Assist in communicating and implementing the diversification decisions of management during transition periods.
14. Prepare necessary reports to keep management informed.

on what should be done in the future. He or she keeps management informed so that action can be taken when necessary. The planner assists management not only in determining appropriate future action but also in ensuring that the timing of that action is appropriate. In the end, the possibility always exists that the manager may not accept the recommendations of the planner.

Evaluation of Planners

As with all other organization members, the performance of the planner must be evaluated against the contribution he or she makes toward helping the organization achieve its objectives. The quality and appropriateness of the system for planning and the plans that the planner develops for the organization should be the primary considerations in this evaluation. Because the organizing, influencing, and controlling functions of the manager are based on the fundamental planning function, the evaluation of the planner becomes critically important.

Importance of Evaluation

Although assessment of the "quality and appropriateness" of the system for planning is somewhat subjective, a number of objective indicators do exist. For example, the extent to which the planner uses aproprate techniques is one objective indicator. If appropriate techniques are being used, the probability increases that the planner is doing an acceptable job. If appropriate techniques are not being used, the probability decreases that the planner is doing an acceptable job. The degree of objectivity displayed by the planner is another objective indicator. To a great extent, the planner's advice should be based on a rational analysis of appropriate information.[9] This is not to say that subjectivity and judgment should be excluded by the planner. This subjectivity and judgment, however, typically should be based on specific and appropriate information.

Malik suggests that some objective evidence that the planner is doing a reputable job exists if:

1. Organizational plans are in writing.
2. The plan is the result of all elements of the management team working together.
3. The plan defines present and possible future businesses of the organization.
4. The plan specifically mentions organizational objectives.
5. The plan includes future opportunities and suggestions on how to take advantage of them.
6. The plan emphasizes both internal and external environments.
7. The plan describes the attainment of objectives in operational terms when possible.
8. The plan includes both long- and short-run recommendations.[10]

These eight points furnish managers with some objective guidelines for evaluating the performance of the planner. This evaluation, however, never should be completely objective. More subjective considerations include how well the planner gets along with key members of the organization, the amount of organizational loyalty the planner displays, and the amount of potential the planner possesses.

Back to the Case

Regardless of who will finally be the primary planning officer at Bluestone, the individual should possess certain qualifications. Ideally, Bluestone's planner should have some experience at Bluestone, be able to see Bluestone as an entire organization, have some ability to gauge and react to major trends that will probably affect Bluestone's future, and be able to work well with others. The planning officer at Bluestone will have the responsibilities of overseeing the planning process, evaluating developed plans, and solving planning problems. Bluestone's planner will be evaluated like all other Bluestone employees. Although some objective indicators can help in this analysis, subjective indicators should also be considered. Overall, Bluestone's chief planning officer should be the individual who possesses the best qualifications, can best perform planning duties, and would have the best performance evaluation as a planner.

Plan for Planning

To be successful, the organization planner must have a comprehensive "plan for planning" that outlines the necessary planning steps. Many planners are unsuccessful simply because they do not have such a plan. Overall, the plan for planning should demonstrate that the planner has a firm understanding of what management wants to achieve, and it should clearly outline the specifics of activities involved in the planning process.

Although details vary somewhat from organization to organization, every plan for planning should include sections that stress (1) evaluating the present planning process, (2) assessing planning needs, (3) projecting planning benefits, (4) designing the planning organization, and (5) developing a work timetable.[11]

Evaluating the Present Planning Process

Planning Activities Inventory

To evaluate the present planning process, the planner should take an inventory of planning activities being performed within the organization, paying attention to the type of forecasting being done and the existing internal system for gathering pertinent information. The planner should be particularly aware of the extent to which the planning process uses such planning techniques as the Program Evaluation and Review Technique (PERT), decision trees, Gantt charts, and expected values based on probability analysis. Any weaknesses in the present planning process, as indicated by this evaluation, should be dealt with in the new plan for planning. Any strengths should be reinforced whenever possible.

Assessing Planning Needs

The main factor in determining how much planning an organization needs is the extent to which the organizational environment is expected to change. The greater the probability of environmental change, the greater the need for organizational planning. As an example, an organization that manufactures home appliances powered by natural gas probably will face a changing external environment in the near future. Namely, the natural gas that powers its products probably will not be as available to consumers as it has in the past. This virtually inevitable change in environment should be a cue that the organization must undertake a comprehensive planning program. The plan for planning should reflect the degree of expected change of the organizational environment.

Projecting Planning Benefits

Any planner knows that planning activities are time consuming and require hard work. If individuals involved in the planning process have unrealistic expectations about the benefits resulting from planning, the process can become very frustrating. Walter B. Schaffir suggests that the realistic benefits of planning include a discovery of problems that might face the organization in the future, an uncovering of opportunities that could enhance profitability, and an analysis of various alternatives for coping with and taking advantage of these problems and opportunities.[12] Unrealistically high expectations regarding the results of the planning process can cause planning participants to be disappointed and to neglect planning duties. The planner should take the time to communicate clearly in the plan for planning exactly what benefits planning participants should expect from the planning process.

Molding Realistic Expectations

Designing the Planning Organization

The design for the planning organization primarily outlines which organization members will be involved in the planning process and what their respective roles will be. Personnel such as department heads, supervisors, and even the chief executive should not only know where they fit in the planning process but also what they are expected to do in the planning effort. Karger advises the development of a planning manual for each planning participant. A planning manual would organize the considerable flow of information involved in planning, thereby also organizing the entire planning organization.[13]

Developing a Work Timetable

A plan for planning should include a work timetable that designates the date by which the first planning cycle is to be completed. In addition, the planner should incorporate into the timetable the deadlines by which various members of the planning organization must have their specific planning tasks completed. To do this, the planner assembles and combines the output of these specific tasks and formulates a plan for the organization as a whole.

Completion Dates for Planning Activities

The planning alternatives available to the Bluestone Dairy Company also can be analyzed from the viewpoint of each alternative's plan for planning. How easily various plans can be implemented, the costs of implementing the plans, and projected benefits from implementation are primary considerations in this analysis. At a minimum these plans for planning should contain an assessment of Bluestone's planning process, a projection of how much planning Bluestone will need, an estimate of the benefits that will accrue to Bluestone as a result of planning, an outline of the planning organization that will be necessary to implement each plan for planning, and a timetable showing when planning will be completed.

Maximizing the Effectiveness of the Planning Process

Success in implementing a planning subsystem is not easily attainable. As the size of the organization increases, the planning task becomes more complicated.[14] The planning process in larger organizations typically requires more people, more information, and more complicated decisions. Regardless of the planning situation, however, several safeguards can ensure the success of an organizational planning effort. These safeguards include (1) top management support, (2) an effective and efficient planning organization, (3) an implementation-focused planning orientation, and (4) inclusion of the right people.

Top Management Support

Concern for Planning

The chief executive must show support of the planning effort.[15] Organization members may not take the planning effort seriously unless top management clearly demonstrates interest in planning activities. The responsibility for organizational planning is ultimately the responsibility of top management, and all individuals within the organization should be aware that top management perceives it as such.

Whenever possible, top management should actively help to guide and participate in planning activities. Furnishing the planner with whatever resources are needed to structure the planning organization, encouraging planning as a continuing process and not as a once-a-year activity, and preparing people for changes usually resulting from planning are clear signs that top management is solidly behind the planning effort. The chief executive must give continual and obvious attention to the planning process if it is to be successful.[16] He or she must not be so concerned about other matters that planning is not given the emphasis it deserves.[17]

An Effective and Efficient Planning Organization

A well-designed planning organization is the primary vehicle by which planning is accomplished and planning effectiveness is determined. The planner must take the time to design as efficient and effective a planning organization as possible.

The Planning Organization Should:

The planning organization should have three built-in characteristics. First, it should be designed to use established management systems within the company. As expressed by Paul J. Stonich:

1. Use established systems

> Many organizations separate formal planning systems from the rest of the management systems that include organization, communication, reporting, evaluating, and performance review. These systems must not be viewed as separate from formal planning systems. Complex organizations need a comprehensive and coordinated set of management systems, including formal planning systems to help them toward their goals.[18]

Second, the planning organization should be simple, yet complex enough to ensure a coordinated effort of all planning participants. Planning can be a complicated process requiring a somewhat large planning organization. The planner should strive to simplify the planning organization and make its complex facets as clearly understood as possible.

2. Be simple yet complex

Lastly, the planning organization should be flexible and adaptable. Planning conditions are constantly changing, and the planning organization must be able to respond to these changing conditions.

3. Be flexible and adaptable

An Implementation-Focused Planning Orientation

Because the end result of the planning process is some type of action that will help achieve stated organizational objectives, planning should be aimed at implementation.[19] As Drucker points out, a plan is effective only if its implementation helps attain organizational objectives.[20] Plans should be developed and scrutinized after looking ahead to when they are to be implemented.[21] Ease of implementation is a positive feature of a plan that should be built in whenever possible.

Plans Precede Action

The marketing plan of the Edsel automobile introduced by Ford in the 1950s is an example of how a sound plan can become unsuccessful simply because of ineffective implementation.[22] The rationale behind the Edsel was complete, logical, and defensible. Three consumer trends at that time solidly justified the automobile's introduction: (1) a trend toward buying higher-priced cars; (2) a general income increase for consumers had resulted in all income groups purchasing higher-priced cars; and (3) people who bought lower-priced Fords were trading them in on Buicks, Oldsmobiles, or Pontiacs after they become more affluent. Conceptually, these trends were so significant that Ford's plan to introduce the larger and more expensive Edsel appeared virtually risk free.

Implementation Can Doom Plans

Two factors in the implementation of this plan, however, turned the entire Edsel situation into a financial disaster. First, the network of controllers, dealers, marketing managers, and industrial relations managers created within Ford to get the Edsel to the consumer became very complicated and inefficient. Second, because Ford pushed as many Edsels as possible on the road immediately after introduction, the quality of the Edsel suffered and consumers bought poorly manufactured products. Although the plan to make and market the Edsel was completely defensible, the long-run influence of the organization and manufacturing processes created to implement the plan doomed it to failure.

Inclusion of the Right People

Planning must include the right people.[23] Whenever possible, the planner should obtain input from the managers of the functional areas for which she or he is planning. These managers are close to the everyday activity of their segments of the organization and can provide the planner with invaluable information. These managers probably also will be involved in implementing whatever plan develops and, therefore, can furnish the planner with feedback on how easily various plans are being implemented.

Planner Seeks Opinions

Exhibit 7 illustrates how Carolyn Dunn, a product manager at Welch Foods, includes such people as marketing research specialists, finance specialists, and advertising specialists in developing her plan to market Welch's grape juice, Swanson's chicken spread, Kraft's sliced cheese, and Nabisco Chips Ahoy cookies. It is also interesting to note in this exhibit that Dunn definitely stresses the implementation of planning as emphasized in the previous section.

Exhibit 7

Carolyn Dunn Plans to Sell at Welch Foods

Carolyn Dunn (Photo: Vincent Frye)

Grapes. The word is on Carolyn Dunn's mind as she drives to work past the Concord vineyards dotting the route into the village of Westfield, New York, home of Welch Foods—the world's largest producer of grape-derived food products. Dunn is one of the company's pivotal employees: she is product manager of bottled juices—Welch's most important line.

Part ad executive, part saleswoman, part numbers cruncher, and part entrepreneur, Carolyn Dunn, 31, helps ensure that Welch Foods ($238 million in sales in 1980) maintains its profitable 70 percent share of the U.S. grape juice market. As product manager, Dunn must market her high quality grape (and one tomato) juice products, by coordinating the diverse efforts of numerous Welch employees. She must work with in-house and independent advertisers to convince people to buy Welch, and with salespeople and store owners to get them to carry her products. At the same time she must track her less expensive "non-premium" competitors, in order to protect her line from their strengths and to exploit their weaknesses. In addition, she must strive to minimize production costs.

When Dunn came on board at Welch, following a two and one-half year stint as an assistant product manager at Standard Brands, she inherited a marketing plan calling for a major promotion of purple grape juice. "It was only a paper plan when I came in," Dunn says from behind the desk in her powder-blue second-floor office. "It was my job to flesh it out in seven months."

The plan involved selling the 40-oz. economy-size bottle of grape juice—the biggest seller among Welch's ten sizes—along with three complementary national food products: Swanson's chicken spread, Kraft's sliced cheese, and Nabisco's Chips Ahoy cookies. The combination would be promoted as the ideal lunch. In addition, the promotion would feature coupons which consumers could redeem for fresh fruit. "It's called thematic marketing," says Dunn. "It's a growing trend in the industry." The idea is that promoting several independently identifiable products together creates an impact on the consumer greater than the impact of any one of the separate items.

January. Carolyn is settling into her office, getting to know the managers for the other lines of Welch products. Despite the intensity, informality is the corporate style. Shirt sleeved managers stop in their supervisors' offices to kick around ideas and get advice. Dunn consults regularly with hers. She needs to be briefed in detail about the marketing plans for fiscal year 1981 [the year this article was written], including the status of the special 40-oz. promotion. (The fiscal year at Welch begins on the first of September.) In addition, Carolyn has to start drawing up her own marketing plan for fiscal year 1982.

Dunn begins the heavy work at her desk. She exhaustively pores over previous marketing plans and research data prepared by Welch and by outside market analysis companies. She's acquiring a feel for how Welch operates. The past is becoming concrete, her future choices clear.

February. Dunn moves into high gear as she begins the preliminary design of her marketing plan. She meets with the bottled juice support group—co-workers from the finance, legal, purchasing, and corporate planning departments—to discuss costs and pricing.

"The marketing plan is your bible," says Dunn. Hence, its preparation is the most important thing that the product manager does. What she plans will ultimately depend on how much or how little juice is produced. Carolyn is also made aware of rising production costs by corporate planning. In 1980 the company couldn't pass along costs to consumers for fear that the juices might be too expensive. Will that situation occur again? A lot depends on the "profit contribution" the company expects from her line.

She gets the preliminary information from the finance department. She can live with it. Now that she has cost projections and profit expectations, Dunn looks at how her products compare with her competition. She must be satisfied that her products are of the highest quality.

"There are such things as key business factors," says Dunn. "For IBM the key is service. For Welch the key is quality."

In the meantime, Dunn continues to execute the special promotion. She meets with the tie-in partners in New York City at the headquarters of the firm they have hired to carry the promotion—Synergistic Marketing, Inc. They hash out the details. They haggle over, then agree on, the size and position of their products in the illustrations. Dunn informs the partners that she must push ahead with a separate promotion of the 40-oz. bottle to satisfy Welch obligations to its regular consumer promotion agency. By the end of the month Dunn and her tie-in partners have their timetable. Now it is time to implement it.

March. Dunn's marketing plan is taking shape. Dunn brought with her to Welch the knowledge that companies have varying ways of doing business. "Each company has its own managerial style," says Dunn. "For example, the product manager at one company won't have the same routine as the product manager at another." Dunn says that Welch is particularly strong in the area of market research, and she devotes much time to getting to know it better. In outline, what she discovers is a market of homemakers, aged 25 to 54, in households of 3 or more people, with a household income of more than $10,000. Research reveals they want pure juices for their children to drink, and that they are particularly conscious of vitamin C content. Welch juices are pure, with no sugar added, and are vitamin enriched.

Welch's market research also reveals that 20 percent of its bottled grape juice bought in the U.S. is consumed by blacks. "The company realized how significant that was and decided to concentrate on that market," says Dunn. Before she came on board, the company had hired the black New York City firm of Uniworld Group, Inc. to handle advertising directed at the black market. Carolyn sees opportunities to strengthen and expand this segment of the market in her own plan.

All the data shows Dunn that she should be able to maintain her market share and profit contribution. But she will need to use more consumer promotions as a fundamental part of her marketing plan. She is not yet sure what type, but knows she's got flexibility. "Grape juice is the kind of juice that can be drunk at any time of the day, unlike something like orange juice, which most people still identify as a breakfast drink," she says.

In the meantime, Carolyn continues to monitor the special September promotion. Things are running smoothly—and on time. She feels good.

April. Dunn's marketing plan is becoming more concrete. And she is getting accustomed to life in western New York. She had known what working 10 hours a day and on weekends was like from her previous jobs. But living in Jamestown (pop. 40,000) the largest town in Chautauqua County, 20 miles south of Westfield, isn't exactly the same thing as living in Newark. "Slower paced" is Carolyn's phrase for it. And whatever loneliness she feels is mitigated by the friendships she is forming with her co-workers, especially those without families. Welch is a small company without a management trainee program. Consequently, they hire their managers from other companies. Many find themselves, like Carolyn, without family and friends nearby. They understand the dislocation—and they do their best to do things together: going to concerts, riding bicycles, playing backgammon.

May. Work goes on. Dunn begins to notify her manufacturing plants and sales brokers about the upcoming special promotion. She provides the manufacturing plants with production quotas. She meets with the regional sales managers. Unlike some companies which have their own sales force, Welch contracts with food store brokers to sell their products. The sales force likes what Dunn presents them. She is pleased.

In the meantime, Dunn receives weekly sales reports from the sales department. The figures are helping her fine-tune the projections for the second draft of the 1982 marketing plan. And they help her spot potential problems before her superiors do. If there are problems, she will have explanations and solutions. None develop.

June/July. Dunn's final draft of the 1982 marketing plan is before her superiors for approval. She's slightly nervous but knows there is little reason to be. She's covered everything: the market analysis of the bottled grape juice industry; the strengths and weaknesses of her line versus her competitors; her specific business objectives; her promotional plan and advertising strategy; and her preliminary budget.

In the meantime, she makes final preparations for the special 40-oz. promotion. The displays should be in the stores and the advertisements in women's magazines by mid-August.

From Elliot D. Lee, "The Grape Expectations of Carolyn Dunn," *Black Enterprise,* October 1981, pp. 55–59. Copyright 1981, The Earl G. Graves Publishing Co., Inc., 295 Madison Avenue, New York, N.Y. 10017. All rights reserved.

Input from individuals who will be directly affected by the plans can also be helpful to the planner. These individuals actually do the work in the organization and can give opinions on how various alternative plans will influence work flow. Although it is extremely important that the planner involves others in the planning process, all organization members cannot and should not be involved. Stonich offers the following advice on the involvement of organization members in the planning process:

> In many corporations the wrong sets of people participate in particular planning activities. Planning requires not only generation of information for making decisions, but decision making itself. The kinds of decisions and types of data needed should dictate the choice of who is involved in what aspects of planning within an organization.[24]

Back to the Case

Once Bluestone has developed a planning process, four safeguards can be taken to ensure that this process will be successful. First, top management should encourage the serious pursuit of planning activities by showing its support of the planning process. Second, the organization designed to implement the planning process should use established systems at Bluestone, be simple yet complex, and be flexible and adaptive. Third, the entire planning process should be oriented toward easing the implementation of generated plans. Lastly, all key people at Bluestone should be included in the planning process.

Summary

The following points are stressed within this chapter:

1. To use what they know about plans and planning, managers must be able to implement an effective planning process. Viewing planning as a subsystem of the overall management system is one way to approach this implementation.

2. Top management typically is responsible for performing many roles in addition to planning. As a result, many chief executives seek planning help by establishing a position called "planner." This planner is the individual within the organization who is primarily responsible for advising top management on organizational plans.

3. The organization planner usually possesses the qualifications of past experience within the organization along with the abilities to see the organization as a whole, detect and react to trends, and work well with people. The planner's duties include overseeing the planning process, evaluating developed plans, and solving planning problems.

4. To be successful, the organization planner must have a detailed plan for planning. This plan outlines what must be done during the planning process and involves evaluating the existing planning process, assessing organizational planning needs, projecting planning benefits, designing the planning organization, and developing a work timetable.

5. To maximize the effectiveness of a planning process, top management must show its support, an effective and efficient planning organization must exist, an implementation-focused planning orientation must be used, and the right people should be included in planning activities.

1. What is an organizational subsystem?
2. List the ingredients of the planning subsystem.
3. How do the many roles of organization chief executives relate to their role as organization planner?
4. Explain the basic qualifications necessary to be an organization planner.
5. Give a detailed description of the general duties the planner must perform within the organization.
6. Present a detailed explanation of the "narrowing of the planning process" shown in figure 7.3.
7. If someone asked you how to evaluate the performance of an organization planner, how would you answer?
8. What is the significance of a "plan for planning"?
9. Why is an evaluation of the present planning process an important ingredient of the plan for planning?
10. Explain the relationship between the need for organizational planning and the probability that the organizational environment will change.
11. Why should the planner be concerned with the benefits planning participants expect from their planning activities?
12. What is the significance of having a design for the planning organization?
13. Should a work timetable for completing the first planning cycle contain numerous deadlines or just one? Why?
14. How can top management show its support for the planning process?
15. Describe the characteristics of an effective and efficient planning organization.
16. Why should the planning process emphasize the implementation of organizational plans?
17. Explain why the Edsel automobile failed to generate consumer acceptance.
18. Which people in an organization typically should be included in the planning process? Why?

Banfield, Edward C. "Ends and Means in Planning." In *Concepts and Issues in Administrative Behavior*, edited by Sidney Mailick and Edward H. Van Ness. Englewood Cliffs, N.J.: Prentice-Hall, 1962.

Christopher, William F. "Is the Annual Planning Cycle Really Necessary?" *Management Review* 70, no. 8 (August 1981): 38–42.

Cotton, Donald B. *Organizing for Company-wide Planning*. New York: Macmillan, 1969.

Ewing, D. W. *The Human Side of Planning*. New York: Macmillan, 1969.

Feinberg, Mortimer R. "Preparing Contingency Plans." *Restaurant Business* 80 (May 1981): 3–8, 16.

Glueck, W. F. *Organization Planning and Development*. New York: American Management Association, 1971.

Heroux, Richard L. "How Effective Is Your Planning?" *Managerial Planning* 30, no. 2 (September/October 198): 3–8ff.

Hutchinson, J. D. *Management Strategy and Tactics*. New York: Holt, Rinehart & Winston, 1971.

Naylor, Thomas H. "Organizing for Strategic Planning." *Managerial Planning* 28 (July/August 1979): 3–9, 17.

Payne, B. *Planning for Company Growth*. New York: McGraw-Hill, 1963.

Ross, Joel E., and Kami, Michael J. *Corporate Management in Crisis: Why the Mighty Fall*. Englewood Cliffs, N.J.: Prentice-Hall, 1973.

Sawyer, George C. "The Hazards of Goal Conflict in Strategic Planning." *Managerial Planning* 28 (May/June 1980): 11–13, 27.

Sord, Burnard H., and Welsch, Glenn A. *Managerial Planning and Control*. Austin, Texas: University of Texas, Bureau of Business Research, 1964.

Sweet, F. H. *Strategic Planning*. Austin, Texas: University of Texas, Bureau of Business Research, 1964.

Warren, E. K. *Long-Range Planning: The Executive Viewpoint*. Englewood Cliffs, N.J.: Prentice-Hall, 1966.

Wortman, Leon A. *Successful Small Business Management*. New York: American Management Association, 1976.

Notes

1. Excerpted, by permission of the publisher, from 1974–75 Exploratory Planning Briefs: Planning for the Future by Corporations and Agencies, Domestic and International, © 1975 by AMACOM, a division of American Management Associations, pp. 10–11. All rights reserved.

2. Henry Mintzberg, "A New Look at the Chief Executive's Job," *Organizational Dynamics,* Winter 1973, pp. 20–40.

3. Adapted from J. F. R. Perrin, *Focus on the Future* (London: Management Publications, 1971).

4. James M. Hardy, *Corporate Planning for Nonprofit Organizations* (New York: Association Press, 1972), p. 37.

5. Milton Leontiades, "The Dimensions of Planning in Large Industrialized Organizations," *California Management Review* 22, no. 4 (Summer 1980): 82–86.

6. The section Qualifications of Planners is adapted from John Argenti, *Systematic Corporate Planning* (New York: John Wiley & Sons, 1974), p. 126.

7. These three duties are adapted from Walter B. Schaffir, "What Have We Learned about Corporate Planning?" *Management Review,* August 1973, pp. 19–26.

8. Peter Lorange and Richard F. Vancil, "How to Design a Strategic Planning System," *Harvard Business Review,* September–October 1976, pp. 75–81.

9. Edward J. Green, *Workbook for Corporate Planning* (New York: American Management Association, 1970).

10. Z. A. Malik, "Formal Long-Range Planning and Organizational Performance" (Ph.D. diss., Rensselaer Polytechnic Institute, 1974).

11. The section Plan for Planning is based on Patrick H. Irwin, "Romulus and Remus: Two Studies in Corporate Planning," *Management Review,* October 1976, pp. 24–36.

12. Schaffir, "What We Have Learned about Corporate Planning?" *Management Review,* August 1973, pp. 23–24.

13. Delmar W. Karger, "What Effective Planning Is All About!" *Industrial Management,* July–August 1976, pp. 1–10.

14. James Brian Quinn, "Managing Strategic Change," *Sloan Management Review* 21, no. 4 (Summer 1980): 3–20.

15. Kamal E. Said and Robert E. Seiler, "An Empirical Study of Long-Range Planning Systems: Strengths—Weaknesses—Outlook," *Managerial Planning* 28, no. 1 (July/August 1979): 24–28.

16. George A. Steiner, "The Critical Role of Management in Long-Range Planning," *Arizona Review,* April 1966.

17. Myles L. Mace, "The President and Corporate Planning," *Harvard Business Review,* January–February 1965, pp. 49–62.

18. Paul J. Stonich, "Formal Planning Pitfalls and How to Avoid Them," *Management Review,* June 1975, pp. 5–6.

19. Thomas A. Ratcliffe and David J. Logsdon, "The Business Planning Process—A Behavioral Perspective," *Managerial Planning,* March/April 1980, pp. 32–37.

20. Peter F. Drucker, *Management: Tasks, Responsibilities, Practices* (New York: Harper & Row, 1973).

21. Bernard W. Taylor, III and K. Roscoe David, "Implementing an Action Program Via Organizational Change," *Journal of Economics and Business,* Spring/Summer 1976, pp. 203–8.

22. William H. Reynolds, "The Edsel: Faulty Execution of a Sound Marketing Plan," *Business Horizons,* Fall 1967, pp. 39–46.

23. To see how various management positions are typically involved in U.S. human resource planning, see Guvenc G. Alpander, "Human Resource Planning in U.S. Corporations," *California Management Review* 22, no. 2 (Spring 1980): 24–32.

24. Stonich, "Formal Planning Pitfalls and How to Avoid Them," p. 5.

Concluding Case 7
Scott Paper: No Longer King of Consumer Paper Goods

(Photo: © 1981 Andrew Popper)

Scott Paper Company has recently found itself in one of the most crucial positions in its 101-year history. The company is faced with unstable earnings, a declining market share, management turmoil, and rumors of a takeover. In order to stabilize its position in the market and recover lost markets while it selects a long-range plan, Scott management is trying to implement a short-term plan that is dictated by its antiquated equipment.

Many of Scott's problems can be traced to its equipment. During the late 1970s, Scott's Packaged Products Division was faced with the realization that most of its plants were too old to produce high-quality goods at competitive costs. Contrary to acceptable marketing standards (the approach that identifies customer's needs and attempts to satisfy them), the company decided to produce those products that its existing machinery could make efficiently.

After a careful analysis of the business it was decided that the company had to change its perspective. According to Philip E. Lippincott, the president of Scott, the business was literally taken apart piece by piece and then rebuilt. The result: Scott found that it had to rely on low-cost goods rather than on high-price, quality items. With the strategy determined, Scott began advertising and promoting more heavily.

The emphasis on low-cost goods has put tremendous pressure on profit margins, but Scott sales have been helped. Scott introduced some reformulated brands in 1979; by mid-1980, the company had reestablished itself as the market leader in toilet tissue sales. An analyst for Smith Barney, Harris Upham & Co. estimated Scott's toilet tissue sales to hold 29 percent of the market, just slightly above Proctor & Gamble's 28 percent. This surge in Scott's toilet tissue sales was, to a great extent, a result of a change in philosophy and upgraded promotional activity. Scott is getting away from the theory that it is "king" of the sanitary paper market, and Scott's $37 million advertising expenditure in 1979 was a challenge to even Proctor & Gamble, who had a $34 million advertising budget.

Scott's strategy to recapture its share of the market included adjustments in paper composition and lower prices for three top brands. These changes brought Scott 30 percent of the paper towel market, a market share 10 percent higher than that of Proctor & Gamble. In addition, Scott has entered the attractive market of the unbranded and generic-type product. More than 20 percent of all tissue sales are in unbranded items. This makes unbranded tissue items extremely attractive since the entire sanitary paper market increases at a slight 3 percent a year.

The short-term program Scott has developed has gained the company some time, but it has also precipitated some problems. The redesign of high-quality products to those of lesser quality, while maintaining the same product name, can confuse and anger consumers. This may eventually lead to a lack of consumer confidence and a reduction of sales. Because of these factors, Scott is working diligently with the Boston Consulting Group to formulate a long-range strategy.

Many observers believe that Scott must undergo some major rebuilding. An analyst for Drexel Barnham Lambert, Inc. estimates that 70 percent of Scott's capacity is "old technology," as compared with 50 percent at Kimberly-Clark and only 20 percent at Proctor & Gamble. Charles D. Dickey, Jr., Scott's chairman and chief executive, agrees that the company faces great challenges to become the leading low-cost producer in the industry. Nevertheless, Dickey believes that Scott is currently in a better position than they have been in for a long time. During the 1960s, Scott began diversifying and neglected its main business (paper products). Furthermore, the company did not reinvest the bulk of its profits. Instead, they paid 63 percent of annual earnings in dividends to stockholders and basically ignored the development of new technology by not investing in the Research and Development Division. In 1971, dividend payments were chopped and capital spending increased. While today Scott faces challenges from all sides, Chairman Dickey hopes to once again make Scott "the undisputed ruler of the industry."

"Scott Paper Fights Back, At Last." *Business Week,* February 16, 1981, pp. 104, 108.

Discussion Issues

1. What is Scott's primary objective for long-range planning?
2. How might the company invest its funds in order to prepare for the future? Explain.
3. What divisions should a planner work with in preparation for Scott's future development?
4. How might the effectiveness of any short-range or long-range plan be maximized? How well is Scott progressing in its long-range planning effort?

Organizing is one of the four major management functions that must be performed for organizations to have long-run success. The material in this section flows naturally from section 2, "Planning," because organizing is the primary mechanism managers have for putting plans into action. In essence, organizing follows planning.

Chapter 8, "Fundamentals of Organizing," defines organizing as the process of establishing orderly uses for all organizational resources. This process is presented as being comprised of five main steps: (1) reflecting on plans and objectives, (2) establishing major tasks, (3) dividing major tasks into subtasks, (4) allocating resources for subtasks, and (5) evaluating implemented organizing strategy. The organizing function is identified as a subsystem of the overall management system and is shown to be influenced by classical organizing principles concerning structure, division of labor, span of control, and scalar relationships.

Chapter 9, "Organizing the Activity of Individuals," defines responsibility as the obligation to perform assigned activity and credits it with being the most fundamental ingredient for channeling the activity of individuals within organizations. The point is made in this chapter that once individuals are assigned some organizational responsibility, they also must be granted a corresponding amount of authority that will enable them to perform this obligation. Authority is defined as the right to perform or command. Delegation, another important management topic covered in this chapter, is explained as the process of assigning responsibility and authority to individuals within organizations. An organization is said to be centralized when its management delegates little authority and responsibility, and decentralized when its management delegates significant amounts of authority and responsibility.

Chapter 10, "Providing Appropriate Human Resources for the Organization," focuses on the task of furnishing people for the organization who will make desirable contributions to attaining organizational objectives. The process of furnishing such people is discussed as involving recruitment, selection, training, and performance evaluation. Recruiting entails screening the total supply of people available to fill a position, and selection involves choosing to hire one of those individuals. Once an individual has been selected or hired, she or he typically undergoes some type of training. Training is the process of developing in human resources qualities that ultimately will enable them to be more productive and thus contribute more to organizational goal attainment. This chapter also suggests that for individuals to be made as productive as possible, their performance should be evaluated after they have been recruited, selected, and trained. This evaluation helps the employees to know what they are doing right, what they are doing wrong, and how they can improve. Lastly, this chapter presents the issue of integrating female blue-collar workers into the organization as a special management problem in providing appropriate human resources for the organization.

Over time, most managers find that they must make some changes in the way their organizations operate. The purpose of making such modifications, of course, is to increase organizational effectiveness—the extent to which an organization attains its organizational objectives. Chapter 11, "Changing an Organization," defines changing an organization as the process of modifying an existing organization. How managers decide who will make the change, what should be changed, what effect the change will have on people in the organization, and how to evaluate the change are discussed. The collective influence of all of these issues is presented as ultimately determining how successful a particular organizational change will be.

Section 3
Organizing

Student Learning Objectives

From studying this chapter I will attempt to acquire:

1. An understanding of the organizing function
2. An appreciation for the complications of determining appropriate organizational structure
3. Insights on the advantages and disadvantages of division of labor
4. A working knowledge of the relationship between division of labor and coordination
5. An understanding of span of management and the factors that influence its appropriateness
6. An understanding of scalar relationships

Chapter Outline

Fundamentals of Organizing

Introductory Case 8
Consolidating Bakeries

Dianne Elmort, a management consultant in Baltimore, is in a meeting with a client. The telephone rings and Elmort's secretary tells her that she has a long-distance call from Los Angeles. The individual placing the call is Ralph Zacarachy, the owner of Bakeall, a small bakery. Elmort excuses herself for a moment and accepts the call privately. The following conversation takes place:

ELMORT: Hello, this is Dianne Elmort speaking.

ZACARACHY: Ms. Elmort, this is Ralph Zacarachy. A friend of mine, James Earl, suggested that I call you for advice concerning a management problem I am presently facing. As you may recall, Earl was one of your past clients.

ELMORT: Yes, I remember Earl's situation very clearly. Before we finished, Jim and I developed a very good working relationship. Fortunately, we were able to solve his problem with minimum difficulty. Is your problem similar to the one Jim had?

ZACARACHY: No. I wish it were. In fact, I think my problem is completely different. You see, for several years I have owned a small bakery in downtown Los Angeles. I have been doing well downtown, and I recently decided to purchase another bakery in a suburban shopping center.

Now, I'm faced with the problem of trying to organize my two bakeries in the best possible way. I'm calling you to ask if you might have time to assist me in developing my organizing strategy. I've been a baker all of my life, and I'm not too sure how to handle this situation. Can you help me?

ELMORT: I have experience handling the type of situation you describe and would be pleased to help if you so desire. Don't worry about the fee. I'm sure we can arrive at some mutually agreeable figure.

I have a list of standard questions regarding organizing that I usually ask clients with your kind of problem. Actually, these questions will only lay the rough groundwork for solving your problem. After you answer the questions, I should spend approximately a week thinking about your answers and then fly to Los Angeles to spend a couple of days with you to finalize your organizing strategy.

Since I am in a meeting right now, it would be difficult for me to talk too much longer. If you want, I'll call you back this afternoon to ask you these questions.

ZACARACHY: Your suggestion sounds fine, and I'm pleased you'll be able to work with me. I'll be in the bakery all afternoon so call at your convenience.

Discussion Issues

1. How would you define organizing?
2. List as many questions as you can that you think Elmort will ask Zacarachy to lay the foundation for solving the organizing situation mentioned in the case.
3. Explain why it would be important for Elmort to ask each of the questions you listed in number 2.

What's Ahead

The ending of the introductory case leaves Ralph Zacarachy, a bakery owner, waiting for a call from Dianne Elmort, a management consultant. Elmort will be calling to ask Zacarachy some questions whose answers will provide the basis for organizing Zacarachy's old bakery and a new one that he just purchased. For these questions to be worthwhile they must focus on the organizing function and furnish information that will help Elmort recommend a specific organizing strategy for Zacarachy's situation. The material in this chapter emphasizes both a definition of organizing and principles of classical organizing theory so that the types of questions Elmort should ask will be better understood.

Organizing is the process of establishing orderly uses for all resources within the management system. These orderly uses emphasize the attainment of management system objectives and assist managers not only in making objectives apparent but also in clarifying which resources will be used to attain them.[1] Organization, as used in this chapter, refers to the result of the organizing process.

> **A Definition of Organizing**
> Orderly Uses for All Management System Resources

In essence, each organizational resource represents an investment from which the management system must get a return. Appropriate organization of these resources increases the efficiency and effectiveness of their use. Henri Fayol has developed sixteen general guidelines that can be used when organizing resources.[2] Although these guidelines were published in English in 1949, they are still valuable recommendations for managers today.

1. Judiciously prepare and execute the operating plan.
2. Organize the human and material facets so that they are consistent with objectives, resources, and requirements of the concern.
3. Establish a single, competent, energetic, guiding authority (formal management structure).
4. Coordinate all activities and efforts.
5. Formulate clear, distinct, and precise decisions.
6. Arrange for efficient selection so that each department is headed by a competent, energetic manager and each employee is placed where she or he can render the greatest service.
7. Define duties.
8. Encourage initiative and responsibility.
9. Have fair and suitable rewards for services rendered.
10. Make use of sanctions against faults and errors.
11. Maintain discipline.
12. Ensure that individual interests are consistent with general interests of the organization.
13. Recognize the unity of command.
14. Promote both material and human coordination.
15. Institute and effect controls.
16. Avoid regulations, red tape, and paperwork.

© 1966 United Feature Syndicate.

The Importance of Organizing

Mechanism to Activate Plans

The organizing function is extremely important to the management system because it is the primary mechanism with which managers activate plans. Organizing creates and maintains relationships between all organizational resources by indicating which resources are to be used for specified activities, and when, where, and how the resources are to be used. A thorough organizing effort helps managers to minimize costly weaknesses, such as duplication of effort and idle organizational resources.

Organizing Department?

Some management theorists consider the organizing function so important that they advocate the creation and use of an organizing department within the management system.[3] Typical areas of responsibilities of this department would include (1) developing reorganization plans that will make the management system more effective and efficient, (2) developing plans to improve managerial skills to fit current management system needs, and (3) attempting to develop an advantageous organizational climate within the management system.[4]

The Organizing Process

The five main steps of the organizing process, as presented in figure 8.1, are (1) reflecting on plans and objectives, (2) establishing major tasks, (3) dividing major tasks into subtasks, (4) allocating resources and directives for subtasks, and (5) evaluating the results of implemented organizing strategy. As this figure implies, managers should continually repeat these steps. Through this repetition, they will obtain feedback that will help them improve the existing organization.

How Do You Organize?

The manager of a restaurant can illustrate how the organizing process might work. The first step the manager would take to initiate the organizing process would be reflecting on restaurant plans and objectives. Since plans involve determining how the restaurant will obtain its objectives, and organizing involves determining how restaurant resources will actually be used to activate plans, the restaurant manager must start to organize by understanding planning.

The second and third steps of the organizing process focus on tasks to be performed within the management system. After the manager understands restaurant plans and objectives, she must designate major task areas or jobs that must be performed within the restaurant. In this particular restaurant, two of these areas might be waiting on the customer and cooking food. Then she must divide major task areas into subtasks. For example, she might decide that the subtasks of waiting on the customer are taking orders and clearing the table.

The fourth organizing step the restaurant manager must perform is determining who will take orders, who will clear tables, and the details of the relationship between these individuals. The type of tables or booths and the type of silverware to be used would also be factors to be considered at this point.

Step five, evaluating the results of a particular organizing strategy, necessitates that the restaurant manager gathers feedback on how well her implemented organizing strategy is working. This feedback should furnish the manager with information she

Figure 8.1 Five main steps of the organizing process.

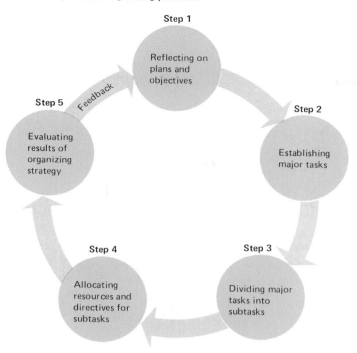

Reflecting on plans and objectives

Step 5

Feedback

Evaluating results of organizing strategy

Step 2

Establishing major tasks

Step 4

Allocating resources and directives for subtasks

Step 3

Dividing major tasks into subtasks

can use to improve the existing organization. For example, she may find that a particular type of booth is not large enough and that larger ones must be purchased if her restaurant is to attain its goals.

The Organizing Subsystem

The organizing function, like the planning function, can be visualized as a subsystem of the overall management system. Figure 8.2 shows the relationship between the overall management system and the organizing subsystem. The primary purpose of the organizing subsystem is to enhance the goal attainment of the general management system by providing a rational approach for using organizational resources. Figure 8.3 presents the specific ingredients of the organizing subsystem. Input is comprised of a portion of the total resources of the organization; process is made up of the steps of the organizing process; and output is organization.

Output Is Organization

Back to the Case

Elmort's questions should be aimed at establishing an orderly use of Zacarachy's organizational resources. Zacarachy's resources represent an investment on which he must get a return, and the information obtained from Elmort's questions eventually will be used to maximize this return. Elmort's questions should reflect the organizing process and focus on Zacarachy's present plans and objectives, establish major baking task areas, divide major baking tasks into subtasks, and create some mechanism for evaluating the effectiveness of the organizing strategy developed for

Zacarachy. Appropriate preliminary questions Elmort should ask include:

1. What objectives do you have for your bakeries?
2. What plans do you have to accomplish those objectives?
3. What are the major tasks or steps you go through to bake your products?
4. Can these major tasks be broken into smaller tasks or steps?
5. What resources do you have to run your bakeries? I need specific information regarding people, money, materials, and machines.

Figure 8.2 Relationships between overall management system and organizing subsystem.

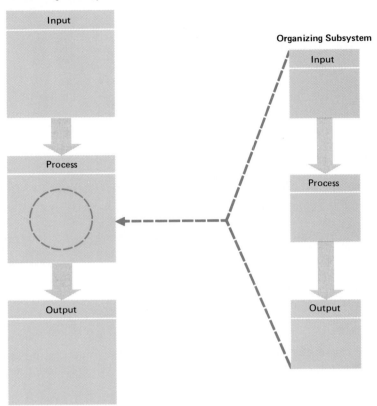

Classical Organizing Theory

How Can Organizational Resources Best Be Used to Reach Goals?

What Is Bureaucracy?

Classical organizing theory is the cumulative insights of early management writers on how organizational resources can best be used to enhance goal attainment. Perhaps the one writer who has had the most profound influence on classical organizing theory is Max Weber.[5] According to Weber, the main components of an organizing effort include detailed procedures and rules, a clearly outlined organizational hierarchy, and mainly impersonal relationships between organization members.

Weber used the term *bureaucracy* to label the management system that contains these components. Although Weber firmly believed in the bureaucratic approach to organizing, he became concerned when managers seemed to overemphasize the merits of a bureaucracy.[6] He cautioned that a bureaucracy is not an end in itself but a means to the end of management system goal attainment.

The main criticism of Weber's bureaucracy, as well as the concepts of other classical organizing theorists, is the obvious lack of concern they show for the human variable within the organization.[7] Considerable discussion on this human variable is presented in part 4 of this text. The following paragraphs summarize four main considerations from classical organizing theory that all modern managers should include in their organizing efforts: (1) structure, (2) span of control, (3) division of labor, and (4) scalar relationships.[8]

Figure 8.3 Organizing subsystem.

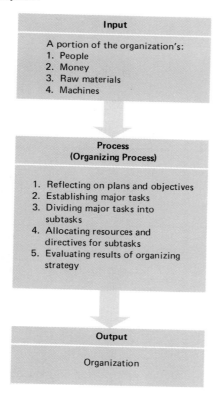

Input

A portion of the organization's:
1. People
2. Money
3. Raw materials
4. Machines

**Process
(Organizing Process)**

1. Reflecting on plans and objectives
2. Establishing major tasks
3. Dividing major tasks into subtasks
4. Allocating resources and directives for subtasks
5. Evaluating results of organizing strategy

Output

Organization

Structure

In any organizing effort managers must choose an appropriate structure.[9] **Structure** refers to designated relationships among resources of the management system. The purpose of structure is to facilitate the use of each resource, both individually and collectively, as the management system attempts to attain its objectives.[10]

Organization structure is represented primarily by means of a graphic illustration called an **organization chart.** Traditionally, an organization chart is constructed in pyramid form, with individuals toward the top of the pyramid having more authority and responsibility than individuals toward the bottom.[11] The relative positioning of individuals within boxes on the chart indicates broad working relationships, while lines between boxes designate formal lines of communication between individuals.

Figure 8.4 is an example of an organization chart. The dotted line in this figure is not part of the organization chart but has been added to illustrate the pyramidal shape of the chart. Positions close to the restaurant manager's have more authority and responsibility; positions farther away from the restaurant manager's have less authority and responsibility. Also, the location of positions on this chart indicates broad working relationships. For example, the positioning of the head chef over the three other chefs indicates that the head chef has authority over them and is responsible for their productivity. The lines between individual chefs and the restaurant manager indicate that formal communication from chef one to the restaurant manager must go through the head chef.

Relationships between Resources

What Is an Organization Chart?

Figure 8.4 Sample organization chart for small restaurant.

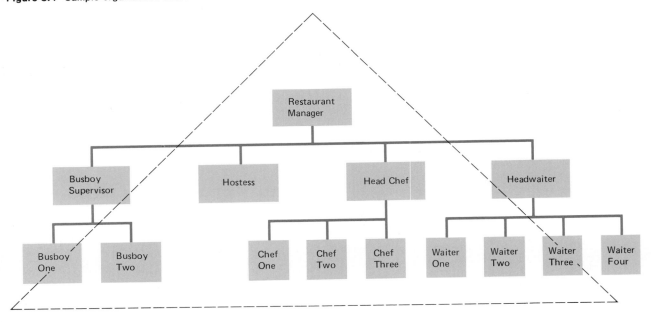

Formal and Informal Structure

Relationships Outlined by Management

In reality, two basic types of structure exist within management systems: formal structure and informal structure. **Formal structure** is defined as relationships between organizational resources as outlined by management. Formal structure is represented primarily by the organization chart.

Informal structure, on the other hand, is defined as patterns of relationships that develop because of the informal existence of organization members. Informal structure evolves naturally and tends to be molded by individual norms, values, and/or social relationships. Informal structure coexists with formal structure but is not necessarily identical to it.[12] The primary focus of this chapter is formal structure. More details on informal structure and how to manage it are covered in chapter 15.

Informal Relationships That Develop between Organization Members

Departmentalization and Formal Structure: A Contingency Viewpoint

What Is a Department?

What Is Departmentalization?

The most common method of establishing formal relationships between resources is by establishing departments. Basically, a **department** is a unique group of resources established by management to perform some organizational task. The process of establishing departments within the management system is called **departmentalization.** The creation of these departments typically is based on, or contingent upon, such situational factors as the work functions being performed, the product being assembled, the territory being covered, the target customer, and the process designed to manufacture the product.* A further explanation of each of these factors is presented in the paragraphs that follow.

*For a quick review of the contingency approach to management, refer to page 38.

Figure 8.5 Organization structure based primarily on function.

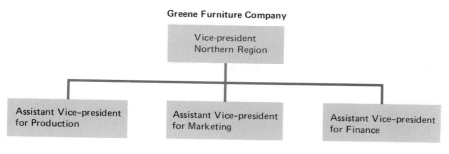

Greene Furniture Company

Function

Perhaps the most widely used base for establishing departments within the formal structure is the type of functions being performed within the management system.[13] A **function** is a type of activity being performed. The major categories into which functions typically are divided include marketing, production, and finance. Structure based on function departmentalizes workers and other resources according to the types of activities being performed. An example portion of an organization chart for a hypothetical organization, Greene Furniture Company, is based primarily on function and is presented in figure 8.5.

Product

Organization structure based primarily on **product** departmentalizes resources according to the product(s) being manufactured. As the management system manufactures more and more products it becomes increasingly difficult to coordinate activities across products. Organizing according to product allows managers to logically group resources necessary to produce each product. An example of Greene Furniture Company's structure based primarily on product is presented in figure 8.6.

Territory

Structure based primarily on **territory** departmentalizes according to the place where the work is being done or the geographic market area on which the management system is focusing. As market areas and work locations expand, physical space between various places can make the management task extremely cumbersome. These distances can range from a relatively short span between two points in the same city to a rela-

Figure 8.6 Organization structure based primarily on product.

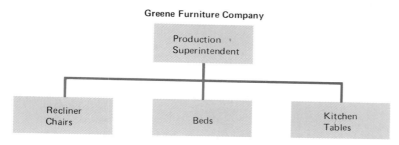

Greene Furniture Company

Organization Design Is Contingent Upon:

1. *Type of activity*

2. *Goods produced*

3. *Work or market locations*

Figure 8.7 Organization structure based primarily on territory.

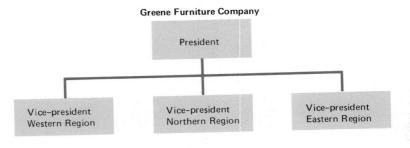

Greene Furniture Company

President

Vice-president Western Region

Vice-president Northern Region

Vice-president Eastern Region

Figure 8.8 Organization Structure Based Primarily on Customers

Greene Furniture Company

Sales Manager

Sales Representative for Educational Sales

Sales Representatives for Residential Sales

Sales Representatives for Commercial Sales

tively long span between two points in the same state or different states.[14] To minimize the effects of distances, resources can be departmentalized according to territory. An example of Greene Furniture Company's structure based primarily on territory is presented in figure 8.7.

Numerous companies also organize by territories within different countries. For example, Xerox has organized its operation by establishing a Latin American division, a Canadian division, and a division that covers Europe, Africa, and Asia.[15] As another example of organizing by territory across national borders, Bendix has a diesel company in France, an electronics company in France, and a brake company in Mexico. A simplified version of the Bendix organization chart showing this international emphasis is shown in figure 8.9.[16]

Customers

4. Who buys products?

Structure based primarily on the **customer** establishes departments in response to major customers of the management system. This structure, of course, assumes that major customers can be identified and divided into logical categories. An example of Greene Furniture Company's structure based primarily on customers is shown in figure 8.8. Greene Furniture obviously can clearly identify its customers and divide them into logical categories.

Manufacturing Process

5. How products are made

Structure based primarily on **manufacturing process** departmentalizes according to major phases of the process used to manufacture products. In the case of the Greene Furniture Company, major phases of the manufacturing process might be wood cutting, sanding, glueing, and painting. A portion of the organization chart that would reflect these phases is presented in figure 8.10.

Figure 8.9 Territories in Different Countries.

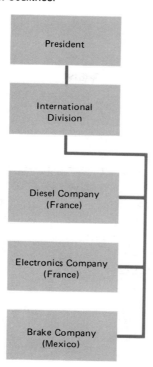

Figure 8.10 Organization structure based primarily on manufacturing process.

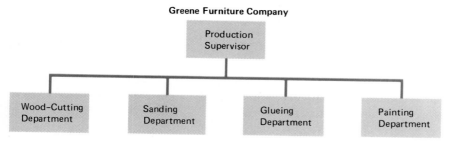

Figures 8.5, 8.6, 8.7, 8.9, and 8.10 all use a portion of an organization chart to illustrate a basis for establishing formal structure. If a situation warrants, organization charts can be combined to use all of these factors for the benefit of the management system. Figure 8.11 integrates the previous figures to show how all of these factors might be included on the same organization chart for the Greene Furniture Company.

Forces Influencing Formal Structure

The previous section described various forms of formal structure. According to Shetty and Carlisle, the formal structure of a management system is not actually fixed over time but is continually evolving. These authors indicate that four primary forces in-

Figure 8.11 Organization structure based primarily on function, product, territory, customers, and manufacturing process.

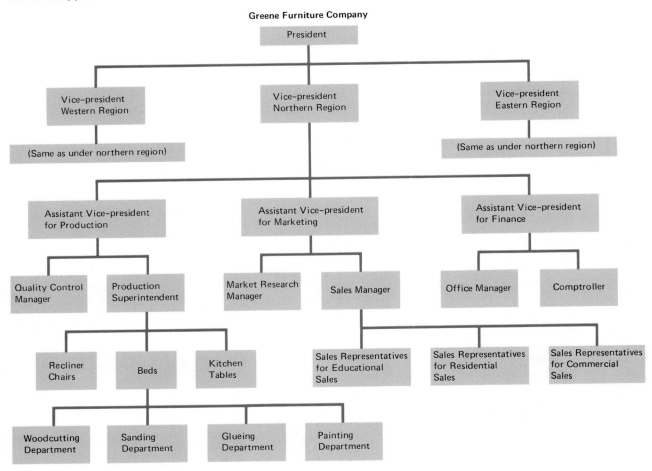

fluence this evolution: (1) forces in the manager, (2) forces in the task, (3) forces in the environment, and (4) forces in the subordinates.[17] The evolution of a particular organization is actually the result of a complex and dynamic interaction between these forces. Figure 8.12 illustrates this interaction.

In addition, exhibit 8 illustrates how this evolution probably took place too quickly at American Telephone and Telegraph and thereby resulted in a set of people problems with which management is now dealing.

Forces in the manager are comprised of the unique way in which managers perceive organizational problems. Naturally, a manager's background, knowledge, experience, and values influence his or her perception of how formal structure should exist or be changed. Forces in the task include the degree of technology involved in the task and the complexity of the task. As task activities change, a force is created to change the organization that exists. Forces in the environment include the customers

Ingredients of Forces

Figure 8.12 Forces influencing the evolution of organizational structure.

and suppliers of the management system, along with existing political and social structures. Forces in subordinates include the needs and skill levels of subordinates. Obviously, as the environment and subordinates vary, forces are created simultaneously to change the organization.

Back to the Case

Taking classical organizing theory into consideration, Elmort should ask questions that will enable her to recommend to Zacarachy: (1) a specific organization structure, (2) various spans of management appropriate for Zacarachy's situation, (3) a division of labor appropriate for Zacarachy's situation, and (4) specific scalar relationships among Zacarachy's human resources.

Elmort's questions regarding structure should be aimed at creating working relationships among all bakery resources. Whatever structure she develops should be presented and explained to Zacarachy with an organization chart. The chart itself should be composed of various departments derived from an analysis of bakery functions, bakery products, geographic locations of the old bakery and the new bakery, customers served by the bakery, and the processes used to bake the products. Elmort must understand these topics as they relate to Zacarachy's situation before she will be able to recommend a specific organization structure.

Division of Labor

The second main consideration of any organizing effort is how to divide labor. The concept *division of labor* is the assignment of various portions of a particular task among a number of organization members. Rather than one individual doing the entire job, several individuals perform different parts of the total activity. Production is divided into a number of steps, with the responsibility for completion of various steps assigned to specific individuals.[18] In essence, individuals specialize in doing part of the task rather than the entire task.

A commonly used illustration of division of labor is the automobile production line. Rather than one individual assembling an entire car, specific portions of the car are assembled by various individuals. The following sections discuss the advantages and disadvantages of division of labor and the relationship between division of labor and coordination.

Specialization

Exhibit 8

Quick Evolution at AT&T Results in Employee Stress

(Photo: © 1982 Rose Stork)

Officially, the company insists that it is just a coincidence. But the fact is that less than a year after American Telephone & Telegraph Co. announced the most sweeping reorganization in the Bell System's history (BW—Nov. 6), medical directors throughout the system are reporting higher levels of anxiety among employees coming in for routine physicals. The anxiety follows a shake-up that is changing job titles, duties, and whole methods of working for about 250,000 employees, or a third of Bell's work force.

Most of the in-house doctors echo the explanation by Dr. Robert S. Hockwald of Pacific Telephone & Telegraph Co. "The Bell System is under stress because of external influences, but other industries are too," he says. "It's the life we live nowadays." Still, there is a pervasive uneasiness that the reorganization is tipping the scales from normal amounts of employee stress to truly deleterious anxiety reactions. Notes Edward Mahler, assistant vice-president of personnel relations for Bell Telephone Co. of Pennsylvania: "Even the smallest change creates quite a churn, and this [reorganization] is a significant change."

In truth, it is affecting the jobs of almost every AT&T manager. Most of Bell's 22 operating telephone companies until recently had been structured along functional lines, such as marketing, operations, engineering, and plant supervision. Now those divisions are being realigned along market segments, such as residential, business, and network services. For example, a manager who previously was in charge of installation of both residential and business phones may now find himself focusing only on the residential customers. Nevertheless, his duties may be broadened, since his department serves all of the residential customer's requirements, from equipment installation and repair to designing new systems and developing new business. The reorganization is causing thousands of Bell managers to be retrained and then to begin making decisions in formerly unfamiliar areas of operations.

Apparently, Bell's top management is starting to recognize that announcing such massive organizational changes and getting employees to accept them sanguinely are two different things. As a result, about a dozen Bell System companies have either beefed up existing programs or developed new ones to help employees cope with change in the workplace and with the stress that accompanies it. Kerry A. Bunker, AT&T's supervisor of basic human resources research, says such programs are "growing like Topsy everywhere."

Pacific Telephone, for one, recently started a noontime discussion program in which some 200 employees a month meet in small groups to talk about stress. The company has also undertaken a pilot stress reduction class that teaches groups of some 10 to 15 managers such "coping" methods as muscle relaxation. And at Illinois Bell Telephone Co., Dr. Robert R. J. Hilker, corporate medical director, concedes that the company's seven-year-old program for studying stress in its top 700 executives was not enough to handle this year's stress problems. "Everything in their [the managers'] whole darn life seems upset," he explains. Since January, all 850 of Illinois Bell's middle managers have completed a new seminar on "managing change" that Hilker says "seems to be effective" in helping them cope.

Personal problems. Although Bell's own internal reorganization is certainly the major change managers are facing, most of the seminars deal with all types of change. The Illinois Bell managers met in groups of 50 over a three-day period and heard speeches from government officials, consumer advocates, business professors, and management consultants regarding general changes in the business environment. A Bell vice-president then discussed the reorganization specifically, and President Charles Marshall made himself available to answer questions. Finally, Hilker gave a 90-minute talk on coping with stress. Several times during the three days, the managers split into groups of about a dozen people to discuss what they had learned.

At a few of the Bell companies, though, the focus of training this year is squarely on personal stress. Possibly the most dramatic examples are Bell of Pennsylvania and Diamond State Telephone Co. in Delaware. Since 1974 the two companies have jointly run annual seminars for middle managers, covering topics such as corporate social responsibility or financial planning. Pennsylvania Bell's Mahler suggests that the sessions were degenerating into company "messages" and that he was already "looking for something different to do" this year. But instead of figuring out how to improve the old management training program, the two companies eliminated it for this year. In its place, 550 middle managers took part in a 2½-day program of small-group discussions and psychological exercises designed specifically to help them deal with change, both in their personal and in their corporate lives.

"It's really a program to teach them to cope better with life," says Peter L. Bell, director of the Center for the Study of Adult Development, a nonprofit group affiliated with the University of Pennsylvania, which was selected by the two Bell companies to conduct the seminars. Adds Pennsylvania Bell's medical director, Dr. Robert S. Ayerle, "It helps people review their lives, focus on problem areas, and . . . see some solutions for those problems."

Advantages and Disadvantages

Why Divide Labor?

Several generally accepted reasons have been offered for why division of labor should be employed within organizing strategy. First, since workers specialize in a particular task, their skill for performing that task tends to increase. Second, workers do not lose valuable time in moving from one task to another. Since they typically have one job and one place in which to do it, time is not lost changing tools or locations. Third, because workers concentrate on performing only one job, they naturally tend to try making their job easier and more efficient. Lastly, division of labor creates a situation in which workers only need to know how to perform their part of the work task rather than the process for the entire product. The task of understanding their work, therefore, typically does not become too much of a burden.

Perhaps Labor Shouldn't Be Divided

Arguments have also been presented, however, that seem to discourage the use of extreme division of labor or specialization.[19] Overall, these arguments stress that the advantages of division of labor focus solely on efficiency and economic benefit and overlook the human variable. Work that is extemely specialized tends to be very boring and therefore usually causes production rates to go down. Clearly, some type of balance is needed between specialization and human motivation. Arriving at this balance is discussed further in chapter 14.

Division of Labor and Coordination

Synchronization

In a division of labor situation with different individuals doing portions of a task, the importance of effective coordination within the organization becomes obvious. Mooney defines **coordination** as "the orderly arrangement of group effort to provide unity of action in the pursuit of a common purpose."[20] Coordination involves encouraging the completion of individual portions of a task in a synchronized order that is appropriate for the overall task. Part of the synchronized order for assembling an automobile entails installing seats only after the floor has been installed. Adhering to this order of installation is coordination. Not adhering to this order of installation illustrates a lack of coordination.

Various Coordinative Roles

Establishing and maintaining coordination may, but does not always, involve close supervision of employees. Managers can also establish and maintain coordination through the performance of such diverse roles as bargaining, formulating common purpose, and/or improving upon specific problem solutions.[21] Each of these roles can help achieve coordination and can be considered specific management tools. Managers must break away from the idea that coordination is only achieved through close employee supervision.

Follett on Coordination

Mary Parker Follett has furnished concerned managers with valuable advice on how to establish and maintain coordination within the organization. First, Follett indicates that coordination can be attained with the least difficulty through direct horizontal relationships and personal communications. When a coordination problem arises, speaking with peer workers may be the best way to solve it. Second, Follett suggests that coordination be a discussion topic throughout the planning process. In essence, managers should plan for coordination. Third, maintaining coordination is a continuing process and should be treated as such. Managers cannot assume that because their management system shows coordination today that it will show coordination tomorrow. Follett also said that managers should not leave the existence of coordination up to chance. Coordination can be achieved only through purposeful managerial action. Lastly, according to Follett, the importance of the human element and the communication process should be considered when attempting to encourage coordination. Employee skill levels and motivation levels are primary considerations as is the effectiveness of the human communication process used during coordination activities.[22]

Elmort also must propose how work should be divided within Zacarachy's bakery. In this instance, division of labor is the assignment of various portions of bakery tasks among a number of organization members. Her suggested division of labor also should include a mechanism for enhancing coordination. Elmort's questions to Zacarachy regarding these issues should deal with developing a thorough understanding of how the work is done so that she can recommend the best way to divide it and to maintain coordination within the suggested division.

Span of Management

The third main consideration of any organizing effort is span of management. **Span of management** refers to the number of individuals a manager supervises. The more individuals a manager supervises, the greater the span of management. Conversely, the fewer individuals a manager supervises, the smaller the span of management. Span of management is also called span of control, span of authority, span of supervision, and span of responsibility.

The central concern of span of management is a determination of how many individuals a manager can effectively supervise.[23] To use human resources efficiently, managers should supervise as many individuals as they can best guide toward production quotas. If they are supervising too few individuals, they are wasting a portion of their productive capacity. On the other hand, if they are supervising too many individuals, they necessarily lose part of their effectiveness and probably will become extremely frustrated.

Designing Span of Management: A Contingency Viewpoint

As reported by Harold Koontz, the main situational factors that influence the appropriateness of the size of an individual's span of management include (1) similarity of functions, (2) geographic contiguity, (3) complexity of functions, (4) coordination, and (5) planning.[24]

Similarity of Functions

Similarity of functions is the degree to which activities performed by supervised individuals are similar or dissimilar. As the similarity of subordinate activities increases, the wider the span of management appropriate for the situation becomes. The converse of this statement is also generally accurate.

Geographic Contiguity

The degree to which subordinates are physically separated is **geographic contiguity.** In general, the closer subordinates are physically, the more individuals managers can supervise effectively.

Complexity of Functions

Complexity of functions refers to the degree to which activities of workers are difficult and involved. The more difficult and involved these activities are, the more difficult it is to manage a large number of individuals effectively.

Coordination

In this sense, coordination refers to the amount of time managers must spend to synchronize the activities of their subordinates with the activities of other workers. The greater the amount of time managers must spend on coordination, the smaller their span of management should be.

Figure 8.13 Major factors that influence the span of management.

Factor	Factor Has Tendency to Increase Span of Management When—	Factor Has Tendency to Decrease Span of Management When—
1. Similarity of function 2. Geographic contiguity 3. Complexity of functions 4. Coordination 5. Planning	1. Subordinates have similar functions. 2. Subordinates are physically close. 3. Subordinates have simple tasks. 4. Work of subordinates needs little coordination. 5. Manager spends little time planning.	1. Subordinates have different functions. 2. Subordinates are physically distant. 3. Subordinates have complex tasks. 4. Work of subordinates needs much coordination. 5. Manager spends much time planning.

Figure 8.14 Geometric increase of possible management-subordinate relationships.

Number of Subordinates	Number of Relationships
1	1
2	6
3	18
4	44
5	100
6	222
7	490
8	1,080
9	2,376
10	5,210
11	11,374
12	24,708
18	2,359,602

From PRINCIPLES OF MANAGEMENT by Koontz & O'Donnell. Copyright © 1972 by McGraw-Hill, Inc. Used with permission of McGraw-Hill Book Co.

Planning

5. Planning required for subordinates' jobs

Planning refers to the amount of time managers must spend developing management system objectives and plans and integrating them with the activities of their subordinates. The more time they must spend with planning activities, the fewer individuals they can manage effectively. Figure 8.13 summarizes the factors that tend to increase and decrease span of management.

Graicunas and Span of Management

What is Graicunas's Formula?

Perhaps the best known contribution to span of management literature was made by V. A. Graicunas,[25] a management consultant.[26] Basically, this contribution is the development of a formula for determining the number of *possible* relationships between a manager and his or her subordinates when the number of subordinates is known. **Graicunas's formula** is as follows:

$$C = n\left(\frac{2^n}{2} + n - 1\right)$$

Figure 8.15 Six possible relationships between manager *M* and two subordinates *X* and *Y*.

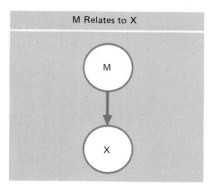

M Relates to X

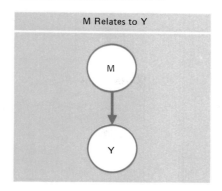

M Relates to Y

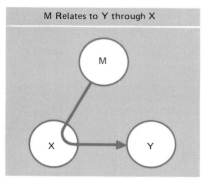

M Relates to Y through X

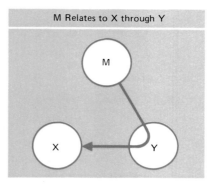

M Relates to X through Y

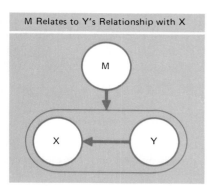

M Relates to Y's Relationship with X

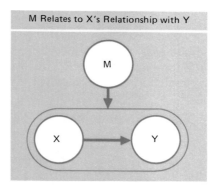

M Relates to X's Relationship with Y

C is the total number of possible relationships between manager and subordinates, while *n* is the known number of subordinates. Figure 8.14 contains the results of what happens to the total possible number of manager-subordinate relationships as the number of subordinates increases from 1 to 18. As the number of subordinates increases arithematically, the number of possible relationships between the manager and those subordinates increases geometrically. Figure 8.15 is an illustration of the six possible relationships between a manager and two subordinates.

A number of criticisms have been leveled at Graicunas's work. Arguments that Graicunas did not take into account a manager's relationships outside the organization and that he only considered potential relationships rather than actual relationships have some validity. The real significance of Graicunas's work, however, does not lie within the realm of these criticisms. His main contribution was pointing out that span of management is an important consideration that can have far-reaching organizational impact.[27]

Is Graicunas's Contribution Valuable?

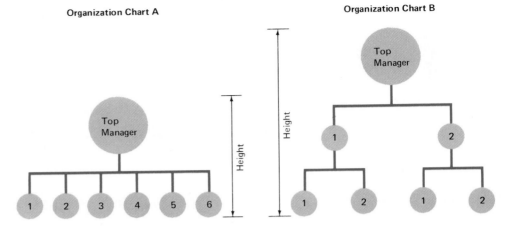

Figure 8.16 Relationship between organization chart height and span of management.

Organization Chart A

Organization Chart B

Height of Organization Chart

Flat and Tall Organization Charts

A definite relationship exists between span of management and the height of an organization chart. Normally, the greater the height of the organization chart, the smaller the span of management within that organization. It also follows that the lower the height of the organization chart, the greater the span of management. Organization charts with little height are usually referred to as **flat,** while organization charts with much height are usually referred to as **tall.**

Figure 8.16 is a simple example of the relationship between organization chart height and span of management. Organization chart *A* has a span of management of six, and organization chart *B* has a span of management of two. As a result, chart *A* is flatter than chart *B*. Both charts *A* and *B* have the same number of individuals below the top manager. The larger span of management in *A* is reduced in *B* simply by adding a level to *B*'s organization chart.

Scalar Relationships

Chain of Command

The fourth main consideration of any organizing effort is scalar relationships. **Scalar relationships** refer to a chain of command. Organization is built upon the premise that the individual at the top possesses the most authority and that other individuals' authority is scaled downward according to the individual's relative position on the organization chart. The lower the individual's position on the organization chart, the less authority she or he possesses.

The scalar relationship concept, or chain of command, is related to the unity of command concept. The **unity of command** concept recommends that an individual should

One Boss

have only one boss. If too many bosses give orders, the most probable result is confusion, contradictory orders, and frustrated workers, a situation that probably will result in ineffectiveness and inefficiency.

Fayol indicates that always adhering to the chain of command is not advisable.[28] Figure 8.17 serves to explain Fayol's rationale. If individual *F* needs information from individual *G* and follows the concept of scalar relationships or chain of command, *F* has to go through individuals *D, B, A, C,* and *E* before reaching *G*. The information would get back to *F* only by going from *G* through *E, C, A, B,* and *D*. Obviously, this long and involved process can be very expensive for the organization in terms of time spent getting the information.

To decrease this expense, Fayol recommends that in some situations a bridge or **"gangplank"** should be used to allow *F* to go directly to *G* for information. This bridge

Figure 8.17 Example organization chart showing that always adhering to the chain of command is not advisable.

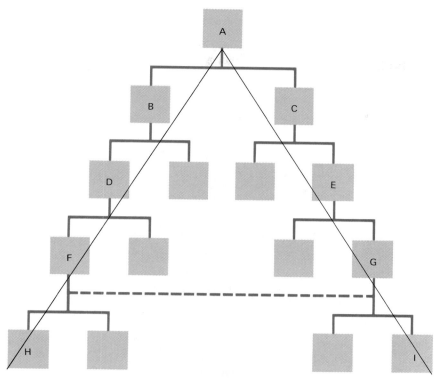

From H. Fayol, *General and Industrial Management,* trans. Constance Storrs (London: Sir Isaac Pitman & Sons, Ltd., 1963), p. 34. Used with permission.

is represented in figure 8.17 by the dotted line that goes directly from F to G. Managers should use these organizational bridges with great care, however, because although F might get the information from G more quickly and cheaply, individuals D, B, A, C, and E are left out of the communication channel. This lack of information caused by using Fayol's bridge might be more costly in the long run than going through the established chain of command. If managers do use an organizational bridge, they must be extremely careful to inform all other appropriate individuals within the organization as to the information they received.

Bridge or Gangplank

Back to the Case

Span of management, another of Elmort's major areas for recommendations to Zacarachy, focuses on the number of subordinates managers can supervise in the bakery. Elmort's questions regarding span of management should be designed to help her understand the degree of similarity between various baking activities, the extent to which managers will be separated from subordinates, the degree of complexity of baking functions, the amount of time managers must spend coordinating subordinates' activities, and the amount of time managers must spend planning. Zacarachy's answers to such questions will help Elmort to suggest appropriate spans of management for the managers in Zacarachy's bakery.

Elmort's recommendations to Zacarachy also should relate to designating scalar relationships within Zacarachy's bakery and suggesting when, if ever, her proposed chain of command should be bridged. Elmort's questions to Zacarachy relative to this recommendation should be aimed at helping her understand the relationships between the tasks individuals within the chain of command are performing and when it is important for one individual within the chain to know what other individuals within the chain are doing.

Summary

The following points are stressed within this chapter:

1. Organizing is the process of establishing orderly uses for all management system resources. Establishing these uses is very important because they represent how plans will be activated.

2. Steps in the organizing process include reflecting on established plans and objectives, establishing major task areas, dividing major tasks into subtasks, allocating resources and directives to perform subtasks, and evaluating the results of the organizing strategy.

3. The organizing function can be visualized as a subsystem of the overall management system. Input is comprised of a portion of the total resources of the organization; process consists of the steps of the organizing process; and output is organization.

4. One of the four main ingredients of classical organizing theory is structure, the designation of relationships between resources of the management system. Structure can be formal or informal, and can be based on, or contingent upon, function, product, territory, customers, or manufacturing process. Forces influencing formal structure include forces in the manager, forces in the task, forces in the environment, and forces in subordinates.

5. The second main ingredient of classical organizing theory is division of labor, or the assignment of various portions of a task, among different organization system members. Division of labor creates the need for coordination and has both advantages and disadvantages.

6. The third main ingredient of classical organizing theory is span of control, or the number of subordinates a manager has. The appropriate number of subordinates for a manager is contingent upon similarity of functions, geographic contiguity, complexity of functions, coordination, and planning. The span of management and the height of an organization chart are inversely related.

7. The last main ingredient of classical organizing theory is scalar relationships, the chain of command. In certain situations, Fayol's organizational bridge can be used to overcome the inefficiencies of the established chain of command.

Issues for Review and Discussion

1. What is organizing?
2. Explain the significance of organizing to the management system.
3. List the steps in the organizing process. Why should managers continually repeat these steps?
4. Can the organizing function be thought of as a subsystem? Explain.
5. Fully describe what Max Weber meant by the term *bureaucracy*.
6. Compare and contrast formal structure with informal structure.
7. How are the degrees of management system diversification and interdependency related to formal structure?
8. List and explain three additional factors which management structure is based on, or contingent upon. Draw three sample portions of organization charts that illustrate the factors you listed.
9. Describe the forces that influence formal structure. How do these forces collectively influence structure?

10. What is division of labor?
11. What are the advantages and disadvantages of employing division of labor within a management system?
12. Define coordination.
13. Does division of labor increase the need for coordination? Why?
14. Summarize Mary Parker Follett's thoughts on how to establish and maintain coordination.
15. Is span of management an important management concept? Explain.
16. Do you think that similarity of functions, geographic contiguity, complexity of functions, coordination, and planning influence appropriate span of control in all management systems? Explain.
17. Summarize and evaluate Graicunas's contribution to span of management literature.
18. What is the relationship between span of management and *flat* and *tall* organizations?
19. What are scalar relationships?
20. Explain the rationale behind Fayol's position that always adhering to the chain of command is not necessarily advisable.
21. What caution should managers exercise when they use the "bridge" Fayol described?

Sources of Additional Information

Albers, H. H. *Organized Executive Action.* New York: John Wiley & Sons, 1961.

Allen, Louis A. "Managerial Planning: Back to Basics." *Management Review*, no. 4 (April 1981): 15–20.

Argyris, C. *Integrating the Individual and the Organization.* New York: John Wiley & Sons, 1964.

Arnold, Mark R. "Unleashing Middle Managers." *Management Review*, no. 5 (May 1981): 58.

Brown, A. *Organization.* New York: Hibbert, 1945.

Dennison, H. S. *Organization: Engineering.* New York: McGraw-Hill, 1931.

Etzioni, A. *A Comparative Analysis of Complex Organizations.* Glencoe, Ill.: The Free Press, 1961.

Giblin, Edward J. "Differentiating Organizational Problems." *Business Horizons* 24, no. 3 (May/June 1981): 60–64.

Lorsch, J. W., and Lawrence, P. R. *Studies in Organization Design.* Georgetown, Ont.: Irwin-Dorsey, 1970.

Lorsch, J. W., and Morse, John J. *Organizations and Their Members: A Contingency Approach.* New York: Harper & Row, 1974.

March, J. G., and Simon, H. A. *Organizations.* New York: John Wiley & Sons, 1958.

Merrill, H. F., ed. *Classics in Management.* New York: American Management Association, 1960 p. 403.

Mintzberg, Henry. "Organization Design: Fashion or Fit?" *Harvard Business Review*, January/February 1981, pp. 103–16.

Petersen, E.; Plowman, E. G.; and Trickett, J. M. *Business Organization and Management.* Homewood, Ill.: Richard D. Irwin, 1962.

Rubenstein, A. H., and Haberstroh, C. J., eds. *Some Theories of Organization.* Homewood, Ill.: Richard D. Irwin, 1966.

Slocum, John W. Jr., and Hellriegel, Don. "Using Organizational Designs to Cope with Change." *Business Horizons* 22 (December 1979): 65–76.

Summer, C. E., Jr. *Factors in Effective Administration.* New York: Columbia University, Graduate School of Business, 1956.

Swinth, R. *Organizational Systems for Management: Designing, Planning and Implementation.* Columbus, Ohio: Grid, 1974.

Woodward, J. *Industrial Organization.* London: Oxford University Press, 1965.

Notes

1. Douglas S. Sherwin, "Management *of Objectives*," *Harvard Business Review,* May–June 1976, pp. 149–60.

2. Henri Fayol, *General and Industrial Management* (London: Sir Isaac Pitman and Sons, 1949), pp. 53–54.

3. William F. Glueck, "Who Needs an Organization Department?" *California Management Review* 4, no. 2 (Winter 1972): 77–82.

4. Burt K. Scanlan, "Managerial Leadership in Perspective: Getting Back to Basics," *Personnel Journal,* March 1979, pp. 168–70.

5. Max Weber, *Theory of Social and Economic Organization,* trans. and ed. by A. M. Henderson and Talcott Parsons (London: Oxford University Press, 1947).

6. Richard Bendix, *Max Weber: An Intellectual Portrait* (New York: Doubleday & Co., 1960).

7. Charles Perrow, "The Short and Glorious History of Organizational Theory," *Organizational Dynamics,* Summer 1973, pp. 2–15.

8. William G. Scott, "Organization Theory: An Overview and Appraisal," *Academy of Management Journal,* April 1961, pp. 7–26.

9. George H. Rice, Jr., "A Set of Organizational Models," *Human Resource Management* 19, no. 2 (Summer 1980): 21.

10. Lyndall Urwich, *Notes on the Theory of Organization* (New York: American Management Association, 1952).

11. For an interesting discussion of a non-traditional organization structure, see Pamela M. Banks and David W. Ewing, "It's Not Lonely Upstairs," *Harvard Business Review,* November/December 1980, pp. 111–32.

12. Fred A. Katz, "Explaining Informal Work Groups in Complex Organizations: The Case for Autonomy of Structure," *Administrative Science Quarterly* 10, no. 2 (September 1965): 204–23.

13. Gerald C. Werner, "Organizing for Innovation: Does a Product Group Structure Inhibit Technological Developments?" *Management Review,* March 1981, pp. 47–51.

14. For information regarding steps to handle international organizing problems, see Gilbert H. Clee and Wilber M. Sachtjen, "Organizing a Worldwide Business," *Harvard Business Review,* November–December 1964, pp. 55–67.

15. Michael G. Dyers and John M. Roach, *Organization and Control of International Operations,* The Conference Board, 1973, pp. 68–69.

16. For more information on organization charts and international involvement, see Daniels, Ogram, and Radebaugh, *International Business* (Reading, Mass: Addison-Wesley, 1979), chapter 18.

17. Y. K. Shetty and Howard M. Carlisle, "A Contingency Model of Organization Design," *California Management Review* 15 (1972): 38–45.

18. Adam Smith, *The Wealth of Nations* (New York: Random House, 1937).

19. C. R. Walker and R. H. Guest, *The Man on the Assembly Line* (Cambridge: Harvard University Press, 1952).

20. J. Mooney, "The Principles of Organization," in *Ideas and Issues in Public Administration,* ed. D. Waldo (New York: McGraw-Hill, 1953), p. 86.

21. George D. Greenberg, "The Coordinating Roles of Management," *Midwest Review of Public Administration* 10, no. 2 (1976): 66–76.

22. Henry C. Metcalf and Lyndall F. Urwich, eds., *Dynamic Administration: The Collected Papers of Mary Parker Follett* (New York: Harper & Row, 1942), pp. 297–99.

23. Gerald G. Fisch, "Stretching the Span of Management," *Harvard Business Review,* no. 5 (1963): 74–85.

24. Harold Koontz, "Making Theory Operational: The Span of Management," *The Journal of Management Studies,* October 1966, pp. 229–43.

25. V. A. Graicunas, "Relationships in Organization," *Bulletin of International Management Institute,* March 1933, pp. 183–87.

26. For more on the life of Graicunas, see Arthur G. Bedeian, "Vytautas Andrius Graicunas: A Biographical Note," *Academy of Management Journal* 17, no. 2 (June 1974): 347–49.

27. Lt. Col. L. F. Urwick, "V. A. Graicunas and the Span of Control," *Academy of Management Journal* 17, no. 2 (June 1974): 349–54.

28. Henri Fayol, *General and Industrial Administration* (Belmont, Calif.: Pitman Publishing Corporation, 1949).

Concluding Case 8
3M Company Overhauls Its Organization Structure

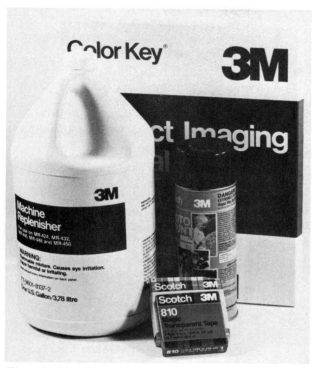

(Photo: David A. Corona)

The 3M Company is presently changing an organizational structure that carried it from sales of $100 million in 1947 to $6.1 billion in 1980. The company, long praised as a fertile breeding ground for product innovation, is in the process of restructuring its management hierarchy because of an unexpected decrease in its growth trend and problems resulting from entrance into the office-automation market. A new layer of management has been developed to formulate and execute long-range strategies for a company that has traditionally grown as a result of its ability to make quick profits on "home-grown" inventions. In the past, a somewhat more expedient approach to planning was taken; however, not all plans were examined as thoroughly as they should have been. Now, with the new management level, each plan can be examined in detail before action is taken.

The new organization will put 3M's ten business groups (each with three to six divisions) into one of four sectors. One objective is to improve the effectiveness of 3M's research, marketing, and production efforts by grouping products according to technologies and markets. The sectors will consist of "industrial and consumer" products, "life sciences," "electro and communications technologies" and "imaging sciences." In addition, the number of executives reporting to top management has been reduced by

more than half, with more authority being given to lower levels of management—a pragmatic response spawned by a span of control problem.

Traditionally, 3M has had a "vertical" structure as each division and many of the company's fifty product lines have had their own research, marketing, and production operations. In the past, someone with a good idea could set up a minicompany, of sorts, within the giant corporation. This approach has been found to be inefficient in the automated-office-equipment market that 3M has declared one of its primary objectives. Even though 3M presently offers a wide variety of copiers, facsimile machines, and microfilm, the fragmented structure has hindered the development of integrated office systems; the old structure made it virtually impossible to move across division lines for funding and integration of product ideas.

Typical of the problems associated with 3M's old vertical structure is that of Linolex. In 1975, 3M Company acquired Linolex, a word-processing company. The acquisition of Linolex was 3M's first attempt to enter the office-automation market. Funding was not sufficient, nor was management attention to the company adequate; the company was left stranded and ceased operation in late 1979.

3M's new organization structure should enable the company to recognize the most important growth markets and nurture them along. However, for some markets it may already be too late. By failing to identify the important markets, such as the word-processing market, 3M has probably been passed by in the office-machine area. According to Kenneth G. Bosomworth, president of International Resource Development Inc., "The window for getting in and effectively participating is nearly closed and 3M isn't anywhere near having its ducks in a row." Hopefully, 3M's new structure will rectify similar problems in future markets.

This case is adapted from "3M Looks Beyond Luck and Fast Profits," *Business Week*, February 23, 1981, p. 44.

Discussion Issues

1. On what factors are the new sectors being organized? What management terminology expresses the basis of new sector organization? Explain.
2. What forces led to the reorganization of 3M's structure? Explain.
3. How might this new organization lead to an improved integration for the development of new products? Do you see any potential problems with this new organization structure?
4. What factors in the case support a narrower span for top management?

Student Learning Objectives

From studying this chapter I will attempt to acquire:

1. An understanding of the relationship between responsibility, authority, and delegation
2. Information on how to divide and clarify job activities of individuals within an organization
3. Knowledge of the differences between line authority, staff authority, and functional authority
4. An appreciation for the issues that can cause conflict in line and staff relationships
5. Insights on the value of accountability to the organization
6. An understanding of how to delegate
7. A strategy for eliminating various barriers to delegation
8. A working knowledge of when and how an organization should be decentralized

Chapter Outline

Organizing the Activity of Individuals

Introductory Case 9
Redesigning Job Activities

Leo Mercer has recently been appointed manager of the student employment department in the financial aids division of Athens University. The purpose of the student employment department is to help students who need part-time work to compete effectively in the community labor market. This help includes such activities as assistance in finding a position, guidance in writing résumés, and suggestions on how to interview. Mercer graduated from the school of business and administration at Central University six months ago.

During his first week on the job, Mercer's only official responsibility was reading a policy manual that familiarized him with the student financial aids division. According to this manual, Mercer was under the direct supervision of the manager of the student financial aids division and at the same level as the manager of student loans and the manager of scholarships and grants. The formal relationship between these four individuals is presented in case figure 9.1.

On the first day of Mercer's second week on the job, he called a meeting with his eight subordinates to introduce himself and to begin orienting himself to his new position. During the meeting Mercer admitted that to do his job well he would have to become familiar with the job each individual was performing, the relationship of the student employment department to other departments in the student financial aids division, and the student employment situation within the community.

The meeting ended with Mercer stressing that his first priority was to learn how the student employment department operated. To this end, Mercer asked each person at the meeting to submit within two weeks a detailed, written summary of his or her activities during a normal working week.

At the end of two weeks Mercer was pleased to discover that all eight performance summaries had been submitted. After analyzing the summaries, however, he was somewhat puzzled that no one was responsible for performing certain job activities that seemed fundamental to a student employment department. For example, no one from the student employment department ever followed up to see how well a student performed in a job. Mercer reasoned that this follow-up could be of significant help in convincing certain employers of the value of student employees. If this follow-up and the other neglected fundamental activities that Mercer found were to be added to the present normal operation of the student employment department, some individuals within the department would have an increased work load.

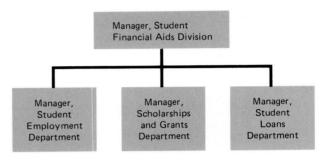

Case figure 9.1 The formal relationship between managers of the financial aids division.

Discussion Issues

1. What should Mercer do now?
2. Assuming that certain fundamental functions have been excluded from the present job activities of the subordinates, what mistakes probably were made by the previous manager that allowed such exclusions to exist?

What's Ahead

Leo Mercer, the lower-level manager in the introductory case, is faced with the task of modifying the job activities of certain individuals within the student employment department. In essence, Mercer must change the way in which his department operates. The information in this chapter should be of great value to Mercer or to anyone he confronted with a similar task. Organizing the job activities of individuals within an organization is the principal topic of discussion in this chapter. Three major elements of organizing are presented: (1) responsibility, (2) authority, and (3) delegation. Explanation of each element and how it relates to Mercer's task follows.

Chapter 8 dealt with using principles of organizational structure, division of labor, span of management, and scalar relationships to establish an orderly use of resources within the management system. Productivity within any management system, however, results from specific activities performed by various individuals within the organization. An effective organizing effort, therefore, includes not only a rationale for the orderly use of management system resources, but also three other elements of organizing that specifically channel the activities of organization members. These three elements are responsibility, authority, and delegation.

Responsibility is perhaps the most fundamental method of channeling the activity of individuals within an organization. **Responsibility** is the obligation to perform assigned activity. It is a person's self-assumed commitment to handle a job to the best of his or her ability. The source of this responsibility lies within the individual. If a person accepts a job, he or she agrees to carry out a series of duties or activities or to see that someone else carries them out. The act of accepting the job means that the person is obligated to a superior to see that job activities are successfully completed. Since responsibility is an obligation that a person *accepts,* there is no way it can be delegated or passed on to a subordinate.

A summary of an individual's job activities within an organization is usually in a formal statement called a job description. A **job description** is simply a listing of specific activities that must be performed by whoever holds the position. Managers should keep in mind that unclear job descriptions can confuse employees and may cause them to lose interest in their jobs.[1]

Job activities, of course, are delegated by management to enhance the accomplishment of management system objectives. Management analyzes its objectives and assigns specific duties that will lead to reaching those objectives. A sound organizing strategy includes specific job activities for each individual within the organization. As objectives and other conditions within the management system change, however, individual job activities within the organization may have to be changed.

Three areas related to responsibility are (1) dividing job activities, (2) clarifying job activities of management, and (3) being responsible. Each of these topics is discussed in the sections that follow.

Responsibility

Obligation

Specific Activities

Job Activity Is Related to Objectives

Figure 9.1 Sequence of activities for the similarity of function method of dividing responsibility.

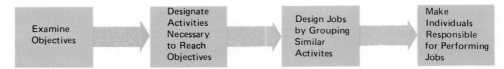

| Examine Objectives | Designate Activities Necessary to Reach Objectives | Design Jobs by Grouping Similar Activites | Make Individuals Responsible for Performing Jobs |

Dividing Job Activities

Since, typically, many individuals work within a given management system, organizing necessarily involves dividing job activities among a number of people. One individual cannot be obligated or responsible for performing all of the activities within an organization. Some method of distributing job activities and thereby channeling the activities of several individuals must be developed.

The phrase *functional similarity* refers to what many management theorists believe to be the most basic method of dividing job activities. Stated simply, the **functional similarity** method suggests that management should take four basic interrelated steps to divide job activities. These steps and the sequence in which they should be taken are (1) management examines management system objectives; (2) management designates appropriate activities that must be performed to reach those objectives; (3) management designs specific jobs by grouping similar activities; and (4) management makes specific individuals responsible for performing those jobs. Figure 9.1 illustrates the sequence of activities suggested by the similarity of function method.

Thierauf, Klekamp, and Geeding have indicated that at least three additional guides can be used to supplement the similarity of function method.[2] The first of these supplemental guides suggests that overlapping responsibility should be avoided when making job activity divisions. **Overlapping responsibility** exists when more than one individual is responsible for the same activity. Generally speaking, only one individual should be responsible for completing any one activity. The second supplemental guide for dividing job activities within an organization recommends avoiding responsibility gaps. A **responsibility gap** exists when certain tasks are not included in the responsibility area of any individual. In essence, a responsibility gap creates a situation in which nobody within the organization is obligated to perform certain necessary activities. The third supplemental guide for dividing job activities within an organization suggests that creating job activities for accomplishing tasks that do not enhance goal attainment should be avoided. Organization members should be obligated to perform only those activities that lead to goal attainment.

Four Interrelated Steps

Individuals Responsible for The Same Activity

What Is a Responsibility Gap?

Undesirable Job Activities

Back to the Case

In management language, Leo Mercer is faced with modifying required activities of various individuals within the student employment department. These activity modifications should help his department to become more successful if he derives them directly from student employment objectives. Mercer's specific steps to make these modifications should include the analysis of departmental objectives, the outlining of specific student employment activities that must be performed to reach those objectives, the designing of student employment jobs by grouping similar activities, and the assigning of these jobs to student employment personnel. To supplement these steps, Mercer must be careful not to create overlapping responsibilities, responsibility gaps, or responsibilities for activities that do not lead directly to goal attainment.

Figure 9.2 Seven responsibility relationships between managers, as used in the management responsibility guide.

1. *General Responsibility* — The individual guides and directs the execution of the function through the person delegated operating responsibility.
2. *Operating Responsibility* — The individual is directly responsible for the execution of the function.
3. *Specific Responsibility* — The individual is responsible for executing a specific or limited portion of the function.
4. *Must Be Consulted* — The individual, if the decision affects his or her area, must be called upon before any decision is made or approval is granted, to render advice or relate information, but not to make the decision or grant approval.
5. *May Be Consulted* — The individual may be called upon to relate information, render advice, or make recommendations.
6. *Must Be Notified* — The individual must be notified of action that has been taken.
7. *Must Approve* — The individual (other than persons holding general and operating responsibility) must approve or disapprove.

Clarifying Job Activities of Management

Clarification of the job activities of managers is as important, if not more important, than dividing the job activities of nonmanagers. The importance of this clarification is supported by the fact that managers affect greater portions of resources within the management system than do nonmanagers. Hence, such factors as responsibility gaps usually have more significant impact on the management system when they relate to managers as opposed to nonmanagers.

One process used to clarify management job activities "enables each manager to actively participate with his or her superiors, peers, and subordinates in systematically describing the managerial job to be done and then clarifying the role each manager plays in relationship to his or her work group and to the organization."[3] The purpose of this interaction is to assure that no overlaps or gaps in perceived management responsibilities exist and that managers are performing only those activities that lead to the attainment of management system objectives. Although this process typically has been used to clarify the responsibilities of managers, it may also be effective in clarifying the responsibilities of nonmanagers.

A specific tool developed to implement the interaction process described in the preceding paragraph is a **management responsibility guide.**[4] The management responsibility guide assists organization members in (1) describing the various responsibility relationships that exist in their organization and (2) summarizing how the responsibilities of various managers within their organization relate to one another.

An Organizing Tool

The seven main organizational responsibility relationships described by this tool are listed in figure 9.2. Once organization members have decided which of these management responsibility relationships exist within their organization, they then define the relationships between these responsibilities.

Figure 9.3 contains a sample completed management responsibility guide for a division of an aerospace company. This sample exhibit summarizes existing management responsibility relationships within the division and shows how these relationships complement one another. The actual members of this aerospace division, of course, were the individuals who completed this management responsibility guide.

Figure 9.3 Sample page of management responsibility guide for division of aerospace company.

Number	Function	Vice-president Aerospace	Vice-president Manufacturing	Director Engineering	Manager Industrial Technology	Manager Quality Assurance	Manager Marketing	Manager Contracts	Manager Master Scheduling	Manager Financial Services
101	Coordinate division budgeting and financial planning activities and communicate financial information to division management	A A-F	E-F D-F	E-F E	E-F F	E-F F	E-F F	E-F E-F	E E	B D
102	Develop project and program schedule requirements; establish, coordinate, and control schedules and report on status	A A	E-F D	E-F D	E-F D-F	E-F C	E-F D	E-F D	B	 F
103	Direct contract activities and evaluate and approve contract provisions of all division sales proposals and contract documents	A A		 E			E-F D	B	E-F D-F	F C
104	Plan and coordinate divisional marketing activities so as to secure the business necessary to maximize division's capabilities	A A-D	E-F F	E-F	E-F	 E	B	D-F C-G	E-F C-D	F F
105	Develop and design new and improve existing electronic and electromechanical aerospace products and processes	A A-F	F E	B	 E		E D-G			
106	Secure materials and tools, coordinate human resources, and manufacture products to specified quantity, quality, time, and cost requirements	A A	B	 E	 E	F C-D		E-F E	 F	E-F E
107	Establish quality assurance policies, procedures, and controls to insure that products meet applicable standards and specifications	A A	D-F D-G	D-F E-F	E E	B	F E	E-F D	E-F	 F
108	Develop and design propriety products and processes utilizing proven technology specifically adapted to industrial automation	A A-F A	D-F E-F E	C B	B D-F	E	E E E-F	D E D-F	F E F	F F

Relationship Code

A General Responsibility

B Operating Responsibility

C Specific Responsibility

D Must Be Consulted

E May Be Consulted

F Must Be Notified

G Must Approve

Organization identification Aerospace Aerospace division	Number 200	Management responsibility guide Approval	Date	Page No. 1 of 1

Reprinted, by permission of the publisher, from "Roles and Relationships: Clarifying the Manager's Job," by Robert D. Melcher, *Personnel,* May/June 1967. © 1967 by American Management Association, Inc. All rights reserved.

Figure 9.4 Four key dimensions of responsible management behavior.

Behavior with Subordinates	Behavior with Upper Management	Behavior with Other Groups	Personal Attitudes and Values
Responsible managers — 1. Take complete charge of their work groups. 2. Pass praise and credit along to subordinates. 3. Stay close to problems and activities. 4. Take action to maintain productivity and are willing to terminate poor performers if necessary.	Responsible managers — 1. Accept criticism for mistakes and buffer their groups from excessive criticism. 2. Ensure that their groups meet management expectations and objectives.	Responsible managers make sure that any gaps between their areas and those of other managers are securely filled.	Responsible managers — 1. Identify with the group. 2. Put organizational goals ahead of personal desires or activities. 3. Perform tasks for which there is no immediate reward but which help subordinates, the company, or both. 4. Conserve corporate resources as if the resources were their own.

Being Responsible

Managers can be described as responsible if they perform the activities they are obligated to perform.[5] Since managers typically can have more impact on an organization than nonmanagers, responsible managers are a prerequisite for management system success. Several recent studies have shown that responsible management behavior is highly valued by top executives because the responsible manager guides many other individuals within the organization in performing their duties appropriately.

The degree of responsibleness that managers possess can be determined by analyzing their (1) attitude toward and conduct with subordinates, (2) behavior with upper management, (3) behavior with other groups, and (4) personal attitudes and values. Figure 9.4 summarizes what each of these dimensions includes for the responsible manager.

When Is a Manager Acting Responsibly?

Back to the Case

Mercer must recognize that his own job activities within the student employment department, not only with those of his subordinates, will be a major factor in determining departmental success. Because Mercer's actions have an impact on all personnel within the student employment department, it is extremely important that his job activities are well designed. From the viewpoint of the student financial-aids division as a whole, Mercer's job activities should be well coordinated with those of the manager of scholarships and grants and the manager of student loans. Perhaps the manager of the student financial-aids division could use the management responsibility guide process to achieve this coordination of responsibilities. Overall, for Mercer to be a responsible manager, he must respond appropriately to his subordinates, the manager of the student financial-aids division, and his peer managers.

Authority

Individuals are delegated job activities to channel their behavior appropriately. Once they have been delegated these activities, however, they also must be delegated a commensurate amount of authority to perform the obligations.

Authority is the right to perform or command. Authority allows its holder to act in certain designated ways and to influence directly the actions of others through orders which she or he issues.

Right to Command

Authority Must Reflect
Responsibility

The following example illustrates the relationship between job activities and authority. Two primary tasks for which a service station manager is responsible are pumping gasoline and repairing automobiles. In this example the manager has the complete authority necessary to perform either of these tasks. If this manager chooses, however, he or she can delegate the activity of automobile repair to the assistant manager. Along with this activity of repairing, however, the assistant also should be delegated the authority to order parts, to command certain attendants to help when necessary, and to do anything else necessary to perform the obligated repair jobs. Without this authority the assistant manager may find it impossible to complete the delegated job activities.

Authority May Not Be
Obeyed

Practically speaking, authority is a factor that only increases the probability that a specific command will be obeyed.[6] The following excerpt emphasizes that authority does not always exact obedience:

> People who have never exercised power have all kinds of curious ideas about it. The popular notion of top leadership is a fantasy of capricious power: the top man presses a button and something remarkable happens; he gives an order as the whim strikes him, and it is obeyed. Actually, the capricious use of power is relatively rare except in some large dictatorships and some small family firms. Most leaders are hedged around by constraints—tradition, constitutional limitations, the realities of the external situation, rights and privileges of followers, the requirements of team work, and most of all, the inexorable demands of large-scale organization, which does not operate on capriciousness. In short, most power is wielded circumspectly.[7]

Acceptance Creates
Obedience

As shown in chapter 8, the positioning of individuals on an organization chart indicates the relative amount of authority delegated to each individual. Individuals toward the top of the chart possess more authority than individuals toward the bottom. Chester Barnard writes, however, that in reality the source of authority is not determined by decree from the formal organization but by whether or not authority is accepted by those existing under the authority. According to Barnard, authority exists and will exact obedience only if it is accepted.

In line with this rationale Barnard defines authority as the character of communication by which it is accepted by an individual as governing the actions the individual takes within the system. Barnard indicates that authority will be accepted only if (1) an individual can understand the order being communicated; (2) an individual believes that the order is consistent with the purpose of the organization; (3) an individual sees the order as compatible with his or her personal interests; and (4) an individual is mentally and physically able to comply with the order. The fewer of these four conditions that exist, the smaller the probability that authority will be accepted and that obedience will be exacted.

Increasing Acceptance of
Authority

Barnard also offers some guidance on what action managers can take to raise the odds that their commands will be accepted and obeyed. According to Barnard, more and more of a manager's commands will be accepted over the long run if:

1. Formal channels of communication are used by the manager and are familiar to all organization members.
2. Each organization member has an assigned formal communication channel through which he or she receives orders.
3. The line of communication between manager and subordinate is as direct as possible.
4. The complete chain of command is used to issue orders.
5. Managers possess adequate communication skills.
6. Managers use formal communication lines only for organizational business.
7. A command is authenticated as coming from a manager.[8]

HERMAN

"You're fighting the King in the semi-finals, so just duck once and he won't get too tired."

Copyright, 1976, Universal Press Syndicate.

Individuals within the student employment department who are delegated additional job activities also should be delegated a commensurate amount of authority to give related orders and to accomplish their obligated activities. Student employment personnel must recognize, however, that the mere possession of authority does not necessarily exact obedience. Only if the authority is accepted will it exact obedience. To increase the probability that commands will be accepted and therefore obeyed, care should be taken to ensure that student employment personnel understand internal orders, see orders as being consistent with both the objectives of the student employment department and the student financial-aids division, perceive orders as being compatible with their individual interests, and see themselves as being physically able to follow the orders.

Back to the Case

Types of Authority

Three main types of authority can exist within an organization: (1) line authority, (2) staff authority, and (3) functional authority. Each type exists only to enable individuals to carry out different types of responsibilities with which they have been charged.

Line and Staff Authority

Line authority is the most fundamental authority within an organization and reflects existing superior-subordinate relationships. **Line authority** is the right to make decisions and to give orders concerning the production, sales, or finance-related behavior of subordinates. Overall, line authority pertains to matters directly involving management system production, sales, and finance and, as a result, the attainment of objectives. Individuals directly responsible for these areas within the organization are delegated line authority to assist them in performing their obligated activities.

Superior-Subordinate Relationships

Organizing the Activity of Individuals

Figure 9.5 Basic relationships between line and staff personnel in most organizations.

1. The units that are designated as line have ultimate responsibility for successful operation of the company. Therefore, the line must also be responsible for operating decisions.
2. Staff elements contribute by providing advice and service to the line in accomplishing the objectives of the enterprise.
3. Staff is responsible for providing advice and service to appropriate line elements when requested to do so. However, staff also has the responsibility of proffering advice and service where it is not requested, but where it believes it is needed.
4. The solicitation of advice and the acceptance of suggestions and counsel is usually at the option of the line organization. However, in some cases, it must be recognized that only the top level of the line organization has this option and that its decision on the use of staff advice or service is binding throughout lower levels. In these cases, subordinate levels in the line may have no option in the use of specialized staff services, but may be required to use them.

   For example, the engineering department may analyze the use of machines, tools, jigs, and fixtures and present recommendations to the line. The operating line organization does not ask for this advisory service. Higher management provides it as a means of improving operations by bringing to the problem the most highly skilled and best informed specialists.

   In this case, it is the line managers' responsibility to make most effective use of this advice. If they disagree with it, they should have the opportunity to appeal to higher authority.

   The same holds true with certain services. Because line managers cannot possibly equip themselves to perform highly specialized parts of their job, staff units may perform these services for them. For example, the services of cost accountants are provided to help line managers determine their costs. If the line managers disagree with the methods of collecting this data or with the figures themselves, they may appeal to higher authority. But since they are not equipped to gather and analyze this data themselves, and since cost standards are necessary to effective operation, they must use the services of the accountants.
5. Line should give serious consideration to offers of advice and service made by staff units and should follow it if it is to the company's best interest to do so. However, except in those cases where the use of staff advice and service is compulsory and subject only to appeal to higher authority, it is not mandatory that the advice of staff should be followed unfailingly. Except as noted above, line managers have the authority to modify, reject, or accept such advice.
6. Both line and staff should have the right of appeal to higher authority in case of disagreement as to whether staff recommendation should be followed. However, this right to appeal should not be permitted to supersede the line's responsibility for making immediate decisions when required by the operating situation.

From Louis A. Allen, "Developing Sound Line and Staff Relationships," from *Studies in Personnel Policy No. 153*, National Industrial Conference Board, 1956. Used with permission.

What Is Staff Authority?

Whereas line authority involves giving orders concerning production activities, **staff authority** is the right to advise or assist those who possess line authority and other staff personnel. Staff authority exists to enable those responsible for improving the effectiveness of line personnel to perform their required tasks. Examples of organization members with staff authority would be members of accounting and personnel departments. Obviously, line and staff personnel must work closely together to improve the efficiency and effectiveness of the organization. The relationship that exists between line and staff personnel in most organizations is presented in figure 9.5.

Larger Organizations Need Staff Personnel

Size is perhaps the most significant factor in determining whether or not staff personnel will be used within an organization. Generally, the larger the organization, the greater the need for staff personnel. As an organization grows, management generally finds a greater need for more expertise in more diversified areas. Although the small organization may also need this expertise, hiring part-time consultants when a need arises may be more practical than hiring a full-time staff individual who may not always be kept busy.

Figure 9.6 Possible line-staff relationships in selected organizational areas.

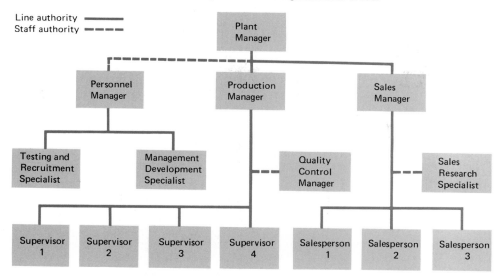

Figure 9.6 shows how line-staff relationships can be presented on an organization chart. The plant manager on this chart has line authority over each immediate subordinate—personnel manager, production manager, and sales manager. The personnel manager also has staff authority in relation to the plant manager. This simply means that the personnel manager possesses the right to do whatever is necessary to advise the plant manager on personnel matters. Final decisions concerning personnel matters, however, are in the hands of the plant manager, the individual holding line authority. Similar relationships exist between the sales manager and the sales research specialist as well as between the production manager and the quality control manager. To carry the example of the personnel manager's staff authority one step further, figure 9.7 contains a detailed listing of the types of decisions over which a personnel manager generally has jurisdiction. These decision areas are not directly related to production but could ultimately have a favorable influence on production.

Roles of Staff Personnel

Harold Steiglitz has pinpointed three main roles that staff personnel typically perform in organizations.[9] Although somewhat different, each of the roles has the purpose of assisting line personnel in some way. These three roles and their corresponding definitions are set forth as follows:

1. *The advisory or counseling role*   The professional expertise of staff personnel in this role is aimed at solving organizational problems. In this role, staff personnel are seen as internal consultants, with the relationship between line and staff being similar to that between a professional and a client. An example of this role might be the staff quality-control manager who advises the line production manager on possible technical modifications to the production process that will help to maintain the quality of products produced.

Professional and Client Relationship

Figure 9.7 Typical decision areas for a personnel director.

Hiring	Wage and Salary Administration (continued)
Hiring requisitions (new positions)	Determining profit–bonus ratio
Hiring requisitions (present positions)	Grouping jobs for pay grades
Approving individual job specifications	Determining number of pay grades
Use of psychological tests	Determining dollar amount of rate
Physical examinations	or range
Use of reference checks	Exceptions to rate or range
Final approval in hiring	Using merit vs. seniority within grades
Initial hiring rates	Using merit vs. seniority for promotion
	Determining merit of individual employee
Promotions, Transfers, Demotions	Granting extra time off
Promotions within a department	Granting fringe benefits exceeding policy
Promotions between departments	
Approving transfers	*Collective Bargaining*
Adopting transfer procedures	Maximum bargaining concessions
Approving pay/rank cuts	Determining negotiation goals
Adopting discharge procedures	Determining bargaining strategy
Approving employee discharge	Taking grievances to arbitration
Wage and Salary Administration	*Training and Development*
Adopting wage-level policy	Adopting training programs
Adopting special wage policies for	Determining training objectives
special groups	Selecting employees for training
Jobs covered by evaluation program	
Method of job evaluation	*Miscellaneous*
Approving job description	Allocation of budgeted funds
Appointing evaluation committee	Determining areas or equipment unsafe
Making actual job evaluation	Establishing output standards
Coverage of wage-incentive plan	
Type of wage-incentive plan	

From Wendell French and Dale A. Henning, "The Authority-Influence Role of the Functional Specialist in Management," *Academy of Management Journal* 9, no. 8 (Sept. 1966).

Supplier and Customer Relationship

2. *The service role*   Staff personnel in this role provide services that can more efficiently and effectively be provided by a single centralized staff group as opposed to many individuals within the organization attempting to provide these services themselves. This role can probably best be understood by viewing staff personnel as suppliers and line personnel as customers. For example, members of a personnel department recruit, employ, and train workers for all organizational departments. In essence, they are the suppliers of workers and the various organizational departments needing workers are their customers.

Agent Relationship

3. *The control role*   This role finds the expertise of staff personnel called upon to help establish and develop a mechanism for evaluating the effectiveness of organizational plans. Staff personnel exercising this role are seen as representatives or agents of top management.

These three are not the only roles performed by staff personnel within organizations, but they do represent the main ones. In the final analysis, the role of staff personnel in any organization should be specially designed to best meet the needs inherent within that organization. It is entirely possible that to meet the needs of a particular organization, staff personnel within that organization must perform some combination of the three main roles.

Conflict in Line-Staff Relationships

Most management practitioners readily admit that a noticeable amount of conflict usually centers around line-staff relationships.[10,11] Identification of the factors that can cause this conflict and a strategy for minimizing their effect follow.

From the viewpoint of line personnel, conflict is created between line and staff personnel because staff personnel (1) tend to assume line authority; (2) do not give sound advice; (3) steal credit for success; (4) do not keep line personnel informed; and (5) do not see the whole picture. In essence, line personnel see staff personnel as overstepping their bounds, incapable of giving good advice, overrated in terms of their potential positive influence on production, noncommunicative, and narrow in scope. Staff Creates Conflict

From the viewpoint of staff personnel, conflict is created between line and staff personnel because line personnel (1) do not make proper use of staff personnel, (2) resist new ideas, and (3) do not give staff personnel enough authority. Staff personnel seem to perceive line personnel as unaware of how to use staff personnel best, nonreceptive, and as depriving staff personnel of the free rein needed to do their job. Line Creates Conflict

To overcome these potential conflicts in line-staff relationships, both line and staff personnel must make a serious and continuing effort. Staff personnel must strive to emphasize the objectives of the organization as a whole, encourage and educate line personnel in the appropriate use of staff personnel, obtain needed skill if it is not already possessed, and deal with resistance to change rather than view this resistance as an immovable barrier. Line personnel's effort in minimizing line-staff conflict should include using staff personnel wherever possible, making proper use of the abilities of staff personnel, and keeping staff personnel appropriately informed.[12, 13] Overcoming Conflict

---

Back to the Case

Assuming that the main objective of the student employment department is to help students to compete more effectively in the community labor market, student employment personnel who are directly responsible for achieving this objective must possess line authority to perform their responsibilities. For example, individuals responsible for contacting prospective employers must be given the right to do everything necessary to develop these contacts to the best benefit of students. Although the student employment department is relatively small, it may be possible that at least one individual is charged with the responsibility of assisting the line in a staff position. Perhaps this individual is responsible for advising Mercer on various surveys that could be conducted to convince prospective employers that part-time university students do make good workers. Any individuals responsible for advising the line should be delegated appropriate staff authority. As in all organizations, the potential for conflict in the relationship between student employment line and staff personnel probably would be significant. Mercer should be aware of this potential and encourage both line and staff personnel to minimize it.

Functional Authority

Functional authority is the right to give orders within a segment of the organization in which this right is normally nonexistent. This authority is usually assigned to individuals to complement the line or staff authority already possessed. Functional authority is generally established to cover only specific task areas and is operational only for designated amounts of time. It typically is possessed by individuals who, in order to meet their responsibilities, must be able to exercise some control over organization members in other areas. What Is Functional Authority?

The vice-president for finance in an organization could be an example of someone with functional authority. Among her basic responsibilities she is obligated to monitor the financial situation within the management system. To accomplish this monitoring, however, she must have appropriate financial information continually flowing to her from various segments of the organization. The vice-president for finance is usually delegated the functional authority to order various departments to furnish her with

Figure 9.8 Advantages and disadvantages of line authority, staff authority, and functional authority.

Advantages	Disadvantages
Line Authority	
Maintains simplicity	Neglects specialists in planning
Makes clear division of authority	Overworks key people
Encourages speedy action	Depends on retention of a few key people
Staff Authority	
Enables specialists to give expert advice	Confuses organization if functions are not clear
Frees the line executive of detailed analysis	Reduces power of experts to place recommendations into action
Affords young specialists a means of training	Tends toward centralization of organization
Functional Authority	
Relieves line executives of routine specialized decisions	Makes relationships more complex
Provides framework for applying expert knowledge	Makes limits of authority of each specialist a difficult coordination problem
Relieves pressure of need for large numbers of well-rounded executives	Tends toward centralization of organization

Reprinted with permission of Macmillan Publishing Co., Inc. from THE NEW MANAGEMENT by Robert M. Fulmer. Copyright © 1974. Robert M. Fulmer.

the kinds and amounts of information she needs to perform her analysis. In reality, the functional authority this vice-president possesses allows her to give orders to personnel within departments in which she normally cannot give orders.

From the previous discussion on line authority, staff authority, and functional authority, it is reasonable to conclude that although authority can exist within an organization in various forms, these forms should be used in a combination that will best enable individuals to carry out their assigned responsibilities and thereby best help the management system to accomplish its objectives. When trying to decide what authority combination is best for a particular organization, managers must keep in mind that the use of each type of authority naturally has both advantages and disadvantages. These advantages and disadvantages are presented in figure 9.8.

As an example of how these authority combinations can be developed, figure 9.9 is an organization chart that shows how David B. Starkweather believes that these three types of authority should be combined for the overall benefit of a hospital management system.

Accountability

An analysis of activities necessary to accomplish management system objectives results in specific individuals accepting responsibility for performing those activities. The individuals obligated to perform these activities are correspondingly delegated the necessary authority to do their jobs.

Accountability is a management philosophy whereby individuals are held liable or accountable for how well they use their authority and live up to their responsibility of performing predetermined activities.[14] The concept of accountability implies that if predetermined activities are not performed, some type of penalty or punishment will be justifiably forthcoming.[15] Also implied within the accountability concept, however, is the notion that some kind of reward will follow if predetermined activities are performed well. One company executive has summed up the punishment theme of accountability by indicating that "individuals who do not perform well simply will not be around too long."[16]

Authority Combinations

Rewards and Punishments

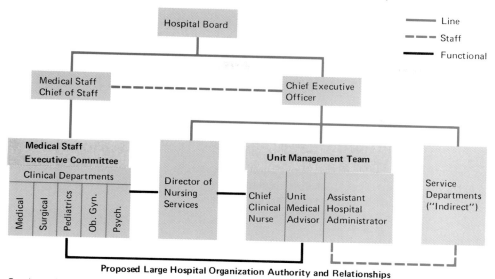

Figure 9.9 Proposed design for incorporating three types of authority in a hospital.

Proposed Large Hospital Organization Authority and Relationships

Courtesy of Dr. P. N. Ghei, Secretary General, Indian Hospital Association, New Delhi.

Functional authority and accountability are two additional factors that must be considered when modifying responsibilities within the student employment department. Some student employment personnel may have to be delegated functional authority to supplement the line or staff authority already possessed. The staff person who advises Mercer on conducting possible surveys to support the hiring of part-time students may need some functional authority to complete her assigned responsibilities. This individual may need information from various student employment personnel on what types of students seem to be performing well in certain kinds of jobs. Functional authority would enable this staff individual to command that this information be channeled to her.

Student employment personnel also should understand that living up to assigned responsibilities brings rewards, while not living up to assigned responsibilities brings punishments. The use of the accountability concept within the student employment department would probably encourage most department members to live up to their responsibilities.

Back to the Case

Previous sections of this chapter have discussed responsibility and authority as complementary factors that channel activity within the organization. **Delegation** is the actual process of assigning job activities and corresponding authority to specific individuals within the organization. This section focuses on the delegation process by discussing (1) steps in the delegation process, (2) obstacles to the delegation process, (3) elimination of obstacles to the delegation process, and (4) centralization and decentralization.

Delegation

Assigning Jobs and Authority to Others

Steps in the Delegation Process

According to Newman and Warren, there are three steps in the delegation process, any of which may be either observable or implied. The first of the three steps is assigning specific duties to the individual. In all cases the manager must be sure that the subordinate has a clear understanding of what these duties entail. Whenever possible,

Assignments, Authority, and Obligations

care should be taken to state the activities in operational terms so that a subordinate knows exactly what action must be taken to perform the assigned duties. The second step of the delegation process involves granting appropriate authority to the subordinate. The subordinate must be given the right and power within the organization to accomplish the duties assigned. The last step of the delegation process involves creating the obligation for the subordinate to perform the duties assigned. The subordinate must be aware of the responsibility to complete the duties assigned and his or her acceptance of that responsibility.[17]

Obstacles to the Delegation Process

The term *obstacle* is used here to represent a variable that can make delegation within an organization difficult or even impossible. These obstacles can be classified in three general categories: (1) obstacles related to superiors, (2) obstacles related to subordinates, and (3) obstacles related to organizations.

Obstacles Related to the Supervisor

Supervisors Make Delegation Difficult

One supervisor-related obstacle to delegation is that some supervisors may resist delegating some of their authority to subordinates because they may find using their authority very satisfying. Two other such obstacles are that supervisors may be afraid that their subordinates will not do a job well or that surrendering some of their authority may be seen by others as a sign of a weak manager. Also, if supervisors are insecure in their job or see specific activities as being extremely important to their personal success, they may find it difficult to put the performance of these activities into the hands of others.

Obstacles Related to Subordinates

Subordinates Make Delegation Difficult

Even if supervisors wish to delegate to subordinates, they may encounter several subordinate-related roadblocks. First, subordinates may be reluctant to accept delegated authority for fear of failure or because of a lack of self-confidence. These two obstacles probably will be especially apparent if subordinates have not experienced the use of delegated authority previously. Other obstacles include the feeling that the supervisor will not be available for guidance once the delegation is made or that being a recipient of additional authority may complicate comfortable working relationships that presently exist.

Obstacles Related to Organizations

Organizations Make Delegation Difficult

Characteristics of the organization itself also may make delegation difficult. For example, a very small organization may present the supervisor with only a minimal number of activities to be delegated. In addition, organizational history can be a roadblock to delegation. If very few job activities and little authority have been delegated over several years in an organization, attempting to initiate the delegation process could make individuals very reluctant and apprehensive. In essence, the supervisor would be introducing a change in procedure that some members of the organization may resist very strongly.[18]

Eliminating Obstacles to the Delegation Process

Eliminating obstacles to delegation becomes important to the manager because delegation usually results in several organizational advantages. These advantages include improved subordinate involvement and interest, more free time for the supervisor to

Figure 9.10 Centralized and decentralized organizations on delegation continuum.

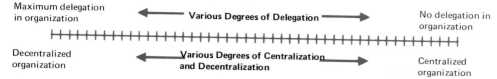

Maximum delegation in organization — ← Various Degrees of Delegation → — No delegation in organization

Decentralized organization — ← Various Degrees of Centralization and Decentralization → — Centralized organization

accomplish tasks, and as the organization gets larger, assistance from subordinates in completing tasks the manager simply wouldn't have time for otherwise.

Although delegation also has potential disadvantages, most managers would probably concur that the potential advantages of some degree of delegation generally outweigh its potential disadvantages. One potential disadvantage is the possibility of the manager losing track of the progress of a task once it has been delegated.[19]

What can managers do to minimize the effect of these obstacles to the delegation process? First of all, they must continually remind themselves that obstacles to delegation may exist in their organization and that they should continually strive to uncover any obstacle relative to their special situation. Next, specific action then should be taken to minimize the effects of any obstacles managers identify. Managers should approach specific action with the understanding that the obstacle may be deeply engrained in the situation and, therefore, require long-run time and effort. Specific managerial action usually necessary to overcome obstacles include building subordinate confidence in the use of delegated authority, minimizing the impact of delegated authority on established working relationships, and helping the subordinate to whom authority has been delegated with any problems whenever necessary.

Besides taking this type of appropriate action, Koontz and O'Donnell imply that for managers to overcome obstacles to delegation, they must possess certain critical characteristics. These characteristics include the willingness to consider seriously the ideas of others, the insight to allow subordinates the free rein necessary to carry out their responsibilities, trust in the abilities of subordinates, and the ability to allow people to learn from their mistakes without suffering unreasonable penalties for making them.[20]

Characteristics of a Good Delegator

Back to the Case

To delegate effectively within the student employment department, Mercer must assign specific duties to individuals, grant corresponding authority to these individuals, and create the awareness within these individuals that they are obligated to perform these activities. Certainly, Mercer must be aware that obstacles to delegation may exist within himself, his subordinates, or the student employment department itself. Discovering which obstacles exist and then taking steps to eliminate them is a prerequisite for successful delegation. If Mercer is to be a successful delegator, he also must be willing to consider the ideas of his subordinates, allow them the free rein necessary to perform their assigned tasks, trust them, and help them to learn from their mistakes without suffering unreasonable penalties.

Centralization and Decentralization

Noticeable differences exist in the relative number of job activities and the relative amount of authority delegated to subordinates from organization to organization. In practice, it is not a case of delegation either existing or not existing within an organization. Delegation exists in most organizations but in varying degrees.

Exhibit 9

Delegation Problems at the Bulova Watch Company

Bob Tisch (Photo: Patrick D. Pagnano)

For the last four years, corporate punsters have had a field day with Bulova Watch Co.'s sorry performance. Among other things, they suggested that Bulova was a company "whose time is running out," a place where "the main ticking is that of a time bomb." But now, just a couple of months after Loews Corp. acquired control of the ailing watchmaker, it is clear that time was running out on Bulova's top management, not necessarily on the company itself.

The Tisches—Laurence A., Loews's chairman; Preston R. (Bob), Loews's president; and Andrew H., the 29-year-old son of Laurence—entered their newest company wielding axes. By the end of April, most of Bulova's veteran top managers were forced to take early retirement. The list of those who have left includes Sol E. Flick, 64, whose main role during his 38 years with the company was as general counsel but whose last year was spent as chief executive officer; Leo Gale, 63, vice-president of merchandising for the last 8 of his 19 years with Bulova; David Anderson, 61, executive vice-president of manufacturing for 13 of his 37 years with the company; and a host of lower-level managers. Although Harry Bulova Henshel, 60, remains chairman, his influence over operations is virtually nil. In an unusual display of corporate candor, Bob Tisch says Henshel now "has an assignment to make 500 phone calls to top customers over the next 20 days and spend time with division managers."

Gone, too, are Bulova's four outside directors, including, most notably, George C. Sheinberg, Bulova's

Former Bulova CEO Sol E. Flick (Photo: Patrick D. Pagnano)

former chief financial officer. Although he left the company in 1977 to join Shearson Hayden Stone Inc., Sheinberg continued to be influential as a director in trying to stem the company's downward financial spiral. The power at Bulova now resides in an executive committee comprising the three Tisches, Loews's Vice-President Herbert C. Hofmann, Henshel, and R. Mark Bourquin, who remains Bulova's president. Technically, there is no chief executive officer at the moment.

Stressing Communication. Loews's goal, apparently, is to transform Bulova's management style from one that was decentralized to a debilitating extreme into one that emphasizes interdepartmental communication. Sources close to Bulova confirm that such communications were certainly lacking, with managers operating almost in total isolation from one another. Anderson, for one, is referred to by one Bulova executive as "an autocratic manager who always knew more than his staff because he didn't communicate," a charge that Anderson, not surprisingly, hotly denies. And Flick "was a lawyer—not a marketing man, or a merchandising man, or a technical man, but a lawyer," notes a watch-industry expert. Bob Tisch says that "Flick couldn't communicate with his own people, and he just couldn't integrate the company." Other Bulova insiders note that while Henshel and Flick had been virtually inseparable for most of their years at the company, even communications between them broke down when Flick was named CEO last year, effectively stripping Henshel of operating authority.

The lack of cooperation at the top filtered down throughout the company, Bob Tisch insists. When Loews took over, he says, "no one could give me a count of the number of employees in the company or where they worked. Every executive ran his own show without telling anyone what was going on."As an example, Tisch says he recently visited a Bulova assembly plant in St. Croix when a shipment of about 6,000 watch assemblies—10 days' worth of work—arrived from Switzerland. "No one was expecting it," he says incredulously.

The Loews penchant for much tighter management is already evident at Bulova. For the first time, a committee of executives from the manufacturing, marketing, and sales departments is meeting regularly. Both Andrew Tisch and Hofmann have set up offices at the company's Flushing (N.Y.) headquarters, and Bob Tisch visits frequently. Loews has also tapped management talent for Bulova from the executive ranks at Lorillard, the tobacco company Loews acquired 10 years ago. James S. Waterwash, 40, until recently general manager of Lorillard's Louisville (Ky.) facilities, is Anderson's replacement in the manufacturing slot. And Alexander W. Spears, Lorillard's executive vice-president for operations and research, is spending several days each week assessing which Bulova operations need changing.

The terms *centralization* and *decentralization* describe the general degree to which delegation exists within an organization. These terms can be visualized at opposite ends of a delegation continuum. Figure 9.10 shows this delegation continuum and indicates the relative positioning of complete centralization and complete decentralization. From this figure it is apparent that centralization implies that a minimal number of job activities and a minimal amount of authority have been delegated to subordinates by management, while decentralization implies the opposite.

Exhibit 9 tells how the inability of top management at the Bulova Watch Company to decentralize was a major factor in its firing.

The problems usually facing practicing managers are determining whether to further decentralize an organization and deciding how to decentralize if that course of action is advisable. The following paragraphs contain practical suggestions on whether or not an organization should be decentralized and how decentralization should take place.

Decentralizing an Organization: A Contingency Viewpoint

The degree of decentralization managers should employ depends on, or is contingent upon, their own unique organizational situation. Every managerial situation is somewhat different, and attempting to fit one specific level of decentralization to all organizational situations is impossible. There are, however, some specific questions that can be asked to determine the amount of decentralization appropriate for a situation. Several of these questions along with an explanation of how managers should relate corresponding answers to the issue of decentralization are:

1. *What is the present size of the organization?*   As indicated earlier, the larger the organization, the greater the likelihood that decentralization would be advantageous. As the organization increases in size, managers probably will have to assume more and more responsibility and different types of tasks. Delegation is typically an effective means of helping managers to keep up with this increased work load.

2. *Where are the organization's customers located?*   The organization's customers can range from being very close together to being separated by great distances. As a general rule, the more physically separated the customers of the organization, the more viable the situation for a significant amount of decentralization. Decentralization would place appropriate management resources close to the customers and thereby allow for quicker customer service.

3. *How homogeneous is the product line of the organization?*   As the product line becomes more heterogeneous or diversified, the appropriateness of decentralization generally increases. Different kinds of decisions, talents, and resources are needed to manufacture different products. Decentralization usually minimizes the potential confusion that can result from diversification by separating organizational resources by product and keeping pertinent decision making close to the manufacturing process.

4. *Where are organizational suppliers?*   The location of raw materials from which organization products are manufactured is another important consideration. Time loss and perhaps even transportation costs associated with shipping raw materials over great distances from supplier to manufacturer could support the need for decentralization of certain functions.

For example, the wood necessary to manufacture a certain type of bedroom set may only be available from tree growers in certain extreme northern states. If the bedroom set is an important enough product line for a furniture company and if costs of transporting the lumber are substantial, a sound basis for a decision to decentralize probably exists. The effects of this decision might be the building of a plant that produces only bedroom sets in a northern state close to where the necessary wood is readily available. The advantages of such a costly decision, of course, would only accrue to the organization over the long run.

5. *Is there a need for quick decisions in the organization?*   If there is a need for speedy decision making within the organization, a considerable amount of decentralization is probably in order. Decentralization avoids red tape and allows the subordinate to whom authority has been delegated to make on-the-spot decisions if necessary.[21] This delegation is advisable only if the delegatees in question have the ability to make sound decisions. If they don't, the increased decision-making speed via delegation has no advantage. Quick or slow, a decision cannot reap benefits for the organization if it is unsound.

5. Quick decisions are necessary

6. *Is creativity a desirable feature of the organization?*   If the answer to this question is yes, then some decentralization probably is advisable. Decentralization allows delegatees the freedom to find better ways of doing things. The mere existence of this freedom can encourage the incorporation of new and more creative techniques within the task process.[22]

6. Creativity is needed

Back to the Case

Centralization implies that few job activities and little authority have been delegated to subordinates, while decentralization implies that many job activities and much authority have been delegated. Mercer will have to determine the degree of delegation best for the student employment department. For guidelines he can use the rules of thumb that greater degrees of delegation probably will be appropriate for the student employment department as the department becomes larger, as the hired students with whom the department deals become more physically separated, as potential employers and student clients become more diversified, and as the needs for quick decision making and creativity increase.

Decentralization at Massey-Ferguson

Positive decentralization can be defined as decentralization that is advantageous for the organization in which it is being implemented. Conversely, negative decentralization is decentralization that is disadvantageous for the organization in which it is being implemented. Perhaps the best way to ascertain how an organization should be decentralized is to study the efforts of an organization with positive decentralization: Massey-Ferguson.[23]

Positive and Negative Decentralization

Massey-Ferguson is a worldwide farm equipment manufacturer that has enjoyed noticeable success with decentralization over the past several years.[24] At Massey-Ferguson there are three definite guidelines for determining the degree of decentralization of decision making appropriate for a situation. These three guidelines are:

Delegation Guidelines

1. The competence to make decisions must be possessed by the person to whom authority is delegated. A derivative of this is that the superior must have confidence in the subordinate to whom authority is delegated.

2. Adequate and reliable information pertinent to the decision is required by the person making the decision. Decision-making authority, therefore, cannot be pushed below the point at which all information bearing on the decision is available.
3. If a decision affects more than one unit of the enterprise, the authority to make the decision must rest with the manager accountable for the most units affected by the decision.[25]

Attitude Toward Decentralization

Massey-Ferguson also encourages a definite attitude toward decentralization. The organization manual of Massey-Ferguson indicates that delegation is not delegation in name only, but is a frame of mind that includes both what a supervisor says to subordinates and the way he or she acts toward them. Managers at Massey-Ferguson are encouraged to allow subordinates to make a reasonable number of mistakes and to help subordinates learn from these mistakes.

Centralization Complements Decentralization

Another feature of the positive decentralization at Massey-Ferguson is that decentralization is complemented with centralization.

> The organization plan that best serves our total requirements is a blend of centralized and decentralized elements. Marketing and manufacturing responsibilities, together with supporting service functions, are located as close as possible to local markets. Activities that determine the long-range character of the company, such as the planning and control of the product line, the planning and control of facilities and money, and the planning of the strategy to react to changes in the patterns of international trade, are highly centralized.[26]

Massey-Ferguson management recognizes that decentralization is not necessarily an either/or decision and uses the strengths of both centralization and decentralization to its own advantage.

Not all activities at Massey-Ferguson, however, are eligible for decentralization consideration. Only management can follow through on some responsibilities. These responsibilities are:

Some Activities Cannot Be Delegated

1. The responsibility for determining the overall objectives of the enterprise
2. The responsibility for formulating the policies that guide the enterprise
3. The final responsibility for the control of the business within the total range of the objectives and policies, including control over any changes in the nature of the business
4. The responsibility for product design, where a product decision affects more than one area of accountability
5. The responsibility for planning for the achievement of overall objectives and for measuring actual performance against those plans
6. The final approval of corporate plans or budgets
7. The decisions pertaining to the availability, and the application, of general company funds
8. The responsibility for capital-investment plans.[27]

The Massey-Ferguson decentralization situation could give Mercer many valuable insights on what characteristics the decentralization process in the student employment department should assume. First, Mercer should use definite guidelines to decide whether or not his situation warrants added decentralization. In general, additional delegation will probably be warranted in the student employment department as the competence of subordinates increases, as Mercer's confidence in the subordinates increases, and as more adequate and reliable decision-making information becomes available to subordinates. For delegation to be advantageous for the student employment department, Mercer must also help subordinates to learn from their mistakes, and he must supplement decentralization with centralization.

Summary

The following points are stressed within this chapter:

1. Organizing individual activity within the management system is extremely important since the actual production of any such system ultimately comes from this activity. Three factors are primarily responsible for organizing individual activity within a management system: responsibility, authority, and delegation.

2. Responsibility is the obligation to perform activity assigned by management to enhance the attainment of management system objectives. To divide job activities among various individuals within the management system, management examines management system objectives, outlines activities necessary to reach objectives, and designs specific jobs by grouping similar activities, and then makes various individuals responsible for performing those jobs.

3. Authority is the right to perform or command. Once individuals are assigned certain job activities, they must also be granted a corresponding amount of authority to perform their required activities. Authority, however, does not always exact obedience. Obedience is exacted only when authority is accepted by those living under it.

4. Three types of authority normally exist in management systems: line authority, staff authority, and functional authority. Line authority is the right to make decisions and to give orders concerning the production, sales, or finance-related behavior of subordinates, while staff authority is the right to advise or assist those possessing line authority and other staff personnel. Functional authority is the right to give orders within a section of the organization in which this right is normally nonexistent. Functional authority is usually delegated to supplement line or staff authority that an individual already possesses.

5. Accountability is a management philosophy that accompanies the delegation of activities and authority in the management system. This philosophy simply indicates that those who carry out assigned responsibilities are rewarded and those who do not are punished.

6. Delegation is the process of assigning job activities and corresponding authority to individuals within the management system. Steps in the delegation process include assigning duties to individuals, granting the individuals an adequate amount of authority to perform these duties, and making the individuals aware that they are obligated to perform their duties. The term *centralization* is used to indicate that little delegation exists within the management system, while *decentralization* indicates that much delegation exists.

Issues for Review and Discussion

1. What is responsibility and why does it exist in organizations?
2. Explain the process a manager would go through to divide responsibility within an organization.
3. What is a management responsibility guide and how is it used?
4. List the four main dimensions of responsible management behavior.
5. Summarize the behaviors that each of the four dimensions of responsible management includes for the responsible manager.
6. What is authority and why does it exist in organizations?
7. Describe the relationship between responsibility and authority.
8. Explain Barnard's notion of authority and acceptance.
9. What steps can managers take to increase the probability that subordinates will accept their authority? Be sure to explain how each of these steps increases the probability.
10. Summarize the relationship that generally exists between line and staff personnel.
11. Explain three roles that staff personnel can perform in organizations.
12. List five possible causes of conflict in line-staff relationships and suggest appropriate action to minimize the effect of these causes.
13. What is functional authority?
14. Give an example of how functional authority actually works in an organization.
15. Compare the relative advantages and disadvantages of line, staff, and functional authority.
16. Define delegation and list the steps of the delegation process.
17. List four obstacles to the delegation process and suggest action for eliminating them.
18. What is the relationship between delegation and decentralization?
19. What is the difference between decentralization and centralization?

Sources of Additional Information

Avots, Ivars. "Why Does Project Management Fail?" In *Dimensions in Modern Management,* edited by Patrick E. Connor. Boston: Houghton Mifflin, 1974.

Chandler, A. D., Jr. *Strategy and Structure.* Garden City, New York: Anchor Books, Doubleday & Company, 1966.

Clark, P. A. *Organizational Design: Theory and Practice.* London: Tavistock Publishing, 1972.

Dale, E. *Planning and Developing the Company Organization Structure.* Research report no. 20. New York: American Management Association, 1952.

Dale, E. *The Great Organizers.* New York: McGraw-Hill, 1960.

Fotilas, Panagiotis N. "Semi-Autonomous Work Groups: An Alternative in Organizing Production Work?" *Management Review* 70, no. 7 (July 1981): 50–54.

Gibson, James L.; Ivancevich, John M.; and Donnelly, James H., Jr. *Organizations, Behavior, Structure, Processes.* Dallas: Business Publications, 1976.

Kets de Vries, Manfred F. R. "Managers Can Drive Their Subordinates Mad." *Harvard Business Review,* no. 4 (July/August 1979): 125–34.

Leavitt, Harold J.; Dill, William R.; and Eyring, Henry B. *The Organizational World.* New York: Harcourt Brace Jovanovich, 1973.

Litterer, J. A. *Analysis of Organizations.* 2d ed. New York: John Wiley & Sons, 1973.

Pfiffner, John M., and Sherwood, Frank P. *Administrative Organization.* Englewood Cliffs, N.J.; Prentice-Hall, 1965.

Rhenman E.; Stromberg, L.; and Westerlund, G. *Conflict and Cooperation in Business Organizations.* New York: John Wiley & Sons, 1970.

Roos, Leslie L., Jr., and Hall, Roger I. "Influence Diagrams and Organizational Power." *Administrative Science Quarterly* 25 (March 1980): 57–71.

Scott, William G., and Mitchell, Terence R. *Organization Theory.* Homewood, Ill.: Richard D. Irwin, 1972.

Shrode, William A., and Voich, Dan, Jr. *Organization and Management: Basic Systems Concepts.* Homewood, Ill.: Richard D. Irwin, 1974.

Smith, Howard R. "The Uphill Struggle for Job Enrichment." *California Management Review* 23, no. 4 (Summer 1981): 33–38.

Tavernier, Gerard. " 'Awakening a Sleeping Giant': Ford's Employee Involvement Program." *Management Review* 70, no. 6 (June 1981): 15–20.

Worthy, James C. *Big Business and Free Men.* New York: Harper & Row, 1959.

1. Stephen X. Doyle and Benson P. Shapiro, "What Counts Most in Motivating Your Sales Force?" *Harvard Business Review,* May/June 1980, pp. 133–40.

2. Robert J. Thierauf, Robert C. Klekamp, and Daniel W. Geeding, *Management Principles and Practices: A Contingency and Questionnaire Approach* (New York: John Wiley & Sons, 1977), p. 334.

3. Robert D. Melcher, "Roles and Relationships: Clarifying the Manager's Job," *Personnel* 44, no. 3 (May–June 1967): 34.

4. For more information on management responsibility guides, see Melcher, "Roles and Relationships," pp. 34–41.

5. This section is based primarily on John H. Zenger, "Responsible Behavior: Stamp of the Effective Manager," *Supervisory Management,* July 1976, pp. 18–24.

6. Max Weber, "The Three Types of Legitimate Rule," trans. Hans Gerth, *Berkeley Journal of Sociology* 4 (1953): 1–11.

7. John Gardner, "The Anti-Leadership Vaccine," *Carnegie Foundation Annual Report,* 1965.

8. Chester I. Barnard, *The Functions of the Executive* (Cambridge, Mass.: Harvard University Press, 1938).

9. Harold Stieglitz, "On Concepts of Corporate Structure," *The Conference Board Record* 11, no. 2 (February 1974): 7–13.

10. This section is based primarily on Louis A. Allen, "Developing Sound Line and Staff Relationships," from *Studies in Personnel Policy no. 153,* National Industrial Conference Board, 1956, pp. 70–80.

11. John R. Simon, Curt Norton, and Neil J. Lonergan, "Accounting for the Conflict Between Line Management and the Controller's Office," *S.A.M. Advanced Management Journal,* Winter 1979, pp. 4–14.

12. Derek Sheane, "When and How to Intervene in Conflict," *Personnel Management,* November 1979, pp. 32–36.

13. For additional information on how to handle conflict, see Andrew K. Hoh, "Consensus-Building: A Creative Approach to Resolving Conflicts," *Management Review,* March 1981, pp. 52–54.

14. Otto Forchheimer, "Accountability for Functional Executives," *Advanced Management Journal,* April 1972, pp. 15–20.

15. For an excellent review of the punishment literature, see Henry P. Sims, Jr., "Further Thoughts on Punishment in Organizations," *The Academy of Management Review* 5, no. 1 (January 1980): 133.

16. "How Ylvisaker Makes 'Produce or Else' Work," *Business Week,* 27 October 1973, p. 112.

17. William H. Newman and E. Kirby Warren, *The Process of Management: Concepts, Behavior, and Practice,* 4th ed. (Englewood Cliffs, N.J.: Prentice-Hall, 1977), pp. 39–40.

18. For organizational barriers unique to a family business, see Louis B. Barnes and Simon A. Hershon, "Transferring Power in the Family Business," *Harvard Business Review,* July-August 1976, pp. 105–14.

19. Ted Pollock, "You Must Delegate . . . But You're Still Responsible," *Industrial Supervision,* February 1976, pp. 10–11.

20. Harold Koontz and Cyril O'Donnell, *Principles of Management,* 4th ed. (New York: McGraw-Hill, 1968), pp. 71–72.

21. Ernest Dale, "Centralization Versus Decentralization," *Advanced Management Journal,* June 1955, pp. 11–16.

22. Donald O. Harper, "Project Management as a Control and Planning Tool in the Decentralized Company," *Management Accounting,* November 1968, pp. 29–33.

23. For further discussion on positive and negative centralization and decentralization, see Anthony Jay, *Management and Machiavelli* (New York: Holt, Rinehart & Winston, 1967), pp. 60–69.

24. Information for this section is mainly from John G. Staiger, "What Cannot Be Decentralized," *Management Record* 25, no. 1 (January 1963): 19–21. At the time this article was written, Staiger was vice-president, administration, North American Operations, Massey-Ferguson, Limited.

25. Staiger, "What Cannot Be Decentralized," p. 19.

26. Staiger, "What Cannot Be Decentralized," p. 21.

27. Staiger, "What Cannot Be Decentralized," p. 21.

Concluding Case 9
Problems at Data General Corporation

Edison D. deCastro (Photo: Patrick D. Pagnano)

During its first twelve years, Data General Corporation appeared to be one of the impressive leaders in the minicomputer market. However, as Data General Corporation reached its thirteenth year, it was faced with a series of problems ranging from slow product development to weakening sales and marketing-support staffs. According to observers internal and external to the company, these problems were only symptoms of more serious management difficulties. Specifically, the observers point to an outmoded management structure that worked well for a developing business but was very inadequate for a company of Data General's present size.

In an attempt to resolve some of the more major problems at Data General a number of changes were initiated. For the first time, for instance, the company instituted formal long-term strategic planning. This, in addition to other changes, necessitated the need for some restructuring of the management hierarchy. However, company officials planned to keep these changes to the bare minimum. According to Edison D. de Castro, Data General's president, the company considered a number of strategies to facilitate decision making. However, he still insisted that the management structure had kept pace with the growth of the company.

Contrary to de Castro's opinion, industry analysts pointed out significant declines in a number of areas. Experts were suggesting that Data General had lost the ability to take advantage of emerging technology and develop new products quickly enough. Other indicators also support this contention. Data General reported a 30 percent decline in fourth-quarter earnings in 1980, while competitors Digital Equipment Corporation and Prime Computer Incorporated reported gains of 18 percent and 74 percent respectively. Operating margins for Data General dropped to 13 percent, far below the 20 percent mark the company had historically maintained. While the company asserted that its profit problems were caused by currency fluctuations, lagging European order rates, weak sales in smaller systems, higher inventories, and a reorganization of its sales force, these explanations, in the view of industry analysts, failed to reveal why Data General suffered more than the other two makers of minicomputers.

During its first few years of existence, Data General was able to react quickly to changes in the minicomputer field. This was due primarily to the guidance of de Castro, Data General's founder and chief executive. De Castro had built the company by being a tough, control-oriented manager who kept the company on its fast-growth track by retaining most decision-making authority. But as the company approached its thirteenth birthday, observers of Data General indicated that many executives in this growing company were becoming apprehensive about making decisions on their own without de Castro's approval. This centralized form of decision making led to the resignation of twelve high-level managers in 1979 and 1980. In the same two-year period, the company's reorganized sales operation resulted in an estimated loss of 40 percent of Data General's managers in the sales area.

Former employees indicate that many of the problems at Data General stemmed from a lack of top management guidance and direction. These problems seemed to be magnified by the fact that the majority of the company's vice-presidents had been with Data General less than two years. Lack of guidance and seniority in the VP ranks appears to have resulted in intense competition among the vice-presidents for de Castro's attention and budget support; observers reported a great deal of in-fighting as VPs jockeyed for position.

According to some analysts, the company may weather these stormy times. But Data General's long-run success, company watchers suggest, will be dependent upon how rapidly de Castro can implement changes in the decision-making hierarchy. A former executive under de Castro suggests that these changes will only be effective if de Castro actually delegates responsibility, and that this may be extremely difficult for him to do as he will have to change before he can hope to make any changes successfully in the company's structure.

This case is adapted from "Computers: Data General Management Trouble," *Business Week* (February 9, 1981), p. 58.

Discussion Issues

1. What seems to be causing the major problems at Data General?
2. Assume that you were hired as a consultant to help Data General resolve its problems. What action would you recommend? Justify your recommendations.
3. Interpret the meaning of the following statement from the case:
   A former executive under de Castro suggested that these changes will only be effective if de Castro actually delegates responsibility.
4. Assume that Mr. de Castro permits subordinates three or four levels below him in the management hierarchy to come directly to him when they have problems or need advice. Explain the managerial implications (from an organizational relationship perspective) of such action for:
   a. the managers that were by-passed.
   b. Mr. de Castro (in this hypothetical situation).
   c. the subordinates that have by-passed their immediate superiors.
   d. the subordinates that have by-passed their immediate superiors to resolve a problem that their superior was not willing to deal with (assume that neither de Castro nor the immediate superior has given permission to "skip levels").

Student Learning Objectives

From studying this chapter I will attempt to acquire:

1. An overall understanding of how appropriate human resources can be provided for the organization

2. An appreciation for the relationship among recruitment efforts, an open position, sources of human resources, and the law

3. Insights on the use of tests and assessment centers in employee selection

4. An understanding of how the training process actually operates

5. A concept of what performance appraisals actually are and how they best can be conducted

6. An appreciation of the complex situation involving women who are blue-collar workers.

Chapter Outline

Providing Appropriate Human Resources for the Organization

Introductory Case 10
Gamble Transportation

Gamble Transportation is an interstate airline company with headquarters in Dallas, Texas. Gamble Transportation has eight medium-sized airplanes and specializes in charter passenger flights and air freight transportation.

In the past Martin Massie, general manager of Gamble Transportation, has had very little difficulty obtaining enough quality people to work for him. In fact, he has always been able to fill open positions through a constant stream of unsolicited applicants looking for work. Openings in his company have occurred mostly in three positions: stewardess, freight handler, and airplane mechanic.

Recently, however, Massie has begun to worry somewhat about filling openings in his organization. The stream of unsolicited applicants has been steadily dwindling. Overall, Massie feels that the general population's intrinsic interest in working for airline companies is decreasing. In his opinion, with a national move toward energy conservation and environmental protection, many people feel that the airlines are on the decline and are, therefore, insecure employers. Because of this situation, Massie has just begun to develop a strategy for obtaining people to fill future open positions.

Discussion Issues

1. In your opinion, how important is this situation to Gamble Transportation?
2. What strategy would you recommend to Massie?

What's Ahead

This chapter focuses on how to provide appropriate human resources for the organization. Martin Massie, the general manager of the airline company in the introductory case, would find the information in this chapter helpful in handling the dilemma he presently faces. The chapter is divided into two main sections: (1) defining appropriate human resources and (2) steps in providing appropriate human resources.

The emphasis in chapter 9 is on organizing the activity of individuals within the management system. To this end, responsibility, authority, and delegation are discussed in detail. This chapter continues to explore the relationship between individuals and organizing by discussing how appropriate human resources can be provided for the organization.

The phrase **appropriate human resources** refers to those individuals within the organization who make a valuable contribution to management system goal attainment. This contribution, of course, is a result of productivity in the positions they hold. On the other hand, *inappropriate human resources* refers to those organization members who do not make a valuable contribution to the attainment of management system objectives. In essence, these individuals are ineffective in their jobs.

The task of providing appropriate human resources is very important to managers. Productivity in all organizations is determined by how human resources interact and combine to use all other management system resources. Such factors as background, age, job-related experience, and level of formal education all have some role in determining the degree of appropriateness of the individual to the organization. Although the process of providing appropriate human resources for the organization is involved and somewhat subjective, the following section offers insights on how to increase the success of this process.

Defining Appropriate Human Resources

Attaining Management System Objectives

Human Resources Determine Management System Success

"You've got style, Fenley. Unfortunately, that's not one of our priorities at the moment."

From the *Wall Street Journal*.

Figure 10.1 Four sequential steps to provide appropriate human sources for an organization.

Step 1	Step 2	Step 3	Step 4
Recruitment	Selection	Training	Performance appraisal

Steps in Providing Appropriate Human Resources

To provide appropriate human resources successfully for the organization as various positions become open, managers should follow four sequential steps: (1) recruitment, (2) selection, (3) training, and (4) performance appraisal. Figure 10.1 illustrates the relationship among these steps. This process can be used to fill either managerial or nonmanagerial openings. Each step is discussed in detail in the paragraphs that follow.

Recruitment

Initial Screening

Recruitment is the first step in providing appropriate human resources for the organization once a position becomes open. **Recruitment** is the initial screening of the total supply of prospective human resources available to fill a position. The purpose of recruitment is to narrow a large field of prospective employees to a relatively small number of individuals from which someone eventually will be hired. To be effective at recruiting, recruiters must know (1) the job they are trying to fill, (2) where sources of potential human resources can be located, and (3) how the law influences recruiting efforts. Discussion on each of these topics follows.

Knowing the Job

What Is a Job Analysis, a Job Description, a Job Specification?

Recruitment activities begin with a thorough understanding of the position to be filled. Only after this understanding exists can the broad range of potential employees be narrowed intelligently. Job analysis is a technique commonly used to gain an understanding of a position. Basically, job analysis is a procedure aimed at determining (1) what activities a job entails and (2) what type of individual should be hired to perform the job. *Job description* is the term used to refer to the activities a job entails, while the term *job specification* refers to the characteristics of the individual who should be hired for the job. Figure 10.2 shows the relationship between job analysis, job description, and job specification.

Information Gathering

The U.S. Civil Service Commission has developed a procedure for performing a job analysis.[1] As with all job analysis procedures, the Civil Service procedure uses information gathering as the primary means of determining what workers do, and how and why they do it. This information then is used to develop both a job description and a job specification. Figure 10.3 shows the kinds of information Civil Service recommends be gathered to perform a job analysis.

Back to the Case

Martin Massie must be concerned not merely with obtaining human resources for Gamble Transportation but with obtaining appropriate human resources. Appropriate human resources are those individuals who make a valuable contribution to the attainment of objectives at Gamble Transportation. To find appropriate human resources, Massie must follow four steps:

(1) recruitment, (2) selection, (3) training, and (4) performance appraisal. Basically, recruitment entails Massie's initial screening of individuals available to fill open positions. For Massie's recruitment effort to be successful, he must know the job he is trying to fill, where sources of potential human resources can be located, and how the law influences his recruiting

Figure 10.2 Relationship between job analysis, job description, and job specification.

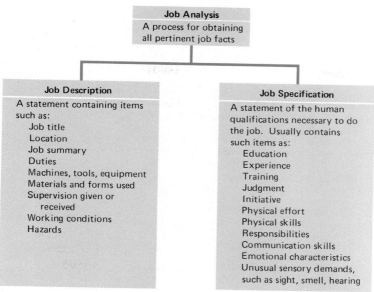

Job Analysis
A process for obtaining all pertinent job facts

Job Description
A statement containing items such as:
- Job title
- Location
- Job summary
- Duties
- Machines, tools, equipment
- Materials and forms used
- Supervision given or received
- Working conditions
- Hazards

Job Specification
A statement of the human qualifications necessary to do the job. Usually contains such items as:
- Education
- Experience
- Training
- Judgment
- Initiative
- Physical effort
- Physical skills
- Responsibilities
- Communication skills
- Emotional characteristics
- Unusual sensory demands, such as sight, smell, hearing

Reprinted with permission of Macmillan Publishing Co., Inc., from *Personnel* by Dale S. Beach. Copyright © 1965, 1970 by Dale S. Beach.

efforts. Massie can acquire an understanding of an open position at Gamble Transportation by performing a job analysis. The job analysis would force Massie to determine the job activities of the open position—the job activities of a stewardess, freight handler, or airplane mechanic, for example—and what type of individual should be hired to fill that position. In essence, Massie's job analysis would result in a job description and a job specification regarding the position.

Knowing Sources of Human Resources

The Changing Labor Supply

Besides a thorough knowledge of the position the organization is trying to fill, the recruiter must be able to pinpoint sources of human resources. A barrier to this pinpointing is the fact that the supply of individuals from which to choose in the labor market is continually changing; in essence, there are times when finding appropriate human resources is much harder than other times. For example, an article that appeared approximately fifteen years ago indicated that organizations should prepare for a frantic scramble to obtain managers from a very low supply in the labor market.[2] In discussing the same managerial recruitment issue, however, a much more recent article indicates that the situation has changed dramatically:

> For the past couple of years, a few thoughtful observers of new business trends have been warning that a glut of corporate executives is imminent. The reason, of course, is the U.S. baby boom of the late 1940s and 1950s.[3]

Overall, sources of human resources available to fill a position can be categorized in two ways: (1) sources inside the organization and (2) sources outside the organization.

Figure 10.3 Information to obtain when performing a job analysis.

Identifying Information (Such as):
    Name of incumbent
    Organization/unit
    Title and series
    Date
    Interviewer

Brief Summary of Job: (This statement will include the primary duties of the job. It may be prepared in advance from class specifications, job descriptions, or other sources. However, it should be checked for accuracy using the task statements resulting from the analysis.)

Job Tasks:
    What does the worker do? How does the worker do it? Why? What output is produced? What tools, procedures, aids are involved? How much time does it take to do the task? How often does the worker perform the task in a day, week, month, or year?

Knowledge, Skills, and Abilities Required:
What does it take to perform each task in terms of the following?
1. Knowledge required
    a. What subject matter areas are covered by the task?
    b. What facts or principles must the worker have an acquaintance with or understand in these subject matter areas?
    c. Describe the level, degree, and breadth of knowledge required in these areas or subjects.
2. Skills required
    a. What activities must the worker perform with ease and precision?
    b. What are the manual skills required to operate machines, vehicles, equipment, or to use tools?
3. Abilities required
    a. What is the nature and level of language ability, written or oral, required of the worker on the job? Are there complex oral or written ideas involved in performing the task, or simple instructional materials?
    b. What mathematical ability must the worker have? Will the worker use simple arithmetic, complex algebra?
    c. What reasoning or problem-solving ability must the worker have?
    d. What instructions must the worker follow? Are they simple, detailed, involved, abstract?
    e. What interpersonal abilities are required? What supervisory or managing abilities are required?
    f. What physical abilities such as strength, coordination, visual acuity must the worker have?

Physical Activities:
    Describe the frequency and degree to which the incumbent is engaged in such activities as: pulling, pushing, throwing, carrying, kneeling, sitting, running, crawling, reaching, climbing.

Environmental Conditions:
    Describe the frequency and degree to which the incumbent will encounter working under such conditions as these: cramped quarters, moving objects, vibration, inadequate ventilation.

Typical Work Incidents:
1. Situations involving the interpretation of feelings, ideas, or facts in terms of personal viewpoint
2. Influencing people in their opinions, attitudes, or judgments about ideas or things
3. Working with people beyond giving and receiving instructions
4. Performing repetitive work, or continuously performing the same work
5. Performing under stress when confronted with emergency, critical, unusual, or dangerous situations; or in situations in which work speed and sustained attention are make-and-break aspects of the job
6. Performing a variety of duties often changing from one task to another of a different nature without loss of efficiency or composure
7. Working under hazardous conditions that may result in: violence, loss of bodily members, burns, bruises, cuts, impairment of senses, collapse, fractures, electric shock

Worker Interest Areas:
    Identify from the list below, the preferences for work activities suggested by each task.
    A preference for activities:
      1. Dealing with things and objects
      2. Concerning the communication of data
      3. Involving business contact with people
      4. Involving work of a scientific and technical nature
      5. Involving work of a routine, concrete, organized nature
      6. Involving work of an abstract and creative nature
      7. Involving work for the presumed good of people
      8. Relating to process, machine, and technique
      9. Resulting in prestige or the esteem of others
     10. Resulting in tangible, productive satisfaction

From U.S. Civil Service Commission.

Figure 10.4 Management inventory card.

Name	Age	Employed
Murray, Mel	47	1945

Present Position	On Job
Manager, sales (House Fans division)	6 years

Present Performance
Outstanding—exceeded sales goal in spite of stiffer competition.

Strengths
Good planner—motivates subordinates very well—excellent communication.

Weaknesses
Still does not always delegate as much as situation requires. Sometimes does not understand production's problems.

Efforts to Improve
Has greatly improved in delegating in last two years; also has organized more effectively after taking a management course on own time and initiative.

Could Move to	When
Vice-president, marketing	1963

Training Needed
More exposure to problems of other divisions (attend top staff conference?) Perhaps university program stressing staff role of corporate marketing versus line sales.

Could Move to	When
Manager, House or Industrial Fans division	1964 1965

Training Needed
Course in production management; some project working with production people; perhaps a good business game somewhere.

From Walter S. Wikstrom, "Developing Managerial Competence: Concepts, Emerging Practices," *Studies in Personnel Policy No. 189*, p. 14. Used with permission.

Sources Inside the Organization

The existing pool of employees presently within an organization is one source of human resources. Individuals already within an organization might possess excellent qualifications for an open position. Although existing personnel are sometimes moved laterally within an organization, most internal movements are usually promotions. Promotion from within typically has the advantages of (1) building morale, (2) encouraging employees to work harder in hopes of being promoted, and (3) making individuals inclined to stay with a particular organization because of possible future promotions.[4] Companies like Exxon and General Electric find it very rewarding to train managers themselves for moving up within the organization.[5]

Why Promote from Within?

Some type of human resources inventory is usually helpful to a company to keep current with possibilities for filling a position from within. The inventory should indicate which individuals within an organization would be appropriate for filling a position if it became available. An article by Walter S. Wikstrom shows three good examples of types of records that can be combined to maintain a useful human resources inventory within an organization.[6] Although Wikstrom's article focuses on filling managerial positions, slight modifications to his inventory forms would make his records equally applicable to nonmanagerial positions.

Who Is in the Organization Now?

Figure 10.4 presents the first of these three record-keeping forms for a human resources inventory. This particular form is called a **management inventory card.** This card is typical of the records kept for maintaining an inventory of people-centered

People-Centered Information

Figure 10.5 Position replacement form.

Position			
	Manager, sales (House Fans division)		
Performance	**Incumbent**	**Salary**	**May Move**
Outstanding	Mel Murray	$22,000	1 year
Replacement 1		**Salary**	**Age**
Earl Renfrew		$17,000	39
Present Position		**Employed:**	
Field sales manager, House Fans		Present job 3 years	Company 10 years
Training Needed Special assignment to study market potential for air conditioners to provide forecasting experience.			**When ready** now
Replacement 2		**Salary**	**Age**
Bernard Storey		$16,500	36
Present Position		**Employed:**	
Promotion manager, House Fans		Present Job 4 years	Company 7 years
Training Needed Rotation to field sales. Marketing conference in fall, 1963.			**When ready** 2 years

From Walter S. Wikstrom, "Developing Managerial Competence: Concepts, Emerging Practices," *Studies in Personnel Policy No. 189*, p. 9. Used with permission.

human resources information. The card in figure 10.4 has been completed for a fictional manager named Mel Murray. The card indicates Murray's age, year of employment, present position and length of time held, performance ratings, strengths and weaknesses, the positions to which he might move, when he would be ready to assume these positions, and additional training he would need to fill these positions. In short, this card is both an organizational history of Murray and an explanation of how he might be used in the future.

Job-Centered Information

Figure 10.5 shows a **position replacement form,** the second human resources inventory form presented by Wikstrom. This form focuses on maintaining position-centered information rather than the people-centered information on the management inventory card. This particular form, therefore, indicates very little about Murray as a person but very much about individuals who could replace him. The position replacement form is helpful in determining what would happen to Murray's present position if he were selected to be moved within the organization or if he left the organization altogether.

What Is a Management Manpower Replacement Chart?

Wikstrom's third sample human resources inventory form is shown in figure 10.6 and is called a **management manpower replacement chart.** This chart presents a composite view of those individuals that management considers significant for manpower planning. The performance rating and promotion potential of Murray easily can be compared with human resources of others when trying to determine which individual would most appropriately fill a particular position.

The management inventory card, the position replacement form, and the management manpower replacement chart are three separate record-keeping devices for a human resources inventory. Each form, however, furnishes different data upon which to base a hiring-from-within decision. The questions these forms help to answer are: (1) What is the organizational history of an individual and what potential does he or she possess? (management inventory card); (2) If a position becomes vacant, who might be eligible to fill that position? (position replacement form); and (3) What are the

Figure 10.6 Management manpower replacement chart.

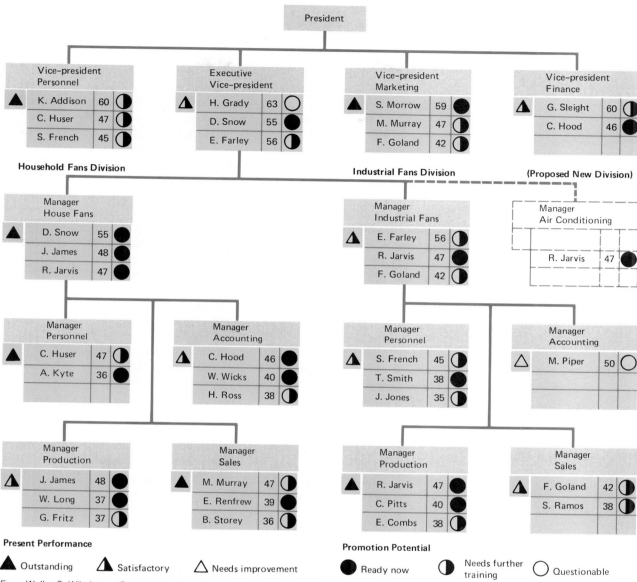

From Walter S. Wikstrom, "Developing Managerial Competence: Concepts, Emerging Practices," *Studies in Personnel Policy No. 189*, p. 9. Used with permission.

relative merits of one individual filling the position as compared to another? (management manpower replacement chart). Considering the answers to these three questions collectively should help to ensure the success of hiring-from-within decisions.

All Inventory Information Should Be Considered Collectively

Sources Outside the Organization

If for some reason a position cannot be filled by someone presently within the organization, numerous sources of prospective human resources are available outside the organization. Several of these sources are:

> 1. *Competitors*   One commonly tapped external source of human resources is competing organizations. Since there are several advantages to luring human resources away from competitors, this type of piracy has become a

Recruitment from Competition

common practice. Among the advantages are: (1) the competitor will have paid for the individual's training up to the time of hire; (2) the competing organization will probably be weakened somewhat by the loss of the individual; and (3) once hired, the individual becomes a valuable source of information regarding how to best compete with his or her former organization.

2. *Employment agencies*   An employment agency is an organization that specializes in matching individuals with organizations. These agencies help people to find jobs and organizations to find people. Employment agencies can be classified into two general types: public and private. Through the Wagner-Peyser Act of 1933, public employment agencies were created to assist the public in the employment process. The private employment agency, however, being a private enterprise, exists to make a profit. The private agency collects a fee from either the person hired or the organization once a hiring has been finalized.

3. *Readers of certain publications*   Perhaps the most widely addressed source of potential human resources is the readership of certain publications. To tap this source, recruiters simply place an advertisement in a suitable publication. The advertisement should describe the open position in detail and announce that the organization is accepting applications from qualified individuals. The type of position to be filled determines the type of publication in which the advertisement should be placed. The objective is to advertise in a publication whose readers would likely be interested in filling the position. An opening for a top-level executive might be advertised in *The Wall Street Journal,* whereas a training director opening might be advertised in the *Journal of Training and Development,* and an educational opening might be advertised in the *Chronicle of Higher Education.*

4. *Educational institutions*   Several recruiters go directly to educational campuses to interview students close to graduation. Liberal arts schools, business schools, engineering schools, junior colleges, and community colleges all have somewhat different human resources to offer. Recruiting efforts should focus on those schools with the highest probability of providing human resources appropriate for the open position.

Knowing the Law

Modern legislation has a major impact on organizational recruitment practices. For a recruitment effort to be successful, it must reflect the laws that govern it. In part, the Civil Rights Act passed in 1964 and amended in 1972 created the **Equal Employment Opportunity Commission (EEOC)** to enforce the laws established to prohibit discrimination on the basis of race, color, religion, sex, or national origin in employment practices. These practices include recruitment, hiring, firing, layoffs, and all other factors involved in employment. Although the Civil Rights Act and the EEOC are discussed in this section on recruitment, the effects of these two factors obviously extend too far beyond recruitment activities to be included here.

Equal opportunity legislation protects the rights of a citizen to work and to get a fair wage rate based primarily on merit and performance. The EEOC seeks to maintain the existence of these rights by holding labor unions, private employers, educational institutions, and governmental bodies responsible for their continuance. The four steps usually followed by the EEOC to hold organizations accountable are presented in figure 10.7.

In response to equal opportunity legislation, many organizations have begun **affirmative action programs.** Translated literally, affirmative action can be defined as positive movement. "In the area of equal employment opportunity, the basic purpose

Figure 10.7 Four steps followed by the EEOC to uphold equal opportunity legislation.

1. The EEOC receives a charge alleging employment discrimination. Such a charge can be filed by an individual, by a group on behalf of an individual, or by any of the EEOC commissioners. Primary consideration for processing the charge is given to an approved state or local employment practices agency, if one exists. This agency has 60 days in which to act on the charge (120 days if the agency has been in operation less than a year). In the absence of such an agency, the EEOC is responsible for processing the charge. If neither the local agency nor the EEOC has brought suit within 180 days of the official filing date, the charging party may request a right-to-sue letter by which to initiate private civil action.

2. The EEOC investigates the charge to gather sufficient facts to determine the precise nature of the employer or union practice. If these facts show *probable cause* to believe that discrimination exists, the EEOC initiates step 3.

3. The EEOC conciliates or attempts to persuade the employer to voluntarily eliminate the discrimination. In this regard, the EEOC will provide extensive technical aid to any employer or union in voluntary compliance with the law. If conciliation fails, the EEOC initiates step 4.

4. The EEOC files suit in federal court (or the aggrieved parties may initiate their own private civil action). Court-ordered compliance with Title VII usually results in large expenses for the employer, often exceeding the cost of voluntary affirmative action.

Gene E. Burton, Dev. S. Pathak, David B. Burton, "Equal Employment Opportunity: Law and Labyrinth," *Management World*, published by Administrative Management Society, Sept. 1976, pp. 29, 30.

of positive movement or affirmative action is to eliminate barriers and increase opportunities for the purpose of increasing the utilization of underutilized and/or disadvantaged individuals."[7] The organization can determine how well it is eliminating these barriers by (1) determining how many minority and disadvantaged individuals it presently employs, (2) determining how many minority and disadvantaged individuals it should employ according to EEOC guidelines, and (3) comparing how many minority and disadvantaged individuals are presently employed to how many the EEOC suggests should be employed.[8] If the two numbers compared in this third step are equivalent, employment practices within the organization probably should be maintained. If the two numbers are not equivalent, employment practices should be modified accordingly.

Back to the Case

As indicated earlier, a successful recruitment effort by Massie requires that he know where to locate sources of potential human resources to fill his open positions. These sources are both within Gamble Transportation and outside Gamble Transportation. To keep current on the possibilities for filling positions from within, Massie should maintain some type of human resources inventory. This inventory would help Massie to organize information regarding (1) the organizational histories and potential of various individuals at Gamble Transportation, (2) who at Gamble Transportation might be eligible to fill specific positions should the positions become open, and (3) the relative abilities of various individuals at Gamble Transportation to fill an opening. Sources of potential human resources outside Gamble Transportation that Massie should be aware of are competitors, public and private employment agencies, the readership of various flight-related publications, and various types of educational institutions. In addition to knowing these sources, Massie should also be aware of how the law should influence his recruitment efforts. Basically, the law says that recruitment practices at Gamble Transportation cannot discriminate on the basis of race, color, religion, sex, or national origin between sources of potential human resources. If Massie's recruitment practices are discriminatory, Gamble Transportation is subject to prosecution by the EEOC.

Figure 10.8 Summary of major factors involved in the selection process.

Stages of the Selection Process	Reasons for Elimination	Available potential personnel from inside or outside company
Preliminary screening from records, data sheets, etc.	Lack of adequate educational and performance record	
Preliminary interview	Obvious misfit from outward appearance and conduct	
Intelligence test(s)	Failure to meet minimum standards	
Aptitude test(s)	Failure to have minimum necessary aptitude	Rejection of potential employees
Personality test (s)	Negative aspects of personality	
Performance references	Unfavorable or negative reports on past performance	
Diagnostic interview	Lack of necessary innate ability, ambition, or other qualities	
Physical examination	Physically unfit for job	
Personal judgment	Remaining candidate placed in available position	Employee

L. C. Megginson, *Providing Management Talent for Small Business* (Baton Rouge, La.: Division of Research, College of Business Administration, Louisiana State University, 1961), p. 108.

Selection

Selection Follows Recruitment

The second major step involved in furnishing appropriate human resources for the organization is selection. **Selection** is choosing an individual to hire from all those who have been recruited. Hence, selection is dependent upon and follows recruitment.

The selection process typically is represented as a series of stages through which prospective employees must pass to be hired.[9] Each successive stage reduces the total group of prospective employees until, finally, one individual is hired. Figure 10.8 lists specific stages of the selection process; indicates reasons for eliminating prospective human resources at each stage; and illustrates how the group of potential personnel for an organization is narrowed down to the individual who ultimately becomes the employee. Two tools often used to aid the selection process are (1) testing and (2) assessment centers. A discussion of each of these tools follows.

Testing

Examining People

Testing can be defined as examining human resources for qualities relevant to performing available jobs. The purpose of testing is to increase the success of selecting human resources that are appropriate for the organization. Although many different kinds of tests are available for organizational use, they generally can be divided into four categories: aptitude tests, achievement tests, vocational interest tests, and personality tests.[10] The following paragraphs describe each type of test.[11]

Potential

Aptitude tests   These tests measure the potential of an individual to perform some task. Aptitude tests are diversified in that some measure general intelligence while others measure special abilities, such as mechanical, clerical, or sight. Figure 10.9 describes the eleven information areas covered by one aptitude test, the Wechsler Adult Intelligence Scale.

Skill Level

Achievement tests   Tests that measure the level of skill or knowledge an individual possesses in a certain area are called achievement tests. This skill or knowledge may have been acquired through various training activities or actual experience in the area.

Figure 10.9 The eleven information areas covered by the Wechsler Adult Intelligence Scale.

Verbal

1. Information. A series of open-ended questions dealing with the kinds of factual data people normally pick up in their ordinary contacts.
2. Comprehension. Another series of open-ended questions covering the individual's understanding of the need for social rules.
3. Arithmetic. All the questions are of the story or problem type. Scoring is for correctness of solutions and time to respond.
4. Digit Span. A group of numbers is read and the subject repeats them from memory, sometimes backward.
5. Similarities. Pairs of terms are read and a common property or characteristic must be abstracted.
6. Vocabulary. A series of words must be defined in the subject's own terms.

Performance

7. Picture Completion. A number of pictures are presented in which the subject must identify the missing component.
8. Picture Arrangement. Items require that a series of pictures be arranged as rapidly as possible in the order that makes the most sense.
9. Object Assembly. Jigsaw puzzles must be put together within a given time limit.
10. Block Design. Working with a set of small blocks having red, white, or red and white faces, the subject attempts to duplicate various printed designs as quickly as possible.
11. Digit Symbol. The subject is given a series of paired symbols and numbers as a code. The subject is then to write as many correct numbers as he or she can for each of a series of scrambled symbols within a set time period.

From *Personnel Psychology* by John B. Miner, 1969. Used by courtesy of the author.

Vocational interest tests   These tests attempt to measure an individual's interest in performing various kinds of activities and are administered on the assumption that certain people perform jobs well because the job activities are interesting to them. The basic purpose of this type of test is to help select those individuals who find certain aspects of an open position interesting.

> Activity Desirability

Personality tests   Personality tests attempt to describe an individual's personality dimensions, such as emotional maturity, subjectivity, or objectivity. Personality tests can be used advantageously if (1) the personality characteristics needed to do well in a particular job are well defined and if (2) individuals possessing those characteristics can be pinpointed and selected.

> Describing People

Several guidelines should be employed when using tests as part of the selection process. First, care should be taken to ensure that the test being used is both valid and reliable. A test is valid if it measures what it is designed to measure and reliable if it measures similarly time after time. Second, test results should not be used as the sole source of information to determine whether or not someone is hired. People change over time, and someone who doesn't score well on a particular test might still be developed into a productive future employee. Such factors as potential and desire to obtain a position should be assessed subjectively along with test scores in making the final selection decision. As a third guideline in using tests as part of the selection process, care should be taken to determine that tests used are nondiscriminatory in nature. "Many tests contain language or cultural biases which may discriminate against minorities."[12] This third guideline is especially important in that the EEOC has the authority to prosecute discriminatory testing practices within organizations.

> Using Tests Correctly

Assessment Centers

Another tool often used to help increase the success of employee selection is the assessment center. Although the assessment center concept is discussed in this chapter primarily as an aid to selection, it also has been used as an aid in such areas as human resources training and organization development. The first industrial use of the assessment center is usually credited to AT&T.[13] Since AT&T's initial efforts, the assessment center concept has been growing quickly and has been adopted by such companies as Merrill Lynch; Pierce, Fenner & Smith; Prudential Life Insurance; IBM; General Electric; and the J. C. Penney Company.[14]

Activities Are Performed   "An **assessment center** is a program, not a place, in which participants engage in a number of individual and group exercises constructed to simulate important activities at the levels to which participants aspire."[15] These exercises might include such activities as participating in leaderless discussion, giving some type of oral presentation, or leading a group in solving some assigned problem. Following the assessment center concept, individuals performing these activities are observed by managers or trained observers to evaluate both their ability and potential.[16] In general, participants are assessed on the basis of:

(1) leadership, (2) organizing and planning, (3) decision making, (4) oral and written communication skills, (5) initiative, (6) energy, (7) analytical ability, (8) resistance to stress, (9) use of delegation, (10) behavior flexibility, (11) human relations competence, (12) originality, (13) controlling, (14) self-direction, and (15) overall potential.[17]

Back to the Case

After Massie's initial screening of potential human resources, he is faced with selecting or choosing the individuals he wishes to hire from those who have been screened. Two tools that Massie can use to help him in this selection process are (1) testing and (2) assessment centers. Test results would tell Massie whether any individuals in his group of potential employees have the qualities relevant to being a good stewardess, freight handler, or airline mechanic. These tests could be aptitude tests, achievement tests, vocational interest tests, or personality tests. In using the tests, Massie must make sure that they are both valid and reliable, that they are not the sole basis on which he makes his selection decision, and that they are nondiscriminatory. The second selection tool, assessment centers, can be used by Massie to simulate tasks to be performed in the open positions. Individuals who perform these tasks the best would show some evidence of being more appropriate for Gamble Transportation than those individuals who do poorly.

Training

Developing Productive Abilities
After recruitment and selection, the next step in providing appropriate human resources for the organization is training. **Training** is the process of developing qualities in human resources that ultimately will enable them to be more productive and, thus, contribute more to organizational goal attainment. Hence, the purpose of training is to increase the productivity of individuals in their jobs by influencing their behavior. "Governmental agencies, industrial firms, volunteer organizations, educational institutions, and other segments of our society are placing more and more emphasis on the need to "train" human resources."[18]

Steps in the Training Process
The training of individuals is essentially a four-step process: (1) determining training needs, (2) designing the training program, (3) administering the training program, and (4) evaluating the training program. The relationship among these steps is presented in figure 10.10. Each of these steps is described in more detail in the paragraphs that follow.

Figure 10.10 Steps of the training process.

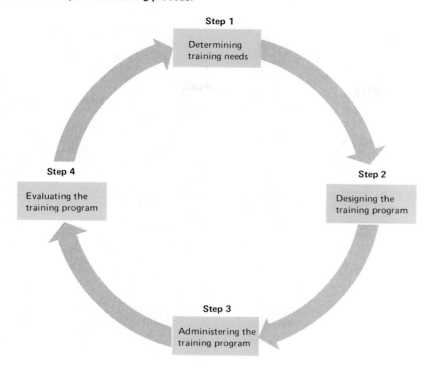

Determining Training Needs

The first step of the training process is determining the training needs that exist in an organization. **Training needs** are the information areas or skill areas of an individual or group that require further development to increase the organizational productivity of that individual or group. Only if training focuses on these needs can it be of some productive benefit to the organization.

What Are Training Needs?

Training organization members is typically a continuing activity. Even after individuals have been with an organization for some time and have undergone initial orientation and skills training, the need for continued human resources training cannot be overemphasized. Training at this stage is aimed at continually improving human resources skills.

Several methods of determining which skills to focus on for more established human resources are available. The first method is evaluating the production process within the organization. Such factors as excessive rejected products, deadlines that are not met, and high labor costs are clues to existing levels of production-related expertise. Another method for determining training needs is direct feedback from employees on what they feel are the organization's training needs. Organization members may be able to verbalize clearly and accurately exactly what types of training they need to help them do a better job. A third way of determining training needs involves looking into the future. If manufacturing new products or using newly purchased equipment is predicted, some type of corresponding training almost certainly will be needed.

How to Determine Training Needs

Designing the Training Program

Once training needs have been determined, a training program aimed at meeting those needs must be designed. Basically, designing a program entails assembling various types of facts and activities that will meet the established training needs. Obviously, as training needs vary, the facts and activities designed to meet those needs will vary.

Back to the Case

After Massie hires the individuals he wishes to employ, he must train them to be productive organization members. To train effectively, Massie must determine training needs, design a corresponding training program, and administer and evaluate the training program. Designing his training program requires that Massie assemble facts and activities that address training needs at Gamble Transportation. These training needs are simply information or skill areas that need to be further developed in individuals at Gamble Transportation to make them more productive. Massie also must realize, however, that, in the long run, training at Gamble Transportation should focus on the more established employees, rather than only on newer employees.

Administering the Training Program

The next step of the training process is administering the training program, or actually training the individuals. Various techniques exist for both transmitting necessary information and developing needed skills in training programs. Several of these techniques are discussed in the following section.

Techniques for Transmitting Information
Two main techniques for transmitting information in training programs are (1) lectures and (2) programmed learning. Although it probably could be argued that these techniques develop some skills in individuals as well as transmit information to them, they are presented in this chapter primarily as devices for the dissemination of information. Relative advantages and disadvantages of each technique are discussed.

Lectures   Perhaps the most widely used technique for transmitting information in training programs is the lecture. Bass and Vaughn define the **lecture** as a primarily one-way communication situation in which an instructor presents information to a group of listeners.[19] The instructor typically does most of the speaking in this type of training situation. Trainees participate primarily by listening and note taking.

An advantage of the lecture is that it allows the instructor to expose trainees to a maximum amount of information within a given time period. The disadvantages of the lecture have been stated as follows:

> The lecture generally consists of a one-way communication: the instructor presents information to the group of passive listeners. Thus, little or no opportunity exists to clarify meanings, to check on whether trainees really understand the lecture material, or to handle the wide diversity of ability, attitude, and interest that may prevail among the trainees. Also, there is little or no opportunity for practice, reinforcement, knowledge of results, or overlearning.
>
> Ideally, the competent lecturer should make the material meaningful and intrinsically motivating to his or her listeners. However, whether most lectures achieve this goal is a moot question.
>
> These limitations, in turn, impose further limitations on the lecture's actual content. A skillful lecture may be fairly successful in transmitting conceptual knowledge to a group of trainees who are ready to receive it; however, all the evidence available indicates that the nature of the lecture situation makes it of minimal value in promoting attitudinal or behavioral change.[20]

Programmed Learning   Another commonly used technique for transmitting information in training programs is called programmed learning. According to Silvern, **programmed learning** is a technique for instructing without the presence or intervention of a human instructor.[21] Small parts of information that necessitate related responses are presented to individual trainees. Trainees can determine from the accuracy of their responses whether their understanding of the obtained information is accurate. The types of responses required of trainees vary from situation to situation but usually are multiple choice, true-false, or fill-in-the-blank. Figure 10.11 shows a portion of a programmed learning training package that could be used to familiarize trainees with PERT (Program Evaluation and Review Technique).

Learning Independently

As with the lecture method, programmed learning has both advantages and disadvantages. Among the advantages are that students can learn at their own pace, know immediately if they are right or wrong, and participate actively. The primary disadvantage of this method is that there is nobody to answer a question for the learner should a question arise.

Advantages and Disadvantages of Using Programmed Learning

Techniques for Developing Skills

Techniques for developing skills in training programs can be divided into two broad categories: (1) on-the-job techniques for developing skills and (2) classroom techniques for developing skills. Techniques for developing skills on the job usually are listed under the title **on-the-job training.** These techniques are a blend of job-related knowledge and experience in using that knowledge and include coaching, position rotation, and special project committees. Coaching is direct critiquing of how well an individual is performing a job, while position rotation involves moving an individual from job to job to obtain an understanding of the organization as a whole. Special project committees involve assigning a particular task to an individual to furnish the individual with experience in a designated area.[22]

Coaching, Position Rotation Special Project Committees

Techniques for developing skills in the classroom are also a blend of both job-related knowledge and experience in using that knowledge. The skills addressed via these techniques can range from technical skills, such as computer programming, to interpersonal skills, such as leadership. Specific techniques aimed at developing skills in the classroom include various types of management games and a diversity of role-playing activities. The most common format for management games requires small groups of trainees to make and then evaluate various management decisions. The role-playing format typically involves acting out and then reflecting upon some people-oriented problem that must be solved in the organization.

Knowledge and Experience in the Classroom

Contrary to the typical one-way communication role in the lecture situation, the skills instructor in the classroom encourages high levels of discussion and interaction among trainees; develops a climate in which trainees learn new behavior from carrying out various activities; acts as a resource person in clarifying related information; and facilitates learning via job-related knowledge and experience in applying that knowledge.[23] The difference between the instructional role used in information dissemination and the instructional role used in skill development is dramatic.[24]

Evaluating the Training Program

After the training program has been completed, it should be evaluated for its effectiveness. Because training programs represent a cost investment, management should obtain some reasonable return. Costs include materials, trainer time, and production loss due to individuals being trained rather than doing their job.

Does Training Pay?

Figure 10.11 Portion of a programmed learning training package emphasizing PERT.

Frame 3²⁴

Program evaluation and review technique, PERT, is performed on a set of time-related activities and events which must be accomplished to reach an objective. The evaluation gives the expected completion time and the probability of completing the total work within that time. By means of PERT, it is possible not only to know the exact schedule, but also to control the various activities on a daily basis. Overlapping and related activities are reviewed. PERT is more practical for jobs involving a one-time effort than for repeat jobs. It is a planning-controlling medium designed to: (1) focus attention on key components, (2) reveal potential problem areas, (3) provide a prompt reporting on accomplishments, and (4) facilitate decision making.

The time-related activities and events are set forth by means of a PERT network (see figure 17). In this illustration, the circles represent events that are sequential accomplishment points; the arrows represent activities or the time-consuming elements of the program. In this type of network, an arrow always connects two activities. All of the activities and events must be accomplished before the end objective can be attained. The three numbers shown for each arrow or activity represent its estimated times, respectively, for the optimistic, most likely, and pessimistic times. The program starts with event no. 1 and ends with event no. 12. From calculations for the time required for each path

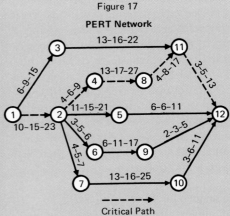

Figure 17

PERT Network

Critical Path

from no. 1 to no. 12, it is found that path 1-2-4-8-11-12 requires the *longest time* and, hence, is the *critical path* because it controls the time required to complete the program. Toward it, managers would direct their attention in order to: (1) ensure that no breakdowns occur in it; (2) better the current times required, if possible; and (3) trade off time from the noncritical paths to the critical path, if the net effect is to reduce total time of the critical path.

Indicate whether each of the following statements is true or false by writing "T" or "F" in the space provided.

_____1. PERT centers its attention on social constraints.
_____2. PERT is best applied to assembly-line operations.
_____3. In PERT, the *critical path* is the path that requires the longest time.
_____4. In the PERT network, circles represent events and the arrows represent activities.

Now turn to Answer Frame 3²⁴, page 146.

Answer frame 3²⁴

1. False. PERT centers its attention on *time* constraints.
2. False. PERT is more practical for jobs involving a one-time effort than for repeat jobs.
3. True. In PERT, the critical path is the path that requires the *longest* time. If this path can be shortened, the program can be completed in a shorter time period.
4. True. Circles represent events that are sequential accomplishment points, and arrows represent activities or the time-consuming elements for the program.

You have completed chapter 24. Now turn to chapter 25.

Figure 10.12 Descriptions of several methods of performance appraisal.

Name of Appraisal Method	Description
Rating scale	Individuals appraising performance use a form containing several employee qualities and characteristics to be evaluated (e.g., dependability, initiative, leadership). Each evaluated factor is rated on a continuum or scale ranging, for example, from one to seven or more points.
Employee comparisons	Appraisers rank employees according to such factors as job performance and value to the organization. Only one employee can occupy a particular ranking.
Free-form essay	Appraisers simply write down their impressions of employees in paragraph form.
Critical–form essay	Appraisers write down particularly good or bad events involving employees as these events occur. Records of all documented events for any one employee are used to evaluate his or her performance.

Compiled from *Personnel Administration and Human Resource Management* by Andrew F. Sikula (New York: John Wiley & Sons, Inc., 1976), pp. 208–11.

Basically, the training program must be evaluated to determine if it meets the needs for which it was designed. Perhaps answers to such questions as the following will help to determine training program effectiveness:

1. Has the excessive reject rate declined?
2. Are deadlines being met more regularly?
3. Are labor costs per unit produced decreasing?

If the answer to questions such as these is yes, the training program would seem successful, but perhaps its effectiveness could be enhanced through certain selective changes. If, on the other hand, the answer is no, some significant modification to the training program certainly is warranted.

Back to the Case

After Massie has determined training needs and designed his training program, he must administer and evaluate the program. To administer the program Massie can use either the lecture or programmed learning technique for transmitting information to his trainees. For actually developing skills in his trainees he could use on-the-job training methods, such as coaching or position rotation. For developing skills in the classroom he could use various techniques, such as role-playing activities. For example, he could place future stewardesses in the roles of specific situations involving customers. These situations could then be acted out and analyzed from the viewpoint of how to improve stewardess-customer relationships. Once the training program is over, Massie must determine if it met the training needs for which it was designed. Massie's approach during this evaluation should always emphasize improving the training program.

After individuals have been recruited, selected, and trained, the task of making them productive individuals within the organization is not finished. The fourth step in the process of providing appropriate human resources for the organization is performance appraisal. **Performance appraisal** is the process of reviewing individuals' past productive activity to evaluate the contribution they have made towards attaining management system objectives. As with training, performance appraisal is a continuing activity and focuses on the relatively new as well as the more established human resources within the organization. One of its main purposes is to furnish feedback to organization members about how they can become more productive. Performance appraisal also has been called performance review or performance evaluation. Names and descriptions of several methods of performance appraisal are shown in figure 10.12.

Why Use Performance Appraisals?

Better than three out of every four firms in the United States use some type of performance appraisal system.[25] This use of performance appraisals in the overwhelming majority of firms can be considered some indication of the high importance that most managers place on them. Douglas McGregor has set forth the following three reasons for performance appraisals in an organization:

1. They provide systematic judgments to support salary increases, promotions, transfers, and sometimes demotions or terminations.
2. They are a means of telling a subordinate how he or she is doing and of suggesting needed changes in behavior, attitudes, skills, or job knowledge; they let the subordinate know where he or she stands with the boss.
3. They also are being used increasingly as a basis for the coaching and counseling of the individual by the superior.[26]

Handling Performance Appraisals

If performance appraisals are not handled well, their benefit to the organization is minimized. Fortunately, several guidelines can assist in increasing the appropriateness of the way in which performance appraisals are conducted.[27] The first of these guidelines is that performance appraisals should stress both performance within the position the individual holds and the success with which the individual is attaining objectives. Performance and objectives should become inseparable topics of discussion during performance appraisals. As a second guideline, appraisals should emphasize the individual in the job and not the evaluator's impression of observed work habits. In other words, emphasis should be more on the objective analysis of performance than on the subjective evaluation of habits. Guideline three is that the appraisal should be acceptable to both the evaluator and the evaluatee. Both individuals should agree that the appraisal can be of some benefit both to the organization and the worker. The last guideline is that performance appraisals should be used as the basis for improving individual productivity within the organization.[28] Emphasis on performance appraisal should be on making individuals more valuable to the organization by making them better equipped to produce.[29]

Potential Weaknesses of Performance Appraisals

To maximize the potential payoff of performance appraisals to the organization, several potential weaknesses of the appraisal process should be avoided. As indicated by George A. Rider, these potential *weaknesses* are that (1) individuals involved in performance appraisals could view them as a reward-punishment situation; (2) the emphasis of performance appraisal could be put on completing paperwork rather than critiquing individual performance; and (3) some type of negative reaction from a subordinate could be generated when the evaluator offers any unfavorable comments.[30] Exhibit 10 complements this discussion on potential weaknesses of performance appraisal by focusing on several related issues that managers like Bill N. Rutherford of the Sun Company battle continually.

Management can avoid these potential weaknesses of the appraisal process. First, supervisors and employees must view the performance appraisal process as an opportunity to increase the worth of the individual through constructive feedback, not as a means of rewarding or punishing individuals through positive or negative comments. Second, paperwork should be seen only as a tool to aid in providing this feedback and not as an end in itself. Third, care should be taken to make appraisal feedback as tactful and objective as possible. This tact and objectivity should help to minimize any negative reactions of the evaluatee.[31]

Women are being hired in increasing numbers to fill blue-collar positions in organizations.[32] One reason women desire to fill such jobs is that pay for performing them is typically well above pay for performing jobs more traditionally held by women. Naturally, organizations are increasing their hiring of women to fill such positions for many varied reasons. One important reason may be that the Office of Federal Contract Compliance Programs has set a mandatory guideline that requires that a proportion of women must work on all federally financed construction projects.[33]

Regardless of the reasons for this emerging movement of women working in blue-collar jobs that traditionally were held by men, managers must cope with the problem of how to integrate such women workers successfully into the organization. One program aimed at handling this problem was developed by Nancy R. Brunner.[34] According to Brunner, such a program should include two primary phases: (1) pre-hire preparation and (2) post-hire activities. Each of these elements is discussed here.

Pre-Hire Preparation

Phase one of this program to integrate women workers into the organization successfully is called pre-hire preparation. Pre-hire preparation involves getting the women ready to come into the organization as well as making the organization ready for women's entry. Included in this preparation are the following:

Job analysis—to define job responsibilities clearly, identify specific training needs, and develop job-proficiency guides. The guides outline expected increases in performance competence and the skills that must be demonstrated at each successive level of improvement.

Interview/selection training—to prepare supervisors for involvement in the selection of women and enable them to help define the job-related dimensions that candidates capable of performance and growth in the organization should have.

Workshops for the men (first-line supervisors and craft workers)—to begin to dispel myths about women workers and develop positive solutions for overcoming barriers.

Pre-selection counseling and tour for women candidates—to familiarize women with the specific nature of craft work, to show them the areas in which they would be working, and to provide them an opportunity for self-assessment of their readiness for entering the trades.

Planning for technical training and for followup—to provide the women with structured training experiences immediately upon reporting to work, and to prepare to offer them needed support services.[35]

Integrating Blue-Collar Women: A Special Problem

Women Working New Jobs

Phases of Integration

Getting Women and Organizations Ready

Exhibit 10

Managers and Consultants Appraise Performance Appraisals

Bill N. Rutherford (Photo: Steven Goldblatt)

Consulting psychologist Harry Levinson tells the story of the newly appointed executive who was told to get a floundering division into the black. This he accomplished with alacrity, only to find himself passed over for promotion because top management felt that his managerial style had been too high-handed. The problem, Levinson says, was that the executive expected to be judged on results, while his superiors judged him on the means by which those results were achieved.

Levinson's story may be apocryphal, but it illustrates one of the major problems plaguing human resources specialists: how to get the mixed signals out of performance appraisal. Although few experts say that appraisal systems should ignore whether specific job goals are achieved, most are wrestling with ways to assure that performance appraisal does more than simply determine salaries. They want a system that will pinpoint specific managerial behavior that should be reinforced or discontinued, serve as a personnel development tool, provide realistic assessment of an employee's potential for advancement, and—a particularly hot issue in the 1980s—stand up in court as a valid defense in discrimination suits.

Finding expertise. Developing such systems is no easy task. "We've struggled with performance appraisal more than with any other process in the company," says Bill N. Rutherford, human resources vice-president for Sun Co. Selig M. Danzig, program manager for human resources systems development at General Electric Co., wonders whether "looking for a truly effective system is the same as pursuing the Holy Grail." Many companies are seeking expert help to get their systems on the right track. "Over the last three years I've done nearly 70 [assignments to set up] performance appraisals, where I used to do no more than six a year," notes Daniel E. Lupton, a principal at Towers, Perrin, Forster & Crosby Inc. . . .

Wider involvement. To Sun's Rutherford, simply adding one more opinion does not go nearly far enough. To obtain a performance appraisal on one select group of executives, he sounded out their subordinates, peers, and bosses. "Performance appraisal is really about telling people how they are perceived," he maintains, adding that the immediate superior's view of the subordinate's work and image is often too narrow. Rutherford hopes to create a similar comprehensive appraisal program for approximately 200 high-level Sun executives by the end of this year. He believes it will take much longer than that for the system to filter down to lower levels.

Not surprisingly, few companies are as ambitious as Sun or GE in developing new approaches to appraisal. But quite a few are looking to "hybrid systems" that are neither overly costly to develop nor difficult to administer. These would include more than simple checklists of personality traits for supervisors to rattle off, and combine the best of both job-result and behavioral appraisals.

By far the most common are the type of goal-setting and review systems that Rohrer's Chinnici espouses. As recently as three years ago, Rohrer rated employees as either outstanding, satisfactory, or marginal, and nitpicked over such issues as whether they came to work on time. "We didn't get into what the real expectations were," he says.

Similarly, V. N. Anderson, sales vice-president for E. R. Squibb & Sons Inc., introduced a goal-based system for his sales force in April. "Our performance reviews had always been historic," he explains. "Now we're looking to the future, making the appraisal system provide employees with tools to help them perform better." For example, if a sales representative's over-the-counter drug sales are low, the appraisal process would establish a quota of in-store presentations for him or encourage him to meet six new store clerks each month.

Evaluating appraisers. Such systems put a large part of the developmental onus on the appraising manager, of course. The manager is motivated, proponents of the goal systems say, by the realization that his superior's appraisal of his own performance will take into account how well he or she evaluates and develops his own staff. At Dover Corp.'s Elevator Div., appraisers are expected to list the most important tasks their subordinates perform and evaluate how well they do them, describe strengths and weaknesses in relative detail, and lay out specific agendas to improve performance in the employee's current job and prepare him or her for promotion. It is a formidable task, but the personnel director Jurgensen notes, "The form evaluates the appraiser as well as the appraisee." Jurgensen's staff reviews more than 400 appraisals each year, and the company's president looks at close to 100. "Supervisors know they are 'graded' on the appraisals, and it makes them think and express themselves in ways that are almost competitive," Jurgensen says.

One factor favoring the goal-setting appraisal technique is that its own objectives are built in. Many attempts at appraisal bog down, psychologists say, when the system developers are not quite sure what they want to accomplish. "A good part of the problem with existing systems," notes Booz's Carlson, "is that people don't know why they're doing them—whether it is to make compensation decisions, to do succession planning, career planning, or instant promotion decisions." GE's Danzig states it another way: "The appraisal process can be improved significantly if you decide whether it is there to satisfy the manager's needs or the subordinate's. You can't ask a manager to be a judge and mentor at the same time." He notes that an appraisal system geared to career development should probably give the subordinate an opportunity to participate in filling out his or her own appraisal form. An appraisal designed essentially for salary increases can be conducted solely by the supervisor without the employee's participation.

The blank sheet. The perfect appraisal system has not been developed, largely because no one yet knows how to factor out human error. The behavioral systems run the risk of a "halo effect"—supervisors basing a summary judgment on one or two dramatic quirks or habits of the employee. Goal-oriented systems often ignore external factors—for example, a windfall order that helps a salesman exceed a quota or adverse economic conditions that prevent him from fulfilling a quota. Even the much-maligned checklist

Judging behavior is harder and more costly than judging results

systems, in which employees are rated on specific traits, run the risk that supervisors may feel they must give all their subordinates high ratings.

Perhaps Arthur W. Alexander, vice-president and director of personnel at Schlumberger Ltd., sums up the problems best. He and the company's chief operating officer have made a big point of discussing the importance of performance appraisal at general management meetings, and the systems used in his company seem to have an enviable mix of concrete goals and behavioral evaluations. "We've tried to whittle away at the third-grade report-card evaluation of 'works and plays well with others,' but we still do not have the best forms," he says. "The best form would be a blank sheet of paper."

Reprinted from the May 19, 1980 issue of *Business Week* by special permission, © 1980 by McGraw-Hill, Inc., New York, NY 10020. All rights reserved.

Post-Hire Activities

Phase two of this program to integrate women workers successfully into the organization is called post-hire activities. This phase focuses on women after they have been hired. In essence, activities in this phase are aimed at helping newly hired women workers adapt to their new environment. Management designs these activities and requires the involvement of both men and women from various organizational positions and levels. These activities include the following:

What to Do after Hiring

Orientation for women selected—to orient them to the job environment, connect them with women already in non-traditional work, and acquaint them with available support services (such as counseling).

General technical training—to enable the women to meet basic job requirements.

On-the-job craft training—to facilitate the development of task-specific job skills needed to improve performance at each stage or skill level.

Periodic counseling for the women—to monitor the progress of their entry into the workplace and provide guidance as needed.

Followup sessions with the men—to monitor adaptation of male workers to having women on board and to provide guidance as needed.

Rap sessions with both men and women—to discuss and solve possible tensions between men and women workers and other problems as needed.

Periodic management discussions with the women, their trainers, and supervisors—to monitor individual and group progress and to demonstrate ongoing support.

Periodic evaluation and revision—to measure results and identify program elements that need to be changed or strengthened.[36]

The main focus of this chapter has been on explaining the generally accepted steps in providing appropriate human resources for the organization: (1) recruitment; (2) selection; (3) training; and (4) performance appraisals. This section implies that managers periodically will face special human resource problems that force them to complement these steps with additional activities. Naturally, integrating female blue-collar workers into the organization is one such problem that managers are presently facing.

Massie's last step in providing appropriate human resources for Gamble Transportation is performance appraisal. This means that Massie must evaluate the contributions that organization members make to the attainment of management system objectives. As with the training effort, Massie should focus performance appraisal effort on more established employees as well as on new employees. His performance appraisals should stress both an individual's activity on the job as well as the individual's effectiveness in accomplishing job objectives. Massie also should design his appraisals to be as objective as possible and should strive to increase the productivity of his stewardesses, freight handlers, and airplane mechanics with tactfully given constructive criticism. Massie must understand that performance appraisals should not be used as a chance to reward or punish an individual but as an opportunity to make the individual more valuable to the organization. In addition, Massie will probably have to take special pre-hire as well as post-hire steps to get maximum organizational benefit from blue-collar workers who are women.

Back to the Case

The following points are stressed within this chapter:

Summary

1. Providing appropriate human resources means that individuals who can make a valuable contribution to organizational goal attainment are furnished for the organization. Basically, providing these resources entails four sequential and related steps: (1) recruitment, (2) selection, (3) training, and (4) performance appraisal.

2. Recruitment involves the initial screening of prospective employees and necessitates an understanding of the job to be filled, where potential sources of human resources can be located, and how the law influences recruiting efforts.

3. Selection, the second major step in providing appropriate human resources for the organization, is choosing an individual to hire from those who have been recruited. Tests and assessment centers are often used as aids in the selection process. Tests can be divided into four types: (1) aptitude tests, (2) achievement tests, (3) vocational interest tests, and (4) personality tests. Assessment centers engage trainees in various activities. Their performance is then judged to determine the degree of appropriateness of the trainee to the organization.

4. Training, the third major step in providing appropriate human resources for the organization, is the process of developing individual characteristics that ultimately will enable employees to be more productive and, thus, contribute more to organizational goal attainment. The training process involves determining training needs, designing the training program, administering the training program, and evaluating the training program.

5. Performance appraisal is the fourth major step in providing appropriate human resources for the organization. Performance appraisal is the process of reviewing an individual's activity to evaluate his or her contribution to reaching organizational objectives. One of the most important purposes of performance appraisals is to furnish feedback to organization members on how they can become more productive.

6. Integrating female blue-collar workers is a special human resource problem modern managers currently face. Both pre-hire preparation and post-hire activities should be performed to ensure that these women are integrated smoothly within the organization.

Issues for Review and Discussion

1. What is the difference between "appropriate" and "inappropriate" human resources?
2. List and define the four major steps in providing appropriate human resources for the organization.
3. What is the purpose of recruitment?
4. How are job analysis, job description, and job specification related?
5. List the advantages of promotion-from-within.
6. Compare and contrast the management inventory card, the position replacement form, and the management manpower replacement chart.
7. List three sources of human resources outside the organization. How can these sources be tapped?
8. Does the law influence organizational recruitment practices? If so, how?
9. Describe the role of EEOC.
10. Can affirmative action programs be useful in recruitment? Explain.
11. Define selection.
12. What is the difference between aptitude tests and achievement tests?
13. Discuss three guidelines for using tests in the selection process.
14. What are assessment centers?
15. List and define the four main steps of the training process.
16. Explain two possible ways of determining organizational training needs.
17. What are the differences between the lecture and programmed learning as alternative methods of transmitting information in the training program?
18. On-the-job training methods include coaching, position rotation, and special project committees. Explain how each of these methods works.
19. What are performance appraisals and why should they be used?
20. If someone asked your advice on how to conduct performance appraisals, describe in detail what you would say.
21. What pre-hire preparation and post-hire activities can be performed to integrate female blue-collar workers into the organization?

Sources of Additional Information

Belasco, James A., and Trice, Harrison M. *The Assessment of Change in Training and Therapy.* New York: McGraw-Hill, 1969.

Brinkerhoff, Derick W., and Kanter, Rosabeth Moss. "Appraising the Performance of Performance Appraisal." *Sloan Management Review,* Spring 1980, pp. 3–16.

Broadwell, Martin M. *The Supervisor and On-The-Job Training.* Reading, Mass.: Addison-Wesley, 1969.

Bursk, Edward C., and Blodgett, Timothy B., eds. *Developing Executive Leaders.* Cambridge, Mass.: Harvard University Press, 1971.

Cronback, Lee J. *Essentials of Psychological Testing.* 3d ed. New York: Harper & Row, 1970.

Drucker, Peter F. *The Effective Executive.* New York: Harper & Row, 1967.

Dunnette, Marvin D. *Personnel Selection and Placement.* Belmont, Calif.: Wadsworth Publishing Company, 1966.

Franklin, William H., Jr. "Why Training Fails." *Administrative Management* 42, no. 7 (July 1981): 42–43, 72–74.

Guion, Robert M. *Personnel Testing.* New York: McGraw-Hill, 1965.

Henderson, Richard. *Compensation Management.* Reston, Va.: Reston Publishing Co., 1976.

Holland, Joan, and Curtis, Theodore. "Orientation of New Employees." In *Handbook of Modern Personnel Administration,* edited by Joseph Famularo. New York: McGraw-Hill, 1972.

Jennings, Eugene Emerson. *Executive Success.* New York: Appleton-Century-Crofts, 1967.

Lebreton, Preston. "The Management Awareness Concept: A Missing Link in the Evolving Science of Management." *Managerial Planning* 30, no. 1 (July/August 1981): 12–17.

Lopez, Felix M., Jr. *Personnel Interviewing: Theory and Practice.* New York: McGraw-Hill, 1965.

Mandell, Milton M. *The Selection Process: Choosing the Right Man for the Job.* New York: American Management Association, 1964.

O'Callaghan, John C., Jr. "Human Resource Development." *Managerial Planning* 30, no. 1 (July/August 1981): 38–42.

Odiorne, George A. *Training by Objectives.* New York: Macmillan, 1960.

Teel, Kenneth S. "Performance Appraisal: Current Trends, Persistent Progress." *Personnel Journal,* April 1980, pp. 296–301, 316.

Tracey, William R. *Evaluating Training and Development Systems.* New York: American Management Association, 1968.

1. "Job Analysis," *Bureau of Intergovernmental Personnel Programs,* December 1973, pp. 135–52.

2. Arch Patton, "The Coming Scramble for Executive Talent," *Harvard Business Review* 45, no. 3 (May/June 1967): 155–71.

3. Thomas J. Murray, "The Coming Glut in Executives," *Dun's Review,* May 1977, p. 64.

4. Fred K. Foulkes, "How Top Nonunion Companies Manage Employees," *Harvard Business Review,* September/October 1981, p. 90.

5. John Perham, "Management Succession: A Hard Game to Play," *Dun's Review,* April 1981, pp. 54–55, 58.

6. Walter S. Wikstrom, "Developing Managerial Competence: Concepts, Emerging Practices," *Studies in Personnel Policy no. 189,* National Industrial Conference Board, pp. 95–105.

7. Ray H. Hodges, "Developing an Effective Affirmative Action Program," *The Journal of Intergroup Relations* 5, no. 4 (November 1976): 13.

8. James M. Higgins, "The Complicated Process of Establishing Goals for Equal Employment," *Personnel Journal,* December 1975, pp. 631–37.

9. Everett Dillman, "A Behavioral Science Approach to Personnel Selection," *Academy of Management Journal,* June 1967, pp. 185–98.

10. For information on various tests available, see O. K. Buros, ed., *The Sixth Mental Measurements Yearbook* (Highland Park, N.J.: Gryphon Press, 1965).

11. This section is based on Andrew F. Sikula, *Personnel Administration and Human Resource Management* (New York: John Wiley & Sons, 1976), pp. 188–90.

12. Gene E. Burton, Dev S. Pathak, and David B. Burton, "Recruiting, Testing and Selecting: Delicate EEOC Areas," *Management World,* October 1976, p. 30.

13. D. W. Bray and D. L. Grant, "The Assessment Center in the Measurement of Potential for Business Management," *Psychological Monographs* 80, no. 17 (1966): 1–27.

14. James C. Hyatt, "More Concerns Use 'Assessment Centers' to Gauge Employees' Managerial Abilities," *The Wall Street Journal,* 3 January 1974, p. 15.

15. Barry M. Cohen, "Assessment Centers," *Supervisory Management,* June 1975, p. 30.

16. For information about strengths and weaknesses of assessment centers, see C. W. Millard and Sheldon Pinsky, "Assessing the Assessment Center," *Personnel Administrator,* May 1980, pp. 85–88.

17. Ann Howard, "An Assessment of Assessment Centers," *Academy of Management Journal* 17, no. 1 (March 1974): 117.

18. Gordon L. Lippitt, "Criteria for Evaluating Human Resource Development," *Training and Development Journal,* October 1976, p. 3.

19. Bernard Bass and James Vaughn, *Training in Industry: The Management of Learning* (Belmont, Calif.: Wadsworth Publishing Co., 1966).

20. Bass and Vaughn, *Training in Industry.*

21. Leonard Silvern, "Training: Man-Man and Man-Machine Communications," in *Systems Psychology,* ed. Kenyon DeGreen (New York: McGraw-Hill, 1970), pp. 383–405.

22. For more information on these and other on-the-job training techniques, see Edwin B. Flippo, *Principles of Personnel Management* (New York: McGraw-Hill, 1971), pp. 211–16.

23. Samuel C. Certo, "The Experiential Exercise Situation: A Comment on Instructional Role and Pedagogy Evaluation," *The Academy of Management Review,* July 1976, pp. 113–16.

24. For more information on instructional roles in various situations, see Bernard Keys, "The Management of Learning Grid for Management Development," *Academy of Management Review,* April 1977, pp. 289–97.

25. Winston Oberg, "Making Performance Appraisal Relevant," *Harvard Business Review,* January/February 1972, pp. 61–67.

26. Douglas McGregor, "An Uneasy Look at Performance Appraisal," *Harvard Business Review,* September/October 1972, pp. 133–34.

27. Harold Koontz, "Making Managerial Appraisal Effective," *California Management Review* 15, no. 2 (Winter 1972): 46–55.

28. Thomas L. Whisler, "Appraisal as a Management Tool," in *Performance Appraisal: Research and Practice,* eds. Thomas L. Whisler and Shirley F. Harper (New York: Holt, Rinehart & Winston, 1962).

29. William J. Birch, "Performance Appraisal: One Company's Experience," *Personnel Journal,* June 1981, pp. 456–60.

30. George A. Rider, "Performance Review: A Mixed Bag," *Harvard Business Review,* July/August 1973, pp. 61–67.

31. John D. Colby and Ronald L. Wallace, "The Art of Leveling with Subordinates about Their Performance," *Supervisory Management,* December 1975, pp. 26–29.

32. Women's Bureau, New York City, U.S. Department of Labor, 1980.

33. "The Hardships That Blue-Collar Women Face," *Business Week,* 14 August 1978, p. 88.

34. The remainder of this section is primarily based on Nancy R. Brunner, "Blue-Collar Women," *Personnel Journal,* April 1981, p. 279–82.

35. Ibid., p. 281.

36. Ibid.

Notes

Concluding Case 10
Spotting Potential "Superstars" at NCR, Entex, and Sun Oil

A psychological test probes whether your personality is "adventurous." A questionaire assesses your opinion of your driving skills. An interview with a psychologist and a mental-ability test reveal even more. Is all of this activity a screening process for would-be astronauts? No, these are just some of the techniques being used by business organizations today to spot employees that are executive material; those young employees who can move quickly into upper-management positions.

According to Donald G. Carlson, vice-president of Booz, Allen & Hamilton Inc., management consultants, many companies are recognizing the importance of identifying potential superstars early. Some companies have devised elaborate methods of finding executive material among their great numbers of employees. According to Carlson, top management became interested in this area after the 1974 recession. During 1979 and 1980, interest in devising methods of finding in-house executive material picked up to a greater extent. This search for young executives has come about in part due to the high expense of recruiting managers from outside of the company. As a result, companies are attempting to develop their own executives. Development Dimensions International, a Pittsburgh consulting firm, believes, in addition, that higher-level jobs have become increasingly complex. In order to meet the demands of such jobs, people must be identified early and groomed to fit the job. If not, they will not have the appropriate preparation in order to survive.

NCR Corporation of Dayton, Ohio, is one of those firms trying to find young employees who can move quickly into upper-management positions. In the last two years, NCR has selected twenty-four people and has made a special effort to move them through a series of managerial positions to diversify their training. The program is described as an early-identification program. NCR is attempting to find as early as possible those individuals with a strong potential for general management. Very few of the twenty-four individuals are aware that they have been selected, even though NCR is watching their careers carefully.

Entex Inc. of Houston attempts to identify candidates with top executive potential during their campus-recruiting process. According to Tom Burke, vice-president of personnel, the company's main concern is a candidate's I.Q. If they find a student with a 4.0 grade point average, they know she or he most likely has a high I.Q. If an individual is hired and his or her personality is not appropriate, then they let that person go.

NCR has used a different approach. Rather than selecting high-potential managers directly out of school, they identify them after they have been working for awhile. NCR searched through the records of 4,000 young employees to find 828 whose performance was high. Each was mailed a letter that identified them as a top performer. They were then asked to fill out and return a biographical questionnaire and a psychological exercise entitled the Strange Interest Inventory. The biographical questionnaire was designed to associate the employee's background and interest in relationship to those of successful NCR managers. For example, in a biological questionnaire given to NCR executives, it was found they had few hobbies in high school but led an active social life. The psychological test was designed to demonstrate whether or not an individual could move from a specialty job (engineering or salesman) to a more general position (upper management). In addition, the company continues to use tests and a program called the assessment center to help spot promotable people. The assessment center uses a series of tests, communication groups, and job simulation experiences to assess people's advancement potential.

After NCR found the 828 high performers, it then used these tests, interviews, and assessment center results to reduce the number to 100. The program was developed in the 1970s with the help of a Minneapolis consulting firm. The assessment center program has been administered to over one thousand middle and upper-level managers at NCR. Not only does it help select "superstars" it also helps the managers identify their strengths and weaknesses.

Sun Co., an oil company in Radnor, Pennsylvania, has taken a different approach. The company compiles a dossier on each of the top 150 managers in the company to identify candidates for key jobs. Bill N. Rutherford, vice-president of human resources, interviewed subordinates, peers, and superiors who know the person well and then compiled a report on each manager. Questions such as the following were asked (1) How does he react when things don't go well? (2) How strong is she conceptually? (3) What does he seem to stand for?

After the interviews were completed, a copy of the manager's composite report was given to top management. It was also made available to the employee. According to Rutherford, in many cases the data confirmed hunches of the top executives and only made them more comfortable with their decisions.

This case is adapted from Bernard Wysoki, "Talent Hunt: More Companies Try to Spot Leaders Early and Guide Them to the Top," *Wall Street Journal,* 25 February 1981, pp. 1, 23.

Discussion Issues

1. At which step in the providing of appropriate human resources does NCR identify potential "superstars?" Entex? Sun Oil?
2. Are there other steps in which these people could be identified? Explain.
3. How successful do you think NCR's method is for identifying potential top managers?
4. What other methods would you suggest to select potential top managers?

Student Learning Objectives

From studying this chapter I will attempt to acquire:

1. A working definition of "changing an organization"
2. An understanding of the relative importance of change and stability to an organization
3. An appreciation for both internal and external diagnoses of what should be changed in an organization
4. Some ability to know what type of change should be made within an organization
5. An appreciation for why individuals affected by a change should be considered when making the change
6. Some facility in evaluating change

Chapter Outline

Changing an Organization

Introductory Case 11
A Change in the Editorial Department

Jackson Company is a small New York City publisher. The company produces a monthly technical magazine aimed at approximately 28,000 design engineers who receive the magazine free of charge. In other words, the circulation is controlled and fixed. This magazine requires the coordination of personnel in advertising, sales, research, promotion, circulation, and editing. Because the magazine is distributed free, advertising provides all revenue. The main concern is with the activities of the editorial department.

The general atmosphere that prevailed in the editorial department was one of informality and casualness. There was considerable freedom from formal controls despite the monthly deadline dates for completion of manuscripts. Each of the nine editors was a highly skilled engineer-writer with extensive specialized experience in one or more distinct fields of engineering. Aside from editing and revising articles received from outside authors, a good deal of original work was done by individual editors.

Top management recognition of the editors' technical superiority and encouragement of their individual abilities resulted in their preferential treatment—freedom of movement, choice offices, individual secretaries—which enhanced their feeling of superiority and set the editorial group apart from the rest of the company. Interaction with the other departments was kept at a minimum. Within the small editorial group, however, there was considerable solidarity and cooperation, and the nature of their duties required continuous interaction.

The editor-in-chief, Alistair King, solicited, accepted or rejected articles from outside authors, coordinated and directly supervised his department, revised manuscripts, scheduled and allocated work among his editors, and performed other administrative tasks. No systematic method of planned scheduling or follow-up of written material had been devised to handle the flow of work in and out of the department. Deadlines were frequently ignored, monthly issues of the magazine were consistently coming out late, complaints were received from the readers, advertisers, company salespeople, and other departments in which work had been delayed. The editorial department, for the most part, ignored these complaints.

To correct this situation, an editorial programmer, Douglas Niles, was hired to serve as the right-hand man to King. Niles's duties were to relieve King and the technical editors of production scheduling details and routines. He was to supervise the editorial production section and to have overall supervision of the editorial secretaries as a group, reporting absences, tardiness, and general deportment of the secretaries directly to the personnel department. However, it was made clear to the editors at the beginning that the new programmer was not to supervise them but to work with them in facilitating the flow of copy to production. He would have no authority to issue orders to them; suggestions and proposed changes in methods or procedures would be presented to the editor-in-chief, and all instructions would be issued only through Alistair King.

A systematic routing and scheduling procedure was devised. A schedule board of articles, dates, and names of editors was set up to show the stage of progress of each article. Editors were required to report proposed field trips well in advance and to keep Niles informed as to manuscript progress. Copyreading for style uniformity; checking dummy pages, galleys, and page proofs; issuing reminders to editors on due dates for copy; and maintenance of editor production records were some of the additional duties of Doug Niles.

Briefly, the procedure worked something like this. An article came in from an author and was accepted by King. The manuscript was passed to Niles, who recorded it and assigned it to a particular editor. Manuscript and artwork were then edited and returned to Niles, who read them for uniformity of style and then either returned them to the editor for revision or sent them to King for checking and approval. The manuscript was then returned to Niles, who expedited it through production, checked dummies, page proofs, and artwork, and then released it to the printers.

In September and October, the first two months following the installation of the new system, no appreciable change in work-flow speed was evident. The magazine was still being held up on account of late manuscripts and other difficulties. But after Niles had oriented the editors in the procedures and had had a chance to put the new system into operation, the editors found that a good part of their routine work was being relieved and they were able to concentrate on the more important aspects of their jobs. They found themselves able to handle their work more efficiently and without sacrificing good-quality standards. Therefore, in November, December, and January, the magazine came out on the first day of each month, or even one or two days before the first. In February, however, and in subsequent months, a reversion to the old pattern of lateness and overstepped deadlines took place and persisted despite the heroic efforts of Niles to correct the situation.

Management was baffled by this latest turn of events. No one seemed able to pinpoint the problem.

Robert E. C. Wegner, Leonard Sayles, CASES IN ORGANIZATIONAL AND ADMINISTRATIVE BEHAVIOR, © 1972, pp. 30–32. Reprinted by permission of Prentice-Hall, Inc., Englewood Cliffs, New Jersey.

Discussion Issues

1. Did the editorial department need to be changed? Why?
2. Evaluate the change made in the editorial department.
3. Evaluate the process used to make this change.
4. In your opinion, why did ''the old pattern of lateness and overstepped deadlines'' eventually return to the editorial department?

What's Ahead

Alistair King, the editor-in-chief of Jackson Company in the introductory case, had the main role in both deciding upon what change to make in the editorial department and actually making the decided-upon change.

In this regard, King and any other manager who has faced the task of modifying an organization would have found the information in this chapter extremely valuable. The major issues involved in changing an organization are discussed in two sections: (1) "Fundamentals of Changing an Organization" and (2) "Factors to Consider When Changing an Organization."

Fundamentals of Changing an Organization

Thus far, discussion in this section of the text has centered on the fundamentals of organizing, furnishing appropriate human resources for the organization, authority, delegation, and responsibility. This chapter focuses on changing an organization. The fundamental principles involved in changing an organization are discussed in the paragraphs that follow.

Defining "Changing an Organization"

Change for Organizational Effectiveness

"Changing an organization" is the process of modifying an existing organization. The purpose of organization modifications is to increase organizational effectiveness; that is, the extent to which an organization accomplishes its objectives. These modifications can involve virtually any organizational segment and typically include changing the lines of organizational authority, the levels of responsibility held by various organization members, and the established lines of organizational communication.

Managers Must Make Changes

Most managers agree that if an organization is to be successful, it must change continually in response to significant developments, such as changes in customer needs, technological breakthroughs, and new government regulations. The study of organizational change is extremely important because all managers at all organizational levels are faced throughout their careers with the task of changing an organization. According to a study by Ronald Daniel, major American manufacturers make major changes in their organizations approximately once every two years.[1] Managers who can make changes successfully are highly valued in organizations of all types.[2]

Employees Can Provide Ideas for Change

Many managers consider change to be so critical to the success of the organization that they encourage employees to continually search for areas in which beneficial organizational change can be made. Within the General Motors Corporation, for example, employees are provided with a "think list" to encourage them to develop ideas for organizational change and to remind them that change is extremely important to the continued success of GM. The "think list" contains the following questions:

1. Can a machine be used to do a better or faster job?
2. Can the fixture now in use be improved?
3. Can materials handling for the machine be improved?
4. Can a special tool be used to combine the operations?
5. Can the quality of the part being produced be improved by changing the sequence of the operation?
6. Can the material used be cut or trimmed differently for greater economy or efficiency?

Figure 11.1 Adaption, stability, and organizational survival.

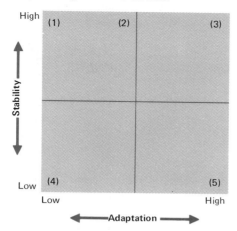

(1) High death probability (slow)
(2) High survival probability
(3) High survival and growth probability
(4) Certainty of death (quick)
(5) Certainty of death (quick)

7. Can the operation be made safer?
8. Can paperwork regarding this job be eliminated?
9. Can established procedures be simplified?[3]

Change vs. Stability

In addition to organizational change, some degree of stability is a prerequisite for long-run organizational success. Figure 11.1 presents a model developed by Hellriegel and Slocum that shows the relative importance of change and stability to organizational survival. Although these authors use the word *adaption* in their model rather than *change,* the two terms are essentially synonymous. This model stresses that an organization has the greatest probability of survival and growth when both stability and adaption are high within the organization (number 3 on the model). The organization without stability to complement or supplement change is at a definite disadvantage. When stability is low, the probability for organizational survival and growth declines. Change after change without stability typically results in confusion and employee stress.[4]

Stability Should Complement Change

Back to the Case

Assuming that Alistair King followed the recommendations made in this first section of the chapter, some of the events that preceded and eventually resulted in King changing the editorial department could be described as follows: in his deliberations on changing the department, King considered only those modifications that would further facilitate the accomplishment of Jackson Company objectives. King realized that if the editorial department was to have continued success, he would probably have to modify it a number of times over the long run. In fact, appropriate change is so important to the editorial department and to Jackson Company as a whole that King considered initiating some type of program that would encourage employees to submit their ideas on how the effectiveness of the editorial department could be increased. When considering possible changes, however, King realized that some level of stability was also necessary if both his department and Jackson Company were to survive and grow over the long run.

Figure 11.2 The collective influence of five major factors on the success of changing an organization.

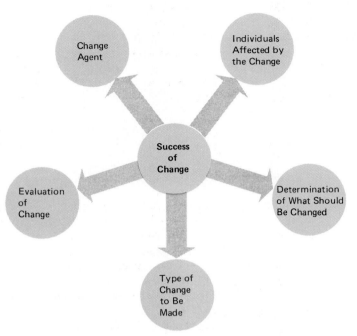

Factors to Consider When Changing an Organization

How managers deal with the major factors to be considered when changing an organization determines to a great extent how successful an organizational change will be. These major factors are (1) the change agent, (2) determination of what should be changed, (3) the type of change to make, (4) individuals affected by the change, and (5) evaluation of change. Although the following sections discuss each of these factors individually, figure 11.2 makes the point that their collective influence ultimately determines the success of a change.

The Change Agent

What Is a Change Agent?

Perhaps the most important factor to be considered by managers when changing an organization is determining who will be the change agent. The term *change agent* refers to anyone inside or outside the organization who tries to effect change.[5] The change agent might be a self-designated manager within the organization or possibly an outside consultant hired because of a special expertise she or he possesses in a particular area. Although in reality the change agent may not be a manager, the terms *manager* and *change agent* are used synonymously throughout this chapter.

Skills of a Change Agent

Several special skills are necessary to be a successful change agent. The most often discussed of these skills include the abilities to (1) determine how a change should be made, (2) solve change-related problems, and (3) use behavioral science tools to influence people appropriately during the change. Perhaps the most overlooked skill necessary to be a successful change agent is deciding how much change organization members can withstand. As indicated by the following excerpt, too much change can be very disturbing to people:

> Millions of psychologically normal people will experience an abrupt collision with the future when they fall victim to tomorrow's most menacing malady—the disease of change. Unable to keep up with the supercharged pace of change, brought to the edge of breakdown by insistent demands to adapt to novelty, many will plunge into future shock. For them, the future will arrive too soon.[6]

Overall, managers should choose change agents who possess the most expertise in areas suggested by the special skills mentioned in the preceding paragraph. A potentially beneficial change for the organization might not result in any advantages if the wrong person is designated to make the change.

Back to the Case

Since King is assumed to have the main role in both deciding upon what changes to make in his department and actually making the changes, he was the change agent in the case. King designated himself as change agent because of his abilities to determine how a change in the editorial department should be made, solve departmental problems that could arise because of the change, use behavioral science tools to influence department members appropriately during the change, and determine how much change department members could withstand. King thought that these abilities would enable him to make successful changes in the editorial department.

Determination of What Should Be Changed

Another major factor managers should consider is exactly what should be changed within the organization. In general, managers should make changes that increase organizational effectiveness.

According to Giegold and Craig, organizational effectiveness is primarily the result of organizational activities centering around three main classes of factors: (1) people, (2) structure, and (3) technology.[7] **People factors** are defined as attitudes, leadership skills, communication skills, and all other characteristics of the human resources within the organization. Organizational controls, such as policies and procedures, constitute **structural factors,** while **technological factors** are any types of equipment or processes that assist organization members in the performance of their jobs.

What Are People, Structural, and Technological Factors?

For an organization to maximize effectiveness, appropriate people must be matched with appropriate technology and appropriate structure. Thus, people factors, technological factors, and structural factors are not independent determinants of organizational effectiveness. Instead, as shown in figure 11.3, organizational effectiveness is determined by the relationship among these three factors.

To increase organizational effectiveness, then, managers must increase the appropriateness of the relationship among people, structure, and technology within the organization. Two commonly used steps managers can take to help determine what changes would increase the appropriateness of this relationship are conducting (1) an internal organizational diagnosis and (2) an external organizational diagnosis.

Increasing Organizational Effectiveness

Figure 11.3 Determination of organizational effectiveness by interrelationship between people, technological, and structural factors.

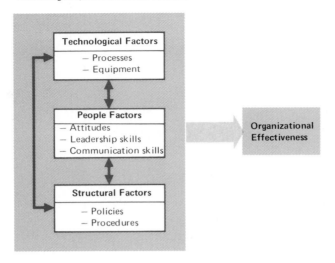

Internal Organizational Diagnosis

Looking within an Organization

An **internal organizational diagnosis** is the examination of all factors within an organization that relate to the effectiveness of the organization. People, technology, and structure, as discussed earlier, are the primary focus of this examination. The relationship among these three variables is studied in an attempt to pinpoint and implement changes that will make the relationship more appropriate for the organization. Increasing the appropriateness of this relationship will enhance organizational effectiveness.

Gathering Information

Gathering information on the appropriateness of this people-structure-technology relationship is the key to conducting an internal diagnosis. In practice, managers can adopt many different strategies to gather this information. For example, they can design and conduct special interviews with various organization members. The purpose of the interviews would be to determine how organization members perceive the people-structure-technology relationship within the organization and to gather suggestions on how to make this relationship more appropriate. Another strategy managers might use is reviewing various types of recorded organizational documents. Organization charts, job descriptions, policies, and procedures can furnish managers with information vital to determining how a people-structure-technology relationship can be improved. A third often-used strategy for gathering this information is to ask organization members to fill out specially designed questionnaires. As with the selection tests discussed in chapter 10, these questionnaires must be both valid and reliable. Figure 11.4 is an example of a questionnaire designed to investigate employee interest in work innovation.

External Organizational Diagnosis

Looking outside the Organization

An **external organizational diagnosis** is the process of examining all outside factors that relate to organizational effectiveness. External diagnosis is essentially an analysis of the environment in which the organization functions. The purpose of external diagnosis is to ascertain the potential impact of organizational environment on organizational effectiveness. Managers use this assessment when deciding how to best increase the appropriateness of the relationship among people, structure, and technology within the organization.

Figure 11.4 Questionnaire designed to investigate employee interest in work innovation.

Interest in Work Innovation Index

The first characteristic of people at work which we wished to assess is interest in work innovation. From an organizational point of view, much benefit can come from a search by employees at all levels for better ways to do things. For individuals, a continuing interest in innovation may represent an alertness which permits them to use well their minds and their abilities. For employees, interest in innovation may be also an indicator of general interest and involvement in their job.

Questionnaire Items

The following items appear to be the best indicators of interest in innovation (numbers in parentheses preceding each response category indicate the score assigned to each response):

1. In your kind of work, if a person tries to change his or her usual way of doing things, how does it generally turn out?
   (1)___Usually turns out worse; the tried and true methods work best in my work.
   (3)___Usually doesn't make much difference.
   (5)___Usually turns out better; our methods need improvement.

2. Some people prefer doing a job in pretty much the same way because this way they can count on always doing a good job.
   Others like to go out of their way in order to think up new ways of doing things. How is it with you on your job?
   (1)___I always prefer doing things pretty much in the same way.
   (2)___I mostly prefer doing things pretty much in the same way.
   (4)___I mostly prefer doing things in new and different ways.
   (5)___I always prefer doing things in new and different ways.

3. How often do you try out, on your own, a better or faster way of doing something on the job?
   (5)___Once a week or more often.
   (4)___Two or three times a month.
   (3)___About once a month.
   (2)___Every few months.
   (1)___Rarely or never.

4. How often do you get chances to try out your own ideas on your job, either before or after checking with your supervisor?
   (5)___Several times a week or more.
   (4)___About once a week.
   (3)___Several times a month.
   (2)___About once a month.
   (1)___Less than once a month.

5. In my kind of job, it's usually better to let your supervisor worry about new or better ways of doing things.
   (1)___Strongly agree.
   (2)___Mostly agree.
   (4)___Mostly disagree.
   (5)___Strongly disagree.

6. How many times in the past year have you suggested to your supervisor a different or better way of doing something on the job?
   (1)___Never had occasion to do this during the past year.
   (2)___Once or twice.
   (3)___About three times.
   (4)___About five times.
   (5)___Six to ten times.
   (6)___More than ten times had occasion to do this during the past year.

From Martin Patchen, *Some Questionnaire Measures of Employee Motivation and Morale*, pp. 15–16. Copyright © 1965 by the Institute for Social Research, The University of Michigan. Used with permission.

For an external diagnosis, the environment is typically divided into and analyzed at two distinct levels: (1) the operating environment and (2) the general environment.[8] Figure 11.5 depicts the relationship among the general environment, the operating environment, and the organization. The **operating environment** is usually of more immediate concern to managers and contains such factors as organization customers,

More Immediate Concern

Figure 11.5 Relationship between the organization, the operating environment, and the general environment.

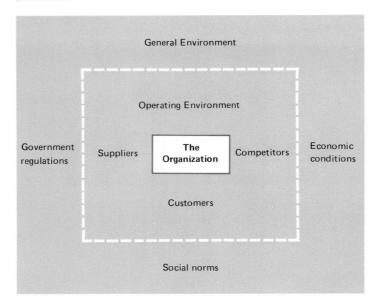

suppliers, competitors, and investors. The organization has direct interaction with and is directly influenced by factors in the operating environment.

The **general environment** is the secondary organizational environment and contains such variables as social norms, economic conditions, and government regulations. Factors in the general environment influence the organization indirectly and can also influence factors in the operating environment. Although the general environment is typically of less immediate concern to managers than the operating environment, it still can have a significant impact on organizational effectiveness and therefore should be considered carefully when deciding what changes to make within an organization. As an example, exhibit 11(a) presents an attempt by Lee A. Iacocca, chairman of the board of Chrysler Corporation, to explain the detrimental impact of various factors in Chrysler's general environment on the effectiveness of internal changes that are being made within the organization itself. According to Iacocca, high interest rates on borrowed money and the social norms regarding free trade and the limited role of government in foreign competition within the automobile industry are immediate barriers to Chrysler's success.

As the internal organizational diagnosis, the external organizational diagnosis requires managers to gather pertinent information. The methods of gathering this information are highly diversified and include such activities as (1) reviewing governmental reports relating to unemployment and economic conditions, (2) analyzing consumer satisfaction with products sold, and (3) comparing the major products of the organization to those of competitors.

It is extremely important that managers weigh the results of both the internal and external organizational diagnoses when finally deciding on how to change the organization to increase organizational effectiveness.

King considered changing only three departmental factors that could increase organizational effectiveness. He finally decided upon which factors to change as a result of information gathered during internal organizational diagnosis and external organizational diagnosis. The internal diagnosis focused on the appropriateness of the people-structure-technology relationship within the editorial department and emphasized such information-gathering techniques as interviewing editors, reviewing organizational documents, and using properly designed and administered questionnaires. External diagnosis, on the other hand, assessed Jackson Company's environment to determine its potential impact on organizational effectiveness and stressed such information-gathering techniques as reviewing appropriate government reports, analyzing consumer satisfaction with Jackson's publications, and comparing Jackson's publications with those of its competitors. As a result of the analysis of information from these diagnoses, King finally decided (as seen in the introductory case opening this chapter) to implement and maintain more of an emphasis within the editorial department on production scheduling and supervision.

The Type of Change to Make

Three Types of Change

The type of change to make is a third major factor managers should consider when changing an organization. Although managers can choose to change an organization in many different ways, most changes can be categorized as one of three types: (1) people change, (2) structural change, and (3) technological change. These three types obviously correspond to the three main determinants of organizational effectiveness and are named for the one determinant that the change emphasizes over the other two. For example, **technological change** emphasizes modifying the level of technology within a management system. In general, a manager's choice of the type of change to make within an organization should be based on the results of internal and external organizational diagnosis. For example, if information gathered by conducting organizational diagnoses suggests that organizational structure is the main cause of organizational ineffectiveness, managers should choose to emphasize structural changes within the organization. Since technological change most often involves outside experts and highly technical language, structural change and people change are the two types discussed in more detail here.

Structural Change

Structural change primarily emphasizes increasing organizational effectiveness by changing controls that influence organizational members during the performance of their jobs. The following sections further describe this approach and discuss matrix organizations (organizations modified to complete a special project) as an example of structural change.

Describing Structural Change
Structural change is aimed at increasing organizational effectiveness through modifications to existing organizational structure. These modifications can take several forms: (1) clarifying and defining jobs; (2) modifying organizational structure to fit the communication needs of the organization; and (3) decentralizing the organization to reduce the cost of coordination, increase the controllability of subunits, increase motivation, and gain greater flexibility.[9] Although structural change must include some consideration of people and technology to be successful, its primary focus is obviously on changing organizational structure. In general, managers would choose to make structural changes within the organization if information gathered from internal and

Emphasis on Organization Structure

Exhibit 11(a)

Give Us a Chance to Compete

Iococca is chairman of the board of the Chrysler Corp. (Photo: UPI Photos)

Everybody these days is an expert on automobile imports. We welcome the debate, but some of the ivory-tower stuff I've been reading lately needs an answer. I read that if our government does anything at all to reduce the flood of Japanese cars into this country, it will stand as a violation of the sacred principles of free trade, and will take away the basic right of all Americans to buy anything they want, no matter where it's produced.

The fact is that they don't have that right now, nor does any nation on earth grant it to its people—especially when it devastates a basic domestic industry and puts hundreds of thousands out of work.

Everybody misses that point. There is something wrong when Americans are laid off and the Japanese are working overtime. There is something wrong when this nation pays $2 billion in special welfare (the Trade Readjustment Allowance) so we can all buy Japanese cars. There is something wrong when they can ship cars here but we can't ship cars there.

The answer is not tariffs or a trade war. And it certainly is not more of what we have now. The answer is a little voluntary recovery time so we can get back on our feet and compete head to head with anybody in the world.

Oil: Let's face the fact that the automobile industry is in trouble largely on account of United States Government actions such as keeping the price of gasoline artificially low, and piling on regulations that are costly to comply with. But it is not a fact that a cold-turkey withdrawal from every kind of government intervention is necessarily good for the industry's health.

It is important to remember that the government changed the oil-price rules in the middle of the game, throwing us all into a five-year, $80 billion rebuilding program. That's how long it takes and that's how much it costs to convert to a whole new fleet of smaller, fuel-efficient cars that will offset the overnight doubling of gasoline prices.

We can complete that transition and meet the market. But we can't stay alive in the meantime if our market is handed over to an importer who lives by the rules of one-way trade. I know the conventional wisdom says that the Japanese simply work harder for less pay, taking breaks only to sing the company song—with the result that the United States buyer gets cheaper cars.

The fact is that the Japanese give their car makers a tax break on the cars they ship into this country. Through this tax break alone, a Japanese car that sells for about $7,000 in Japan can be sold in this country for about $6,300. Try doing that with one of our cars over there. The price doubles.

Japan has given the stiff-arm to United States cars for the last twenty years. In addition to a variety of hidden trade barriers, they slap a 20 percent "indirect" commodity tax on cars sold in Japan—a tax that is scheduled to increase to 22.5 percent in May.

There is something wrong when American workers are laid off and the Japanese are working overtime.

That's not free trade. That's a one-way street that has created an annual trade deficit with Japan of $11.2 billion on cars and trucks alone, and has cost us $2 billion a year in TRA payments to laid-off workers.

The rest of the world won't have that. *No other country gives imported vehicles a tax-related price advantage over its own.* The Common Market countries hang a 10.8 percent tariff on imported cars, plus a value-added tax ranging from 13 percent in Germany to 33 percent in France.

We're the only country that says: let them in, the more the better! As a result, the United States leads all industrialized nations in the size of its trade deficits, the number of workers unemployed and the number of large corporations in basic industries fighting for their lives.

Some people argue that restricting the number of Japanese cars sold in this country would hype the price of United States cars. That's just not so. We sell cars in a very tough market. We had competitive pricing over here long before the first boatload of Japanese cars docked in California. And we'll continue to have it in the future.

Others argue that cutting down the flood of Japanese cars would help only the workers in Detroit. Do we still have to be reminded that the automobile industry accounts for one out of every six jobs across the country? Not just the jobs of autoworkers, but hundreds of thousands of jobs in America's basic industries: steel, iron, rubber, aluminum, glass, machine tools, plastics and electronics. Thousands of small companies—suppliers and dealers— depend on the auto industry.

Free Enterprise: They're all sick, and they need help. The help should come in the form of a voluntary marketing agreement to hold imports to 1977–78 levels for two or three years. After that, take the gloves off. Free enterprise forever. We can compete. Yankee ingenuity is still alive and well. But we do need time to get up off the canvas and catch our breath.

Import restraint is not the full answer to the industry's problems. A lower prime rate would be even better. But it is time for a little common sense. We ought to ask the Japanese to voluntarily limit the number of cars they ship here while our nation's largest industry gets back on its feet. If we don't, I think we'll face a demand by the people for a much more restrictive and damaging system of import controls from which we can never retreat.

Evidently President Reagan thinks so, too. Last fall, when he visited Detroit, I stood beside him when he said: "There is a place where government can be legitimately involved—and this is where I think government has a role that has been shirked so far, and that is, to convince the Japanese that, in one way or another and in their own best interest, the deluge of their cars into the United States must be slowed while our industry gets back on its feet."

I think the man meant what he said. And he does have a way of cutting through the philosophical baloney. It's time for the rest of us to leave the ivory tower too. Like all Americans, the people in the auto industry want a fair shot at keeping their jobs. I think they ought to have that chance.

Figure 11.6 Portion of a traditional organizational structure based primarily on product.

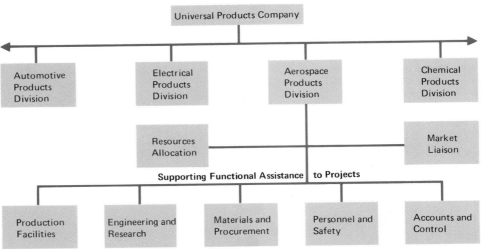

Copyright, 1964, by the Foundation for the School of Business at Indiana University. Reprinted by permission.

external organizational diagnoses indicates that the present organizational structure is the main cause of organizational ineffectiveness. The precise structural change managers should make would vary from situation to situation of course.

Matrix Organizations

Special Projects

Perhaps structural change is best illustrated by describing matrix organizations. According to C. J. Middleton, a **matrix organization** is a more traditional organization that is modified primarily for the purpose of completing some type of special project.[10] For this reason, matrix organizations are also called project organizations. The project itself may be either long run or short run, with employees needed to complete the project borrowed from various organizational segments.

An Example of Matrix Organizations

John F. Mee has developed an excellent example showing how a more traditional organization can be changed into a matrix organization.[11] Figure 11.6 presents a portion of a traditional organizational structure divided primarily according to product line. Although this organizational design might be generally useful, managers could learn through internal organizational diagnosis that this design makes it impossible for organization members to give adequate attention to three government projects of extreme importance to long-run organizational success.

Figure 11.7 presents one way of changing this more traditional organizational structure into a matrix organization to facilitate completion of these three government projects. A manager would be appointed for each of the three projects and allocated personnel with appropriate skills to complete the project. The three project managers would have authority over personnel assigned to them and be accountable for the performance of those personnel. Each of the three project managers would be placed on the chart in figure 11.7 in one of the three boxes labeled Venus Project, Mars Project, and Saturn Project. As a result, work flow related to each project would go from right to left on the chart. After the projects are completed, the organization chart could be changed back to its original design, if more advantageous.

Advantages and Disadvantages

Several advantages and disadvantages to making structural changes such as those reflected by the matrix organization can be cited. Among the major advantages are the claims that such structural changes generally result in better control of a project, better customer relations, shorter project-development time, and lower project costs.

Organizing

Figure 11.7 Traditional organization chart transformed into matrix organization.

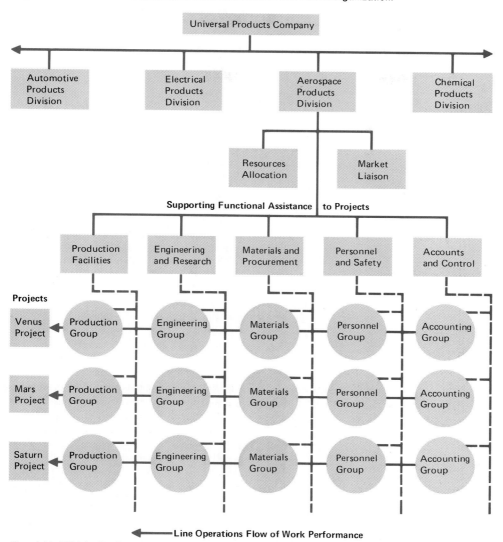

Line Operations Flow of Work Performance

Accompanying these advantages, however, are the claims that such structural changes also generally create more complex internal operations, encourage inconsistency in the application of company policy, and actually result in an overall more difficult situation to manage.[12] One point, however, is clear. In order for a matrix organization to be effective and efficient, organization members must be willing to learn and execute somewhat different organizational roles.[13] The significance of these advantages and disadvantages relative to the success of changing a specific organization obviously vary from situation to situation.

Exhibit 11(b) presents an example of how Andrew O. Manzini, vice-president at Ebasco Services, Inc., has developed an approach to minimize such disadvantages.

Exhibit 11(b)

Andrew O. Manzini (Photo: Thom O'Connor)

Matrix management, a system that adds horizontal reporting rquirements to the traditional vertical chain of command, has become increasingly popular at companies that manage complex construction projects. Under a matrix system an engineer, for example, may have to satisfy several bosses. For the construction manager, he must design products that perform well. For the project manager, he must consider scheduling necessities, component costs, and other bottom-line factors. Reconciling the obvious clashes that erupt from such conflicting priorities is a formidable task. Indeed, many companies have abandoned matrix management for that reason.

But Andrew O. Manzini, vice-president for human resources for Ebasco Services, Inc., Enserch Corp.'s energy-oriented engineering and consulting arm, has developed an approach to minimize the confusion. Three years ago an extensive internal study turned up mounting friction caused by the matrix system at Ebasco's nuclear sites. Since then, Manzini and his organizational development (OD) staff have been implementing a veritable laundry list of training and troubleshooting programs to lessen the chaos. And while follow-up surveys of Ebasco

How Manzini Makes the Matrix Method Work at Ebasco Services, Inc.

managers show that matrix-caused problems have by no means been eradicated, they also show that tensions at the project sites have been reduced dramatically.

'Facilitators' intervene to resolve disputes over conflicting priorities

That is no mean feat in light of the problems peculiar to nuclear power-plant projets. Most such projects take more than a decade from start to finish, and changing government regulations and roadblocks can throw schedules awry at any point. Moreover, reporting requirements constantly change as the project moves from one stage to another. For example, project engineers, construction supervisors, and the like can find themselves responsible to the reactor building manager while they are working on that section of the project, and to the manager of another physical area the following month. To compound the confusion, Ebasco's employees must also interrelate with the client's employees at every step along the way.

Defusing conflicts. Although these multiple pressures make cooperation essential, team members tend to be protective of their specialties and can be resentful and suspicious of colleagues with different priorities. Much of Manzini's effort has gone to defusing the emotional side of the conflicts, paving the way for the basic issues to be resolved.

Although dollar-and-cents results of Manzini's programs remain almost impossible to quantify, accolades from Ebasco insiders and outsiders alike clearly show that he has been on the right track. Ebasco's new 45-hour supervisory development course has so impressed the New York State Board of Regents that "graduates" receive college credit. The success of the company's "facilitators" in smoothing relations among Ebasco personnel has led clients to ask Manzini to intervene in their own staff conflicts. Indeed, President and Chief Executive Officer William Wallace III is using organizational development people to run some of his own meetings.

The OD-sponsored programs have been as diverse as the problems they were developed to solve. Since the original study highlighted the misunderstandings both from and about matrix systems, the OD staff has held more than 100 formal seminars to explain that structure to employees. It has put in a dual-performance evaluation program to ensure that employees who report to two bosses are evaluated by both. That way the employee cannot be penalized by a supervisor who says he has been recalcitrant in following orders, for example, when in fact he was given conflicting instructions by another supervisor.

Employees are also receiving a measure of reassurance from a complex computerized career tracking program in which their skills are matched against Ebasco's projected staffing needs. The program will give Ebasco early warning of manpower shortages. And it will give employees the comfort of knowing that their strengths are on record in a skills bank, ready to be tapped as promotions become available.

The hands-on way. While most of these programs are easily directed from Manzini's New York office, the OD staff is also taking a hands-on approach to solving problems in the field. The group has conducted some 60 "team-building interventions" in which an OD facilitator meets with project personnel who are in conflict. He asks each person for his or her perception of the cause of conflict and then leads a meeting in which those conflicts are resolved. Manzini notes that more than once facilitators have been called in to resolve "personality conflicts" between construction and project managers—and found that the trouble stemmed from faulty scheduling of materials. In those cases, the facilitator helps the managers work out a new scheduling system.

Of course, attitudes and behavior sometimes are the source of trouble. And when this kind of problem is brewing, Ebasco managers are increasingly calling facilitators in as preventive medicine. Robert K. Stemple, project manager for a nuclear power plant Ebasco is building for Louisiana Power & Light Co. in New Orleans, had been directing the project from New York, leaving the on-site management to the construction manager in New Orleans. Then the construction manager resigned, and LP&L requested that Stemple move down to the site. "Project managers are rarely located on-site, and I knew the construction people would consider my presence a threat," he recalls.

Stemple's solution was to involve the project's top 15 people in a two-day team-building session with Manzini. "He started off the meeting by giving us one of those brain-teaser questions that nobody could solve," Stemple recalls. "With all of us feeling dumb, a nonthreatening atmosphere was established." In that atmosphere, both sides relaxed and were able to exorcise some of their prior resentments and fears. The net result made Stemple more comfortable with the move.

Following the example. David B. Lester, LP&L's project manager at the plant, also has used Ebasco's OD people to facilitate meetings. "Not only can outside facilitators keep a meeting on track, but when there is friction, the participants can get angry at the facilitator, not at each other," he says.

Indeed, Ebasco's top echelon has started to use a team-building approach of its own. As part of an "executive development program," OD facilitators periodically interview Wallace and some 12 members of his senior corporate staff to ask about areas in Ebasco that need improvement, then coordinate a two-day meeting to

discuss what actions can be taken on problems that had been pinpointed during the interviews. Although this program was originally meant to be a vehicle to "educate top executives on personnel issues," Wallace recalls, it has so far concentrated more on getting regional offices involved in long-range planning and other strategic areas. "We will eventually look at matters of motivation, but for now we can't really let personnel development take priority over discussions on how to proceed in synfuels and the like," he explains.

The benefits. Few Ebasco managers are complaining that personnel development is suffering from neglect, however. The new supervisory development program is getting high marks from graduates, for example. It combines lectures on planning, delegating, communicating, and other people-oriented aspects of management with self-scored tests that help supervisors learn to handle hypothetical management problems. Graduates say they gain a better understanding of how their management styles affect their employees.

Dual evaluation: a fair shake for the worker who reports to two bosses

For example, Merrill W. Grogel, an expediting supervisor, notes that during the course he was able to analyze the persistent conflicts he had been having with one of his subordinates. He came to realize that he had been looking over the man's shoulder constantly and that this was the cause for the antagonism. "I thought I was giving him the benefit of my knowledge, but he thought I was belittling him," Grogel admits. Since then, Grogel says, he has given the subordinate a longer leash and now has a smoother running department.

Still, none of the new programs has proved to be a panacea for resolving all conflicts, and the matrix system remains not only a fuzzy concept but also a thorny one to many employees. "Technical employees still feel a good technical job is most important, and engineers feel they're spending too much time reporting, planning, scheduling, and budgeting," admits Wallace. Indeed, even Stemple, an obvious OD enthusiast, notes that "you lose enthusiasm with time. The problem is keeping up everyone's commitment to [cooperation]."

Manzini and the OD staff have a long way to go before their human-resource innovations can make all aspects of the matrix system trouble-free. But it is clear that even if the trouble-free point is never reached, the OD programs have made the system significantly less trouble-prone.

Figure 11.8 The organizational iceberg.

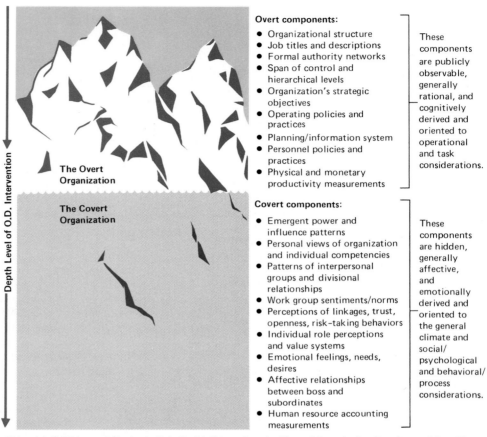

Overt components:

- Organizational structure
- Job titles and descriptions
- Formal authority networks
- Span of control and hierarchical levels
- Organization's strategic objectives
- Operating policies and practices
- Planning/information system
- Personnel policies and practices
- Physical and monetary productivity measurements

These components are publicly observable, generally rational, and cognitively derived and oriented to operational and task considerations.

Covert components:

- Emergent power and influence patterns
- Personal views of organization and individual competencies
- Patterns of interpersonal groups and divisional relationships
- Work group sentiments/norms
- Perceptions of linkages, trust, openness, risk-taking behaviors
- Individual role perceptions and value systems
- Emotional feelings, needs, desires
- Affective relationships between boss and subordinates
- Human resource accounting measurements

These components are hidden, generally affective, and emotionally derived and oriented to the general climate and social/psychological and behavioral/process considerations.

The Overt Organization

The Covert Organization

Depth Level of O.D. Intervention

Richard J. Selfridge and Stanley L. Sokolik, "A Comprehensive View of Organization Development," p. 47, *MSU Business Topics*, Winter 1975.

Back to the Case

Once King decided that the change needed within the editorial department primarily concerned structural factors and should emphasize implementing and maintaining more of an emphasis within the editorial department on both production scheduling and supervision, he decided to make this change by making a structural type of modification within the department. Accordingly, he created a new position within the organization, hired Douglas Niles as his right-hand man, and made Niles responsible for setting up production schedules and generally supervising the editorial-production section.

People Change

Although successful people change involves some consideration of people, structure, and technology, its primary emphasis is on people. The following sections discuss people change and present grid organization development, one commonly used means of attempting to change organization members.

Describing People Changes

Modifying People

People change emphasizes increasing organizational effectiveness by changing organization members. The focus of this type of change is on such factors as modifying attitudes and leadership skills of employees. In general, managers should attempt to

Figure 11.9 The managerial grid.

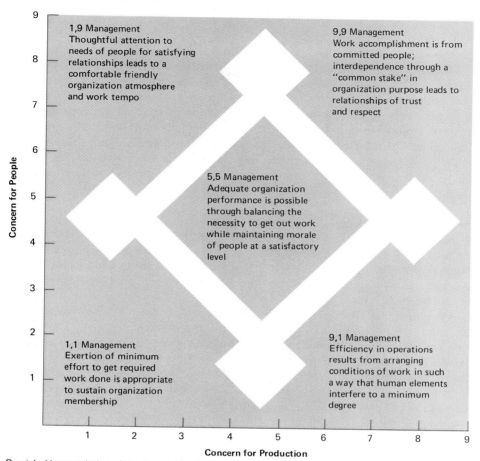

1,9 Management
Thoughtful attention to needs of people for satisfying relationships leads to a comfortable friendly organization atmosphere and work tempo

9,9 Management
Work accomplishment is from committed people; interdependence through a "common stake" in organization purpose leads to relationships of trust and respect

5,5 Management
Adequate organization performance is possible through balancing the necessity to get out work while maintaining morale of people at a satisfactory level

1,1 Management
Exertion of minimum effort to get required work done is appropriate to sustain organization membership

9,1 Management
Efficiency in operations results from arranging conditions of work in such a way that human elements interfere to a minimum degree

Concern for People (vertical axis, scaled 1 through 9)

Concern for Production (horizontal axis, scaled 1 through 9)

make this type of change when the results of organizational diagnoses indicate that human resources are the main cause of organizational ineffectiveness.

The process of people change can be referred to as **organization development (OD).** Although OD focuses mainly on changing people, these changes are based on an overview of structure, technology, and all other organizational ingredients.[14] To demonstrate this organizational overview approach, figure 11.8 shows both overt and covert organizational components considered during OD efforts. Overt factors are generally easily detectable and pictured as the tip of an organizational iceberg, while covert factors are usually more difficult to assess and therefore displayed as that part of the organizational iceberg that is "under water."

What is Organization Development?

Grid OD

One commonly used OD technique for changing people in organizations is called **Grid OD.**[15, 16] The managerial grid is a basic model describing various managerial styles and is used as the foundation for Grid OD. The **managerial grid** is based on the premise that various managerial styles can be described by means of two primary attitudes of the manager: (1) concern for people and (2) concern for production. Within this model, each attitude is placed on an axis scaled 1 through 9 and is used to generate five managerial styles. Figure 11.9 shows the managerial grid, its five managerial styles, and the factors that characterize each of these styles.

An OD Technique

The central theme of this managerial grid is that 9,9 Management (as shown on the grid) is the ideal managerial style. Managers using this style have both high concern for people and high concern for production. Managers using any other style have lesser degrees of concern for people or production and are thought to reduce organizational success accordingly. The purpose of Grid OD is to change organization members so that they approximate the 9,9 Management style.

How is a Grid OD program actually conducted? The program itself has six main training phases conducted for all managers within the organization. The first two of these phases focus on acquainting managers with the managerial grid concept and assisting them in determining which managerial style they most commonly use. The last four phases of the Grid OD program concentrate on encouraging managers to adopt the 9,9 Management style and showing them how to use this style within their specific job situation. Emphasis throughout the program is on developing teamwork within the organization.

The Status of People Change

Some evidence suggests that Grid OD is a useful technique because it is effective in enhancing profit, positively changing managerial behavior, and positively influencing managerial attitudes and values.[17] Grid OD probably will have to undergo more rigorous testing for an extended period of time, however, before more conclusive statements can be made.[18]

If the entire OD area is taken into consideration changes that emphasize both people and the organization as a whole seem to have inherent strength. There are, however, several commonly voiced weaknesses of OD efforts. These weaknesses indicate that (1) the effectiveness of an OD program is difficult to evaluate; (2) OD programs are generally too time consuming; (3) OD objectives are commonly too vague; (4) total costs of an OD program are difficult to pinpoint at the time the program starts; and (5) OD programs are generally too expensive.[19]

Strengths and Weaknesses of OD

Despite these weaknesses, however, the use of OD techniques probably will continue to grow in the future.[20] Therefore, these weaknesses should not eliminate OD but indicate areas to perfect within it. Common guidelines that managers can use to improve the quality of OD efforts are (1) systematically tailoring OD programs to meet the specific needs of the organization, (2) continually demonstrating as part of the program exactly how people should change their behavior, and (3) conscientiously changing organizational reward systems so that organization members who change their behavior as suggested by an OD program are rewarded.[21]

Back to the Case

The change as conceived and implemented by Alistair King in the editorial department of Jackson Company would not be classified as people change. Although the people involved in the change inevitably were considered to some extent, the main emphasis of the change was not on such issues as modifying attitudes or leadership skills. If the information gathered from the diagnoses conducted by King had indicated that human resources were the main cause of organizational ineffectiveness, people change would have been more appropriate for the Jackson Company than the structural change made. In this case, Grid OD possibly could have been used to attempt to modify people's management styles and mold organization members into a more cooperative work team.

Individuals Affected by Change

Increasing Support for a Change

A fourth major factor to be considered by managers when changing an organization is the people affected by the change. A good assessment of what to change and how to make the change probably will be wasted if the organization members do not support the change. To raise the chances of employee support of a change, managers should be aware of (1) the usual employee resistance to change, (2) how this resistance can be reduced, and (3) the three phases usually present when behavioral change occurs.

Resistance to Change

Resistance to change within an organization is as common as the need for change. Managers have an especially difficult job because after they decide on making some organizational change, they typically meet with resistance aimed at preventing the change from occurring from organization members. This resistance generally exists because organization members fear some personal loss as a result of the proposed change. Examples of this feared personal loss include the possibilities of a reduction in personal prestige, a disturbance of established social and working relationships, and personal failure due to an inability to carry out new job responsibilities.

Feared Personal Loss

Reducing Resistance to Change

Since resistance typically accompanies proposed change, managers must be able to reduce the effects of this resistance to ensure the success of needed organizational modifications. Resistance usually can be reduced by following several generally accepted guidelines and by considering implementing change on a tentative basis. Each of these strategies is discussed in the material that follows.

General Guidelines

Fortunately, managers have some general guidelines they can follow to help reduce resistance to change. Among these guidelines are the following recommendations to managers:[22]

1. **Avoid surprises** People typically need time to evaluate proposed change before management implements it. Elimination of this time to evaluate how proposed change may affect individual situations usually results in automatic opposition to change. Whenever possible, individuals who will be affected by a change should be kept informed of the type of change being considered and the probability that the change will be adopted.

2. **Promote real understanding** When fear of personal loss related to a proposed change is reduced, opposition to the proposed change is reduced.[23] Most managers would agree that having organization members thoroughly understand a proposed change is a major step in reducing this fear. This understanding may even generate support for the proposed change by focusing attention on possible individual gains that could materialize as a result of the change. Individuals should receive information that will help them to answer the following change-related questions that they invariably will be asking themselves:

   1. Will I lose my job?
   2. Will my old skills become obsolete?
   3. Am I capable of producing effectively under the new system?
   4. Will my power and prestige decline?
   5. Will I be given more responsibility than I care to assume?
   6. Will I have to work longer hours?
   7. Will it force me to betray or desert my good friends?[24]

3. **Set the stage for change** Perhaps the most powerful tool for reducing resistance to change is management's positive attitude toward change. This attitude should be displayed openly by top and middle management as well as by lower management. In essence, management should demonstrate its

appreciation for change as one of the basic prerequisites necessary for a successful organization. Management also should strive to be seen not as encouraging change for the sake of change, but as encouraging change only to increase organizational effectiveness. To emphasize this attitude toward change, some portion of organizational rewards should be earmarked for those organization members most instrumental in implementing constructive change.

Tentative Change

Trial Change

Besides following the preceding guidelines, making changes on a temporary basis can help to reduce resistance to change. This approach establishes a trial period during which organization members spend some time working under a proposed change before voicing support or nonsupport of the change. Tentative change is based on the assumption that a trial period during which organization members "live under" a change is the best way of reducing feared personal loss. Judson has summarized benefits to using the tentative approach as follows:

1. Those involved are able to test their reactions to the new situation before committing themselves irrevocably.
2. Those involved are able to acquire more facts on which to base their attitudes and behavior toward the change.
3. Those involved with strong preconceptions are in a better position to regard the change with greater objectivity. Consequently, they could review their preconceptions and perhaps modify some of them.
4. Those involved are less likely to regard the change as a threat.
5. Management is better able to evaluate the method of change and make any necessary modifications before carrying it out more fully.[25]

The Behavioral Side of Change

Almost any change will require that organization members modify the way in which they are accustomed to behaving or working. Therefore, managers must not only be able to decide upon the best people-structure-technology relationship for the organization but also be able to make corresponding changes in such a way that related human behavior is changed most effectively. In essence, positive results of any change will materialize only if organization members change their behavior as necessitated by the change.

Change and Work Habits

Lewin's theory about what causes behavioral change can be invaluable to managers. According to Lewin, behavioral change is caused by three distinct but related conditions experienced by an individual: (1) unfreezing, (2) changing, and (3) refreezing.[26] The first condition, **unfreezing,** is a state in which individuals become ready to acquire or learn new behaviors—they experience the ineffectiveness of their present mode of behavior and are ready to attempt to learn new behavior that will make them more effective. It may be especially difficult for individuals to "thaw out" because of positive attitudes they traditionally associated with their past behavior.

Ready to Change

Experimenting with New Behaviors

Changing, the second of Lewin's conditions, is a situation in which individuals, now unfrozen, begin experimenting with new behavior. They try new behaviors they hope will increase their effectiveness. According to Schein, this changing is best effected if it involves both identification and internalization.[27] Identification is a process in which individuals performing new behaviors pattern themselves after someone who already has expertise in those behaviors—that is, individuals model themselves after an expert. Internalization is a process in which individuals performing new behaviors attempt to use those behaviors as part of their normal behavioral pattern. In other words, individuals consistently try to make the new behaviors useful over an extended period of time.

Refreezing, the third of Lewin's conditions, is a situation in which individuals see that the new behavior they have experimented with during "changing" is now part of themselves. They have developed attitudes consistent with performing the new behaviors and now see those behaviors as part of their normal mode of operations. Rewards individuals receive as a result of performing the new behavior are very instrumental in refreezing.

What is Refreezing?

For managers to increase their success as change agents, they must be able to make their changes in such a way that individuals who will be required to modify their behavior as a result of the change live through Lewin's three conditions. A manager might do this in the following way. A middle-level manager named Ed Clark has gathered information through an internal organizational analysis that indicates that Terry Lacey, a lower-level manager, must change his technique for transmitting memos within the organization. Clark knows that Lacey firmly believes that he can save time and effort by simply writing out his intracompany memos longhand rather than having them typed, proofread, corrected if necessary, and then sent out. Lacey also believes that an added benefit to this strategy is the fact that it frees his secretary to do other kinds of tasks.

Using Lewin's Theory: An Example

In support of the internal organizational diagnosis information, Clark himself is getting several requests for help in reading Lacey's sometimes illegible handwriting and knows for a fact that some of Lacey's memos are written so poorly that words and sentences are misinterpreted. Clearly, some change seems necessary. As his superior, Clark simply could mandate change by telling Lacey to write more clearly or to have his memos typed. This strategy, however, may not have enough impact to cause a lasting behavioral change and could conceivably result in the additional problem of personal friction between the two managers.

By using the change theory just discussed, Clark could increase the probability of Lacey changing his behavior in a more lasting way. Clark must make his change in such a way that Lacey experiences unfreezing, changing, and refreezing. To encourage unfreezing Lacey, Clark could direct all questions he receives concerning Lacey's memos back to Lacey himself and make sure that Lacey is aware of all memo misinterpretations and resulting mistakes that have occurred. This strategy should demonstrate to Lacey that there is some need for change.

Once Lacey recognizes this need for changing the way in which he writes his memos, he will be ready to try alternative memo-writing methods. Clark can then offer suggested methods to Lacey, taking special care to give him examples of what others do to write intracompany memos (identification). Over time, Clark should also help Lacey to develop the method of transmitting the memos that best suit his talents (internalization).

After Lacey has developed an effective method of writing memos, Clark should take steps to ensure that positive feedback concerning his method reaches Lacey. This feedback, of course, will be instrumental in refreezing Lacey's new method. The feedback can come from Clark, Lacey's subordinates and peers, and from Lacey's own observations.

Back to the Case

Perhaps the main reason why the change made in Jackson Company's editorial department failed is that Alistair King did not appropriately consider the individuals affected by the change. King's overall strategy for encouraging the editors to change their behavior and thereby meet deadlines seemed to consist primarily of appointing Douglas Niles as his right-hand man. King seemed to think that Niles, although lacking the power to give direct orders to the editors, would be able to change the work habits of the editorial group.

King's biggest problem probably was his failure to assist the editors in experiencing the conditions of unfreezing, changing, and refreezing. To ensure the success of this change, King should have developed and implemented a strategy through which the editors recognized the need for change, experimented with new behaviors, and were then given positive feedback on the development of appropriate new behaviors. Making the editors aware that their publication was in danger of failing because of unmet deadlines would have helped to unfreeze the editors. Perhaps Niles's production system could have then been presented to help the editors to experience changing or to find a new way of working more productively.

To refreeze the editors, King should have ensured that positive feedback reached the editors when they began to meet deadlines. When the editors did meet their deadlines but received no related positive feedback, they probably perceived themselves as getting more positive feedback in the form of preferential treatment when they didn't meet deadlines. This may have been the reason why the editors reverted back to their old behavior after some time.

No overt resistance to the change was obvious among the editors, probably because King had reduced the feelings of feared personal loss by following the general guidelines of avoiding surprise change, promoting real understanding of the change, and setting the stage for change. Various forms of tentative change may have even been used prior to Niles's arrival.

Evaluation of Change

Why Evaluate Change?

As with all other action managers take, they should spend some time evaluating the changes they make. The purpose of this evaluation is not only to gain insights on how the change itself might be modified to further increase organizational effectiveness, but also to determine if the steps taken to make the change can be modified to increase organizational effectiveness the next time they are used.

This evaluation is not as easy to conduct as it may seem at first glance. According to Margulies and Wallace, the difficulty of making this evaluation is partly created because it is often difficult to achieve reliable outcome data from individual change programs.[28] Regardless of the level of this difficulty, however, the responsibility of managers seems clear. They must do their best to evaluate change to increase the organizational benefit from the change.

Symptoms and Change

One commonly used method for evaluating change is to be on the alert for symptoms that indicate that further change is necessary. Examples of these symptoms are continued management behavior that (1) is oriented more to the past than to the future, (2) recognizes the obligations of rituals more than the challenges of current problems, or (3) owes allegiance more to departmental goals than to overall company objectives.[29] If these behaviors are observed within an organization, the probability is relatively high that further change is necessary.

A word of caution, however, is needed at this point. Although symptoms such as those listed in the preceding paragraph generally indicate that further change is warranted, this is not necessarily the case. The decision to make additional changes should not be made solely on the basis of observing symptoms; it also should consider more objective information resulting from repeated and well-executed internal and external organizational diagnoses. In general, additional change is justified if it further

(1) improves the means for satisfying someone's economic wants, (2) increases profitability, (3) promotes human work for human beings, or (4) contributes to individual satisfaction and social well-being.[30]

Back to the Case

The change in the editorial department at Jackson Company needs to be evaluated to see (1) if further departmental change is necessary and (2) if the process King used to make the change might be improved in the future. Since the editors have reverted to their old pattern of lateness and overstepped deadlines, additional departmental change certainly seems necessary. The key to making additional changes successful probably lies in the analysis of the process used to make the initial changes. This analysis shows that additional changes should put more emphasis on considering individuals affected by the change, with a special focus on assisting these individuals to experience unfreezing, changing, and refreezing.

Summary

The following points are stressed within this chapter:

1. Changing an organization is defined as the process of modifying an existing organization. The purpose of making these modifications is to increase the probability of organizational success. Change is an inevitable part of management and considered so important to organizational success that some managers encourage employees to suggest needed changes. The organization with the highest probability of survival and growth is characterized by both change and stability.

2. The change agent is anyone inside or outside the organization who tries to make changes. Skills necessary to be a successful change agent include determining if change is needed and how much change is appropriate for the human resources of the organization.

3. Determining what should be changed within an organization is a process that includes an evaluation or organizational effectiveness and an organizational diagnosis. Organizational effectiveness is the degree to which an organization accomplishes its objectives and is primarily determined by the relationship among people, technology, and structure within the management system. Organizational diagnosis is examining the functioning of an organization to determine what specific changes should be made to enhance organizational effectiveness.

Issues for Review and Discussion

1. What is meant in this chapter by the phrase *changing an organization*?
2. Why do organizations typically undergo various changes?
3. Does an organization need both change and stability? Explain.
4. What major factors should a manager consider when changing an organization?
5. Define "change agent" and list the skills necessary to be a successful change agent.
6. Explain the term *organizational effectiveness* and describe the major factors that determine how effective an organization will be.
7. Outline the roles of internal organizational diagnosis and external organizational diagnosis in determining what should be changed within an organization.
8. What should be done to perform an internal organizational diagnosis?
9. What should be done to perform an external organizational diagnosis?

10. Describe the relationship between "determining what should be changed within an organization" and "choosing a type of change for the organization."
11. What is the difference between structural change and people change?
12. Is matrix organization an example of a structural change? Why?
13. What is the difference between the overt and covert factors considered during organizational development?
14. Draw and explain the managerial grid.
15. Is Grid OD an example of a technique used to make structural change? Why?
16. What causes resistance to change?
17. List and explain the steps managers can take to minimize this resistance.
18. Explain the significance of "unfreezing," "changing," and "refreezing" to changing the organization.
19. How and why should managers evaluate the changes they make?

Sources of Additional Information

Argyris, C. *Management and Organization Development*. New York: McGraw-Hill, 1972.

Barnes, Louis B. "Managing the Paradox of Organizational Trust." *Harvard Business Review*, March/April 1981, pp. 107–16.

Basil, Douglas C., and Cook, Curtis W. *The Management of Change*. New York: McGraw-Hill, 1974.

Beckhard, Richard. *Organizational Development: Strategies and Models*. Reading, Mass.: Addison-Wesley, 1969.

Bennis, Warren. *Organization Development: Its Nature, Origins, and Prospects*. Reading, Mass.: Addison-Wesley, 1969.

Blake, R. R., and Mouton, J. S. *The Managerial Grid*. Houston: Gulf Publishing, 1964.

Dalton, G. W.; Lawrence, P. R.; and Greiner, L. E. *Organizational Change and Development*. Homewood, Ill.: Irwin-Dorsey, 1970.

Filley, Alan; House, Robert J.; and Kerr, Steven. *Managerial Process and Organizational Behavior*. Chicago: Scott, Foresman and Company, 1976.

Guest, Robert H.; Hersey, Paul; and Blanchard, Kenneth H. *Organizational Change through Effective Leadership*. Englewood Cliffs, N.J.: Prentice-Hall, 1977.

Huse, Edgar F. *Organization Development and Change*. St. Paul: West Publishing, 1975.

Lawrence, Paul R. *The Changing of Organization Behavior Patterns*. Cambridge, Mass.: Harvard University Press, 1958.

Leavitt, Harold. "Applied Organization Change in Industry." In *Handbook on Organizations*, edited by James March. Chicago: Rand McNally, 1965.

Lorsch, Jay. *Organizational Behavior and Administration*. Homewood, Ill.: Irwin-Dorsey, 1976.

Marchington, Mick. "Employee Participation—Consensus or Confusion?" *Personnel Management* 13, no 4 (April 1981): 38–41.

Margulies, N., and Raia, A. P. *Organization Development: Values, Process, and Technology*. New York: McGraw-Hill, 1972.

Sibbins, Gerald J. *Organizational Evolution: A Program for Managing Radical Change*. New York: American Management Association, 1974.

Umstot, Denis D. "Organization Development Technology and the Military: A Surprising Merger?" *Academy of Management Review* 5, no. 2 (1980): 189–201.

Zierden, William E. "Managing Workplace Innovations: A Framework and a New Approach." *Management Review* 70, no. 6 (June 1981): 57–61.

Notes

1. Ronald D. Daniel, "Reorganization for Results," *Harvard Business Review,* November/December 1966, pp. 96–104.

2. Bridgford Hunt, "Managers of Change: Why They Are in Demand," *S.A.M. Advanced Management Journal,* Winter 1980, pp. 40–44.

3. John S. Morgan, *Managing Change: The Strategies of Making Change Work for You* (New York: McGraw-Hill, 1972), p. 99.

4. Oliver L. Niehouse and Karen B. Massoni, "Stress—An Inevitable Part of Change," *S.A.M. Advanced Management Journal,* Spring 1979, pp. 17–25.

5. Warren C. Bennis, K. D. Benne, and R. Chin, eds., *The Planning of Change: Readings in the Applied Behavioral Sciences* (New York: Holt, Rinehart & Winston, 1961), p. 69.

6. Alvin Toffler, *Future Shock* (New York: Bantam Books, 1971).

7. William C. Giegold and R. J. Craig, "Whatever Happened to OD?" *Industrial Management,* January/February 1976, pp. 9–12.

8. For more details on these two environmental levels and how to analyze them, see Phillip S. Thomas, "Environmental Analysis for Corporate Planning," *Business Horizons,* October 1974, pp. 27–38.

9. W. F. Glueck, "Organization Change in Business and Government," *Academy of Management Journal* 12 (1969): 440–41.

10. C. J. Middleton, "How to Set Up a Project Organization," *Harvard Business Review,* March/April 1967, p. 73.

11. John F. Mee, "Matrix Organization," *Business Horizons,* Summer 1964.

12. Middleton, "How to Set Up a Project Organization," p. 74.

13. Harvey F. Kolodny, "Managing in a Matrix," *Business Horizons* 24, no. 2 (March/April 1981): 17–24.

14. John C. Alpin and Duane E. Thompson, "Successful Organizational Change," *Business Horizons,* August 1974, pp. 61–66.

15. This section is based primarily on R. Blake, J. Mouton, and L. Greiner, "Breakthrough in Organization Development," *Harvard Business Review* (1964): 133–55.

16. For discussion on other methods for implementing OD change, see William F. Glueck, *Organization Planning and Development* (New York: American Management Association, 1971).

17. Blake, Mouton, and Greiner, "Breakthrough in Organization Development."

18. L. G. Malouf, "Managerial Grid Evaluated," *Training Development Journal* 20 (1966): 6–15.

19. W. J. Heisler, "Patterns of OD in Practice," *Business Horizons,* February 1975, pp. 77–84.

20. William E. Halal, "Organization Development in the Future," *California Management Review* 16, no. 3 (Spring 1974): 35–41.

21. Martin G. Evans, "Failures in OD Programs—What Went Wrong," *Business Horizons,* April 1974, pp. 18–22.

22. This strategy for minimizing the resistance to change is based on "How Companies Overcome Resistance to Change," *Management Review,* November 1972, pp. 17–25.

23. John P. Kotter and Leonard A. Schlesinger, "Choosing Strategies for Change," *Harvard Business Review,* March/April 1979, pp. 106–13.

24. "How Companies Overcome Resistance," p. 25.

25. Arnold S. Judson, *A Manager's Guide to Making Changes* (New York: John Wiley & Sons, 1966), p. 118.

26. Kurt Lewin, "Frontiers in Group Dynamics: Concept, Method, and Reality of Social Sciences: Social Equilibria and Social Change," *Human Relations* 1, no. 1 (June 1947): 5–14.

27. Edgar H. Shein, "Management Development as a Process of Influence," *Industrial Management Review,* May 1961, pp. 59–76.

28. Newton Margulies and John Wallace, *Organizational Change: Techniques and Applications* (Chicago: Scott, Foresman & Co., 1973), p. 14.

29. Larry E. Greiner, "Patterns of Organizational Change," *Harvard Business Review,* May/June 1967, pp. 119–30.

30. Edgar C. Williams, "Changing Systems and Behavior: People's Perspectives on Prospective Changes," *Business Horizons* 12, no. 4 (August 1969): p. 53.

Concluding Case 11
Checking Out at Great Scot

John Holdren, owner-president of Great Scot

John R. Holdren was an owner-manager in the grocery business in his early twenties. Holdren's father had opened a corner "Mom and Pop" store in Anderson, Indiana, after ill health had forced him to quit his job as a mail carrier. This store was so successful that the elder Holdren made plans to open a second, larger store, with backing from some acquaintances. When these backers pulled out at the last minute, Holdren's son John quit school, pitched in his army savings, and began a new career. Since then, John Holdren's operation has grown steadily. Now, over twenty years later, he is owner-president of Great Scot, a chain of six giant supermarkets in Indiana—two in Terre Haute and four in Evansville. It has been Holdren's abilities to offer high-quality products at competitive prices and to provide good customer service that have allowed Great Scot to compete very successfully with such supermarket giants as Kroger and A & P.

Over the years Holdren has acquired and maintained a strong desire to uncover and implement improvements in his supermarkets that have the potential of raising the quality of goods and services Great Scot offers to the public. It was almost certainly the intensity of this desire that made Holdren take special note of the following article that appeared in his morning newspaper.

The author would like to express sincere appreciation to John R. Holdren for allowing this material about himself and Great Scot Supermarkets to appear in this text.

Code Machines At Checkouts

By Louise Cook Associated Press Writer

Those funny little lines that started appearing on boxes and cans in the supermarket four years ago have spread steadily along the supermarket shelves, and the machines that read the code are beginning to make their way to the checkout counter in growing numbers.

The number of stores using electronic scanners to read the Universal Product Code and automatically enter the correct price is still relatively small, but it has more than doubled in the past year.

Victor Hersh of the Food Marketing Institute said 415 of the nation's 33,000 supermarkets had scanning systems as of the end of September, up from 180 stores in September 1977.

The UPC was introduced on an experimental basis in 1974. Manufacturers were quick to accept the idea. More than 90 percent of all frozen foods and dry grocery items are marked with the UPC; 60 percent of health and beauty aids are coded.

Here's how the system works:

Each product is marked with a combination of lines, bars, and numbers. There is a different combination for each item, brand, and size.

A computer is programmed to translate the code into a specific price. When a customer reaches the checkout, each item in his or her order is passed over a scanner which "reads" the code. The scanner transmits the information to the computer. The computer identifies the product, "rings" it up, and prints the price and other appropriate information on the receipt.

By using the Universal Product Code, the computer also can help a store keep track of its inventory. Store personnel can find out how much of a specific item is on hand, how fast it is being sold, and when it is time to reorder.

For the customer, the scanning system means less time spent at the checkout. As a general rule, it also means more information on the receipt since each item can be identified by name and price. Scanning also is designed to eliminate the possibility of a customer being charged too much or too little because of a clerk's error in ringing up a price.

The introduction of electronic scanning has been controversial. The idea brought protests from labor unions who feared that jobs would be lost. Consumer activists, meanwhile, objected to the stores' plans to eliminate price markings on individual items. They argued that customers would find it difficult to compare prices and keep track of costs. A number of states and cities enacted laws making such markings mandatory.

The industry, which had argued that eliminating individual prices offered substantial savings to the store and ultimately the shopper, agreed to continue stamping the cans and boxes with prices, and consumer resistance abated.

Hersh said that among customers who shop in stores with a scanning system, "it is exceedingly popular." He said the system is "well on its way and will become commonplace."

The cost of the systems has been a major factor delaying their introduction. Hersh said installation of a scanning system costs from $110,000 to $275,000. The large capital investment required is a deterrent for many retailers, even though they can recover their money through increased operating efficiency and reduced labor costs.

Many supermarkets are moving toward scanning on a step-by-step basis. They are installing electronic cash registers which can be either manually operated or connected to a scanning system. Eighty-five percent of the new stores opened in 1977 had electronic registers; three-fourths of them were designed so they could be upgraded to scanning.

Food Marketing Institute studies show that most supermarket operators expect to introduce scanning systems sooner or later. Almost one-third of the store owners who had no scanning operations in 1977 said they planned some sort of installation within two years; an additional 20 percent said they expected to introduce at least one scanner before 1980. Only 3 percent of the retailers said they had no intention of ever using the technology.

Discussion Issues

1. Assuming that Holdren decides to put scanners in his supermarkets, how do you think he should make this change?
2. As Holdren performs an external organizational diagnosis, what factors do you think he will find to support installing the scanners? to not support installing the scanners?
3. What kinds of resistance could Holdren meet in attempting to make this change? How could this resistance be reduced or eliminated?

Influencing is the third of the four major management functions that must be performed for organizations to have long-run success. The previous two sections—"Planning" and "Organizing"—dealt with determining how the organization will get where it wants to go and establishing working relationships among organizational resources that will help the organization to get there. This section focuses on people variables managers must consider to get organization members to become and remain productive within the organization. Major topics in this section include communication, leadership, motivation, and management of groups, as well as a definition of influencing.

Chapter 12, "Fundamentals of Influencing and Communication," defines influencing as the process of guiding the activities of organization members in appropriate directions. Influencing is presented as a subsystem of the overall management system. This subsystem is discussed as involving issues primarily relating to communication, motivation, leadership, and consideration of groups. Communication is defined in chapter 12 as the process of sharing information with other individuals. Such topics as the elements of the interpersonal communication situation, the interpersonal communication process, successful and unsuccessful communication attempts, and verbal and nonverbal communication are discussed. Interpersonal communication that takes place in organizations is called organizational communication, which is presented as being either formal or informal.

Chapter 13, "Leadership," defines leadership as the process of directing the behavior of others toward the accomplishment of some objective and emphasizes that leadership is not another word for management. The point also is made in this chapter that individuals' ability to match appropriately their leadership style with both the leadership situation and their followers is a primary determinant of successful leadership. Specific leadership strategies as they relate to managerial decision making, the level of follower maturity, and engineering a situation to fit leadership style are discussed in detail.

Chapter 14, "Motivation," defines motivation as an inner state of an individual that causes him or her to behave in a way that ensures the accomplishment of some goal. Three models used to discuss motivation are the needs-goal model, the Vroom expectancy model, and the Porter-Lawler model. Human needs, an integral part of motivation theory, are described through Maslow's hierarchy of needs, Argyris's maturity-immaturity continuum, and McClelland's achievement theory. Strategies presented in this chapter that managers can use to motivate organization members include appropriate managerial communication, Theory Y, job enrichment, flexitime, behavior modification, and Likert's management systems. Included also in this chapter is a special section that describes Japanese management strategy for motivating organization members. But caution in using one country's management strategy in another country is emphasized.

Chapter 15, "Managing Groups," stresses that for managers to influence organization members successfully they must be able to manage groups of people. A group is defined as any number of people who interact with one another, are psychologically aware of one another, and perceive themselves to be a group. Organizational groups are explained as being divided into two types: formal groups and informal groups. Formal groups are work groups established by management decree, while informal groups develop naturally as organization members interact with one another. Chapter 15 suggests that managers can maximize the effectiveness of a work group by understanding and appropriately applying concepts regarding the relationship between work group productivity and (1) the size of a work group, (2) the cohesiveness of a work group, (3) norms of a work group, and (4) the status of work group members.

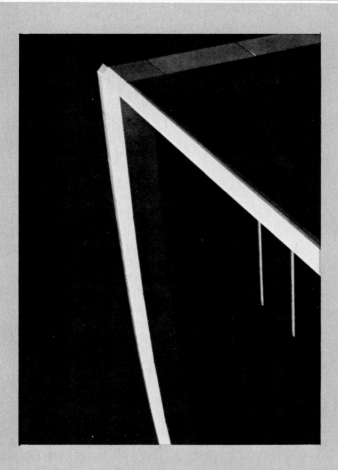

Section 4
Influencing

Student Learning Objectives

From studying this chapter I will attempt to acquire:

1. An understanding of influencing
2. An understanding of interpersonal communication
3. A knowledge of how to use feedback
4. An appreciation for the importance of nonverbal communication
5. Insights on formal organizational communication
6. An appreciation for the importance of the grapevine
7. Some hints on how to encourage organizational communication

Chapter Outline

Fundamentals of Influencing and Communication

Introductory Case 12
The Perplexed Manager

Case study figure 12.1 Merchandise manager's area of responsibility within the J-Mart Discount Store.

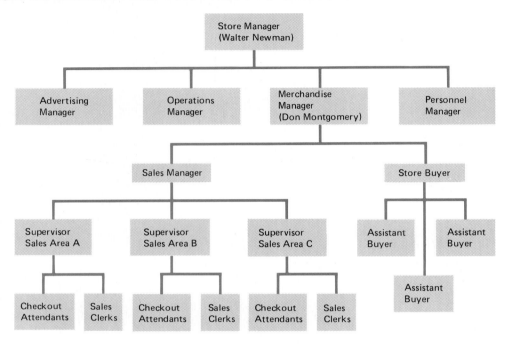

Don Montgomery is the merchandise manager of a J-Mart discount store in New Orleans, Louisiana. He has been with J-Mart for one year and is about to have his second semi-annual performance evaluation interview with Walter Newman, the store manager. Montgomery's last performance evaluation with Newman focused on eliminating reductions in sales in almost all merchandise areas. Although the sales picture has improved somewhat over the last six months, Montgomery knows that the merchandise area, for which he is responsible (see case figure 12.1), still isn't up to par.

Even after spending many hours analyzing various factors that could have caused the sales decrease, Montgomery is somewhat perplexed. He remains uncertain as to what factor or factors are primarily responsible. He has reached the tentative conclusion, however, that ineffective communication among individuals within the merchandise area could be a major part of the problem.

Montgomery has decided to ask Newman during the upcoming interview if Newman thinks ineffective communication could have caused the existing decline in sales. If Newman says yes, Montgomery also wants to ask him what steps he would suggest to increase communication effectiveness within the merchandise area.

Discussion Issues

1. In your opinion, do you think that ineffective communication in the merchandise area could be mainly responsible for Montgomery's sales losses? Why?

2. Assuming that Montgomery is correct, list and explain three examples of communication problems that could exist at J-Mart.

3. If you were Newman, what advice would you give Montgomery for improving the effectiveness of communication within the merchandise area?

What's Ahead

Don Montgomery, the merchandise manager in the introductory case, is perplexed for two reasons. First, he doesn't know for sure if ineffective communication is causing his downward sales trends. Second, he's uncertain about exactly what can be done to increase the effectiveness of communication within his organizational area. The information in this chapter is designed to help a manager such as Montgomery settle these issues. The chapter is divided into two main parts: (1) fundamentals of influencing and (2) communication.

The four basic managerial functions—planning, organizing, influencing, and controlling—were introduced in chapter 1. *Influencing* follows *planning* and *controlling* to be the third of these basic functions that are covered in this text. A definition of influencing and a discussion of the influencing subsystem follow.

Fundamentals of Influencing

Defining Influencing

Influencing is the process of guiding the activities of organization members in appropriate directions. Appropriate directions, of course, are those that lead to the attainment of management system objectives. Influencing involves focusing on organization members as people and dealing with such issues as morale, arbitration of conflicts, and the development of good working relationships among individuals.

Guiding Activities

The Influencing Subsystem

As with the planning and organizing functions, the influencing function can be viewed as a subsystem that is part of the overall management system process. Figure 12.1 presents the relationship between the overall management system and the influencing subsystem. The primary purpose of the **influencing subsystem** is to enhance the attainment of management system objectives by guiding the activities of organization members in appropriate directions.

What Is the Influencing Subsystem?

Figure 12.2 shows the specific ingredients of the influencing subsystem. Input of this subsystem is comprised of a portion of the total resources of the overall management system, and output is appropriate organization member behavior. The process of the influencing subsystem involves the performance of four primary management activities: (1) leading, (2) motivating, (3) considering groups, and (4) communicating. It can be said that managers transform a portion of organizational resources into appropriate organization member behavior mainly by performing these four activities.

Input

Process

Output

As figure 12.2 shows, leading, motivating, and considering groups are related influencing activities, each of which is accomplished, to some extent, by managers communicating with organization members. For example, managers decide what kind of leader they should be only after they analyze the characteristics of various groups with which they will interact and how these groups can best be motivated. Then, regardless of the strategy they adopt, their leading, motivating, and working with groups will be accomplished, at least to some extent, by communicating with other organization members.

In fact, as figure 12.3 implies, essentially all management activities are at least partially accomplished through communication or communication-related endeavors.[1] Since communication is used repeatedly by managers, communication skill is often

The Fundamental Management Skill

Figure 12.1 Relationship between overall management system and influencing subsystem.

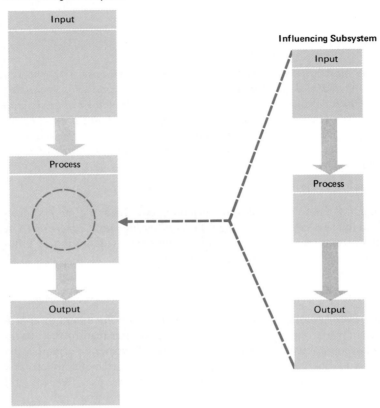

Overall Management System

referred to as the fundamental management skill. Communication is discussed further in the remainder of this chapter, while leading, motivating, and considering groups are discussed in chapters 13, 14, and 15 respectively.

Back to the Case

Given the information in the preceding section, Walter Newman, the store manager, would probably answer Don Montgomery's question about the relationship between ineffective communication and a decline in sales as follows:

"Unfortunately, Don, I do not presently know enough about the effectiveness or ineffectiveness of communication in your area to give you a definite answer. From what I know about communication in general, however, I do think that ineffective communication could be a significant enough factor to be causing your downward sales trends.

"You see, Don, one of the primary functions of a manager such as yourself is called influencing. You perform this function when you guide the activities of people in the merchandise area so that the attainment of store objectives is enhanced. You accomplish this influencing through activities like leading such individuals as the sales manager and the store buyer, motivating them to do better jobs, working well with various groups of merchandise area workers, and communicating successfully with all merchandise area personnel.

"Of all these influencing activities, communication is especially critical. Not only does communication directly affect the behavior of merchandise area personnel through such factors as directions you may give, but it also serves as the primary mechanism through which you activate your strategy to lead them, motivate them, and work with them as groups.

"In essence, communication is the main tool through which you accomplish, at least to some extent, most of your duties as merchandise manager. This is why I think that ineffective communication could cause a store disaster, even if you had the right merchandise on the shelf."

Figure 12.2 The influencing subsystem.

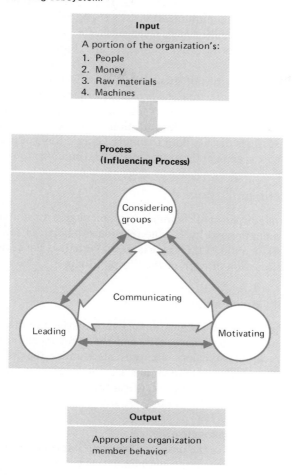

Input

A portion of the organization's:
1. People
2. Money
3. Raw materials
4. Machines

Process
(Influencing Process)

Considering groups

Communicating

Leading

Motivating

Output

Appropriate organization member behavior

Figure 12.3 Managerial activities and communication-related behaviors used, at least partially, to accomplish those activities.

Example Management Activities	Example Communication–Related Behaviors Used to Accomplish Management Activities
Leading	Speaking
Participating	Conducting conferences
Consulting	Evaluating employee participation
Cooperating	Listening
Considering groups	Interviewing
Creating a social climate	
Delegating	
Persuading	
Motivating	

From Harold P. Zelko, "Trends in Oral Communication Training in Business and Industry," *Journal of Communication* 12, no. 2 (1962): 109. Used with permission of *Journal of Communication* and the International Communication Association.

Communication is the process of sharing information with other individuals. Information, as used here, represents any thought or idea that managers desire to share with other individuals. Since communication is a commonly used management skill and often is cited as the one ability most responsible for the success of a manager, it is extremely important that prospective managers are thoroughly familiar with how managers communicate.[2]

The communication activities of managers generally take place within an organization and involve sharing information with other organization members. To be effective communicators, therefore, managers must not merely understand interpersonal communication, but interpersonal communication as it takes place within organizations. The following sections discuss both the more general topic of interpersonal communication and the more specific topic of interpersonal communication in organizations.

Interpersonal Communication

To be successful as an interpersonal communicator, managers must understand (1) how interpersonal communication works, (2) the relationship between feedback and interpersonal communication, and (3) the importance of verbal vs. nonverbal interpersonal communication. A discussion of each of these topics follows.

How Interpersonal Communication Works

To understand interpersonal communication one must understand the steps that occur when two people communicate. These steps and the other mechanics involved in interpersonal communication situations are presented under the following headings: (1) elements of interpersonal communication, (2) the interpersonal communications process, (3) successful and unsuccessful interpersonal communication, and (4) barriers to successful interpersonal communication.[3]

Elements of Interpersonal Communication

Interpersonal communication is the process of sharing information with other individuals. To be complete, the interpersonal communication process must have the following three basic elements.

1. *The source/encoder*   The **source/encoder** is that person in the interpersonal communication situation who originates and encodes information that he or she desires to share with another person. Encoding is the process of putting information in some form that can be received and understood by another individual. Putting thoughts into a letter is an example of encoding. Until information is encoded, it cannot be shared with others. In subsequent discussion the source/encoder will be referred to simply as the source.

2. *The signal*   Encoded information that the source intends to share constitutes a **message.** A message that has been transmitted from one person to another is called a **signal.**

Figure 12.4 Role of the source/encoder, signal, and decoder/destination in the communication process.

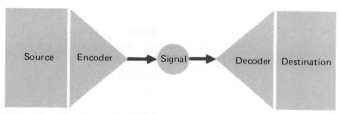

3. *The decoder/destination* The **decoder/destination** is that person with whom the source is attempting to share information. This individual receives the signal and decodes or interprets the message to determine its meaning. Decoding is the process of converting messages back into information. In all interpersonal communication situations, message meaning is a result of decoding. The decoder/destination is referred to as the destination throughout the remainder of this chapter.

Receiver of the Message

The Interpersonal Communication Process

What role does each of the three elements of the interpersonal communication process play? As implied in figure 12.4, the source determines what information he or she intends to share; encodes this information in the form of a message; and then transmits the message as a signal to the destination. The destination decodes the transmitted message to determine its meaning and then responds accordingly.

A manager who desires to assign the performance of a certain task to a subordinate would use the communication process in the following way. First, the manager would determine exactly what task she or he wanted the subordinate to perform. Then the manager would encode and transmit a message to the subordinate that would accurately reflect this assignment. The message transmission itself could be as simple as the manager telling the subordinate what the new responsibilities include. Next, the subordinate would decode the message transmitted by the manager to ascertain its meaning and then respond to it as she or he thinks appropriate.

Successful and Unsuccessful Interpersonal Communication

Successful communication is an interpersonal communication situation in which the information the source intends to share with the destination and the meaning the destination derives from the transmitted message are the same. Conversely, **unsuccessful communication** is an interpersonal communication situation in which the information the source intends to share and the meaning the destination derives from the transmitted message are different.

Intentions of Source

To increase the probability that communication will be successful, a message must be encoded to ensure that the source's experience concerning the way in which a signal should be decoded is equivalent to the destination's experience of the way it should be decoded. If this situation exists, the probability is high that the destination will interpret the signal as intended by the source. Figure 12.5 illustrates these overlapping fields of experience that ensure successful communication.

Figure 12.5 Overlapping fields of experience that ensure successful communication.

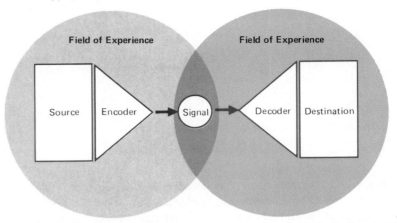

Back to the Case

Montgomery's performance appraisal would probably continue as follows:

MONTGOMERY: Mr. Newman, I didn't realize that communication was so important to a manager. Can you help me learn anything else about communication?
NEWMAN: Communication is sharing ideas with others. For you to be a successful communicator, Don, you must not only understand interpersonal communication in general, but also interpersonal communication as it takes place here in the store.

There are three essential elements of the interpersonal communication process. The first element is the source, or the individual who wishes to share information with another. The second element is the signal, or the message transmitted to another by the source. The third element is the destination, or that person with whom the source wishes to share information.

Assuming that you were the source, Don, you would communicate with one of your subordinates by first determining what information you wanted to share, encoding the information, and then by transmitting the message. Your subordinate would then interpret the message and respond accordingly. Your communication would be successful if the subordinate interpreted the message as you intended.

Barriers to Successful Interpersonal Communication

Factors that decrease the probability that communication will be successful commonly are called communication barriers. A clear understanding of these barriers is helpful to managers in their attempt to maximize communication success. The following sections discuss both communication macrobarriers and communication microbarriers.

Communication Macrobarriers　**Communication macrobarriers** are those that hinder successful communication in a general communication situation.[4] These factors relate primarily to the communication environment and the larger world in which communication takes place. Among these macrobarriers are the following:

The General Environment

　　1. The increasing need for information　Because society is constantly and rapidly changing, individuals have a greater and greater need for information. With individuals searching for more and more information, communication networks tend to overload, and as a result, communication

Limit Amount of Communication

　　is distorted. To minimize the effects of this barrier, managers should take steps to ensure that organization members are not overloaded with too much information. Only information critical to the performance of their jobs should be transmitted to them.

2. *The need for increasingly more complex information*   With the rapid advances in technology, it is virtually impossible for the majority of the population not to be faced with more and more complex communication situations in their everyday lives. If managers took steps to emphasize simplicity in communication, the effects of this barrier might be lessened. Also, furnishing organization members with adequate training to deal with more technical areas might be another strategy for overcoming this barrier.

Make Messages Simple

3. *The reality that individuals in the United States are coming in contact more and more with individuals using other languages besides English* As business becomes international in scope and as organization members travel more, this trend will accelerate. The potential communication barrier of this multi-language situation is obvious. When dealing with foreigners, it becomes important to be familiar not only with their language but also their cultures. Knowledge of a foreign language may be of little value if individuals don't know which words, phrases, and actions are culturally acceptable for use.[5]

Understand Cultures

Communication Microbarriers   **Communication microbarriers** are those that hinder successful communication in a specific communication situation.[6] These factors relate directly to such variables as the communication message, the source, and the destination. Among these microbarriers are:

Specific Situations

1. *The source's view of the destination*   The source in any communication situation has a tendency to view a destination in a specific way and to influence his or her messages by this view. For example, individuals tend to speak differently to people they think are informed about a subject than to those they think are uninformed. The destination (the person receiving the message) can sense these source attitudes, and oftentimes the attitudes block successful communication. Managers should keep an open mind about the people with whom they communicate and be careful not to imply any negative attitudes through their communication behavior.

Beware of Attitudes toward Destination

2. *Message interference*   Stimuli that compete with the communication message for the attention of the destination is called **message interference.** This interference is sometimes called noise.[7] An example of message interference is a manager talking to her secretary while the secretary is trying to correct a typing mistake. Correcting the mistake is message interference because it competes with the manager's communication message for the secretary's attention. Managers should attempt to communicate only when they have the total attention of the individual or individuals with whom they wish to share information.

Monopolize Attention

3. *The destination's view of the source*   Just as the source can have attitudes toward the destination that can hinder successful communication, the destination can have certain attitudes toward the source that can hinder successful communication. If, for example, a destination believes that the source has little expertise in the area about which the source is communicating, the destination may filter out much of the source's message and only slightly consider that part of the message he or she actually receives. When communicating, managers should attempt to consider the worth of messages transmitted to them independent of their personal attitudes toward the source. They may lose many valuable ideas if personal feelings toward others influence which messages they listen to carefully.

Beware of Attitudes toward Source

Make Messages Specific

4. *Perception*   **Perception** is an interpretation of a message as observed by an individual. Because different individuals can perceive the same message in different ways, the interpersonal communication process is extremely complex. One message can be interpreted by two individuals in two very different ways. The two primary factors that influence the way in which a stimulus is perceived are the level of the destination's education and the destination's amount of experience. Since the interpersonal communication situation involves people, it automatically involves the possibility that the destination may perceive a message differently than the source intended. To minimize the negative effects of this perceptual factor on interpersonal communication, managers should try to use messages with precise meanings. Ambiguous words generally tend to magnify the detrimental outcome of the perceptual process on interpersonal communication.

5. *Multi-meaning words*   Many words in the English language have several different meanings. Because of these words, a destination may have difficulty deciding which meaning should be attached to the words of a message. A manager should not assume that a word means the same thing to all people who use it.[8]

   A study by Lydia Strong substantiates this point. Strong concluded that for the 500 most common words in our language there are 4,070 different dictionary definitions. On the average, each of these words has over eighteen usages. The word *run* is an example:

Babe Ruth scored a *run.*
Did you ever see Jesse Owens *run?*
I have a *run* in my stocking.
There is a fine *run* of salmon this year.
Are you going to *run* this company or am I?
You have the *run* of the place.
What headline do you want to *run?*
There was a *run* on the bank today.
Did he *run* the ship aground?
I have to *run* (drive the car) downtown.
Who will *run* for president this year?
Joe flies the New York-Chicago *run* twice a week.
You know the kind of people they *run* around with.
The apples *run* large this year.
Please *run* my bath water.[9]

When encoding information, managers should be careful to define the terms they use whenever possible. They also should try to use words in the same way they see their destination use them.

Define Words in Messages

Montgomery's performance interview with Newman would probably continue as follows:

MONTGOMERY: Mr. Newman, it sounds pretty simple to communicate. Is it?
NEWMAN: Absolutely not! There are many barriers to overcome if you wish to be a successful communicator. These barriers include the merchandise people's need to have more and more information to do their jobs, message interference, your view of the destination as well as the destination's view of you, the perceptual process of people involved in communication, and multi-meaning words. To be a successful communicator, you have to minimize the effects of these barriers when you communicate with others.

Feedback and Interpersonal Communication

Feedback is the destination's reaction to a message. In general, feedback can be used by the source to ensure successful communication.[10] For example, if the destination's message reaction is inappropriate, the source can conclude that communication was not successful and that another message should be transmitted. On the other hand, if the destination's message reaction is appropriate, the source can conclude that communication has been successful. This, of course, assumes that the appropriate reaction did not happen merely by chance. Because of the potentially high value of feedback, managers should encourage feedback whenever possible and evaluate this feedback very carefully.

What Is Feedback?

Feedback can be either verbal or nonverbal.[11] For example, to gather verbal feedback on a message, the source could simply ask the destination pertinent message-related questions. The answers to these questions would probably indicate to the source whether or not the message was perceived as intended. To gather nonverbal feedback, the source merely may have to observe the destination's nonverbal response to a message. An example would be a manager who has transmitted a message to a subordinate indicating new steps that must be taken in the normal performance of the subordinate's job. Assuming that no other problems exist, if the steps are not followed accurately, the manager has nonverbal feedback that indicates she or he should clarify further the initial message.

Gathering Feedback

Robert S. Goyer has suggested other uses for feedback besides determining if a message is perceived as intended.[12] For example, over time this feedback can be used by the source to evaluate his or her personal communication effectiveness. This evaluation is made by determining the proportion of the destination's message reactions that actually were intended by the source. A formula illustrating how this evaluation, the **communication effectiveness index,** can be calculated is shown in figure 12.6. According to this formula, communication effectiveness of the source is determined by the proportion of the destination's reactions that were intended by the source. The higher this proportion, the greater the communication effectiveness of the source.

What Is a Communication Effectiveness Index?

If managers discover that their communication effectiveness index is relatively low over an extended period of time, they should assess their situation to determine how to improve their communication skill. One problem they may discover is that they are repeatedly using a vocabulary confusing to the destination. For example, a study conducted by Group Attitudes Corporation found that if managers tended to use certain words repeatedly in communicating with steelworkers, the steelworkers almost certainly became confused.[13] Figure 12.7 shows thirty words that Group Attitudes Corporation found to be misunderstood frequently by steelworkers and suggested phrases or words that managers should use instead.

Improve Communication Skills

Figure 12.6 Calculation of communication effectiveness.

$$\frac{\text{C E I}}{\text{(Communication Effectiveness Index)}} = \frac{\text{I M R (Intended Message Reaction)}}{\text{T M (Total Number of Messages Transmitted)}}$$

Figure 12.7 Thirty words frequently misunderstood by steelworkers and suggested words or phrases to be used in their place.

1. Accrue — *pile up; collect*
2. Compute — *figure*
3. Concession — *giving up (something)*
4. Contemplate — *think about; expect*
5. Delete — *cancel; take out; remove*
6. Designate — *name; appoint*
7. Deterioration — *breaking down; wearing away*
8. Detriment — *hurt; damage; harm*
9. Economic problem — *a cost problem*
10. Efficiency — *the way it should be (e.g., operating a machine the way it should be operated)*
11. Embody — *contain; include; hold*
12. Equitable — *fair; just*
13. Excerpt — *section; part*
14. Facilitate — *help along*
15. Fortuitously — *by chance; accidentally; luckily*
16. Generate — *create; build; produce*
17. Impediment — *barrier; road block*
18. Inadequate — *not enough*
19. Initiate — *begin; start*
20. Increment — *raise; increase*
21. Inevitably — *in the end; finally*
22. Injurious — *damaging; harmful*
23. Jeopardy — *danger*
24. Magnitude — *size*
25. Modify — *change; alter*
26. Objectivity — *fairness*
27. Pursuant — *in agreement with*
28. Perpetuate — *keep alive; continue*
29. Subsequently — *later*
30. Ultimate — *final; end*

Reprinted, by permission of the publisher, from "Management's Tower of Babel," by Verne Burnett, *Management Review*, June 1961, © 1961 by American Management Association, Inc., p. 7. All rights reserved.

Besides analyzing their vocabulary, managers should attempt to increase their communication effectiveness by trying to determine if they have been following the "ten commandments of good communication" as closely as possible. These commandments are:

1. *Seek to clarify your ideas before communicating* The more systematically you analyze the problem or idea to be communicated, the clearer it becomes. This is the first step toward effective communication. Many communications fail because of inadequate planning. Good planning must consider the goals and attitudes of those who will receive the communication and those who will be affected by it.
2. *Examine the true purpose of each communication* Before you communicate, ask yourself what you really want to accomplish with your message—obtain information, initiate action, change another person's attitude? Identify your most important goal and then adapt your language, tone, and total approach to serve that specific objective. Don't try to accomplish too much with each communication. The sharper the focus of your message, the greater its chances of success.
3. *Consider the total physical and human setting whenever you communicate* Meaning and intent are conveyed by more than words alone. Many other factors influence the overall impact of a communication, and managers must be sensitive to the total setting in which they communicate. Consider, for example, your sense of timing, that is, the circumstances under which

you make an announcement or render a decision; the physical setting—whether you communicate in private or otherwise, for example; the social climate that pervades work relationships within the company or a department and sets the tone of its communications; custom and practice—the degree to which your communication conforms to, or departs from, the expectations of your audience. Be constantly aware of the total setting in which you communicate. Like all living things, communication must be capable of adapting to its environment.

4. *Consult with others, when appropriate, in planning communications* Frequently, it is desirable or necessary to seek the participation of others in planning a communication or developing the facts on which to base the communication. Such consultation often lends additional insight and objectivity to your message. Moreover, those who have helped you plan your communication will give it their active support.

5. *Be mindful, while you communicate, of the overtones as well as the basic content of your message* Your tone of voice, your expression, your apparent receptiveness to the responses of others—all have tremendous impact on those you wish to reach. Frequently overlooked, these subtleties of communication often affect a listener's reaction to a message even more than its basic content. Similarly, your choice of language—particularly your awareness of the fine shades of meaning and emotion in the words you use—predetermine in large part the reactions of your listeners.

6. *Take the opportunity, when it arises, to convey something of help or value to the receiver* Consideration of the other person's interests and needs—trying to look at things from the other person's point of view—frequently points up opportunities to convey something of immediate benefit or long-range value to the other person. Subordinates are most responsive to managers whose messages take the subordinates' interests into account.

7. *Follow up your communication* Your best efforts at communication may be wasted and you may never know whether you have succeeded in expressing your true meaning and intent if you do not follow up to see how well you have put your message across. You can do this by asking questions, by encouraging the receiver to express his or her reactions, by follow-up contacts, and by subsequent review of performance. Make certain that every important communication has feedback so that complete understanding and appropriate action result.

8. *Communicate for tomorrow as well as today* While communications may be aimed primarily at meeting the demands of an immediate situation, they must be planned with the past in mind if they are to maintain consistency in the receiver's view. Most important, however, communications must be consistent with long-range interests and goals. For example, it is not easy to communicate frankly on such matters as poor performance or the shortcomings of a loyal subordinate, but postponing disagreeable communications makes these matters more difficult in the long run and is actually unfair to your subordinates and your company.

9. *Be sure your actions support your communications* In the final analysis the most persuasive kind of communication is not what you say, but what you do. When your actions or attitudes contradict your words, others tend to discount what you have said. For every manager, this means that good supervisory practices—such as clear assignment of responsibility and authority, fair rewards for effort, and sound policy enforcement—serve to communicate more than all the gifts of oratory.

10. *Last, but by no means least: seek not only to be understood but to understand—be a good listener*   When you start talking, you often cease to listen, at least in that larger sense of being attuned to the other person's unspoken reactions and attitudes. Even more serious is the occasional inattentiveness you may be guilty of when others are attempting to communicate with you. Listening is one of the most important, most difficult, and most neglected skills in communication. It demands that you concentrate not only on the explicit meanings another person is expressing, but also on the implicit meanings, unspoken words, and undertones that may be far more significant. Thus, you must learn to listen with the inner ear if you are to know the inner person.[14]

Back to the Case

Montgomery probably would continue the interview with the following question:

MONTGOMERY: Mr. Newman, these communication barriers sound tough to overcome. How can I try to make my communication successful?
NEWMAN: Feedback, or the destination's reaction to your message, is perhaps the most useful tool in making communication successful. Watch this reaction carefully and when it doesn't seem to be appropriate, transmit another message to clarify the meaning of your first message. Remember, feedback can be either verbal or nonverbal. Be on the alert for both types. Over time, Don, if feedback indicates that you are a relatively unsuccessful communicator, analyze your situation carefully to improve your communication effectiveness. You may find, for instance, that you are using a vocabulary that is generally inappropriate for personnel in the merchandise area. On the other hand, you may find that you are not following one or more of the ten commandments of good communication. Keep in mind that you can use feedback to improve your communication skills.

Verbal and Nonverbal Interpersonal Communication

Interpersonal communication is generally divided into two types: (1) verbal and (2) nonverbal. Up to this point the main emphasis of the chapter has been on **verbal communication,** communication that uses either spoken or written words to share information with others.

Encoding without Words

Nonverbal communication is sharing information without using words to encode thoughts. Factors commonly used to encode thoughts in nonverbal communication include gestures, vocal tones, and facial expressions. In most interpersonal communication incidents, verbal and nonverbal communications are not either-or occurrences. Instead, the destination's interpretation of a message generally is based not only on the words in the message but also on such factors as the source's gestures and facial expressions that accompany the words.

Impact of a Message

In an interpersonal communication situation in which both verbal and nonverbal factors are present, nonverbal factors may have more influence on the total impact of a message than verbal factors. Albert Mehrabian has developed a formula that shows the relative contributions of both verbal and nonverbal factors to the total impact of a message. This formula is as follows: Total message impact = .07 words + .38 vocal tones + .55 facial expressions.[15] Of course, both vocal tones and facial expressions are nonverbal factors. Besides vocal tones and facial expressions, gestures,[16] space,[17] and smell[18] can influence the impact of a verbal message.

Given the great potential influence of nonverbal factors on the impact of a message, managers should use nonverbal message ingredients to complement verbal message ingredients whenever possible.[19] For example, nonverbal messages can emphasize or accent the content of a verbal message. Exhibit 12 shows how Franklin M. Jarman used gifts as nonverbal messages to emphasize the importance of the content of a verbal message.

Using Verbal and Nonverbal Messages Together

Nonverbal messages can also be used to add new content to a verbal message. To this end, a head might be nodded or a voice might be toned to show either agreement or disagreement.

Regardless of how managers decide to combine verbal and nonverbal factors, they must be sure that the two do not unknowingly present contradictory messages. For instance, the words of a message might express approval while the nonverbal factors express disapproval. This type of situation creates message ambiguity and leaves the destination frustrated.

Back to the Case

MONTGOMERY: I think I understand, Mr. Newman. Any more tips?

NEWMAN: Yes, one last thing about interpersonal communication. You also can communicate with others without using words. Your facial expressions, gestures, and even the tone of your voice say things to people. Most of your communication situations, Don, will involve the simultaneous sending of both verbal and nonverbal messages to merchandise area personnel. Remember that the total impact of a message may be generated mostly by its nonverbal components and that nonverbal messages should be used to complement your verbal messages. Be sure not to overlook the potential impact of nonverbal communication in the merchandise area.

Interpersonal Communication in Organizations

What Is Organizational Communication?

To be effective communicators, managers must not merely understand the more general interpersonal communication concepts discussed previously but also the characteristics of interpersonal communication within organizations. Interpersonal communication within organizations is called **organizational communication.** In essence, organizational communication directly relates to the goals, functions, and structure of human organizations.[20] Organizational success, to a major extent, is determined by the effectiveness of organizational communication.[21]

Although organizational communication is referred to a number of times by early management writers, only after World War II did the topic begin to receive systematic study and attention.[22] From World War II to the 1950s, organizational communication as a discipline made significant advances in such areas as mathematical communication theory and behavioral communication theory.[23] In more recent times, a trend toward emphasis on organizational communication is growing in colleges of business throughout the nation.[24] The following information focuses on three fundamental organizational communication topics: (1) formal organizational communication, (2) informal organizational communication, and (3) the encouragement of formal organizational communication.

Formal Organizational Communication

Following the Organization Chart

In general, organizational communication that follows the lines of the organization chart is called **formal organizational communication.**[25] As discussed in chapter 8, the organization chart depicts relationships between people and jobs and shows the formal channels of communication between them. Two main aspects of formal organizational communication are discussed in the next sections: (1) types of formal organizational communication and (2) patterns of formal organizational communication.

Exhibit 12

Noose with a Message at Genesco, Inc.

Franklin M. Jarman: Shadow of the hangman (Photo: Seawell Multimedia)

Many chief executives bestow favors on their corporate officers—attaché cases, perhaps, or crystal paperweights. But the souvenirs Franklin M. Jarman gave each member of his management group of Genesco, Inc., two years ago were no run-of-the-desk keepsakes: a genuine rope hangman's noose and a leather belt buckled with the same symbol in gold. There was a blunt message, too: "Tighten your belt, not your noose." Jarman meant that directive to encourage cost-cutting at the troubled conglomerate.

Types of Formal Organizational Communication

In general, there are three basic types of formal organizational communication: (1) downward, (2) upward, and (3) lateral.

Downward Organizational Communication   Communication that flows from any point on an organization chart downward to another point on the organization chart is called **downward organizational communication.** This type of formal organizational communication primarily relates to the direction and control of employees. Job-related information that focuses on what activities are required, when the activities should be performed, and how the activities should be coordinated with other activities being performed within the organization must be transmitted to employees. This downward communication typically includes a statement of organizational philosophy, management system objectives, position descriptions, and other written information relating to the importance, rationale, and interrelationships of various departments.[26]

What Is Downward Organizational Communication?

Upward Organizational Communication   Communication that flows from any point on an organization chart upward to another point on the organization chart is called **upward organizational communication.** This type of organizational communication primarily contains information managers need to evaluate the organizational area for which they are responsible. This type of communication can furnish managers with valuable information on what is going wrong within the organization. Organizational modifications based on this feedback can be made to enable the organization to be more successful in the future. Upward communication generally contains information that relates to production reports, shipping reports, and customer complaints.[27]

Organizational Feedback

Lateral Organizational Communication   Communication that flows from any point on an organization chart horizontally to another point on the organization chart is called **lateral organizational communication.** Communication that flows across the organization usually focuses on coordinating the activities of various departments and developing new plans for future operating periods. Within the organization, all departments are related to all other departments. Only through the successful use of lateral communication can these departmental relationships be coordinated well enough to enhance the attainment of management system objectives.

Planning and Coordinating

Patterns of Formal Organizational Communication

By nature, organizational communication creates patterns of communication among organization members. These patterns essentially evolve from the repeated occurrence of various serial transmissions of information. According to Haney, a **serial transmission** involves passing information from one individual to another. A serial transmission of information occurs when:

> A communicates a message to B; B then communicates A's message (or rather his or her interpretation of A's) to C; C then communicates his or her interpretation of B's interpretation of A's message to D; and so on. The originator and the ultimate recipient of the message are separated by middle people.[28]

What Is a Serial Transmission?

Of course, one of the obvious weaknesses of a serial transmission is that messages tend to become distorted as the length of the serial transmission increases. Research has shown that a serial transmission can distort messages as a result of (1) message details being omitted, (2) message details becoming altered, and (3) message details being added.[29]

Figure 12.8 Relationship between three patterns of organizational communication and group characteristics of speed, accuracy, organization, emergence of leader, and morale.

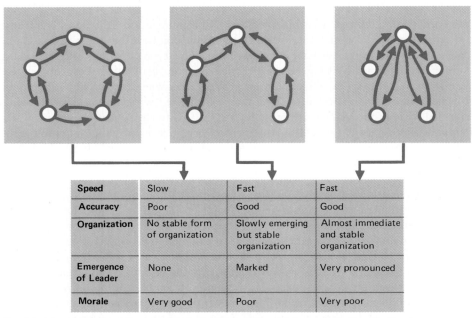

Speed	Slow	Fast	Fast
Accuracy	Poor	Good	Good
Organization	No stable form of organization	Slowly emerging but stable organization	Almost immediate and stable organization
Emergence of Leader	None	Marked	Very pronounced
Morale	Very good	Poor	Very poor

Reprinted, by permission of the publisher, from "An Experimental Approach to Organizational Communication," by Alex Bavelas and Dermot Barrett, *Personnel,* March 1951, © 1951 by American Management Association, Inc., p. 370. All rights reserved.

Formal Patterns and People

As presented in a well-known article by Alex Bavelas and Dermot Barrett,[30] this influence on the accuracy of messages transmitted is not the only weakness of a serial transmission. A serial transmission can also have some influence on morale, the emergence of a leader, and the degree to which individuals involved in the transmission are organized and efficient. Three basic organizational communication patterns studies and their corresponding effects on the variables just mentioned are shown in figure 12.8.

Back to the Case

NEWMAN: OK, Don. I think we've talked about the important factors involved in interpersonal communication. As a manager with J-Mart, though, you also should know something about interpersonal communication as it takes place in organizations.

The success of organizational communication—the interpersonal communication that takes place within J-Mart—will determine primarily how successful this store will be. You can communicate to your people in the merchandise area in either of two basic ways: formally or informally.

In general, your formal organizational communication will follow the lines on our organization chart. When communicating formally, you can communicate downward, like to the sales manager; upward, like to me; or laterally, like to the operations manager. Your downward communication should focus on the activities people below you should be doing, while your upward communication should indicate how well your area is doing. Your lateral communication should emphasize coordinating the merchandise area with other store areas.

Informal Organizational Communication   Organizational communication that does not follow the lines of the organization chart is called **informal organizational communication.** This type of communication typically follows the pattern of personal relationships among organization members. One friend communicates with another friend regardless of their relative positions on the organization chart. Informal organizational communication networks generally exist because organization members have a desire to know information that formal organizational communication does not furnish them. Ignoring the Organization Chart

The informal organizational communication network, or **grapevine,** has several distinctive characteristics: (1) the grapevine springs up and is used irregularly within the organization; (2) it is not controlled by top executives, who may not even be able to influence it; and (3) it is used largely to serve the self-interests of the people within it. What Is the Grapevine?

Another characteristic of the grapevine is that it usually transmits information very quickly. One study of more than four thousand employees of a U.S. naval ordnance test station focused on the speed at which information passes by use of grapevines. The employees were asked the following question: Suppose that the management made an important change in the way the organization would be run—through what channel or means of communication would you get the word first? How various percentages of employees ranked seven communication sources in response to this question is as follows.

1. Grapevine, 38 percent
2. Supervisor, 27 percent
3. Official memo, 17 percent
4. Station newspaper, 7 percent
5. Station directive system, 4 percent
6. Bulletin boards, 4 percent
7. Other, 3 percent[31]

As with the formal organizational communication situation, the informal organizational communication situation involves serial transmissions. Organization members involved in these transmissions, however, are more difficult for managers to identify than those in the formal communication network. As figure 12.9 illustrates, four different patterns of grapevines generally tend to exist in organizations.[32] These grapevine patterns are: Informal Patterns

1. *The single-strand grapevine*   A tells B, who tells C, who tells D, and so on. This type of grapevine generally tends to distort messages more than any other.

2. *The gossip grapevine*   A informs everyone else on the grapevine.

3. *The probability grapevine*   A communicates randomly, for example, to F and D. F and D then continue to inform other grapevine members in the same way.

4. *The cluster grapevine*   A selects and tells C, D, and F. F selects and tells I and B, and B selects and tells J. Information in this grapevine travels only to selected individuals.

Clearly, the grapevine is a factor with which managers must deal.[33] Most managers agree that a grapevine can and often does generate rumors that can be detrimental to organizational success. To minimize the development of such rumors, some managers advise distributing maximum information through formal communication channels. This distribution of information should eliminate some of the rumors generated and carried within grapevines.[34] Other writers argue, however, that managers Handling Grapevines

Figure 12.9 Four types of organizational grapevines.

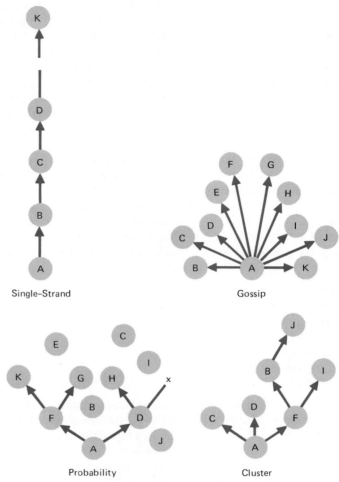

Single-Strand

Gossip

Probability

Cluster

should encourage the development of grapevines and strive to become grapevine members to gain information feedback that could be very valuable in improving the organization. Exactly how individual managers should deal with the grapevine, of course, depends on the specific organizational situation in which the managers find themselves.[35]

Encouraging Formal Organizational Communication   Organizational communication often is called the "nervous system" of the organization. The organization acts only as its "nervous system," or organizational communication, directs it. Since formal organizational communication is generally the most important type of communication that takes place in the organization, managers must encourage its free flow if the organization is to be successful.

Listening, Clear Messages,
Access to Channels

Figure 12.10 Ten commandments for good listening.

1. *Stop talking!*
   You cannot listen if you are talking.
   Polonius (*Hamlet*): "Give every man thine ear, but few thy voice."
2. *Put the talker at ease.*
   Help the talker feel free to talk.
   This is often called a permissive environment.
3. *Show the talker that you want to listen.*
   Look and act interested. Do not read your mail while he or she talks.
   Listen to understand rather than to oppose.
4. *Remove distractions.*
   Don't doodle, tap, or shuffle papers.
   Will it be quieter if you shut the door?
5. *Empathize with the talker.*
   Try to put yourself in the talker's place so that you can see his or her point of view.
6. *Be patient.*
   Allow plenty of time. Do not interrupt the talker.
   Don't start for the door or walk away.
7. *Hold your temper.*
   An angry person gets the wrong meaning from words.
8. *Go easy on argument and criticism.*
   This puts the talker on the defensive. He or she may "clam up" or get angry.
   Do not argue: even if you win, you *lose*.
9. *Ask questions.*
   This encourages the talker and shows you are listening.
   It helps to develop points further.
10. *Stop talking!*
    This is first and last, because all other commandments depend on it.
    You just can't do a good listening job while you are talking.

    Nature gave us two ears but only one tongue,
    which is a gentle hint that we should listen more than we talk.

From HUMAN BEHAVIOR AT WORK by Keith Davis. Copyright © 1972 by McGraw-Hill, Inc. Used with permission of McGraw-Hill Book Company.

Managers can use many different strategies to encourage the flow of formal organizational communication. One strategy is listening attentively to messages that come through formal channels. This listening shows organization members that managers are interested in what subordinates have to say and, as a result, encourages employees to use formal communication channels in subsequent situations. General guidelines managers can use to help them listen are presented in figure 12.10. Another strategy managers can adopt to encourage the free flow of formal organizational communication is to support the flow of clear and concise statements through formal communication channels. Receiving an ambiguous message through a formal organizational communication channel can discourage members from using that channel again. A third strategy managers can use is taking care to ensure that all organization members have free access to the use of formal communication channels within the organization. Obviously, organization members cannot communicate formally within the organization if they don't have access to the formal communication network. A fourth strategy for encouraging the flow of formal organizational communication is assigning specific communication responsibilities to staff personnel. In this capacity, for example, staff personnel could be of enormous help to line personnel in spreading important information throughout the organization.

NEWMAN: Informal organizational communication on the other hand, Don, does not necessarily follow the lines of the organization chart. Instead, individuals communicating informally tend to communicate with various social contacts within the store. Although the store grapevine must be dealt with, you may not be able to significantly influence it. People typically are involved in grapevine messages for self-interests and because the formal organizational communication has not furnished them with the information they feel they need.

You may be able to get feedback through the grapevine by developing various social relationships to try to become part of it. Also, because grapevines can have detrimental effects on store success through the development of rumors, try to ensure that merchandise personnel are given all the information they need to do their jobs well through formal organizational communication. This should eliminate the development of a significant number of rumors.

Also, Don, because formal organizational communication is of such vital importance to this store, you should try to encourage its flow. You can do this through such simple strategies as listening intently to messages that come to you over formal channels, supporting the flow of clear messages through formal channels, and making sure that all merchandise personnel have an opportunity to use formal channels of communication.

Summary

The following points are stressed within this chapter.

1. Influencing is a major management function and is the process of guiding the activities of organization members in appropriate directions. The influencing function can be viewed as a subsystem of the overall management system.
2. Input of the influencing subsystem is comprised of a portion of the total resources of the overall management system and output is appropriate organization member behavior. Four primary activities constitute the process of the influencing subsystem: (1) leading, (2) motivating, (3) considering groups, and (4) communicating.
3. The interpersonal communication process involves the source determining which information he or she wishes to share; encoding this information in the form of a message; and then transmitting the message as a signal to the destination. The destination then decodes the transmitted message to determine its meaning and responds accordingly.
4. Successful communication occurs when the destination interprets a message as the source intended. When message interpretation is different from what the source intended, communication is unsuccessful.
5. To be successful as communicators, managers must be able to use communication feedback and both verbal and nonverbal communication techniques. Feedback is the destination's reaction to a message. Verbal communication involves sharing information with others by using either spoken or written words. Nonverbal communication involves sharing information with others without the use of words.
6. Organizational communication is interpersonal communication within an organization. Formal organizational communication follows the lines of the organization chart and can be either downward, upward, or lateral. Informal organizational communication typically follows the pattern of personal relationships among organization members.
7. Serial transmissions are prevalent in organizations and involve passing messages through chains of individuals. Information transmitted through chains of individuals may be distorted.

1. What is influencing?
2. Describe the relationship between the overall management system and the influencing subsystem.
3. What factors make up the input, process, and output of the influencing subsystem?
4. Explain the relationship between the factors that comprise the process section of the influencing subsystem.
5. What is communication?
6. How important is communication to managers?
7. Draw the communication model presented in this chapter and explain how it works.
8. How does successful communication differ from unsuccessful communication?
9. Summarize the significance of "field of experience" to communication.
10. List and describe three communication macrobarriers and three communication microbarriers.
11. What is feedback, and how should managers use it when communicating?
12. How is the communication-effectiveness index calculated, and what is its significance?
13. Name the ten commandments of good communication.
14. What is nonverbal communication, and explain its significance.
15. How should managers use nonverbal communication?
16. What is organizational communication?
17. How do formal and informal organizational communication differ?
18. Describe three types of formal organizational communication and explain the general purpose of each type.
19. Can serial transmissions and other formal communication patterns influence communication effectiveness and also the individuals using the patterns? If so, how?
20. Draw and describe the four main types of grapevines that exist in organizations.
21. How can managers encourage the flow of formal organizational communication?

Sources of Additional Information

Allport, Gordon, and Postman, Leo. *The Psychology of Rumor.* New York: Henry Holt & Co., 1947.

Argyris, Chris. *Understanding Organizational Behavior.* Homewood, Ill.: Dorsey, 1960.

Barnlund, Dean. *Interpersonal Communication: Survey and Studies.* Boston: Houghton Mifflin, 1968.

Berlo, David K. *The Process of Communication.* New York: Rinehart & Winston, 1960.

Bosmajian, H. A., ed. *The Rhetoric of Nonverbal Communication.* Chicago: Scott, Foresman, 1971.

Davis, Keith. *Human Relations at Work: The Dynamics of Organizational Behavior.* New York: McGraw-Hill, 1967.

Ebenstein, Michael, and Krauss, Leonard I. "Strategic Planning for Information Resource Management." *Management Review* 70, no. 6 (June 1981): 21–26.

Eisenberg, Abne M., and Smith, Ralph R. *Nonverbal Communication.* Indianapolis: Bobbs-Merrill, 1972.

Fast, Julius. *Body Language.* New York: M. Evans, 1970.

Friedman, Selma. "Where Employees Go For Information (Some Surprises!)." *Administrative Management* 42, no. 9 (September 1981): 72–73.

Hall, Edward T. *The Silent Language.* New York: Doubleday, 1959.

Lesikar, Raymond. *Business Communication.* Homewood, Ill.: Richard D. Irwin, 1972.

Lin, Nan. *The Study of Human Communication.* Indianapolis: Bobbs-Merrill, 1973.

Montgomery, Robert L. "Are You a Good Listener?" *Nation's Business* 69, no. 10 (October 1981): 65–68.

Mortensen, C. David. *Communication: The Study of Human Interaction.* New York: McGraw-Hill, 1972.

Newcomb, R., and Sammons, Marg. *Employee Communications in Action.* New York: Harper & Row, 1961.

Redding, W. C., and Sanborn, G. A., eds. *Business and Industrial Communication: A Source Book.* New York: Harper & Row, 1964.

Shatshat, H. M., and Shin, Bong-Gon P. "Organizational Communication—A Key to Successful Strategic Planning." *Managerial Planning* 30, no. 2 (September/October 1981): 37–40.

Notes

1.
   (a) John Machin and Adrian Woolley, "Inter-Manager Communications: Matching Up to Expectations," *Personnel Management,* January 1981, pp. 26–29.

   (b) For a discussion on the relationship between communication and organizational change, see Richard C. Huseman, Elmore R. Alexander, III, and Russell W. Driver, "Planning for Organizational Change: The Role of Communication," *Managerial Planning* 28, no. 6 (May/June 1980): 32–36.

   (c) For discussion on the relationship between organizational communication and strategic planning, see H. M. Shatshat and Bong-Gon P. Shin, "Organizational Communication—A Key to Successful Strategic Planning," *Managerial Planning* 30, no. 2 (September/October 1981): 37–40.

2. James B. Strenski, "Two-Way Communication—A Management Necessity," *Personnel Journal,* January 1970, pp. 29–35.

3. This section on how interpersonal communication works is based on the following classic article on interpersonal communication: Wilbur Schramm, "How Communication Works," in *The Process and Effects of Mass Communication,* ed. Wilbur Schramm (Urbana, Ill.: University of Illnois Press, 1954), pp. 3–10.

4. This section on communication macrobarriers is based primarily on David S. Brown, "Barriers to Successful Communication: Part I, Macrobarriers," *Management Review,* December 1975, pp. 24–29.

5. James A. Lee, "Cultural Analysis in Overseas Operations," *Harvard Business Review,* no. 2 (March-April 1966): 106–14.

6. This section on communication microbarriers is based primarily on David S. Brown, "Barriers to Successful Communication: Part II, Microbarriers," *Management Review,* January 1976, pp. 15–21.

7. Gene E. Burton, "Barriers to Effective Communication," *Management World,* March 1977, pp. 4–8.

8. Sally Bulkley Pancrazio and James J. Pancrazio, "Better Communication for Managers," *Supervisory Management,* June 1981, pp. 31–37.

9. Lydia Strong, "Do You Know How to Listen?" in *Effective Communications on the Job,* eds. Dooher and Marquis (New York: American Management Association, 1956), p. 28.

10. Donald E. Montgomery, "How to Get Your Message Across," *Supervisory Management,* February 1975, pp. 2–10.

11. For more on nonverbal feedback, see James M. Lahiff, "Clear Up Communication Static," *Supervisory Management,* March 1973, pp. 21–29.

12. Robert S. Goyer, "Interpersonal Communication and Human Interaction: A Behavioral View" (paper presented at the 138th annual meeting of the American Association for the Advancement of Science, 1971).

13. Verne Burnett, "Management's Tower of Babel," *Management Review,* June 1961, pp. 4–11.

14. Reprinted by permission of the publisher, © 1955 by American Management Association, Inc. All rights reserved.

15. Albert Mehrabian, "Communication without Words," *Psychology Today* 2 (September 1968): 53–55.

16. The study of gestures is called kinesics. For more information on kinesics, see Ray Birdwhistell, "Background to Kinesics," *ETC* 13 (1955): 10–18.

17. Don Fabun, *Communications: The Transfer of Meaning* (New York: Macmillan, 1968).

18. A. M. Meerioo, *Unobtrusive Communication: Essays in Psycholinguistics* (Assen, Netherlands: Van Gorcum, 1964).

19. Gary M. Grikscheit and William J. E. Crissy, "Improving Interpersonal Communication Skill," *MSU Business Topics,* Autumn 1973, pp. 63–68.

20. Charles W. Redding, "Position Paper: A Response to Discussions at the Ad Hoc Conference on Organizational Communication" (Lafayette, Ind.: Purdue University Communication Research Center, May 1967).

21. Don J. Baxter, "Employee Communication . . . A Matter of Organizational Survival," *Journal of Organizational Communication* 4, no. 1 (1974): 5–7.

22. Paul H. Pietri, "Organizational Communication: The Pioneers," *The Journal of Business Communication* 11, no. 4 (1974): 3–6.

23. Kenneth R. VanVoorhis, "Organizational Communication: Advances Made During the Period from World War II through the 1950s," *Journal of Business Communication* 11, no. 4 (1974): 11–18.

24. Phillip J. Lewis, "The Status of 'Organizational Communication' in Colleges of Business," *The Journal of Business Communication* 12, no. 4 (1975): 25–28.

25. This section on formal organizational communication is based primarily on Paul Preston, "The Critical 'Mix' in Managerial Communications," *Industrial Management,* March-April 1976, pp. 5–9.

26. Arnold E. Schneider, William C. Donaghy, and Pamela J. Newman, "Communication Climate within an Organization," *Management Controls,* October-November 1976, pp. 159–62.

27. Schneider, Donaghy, and Newman, "Communication Climate within an Organization," pp. 159–62.

28. William V. Haney, "Serial Communication of Information in Organizations," in *Concepts and Issues in Administrative Behavior,* eds. Sidney Mailick and Edward H. Van Ness (Englewood Cliffs, N.J.: Prentice-Hall, 1962), p. 150.

29. Haney, "Serial Communication," p. 150.

30. Alex Bavelas and Dermot Barrett, "An Experimental Approach to Organizational Communication," *Personnel* 27 (1951): 366–71.

31. Eugene Walton, "Communicating Down the Line: How They Really Get the Word," *Personnel,* July-August 1959, pp. 78–82.

32. Keith Davis, "Management Communication and the Grapevine," *Harvard Business Review* (January-February 1953): 43–49.

33. Linda McCallister, "The Interpersonal Side of Internal Communications," *Public Relations Journal,* February 1981, pp. 20–23.

34. Eugene Walton, "How Efficient Is the Grapevine?" *Personnel,* March-April 1961, pp. 45–49.

35. Keith Davis, "Cut Those Rumors Down to Size," *Supervisory Management,* June 1975, pp. 2–7.

Concluding Case 12
Improved Communication: One of Labor Secretary Donovan's First Priorities

Raymond G. Donovan (Photo: Wide World Photos)

Raymond G. Donovan was selected by President Reagan to serve as Secretary of Labor in his Cabinet recently. Donovan brings with him both his experience and his instincts that indicate that he will be an excellent manager. Further, previous experience as a bargainer in the building trades suggests that he should do well in promoting smooth and efficient collective bargaining. Managerial ability and collective bargaining skills are only two of the responsibilities pertinent to the position of Labor Secretary. The other major areas of concern are manpower areas in which Donovan sorely lacks skill or experienced subordinates and he must make appointments quickly in order to control the politically sensitive department.

One of Donovan's first priorities when he begins his term is to improve the management of his department. According to Donovan, he wants to "get the lines of communication running out and down into the bowels of the department." However at this point, Donovan and the White House are as yet to appoint the undersecretary and three assistant secretaries to form the basis of his "smoothly communicating" department. *

Donovan carries his management approach over to his bargaining approach. He hopes that his department's approach to collective bargaining will please labor. "Our job is to facilitate bargaining, to lend our offices and services, but not to become a referee," says Donovan. While with Schiavone Construction Company as executive vice-president, he gained a reputation as a skilled bargainer among the building trades. From this experience, he has found that in most cases there is little communication in advance of the actual bargaining process; he hopes to remedy this by pushing for the formation of labor-management committees.

In contrast to this are Donovan's positions on other matters of policy in the Labor Department. He wants to remove more than three hundred thousand public service jobs for the disadvantaged and put more money into business-oriented programs that would train these workers for jobs in private industry. In addition, he plans to rewrite the Comprehensive Employment and Training Act (CETA) and make it more "result oriented." Furthermore, he plans to reduce the Labor Department budget by approximately $6.8 billion, a reduction of 18 percent. These positions are likely to anger labor whose interests he is charged by law to protect. Concerning regulations, he promises to change the Occupational Safety and Health Administration (OSHA) so that it creates less interference with business. In addition, he promises to prosecute union officials that violate federal labor laws.

Some of Donovan's appointments thus far have been highly criticized. For instance, Albert Angrisani, a thirty-one-year-old former loan vice-president for Chase Manhattan Bank, was selected as assistant secretary for employment and training. His appointment was fought by some White House officials, but Donovan's insistence prevailed. In addition, he appointed Thorn G. Auchter, a thirty-five-year-old construction executive, to administer OSHA. Angrisani and Auchter are not recognized as experts in their respective fields; however Donovan selected them both because they are good managers, a trait he considers to be of greater importance than knowledge of their fields.

*Since this article was written, Malcolm Powell has been appointed Undersecretary of Labor. The three assistant secretaries are William Plowden, secretary for veteran's employment; Ford Ford, secretary for mines' safety and health; and James F. Cogan, secretary for policy evaluation and research.

This case is adapted from "A Hard Apprenticeship for Labor's Donovan." *Business Week*, March 9, 1981, pp. 23–24.

Discussion Issues

1. What specifically is Donovan doing to "get lines of communication running out and down into the bowels of the department?"
2. Once positions are staffed and functioning, how could Donovan assess the effectiveness of communication in his department?
3. Do you believe that Donovan is only concerned with downward and outward flow of information? Explain.
4. Which communication microbarriers would you suspect have the greatest impact in the collective bargaining process? Explain.
5. Which of the basic "ten commandments of good communication" seem to be *most* important to Donovan? Explain.

Student Learning Objectives

From studying this chapter I will attempt to acquire:

1. A working definition of leadership
2. An understanding of the relationship between leading and managing
3. An appreciation for the trait and situational approaches to leadership
4. Insights on how to make decisions as a leader
5. A strategy for using the life cycle theory of leadership
6. An understanding of alternatives to leader flexibility

Chapter Outline

Leadership

Introductory Case 13
Becoming a Successful Leader

Case figure 13.1 A comparison of successful and unsuccessful organizational leaders.

Profile of More Successful Leaders	Profile of Less Successful Leaders
People who were usually in the upper 10 percent of their school class.	Less successful people tend to be from the middle or lower half of their school class.
Their favorite subject was probably one of the social sciences or English, even though they may have majored in engineering or business.	Their favorite subject was science or math.
They read the *New York Times*, are familiar with the Bible, and prefer French impressionist paintings and Tchaikovsky's music.	They read the *New York Times* less than their successful counterparts and the *Wall Street Journal* more.
Their TV habits tend towards news programs and sports, with occasional mixing of such programs as "All in the Family."	They prefer sports to news on TV and have limited interest in art and music.
Their most admired leader is Winston Churchill, although Richard M. Nixon rated high with them before Watergate. Dwight D. Eisenhower and John F. Kennedy are lesser choices, but in the top four.	They are politically more independent or neutral than successful people, and three times more often a Republican than a Democrat.
Their average annual income is around $75,000, although their range might be as low as $25,000 or as high as $1,000,000. Their age range is the mid-fifties. More often than not they are Republicans rather than Independents or Democrats (3 to 2).	Their average income is $16,000, and their rate of salary growth over the past ten years was half that of the successful executives. Their choice of a leader was Nixon (pre-Watergate), almost three times over Churchill or Eisenhower.
Successful executives place a high priority on moral standards and integrity, on a sense of fairness to others, and a sense of personal worthfulness. They are less interested in defeating communism or advancing capitalism than in being happy.	They place survival and return on investments on the same par as integrity. They are less interested in helping humanity than helping themselves. They no longer have their hearts set on making a fortune, but are more willing to settle for improving their financial security and their work situation.
In their scale of values, they place power and economics at the top of the list. However, they are significantly higher than less successful executives in their concern for people.	They place a great value on intelligence and place economics at the top of their list of values.

John Rich is a dietitian and manager of a hospital food services department in a large metropolitan hospital. One of Rich's strengths as a manager is that he continually reads management-related articles to improve his managerial effectiveness. Last week he read an article that compared successful and unsuccessful organizational leaders. A summary of the main theme of this article is presented in case figure 13.1.

Rich was somewhat disturbed because as he attempted to evaluate himself in relation to the two profiles, he seemed to have more of the characteristics of the less successful leader than the more successful leader. Rich developed a strategy, based on this article, for becoming a more successful leader. The strategy required that he change his interests and attitudes to be more consistent with the profile of the more successful leader. Rich reasoned that as his interests and attitudes came closer to those of more successful leaders, he would become a more successful leader himself.

Discussion Issues

1. Evaluate John Rich's strategy.
2. How would you have reacted to this article (summarized in case figure 13.1) if you were Rich?

What's Ahead

John Rich, the dietitian-manager in the introductory case, is attempting to become a more successful leader by changing his interests and attitudes. The information in this chapter would be helpful to an individual like Rich as the basis for developing a more useful leadership strategy. This chapter discusses (1) how to define leadership, (2) the difference between a leader and a manager, (3) the trait approach to leadership, and (4) the situational approach to leadership.

Leadership is the process of directing the behavior of others toward the accomplishment of some objective. Directing, in this sense, means causing individuals to act in a certain way or to follow a particular course. Ideally, this course of action is perfectly consistent with such factors as established organizational policies, procedures, and job descriptions. The central theme of leadership is getting things accomplished through people. As indicated in chapter 12, leadership is one of the four main interdependent activities of the influencing subsystem and is accomplished, at least to some extent, by communicating with others. Leadership is of such great importance to organizational success that some management writers recommend that when interviewing candidates to fill an open management position, the interviewer should try to find out the candidate's leadership style to see if it is appropriate for the needs of the organization.[1]

Defining Leadership

Guiding Behavior

Leading is not the same as managing.[2] Although some managers are leaders and some leaders are managers, leading and managing are not identical activities.[3] According to Theodore Levitt, management consists of:

Leader vs. Manager

> the rational assessment of a situation and the systematic selection of goals and purposes (what is to be done); the systematic development of strategies to achieve these goals; the marshalling of the required resources; the rational design, organization, direction, and control of the activities required to attain the selected purposes; and, finally, the motivating and rewarding of people to do the work.[4]

Leadership, on the other hand, as one of the four primary activities comprising the influencing function, is a subset of management. Managing is much broader in scope than leading and focuses on behavioral as well as nonbehavioral issues. Leading emphasizes mainly behavioral issues. Figure 13.1 makes the point that although all managers are not necessarily leaders, the most effective managers, over the long run, are. Figure 13.2 is a list of the primary activities that effective managers/leaders perform.

Leadership is Part of Management

The **trait approach to leadership** is based on early leadership research that seemed to assume that a good leader is born and not made. The mainstream of this research attempted to describe successful leaders as precisely as possible. The reasoning was that if a complete profile of the traits of a successful leader could be summarized, it would be fairly easy to pinpoint those individuals who should and should not be placed in leadership positions.

The Trait Approach to Leadership

Figure 13.1 Most effective managers over the long run are also leaders.

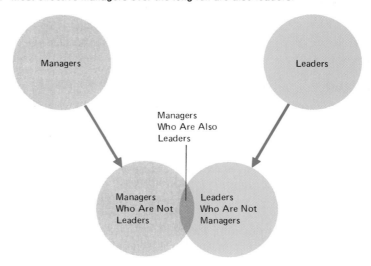

Figure 13.2 Primary activities of the effective manager/leader.

1. *In Terms of Attitudes toward Subordinates:*
   a. Has confidence in subordinates and conveys this confidence.
   b. Is approachable and friendly.
   c. Is eager to help subordinates to be more effective and works at removing obstacles to achievement.
   d. In dealing with subordinates, is emotionally supportive and is careful to avoid ego-threatening behavior.
   e. Tries to minimize stress in relationships with subordinates to avoid diminishing subordinates use of intellectual capabilities.
   f. Permits subordinates to have latitude in the solution of work problems where the subordinate's ingenuity can result in gains and where standardization in method is not imperative.
   g. Is cognizant of the need for leadership styles to be somewhat different in different technological settings, for example, that it is easily possible to overstructure and be too directive in a laboratory setting and to understructure and be too participative in some factory settings.
   h. Encourages the participation of subordinates but only on the basis of a genuine interest in utilizing constructive suggestions and only where subordinates perceive participation as being legitimate.
2. *In Terms of Technology, Planning, and Selection:*
   a. Utilizes, and encourages subordinates to utilize the appropriate technology in attaining these goals — e.g., work simplification, appropriate tools, proper layout, and so on.
   b. Is an effective planner in terms of both short-range and long-range goals and contingencies.
   c. Selects subordinates with appropriate qualifications.
3. *In Terms of Performance Standards and Appraisal:*
   a. Works with subordinates in establishing attainable but high performance standards and high goals — which are consistent with the goals of the enterprise.
   b. Appraises subordinates as nearly as possible on objective, measurable performance but makes compensation and promotion judgments on the basis of total performance.
4. *In Terms of the Linking-Pin Function:*
   a. Is an effective link with higher management and other groups within the enterprise in facilitating task performance.
5. *In Terms of Rewards and Correction:*
   a. Gives recognition to good work.
   b. Uses subordinates' mistakes as an educational opportunity rather than an opportunity for punishment.

From Wendell L. French: PERSONNEL MANAGEMENT PROCESS, 5th ed., pp. 123–124. Copyright © 1982, 1978, 1974 by Houghton Mifflin Company. Used by permission.

Many of the studies that attempted to summarize the traits of successful leaders have been documented.[5] One of these summaries concludes that successful leaders tend to possess the following characteristics:

1. Intelligence, including judgment and verbal ability
2. Past achievements in scholarship and athletics
3. Emotional maturity and stability
4. Dependability, persistence, and a drive for continuing achievement
5. The skill to participate socially and adapt to various groups
6. A desire for status and socioeconomic position[6]

An evaluation of a number of these trait studies, however, concludes that their findings generally tend to be inconsistent.[7] One researcher says that fifty years of study have failed to produce one personality trait or set of qualities that can be used consistently to discriminate leaders from nonleaders.[8] It follows then, that no trait or combination of traits guarantees that a leader will be successful. Thus, leadership is apparently a much more complex issue than simply describing the traits of successful leaders.

Back to the Case

From the preceding material John Rich should be able to see that his leadership activities in the hospital involve directing the behavior of food services employees so that hospital goals are reached. Rich also should recognize that leading and managing are not the same thing. When managing, Rich is involved with planning, organizing, influencing, and controlling within the food services area. When leading, Rich actually is performing an activity that is part of the influencing function of management. To maximize his long-run success, Rich should strive to be both a manager and a leader.

The introductory case concludes with Rich attempting to increase his success as a leader by changing his interests and attitudes. Studies based on the trait approach to leadership should indicate to Rich that merely changing his individual characteristics will not guarantee his success as a leader.

The Situational Approach to Leadership

The emphasis of leadership study has shifted from the trait approach to primarily the situational approach. The more modern **situational approach to leadership** is based on the assumption that all instances of successful leadership are somewhat different and require a unique combination of leaders, followers, and leadership situations. This interaction commonly is expressed in formula form: $SL = f(L,F,S)$. In this formula, SL is *successful leadership*, f stands for *function of*, and L, F, and S are, respectively, the *leader*, the *follower*, and the *situation*. A translation of this formula would be that successful leadership is a function of the leader, the follower, and the situation. In other words, the leader, the follower, and the situation must be appropriate for one another if a leadership attempt is to be successful.

Leadership Situations and Decisions

Tannenbaum and Schmidt wrote one of the first and perhaps most well-known discussions on the situational approach to leadership. This discussion emphasizes situations in which a leader makes decisions.[9] Since one of the most important tasks of a leader is making sound decisions, practical and legitimate leadership thinking should contain some emphasis on decision making. Figure 13.3 presents Tannenbaum and Schmidt's model of leadership behavior that contains such a decision-making emphasis.

Figure 13.3 Continuum of leadership behavior that emphasizes decision making.

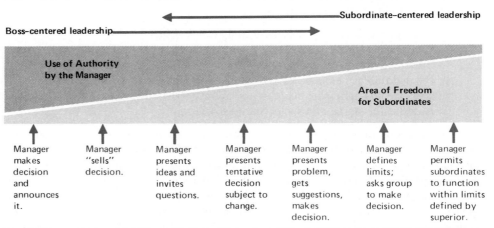

Continuum of Behavior

The model presented in figure 13.3 is actually a continuum, or range, of leadership behavior available to managers in making decisions. Each type of decision-making behavior on this model has both a corresponding degree of authority used by the manager and a related amount of freedom available to subordinates. Management behaviors at the extreme left of the model characterize the leader who makes decisions by maintaining high control and allowing little subordinate freedom, while those at the extreme right characterize the leader who makes decisions by exercising little control and allowing much subordinate freedom and self-direction. Behavior between the extreme right and left of the model reflect a gradual change from autocratic to democratic leadership, or vice versa. Managers displaying leadership behavior toward the right of the model are more democratic and called subordinate-centered leaders, while managers displaying leadership behavior toward the left of the model are more autocratic and called boss-centered leaders. Each type of leadership behavior in this model is explained in more detail in the paragraphs that follow.

The manager makes the decision and announces it   This behavior is characterized by the manager (1) identifying a problem, (2) analyzing various alternatives available to solve the problem, (3) choosing the alternative that will be used to solve the problem, and (4) requiring followers to implement the chosen alternative. Coercion may or may not be used by the leader, but the followers have no opportunity to participate directly in the decision-making process.

The manager "sells" the decision   As before, the manager identifies the problem and independently arrives at a decision. Rather than announce the decision to subordinates for implementation, however, the manager tries to persuade subordinates to accept the decision.

The manager presents his or her ideas and invites questions   Here, the manager makes the decision and attempts to gain acceptance through persuasion. One additional step is taken, however, since subordinates are invited to ask questions about the decision.

"If we knew what conclusions the President wanted our commission to come to, we could come to them, and that would be that."

Drawing by Handelsman; © 1971 The New Yorker Magazine, Inc.

The manager presents a tentative decision subject to change   The manager actually allows subordinates to have some part in the decision-making process. The responsibility for identifying and diagnosing the problem, however, remains with the manager. The manager arrives at a tentative decision that is subject to change based upon subordinate input. The final decision is made by the manager.

The manager presents the problem, gets suggestions, and then makes the decision   This is the first leadership activity described thus far that allows subordinates the opportunity to offer problem solutions before the manager offers a problem solution. The manager still, however, identifies the problem in the first place.

The manager defines the limits and requests the group to make a decision   This behavior is characterized by the manager first defining the problem and setting the boundaries within which a decision must be made. The manager then indicates that she or he and the group are partners in making an appropriate decision. However, if the group does not perceive the manager as genuinely desiring a serious group decision-making effort, it will tend to arrive at conclusions that reflect what the group thinks the manager wants rather than what the group actually thinks.

The manager permits the group to make decisions within prescribed limits   Here the manager actually becomes an equal member of a problem-solving group. The entire group identifies and assesses the problem, develops alternative problem solutions, and chooses an alternative to be implemented. Everyone within the group understands that the group's decision will be implemented.

Back to the Case

The situational approach to leadership can give John Rich more insight on how to develop his leadership skill than the trait approach. The situational approach suggests that successful leadership within the hospital is determined by the appropriateness of a combination of three factors: (1) Rich as a leader, (2) the food services' employees or followers, and (3) the situation within the food services department. Each of these factors will play a significant role in determining whether or not Rich is successful.

One of the most important activities Rich will perform as a leader is making decisions. He can make decisions in any number of ways, ranging from being primarily authoritarian (making a decision and announcing it) to primarily democratic (permitting subordinates to make the decision within defined limits).

Determining How to Make Decisions as a Leader

Although the model developed by Tannenbaum and Schmidt makes for interesting discussion, its true value can be realized only if a leader can use it to make practical and desirable decisions. According to these authors, the three primary factors or forces that influence a manager's determination of which leadership behavior to use to make decisions are (1) forces in the manager, (2) forces in subordinates, and (3) forces in the leadership situation. Each of these forces is discussed in the following in more detail.

Forces in the Manager

Managers should be aware of four forces within themselves that influence their determination of how to make decisions as a leader. The first of these forces is a manager's values, such as the relative importance to the manager of organizational efficiency, personal growth, growth of subordinates, and company profits. For example, if subordinate growth is valued very highly, a manager may want to give the group members the valuable experience of making a decision, even though the manager could have made the same decision much more quickly and efficiently alone.

The second force within the manager is the manager's level of confidence in subordinates. In general, the more confidence a manager has in subordinates, the more likely the manager's style of decision making will be democratic or subordinate-centered. The reverse is also true. The less confidence a manager has in subordinates, the more likely the manager's style of decision making will be autocratic, or boss-centered.

The third force within the manager that influences a manager's determination of how to make decisions as a leader is the manager's own leadership strengths. Some managers are more effective in issuing orders than leading a group discussion and vice versa. A manager must be able to recognize his or her personal leadership strengths and to capitalize on them.

The fourth influencing force within a manager is tolerance for ambiguity. As a manager moves from a boss-centered style to a subordinate-centered style, she or he loses some certainty about how problems should be solved. If this reduction of certainty is disturbing to a manager, it may be extremely difficult for the manager to be successful as a subordinate-centered leader.

Forces in Subordinates

A manager also should be aware of forces within subordinates that influence the manager's determination of how to make decisions as a leader.[10] To understand subordinates adequately, a manager should keep in mind that each subordinate is both somewhat different and somewhat alike. Any cookbook approach for deciding how to lead all subordinates is therefore impossible. Generally speaking, however, a manager probably could increase his or her success as a leader by allowing subordinates more freedom in making decisions, as suggested in the following:

1. If the subordinates have relatively high needs for independence. (People differ greatly in the amount of direction they desire.)
2. If the subordinates have a readiness to assume responsibility for decision making. (Some see additional responsibility as a tribute to their ability; others see it as "passing the buck.")
3. If they have a relatively high tolerance for ambiguity. (Some employees prefer to have clear-cut directives given to them; others prefer a wider area of freedom.)
4. If they are interested in the problem and feel that it is important.
5. If they understand and identify with goals of the organization.
6. If they have the necessary knowledge and experience to deal with the problem.

7. If they have learned to expect to share in decision making. (Persons who have come to expect strong leadership and who suddenly are confronted with the request to share more fully in decision making are often upset by this new experience. On the other hand, persons who have enjoyed a considerable amount of freedom resent the boss who begins to make all the decisions alone.)[11]

If these characteristics of subordinates do not exist in a particular situation, a manager probably should move toward a more autocratic or boss-centered approach to making decisions.

Forces in the Situation

The last group of forces that influence a manager's determination of how to make decisions as a leader are forces in the leadership situation. The first such situational force involves the type of organization in which the leader works. Such organizational factors as the size of working groups and their geographical distribution become especially important in deciding how to make decisions as a leader. Extremely large work groups or a wide geographic separation of work groups, for example, could make a subordinate-centered leadership style impractical.

The Organization

Another such force in the leadership situation is the effectiveness of group members working together. To this end, a manager should evaluate such issues as the experience of the group in working together and the degree of confidence group members have in their ability to solve problems as a group. As a general rule, a manager should only assign decision-making responsibilities to effective work groups.

Effectiveness of Groups

A third situational force that influences a manager's determination of how to make decisions as a leader is the problem to be solved. Before acting as a more subordinate-centered leader, a manager should be sure that a group possesses the expertise necessary to make a decision about the existing problem. As a group loses the necessary expertise to solve a problem, a manager generally should move toward more boss-centered leadership.

Problem to Be Solved

A fourth situational force involves the time available to make a decision. As a general guideline, the less time available to make a decision, the more impractical it becomes to have that decision made by a group. Typically it takes a group more time to reach a decision than an individual.

Time Available to Solve Problem

Figure 13.4 summarizes the main forces that influence a manager's determination of how to make decisions as a leader and stresses the point that this determination is the result of the collective influence of all these forces. As the situational approach to leadership implies, a manager will be successful as a decision maker only if the method used to make those decisions appropriately reflects the leader, the followers, and the situation.

Determining How to Make Decisions as a Leader: An Update

Tannenbaum and Schmidt's original article on leadership decision making was so widely accepted that these two authors were invited by *Harvard Business Review* to update their original work.[12] This update stresses that in modern organizations the relationship among forces within the manager, subordinates, and situation is becoming more complex and more interrelated than ever. As this relationship becomes increasingly complicated, it obviously becomes more difficult for the leader to determine how to lead.

Increasing Interrelatedness and Complexity

This update also stresses both societal and organizational environments as more modern forces to consider when determining how to lead. Such societal and organizational values as the development of minority groups and pollution control should have some influence on the decision making of leaders.

Decision Environment

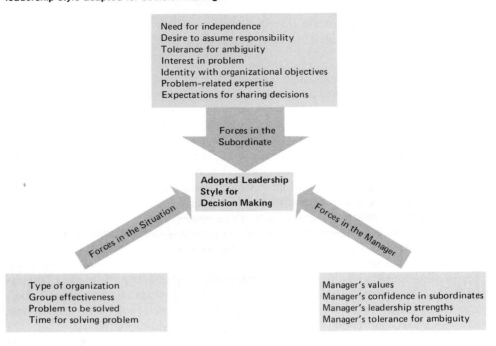

Figure 13.4 Collective influence of forces in the manager, subordinates, and the situation on the leadership style adapted for decision making.

Need for independence
Desire to assume responsibility
Tolerance for ambiguity
Interest in problem
Identity with organizational objectives
Problem-related expertise
Expectations for sharing decisions

Forces in the Subordinate

Adopted Leadership Style for Decision Making

Forces in the Situation

Forces in the Manager

Type of organization
Group effectiveness
Problem to be solved
Time for solving problem

Manager's values
Manager's confidence in subordinates
Manager's leadership strengths
Manager's tolerance for ambiguity

Back to the Case

When trying to decide exactly how to make his decisions as a leader, John Rich should consider forces in himself as manager, forces in subordinates or his food services employees, and forces in the situation or the food services department. Forces within Rich include his own ideas about how to lead, his level of confidence in the food services personnel, and his overall leadership strengths and weaknesses. Forces within the food

services personnel include their need for independence, their readiness to assume responsibility for decision making, and their tolerance for ambiguity. Forces within the food services department include the geographic distribution of personnel and the number of personnel making a decision. Rich must consider all such forces collectively when determining the best way for him to make decisions within his department.

Leadership Situations in General

In addition to Tannenbaum and Schmidt's model of leadership, decision-making behavior is another stream of leadership thought that focuses on leadership situations in more general terms. This stream of thought usually is discussed as beginning with a series of leadership studies affiliated with the Bureau of Business Research at Ohio State University. These studies are called the OSU studies.[13]

The OSU Studies

The OSU studies are a series of leadership investigations that concluded that leaders exhibit two main types of behavior while accomplishing their duties. The first type of behavior is called structure behavior. **Structure behavior** is any leadership activity that (1) delineates the relationship between the leader and the leader's followers or (2) establishes well-defined procedures that followers should adhere to in performing

What Is Structure Behavior?

Figure 13.5 Four fundamental leadership styles based on structure behavior and consideration behavior.

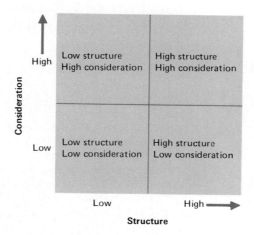

their jobs. Overall, structure behavior limits the self-guidance of followers in the performance of their tasks. Although it would be correct to conclude that structure behavior can be, and sometimes is, relatively firm, it would be incorrect to assume that it is rude and malicious.[14]

Exhibit 13 illustrates how Bennett A. Brown, the chief executive of Citizens & Southern National Bank, seemed to help his organization by performing less structured behavior than did his predecessor. Brown did, however, closely control subordinate behavior through a management by objectives program.[15]

The second main type of leadership behavior described by the OSU studies is consideration behavior. **Consideration behavior** is leadership behavior that reflects friendship, mutual trust, respect, and warmth in the relationship between the leader and the followers. Consideration behavior generally is aimed at developing and maintaining a more human relationship between the leader and the followers.

What Is Consideration Behavior?

The OSU studies resulted in a model that depicts four fundamental leadership styles. A **leadership style** is the behavior a leader exhibits while guiding organization members in appropriate directions. This model is presented in figure 13.5. Each of the four leadership styles in this model is actually a different combination of structure behavior and consideration behavior. Each style represents a leader who emphasizes structure differently than consideration. For example, the high structure/low consideration leadership syle represents a leader who emphasizes structure behavior and deemphasizes consideration behavior.

Behavior Exhibited

Effectiveness of Various Leadership Styles

One investigation of high school superintendents concluded that more desirable leadership behavior seems to be associated with high leader emphasis on both structure and consideration, while more undesirable leadership behavior tends to be associated with low leader emphasis on both dimensions.[16] Similarly, the managerial grid covered in chapter 11 implies that the most effective leadership style is characterized by high consideration and high structure.

One should be extremely careful, however, in concluding that any one leadership style is more effective than any other.[17] The overall leadership situation is so complex that pinpointing one leadership style as the most effective seems to be an oversimplification. In fact, individual managers probably will find that a successful leadership style for them in one situation is ineffective for them in another situation. Recognizing

Which Leadership Style Is Best?

Exhibit 13

Brown Allows His Subordinates Freedom at Citizens & Southern National Bank

McIntyre, Brown, and Poelker (Photo: T. S. England)

When Bennett A. Brown was promoted from assistant president to acting chief executive of Citizens & Southern National Bank in February, 1978, the general reaction was dismay. One veteran C&S-watcher recalls thinking, "Oh, my God, no! Only a complete outsider could clean up this mess." And indeed, "mess" was an understatement to describe C&S's condition then. . . .

Today everyone is singing a different tune. By any standard, Brown has done a miraculous patch-up job. Last year, C&S posted record earnings of $37.2 million on assets of $4.8 billion, and analysts are forecasting a 12% increase in profits this year, to $42 million. Nonperforming assets—foreclosed properties or reduced-rate loans—have been chopped from a high of $212 million in 1977 to $60 million, while net core deposits increased 23% since 1977, to $2 billion. The quarterly dividend has been reinstated at 10¢ per share. And return on average assets was 0.93% in June—still below the 1% average for 20 leading Southern banks but certainly a vast improvement from C&S's negative return of 1977.

To C&S insiders, the change in management style has been as profound as the balance-sheet improvement. Brown himself describes Kattel's method as "strong, one-man rule." By contrast, Brown advocates delegation of authority. But, he says bluntly, "You put a guy in charge, and if he doesn't do it, you get rid of him." Over the last few years, Brown has determinedly implemented that philosophy. For the first time, C&S has a classic management-by-objectives program. All bank officers participate in setting their own goals—and are held accountable for meeting them. A committee of the bank's top 11 managers meets weekly and distributes the minutes of its meeting throughout the C&S system of 11 banks. There is a quarterly review system in which subordinates are evaluated by the senior managers, who in turn are evaluated by Brown. Brown is reviewed by the executive committee of the board, which measures his progress against his plan. Indeed, C&S now has a formal five-year plan along with its first formal planning structure.

Autonomy. While top management takes a major role in setting the goals, subordinates have considerable autonomy in their method of meeting them. For example, in July, 1978, Brown promoted Willard A. Alexander, a 30-year C&S veteran, to general vice-president for credit administration and gave him clear-cut marching orders: Unload bad loans as quickly as possible, and reduce nonperforming assets by 20% annually. "I told Willie that this bank has the worst portfolio, and cleaning up the mess is your responsibility," Brown recalls. Alexander clearly heard the message. "My neck was on the line," he says now. He formed a 30-member staff that for two years concentrated solely on combing out bad loans. The result

was that nonperforming assets were slashed by 25% in 1978, 38% in 1979, and 31% last year—vastly exceeding Brown's hopes.

Brown is equally willing to let new hires run with the ball. In August, 1978, he set aside C&S's promote-from-within tradition and hired John S. Poelker, then senior vice-president of Mercantile Trust Co. in St. Louis, as his new chief financial officer. "I told him that we have the worst accounting system and I want the best," Brown says. "I gave him 18 months to do it, and he did it. It used to take us a month to 45 days to get out quarterly earnings reports. Now they are out in 10 days."

Poelker, who became C&S president in 1979, recalls the period as one of trying to create order out of chaos. "There were, incredibly, millions of numbers flying around, and they overburdened top management to the point of being meaningless," he explains. Poelker and Brown brought in 13 more outside executives with financial backgrounds to strengthen controls. Today, Brown reviews only those reports that show more than a 10% variance from plan.

Figure 13.6 The life cycle theory of leadership model.

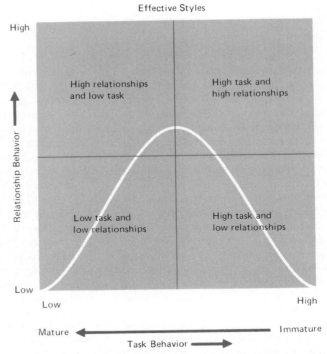

Effective Styles

Paul Hersey, Kenneth H. Blanchard, MANAGEMENT OF ORGANIZATIONAL BEHAVIOR: Utilizing Human Resources, 3rd ed. © 1977, p. 103. Reprinted by permission of Prentice-Hall, Inc., Englewood Cliffs, New Jersey.

the need to link leadership styles to appropriate situations, A. K. Korman indicates that a worthwhile contribution to leadership literature would be a rationale for systematically linking appropriate styles with various situations so as to ensure effective leadership.[18] The life cycle theory of leadership, which is covered in the next section, provides such a rationale.

Life Cycle Theory of Leadership

Linking Style and Situations

The **life cycle theory of leadership** is a rationale for linking leadership styles with various situations so as to ensure effective leadership. This theory uses essentially the same two types of leadership behavior as the OSU leadership studies, but calls these dimensions "task" rather than structure, and "relationships" rather than consideration.

Follower Maturity
Task Behavior
Relationship Behavior

Life cycle theory is based primarily on the relationship between follower maturity, leader task behavior, and leader relationship behavior. In general terms, according to this theory, leadership style primarily should reflect the maturity level of the followers. **Maturity** is defined as the ability of the followers to perform their job independently, to assume additional responsibility, and desire to achieve success. The more of each of these characteristics followers possess, the more mature they are said to be. Maturity, as used in life cycle theory, is not necessarily linked to chronological age.

Matching Leadership Style With Follower Maturity Level

Figure 13.6 shows the life cycle theory of leadership model. The curved line in this model indicates the maturity level of the followers. As the maturity curve runs from right to left, the follower's maturity level increases. In more specific terms, life cycle theory suggests that effective leadership behavior should shift from "(1) high task—low relationships behavior to (2) high task—high relationships behavior to (3) high relationships—low task behavior to (4) low task—low relationships behavior, as one's followers progress from immaturity to maturity."[19]

Figure 13.7 How basic leadership styles are perceived by others as effective and ineffective.

Basic Styles	Effective	Ineffective
High task and low relationships	Often seen as knowing what he or she wants and imposing personal methods for accomplishing this without creating resentment.	Often seen as having no confidence in others, unpleasant, and interested only in short-run output.
High task and high relationships	Often seen as satisfying the needs of the group for setting goals and organizing work, but also providing high levels of socioemotional support.	Often seen as initiating more structure than is needed by the group and spends more time on socioemotional support than necessary.
High relationships and low task	Often seen as having implicit trust in people and as being primarily concerned with developing their talents.	Often seen as primarily interested in harmony and being seen as "a good person," and being unwilling to risk disruption of a relationship to accomplish a task.
Low task and low relationships	Often seen as appropriately permitting subordinates to decide how the work should be done and playing only a minor part in their social interaction.	Often seen as uninvolved and passive, as a "paper shuffler," who cares little about the task at hand or the people involved.

Reprinted from Paul Hersey, Kenneth H. Blanchard, MANAGEMENT OF ORGANIZATIONAL BEHAVIOR: Utilizing Human Resources, 3rd ed., © 1977 by Prentice-Hall, Inc., Englewood Cliffs, New Jersey. Used with permission of Dr. W. J. Reddin, University of New Brunswick.

Life cycle theory suggests, therefore, that a style of leadership will be effective only if it is appropriate for the maturity level of the followers. Figure 13.7 indicates how each of the four main leadership styles is perceived when it is both effective and ineffective, or appropriate and inappropriate, for followers' maturity levels.

Some exceptions to the general philosophy of life cycle theory do exist. For example, if there is a short-run deadline to meet, a leader may find it necessary to accelerate production through a high task—low relationships style rather than a low task—low relationships style even though the leader's followers may be extremely mature. A high task—low relationships leadership style carried out over the long run with such followers, however, typically results in a poor working relationship between leader and followers.

Exceptions to Life Cycle Theory

The following is an example of how life cycle theory would apply in an actual leadership situation. A man has just been hired as a salesperson in a men's clothing store. Immediately upon entrance in the organization, this individual is extremely immature, or in other words, unable to solve task-related problems independently. According to life cycle theory, the appropriate style for leading this salesperson at his level of maturity is high task—low relationships. The leader should tell the salesperson exactly what should be done and how it should be done. The salesperson should be shown how to make cash sales, how to make charge sales, and how to handle merchandise returns. The leader also should begin laying some of the groundwork for developing a personal relationship with the salesperson. Too much relationships behavior at this point, however, should be avoided since it easily can be misinterpreted as permissiveness.

Life Cycle Theory: An Example

As time passes and the salesperson increases somewhat in job-related maturity, the next appropriate style for leading him is high task—high relationships. Although the salesperson's maturity has increased somewhat, the leader needs to watch him closely because he still needs some guidance and direction at various times. The main difference between this leadership style and the first leadership style is the amount of relationships behavior displayed by the leader. Building on the groundwork laid during use of the first leadership style, the leader is now ready to start developing to its utmost an atmosphere of mutual trust, respect, and friendliness between him and the salesperson.

As more time passes, the salesperson's maturity level increases still further. The next style appropriate for leading this individual is high relationships—low task. The leader can now deemphasize task behavior because the salesperson is now of above average maturity in his job and usually can solve job-related problems independently. As with the previous leadership style, the leader still emphasizes the development of a human relationship with his followers.

As the salesperson's maturity level approximates its maximum, the appropriate style for leading him is low task—low relationships. Again, the leader can deemphasize task behavior because the follower is thoroughly familiar with the job. The leader also can deemphasize relationships behavior because he now has a good working relationship with the follower. Here, task behavior is seldom needed, and relationships behavior is used primarily to nurture the good working rapport that has developed between the leader and the follower. The salesclerk, then, is left to do his job without close supervision, knowing that he has a positive working relationship with a leader who can be approached for additional guidance.

Back to the Case

The OSU leadership studies should furnish John Rich with insights on leadership behavior in more general situations. According to these situations, as a leader, Rich could exhibit two general types of behavior: (1) structure and (2) consideration. Rich should use structure behavior when he tells food services personnel what to do and consideration behavior when he attempts to develop a more human rapport with them. Depending on how Rich combines and emphasizes these two behaviors, his leadership style would be called high structure—low consideration, high structure—high consideration, low structure—high consideration, or low structure—low consideration.

Although no one of these leadership styles is more effective than any other in all situations, the life cycle theory of leadership furnishes Rich with a strategy for using various styles in various situations. According to life cycles theory, Rich should make his style consistent primarily with the maturity level of food services personnel. As Rich's followers progress from immaturity to maturity, his leadership style should shift systematically from (1) high task—low relationships behavior to (2) high task—high relationships behavior to (3) high relationships—low task behavior to (4) low task—low relationships behavior.

Leader Flexibility

Obstacles to Changing Leadership Style

Situational theories of leadership such as life cycle theory are based on the concept that successful leaders must change their leadership style as they encounter different situations. This changing of styles as new situations are encountered is called **leader flexibility.** Is it asking too much, however, to demand that leaders be so flexible as to span all major leadership styles? The only answer to this question is that some leaders can be flexible and some cannot. After all, a leadership style may be so ingrained in a leader that it takes years to even approach flexibility. On the other hand, some leaders may have experienced such success in a basically static situation that they believe flexibility is unnecessary. Unfortunately, there are numerous obstacles to leader flexibility.

Figure 13.8 Eight combinations, or octants, of three factors: leader-member relations, task structure, and leader position power.

Octant	Leader–Member Relations	Task Structure	Leader Position Power
I	Good	High	Strong
II	Good	High	Weak
III	Good	Weak	Strong
IV	Good	Weak	Weak
V	Moderately poor	High	Strong
VI	Moderately poor	High	Weak
VII	Moderately poor	Weak	Strong
VIII	Moderately poor	Weak	Weak

From A THEORY OF LEADERSHIP EFFECTIVENESS by F. E. Fiedler. Copyright © 1967 by McGraw-Hill, Inc. Used with permission of McGraw-Hill Book Company.

One strategy, proposed by Fred Fiedler, for overcoming these obstacles is changing the organizational situation to fit the leader's style rather than changing the leader's style to fit the organizational situation.[20] Relating this thought to the life cycle theory of leadership, it may be easier to shift various leaders to situations appropriate for their leadership styles rather than expect leaders to change styles as situations change. It probably would take three to five years to train managers to use effectively a concept such as life cycle theory.[21] Changing the situation a particular leader faces, however, can be done in the short run simply by exercising organizational authority.

According to Fiedler and his **contingency theory of leadership,** leader-member relations, task structure, and the position power of the leader are the three primary factors that should be used as the basics for moving leaders into situations more appropriate for their leadership styles. Leader-member relations is the degree to which the leader feels accepted by his or her followers, and task structure is the degree to which goals, the work to be done, and other situational factors are outlined clearly. The third factor, position power, is determined by the extent to which the leader has control over rewards and punishments the followers receive. How these three factors can be arranged in eight different combinations is presented in figure 13.8. Each of these eight combinations is called an octant.

Figure 13.9 shows how effective leadership varies with these eight octants. From an organizational viewpoint this figure implies that management should attempt to match permissive, passive, and considerate leaders with situations reflecting the middle of the continuum containing the octants. Figure 13.9 also implies that management should try to match a controlling, active, and structuring leader with the extremes of this continuum. Possible actions that Fiedler suggests to modify the leadership situation are:

1. *In some organizations we can change the individual's task assignment. We may assign to one leader very structured tasks which have implicit or explicit instructions telling him what to do and how to do it, and we may assign to another the tasks that are nebulous and vague. The former are the typical production tasks; the latter are exemplified by committee work, by the development of policy, and by tasks which require creativity.*

2. *We can change the leader's position power. We not only can give him a higher rank and corresponding recognition, we also can modify his position power by giving him subordinates who are equal to him in rank and prestige or subordinates who are two or three ranks below him. We can give him subordinates who are experts in their specialties or subordinates who depend upon the leader for guidance and instruction.*

Overcoming Leader Flexibility Obstacles

Leader-Member Relations

Task Structure

Position Power

Changing Situations to Suit Leadership Styles

How Leadership Situations Can Be Changed

Figure 13.9 How effective leadership style varies with Fiedler's eight octants.

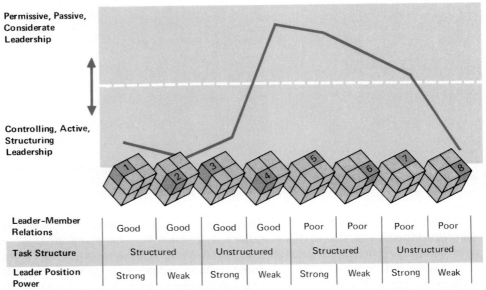

Permissive, Passive, Considerate Leadership

Controlling, Active, Structuring Leadership

Leader–Member Relations	Good	Good	Good	Good	Poor	Poor	Poor	Poor
Task Structure	Structured		Unstructured		Structured		Unstructured	
Leader Position Power	Strong	Weak	Strong	Weak	Strong	Weak	Strong	Weak

We can give the leader the final say in all decisions affecting his group, or we can require that he make decisions in consultation with his subordinates, or even that he obtain their concurrence. We can channel all directives, communications, and information about organizational plans through the leader alone, giving him expert power, or we can provide these communications concurrently to all his subordinates.

3. *We can change the leader-member relations in this group. We can have the leader work with groups whose members are very similar to him in attitude, opinion, technical background, race, and cultural background. Or we can assign him subordinates with whom he differs in any one or several of these important aspects. Finally, we can assign the leader to a group in which the members have a tradition of getting along well with their supervisors or to a group that has a history and tradition of conflict.*[22]

Overall, Fiedler's work helps to destroy the old myths that (1) there is one best leadership style, and (2) that leaders are born, not made. Further, Fiedler's work supports the theory that lmost every manager in an organization can be a successful leader if placed in a situation appropriate for his or her leadership style. This, of course, assumes that someone within the organization has the ability to assess the characteristics of the organization's leaders and of other important organizational variables and then match the two accordingly.[23] Although criticism of Fiedler's work can be found,[24] his leadership research is probably the most rigorous to date, and his works are highly recommended to anyone seeking insights on the challenge and "how-to" of leadership.

Life cycle theory suggests that John Rich should be flexible enough to behave as the situation requires. Rich may find it extremely difficult to be flexible, however. Recognizing his inability to be flexible, Rich should attempt to structure his situation so as to make it appropriate for his style. As suggested by Fiedler, if Rich's leadership style is more high task in nature, he generally will be a more successful leader in situations best described by octants 1, 2, 3, and 8 in figure 13.8. On the other hand, if Rich's leadership style is more relationships oriented, he usually will be a more successful leader in situations representative of octants 4, 5, 6, and 7 in that figure. Overall, Fiedler's works provide Rich with insights on how to engineer situations within the food services department so that they are appropriate for his leadership style.

Summary

The following points are stressed within this chapter:

1. Leadership is the process of directing the behavior of others toward the accomplishment of some objective. Although sound management entails good leadership, management and leadership are not the same.

2. The study of leadership essentially began with an analysis of leadership traits. The results of these trait studies indicated that no single set of traits could guarantee successful leadership in all situations.

3. The situational approach to leadership suggests that successful leadership is the result of the appropriateness of the relationship between the leader, the followers, and the leadership situation. The actual leadership behavior a manager adopts to make decisions should be determined by collectively analyzing forces within the manager, forces within the subordinates, and forces within the leadership situation.

4. The life cycle theory of leadership is a situational approach to leadership that describes leadership behavior in more general terms. Life cycle theory recommends that as the maturity level of the followers increases, a leader should correspondingly change his or her leadership style from high task—low relationships to high task—high relationships to high relationships—low task, to low task—low relationships.

5. Although in concept life cycle theory may seem sound, leaders may find it extremely difficult to change their styles as situations change. Fiedler's contingency theory of leadership suggests that an alternative to successful leadership using life cycle theory is changing the leadership situation to make it more appropriate for the leader's style.

Issues for Review and Discussion

1. What is leadership?
2. How does leadership differ from management?
3. Explain the trait approach to leadership.
4. What relationship exists between successful leadership and leadership traits?
5. Explain the situational approach to leadership.
6. Draw and explain Tannenbaum and Schmidt's leadership model.
7. List the forces in the manager, subordinates, and the situation that ultimately determine how a manager should lead.
8. What contribution did the OSU studies make to leadership theory?
9. Can any one of the major leadership styles resulting from the OSU studies be called more effective than the others? Why?
10. What is meant by "maturity" as used in the life cycle theory of leadership?
11. Draw and explain the life cycle theory of leadership model.
12. What is meant by "leader flexibility"?
13. Describe some obstacles to leader flexibility.
14. In general, how might these obstacles be overcome?
15. In specific terms, how does Fiedler suggest that these obstacles be overcome?

Sources of Additional Information

Costello, T. W., and Zalkind, S. S. *Psychology in Administration*. Englewood Cliffs, N.J.: Prentice-Hall, 1963.

Fiedler, Fred, and Chemers, Martin. *Leadership and Effective Management*. Chicago, Ill.: Scott, Foresman, 1974.

Fleishman, E. A.; Harris, E. F.; and Burtt, H. E. *Leadership and Supervision in Industry*. Columbus, Ohio: Ohio State University Bureau of Education Research, 1955.

Ford, Jeffrey D. "The Management of Organizational Crises." *Business Horizons* 24, no.3 (May/June 1981): 10–16.

Gibb, Cecil. "Leadership." In *Handbook of Social Psychology*, 2d ed., edited by Gardner Lindzey and Elliot Aronson. Reading, Mass.: Addison-Wesley, 1969.

Gordon, Thomas. *Group-Centered Leadership*. Boston: Houghton Mifflin, 1955.

Gouldner, Alvin. *Studies in Leadership*. New York: Harper & Row, 1950.

Guest, David, and Horwood, Robert. "Characteristics of the Successful Performance Manager." *Personnel Management* 13, no. 5 (May 1981): 18–23.

Jennings, Eugene. *An Anatomy of Leadership: Princes, Heroes, and Supermen*. New York: Harper & Brothers, 1960.

Kleiner, Brian H. "Tracing the Evolution of Leadership Styles." *Management World*, March 1981, pp. 18–20.

Lawless, David J. *Effective Management*. Englewood Cliffs, N.J.: Prentice Hall, 1972.

McGregor, Douglas. *Leadership and Motivation*. Cambridge, Mass.: M. I. T. Press, 1966.

Mintzberg, Henry. *The Nature of Managerial Work*. New York: Harper & Row, 1973.

Nord, W. *Concepts and Controversy in Organizational Behavior*. Santa Monica, Calif.: Goodyear, 1972.

Peters, Thomas J. "Leadership: Sad Facts and Silver Linings." *Harvard Business Review* (November/December 1979): 164–72.

Plachy, Roger J. "Leading vs. Managing: A Guide to Some Crucial Distinctions." *Management Review* 70, no. 9 (September 1981): 58–61.

Reddin, Willliam. *Managerial Effectiveness*. New York: McGraw-Hill, 1970.

Stogdill, R. M. *Handbook of Leadership*. New York: The Free Press, 1974.

Vroom, Victor, and Yetton, Philip. *Leadership and Decision Making*. Pittsburgh: University of Pittsburgh Press, 1973.

Wren, D. A. *The Evolution of Management Thought*. New York: Ronald, 1972.

1. Thomas J. Neff, "How to Interview Candidates for Top Management Positions," *Business Horizons,* October 1980, pp. 47–52.

2. For more discussions on leader vs. manager, see Joseph L. Massie and John Douglas, *Managing: A Contemporary Introduction* (Englewood Cliffs, N.J.: Prentice-Hall, 1977), pp. 372–73.

3. Abraham Zaleznik, "Managers and Leaders: Are They Different?" *Harvard Business Review,* May/June 1977, pp. 67–78.

4. Theodore Levitt, "Management and the Post-Industrial Society," *The Public Interest,* Summer 1976, p. 73.

5. As an example, see R. D. Mann, "A Review of the Relationship between Personality and Performance in Small Groups," *Psychological Bulletin* 56, no. 4 (1959): 241–70.

6. Ralph M. Stogdill, "Personal Factors Associated with Leadership: A Survey of the Literature," *Journal of Psychology* 25 (January 1948): 35–64.

7. Cecil A. Gibb, "Leadership," in *Handbook of Social Psychology,* ed. Gardner Lindzey (Reading, Mass: Addison-Wesley, 1954).

8. Eugene E. Jennings, "The Anatomy of Leadership," *Management of Personnel Quarterly* 1, no. 1 (Autumn 1961).

9. Robert Tannenbaum and Warren H. Schmidt, "How to Choose a Leadership Pattern," *Harvard Business Review,* March/April 1957, pp. 95–101.

10. William E. Zierden, "Leading Through the Follower's Point of View," *Organizational Dynamics,* Spring 1980, pp. 27–46.

11. Tannenbaum and Schmidt, "How to Choose a Leadership Pattern," pp. 95–101.

12. Robert Tannenbaum and Warren H. Schmidt, "How to Choose a Leadership Pattern," *Harvard Business Review,* May/June 1973, pp. 162–80.

13. Roger M. Stogdill and Alvin E. Coons, eds., "Leader Behavior: Its Description and Measurement," Research Monograph no. 88 (Columbus, Ohio: Ohio State University Bureau of Business Research, 1957).

14. "How Basic Management Principles Pay Off: Lessons in Leadership," *Nation's Business,* March 1977, pp. 46–53.

15. For other discussion of how a minimal amount of structure behavior of a leader can increase subordinate productivity see David Clutterbuck, "Management by Anarchy," *International Management,* May 1980, pp. 30–32.

16. Andrew W. Halpin, *The Leadership Behavior of School Superintendents* (Chicago: The University of Chicago Midwest Administration Center, 1959).

17. W. J. Reddin, "The Tridimensional Grid," *Training and Development Journal,* July 1964.

18. A. K. Korman, " 'Consideration,' 'Initiating Structure,' and Organizational Criteria—A Review," *Personnel Psychology: A Journal of Applied Research* 19, no. 4 (Winter 1966): 349–61.

19. P. Hersey and K. H. Blanchard, "Life Cycle Theory of Leadership," *Training and Development Journal,* May 1969, pp. 26–34.

20. Fred E. Fiedler, "Engineer the Job to Fit the Manager," *Harvard Business Review* 43, no. 5 (September-October 1965): 115–22. See also Fred E. Fiedler, *A Theory of Leadership Effectiveness* (New York: McGraw-Hill, 1967).

21. Rensis Likert, *New Patterns of Management* (New York: McGraw-Hill, 1961).

22. From A THEORY OF LEADERSHIP EFFECTIVENESS by F. E. Fiedler. Copyright © 1967 by McGraw-Hill, Inc. Used with permission of McGraw-Hill Book Company.

23. Fred E. Fiedler, "How Do You Make Leaders More Effective: New Answers to an Old Puzzle," *Organizational Dynamics,* Autumn 1972, pp. 3–18.

24. Timothy McMahon, "A Contingency Theory: Logic and Method Revisited," *Personnel Psychology* 25, no. 4 (Winter 1972): 697–710.

Concluding Case 13
Matching Managers to a Company's Life Cycle:
From Best Western to Quality Inns

Hazard takes his team and his lavish style to where it is welcome.

Traditionally, it was felt that a competent and knowledgeable executive could successfully run any company in his or her industry. However, this view has been challenged by some management theorists who claim that a manager's skills must be linked to the life cycle stage of the product being managed. Once a product has reached the maturity stage of its life cycle then the entrepreneurial-type person who developed the product is no longer the appropriate person to manage it. At this point, a manager who is cost and productivity conscious should be brought in, while the risk-taking, innovating entrepreneur should be placed in charge of a beginning-product line.

This theory tends to reveal a possible explanation for the departure of Robert C. Hazard and Gerald W. Petitt from Best Western International Inc., and their subsequent association with a competitor, Quality Inns International Inc. From 1974 to 1980, the two men flashed their entrepreneurial skills with flair at Best Western. They increased the Best Western chain from 800 hotels to 2,597, and expanded the chain into 18 countries. Furthermore, they implemented one of the most sophisticated of computerized reservations systems and were praised continually by affiliated hotels for their innovation. But eventually a confrontation arose between the team of Hazard and Petitt and the hotel owner's board. The board wished to slow the growth of the company while Hazard and Petitt continued to push growth. Consequently, animosity developed between the management team and the board.

At the same time the bad feelings developed, Quality Inns, emerging from several years of financial instability, actively sought Hazard to replace their president who had recently resigned. The company saw itself as being in the early stages of its life cycle. The same entrepreneurial skills that were no longer needed by Best Western were now in great demand at Quality Inns. Hazard and Petitt left Best Western to ply their skills at Quality Inns.

Hazard and Petitt had worked together at International Business Machines Corporation and American Express Co. prior to their stint at Best Western in 1974. Hazard became known as the team's outside man and conceptualizer, while Petitt had the reputation of being the insider and implementor. According to Petitt, Hazard formulates a tremendous number of ideas, but many of them are impossible to implement. Hazard says that Petitt's strength is his ability to make decisions at the appropriate time.

Hazard and Petitt have begun to implement their new strategy at Quality Inns. The complicated strategy is composed of several factors. First, they plan to double the number of franchised properties from 345 to 750 by 1983. Secondly, the company's headquarters building and many of the hotels are to be refurbished. Finally, the company's computerized reservations system will be altered from one in which all reservations pass through company headquarters to one that allows intercommunication among the company hotels.

Currently, the team's ideas have been accepted enthusiastically by the Quality Inn board. However, critics of Hazard suggest that such enthusiasm will wane when the board realizes how expensive these plans will be. For instance, the new reservation system proposed by Hazard will exceed the $2 million mark, much greater than the $800,000 originally budgeted. The system was very effective at Best Western, which has approximately 2,600 hotels. It is questionable whether it will be as successful for Quality Inns, whose present membership is 345 hotels.

Contrary to critics' opinions, proponents of Hazard foresee the growth potential of the company off-setting the costly programs to be implemented. Quality Inns is presently a different company then what it was during the years from 1975 to 1977. From 1975 through 1977 it suffered tremendous losses due to an over-ambitious expansion program combined with the losses resulting from the energy crunch and recession. Profits from the franchise fees were devoured by the losses suffered by the forty-five hotels the company owned. During 1976, Joseph W. McCarthy, a new chief executive officer, had been brought in to salvage the damaged company. Under McCarthy's direction seventeen of its forty-five hotels were sold, and staff was consolidated. In 1978, Quality Inns finally moved into the black. In 1979, the net income of Quality Inns was $4.3 million, on revenues of $62 million. Trading was begun in the American Stock Exchange, and the company paid its first dividend in its history.

In the future, Quality Inns will concentrate on heavy expansion of the franchise network. Board Chairman, Stewart Bainum, echoes the confidence he has in Hazard: "It is clear to us now that the franchise business yields the highest return on equity, and that's Hazard's charge—expanding that business heavily in Europe as well as here."

This case is adapted from "Matching Managers to a Company's Life Cycle," *Business Week*, 23 February 1981, p. 62; "Best Western: Ready to Put on the Brakes," *Business Week*, 23 February 1981, pp. 62 and 67; and "Quality Inns: Ready for Fast-track Growth," *Business Week*, 23 February 1981, pp. 70 and 74.

Discussion Issues

1. What appears to be causing Hazard and Petitt to move from one organization to another? Explain.
2. Explain the difference between a management style and a leadership style.
3. Assume the cause of Hazard's and Petitt's movement from one organization to another was a result of leadership style. Which theory of leadership would such movement support? Explain.
4. Substitute the terms: company (or organizational) maturity, cost/productivity consciousness, and risk-taking/innovativeness for the terminology in the Hersey/Blanchard life-cycle theory of leadership model, then diagram this model. Use the model to explain why the value of Hazard's managerial skills diminished as companies or organizations matured.
5. Can a person actually change his or her managerial style? Explain.

Student Learning Objectives

From studying this chapter I will attempt to acquire:

1. A basic understanding of human motivation
2. Insights on various needs that people possess
3. An appreciation for the importance of motivating organization members
4. An understanding of various motivation strategies

Chapter Outline

Motivation

Introductory Case 14
Happiness Is Success!?

Roseland Florist opened for business sixteen years ago as a one-room, privately owned business specializing in occasion floral arrangements. The shop was opened by Mrs. Ann Conrad because, "I wanted to have something to keep me occupied and bring in a few extra dollars." Palos, the town in which the shop was located, had a population of 25,000. However, it and many of the towns in the area were growing rapidly. Two larger florists already were operating in Palos when Roseland opened.

At first, Ann had only one employee, Ellen Holland. Ellen was a neighbor and longtime friend of Ann's. Ellen also was interested in "occupying her time" while her children were in school. Although business was slow at first, their friends in the community constituted a large enough patronage to allow the women to maintain an adequate level of business. Soon, Roseland's reputation for quality service and low prices began to expand its list of customers. By the end of the first year of operation, Ann had added a combination secretary-bookkeeper and another part-time floral arranger.

Roseland's success continued for several years. Sales and profits grew, but Roseland was plagued by one continuous problem: high employee turnover. Three to four months were required to adequately train flower arrangers. And employees often left within five to six months after they were hired. Some took positions in other florist shops, while others sought other types of employment. Since Ann had built the reputation of Roseland on the high quality of its work, she was faced with a serious problem. The volume of business was increasing rapidly; however, the lack of trained personnel had caused the quality of work to fall off badly.

A climax was reached when Ellen, Ann's first employee, quit her job at Roseland and took employment with a rival florist. Ellen explained her reasons for leaving to a fellow employee:

This used to be a pleasant atmosphere to work in, but Ann has changed. All she cares about now is money. Roseland is her whole life. She is so involved in making money that she forgets that people have to work with her. It's made me a nervous wreck; I just can't take it any longer. And frankly, her husband Paul is just as bad. We have been friends and neighbors for years. But he hangs around the shop, gets in the way, criticizes my work, and well, just sticks his nose in where it doesn't belong.

Before leaving Roseland Florist, Ellen and Ann talked about Ellen's reasons for leaving. After listening to what Ellen had to say, Ann replied, "Hard work is the secret to success, and since I opened this business, I have worked hard seven days a week with only a couple of vacations. That is the only way I know to run a business."

From Donald D. White and H. William Vroman, ACTION IN ORGANIZATIONS: CASES AND EXPERIENCES IN ORGANIZATIONAL BEHAVIOR. Copyright © 1977 by Holbrook Press, Inc. Reprinted with permission of Allyn and Bacon, Inc.

Discussion Issues

1. Define the main problem at Roseland Florist.
2. What steps do you think that Ann Conrad should take to solve this problem?

What's Ahead

Ann Conrad, the owner-manager of Roseland Florist in the introductory case, has been plagued in recent years by high employee turnover. This turnover seems to have been caused by the development of a work situation that is very unpleasant for her employees. The material in this chapter is intended to help a manager like Ann Conrad to deal with such a work-related problem.

To be successful in working with other people, managers should have a thorough understanding of both the motivation process and the steps that can be taken to motivate organization members. This chapter, therefore, is divided into two main sections: (1) the motivation process and (2) motivating organization members.

Prospective managers need to understand the motivation process. To this end, a definition of motivation, various motivation models, and descriptions of people's needs are the main topics of discussion in this chapter.

The Motivation Process

Defining Motivation

Motivation is an individual's inner state that causes her or him to behave in a way that ensures the accomplishment of some goal.[1] In other words, motivation explains why people behave the way they do. The more managers understand organization members' behavior, the better able they should be to influence that behavior and make it more consistent with the accomplishment of organizational objectives. Since productivity in all organizations is a result of the behavior of organization members, influencing this behavior is a manager's key to increasing productivity.

Motivation Influences Productivity

Motivation Models

Various models that describe how motivation takes place have been developed. Three of these models are: (1) the needs-goal model, (2) the Vroom expectancy model, and (3) the Porter-Lawler model. These three models build on one another to furnish a description of the motivation process that begins at a relatively simple and easily understood level but culminates at a somewhat more intricate and realistic level.

The Needs-Goal Model of Motivation

The **needs-goal model** of motivation is presented in figure 14.1 and is the most fundamental of the three motivation models discussed in this chapter. As its name implies, needs and goals are the two primary components of this model. As figure 14.1 indicates, motivation begins with an individual feeling a need. This need is then transformed into behavior directed at supporting, or allowing, the performance of goal behavior. The purpose of the goal behavior is to reduce the felt need. Theoretically, goal-supportive behavior and goal behavior continue until a felt need has been reduced significantly.

For example, one individual may feel a hunger need. Typically, this need is transformed first into behavior directed at supporting the performance of the goal behavior of eating. Examples of this supportive behavior could include such activities as buying,

What Is the Needs-Goal Model?

Goal Behavior Reduces Felt Needs

Figure 14.1 The needs-goal model of motivation.

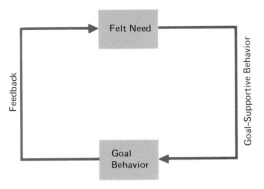

Figure 14.2 Vroom's expectancy model of motivation in equation form.

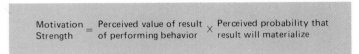

Lyman Porter and Edward Lawler, III, MANAGERIAL ATTITUDES AND PERFORMANCE (Homewood, Ill.: Richard D. Irwin, 1968), p. 165. © 1968 by Richard D. Irwin, Inc.

cooking, and serving the food to be eaten. Goal-supportive behaviors such as these and the goal behavior itself of eating typically continue until the individual's felt hunger need substantially subsides. Once the individual experiences the hunger need again, however, the entire cycle is repeated.

The Vroom Expectancy Model of Motivation

In reality, the motivation process is a more complex situation than depicted by the needs-goal model of motivation. The **Vroom expectancy model** handles some of these additional complexities.[2] As with the needs-goal model, the Vroom expectancy model is based on the premise that felt needs cause human behavior. In addition, however, the Vroom model addresses the issue of motivation strength. **Motivation strength** is an individual's degree of desire to perform a behavior. As this desire increases or decreases, motivation strength is said to fluctuate correspondingly.

Intensity of Desire to Perform Behavior

Vroom's expectancy model is shown in equation form in figure 14.2. According to this model, motivation strength is determined by (1) the perceived value of the result of performing a behavior and (2) the perceived probability that behavior performed by the individual will cause the result to materialize. As both of these factors increase, the motivation strength, or the individual's desire to perform the behavior, increases. In general, individuals tend to perform those behaviors that maximize personal rewards over the long run.

An illustration of how Vroom's model applies to human behavior could be a college student who has been offered the summer job of painting three houses at the rate of $200 a house. Assuming that the student has a need for money, his or her motivation strength or desire to paint the houses is determined by two major factors: (1) the student's perceived value of $600 and (2) the perceived probability that the student actually could paint the houses satisfactorily and, thus, receive the $600. As the perceived

Figure 14.3 The Porter-Lawler model of motivation.

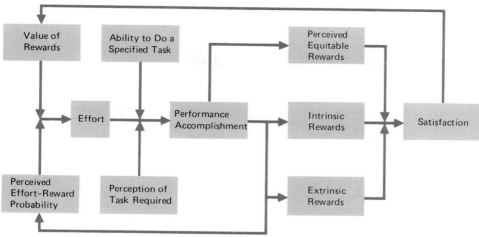

Lyman Porter and Edward Lawler, III, MANAGERIAL ATTITUDES AND PERFORMANCE (Homewood, Ill.: Richard D. Irwin, 1968), p. 165. © 1968 by Richard D. Irwin, Inc.

value of the $600 reward and the probability that the houses could be painted satisfactorily increase, the student's motivation strength to paint the houses increases. Conversely, as the perceived value of the $600 reward and the probability that the house could be painted satisfactorily decreases, the student's motivation strength to paint the houses decreases.

The Porter-Lawler Model of Motivation

Porter and Lawler developed a motivation model that presents a more complete description of the motivation process than either the needs-goal model or the Vroom expectancy model.[3] The **Porter-Lawler model** of motivation is presented in figure 14.3. Obviously, this model is consistent with the prior two models in that it accepts the premises that (1) felt needs cause human behavior; and (2) effort expended to accomplish a task is determined by the perceived value of rewards that will result from the task and the probability that the rewards actually will materialize.

A More Complete Model

In addition, however, the Porter-Lawler motivation model stresses three other characteristics of the motivation process:

1. The perceived value of a reward is determined by both intrinsic and extrinsic rewards that result in need satisfaction when a task is accomplished. **Intrinsic rewards** come directly from performing a task, while **extrinsic rewards** are extraneous to the task itself. For example, when a manager counsels a subordinate about a personal problem, the manager may get some intrinsic reward in the form of personal satisfaction simply from helping another individual. In addition to this intrinsic reward, however, the manager also would receive some extrinsic reward in the form of the overall salary the manager is paid.[4]

Rewards and Jobs

Total Reward = Intrinsic Reward + Extrinsic Reward

2. The extent to which an individual effectively accomplishes a task is determined primarily by two variables: (1) the individual's perception of what is required to perform the task and (2) the individual's actual ability to perform the task. Naturally, an individual's effectiveness at accomplishing a task increases as perception of what is required to perform the task becomes more accurate and as ability to perform the task increases.

Task Requirements and Ability

3. The perceived fairness of rewards influences the amount of satisfaction produced by those rewards. In general, the more equitable an individual perceives rewards to be, the greater the satisfaction the individual will experience as a result of receiving those rewards.

Back to the Case

To thoroughly understand her people-oriented problem at Roseland Florist, Ann Conrad should acquire a thorough understanding of the motivation process. According to the material in this chapter thus far, motivation is an inner state that causes individuals to act in ways that ensure the accomplishment of some goal. An understanding of motivation would give Ann some insights on how to influence the behavior of floral shop personnel to make it more consistent with floral shop objectives.

Ann also should keep in mind five more specific principles of human motivation: (1) felt needs cause behavior aimed at reducing those needs; (2) degree of desire to perform a particular behavior is determined by an individual's perceived value of the result of performing the behavior and the perceived probability that the behavior actually will cause the result to materialize; (3) perceived value of a reward for a particular behavior is determined by both intrinsic and extrinsic rewards that result in need satisfaction when the behavior is accomplished; (4) individuals can effectively accomplish a task only if they understand what the task requires and have the ability to carry out these requirements; and (5) the perceived fairness of a reward influences the degree of satisfaction generated when the reward is received.

Human Needs

The motivation models discussed thus far imply that a thorough understanding of motivation is based on a thorough understanding of human needs. There is some evidence that people in the general population typically possess strong needs for self-respect, respect from others,[5] promotion, and psychological growth.[6] Although the task of precisely pinpointing all human needs is impossible, several theories have been developed to help managers better understand these needs. These theories are (1) Maslow's hierarchy of needs, (2) Argyris's maturity-immaturity continuum, and (3) McClelland's achievement motive. Each of these theories is discussed fully in the sections that follow.

Maslow's Hierarchy of Needs

Perhaps the most widely accepted description of human needs of the general population is the hierarchy of needs concept developed by Abraham Maslow.[7]

Describing the Hierarchy of Needs

Maslow states that human beings possess five basic needs: (1) physiological needs, (2) security needs, (3) social needs, (4) esteem needs, and (5) self-actualization needs. Maslow theorizes that these five basic needs can be arranged in a hierarchy of importance or order in which individuals generally strive to satisfy them. Each need and its relative positioning on the hierarchy of importance are shown in figure 14.4. Definitions of and related discussion on each of these five needs follows.

Physiological Needs **Physiological needs** relate to the normal functioning of the body and include needs for water, rest, sex, and air. Until these needs are met, a significant portion of an individual's behavior is aimed at satisfying them. On the other hand, if these needs are satisfied, behavior becomes aimed at satisfying the security needs on the next level of Maslow's hierarchy.

Figure 14.4 Maslow's hierarchy of needs.

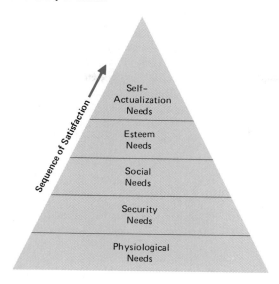

Security Needs   **Security or safety needs** are the needs individuals feel to keep them-selves free from harm. This harm, of course, includes avoiding both bodily and eco-nomic disaster. Management can probably best help employees to satisfy their physiological and security needs through salaries that employees are paid. It is with these salaries that employees can buy such things as food and housing.[8] As security needs are satisfied, behavior tends to be aimed at satisfying social needs.

Freedom from Harm

Social Needs   **Social needs** include an individual's desire for love, companionship, and friendship. Overall, these needs reflect a person's desire to be accepted by others. As these needs are satisfied, behavior shifts to satisfying esteem needs.

Sense of Belonging

Esteem Needs   **Esteem needs** are an individual's desire for respect and generally are divided into two categories: (1) self-respect and (2) respect for others. Until esteem needs are satisfied, they continue to motivate related behavior. Once they are satisfied, however, an individual emphasizes satisfying self-actualization needs.

Respect

Self-Actualization Needs   The need to **self-actualize** is the desire to maximize what-ever potential an individual possesses. For example, a high school principal who seeks to satisfy self-actualization needs would strive to become the best principal possible. Self-actualization needs are on the highest level of Maslow's hierarchy.

Maximizing Potential

Appraising the Hierarchy of Needs

Maslow's hierarchy has gained wide acceptance since its development. Although many management theorists would admit readily that the hierarchy can be useful in under-standing human needs, many concerns have been expressed about the hierarchy. One such concern was expressed by Maslow himself:

> I of all people should know just how shaky this foundation for the theory is as a final foundation. My work on motivation came from the clinic, from a study of neurotic people. The carry-over of this theory to the industrial situation has some support from industrial studies, but certainly I would like to see a lot more studies of this kind before feeling finally convinced that this carry-over from the study of neurosis to the study of labor in factories is legitimate. The same thing is true of my studies of self-actualizing people—there is only this one study of mine available. There were many things wrong with the sampling, so many in fact that it must be considered to be, in the classical sense

Use Maslow's Hierarchy Cautiously

anyway, a bad or poor or inadequate experiment. I am quite willing to concede this—because I'm a little worried about this stuff which I consider to be tentative being swallowed whole by all sorts of enthusiastic people who really should be a little more tentative in the way that I am.[9]

Other concerns related to Maslow's hierarchy include a re-emphasis on its lack of a research base[10] a questioning of whether or not Maslow has pinpointed accurately five basic human needs for his hierarchy,[11] and doubt as to whether human needs actually are arranged in a hierarchy.[12] Despite such concerns, Maslow's hierarchy probably remains the most popular conceptualization of human needs to date. The concerns mentioned, however, indicate that Maslow's hierarchy should be held in its proper perspective as a more subjective statement about human needs rather than an objective description of human needs.

Argyris's Maturity-Immaturity Continuum

Argyris's maturity-immaturity continuum also furnishes insights on human needs.[13] According to Argyris, as people naturally progress from immaturity to maturity, they move:

Natural Maturation Process

1. From a state of passivity as an infant to a state of increasing activity as an adult
2. From a state of dependence on others as an infant to a state of relative independence as an adult
3. From a state of being capable of behaving only in a few ways as an infant to being capable of behaving in many different ways as an adult
4. From having erratic, casual, shallow, and quickly dropped interests as an infant to having deeper interests as an adult
5. From having a short time perspective as an infant to having a much longer time perspective as an adult
6. From being in a superordinate position as an infant to aspiring to occupy an equal and/or subordinate position as an adult
7. From a lack of awareness of self as an infant to awareness and control over self as an adult[14]

Maturity Needs

According to Argyris's continuum, as individuals mature, they have increasing needs for (1) more activity, (2) a state of relative independence, (3) behaving in many different ways, (4) deeper interests, (5) considering a relatively long time perspective, (6) occupying an equal position with other mature individuals, and (7) more awareness of themselves and control over their own destiny. Unlike Maslow's hierarchy, Argyris's needs are not arranged in a hierarchy. Similar to Maslow's hierarchy, however, Argyris's continuum primarily represents a subjective position on the existence of human needs.

McClelland's Achievement Motivation

Doing It Better Than Before

Another theory about human needs focuses on the need for achievement. This theory, popularized primarily by David C. McClelland, defines the **need for achievement ("n Ach")** as the desire to do something better or more efficiently than it has ever been done before.[15] McClelland claims that in some businesspeople the need to achieve is so strong that it is more motivating than a quest for profits.[16] To maximize their satisfaction, individuals with high achievement needs tend to set goals for themselves that are challenging but yet achievable.[17] Although these individuals do not avoid risk completely, they assess risk very carefully. Individuals motivated by the need to achieve do not want to fail and will avoid tasks that involve too much risk. Individuals with a low need for achievement generally avoid challenges, responsibilities, and risk.

Figure 14.5 Unsatisfied needs of organization members resulting in either appropriate or inappropriate behavior.

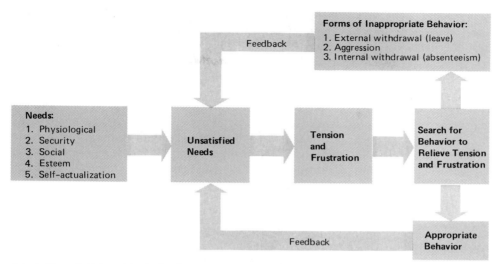

Adapted from B. Kolasa, *Introduction to Behavioral Science in Business* (New York: John Wiley & Sons, 1969), p. 256. Used with permission.

Back to the Case

Once Ann Conrad understands the basic motivation principle, which indicates that felt needs cause behavior, she should attempt to become thoroughly familiar with the various human needs. According to Maslow, people generally possess physiological needs, security needs, social needs, esteem needs, and self-actualization needs. Further, Maslow hypothesizes that these needs are arranged in a hierarchy of importance. Argyris suggests that as people mature, they have increasing needs for activity, independence, flexibility, deeper interests, analyses of longer time perspectives, a position of equality with other mature individuals, and control over personal destiny. Lastly, McClelland indicates that the need for achievement is a common need of people in the general population.

Motivating Organization Members

Satisfying Human Needs through Work

People are motivated or perform behavior to satisfy personal needs. Therefore, from a managerial viewpoint, motivating organization members is the process of furnishing them with the opportunity to satisfy their needs as a result of performing productive behavior within the organization. As discussed in chapter 12, motivating is one of the four primary interrelated activities of the influencing function performed by managers to guide the behavior of organization members toward attainment of organizational objectives. The following sections discuss (1) the importance of motivating organization members and (2) strategies for motivating organization members.

The Importance of Motivating Organization Members

Increasing Appropriate Behavior

Figure 14.5 makes the point that unsatisfied needs of organization members can lead to either appropriate or inappropriate organization member behavior. Managers who are successful at motivating organization members minimize the occurrence of inappropriate organization member behavior and maximize the occurrence of appropriate organization member behavior. Correspondingly, these managers raise the probability that organization member productivity will increase and lower the probability that organization member productivity will decrease. Successful motivation of organization members is extremely important to managers.

Strategies for Motivating Organization Members

Managers have various strategies they can use for motivating organization members. Each strategy is aimed at satisfying organization members' needs consistent with those described by Maslow's hierarchy of needs, Argyris's maturity-immaturity continuum, and McClelland's achievement motive. In essence, these strategies contain general guidelines for what managers can do to ensure that organization members satisfy these needs through the performance of appropriate organization member behavior.[18] These managerial motivation strategies are (1) managerial communication, (2) Theory X-Theory Y, (3) job design, (4) behavior modification, and (5) Likert's management systems. Each strategy is discussed in further detail in the sections that follow.

Exhibit 14(a) illustrates that not only does Mary Kay of Mary Kay Cosmetics recognize that people have esteem as well as other needs but she also understands how to provide opportunities for her employees to satisfy these needs as a result of working productivity.

Managerial Communication

Motivation through Messages

Perhaps the most basic motivation strategy for managers is simply to communicate with organization members. As a result of this communication with managers, organization members can satisfy such basic human needs as recognition, a sense of belonging, and security.[19] For example, such a simple action as a manager attempting to become more acquainted with subordinates could contribute substantially to the satisfaction of each of these three needs. As another example, a communication message from a manager to a subordinate that praises the subordinate for a job well done can help to satisfy recognition and security needs of the subordinate. On the other hand, a communication message from a manager to a subordinate such as the one illustrated in the cartoon from *Changing Times* typically would contribute to the frustration of the subordinate's recognition and security needs and certainly could result in inappropriate or nonproductive behavior. As a general rule, managers should strive to communicate often with other organization members, not only because it is the basic means of conducting organizational activities but also because it is a basic tool for satisfying the human needs of organization members.

Theory X—Theory Y

Assumptions about People

Another strategy a manager can use in motivating organization members involves the assumptions he or she possesses about the nature of people. Douglas McGregor identified two sets of these assumptions and designated one set Theory X and the other Theory Y.[20] **Theory X** involves assumptions that McGregor feels managers often use as the basis for dealing with people, while **Theory Y** represents the assumptions that McGregor feels management constantly should strive to use. Theory X and Theory Y assumptions are presented in figure 14.6.

"...and this, Carstairs, is you, which I think
fully explains why your worth to this organization remains at $75 a week!"

Reprinted with permission from CHANGING TIMES
magazine, © 1973 Kiplinger Washington Editors, Inc.
August 1973.

Figure 14.6 McGregor's Theory X/Theory Y assumptions about the nature of people.

Theory X Assumptions	Theory Y Assumptions
The average person has an inherent dislike for work and will avoid it if he or she can. Because of this human characteristic of dislike of work, most people must be coerced, controlled, directed, and threatened with punishment to get them to put forth adequate effort toward the achievement of organizational objectives. The average person prefers to be directed, wishes to avoid responsibility, has relatively little ambition, and wants security above all.	The expenditure of physical and mental effort in work is as natural as play or rest. People will exercise self-direction and self-control in the service of objectives to which they are committed. Commitment to objectives is a function of the rewards associated with achievement. The average person learns, under proper conditions, not only to accept but to seek responsibility. The capacity to exercise a relatively high degree of imagination, ingenuity, and creativity in the solution of organizational problems is widely, not narrowly, distributed in the population.

From THE HUMAN SIDE OF ENTERPRISE by Douglas McGregor. Copyright © 1960 by McGraw-Hill, Inc. Used with permission of McGraw-Hill Book Company.

Exhibit 14(a)

Mary Kay Understands People's Needs

With a rhinestone tiara perched on her head and a dozen roses clutched to her breast, Patricia Miller sat on a red velvet throne, savoring her moment of glory. Flashing lights spelled out her name while two large video screens beamed her image to the 8,000 people cheering below. Miller, a plump, 38-year-old mother of three, had just been crowned Queen of Personal Sales at the Mary Kay Cosmetics annual convention. "It's something we've all dreamed of," she says. "So what if you get it for selling cosmetics? When you're 38, you've got to get there on more than sheer beauty."

Welcome to the world of Mary Kay Cosmetics, a thriving Dallas-based company whose motivational techniques would make a feminist faint. Owned and operated by Mary Kay Ash, the company sold $54 million in cosmetics last year without a single franchise or distributorship. Instead, Mary Kay has cleverly mobilized a sales force of 46,000 housewives, egging them on with prizes of diamonds, minks and—the prize of prizes—the right to drive one of her 125 pink Cadillacs for an entire year.

Many of these women have never "worked" before. But by skillful use of behavioral psychology, sorority-style rituals and some shrewd husband-stroking, Mary Kay has probably liberated as many women as Gloria Steinem. Says Della Madeley, a Vidor, Texas, housewife: "I'd give up my husband and my microwave before Mary Kay."

Mary Kay's success rides on her sharp understanding of Middle American matronhood. Craftily, she has tailored the "Mary Kay Way of Life" to ease women out of the house and into the business world without creating a fuss at home. By calling her saleswomen "beauty consultants" (what man could object to his wife's being a beauty consultant?) and by requiring them merely to ask neighbors to hold small beauty shows, Mary Kay has built up a formidable work force. Soon the consultant is making a nice little income from her percentage of the sales. She can also recruit new consultants—called "offspring"—and collect a percentage of their sales as well. Though many women work only six hours a week and earn $3,000 a year, others make as much as $100,000 (Queen Patricia made $45,000 last year). All the while, Mary Kay is reminding her charges: "God first, family second, career third."

Though Mary Kay runs her company like a college sorority, it is done with shrewd purpose. The Mary Kay fight song may be silly but it builds esprit de corps. Liquor is forbidden at all Mary Kay functions, because she knows this reassures husbands that their wives won't get into trouble. In fact, she coddles her ladies' men, bringing them onstage when their wives are honored and giving them presents, too. At the Dallas convention, Mary Kay even gave the husbands a special class. "Women need lots of encouragement," she told them. "So give her a pat on the back—but not too low. We want to keep our minds on business." Behind their backs, she advises wives not to flaunt their earnings. "I tell them to just go out and buy things for their home and their family," says Mary Kay. "Men don't know how much things cost."

Mary Kay, a great-grandmother who declines to divulge her age, was a retired saleswoman when she started her company sixteen years ago with $5,000. Her techniques evolved from her years in male-dominated companies. "I never had a chance as a woman," she says. "Every time I got to a plateau in my career, there was some man there to tell me that I couldn't do anything else." But it's not out of vengeance that she discourages men from becoming consultants. "Even if husbands allow a man to come to the house and do a beauty show," she says, "half the women there won't take off their make-up. If they just watch, they don't buy."

COURAGE: For many women, Mary Kay has become a new way of life. Mary Jane Schiavone of Upper Brookville, N.Y., says that with no job and her children grown, "I was a basket case." Now she earns $45,000 and drives a shiny pink Cadillac. Texan Shirley Cormier gained so much confidence with Mary Kay that she shed 108 pounds—and her husband. With the knowledge that she could earn money to support her five children, "I had the courage to get a divorce," she says. But most women are like Patricia Miller, who has ten diamond rings and two minks from her six years with Mary Kay. "Wearing my mink in the A&P," she says, "lets people know I'm a winner."

DIANE K. SHAH with LEA DONOSKY in Dallas

Mary Kay crown Queen Patricia. (Photo: Shelly Katz, Black Star)

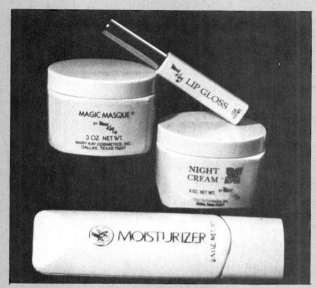

The "Mary Kay Way." (Photo: Shelly Katz, Black Star)

At home in Dallas: A $54 million cosmetics business with a sales force of 46,000 housewives. (Photo: Shelly Katz, Black Star)

Figure 14.7 Theory X, Theory Y, and the effectiveness dimension Z.

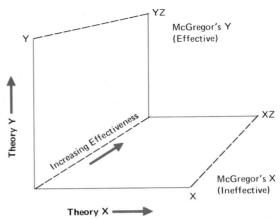

From W. J. Reddin, "The Tri-Dimensional Grid." Reproduced by special permission from the July 1964 TRAINING AND DEVELOPMENT JOURNAL. Copyright 1964 by the American Society for Training and Development Inc.

McGregor implies that managers who use Theory X assumptions are "bad" and those who use Theory Y assumptions are "good." Reddin, however, argues that production might be increased by using either Theory X or Theory Y assumptions, depending on the situation the manager faces:

> Is there not a strong argument for the position that any theory may have desirable outcomes if appropriately used? The difficulty is that McGregor had considered only the ineffective application of Theory X and the effective application of Theory Y.[21]

The Effectiveness Dimension

Use Theory Y in Most Cases

Using this argument, Reddin discusses a **Theory Z.** Theory Z is actually an effectiveness dimension that implies that managers who use either Theory X or Theory Y assumptions when dealing with people can be successful, depending on their situation. Figure 14.7 shows Z as an effectiveness dimension relating to Theory X and Theory Y. The basic rationale for using Theory Y rather than Theory X in most situations, however, is that managerial activity that reflects Theory Y assumptions generally will be more successful in satisfying the human needs of most organization members than management activities that reflect Theory X assumptions. Therefore, management activities based on Theory Y assumptions generally will be more successful in motivating organization members than management activities based on Theory X assumptions.

Back to the Case

Once Ann Conrad understands that felt needs cause behavior and familiarizes herself with the types of needs people possess, she should be ready to apply what she knows to motivating the personnel in her floral shop. From Ann's viewpoint, motivating floral shop personnel is the process of furnishing them with the opportunity to satisfy their human needs from performing their jobs. This is very important to Ann because if she is successful at motivating her employees, the productivity of organization members

within the floral shop probably will increase. If Ann does not furnish her employees with this opportunity to satisfy these human needs while working, absenteeism and turnover probably will be a continual problem for her. From what Ellen says at the beginning of this case, the present work situation in the floral shop does not afford employees the opportunity to satisfy human needs while working. This is probably the main reason why Ellen has decided to work for one of Ann's competitors.

What can Ann do to motivate floral shop personnel? One strategy might be merely taking time to communicate with her employees. Such a simple activity as this can help satisfy employee needs for recognition, a sense of belonging, and security. Another strategy, based on McGregor's Theory X—Theory Y concept, suggests that when dealing with her employees, Ann should adopt the assumptions that floral work is as natural as play; that floral shop personnel can be self-directed in goal accomplishment; that granting rewards encourages the achievement of floral shop objectives; that floral shop personnel seek and accept responsibility; and that most floral shop personnel are creative, ingenious, and imaginative. Ann's adoption of such assumptions probably will lead to the satisfaction of many of Maslow's and Argyris's needs as well as the achievement needs of her employees.

Back to the Case
continued

Job Design

A third strategy managers can use to motivate organization members relates to the design of jobs organization members perform. The following two sections discuss earlier and more recent job design strategies.

Earlier Job Design Strategies

A movement has existed in the more recent history of American business to make jobs simpler and more specialized to increase worker productivity. Theoretically, this movement is aimed at making workers more productive by enabling them to be more efficient. Perhaps the best example of this movement is the development of the automobile assembly line. A negative result that generally accompanies this work simplification and specialization, however, is job boredom. As work becomes simpler and more specialized, it typically becomes more boring and less satisfying to individuals performing the jobs. As a result, productivity suffers.

Job Boredom

Perhaps the earliest major attempt to overcome this job boredom was job rotation. **Job rotation** entails moving individuals from job to job or not requiring individuals to perform only one simple and specialized job over the long run. For example, rather than constantly mowing lawns, a gardener would be shifted to other activities, such as trimming bushes, raking grass, and sweeping sidewalks. Although job rotation programs have been known to increase organizational profitability, they typically are ineffective because over time individuals become bored with all the jobs they are rotated to.[22] Job rotation programs, however, usually are more effective in achieving other objectives, such as the training objective of providing individuals with an overview of how various units of an organization function.

What Is Job Rotation?

Job enlargement is another strategy developed to overcome the boredom of more simple and specialized jobs. **Job enlargement** advocates claim that jobs become more satisfying as the number of operations an individual performs increases. The job enlargement concept, then, claims that the gardener's job would become more satisfying as such activities as trimming bushes, raking grass, and sweeping sidewalks were added to the gardener's initial job responsibility of mowing grass. Some research supports[23] the theory that job enlargement makes jobs more satisfying, while some does not.[24] Job enlargement programs, however, generally have been more successful in increasing job satisfaction than job rotation programs.

What Is Job Enlargement?

More Recent Job Design Strategies

A number of more recent job design strategies have evolved since the development of job rotation and job enlargement programs. Two of these more recent strategies are (1) job enrichment and (2) flextime.

Figure 14.8 Herzberg's hygiene factors and motivators.

Dissatisfaction: Hygiene or Maintenance Factors	Satisfaction: Motivating Factors
1. Company policy and administration 2. Supervision 3. Relationship with supervisor 4. Relationship with peers 5. Working conditions 6. Salary 7. Relationship with subordinates	1. Opportunity for achievement 2. Opportunity for recognition 3. Work itself 4. Responsibility 5. Advancement 6. Personal growth

Reprinted by permission of the *Harvard Business Review,* from "One More Time: How Do You Motivate Employees?" by Frederick Herzberg (January–February 1968). Copyright © 1967 by the President and Fellows of Harvard College; all rights reserved.

Job Enrichment   Frederick Herzberg concludes from his research that the degree of satisfaction and the degree of dissatisfaction that organization members feel as a result of performing a job are two different variables determined by two different sets of items.[25] The set of items that influence the degree of job satisfaction are called **motivating factors,** or motivators, while the set of items that influence the degree of job dissatisfaction are called **hygiene,** or **maintenance, factors.** Hygiene factors relate to the work environment, while motivating factors relate to the work itself. Items that make up Herzberg's motivating and hygiene factors are presented in figure 14.8.

Herzberg indicates that if hygiene factors are undesirable in a particular job situation, organization members will become dissatisfied. Making these factors more desirable by, for example, increasing salary generally will not motivate organization members to do a better job, but it will keep them from becoming dissatisfied. On the other hand, if motivating factors are high in a particular job situation, organization members generally are motivated to do a better job. In general, orgnization members tend to be more motivated and productive as more motivators are built into their job situation.

The process of incorporating motivators into a job situation is called **job enrichment.** Although such companies as Texas Instruments Incorporated[26] and the Volvo Company[27] have reported notable success in motivating organization members through job enrichment programs, experience indicates that for a job enrichment program to be successful, it must be designed and administered very carefully.[28] An outline of a successful job enrichment program is presented in figure 14.9.

Herzberg's overall findings indicate that the most productive organization members are involved in work situations characterized by desirble hygiene factors and motivating factors. The respective needs on Maslow's hierarchy of needs that desirable hygiene factors and motivating factors generally satisfy are shown in figure 14.10. Esteem needs can be satisfied by both types of factors. An example of esteem needs satisfied by a hygiene factor could be private parking space—a status symbol and working condition evidencing the importance of the organization member. On the other hand, an example of esteem needs satisfied by a motivating factor could be an award received for outstanding performance—a display of importance through recognition for a job well done.

Flextime   Another more recent job-design strategy for motivating organization members is based on a concept called flextime. Perhaps the most common traditional characteristic of work performed in the United States is that jobs are performed within a fixed eight-hour workday. Recently, however, this tradition has been challenged. Faced with motivation problems and absenteeism, many managers are turning to scheduling innovations as a possible solution.[29]

Jobs and Environments (margin note)

Incorporating Motivators (margin note)

Motivators, Hygiene Factors, and Maslow's Hierarchy (margin note)

Figure 14.9 Outline of successful job enrichment program.

Specific Changes Aimed at Enriching Jobs	"Motivators"—These Changes Are Aimed at Increasing
1. Removing some controls while retaining accountability	Responsibility and personal achievement
2. Increasing the accountability of individuals for own work	Responsibility and recognition
3. Giving a person a complete natural unit of work (module, division, area, and so on)	Responsibility, achievement, and recognition
4. Granting additional authority to an employee in his or her activity; job freedom	Responsibility, achievement, and recognition
5. Making periodic reports directly available to the worker rather than to the supervisor	Internal recognition
6. Introducing new and more difficult tasks not previously handled	Growth and learning
7. Assigning individuals specific or specialized tasks, enabling them to become expert	Responsibility, growth, and advancement

Figure 14.10 Needs on Maslow's hierarchy of needs that desirable hygiene factors and motivating factors generally satisfy.

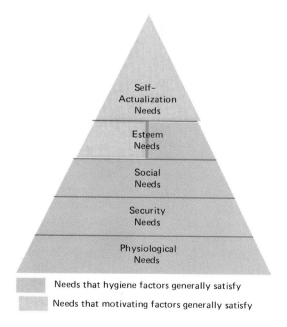

Needs that hygiene factors generally satisfy

Needs that motivating factors generally satisfy

The main purpose of these scheduling innovations is not to reduce the total number of hours during which organization members perform jobs but to provide workers with greater flexibility in the exact hours during which they must perform their jobs. The main thrust of **flextime,** or flexible working hours programs, is that it allows workers to complete their jobs within a forty-hour workweek that they arrange themselves.[30] The choices of starting and finishing times can be as flexible as the organizational situation allows.

Flextime and Motivation

Various kinds of organizational studies have indicated that flextime programs seem to have some positive organizational effects. Douglas Fleuter, for example, has reported that flextime contributes to greater job satisfaction, which typically results in greater production.[31] Other research concludes that flextime programs can result in higher motivation levels of workers.[32] Although many well-known companies, such as Scott Paper, Sun Oil, and Samsonite, have decided to adopt flextime programs,[33] more related research must be conducted to assess conclusively its true worth.

Back to the Case

The preceding material furnishes Ann Conrad with two major job design strategies to help motivate floral shop personnel. The first of these strategies, job enrichment, suggests that Ann incorporate such motivating factors as opportunities for achievement, recognition, and personal growth into the floral shop's work situations. However, for Ann's job enrichment program to have maximum success, hygiene factors within the floral shop must be perceived by floral shop personnel as desirable. Hygiene factors related to Ann's situation would include floral shop policy and administration, supervision, salary, and working conditions.

The second major job design strategy that Ann could use as a basis for motivating floral shop personnel is flextime. Following the flextime concept, Ann would allow floral shop personnel the freedom to schedule the beginning and ending of their workdays whenever they desired. Of course, Ann may have to limit this freedom somewhat depending on such organizational factors as peak selling periods.

Behavior Modification

A fourth strategy that managers can use in motivating organization members is based primarily on a concept known as behavior modification. As stated by B. F. Skinner, **behavior modification** focuses on encourging appropriate behavior as a result of the consequences of that behavior.[34] According to the law of effect,[35] behavior that is rewarded tends to be repeated, while behavior that is punished tends to be eliminated. Although behavior modification programs typically involve the administration of both rewards and punishments, the administration of rewards generally is emphasized since rewards typically are considered to have more effective influence on behavior than punishments. Obviously, the main theme of behavior modification is not new.[36]

Consequences of Behavior

Behavior modification theory asserts that if a manager wants to modify a subordinate's behavior, he or she must ensure that appropriate consequences occur as a result of that behavior.[37] For example, if a particular activity such as a worker arriving on time for work is positively reinforced, or rewarded, the probability increases that the worker will begin arriving on time with greater frequency. In addition, if the worker experiences some undesirable outcome related to arriving late for work, such as a verbal reprimand, the worker will be negatively reinforced when this outcome is eliminated due to the worker coming to work on time. According to behavior modification, positive reinforcement and negative reinforcement are both rewards that increase the likelihood that behavior will continue. **Positive reinforcement** is a desirable consequence of a behavior, while **negative reinforcement** is the elimination of an undesirable consequence of behavior.

Desirable Consequences

Punishment is the presentation of an undesirable behavioral consequence and/or the removal of a desirable behavioral consequence that decrease the likelihood of behavior continuing.[38] Extending the earlier example given, managers could punish employees for arriving late for work by (1) exposing employees to some undesirable consequence, such as a verbal reprimand; and/or (2) removing the desirable consequence of salary by refusing to pay employees wages for the amount of time they are late.[39] Although this punishment would probably quickly cause workers to come to work on time, it might be accompanied by undesirable side effects, such as employee turnover and absenteeism, if emphasized by the manager over the long run.

Undesirable Consequences

Behavior modification programs have been applied both successfully and unsuccessfully in a number of different organizations.[40] The behavior modification efforts of the Emery Air Freight Company resulted in the finding that the establishment and use of an effective feedback system is extremely important in making a behavior modification program successful.[41] This feedback should be aimed at keeping employees informed of the relationship between various behaviors and the consequences associated with them. Other ingredients that successful behavior modification programs include are (1) giving different levels of rewards to different workers depending on the quality of their performance, (2) telling workers what they are doing wrong, (3) punishing workers privately so as not to embarrass them in front of others, and (4) always giving rewards and punishments when earned to emphasize that management is serious about behavior modification efforts.[42]

Ingredients of Successful Behavior Modification Programs

Likert's Management Systems

Another strategy that managers can use for motivating organization members is based on the work of Rensis Likert.[43] As a result of studying several types and sizes of organizations, Likert concludes that management styles in organizations can be categorized into the following systems:

System 1   This style of management involves having no confidence or trust in subordinates. Subordinates do not feel free to discuss their job with superiors and are motivated by fear, threats, punishments, and occasional rewards. Information flow primarily is directed downward, with upward communication viewed with great suspicion. The bulk of all decision making is at the top of the organization.

Treating People Poorly

System 2   This style of management involves having condescending confidence and trust (such as master to servant) in subordinates. Subordinates do not feel very free to discuss their job with superiors and are motivated by rewards and some actual or potential punishment. Information flows mostly downward, while upward communication may or may not be viewed with suspicion. While policies primarily are made at the top of the organization, decisions within a prescribed framework are made at lower levels.

Treating People Less Poorly

System 3   This style of management involves having substantial, but not complete, confidence in subordinates. Subordinates feel rather free to discuss their job with superiors and are motivated by rewards, occasional punishment, and some involvement. Information flows both up and down, while upward communication is often accepted but at times may be viewed with suspicion. While broad policies and general decisions are made at the top of the organization, more specific decisions are made at lower levels.

Treating People Fairly Well

System 4   This style of management involves having complete trust and confidence in subordinates. Subordinates feel completely free to discuss their job with superiors and are motivated by such factors as economic rewards based on a compensation system developed through participation and involvement in goal setting. Information flows upward, downward, and horizontally. Upward

Treating People Extremely Well

Figure 14.11 Comparative long-run and short-run effects of system 1 and system 4 on organizational production.

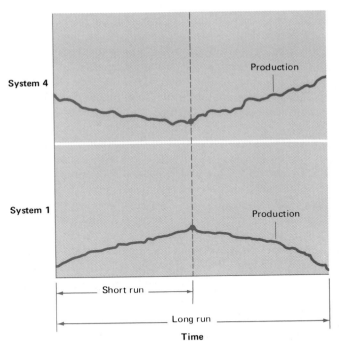

communication is generally accepted; however, if it is not, related questions are asked candidly. Decision making is spread widely throughout the organization and is well coordinated.[44]

Likert suggests that as management style within an organization moves from system 1 to system 4, the human needs of individuals within that organization tend to be more effectively satisfied over the long run. Thus, as management style within an organization moves toward system 4, the organization tends to become more productive over the long run.

Management Systems and Production

Figure 14.11 illustrates the comparative long- and short-run effects of both system 1 and system 4 on organizational production. Managers may increase production in the short run by using a system 1 management style, since motivation by fear, threat, and punishment is generally effective in the short run. Over the long run, however, this style usually causes production to decrease. This long-run effect is due primarily to the long-run nonsatisfaction of organization member needs and poor working relationships that develop between managers and subordinates as a result of using system 1 components.

Conversely, managers who attempt to initiate a system 4 management style probably face some decline in production initially, but an increase in production over the long run. This trend exists over the short run because managers must implement a new system to which organization members must adapt. The production increase over the long run materializes as a result of organization members becoming adjusted to the new management system, greater satisfaction of the human needs of organization members, and good working relationships that tend to develop between managers and subordinates as a result of system 4.

Likert offers his **principle of supportive relationships** as the basis for management activity aimed at developing a system 4 management style. This principle states that:

Personal Worth and Importance

The leadership and other processes of the organization must be such as to ensure a maximum probability that in all interactions and in all relationships within the

Influencing

organization, each member in light of his or her background, values, desires, and expectations will view the experience as supportive and one which builds and maintains his or her sense of personal worth and importance.[45]

In conclusion, this section has discussed many different strategies for motivating organization members. No one of these strategies, however, will necessarily always be more effective for a manager than any other. In fact, a manager may find that some combination of all or any number of these strategies is the most effective strategy, given his or her unique organizational situation.

Comparative Management and Motivation Strategies

In addition to using the strategies for motivating organization members just discussed, one can also gain motivation insight by studying what managers in other countries do to motivate organization members. The study of the management process in different countries in order to examine the potential of management action under different environmental conditions is called **comparative management.** Whereas **international management** focuses on management activities across national borders,[46] comparative management emphasizes analyzing management practices in one country for their possible application in another country.[47]

What Is Comparative Management?

One country that is currently being studied very thoroughly from a comparative management viewpoint is Japan. Although knowledge of the overall success of today's Japanese managers is widespread,[48] perhaps the most analyzed area of this success deals with how Japanese managers effectively motivate organization members. So successful are the Japanese in this area that American managers are traveling to Japan to try to gain insights on how this is accomplished.[49]

Japanese Managers Gain Attention

Japanese managers seem to be able to motivate their organization members in the following ways:

How Japanese Managers Motivate Employees

By hiring an employee for life rather than some shorter period of time. A close relationship between worker and organization is built through this lifetime employment. Since workers know they have a guaranteed job and their future is therefore heavily influenced by the future of the organization, they are very willing to be flexible and cooperative.[50]

By elevating them to a level of organizational status equal to that of management. In Japanese factories, employees at all levels wear similar work clothes, eat in the same cafeteria, and use the same restrooms.[51]

By making them feel that they are highly valued by management and that the organization will provide for their material needs.[52] For example, new workers and their relatives attend a ceremony at which the president welcomes newcomers to the firm and they often live in company-built housing for several years until they can afford to buy their own housing. Also, much employee life outside work is spent in company social clubs. Weddings and wedding receptions are often held in company facilities; some Japanese companies even help pay for wedding expenses.

Such actions taken by Japanese managers indicate that they go to great lengths to build positive working relationships with their employees. In addition, Exhibit 14(b) reveals that similar actions have been successfully applied by Japanese managers in motivating American employees at the Japanese Sony plant in San Diego. Since the general culture of the Japanese worker has been shown to be a significant factor in influencing the success of Japanese management[53] however, managers of other countries should imitate these actions with extreme caution. After all, what Japanese workers feel are desirable or need-satisfying actions by management may not be the same as what those workers from other countries feel are desirable or need satisfying.[54]

Success at Sony

Caution in Imitating Japanese Action

Exhibit 14(b)

Japanese Managers in San Diego

Mike Morimoto in Sony's cafeteria line. (Photo: Robert Burroughs)

Japanese managers are famous for inspiring loyalty, long hours and high-quality production in their workers. But can they carry that management skill with them to other countries? TIME Correspondent D. L Coutu last week visited a Sony television manufacturing plant in San Diego where Japanese executives help supervise 1,800 workers. Her report:

Time clocks are banned from the premises. Managers and workers converse on a first-name basis and eat lunch together in the company cafeteria. Employees are briefed once a month by a top executive on sales and production goals and are encouraged to air their complaints. Four times a year, workers attend company-paid parties. Says Betty Price, 54, an assembly-line person: "Working for Sony is like working for your family."

Her expression, echoed by dozens of other American Sony workers in San Diego, is a measure of the success achieved at the sprawling two-story plant, where both the Stars and Stripes and the Rising Sun fly in front of the factory's glistening white exterior. This year the San Diego plant will turn out 700,000 color television sets, one-third of Sony's total world production. More significantly, company officials now proudly say that the plant's productivity approaches that of its Japanese facilities.

Plant Manager Shiro Yamada, 58, insists that there are few differences between workers in the United States and Japan. Says he, "Americans are as quality conscious as the Japanese. But the question has been how to motivate them." Yamada's way is to bathe his United States employees in personal attention. Workers with perfect attendance records are treated to dinner once a year at a posh restaurant downtown. When one employee complained that a refrigerator for storing lunches was too small, it was replaced a few days later with a larger one. Vice President Masayoshi Morimoto, known as Mike around the plant, has mastered Spanish so he can talk with his many Hispanic workers. The company has installed telephone hot lines on which workers can anonymously register suggestions or complaints.

The firm strives to build strong ties with its employees in the belief that the workers will then show loyalty to the company in return. It carefully promotes from within, and most of the assembly-line supervisors are high school graduates who rose through the ranks because of their hard work and dedication to the company. During the 1973–75 recession, when TV sales dropped and production slowed drastically, no one was fired. Instead, workers were kept busy with plant maintenance and other chores. In fact, Sony has not laid off a single employee since 1972, when the plant was opened. The Japanese managers were stunned when the first employee actually quit within just one year. Says Richard Crossman, the plant's human relations expert: "They came to me and wanted to know what they had done wrong. I had to explain that quitting is just the way it is sometimes in Southern California."

This personnel policy has clearly been a success. Several attempts to unionize the work force have been defeated by margins as high as 3 to 1. Says Jan Timmerman, 22, a parts dispatcher and former member of the Retail Clerks Union: "Union pay was better, and the benefits were probably better. But basically I'm more satisfied here."

Sony has not forced Japanese customs on American workers. Though the company provides lemon-colored smocks for assembly-line workers, most prefer to wear jeans and running shoes. The firm does not demand that anyone put on the uniforms. A brief attempt to establish a general exercise period for San Diego workers, similar to the kind Sony's Japanese employees perform, was dropped when managers saw it was not wanted.

Inevitably, there have been minor misunderstandings because of the differences in language and customs. One worker sandblasted the numbers 1 2 6 4 on a series of parts she was testing before she realized that her Japanese supervisor meant that she was to label them "one to 64." Mark Dempsey, 23, the plant's youngest supervisor, admits that there is still a vast cultural gap between the Japanese and Americans. Says he: "They do not realize that some of us live for the weekend, while lots of them live for the week—just so they can begin to work again." Some workers grumble about the delays caused by the Japanese system of managing by consensus, seeing it instead as an inability to make decisions. Complains one American: "There is a lot of indecision. No manager will ever say do this or do that."

Most American workers, though, like the Japanese management style, and some do not find it all that foreign. Says Supervisor Robert Williams: "A long time ago, Americans used to be more people-oriented, the way the Japanese are. It just got lost somewhere along the way." The Sony experience in San Diego might show Americans how to regain some of their lost skills at employee relations.

Back to the Case

The last two strategies mentioned in this chapter that Ann Conrad can use to help motivate floral shop personnel are behavior modification and Likert's management systems. For Ann to apply behavior modification to her situation, she must reward appropriate behavior performed by floral shop personnel and punish inappropriate behavior. Punishment should be used very carefully, however, because if it is used continually, the working relationship between Ann and floral shop personnel will be destroyed. For Ann's behavior modification program to be successful, she must furnish floral shop employees with feedback on which behaviors are appropriate and inappropriate, give workers different rewards depending on the quality of their performance, tell workers what they are doing wrong, and consistently give rewards and punishments when earned.

If Ann wants to implement Likert's system 4 management style to motivate her employees over the long run, she should demonstrate complete confidence in her workers and encourage them to feel completely free to discuss problems with her. With system 4, communication should flow freely in all directions within the floral shop organization structure. Upward communication generally should be accepted and discussed candidly, and Ann's decision-making process should involve many of the floral shop workers. Ann can use the principle of supportive relationships as the basis of her system 4 management style.

Ann also should consider that no one of the strategies discussed in this chapter for motivating organization members necessarily will be more useful for her than any other. In fact, some combination of all of them may be her most useful strategy. If possible, Ann probably should compare her chosen strategy with strategies used in other countries to see if she can gain additional insight concerning what her final strategy should be.

Summary

The following points are stressed within this chapter:

1. Motivation can be defined as an inner state that causes people to behave in a way that ensures the accomplishment of some goal. The study of motivation provides managers with insights on how to influence the behavior of organization members to make it more consistent with the accomplishment of organizational objectives.

2. Motivation theory is based on the premise that felt needs cause human behavior. Motivation theory also infers that motivation strength or the desire to perform some behavior is determined primarily by the perceived value of the result of performing the behavior and the perceived probability that the behavior performed by the individual will cause the result to materialize. As these factors increase, motivation strength increases.

3. Three additional characteristics of the motivation process are (1) the total perceived value of a reward is determined by both intrinsic and extrinsic rewards received when behavior is performed; (2) effective task accomplishment is determined mainly by an individual's perception of what is required to perform the task and his or her ability to perform the task; and (3) the perceived fairness of rewards influences desire to perform behavior that results in those rewards.

4. Five hypothesized basic human needs, listed in the order in which people generally try to satisfy them, are (1) physiological needs, (2) security needs, (3) social needs, (4) esteem needs, and (5) self-actualization needs.

5. Argyris developed a maturity-immaturity continuum that indicates that as people mature, they naturally feel increasing needs for activity, relative independence, flexibility, deeper interests, analyses of longer time perspectives, a position of equality with other mature individuals in the environment, and more control over personal destiny.

6. From a managerial viewpoint, motivating organization members is the process of furnishing them with the opportunity to satisfy their needs as a result of performing productive behavior within the organization. Strategies managers can use to furnish such opportunities are (1) managerial communication, (2) Theory X—Theory Y, (3) job design, (4) behavior modification, and (5) Likert's management systems.

7. Managers can probably gain some additional motivation strategies by comparing their management styles with those of Japanese managers. By treating workers with respect and dignity, Japanese managers are even enjoying success with workers in the United States.

Issues for Review and Discussion

1. Define motivation and explain why managers should understand it.
2. Draw and explain the needs-goal model of motivation.
3. Summarize Vroom's expectancy model of motivation.
4. List and explain three characteristics of the motivation process contained in the Porter-Lawler motivation model that are not contained in either the needs-goal model or Vroom's model.
5. What does Maslow's hierarchy of needs tell us about the needs people possess?
6. What concerns have been expressed about Maslow's hierarchy of needs?
7. Describe Argyris's maturity-immaturity continuum.
8. What is the achievement motive?
9. Summarize the characteristics of individuals who have high needs for achievement.
10. Define the phrase *motivating organization members*.
11. Is the process of motivating organization members important to managers? Why?
12. How can managerial communication be used to motivate organization members?
13. What are Theory X, Theory Y, and Theory Z? What does each of these theories tell us about motivating organization members?
14. What is the difference between job enlargement and job rotation?
15. Describe the relationship between hygiene factors, motivating factors, and job enrichment.
16. Define flextime.
17. Define behavior modification.
18. What basic ingredients are necessary to make a behavior modification program successful?
19. In your own words, summarize Likert's four systems of management.
20. What effect do systems 1 and 4 generally have on organizational production in both the short and long run? Why do these effects occur?
21. What is comparative management?
22. What Japanese-motivated strategies are discussed in this chapter? Do you think that these strategies would work in a country such as the U.S.A.? Why?

Sources of Additional Information

Alderfer, Clayton P. *Existence, Relatedness, and Growth.* New York: Free Press, 1972.

Argyris, C. *Integrating the Individual and the Organization.* New York: John Wiley & Sons, 1964.

Arnold, Hugh J. "A Test of the Validity of the Multiplicative Hypothesis of Expectancy-Valence Theories of Work Motivation." *Academy of Management Journal* 24, no. 1 (March 1981): 128–41.

Atkinson, J. W. *An Introduction to Motivation.* New York: Van Nostrand, 1964.

Bass, B. M. *Organizational Psychology.* Boston: Allyn & Bacon, 1965.

Costello, T. W., and Zalking, S. S. *Psychology in Administration.* Englewood Cliffs, N.J.: Prentice-Hall, 1963.

Dunnette, Marvin D. *Work and Nonwork in the Year 2001.* Monterey, Calif.: Brooks/Cole Publishing, 1973.

Freedman, Sara M., and Montanari, John R. "An Integrative Model of Managerial Reward Allocation." *Academy of Management Review* 5, no. 3: 381–90.

Gardner, Jerry. "Creating Motivating Workplaces." *Personnel Journal,* May 1981, pp. 406–8.

Gellerman, Saul W. *Motivation and Productivity.* New York: American Management Association, 1963.

Herzberg, F.; Mausner, B.; and Snyderman, B. *The Motivation to Work.* New York: John Wiley & Sons, 1959.

Kanter, Rosabeth Moss, and Stein, Barry A. "Ungluing the Stuck: Motivating Performance and Productivity through Expanding Opportunity." *Management Review* 70, no. 7 (July 1981): 45–49.

Lawler, E. E. *Pay and Organizational Effectiveness.* New York: McGraw-Hill, 1971.

Litwin, G. H., and Stringer, R. A. *Motivation and Organizational Climate.* Cambridge, Mass.: Harvard Business School, Division of Research, 1968.

Locke, Edwin A. "The Nature and Causes of Job Satisfaction." In *Handbook of Industrial and Organizational Psychology,* edited by M. D. Dunnette. Chicago: Rand McNally, 1976.

Magnus, Margaret. "Employee Recognition: A Key to Motivation." *Personnel Journal,* February 1981, pp. 103–7.

Porter, Lyman W., and Lawler, Edward E., III. *Managerial Attitudes and Performance.* Homewood, Ill.: Richard D. Irwin, 1968.

Skinner, B. F. *Beyond Freedom and Dignity.* New York: Alfred A. Knopf, 1971.

Steers, Richard M., and Porter, Lyman W., eds. *Motivation and Work Behavior.* New York: McGraw-Hill, 1975.

Vroom, Victor H. *Work and Motivation.* New York: John Wiley & Sons, 1964.

Notes

1. Bernard Berelson and Gary A. Steiner, *Human Behavior: An Inventory of Scientific Findings* (New York: Harcourt, Brace, and World, 1964), pp. 239–40.

2. Victor H. Vroom, *Work and Motivation* (New York: John Wiley & Sons, 1964).

3. L. W. Porter and E. E. Lawler, *Managerial Attitudes and Performance* (Homewood, Ill.: Richard D. Irwin, 1968).

4. For more information on intrinsic and extrinsic rewards, see Richard A. Guzzo, "Types of Rewards, Cognitions, and Work Motivation," *Academy of Management Review* 4, no. 1 (1979): 75–84.

5. *Work in America: Report of the Special Task Force to the Secretary of Health, Education, and Welfare* (Cambridge, Mass.: M.I.T. Press, 1972).

6. H. Sheppard and N. Herrick, *Where Have All the Robots Gone?* (New York: Free Press, 1972).

7. Abraham Maslow, *Motivation and Personality,* 2d. ed. (New York: Harper & Row, 1970).

8. Allen Flamion, "The Dollars and Sense of Motivation," *Personnel Journal,* January 1980, pp. 51–53.

9. Abraham Maslow, *Eupsychian Management* (Homewood, Ill.: Richard D. Irwin, 1965).

10. Jack W. Duncan, *Esssentials of Management* (Hinsdale, Ill.: Dryden Press, 1975), p. 105.

11. C. P. Adlerfer, "An Empirical Test of a New Theory of Human Needs," *Organizational Behavior and Human Performance* 4, no. 2 (1969): 142–75.

12. D. T. Hall and K. Nougaim, "An Examination of Maslow's Need Hierarchy in an Organizational Setting," *Organizational Behavior and Human Performance* 3, no. 1 (1968): 12–35.

13. Chris Argyris, *Personality and Organization* (New York: Harper & Row, 1957).

14. Argyris, *Personality and Organization.*

15. David C. McClelland, "Power Is the Great Motivator," *Harvard Business Review,* March/April 1976, pp. 100–110.

16. David C. McClelland and David G. Winter, *Motivating Economic Achievement* (New York: Free Press, 1969).

17. Burt K. Scanlan, "Creating a Climate for Achievement," *Business Horizons* 24, no. 2 (March/April 1981): 5–9.

18. William H. Franklin, Jr., "Why You Can't Motivate Everyone," *Supervisory Management,* April 1980, pp. 21–28.

19. Edwin Timbers, "Strengthening Motivation through Communication," *Advanced Management Journal* 31 (April 1966): 64–69.

20. Douglas McGregor, *The Human Side of Enterprise* (New York: McGraw-Hill, 1960).

21. W. J. Reddin, "The Tri-Dimensional Grid," *Training and Development Journal,* July 1964.

22. Dennis J. Sweeney and Thomas A. Williams, "Increased Profitability through Job Rotation Programs," *Industrial Management*, July/August 1976, pp. 15–18.

23. L. E. Davis and E. S. Valfer, "Intervening Responses to Changes in Supervisor Job Designs," *Occupational Psychology*, July 1965, pp. 171–90.

24. M. D. Kilbridge, "Do Workers Prefer Larger Jobs?" *Personnel*, September/October 1960, pp. 45–48.

25. This section is based on Frederick Herzberg, "One More Time: How Do You Motivate Employees," *Harvard Business Review*, January/February 1968, pp. 53–62.

26. Scott M. Myers, "Who Are Your Motivated Workers?" *Harvard Business Review* (January/February 1964): 73–88.

27. John M. Roach, "Why Volvo Abolished the Assembly Line," *Management Review*, September 1977, p. 50.

28. Richard J. Hackman, "Is Job Enrichment Just a Fad?" *Harvard Business Review*, September/October 1975, pp. 129–38.

29. William B. Werther, Jr., "Flexible Working Hours: An Overview," *Arizona Business*, January 1976, p. 19.

30. Paul J. Cathey, "Flexible Hours—An Idea Whose Time Has Come," *Iron Age*, 31 May 1973, pp. 35–37.

31. Douglas L. Fleuter, "Flextime—A Social Phenomenon," *Personnel Journal*, June 1975, pp. 318–19.

32. Lee A. Graf, "An Analysis of the Effect of Flexible Working Hours on the Management Functions of the First-Line Supervisor" (Ph.D. diss., Mississippi State University, 1976).

33. William Wong, "Rather Come in Late or Go Home Earlier? More Bosses Say OK," *Wall Street Journal*, 12 July 1973, p. 1.

34. B. F. Skinner, *Contingencies of Reinforcement* (New York: Appleton-Crofts, 1969).

35. E. L. Thordike, "The Original Nature of Man," *Educational Psychology* 1 (1903).

36. Keith E. Barenklaw, "Behavior Reinforcement," *Industrial Supervisor*, February 1976, pp. 6–7.

37. David E. Terpstra, "Theories of Motivation—Borrowing the Best," *Personnel Journal*, June 1979, pp. 376–79.

38. E. Kazadin, *Behavior Modification in Applied Settings* (Homewood, Ill.: Dorsey Press, 1975).

39. For another practical discussion on punishment, see Bruce R. McAfee and William Poffenberger, *Productivity Strategies: Enhancing Employee Job Performance* (Englewood Cliffs, N.J.: Prentice-Hall, Spectrum, 1982).

40. W. Clay Hamner and Ellen P. Hamner, "Behavior Modification on the Bottom Line," *Organizational Dynamics* 4, no. 4 (Spring 1976): 3–21.

41. "New Tool: Reinforcement for Good Work," *Psychology Today*, April 1972, pp. 68–69.

42. Hamner and Hamner, "Behavior Modification," pp. 6–8.

43. Rensis Likert, *New Patterns of Management* (New York: McGraw-Hill, 1961).

44. These descriptions are based on the table of organizational and performance characteristics of different management systems in Rensis Likert, *The Human Organization* (New York: McGraw-Hill, 1967), pp. 4–10.

45. Likert, *New Patterns of Management*, p. 103.

46. R. N. Farmer, *Contemporary Management Issues and Viewpoints*, ed. J. W. McGuire (Englewood Cliffs: Prentice-Hall, 1974), p. 302.

47. Frank Ching, "China's Managers Get U.S. Lessons," *Wall Street Journal*, 23 January 1981, p. 27.

48. Peter F. Drucker, "Behind Japan's Success," *Harvard Business Review*, January/February, 1981, pp. 83–90.

49. "How Japan Does It," *Time*, 30 March 1981, p. 55.

50. Charles McMillan, "Is Japanese Management Really So Different?" *Business Quarterly*, Autumn, 1980, pp. 26–31.

51. Masaru Ibuka, "Management Opinion," *Administrative Management*, May 1980, p. 86.

52. "How Japan Does It," *Time*, p. 57.

53. Lane Kelly and Reginald Worthley, "The Role of Culture in Comparative Management," *Academy of Management Journal* 24, no. 1 (1981): 164–73.

54. Isaac Shapiro, "Second Thoughts About Japan," *The Wall Street Journal*, 5 June 1981.

55. Muhammad Ali and Richard Durham, *The Greatest: My Own Story* (New York: Random House, Inc., 1975), p. 11.

56. Michael Brennan, "Ali and Hi Educators," *Sports Illustrated*, 22 September 1980, p. 40.

57. Ibid.

58. Jack Slater, "Muhammad Ali: The Loneliness of the Man at the Top," *Ebony*, July 1980, p. 34.

59. Ibid.

60. Ibid.

61. Ibid.

62. Ibid.

63. Ibid., p. 35.

64. Ibid.

65. Ibid.

66. Ibid., p. 42.

67. Ibid.

68. Ibid.

69. Ibid., p. 38.

70. B. J. Phillips, "Requiem for a Heavyweight," *Time*, 13 October 1980, p. 78.

71. Ibid.

72. Slater, "Muhammad Ali," p. 42.

73. Ibid.

Concluding Case 14
Muhammad Ali: World President? Four-Time Champ? Diplomat? Super-Superstar?

(Photo: Howard Bingham for *Sports Illustrated*, © Time, Inc.)

Muhammad Ali, three-time winner of the world heavyweight boxing title, has won fifty-six of sixty fights in a career spanning more than twenty years. Ali was born Cassius Clay, in Louisville, Kentucky, in 1942. Ali first gained national recognition as a boxer when he won the Golden Gloves championship in Chicago in 1959 and then retained that title the following year. In 1960, he won a gold medal at the Olympic Games in Rome; that same year he started his professional career by signing with a Louisville sponsoring group. In 1964, he won the heavyweight championship of the world, joined the Nation of Islam, and was married. When he refused to be drafted into the armed services in 1965, Ali's license was rescinded by the World Boxing Association, and in 1967, he received a five-year jail sentence for his refusal to join the army. Ali remained inactive until the court's decision was reversed in late 1970 and his license was renewed.[55]

During his turbulent career Ali has fought such well-known fighters as Floyd Patterson, Sonny Liston, Joe Frazier, and George Foreman. He has earned several million dollars and has travelled to such exotic places as Manila, Kuala Lampur, and Zaire to fight. While Ali has spoken "most eloquently with his fists,"[56] he is better known for having spoken several million words, most of them spoken at the top of his voice, many in rhyme. Probably more words have been written about, more cameras aimed at, and more arguments raged over Ali than anyone in the history of sports. It's Ali the personality even more than Ali the athlete that has kept him in the public eye.[57]

Over the years, Ali has announced his retirement from the ring more than once and has staged numerous comebacks. Each time he came out of retirement the question most dominant in people's minds was, Why does Ali come back to fight? Why?

It has been gossiped that Ali was in financial straights, forcing him to remain in the ring. Yet, other reliable press reports estimate Ali's net worth and holdings at $2 million to $3.5 million.[58] Some of Ali's close friends, however, suggest that Ali becomes bored when away from the ring and that his feeling of boredom has been further accentuated after his failure to establish a professional life in other fields. His plans to start a fast-food hamburger business have floundered. He has failed to become a successful actor. His initiative to start a philanthropic organization has met with the same fate. His trip to Africa as a representative of President Carter to convince those nations to boycott the Moscow Olympics was unsuccessful. In fact, some suggest that his inability to bring about the African boycott may have been the stimulus for his return to boxing. Within four days of his return from Africa, Ali announced that "he was considering a return to the ring."[59]

Ali has refused to admit that boredom and loneliness could ever enter his life. But his best friend, photographer

Howard Bingham, has stated that boredom is part of the reasons Ali returns to the ring; the other reason, Ali's belief that "Nobody is out there who can beat him."[60] However, another close associate suggests that Ali has trained all his life for one recurring event and that event has vanished, therefore life has become disenchanting, disorienting, adrift, useless, and kind of lonely for him.[61]

Ali himself has given different statements depending on his mood. For example, Ali states that "the money is important, but the main thing is that I will make history."[62] "I want to go down in history as a four-time heavy-weight champion—that's all. It's just that simple."[63] Yet earlier he had argued that the Muslim faith was facing a lot of problems in the United States and that this was forcing some of the mosques and schools to close down. To keep this from occurring he states, "I would return to keep houses of religion and schools open."[64]

In another statement he said he was planning to return to the ring for his philanthropic WORLD group—World Organization for Rights, Liberty, and Dignity. "I want to be the first WORLD president," he declared. "President of the WORLD. I'm serious. I'm the world's most recognized man. Who else could take this job?"[65] Other arguments include: "I want to make a comeback to reach black kids and be their 'Super-Superstar,'[66] so that they can say, 'We look like him,'[67] and I'm doing this one for all the people who've been told, 'You ain't gonna be nothing'."[68]

Ali speaks enthusiastically about his visit to India, China, and Russia and his meetings with leaders like Indira Gandhi, Deng Cio Ping, and Leonid I. Brezhnev. But when questioned on his African Tour and especially his treatment by the news media, he is quoted as saying, "That was the President's thing,"[69] implying that the displeasure shown in Africa was against President Carter, not Ali himself.

In October 1980, after a two-year retirement following his victory over Leon Spinks, Ali was battered by Larry Holmes for ten rounds before his aides in his corner stopped the fight. For the first time in his twenty-year career, Ali could not finish a bout.[70] After the fight, Ali said, "Taking as many punches as I was, I was glad they stopped it. Take your hearts and turn them over to Larry. He's the heavyweight champion—until I return."[71]

Ali accepts that there are limitations like old age, being overweight, and the boxers' limitation of once they lose, "they never come back."[72] But Ali's personal philosophy is: "the hell with them. Don't tell me I'm too old. Some people give up on life. Some people exchange life for a hospital bed. But some say to themselves, I ain't gonna die. And I say, I ain't gonna give up. I ain't gonna give up! I ain't gonna give up!"[73] On September 1, 1981, Muhammad Ali announced a December fight with Treavor Berbick in Jamaica!

Discussion Issues

1. From information in the case, what are the personal goals of Ali? What needs do you feel will be fulfilled if these goals are met?
2. If you were Ali, how would you rank the personal goals identified in question number 1?
3. Using Vroom's expectancy theory, explain why Ali continues to come back to the ring.
4. From the perspective of the Porter-Lawler Model, explain how Ali is motivated.
5. What level of human needs seem to be motivating Muhammad Ali?

Student Learning Objectives

From studying this chapter I will attempt to acquire:

1. A definition of the term *group* as used within the context of management
2. A thorough understanding of the difference between formal and informal groups
3. Knowledge of the types of formal groups that exist in organizations
4. An understanding of how managers can determine which groups exist in an organization
5. An appreciation for how managers must simultaneously evaluate formal and informal groups to maximize work group effectiveness

Chapter Outline

Managing Groups

Introductory Case 15
Giving Advice on Managing Groups

All five vice-presidents of the Crutch Athletic Equipment Company were gathered for a special meeting. From the conversation taking place, it was easy to tell that none of the five knew what the meeting was about. Each had received a memo about the meeting from Jesse Flick, the president of the company, but the memo had given no hint as to the meeting's purpose.

Flick walked into the room; greeted everyone present; sat down; and began the following speech:

As you know, ladies and gentlemen, our company over the past two years has shown only moderate success. After considerable thought as to how we might excel over the next few years, I have determined that a sound strategy should include improving our use of work groups within the company. In this regard, I offer the following advice. . . .

Discussion Issues

1. Do you think that Flick chose an important area in which to give advice to his vice-presidents? Why?
2. List three pieces of advice on the management of work groups that you think Flick probably gave to his vice-presidents.

What's Ahead

Jesse Flick, the company president in the introductory case, is advising his vice-presidents on how to manage work groups. This chapter contains the management theory on which Flick could be basing his advice.

The previous chapters in this section have dealt with three primary activities of the influencing function: (1) communication, (2) leadership, and (3) motivation. This chapter focuses on managing groups, the last major influencing activity to be discussed in this text. As with the other three activities, managing work groups requires guiding the behavior of organization members so as to increase the probability that an organization achieves its objectives. The material in this chapter develops a foundation for group management theory by (1) defining groups, (2) discussing the kinds of groups that exist in organizations, and (3) explaining what steps managers should take to manage groups appropriately.

To deal with groups appropriately, managers must have a thorough understanding of the nature of groups in organizations.[1] As used in management-related discussions, a **group** is not simply a gathering of people, but "any number of people who (1) interact with one another, (2) are psychologically aware of one another, and (3) perceive themselves to be a group."[2] Such a group is characterized by its members communicating with one another over time and being small enough so that each group member is able to communicate with all other members on a face-to-face basis.[3] As a result of this communication, each group member influences and is influenced by all other group members.[4]

Defining Groups

Gathering vs. Group

The study of groups is important to managers since the common ingredient of all organizations is people and since the most common technique for accomplishing work through these people is dividing them into work groups. Cartwright and Lippitt list four additional reasons for the importance of studying groups:

1. Groups exist in all kinds of organizations.
2. Groups inevitably form in all facets of organizational existence.
3. Groups can cause either desirable or undesirable consequences within the organization.
4. Understanding groups can assist managers in increasing the probability that groups with which he or she works will cause desirable consequences within the organization.[5]

Why Study about Groups?

Groups that exist in organizations typically are divided into two basic types: formal and informal.

Kinds of Groups in Organizations

Formal Groups

A **formal group** is one that exists within an organization by virtue of management decree to perform tasks that enhance the attainment or organizational objectives.[6] Figure 15.1 shows an example of a formal group. The placing of organization members in such areas as marketing departments, personnel departments, or production departments could all be examples of establishing formal groups.

Established by Management

Figure 15.1 A formal group.

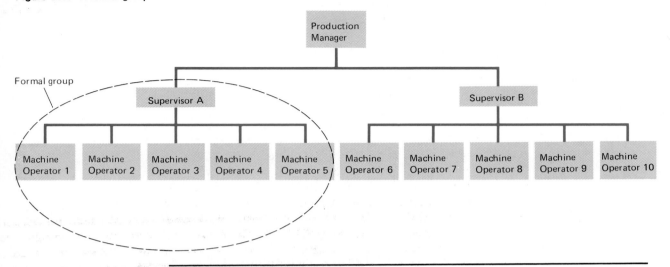

Figure 15.2 Formal groups that can exist within an organization and related linking pins.

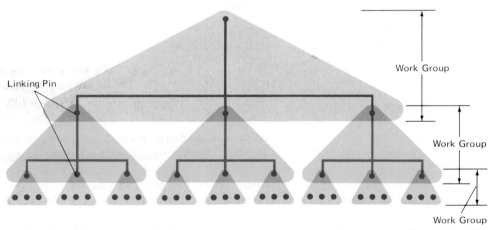

From NEW PATTERNS OF MANAGEMENT by Rensis Likert. Copyright © 1961 by McGraw-Hill, Inc. Used with permission of McGraw-Hill Book Company.

Organizations Have Many Formal Groups

In reality, organizations actually are made up of a number of formal groups that exist at various organizational levels. The coordination of and communication among these formal groups is the responsibility of managers or supervisors commonly called "linking pins." Figure 15.2 shows the various formal groups that can exist within an organization and the linking pins associated with those groups. The linking pins are actually organization members who belong to two formal groups.

In essence, formal groups are clearly defined and structured. The following sections discuss (1) the basic kinds of formal groups, (2) examples of formal groups as they exist in organizations, and (3) the four stages of group development.

Kinds of Formal Groups

What Are Command Groups?

Formal groups commonly are divided into two basic types: (1) command groups and (2) task groups.[7] **Command groups** are formal groups that are outlined on the chain of command on an organization chart. In general, command groups typically handle the more routine organizational activities.

Task groups, on the other hand, are formal groups of organization members who interact with one another to accomplish most nonroutine organizational tasks. Although task groups commonly are considered to be made up of members on the same organizational level, they can consist of people from different levels of the organizational hierarchy. For example, a manager could establish a task group to consider the feasibility of manufacturing some new product. Representatives from various levels of such organizational areas as production, market research, and sales probably would be included as task group members.

What Are Task Groups?

Back to the Case

Considering the information in the preceding section, Jesse Flick, the president in the introductory case, probably would proceed with his speech to his vice-president as follows:

The term group *when used in management-related discussions, has a very specific meaning. A group usually is defined as any number of people who interact with each other, are psychologically aware of each other, and perceive themselves to be a group. These people communicate with each*

other on a face-to-face basis and also influence one another. All of us here have such groups under us, and our success in dealing with these groups is obviously a major determinant of how successful our company is.

As you deal with groups in your areas, be sure to consider both formal groups and informal groups. Formal groups are those represented on an organization chart. Our marketing department would be an example of a formal group.

Examples of Formal Groups

The next two sections discuss two formal groups that can be established in organizations: (1) committees and (2) work teams. Committees represent a more traditionally used formal group, while work teams are formal groups that recently are beginning to gain popular acceptance and support in organizations. Since the organizing section of this text emphasized command groups, the examples in this section emphasize task groups.

Committees

A **committee** is a group of individuals that has been charged with performing some type of activity. A committee, therefore, usually is classified as a task group. From a managerial viewpoint, the major reasons for establishing committees are (1) to allow organization members to exchange ideas, (2) to generate suggestions and recommendations that can be offered to other organizational units, (3) to develop new ideas for solving existing organizational problems, and (4) to assist in the development or organizational policies.[8]

Why Establish Committees?

Committees typically exist within all organizations and at all organizational levels. As figure 15.3 suggests, however, the larger the organization, the greater the probability that committees are used within that organization on a regular basis. The following two sections discuss (1) why managers should use committees and (2) what makes committees successful.

Committees and Larger Organizations

Why Managers Should Use Committees Managers generally agree that committees have several uses in organizations. One reason for their use is that committees can improve the quality of decision making.[9] Generally speaking, as more people become involved in making a decision, the strengths and weaknesses of that decision are discussed in more detail and the quality of the decision tends to increase.

Quality of Decisions, Honest Opinions, Enhance Decision Support, Opportunity to Satisfy Needs, Group Representation

Figure 15.3 More committees on a regular basis in larger organizations than smaller organizations.

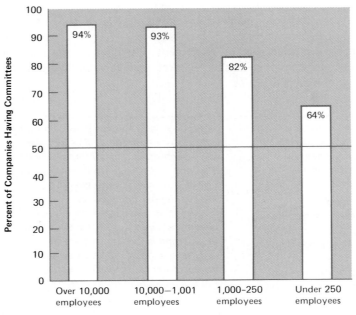

Percent of Companies Having Committees

| Over 10,000 employees | 10,000–1,001 employees | 1,000–250 employees | Under 250 employees |

94% 93% 82% 64%

Size of Company

"Then it's moved and seconded that the compulsory retirement age be advanced to ninety-five."

Drawing by Peter Arno; © 1963 The New Yorker Magazine, Inc.

Another reason for committees is that they encourage honest opinions. Committee members feel protected because the group output of a committee logically cannot be totally associated with any one member of that group.

A third reason why managers generally feel that committees should be used is that committees tend to increase organization member participation in decision making and thereby enhance support of committee decisions. Also, as a result of this increased participation, committee work creates the opportunity for committee members to satisfy their social or esteem needs.

The fourth reason for the use of committees is that they ensure the representation of important groups in the decision-making process. The *New Yorker* cartoon, however, makes the point that merely establishing a committee does not guarantee appropriate group representation. Managers must choose committee members wisely to achieve this representation.

Some top executives show only qualified acceptance of committees as work groups, while still other executives express negative feelings. Figure 15.4 indicates that, in general, the executives who are negative about using committees are fewer in number than those who have positive feelings or display qualified acceptance of them.

What Makes Committees Successful   Although committees have become a commonly accepted management tool, managerial action taken to establish and run committees is a major variable in determining the degree of success a committee achieves. Procedural steps that can be taken to increase the probability that a committee will be successful are:

Committee Procedures

1. The committee's goals should be clearly defined, preferably in writing. This will focus the committee's activities and reduce the time devoted to discussing what the committee is supposed to do.

2. The committee's authority should be specified. Can the committee merely investigate, advise, and recommend, or is it authorized to implement decisions?

3. The optimum size of the committee should be determined. With fewer than five members, the advantages of group work may be diminished. With more than ten or fifteen members, the committee may become unwieldy. While size varies with the circumstances, the ideal number of committee members for many tasks seems to range from five to ten.

4. A chairperson should be selected on the basis of ability to run an efficient meeting—that is, an individual's ability to keep the participation of all committee members from getting bogged down in irrelevancies and to see that the necessary paperwork gets done.

5. Appointing a permanent secretary to handle communications is often useful.

6. The agenda and all supporting material for the meeting should be distributed before the meeting. When members have a chance to study each item beforehand, they are more likely to stick to the point and be ready with informed contributions.

7. Meetings should be started on time, and the time at which they will end should be announced at the outset.[10]

Figure 15.4 Feelings of executives about committees as work groups.

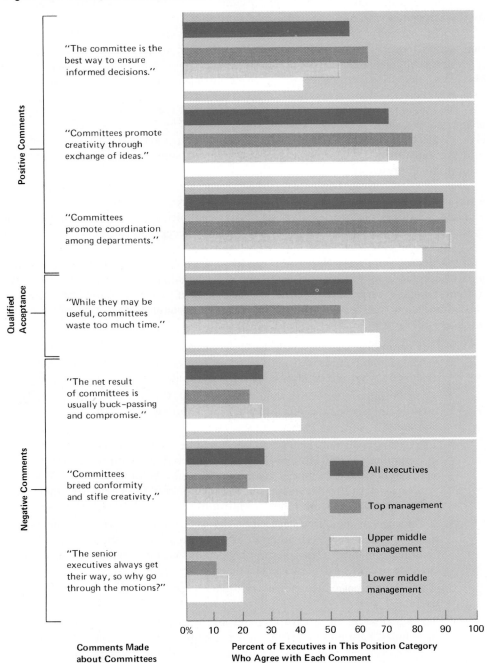

Reprinted by permission of the *Harvard Business Review,* from "Committees on Trial" (Problems in Review) by Rollie Tillman, Jr. (May–June 1960). Copyright © 1960 by the President and Fellows of Harvard College; all rights reserved.

In addition to these more procedurally oriented steps are a number of more people-oriented guidelines managers can follow to increase the probability that a committee is successful. In this regard, a manager can increase the quality of discussion in committees by:

People in Committees

1. *Rephrasing ideas already expressed*   This rephrasing makes sure that the manager as well as other individuals in the committee have a clear understanding of what has been said.

2. *Bringing a member into active participation*   All committee members represent possible sources of information, and the manager should serve as a catalyst to spark individual participation whenever appropriate.

3. *Stimulating further thought by a member*   The manager should encourage committee members to think ideas through carefully and thoroughly. Only this type of analysis generates high quality committee output.[11]

Another people-oriented guideline managers can follow to increase the probability that a committee will be successful is to avoid a phenomenon called "groupthink."[12] **Groupthink** is the mode of thinking that persons engage in when seeking agreement becomes so dominant in a group that it tends to override the realistic appraisal of alternative problem solutions. Groups operate under groupthink when group members are so concerned with being too harsh in their judgments of other group members that objective problem solving is lost. Such groups tend to adopt a softer line of criticism and seek complete support on every issue with little conflict generated to endanger the "we-feeling" atmosphere.

Desire for Unanimous Agreement

Back to the Case

Considering the information in the preceding section, Flick probably would continue his speech to his vice-presidents as follows:

Examples of task groups you can use to assist you in your areas are committees and work teams. Basically, a committee is a group you charge with some activity. You can use committees to exchange ideas in your divisions, to furnish yourself with needed suggestions on solving problems, and to help yourself to develop plans for a subsequent year. Keep in mind that our organization probably is large enough to justify the use of committees on a regular basis.

Try to use committees wherever feasible since committees can improve the quality of our decision making and increase the motivation level of committee members through increased participation in organizational matters. From a procedural viewpoint, you can help to make your committees successful by doing such things as clearly defining the committee's goal, selecting a well-qualified committee chairperson, and appointing a committee secretary to inform other organization members of committee progress. From more of a people viewpoint, you can increase the probability of your committees' success by rephrasing ideas already expressed, bringing members into active participation, and stimulating further thought of committee members. Also, try to avoid groupthink.

Work Teams

Rapid Growth Flexibility

Work teams are another example of task groups used in organizations. A more recently developed management tool than committees, work teams generally are established to achieve greater organizational flexibility or to cope with rapid growth.

A case in point would be a situation faced by William W. George, a corporate vice-president of Litton Industries. George created work teams within the Litton microwave cooking division to manage rapid growth.[13] One such team described by George included members from new product development, manufacturing, marketing, cost-reduction, facilities planning, and new business ventures. As designed by George, the team had a designated leader, representation from several functional departments, and involvement by top management on an "as required" basis.

Back to the Case

Considering the information in the preceding section, Flick probably would continue his speech to his vice-presidents as follows:

> You can also use work teams, another type of task group, to assist in the accomplishment of work in your areas. These work teams can be created to meet special organizational needs, such as rapid growth or needed flexibility. If, for example, our vice-president for production finds out that we can't produce a product as fast as we can sell it, a work team made up of organization members from various key parts of our company could be established to work on expediting the production process. The establishment of such a group typically would result in increased organizational flexibility.
>
> I do want to stress, however, that I am not telling you to go out and start establishing committees and work teams. What I am suggesting is that you seriously consider using these group devices when situations seem to warrant them.

Stages of Group Development

Another facet to managing groups is understanding the stages of group development. Bernard Bass has suggested that group development is a four-stage process influenced primarily by groups learning how to use their resources.[14] Although these stages may not occur sequentially, for purposes of clarity the following discussion assumes that they do. The four stages can be labeled and defined as follows:

How Groups Develop

1. *The acceptance stage*   It is relatively common for new members of a group initially to mistrust each other somewhat. The acceptance stage occurs only after the initial mistrust within a group has been transformed into mutual trust and the general acceptance of group members by one another.

2. *The communication and decision-making stage*   Once the acceptance stage has been passed, group members are better able to communicate frankly with one another. This frank communication actually provides the basis for establishing and using effectively some type of group decision-making mechanism.

3. *The group solidarity stage*   The group solidarity stage flows naturally as the mutual acceptance of group members increases, and communication and decision making continue within the group. This stage is characterized by members becoming more involved in group activities and cooperating, rather than competing, with one another. Group members find being a member of the group extremely satisfying and are committed to enhancing the overall success of the group.

4. *The group control stage*   A natural result of the group solidarity stage is the group control stage. This stage involves group members attempting to maximize group success by matching individual abilities with group activities being performed as well as giving assistance to each other that will ensure group success. Flexibility and informality tend to characterize this group development stage.

In general terms, as a group passes through each of these four stages, it tends to become more mature, more effective, and therefore more productive. The group that reaches maximum maturity and effectiveness is characterized by:

Mature Groups

1. *Members functioning as a unit*   The group works as a team. Members do not disturb each other to the point of interfering with their collaboration.

2. *Members participating effectively in group effort*   Members work hard when there is something to do. They usually do not loaf even if they get the opportunity.

3. *Members being oriented toward a single goal*   Group members work for common purposes and thereby do not waste group resources by moving in different directions.

4. *Members having the equipment, tools, and skills necessary to attain the group's goals*   Group members are taught various parts of their jobs by experts and strive to acquire whatever resources are needed to attain group objectives.

5. *Members asking and receiving suggestions, opinions, and information from each other*   If a member is uncertain about something, he or she stops working and asks another group member for information. Group members generally talk to each other openly and frequently.[15]

Back to the Case

Considering the information in the preceding section, Flick probably would continue his speech to his vice-presidents as follows:

Even though you establish a task group to assist you in your respective areas of responsibility, remember that it may take some time for that group to mature as a productive working unit. Groups generally pass through stages of developing mutual trust among group members, communicating frankly within the group, cooperating as much as possible within the group, and maintaining flexibility and informality to achieve group objectives. As groups pass through these stages, they become more mature and more productive working units. Be patient with groups that seem relatively immature because as these groups mature, they will tend to become more productive and therefore more helpful to you.

Informal Groups

The second major kind of group that can exist within an organization is informal groups. **Informal groups** are those that develop naturally as people interact. As shown in figure 15.5, informal group structures can deviate significantly from formal group structures. As in the case of Supervisor A, an organization member can belong to more than one informal group at the same time. In contrast to formal groups, informal groups typically are not highly structured in terms of procedure and are not formally recognized by management.

People Interaction

Some Groups Develop Naturally

The following sections discuss (1) various kinds of informal groups that can exist in organizations, (2) the benefits usually reaped by membership in informal groups, and (3) encouraging the development of informal groups.

Figure 15.5 Three informal groups that deviate significantly from formal groups within the organization.

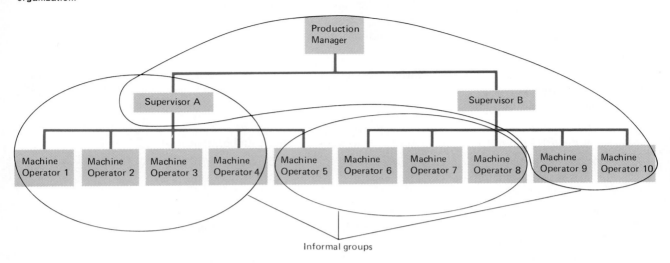

Informal groups

Kinds of Informal Groups

Issues of Common Concern

Informal groups generally are divided into two basic types: (1) interest groups and (2) friendship groups. **Interest groups** are informal groups that gain and maintain membership primarily because of a special concern each member possesses about a specific issue. An example might be a group of workers pressing management for better pay or working conditions. In general, once the interest or concern that caused this informal group to form has been eliminated, the group tends to disband.

Social Relationships

As its name implies, **friendship groups** are informal groups that form in organizations because of the personal affiliation members have for one another. As with interest groups, the membership of friendship groups tends to change over time. Here, however, group membership changes as friendships dissolve or new friendships are made.

Benefits of Informal Group Membership

Rewards of Informal Group Membership

Informal groups tend to develop in organizations because of various benefits that group members obtain. These benefits include (1) perpetuation of social and cultural values that group members consider important, (2) status and social satisfaction that might not be enjoyed without group membership, (3) increased ease of communication between group members, and (4) increased desirability of the overall work environment.[16] These benefits may be one reason why employees who are on fixed shifts or continually work with the same group are sometimes more satisfied with their work than employees whose shifts are continually changing.[17]

Encouraging the Development of Informal Groups

Relations with Unions

One tool managers may be able to use to assist in the development of informal groups is called a quality circle. **Quality circles** are simply small groups of factory workers that meet regularly with management to discuss quality-related problems. Naturally, during these meetings management would have regular opportunities to nurture relationships with various informal groups. In fact, quality circles may actually result in some managers and workers being members of the same informal groups. As exhibit 15 illustrates, union leaders are worrying that management relations with workers may become too good as a result of quality circles. Although managers report good success with the use of quality circles, the circles are so new that much research must be done to assess their long-run impact on the organization.

Back to the Case

Considering the information in the preceding section, Flick probably would continue his speech to his vice-presidents as follows:

> In addition to working with formal groups, you will have to work with and through informal groups in your areas. These groups develop naturally as people in our organization interact. Two examples of these informal groups are interest groups and friendship groups. The former gains and maintains membership because of a special concern or issue that the members share, while the latter gains and maintains membership due to personal affiliations that people have with one another. As you might suspect, the membership of these groups changes over time. In general, individuals belong to informal groups because of the benefits, such as increased desirability of the working environment, that accrue to group members. If you feel the need, try to develop positive informal group relations in your areas through quality circles.

To manage work groups effectively, managers must consider simultaneously the impact of both formal and informal group factors on organizational productivity. This consideration requires three steps: (1) determining group existence, (2) understanding the evolution of informal groups, and (3) maximizing work group effectiveness. Each of these topics is discussed further in the sections that follow.

Managing Work Groups

Consider Both Formal and Informal Groups

Determining Group Existence

Perhaps the most important step that managers should take in managing work groups is determining what groups exist within the organization and who constitutes the membership of those groups. **Sociometry** is an analytical tool that managers can use to help determine such information. Sociometry also can provide information on the internal workings of an informal group. Included in this information are such factors as identification of the leader of an informal group, the relative status level of various members within the informal group, and the communication networks that tend to exist within the informal group.[18] This information on informal groups, along with an understanding of the established formal groups as shown on an organization chart, gives managers a complete picture of the group structure with which they must deal.

What is Sociometry?

The procedure involved in performing a sociometric analysis in an organization is quite basic.[19] Various organization members simply are asked, either through an interview or questionnaire, to state several other organization members with whom they would like to spend some of their free time. Based on results of this information-gathering process, a sociogram then is constructed to summarize the informal relationships among group members that were uncovered. **Sociograms** are diagrams that visually link individuals within the group according to the number of times they were chosen and whether or not the choice was reciprocal.

What are Sociograms?

(Photo: Buick Public Relations)

WASHINGTON—Some labor officials are starting to worry that the growing use of "quality circles," or small groups of factory workers that meet regularly with management to discuss production problems, may turn out to be a potent antiunion tool.

Quality circles, often formed with labor's cooperation, are increasing rapidly. About 1,000 organizations are using them, up from 150 a year ago, estimates the International Association of Quality Circles, a business group.

The goal of such groups is to produce ideas that improve both productivity and conditions in the work place. But some labor leaders are concerned that quality circles are being used by companies either to combat union organizing drives or to diminish a union's authority in a plant. They fear that quality circles will expand to include areas such as work rules and benefits that historically have been covered by collective bargaining.

"A number of well-meaning people believe that quality circles can lead to improvements in the work place," says William Roehl, the AFL-CIO's assistant director of organizing. "But what they don't know is that they can also be part of a company's union-busting strategy." Expressing organized labor's greatest fear, he worries that some companies "will give workers the impression that all their problems will be solved by quality circles, which implies that there's no need for unions."

Unions Advise Cooperation

Nevertheless, the AFL-CIO's emerging strategy is to advise its unions to join the quality circles, rather than fight them. The federation is preparing a detailed manual that will suggest that in unionized plants, labor should push for equal participation in the circles—and an equal share of the credit for any accomplishments.

Sometimes companies beginning quality circles get off to a bad start by bypassing unions. Last spring a consumer-electronics unit of North American Philips Corp. set up several quality circles at its Jefferson City, Tenn., plant. Although 70% of the factory's 1,010 workers are represented by the International Union of Electrical Workers, the union wasn't consulted before the plan was started. Further, the company won't give the union a list of the workers in the quality circles, says Charles Wolfenbarger, local union president.

"My people are afraid that they'll wind up with some cost-saving ideas that will put them out on the street," says Mr. Wolfenbarger.

Bruce Handshu, the company's manager of quality training, concedes that "it's conceivable we made a mistake. In the future, we'll bring the union in from the beginning." He says that management met recently with union officials in an effort to get their support. The union says it's too early to judge the value of the company's circles.

Antiunion Uses Feared

Labor officials say that other companies see quality circles as a way to keep unions weak or to keep them out altogether. A copy of the minutes of a May 1980 meeting of Du Pont Co. executives, in Nashville, Tenn., says the motive "for entering into collaboration with the union" in worker committees "is more likely to be a recognition that the environment within the organization is rife with opportunity for the unions to make an issue of job pressure . . . if the company doesn't take the initiative itself. . . ." The company, which has local unions at some plants, is fighting a major organizing drive by the United Steelworkers union.

A Du Pont spokeswoman confirms that there were meetings during that period involving Du Pont's Old Hickory plant in Tennessee, but she can't vouch for the authenticity of the minutes. A spokesman adds that, to his knowledge, quality circles haven't been discussed as part of a strategy to keep out unions.

Despite labor's worries, some major unions support the quality-circle concept and are working closely with companies that have invited them to join as equal partners. These unions include the steelworkers, the auto workers and the communications workers. "We're not going to stand in the way of progress," says John Oshinski, the steelworkers' organizing director.

Enthusiasm at GM

Even the electrical workers, while suspicious of North American Philips's efforts in Tennessee, are enthusiastic about a plan they participate in at a General Motors Corp. plant in Warren, Ohio. Edward Fire, the union's local president, says the quality circle discovered that high-paid workers were losing production time because of delays in getting them certain materials. The group suggested that four low-paid maintenance workers be hired to move material around the plant more efficiently. The suggestion was adopted by management.

However, some labor experts see quality circles moving from production problems into other areas. Kim Smith, former labor relations director for the National Association of Manufacturers and now a private consultant, predicts "companies using the concept will head slowly towards broader quality-of-worklife programs that include such issues as health and safety."

And, she concludes: "If I were in the unions' shoes, I'd be concerned. Quality circles are trying to achieve a lot of the things that are traditional union objectives."

From Robert S. Greenberger, "Quality Circles Grow, Stirring Union Worries," *Wall Street Journal,* 22 September 1981, p. 33. Reprinted by permission of Wall Street Journal. Copyright Dow Jones and Company, Inc. 1980. All rights reserved.

Figure 15.6 Sample sociograms.

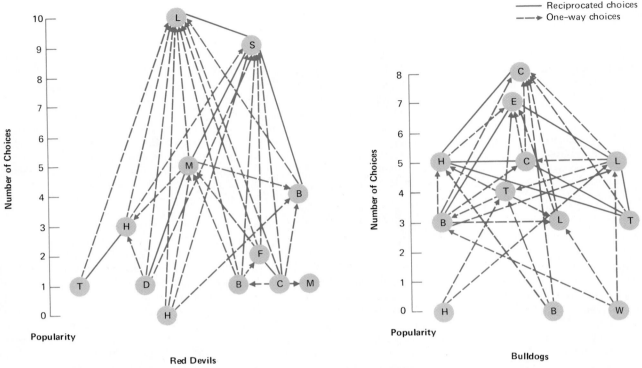

Fig. 11.5 "Sociograms of friendship choices made by Bull Dogs and Red Devils at end of in-groups formation" (p. 238) in SOCIAL PSYCHOLOGY by Muzafer Sherif and Carolyn W. Sherif. By permission of Harper & Row, Publishers, Inc.

Figure 15.6 shows two sample sociograms based on a study of two groups of boys in a summer camp—the Bulldogs and the Red Devils.[20] In analyzing these sociograms several interesting observations can be made. For example, more boys within the Bulldogs were chosen overall as being desirable to spend time with than within the Red Devils. This probably implies that the Bulldogs are a closer-knit informal group than the Red Devils. Also, communication between "L" and most other Red Devils members is likely to occur directly, while communication between "C" and other Bulldogs is likely to pass through other group members. Lastly, the greater the number of times an individual is chosen, the more likely that individual will be the group leader. Thus, individuals "C" and "E" would tend to be Bulldog leaders, while individuals "L" and "S" would tend to be Red Devil leaders.

Sociometric analysis can give managers many useful insights on the existence of informal groups within an organization. Although managers may not desire to perform a formal sociometric analysis within an organization, they can casually gather information that would indicate what form a sociogram might take in a particular situation. This information can be gathered through inferences made in normal conversations that managers have with other organization members and observations of how various organization members relate to one another.

Understanding the Evolution of Informal Groups

Obviously, knowing what groups exist within an organization and what characterizes the membership of those groups is an extremely important prerequisite for managing

Figure 15.7 Homans's ideas on how informal groups develop.

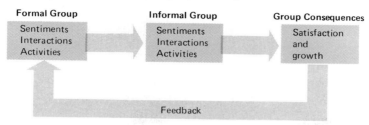

groups effectively. A second prerequisite for managing groups effectively is understanding how informal groups evolve. An understanding of this evolution affords managers some insights on how to encourage informal groups to develop appropriately within an organization. Naturally, encouraging these groups to develop appropriately and maintaining good relationships with work group members can help to ensure that organization members support management in the process of attaining organizational objectives.[21]

Perhaps the most widely accepted framework for explaining the evolution of informal groups was developed by George Homans.[22] Figure 15.7 broadly summarizes his theory. According to Homans, the sentiments, activities, and interactions that emerge as part of an informal group actually result from the sentiments, activities, and interactions that exist within a formal group. In addition, Homans says that the informal group exists to obtain the consequences of satisfaction and growth for informal group members. Feedback on whether or not these consequences are achieved can result in forces that attempt to modify the formal group so as to increase the probability that the informal group achieves these consequences.

An example to illustrate Homans's concept would be twelve factory workers who are members of a formal work group that manufactures toasters. According to Homans, as these workers interact to assemble toasters, they will discover common personal interests that encourage the evolution of informal groups. In turn, these informal groups tend to maximize the satisfaction and growth of informal group members. Once established, these informal groups will probably resist changes or established segments of formal groups that threaten the satisfaction and growth of informal group members.

How Informal Groups Evolve

Considering the information in the preceding section, Flick probably would continue his speech to his vice-presidents as follows:

For you to be successful in managing groups in your areas, you must consider simultaneously the potential impact of both formal and informal groups on productivity. Perhaps the first step you should take in this regard is to determine what informal groups exist in your divisions and who constitutes the membership of those groups. Sociometry is a tool you can use to determine the formation of informal groups in your divisions, identification of the leaders of those informal groups,

and the communication networks that probably exist within those informal groups. To ascertain the complete situation on groups in your areas, compare specifics on the informal groups in your areas to your formal groups as listed on our organization chart.

In addition, remember that informal groups usually are the result of the way in which we force people to interact as a result of the policies, procedures, and all other formal constraints we place on them. Influencing informal groups in your areas, therefore, probably can best be achieved through various modifications to formal dimensions of the organization.

Back to the Case

Figure 15.8 Primary determinants of work group effectiveness.

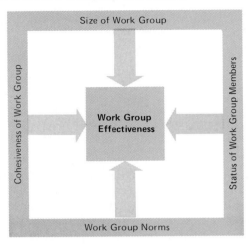

Maximizing Work Group Effectiveness

Once managers determine which groups exist within an organization and understand how informal groups evolve, they should strive to maximize work group effectiveness. As the following discussion emphasizes, maximizing work group effectiveness requires that managers continue to consider both formal and informal dimensions of the organization.[23]

Figure 15.8 indicates the four factors primarily responsible for collectively influencing work group effectiveness: (1) size of work group, (2) cohesiveness of work group, (3) work group norms, and (4) status of work group members. The following sections explain how each of these factors should be considered when attempting to maximize work group effectiveness. The terms *work group* and *formal group* are used synonymously in these sections.

Size of Work Group

Number of People in a Work Group

As work group size or the number of members of a work group increases, forces usually are created within that group that can either increase or decrease its effectiveness.[24] The ideal number of members for a work group depends primarily on the group's purpose.[25] For example, the ideal size for a fact-finding work group usually is set at about fourteen members, while the maximum size for a problem-solving work group is approximately seven members.[26]

Work group size is a significant determinant of group effectiveness because it has considerable impact on three major components of a group: (1) leadership, (2) group members, and (3) group processes. A summary of how these three factors can be influenced by group size is presented in figure 15.9.

Size: Formal and Informal Considerations

When attempting to maximize group effectiveness by modifying formal group size, managers also should consider informal group factors. For example, a manager may decide that a formal work group should be reduced in size to make it more effective. Before making this reduction, however, the manager should consider the existence of informal groups within that formal group. If the manager reduces the size of the formal group by transferring the informal group leader, the possibility exists that the effectiveness of the work group could diminish considerably due to the loss of its informal leader. The manager may conclude that the slight ineffectiveness of the overly large formal work group is more advantageous than the greater ineffectiveness that could result from reducing the formal group size and possibly transferring the informal group leader.

Figure 15.9 Possible effects of group size on group leadership, group members, and group processes.

Dimensions	Group Size 2–7 Members	Group Size 8–12 Members	Group Size 13–16 Members
Leadership			
1. Demand on leader	Low	Moderate	High
2. Differences between leaders and members	Low	Low to moderate	Moderate to high
3. Direction of leader	Low	Low to moderate	Moderate to high
Members			
4. Tolerance of direction from leader	Low to high	Moderate to high	High
5. Domination of group interaction by a few members	Low	Moderate to high	High
6. Inhibition in participation by ordinary members	Low	Moderate	High
Group processes			
7. Formalization of rules and procedures	Low	Low to moderate	Moderate to high
8. Time required for reading decisions	Low to moderate	Moderate	Moderate to high
9. Tendency for subgroup to form	Low	Moderate to high	High

Reprinted with permission from Don Hellriegel and John W. Slocum, Jr.'s "Organizational Behavior Contingency Views," Copyright © 1976 by West Publishing Co.

Cohesiveness of Work Group

Another factor that can influence work group effectiveness is the degree of cohesiveness within the group. **Group cohesiveness** is the attraction group members feel for one another in terms of desires to remain a member of the group and resist leaving it.[27] The greater these desires, the more the cohesiveness within that group. In general, the cohesiveness of a work group is determined by the cohesiveness of the informal groups that exist within that work group. Therefore, to manage the degree of cohesiveness that exists within a work group, managers must manage the degree of cohesiveness that exists within the informal group or groups that constitute that work group.

Group cohesiveness is extremely important to managers since the greater the cohesiveness that exists within a group, the greater the probability the group will accomplish its objectives. In addition, some evidence indicates that groups whose members have positive feelings toward one another tend to be more productive than groups whose members have negative feelings toward one another.[28] This positive feeling or cohesiveness tends to increase within an informal group as the following factors become more important within the group:

1. The members have a broad, general agreement on the goals and objectives of the informal group.
2. A significant amount of communication and interaction is evident among participating members.
3. There is a satisfactory level of homogeneity in social status and social background among the members.
4. Members are allowed to participate fully and directly in the determination of group standards.
5. The size of the group is sufficient for interaction, but is not too large to stymie personal attention. Normally, the optimum size range of an informal group is from four to seven members.

Desire to Remain a Group Member

Importance of Cohesiveness

Indicators of High Cohesiveness

6. The members have a high regard for their fellow members.
7. The members feel a strong need for the mutual benefits and protection the group appears to offer.
8. The group is experiencing success in the achievement of its goals and in the protection of important values.[29]

Cohesiveness: Formal and Informal Dimensions

Since group cohesiveness of informal groups is such an influential determinant of cohesiveness within work groups and, as a result, of work group effectiveness, management should assist in the development of informal group cohesiveness whenever possible. This, of course, assumes that the informal group is attempting to make a constructive contribution to organizational goal attainment. To this end, managers should attempt to enhance the prestige of existing informal group members, design the overall organization to allow the encouragement of informal group development, and eliminate organizational barriers to continuing informal group membership over an extended period of time.

If, however, managers determine that an informal group is attempting to attain objectives that are counterproductive within the organization, an appropriate strategy would be to attempt to reduce informal group cohesiveness. For example, managers could take action to limit the prestige of existing group members and design the overall organization to discourage further group cohesiveness. This type of action, however, should be taken very cautiously since it could result in a major conflict between management and various informal groups that exist within an organization. Overall, managers must keep in mind that as with informal groups with productive objectives, the greater the cohesiveness within informal groups with nonproductive objectives, the greater the probability that those nonproductive objectives will be attained.

Back to the Case

Considering the information in the preceding section, Flick probably would continue his speech to his vice-presidents as follows:

Once you determine the members of various formal and informal groups in your areas and thoroughly understand how informal groups evolve, you can begin to try to increase the effectiveness of your work groups. Two main variables to consider when attempting to increase this effectiveness are group size and group cohesiveness. You may find, for example, that a group's effectiveness as a working unit is being hampered because the group is too large. Before you transfer someone out of that group, consider informal groups within that formal group. Transferring a respected member of the informal group could drastically reduce rather than increase work group productivity.

With regard to cohesiveness, the more cohesive the work group, the more successful it will tend to be. You should attempt to increase the cohesiveness of your formal work groups by enhancing the cohesiveness of informal groups that exist within the formal group structure. Such actions as allowing informal group members to take breaks together and recognizing various members of the informal group for a job well done can help you to enhance the cohesiveness of the formal work group of which the informal group is a part.

Work Group Norms

Required Behavior

A third major determinant of work group effectiveness is group norms. **Group norms,** as used in this chapter, apply only to informal groups and can be defined as appropriate or standard behavior that is required of informal group members. These norms, therefore, have significant influence on the behavior that informal group members perform as members of their formal group. According to Hackman, group norms (1) are structured characteristics of groups that simplify the group influence processes, (2) apply

Figure 15.10 Examples of positive and negative group norms.

	Negative Norms
Factory Workers	Keep your mouth shut when the boss is around.
Factory Workers	We stop working fifteen minutes before quitting time to wash up.
Utility Workers	We always take a nice long coffee break in the morning before climbing those poles.
Typing Pool	Don't rush the work — they'll just give you more to do.
Salesclerks	Don't hurry to wait on a customer — they'll keep.
	Positive Norms
Factory Workers	Do it right the first time.
Typing Pool	Make certain it looks nice — we want to be proud of our work.
Car Salespeople	We want to sell more cars than anyone else in the city.
Grocery Clerks	Go out of your way to satisfy customers — we want them to come back.
Factory Workers	Don't waste materials — they cost money.

Thomas W. Johnson and John E. Stinson, MANAGING TODAY AND TOMORROW © 1978, Addison-Wesley Publishing Co., Reading, Massachusetts, p. 69. Reprinted with permission.

only to behavior and not to private thoughts and feelings of group members, (3) generally develop only in relation to those matters that most group members consider important, (4) usually develop slowly over time, and (5) sometimes apply only to certain group members.[30]

Systematic study of group norms has revealed that there is generally a close relationship between group norms and the profitability of the organization of which that group is a part.[31] Although it would be impossible to state all possible norms that might develop in a group, most group norms relate to one or more of the following ten categories: (1) organizational pride, (2) performance, (3) profitability, (4) teamwork, (5) planning, (6) supervision, (7) training, (8) innovation, (9) customer relations, and (10) honesty or security.

Norms usually are divided into two general types: negative norms and positive norms. **Negative norms** are required informal group behavior that limits organizational productivity, while **positive norms** are required informal group behavior that contributes to organizational productivity. Examples of both positive and negative norms are presented in figure 15.10.

Some managers consider group norms to be of such great importance to the organization that they develop profiles of group norms to assess the norms' organizational impact. Figure 15.11 shows a normative profile developed by one company manager. This particular normative profile is characterized by a number of norm differences. For example, a high level of organizational pride and good customer relations contrasts with a lower concern for profitability. What actually happened in this company was that employees placed customer desires at such a high level that they were significantly dwindling organizational profitability to please customers. Once these norms were discovered, management took steps to make the situation more organizationally advantageous.

Limit Organizational Productivity

Contribute to Organizational Productivity

Normative Profile

Figure 15.11 Sample normative profile.

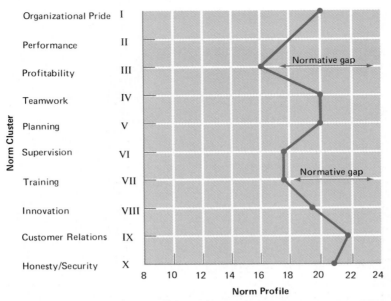

Norms: Formal and Informal Considerations

As the preceding information suggests, a major key to managing the behavior within a formal work group is managing the norms of the informal group or groups that exist within that formal group. More specifically, Homans's framework for analyzing group behavior indicates that informal group norms are mainly the result of the characteristics of the formal work group of which the informal group is a part. As a result, to change existing norms within an informal group, characteristics of the formal work group of which that informal group is a part must be changed.

An illustration of changing informal group norms could involve an informal group that possesses the negative norm: "Don't rush the work—they'll just give you more to do." For a manager to change this norm, the factor in the formal work group from which this norm probably arose should be eliminated. For example, the manager may find that this norm is a direct result of the fact that workers are formally recognized within the organization through pay and awards regardless of the amount of work performed. Changing this formal policy so that the amount of work accomplished is considered in formal organizational recognition should help to dissolve this negative norm. In some situations, norms may be extremely difficult if not impossible to change.

Status of Work Group Members

Position within Group

Status is the position of a group member in relation to other group members. Overall, an individual's status within a group is determined not only by the person's work or role within the group but by the nonwork qualities the individual brings into the group.[32] Work-related determinants of status include titles, work schedules, and amounts of

Figure 15.12 How status symbols vary with various levels of the organizational hierarchy.

Visible Appurtenances	Top Dogs	V.I.P.s	Brass	No. 2s	Eager Beavers	Hoi Polloi
Brief cases	None—they ask the questions	Use backs of envelopes	Someone goes along to carry theirs	Carry their own—empty	Daily—carry their own—filled with work	Too poor to own one
Desks, office	Custom-made (to order)	Executive style (to order)	Type A, "Director"	Type B, "Manager"	Cast-offs from No. 2s	Yellow oak— or cast-offs from eager beavers
Tables, office	Coffee tables	End tables or decorative wall tables	Matching tables, type A	Matching tables, type B	Plain work table	None—lucky to have own desk
Carpeting	Nylon— one-inch pile	Nylon— one-inch pile	Wool-twist (with pad)	Wool-twist (without pad)	Used wool pieces—sewed	Asphalt tile
Plant stands	Several—kept filled with strange, exotic plants		Two—repotted whenever they take a trip	One medium-sized —repotted annually during vacation	Small—repotted when plant dies	May have one in the department or bring their own from home
Vacuum-water bottles	Silver	Silver	Chromium	Plain painted	Coke machine	Water fountains
Library	Private collection	Autographed or complimentary books and reports	Selected references	Impressive titles on covers	Books everywhere	Dictionary
Shoe-shine service	Every morning at 10:00	Every morning at 10:15	Every day at 9:00 or 11:00	Every other day	Once a week	Shine their own
Parking space	Private—in front of office	In plant garage	In company garage —if enough seniority	In company properties— somewhere	On the parking lot	Anywhere they can find a space —if they can afford a car

Reprinted, by permission of the publisher, from "What Raises a Man's Morale," by Morris S. Viteles, from PERSONNEL, January 1954, © 1954 by American Management Associations, Inc., p. 305. All rights reserved.

pay group members receive. Of these three, pay is perhaps the most commonly used.[33] Nonwork-related determinants of status include education level, race, age, and sex. Figure 15.12 is an entertaining but realistic treatment of how status symbols vary within formal groups of an organizational hierarchy. These status symbols generally are used within formal work groups to reward individual productivity and to show clearly different levels of organizational importance.

Status in Formal Groups

To maximize the effectiveness of a work group, however, managers also should consider the status of members of the informal group or groups that exist within that formal group. For example, formal group leaders have higher status within a formal group than other group members. The informal group or groups that exist within that formal group also have informal leaders, who generally are different from the formal leader and of higher status than other informal group members. Management usually finds that to increase productivity within a formal work group, the support of both the formal and informal leaders must be gained. In fact, some evidence suggests that production is more associated with support from informal group leaders than from formal group leaders.[34]

Status in Informal Groups

Status: Formal and Informal Considerations

Back to the Case

Considering the information in the preceding section, Flick probably would conclude his speech to his vice-presidents as follows:

Two other variables you can assess when attempting to increase the effectiveness of your work groups are group norms and group status. The quality of required behavior displayed by formal group members is influenced significantly by the norms of the informal group or groups that exist within the formal group. Norms of the informal group are simply the behavior that informal group members are expected to perform. If the norms of informal groups in your areas seem negative, try to determine what changes might be made in the formal organization to eliminate these norms. On the other hand, if norms of informal groups in your areas seem positive, try to reward their existence or make them stronger in whatever way you possibly can.

You typically will find that various individuals within informal groups tend to achieve different levels of status. The manager who is able to gain the support of both formal leaders and high-status informal group members will increase significantly the probability that his or her work group will be successful.

I realize that I have given you much information in a relatively short period. Let's spend whatever time is necessary to make sure that everyone has a clear understanding of what I have said. Do you have any questions?

Summary

The following points are stressed within this chapter:

1. A group is any number of people who interact with one another, are psychologically aware of one another, and perceive themselves to be a group. Managers should study groups mainly because dividing people into groups is the most common strategy for accomplishing work through people.

2. Groups can be categorized into formal groups and informal groups. Formal groups exist by virtue of management decree to accomplish some activity and are clearly defined and highly structured. Informal groups develop naturally as people interact.

3. Two kinds of formal groups that exist in organizations are command groups and task groups. Command groups reflect the chain of command and handle more routine organizational business, while task groups may deviate significantly from the chain of command and handle more nonroutine organizational business.

4. Two kinds of informal groups are interest groups and friendship groups. Interest groups gain and maintain membership primarily because of mutual concerns that individuals possess about specific issues, while friendship groups form because of personal affiliation individuals develop for one another. Individuals tend to belong to informal groups because informal group members generally obtain such benefits as the perpetuation of a desirable social climate and an increased desirability of the overall work environment. Management tools such as quality circles can encourage the development of informal groups in organizations.

5. To manage work groups appropriately, managers should determine what groups exist in a particular organization, understand the evolution of its informal groups, and strive to maximize work group effectiveness. Sociometry is a tool managers can use to furnish needed information about informal groups, while the organization chart can furnish corresponding information about formal groups.

6. To understand the evolution of informal groups, managers must realize that informal groups are usually the direct result of the characteristics of formal groups to which organization members belong.

7. To maximize the effectiveness of a work group, managers must consider both formal and informal group factors as they attempt to optimize work group cohesiveness, work group norms, work group size, and the support of high-status work group members.

Issues for Review and Discussion

1. How is the term *group* defined in this chapter?
2. Why is the study of groups important to the manager?
3. What is a formal group?
4. Explain the significance of "linking pins" to formal groups in organizations.
5. List and define two types of formal groups that can exist in organizations.
6. Why should managers use committees in organizations?
7. What steps can managers take to ensure that a committee will be successful?
8. Explain how work teams can be valuable to an organization.
9. Describe the stages a group typically goes through as it becomes more mature.
10. What is an informal group?
11. List and define two types of informal groups in organizations.
12. What benefits generally accrue to members of informal groups?
13. What is the relationship between quality circles and informal groups?
14. Are formal groups more important to managers than informal groups? Explain.
15. Describe the sociometric procedure used to study group membership. What can the results of a sociometric analysis tell managers about members of a group?
16. Explain Homans's concept of how informal groups develop.
17. List and define the primary factors that influence work group effectiveness.
18. What is the relationship among formal groups, informal groups, and increasing work group effectiveness?

Sources of Additional Information

Bales, Robert F. *Interaction Process Analysis.* Reading, Mass.: Addison-Wesley, 1951.

Bales, Robert F. *Personality and Interpersonal Behavior.* New York: Holt, Rinehart, & Winston, 1970.

Cartwright, Dorwin, and Zander, Alvin, eds. *Group Dynamics,* 2d ed. Evanston, Ill.: Row, Peterson & Company, 1960.

Collins, B. E., and Guetzkow, H. *A Social Psychology of Group Processes for Decision Making.* New York: John Wiley & Sons, 1964.

Davis, K. *Human Relations in Business.* New York: McGraw-Hill, 1957.

Delbecq, A.; Van de Ven, A. H.; and Gustafson, D. H. *Group Techniques for Program Planning.* Chicago: Scott, Foresman, 1975.

Halal, William E., and Brown, Bob S. "Participative Management: Myth and Reality." *California Management Review* 23, no. 4 (Summer 1981): 20–32.

Hare, A. P. *Handbook of Small Group Research.* New York: Free Press, 1962.

Homans, George C. *The Human Group.* New York: Harcourt Brace Jovanovich, 1950.

Homestead, Michael S. *The Small Group.* New York: Random House, 1969.

Luthans, Fred. *Organizational Behavior.* New York: McGraw-Hill, 1973.

Marsh, Arthur. "Employee Relations—From Donovan to Today." *Pesonnel Management* 13, no. 6 (June 1981): 34–36, 47.

Miner, Frederick C., Jr. "A Comparative Analysis of Three Diverse Group Decision Making Approaches." *Academy of Management Journal* 22, no. 1 (March 1979): 81–93.

Napier, R. W., and Gershenfeld, M. K. *Groups: Theory and Experience.* Boston: Houghton Mifflin, 1973.

Quible, Dr. Zane K. "Quality Circles: A Well-Rounded Approach to Employee Involvement." *Management World* 10, no. 9 (September 1981): 10–11, 38.

Schriesheim, Chester A. "The Similarity of Individual Directed and Group Directed Leader Behavior Descriptions." *Academy of Management Journal* 22, no. 2 (June 1979): 345–55.

Scott, William G. *Organization Theory.* Homewood, Ill.: Richard D. Irwin, 1967.

Seashore, W. E. *Group Cohesiveness in the Industrial Work Group.* Ann Arbor, Mich.: Institute for Social Research, 1964.

Steele, Fred I. *Physical Settings and Organization Development.* Reading, Mass.: Addison-Wesley, 1973.

Thibaut, John W., and Kelley, Harold H. *The Social Psychology of Groups.* New York: John Wiley & Sons, 1959.

Notes

1. Robert L. Masson and Edward Jacobs, "Group Leadership: Practical Points for Beginners," *The Personnel and Guidance Journal,* September 1980, pp. 52–55.

2. Edgar H. Schein, *Organizational Psychology* (Englewood Cliffs, N.J.: Prentice-Hall, 1965), p. 67.

3. George C. Homans, *The Human Group* (New York: Harcourt Brace Jovanovich, 1950), p. 1.

4. Marvin E. Shaw, *Group Dynamics: The Psychology of Small Group Behavior* (New York: McGraw-Hill, 1971), p. 10.

5. Dorwin Cartwright and Ronald Lippitt, "Group Dynamics and the Individual," *International Journal of Group Psychotherapy* 7, no. 1 (January 1957): 86–102.

6. Edgar H. Schein, *Organizational Psychology,* 2d. ed. (Englewood Cliffs, N.J.: Prentice-Hall, 1970), p. 82.

7. For more information on these groups, see Leonard R. Sayles, "Research in Industrial Human Relations," in *Industrial Relations* (New York: Harper & Row, 1957).

8. "Committees: Their Role in Management Today," *Management Review* 46, no. 10 (October 1957): 4–10.

9. Ethel C. Glenn and Elliott Pood, "Groups Can Make the Best Decisions, If You Lead the Way," *Supervisory Management,* December 1978, pp. 2–6.

10. Cyril O'Donnell, "Ground Rules for Using Committees," *Management Review* 50, no. 10 (October 1961): 63–67.

11. These guidelines are taken from "How Not to Influence People," *Management Record,* March 1958, pp. 89–91. This article also can be consulted for additional guidelines not covered in this text.

12. Irving L. Janis, "Groupthink," *Psychology Today,* November 1971, pp. 103–8.

13. For more information on the use of task teams within the Litton microwave cooking division, see William W. George, "Task Teams for Rapid Growth," *Harvard Business Review,* March/April 1977, pp. 71–80.

14. Bernard Bass, *Organizational Psychology* (Boston: Allyn & Bacon, 1965), pp. 197–98.

15. Bass, *Organizational Psychology,* p. 199.

16. Keith Davis, *Human Relations at Work,* 2d. ed. (New York: McGraw-Hill, 1962), pp. 215–16.

17. Muhammad Jamal, "Shift Work Related to Job Attitudes, Social Participation and Withdrawal Behavior: A Study of Nurses and Industrial Workers," *Personnel Psychology* 34, no. 3 (Autumn 1981): 535–47.

18. J. L. Moreno, "Contributions of Sociometry to Research Methodology in Sociology," *American Psychological Review* 12 (June 1947): 287–92.

19. J. H. Jacobs, "The Application of Sociometry to Industry," *Sociometry* 8 (May 1954): 181–98.

20. Muzafer Sherif, "A Preliminary Experimental Study of Intergroup Relations," in *Social Psychology at the Crossroads,* eds. John H. Rohrer and Muzafer Sherif (New York: Harper & Bros., 1951).

21. Edgar H. Schein, "SMR Forum: Improving Face-to-Face Relationships," *Sloan Management Review* 22, no. 2 (Winter 1981): 43–52.

22. Homans, *The Human Group.*

23. For an interesting attempt to analyze characteristics of work groups in a small business, see James Curran and John Stanworth, "The Social Dynamics of the Small Manufacturing Enterprise," *Journal of Management Studies* 18, no. 2 (April 1981): 141–58.

24. James H. Davis, *Group Performance* (Reading, Mass.: Addison-Wesley, 1969), pp. 71–73.

25. B. J. Kolasa, *Introduction to Behavioral Science for Business* (New York: John Wiley & Sons, 1969).

26. Don Hellriegel and John W. Slocum, Jr., *Management: A Contingency Approach* (Reading, Mass.: Addison-Wesley, 1974), p. 377.

27. Stanley E. Seashore, *Group Cohesiveness in the Industrial Work Group* (Ann Arbor, Mich.: University of Michigan Press, 1954).

28. Raymond A. Van Zelst, "Sociometrically Selected Work Teams Increase Production," *Personnel Psychology* 4 (Autumn 1952): 175–85.

29. O. Jeff Harris, *Managing People at Work* (New York: John Wiley & Sons, 1976), p. 122.

30. J. R. Hackman, "Group Influence on Individuals," in *Handbook for Industrial and Organizational Psychology,* ed. M. P. Dunnette (Chicago: Rand McNally, 1976).

31. This section is based primarily on P. C. André De la Porte, "Group Norms: Key to Building a Winning Team," *Personnel,* September/October 1974, pp. 60–67.

32. A. Mazur, "A Cross-Species Comparison of Status in Small Established Groups," *American Sociological Review* 38, no. 5 (1973): 513–30.

33. Peter F. Drucker, "Is Executive Pay Excessive?" *The Wall Street Journal,* 23 May 1977, p. 22.

34. T. N. Whitehead, "The Inevitability of the Informal Organization and Its Possible Value," in *Readings in Management,* ed. Ernest Dale (New York: McGraw-Hill, 1970).

Concluding Case 15
Volvo's Ergonomics Now Being Implemented
at Shaklee Corporation

Hexagonal plant design gives each group its own wall and windows. (Reprinted from PEOPLE AT WORK, by Pehr G. Gyllenhammer, © 1977. By permission of Addison-Wesley Pub. Co., Reading, MA.)

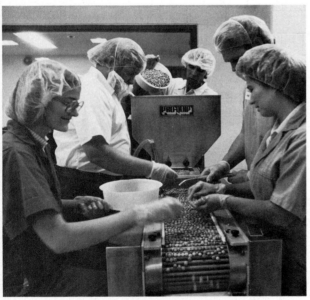

Team workers at Shaklee Corp.'s Norman (Okla.) plant. (Photo: J. Don Cook)

Volvo, an automobile company with twenty factories in Sweden and seven factories in countries as diverse and distant as Iran, Peru, Malaysia, and the United States, was founded in 1927 at Gothensberg, Sweden. Skilled craftsmen working on a single car until it was completed were mainly responsible for the early reputation of the Volvo automobile. Production was managed by foremen who were skilled technicians that were expected to develop authoritarian and paternalistic attitudes toward employees.

By the end of the forties, technology was becoming more important and its growth was beginning to erode the group approach. During the fifties, emphasis was on heavy mechanization and economic growth, and the human side of planning was deemphasized. Volvo maintained its growth pattern during the sixties, but toward the end of this decade it was plagued with wild-cat strikes, a very high rate of employee turnover, and absenteeism. At this time, Volvo's management recognized the need to pay more attention to the social, sociological and psychological aspects of work. One repercussion of this attention was the work council, a joint consultation group of management and workers.

In 1971, Pehr G. Gyllenhammar took over as president of the then volatile company. Gyllenhammar felt that there was a need for a nontraditional approach to management that would combine humanity and efficiency. To merge these concerns, he set up a task force to design a landmark factory as an alternative to the traditional plant. Gyllenhammar felt that instead of a plant with a conveyor moving through the building, the new plant should be based upon stationary work, with the materials brought to the work station. In addition, he felt that each group's work area should accommodate about fifteen employees. Tasks should be rotated among members of the group, and each group should take more responsibility for work quality. Finally, the reputation of the finished product should be reflected more directly back to the employees. The goal of the plan was to make it possible for an employee to see a Volvo being driven down the street and be able to say, "I made that car." Such thinking provided the basis for the new Kalmar plant.

At the heart of the Kalmar technology is the carrier on which assembly takes place. Carriers are self-propelled platforms on which cars are assembled. These carriers are guided around the factory according to a pattern of conductive tape in grooves on the floor. Lower-level carriers are used for most assembly. The higher-level carrier is designed for lower parts of the car (engines, gearboxes, axles, and exhaust assemblies) so that group members can work in normal standing postures.

The design of the building, like the design of the carrier, is based upon working groups. It is a set of one- and two-story interlocking hexagons that permits each group to have its own work area (generally one wall of the hexagon), yet remain visually and socially connected with nearby work groups. The new design also reduced noise levels to about sixty-five decibels, allowing for normal conversation.

Group work areas are airy and have large windows with a view of the countryside. Most teams have their own work areas, entryways and non-work areas. Non-work areas have carpeted coffee areas—rooms looking out over the countryside, furnished with stove, refrigerator, coffeemaker, and pantry, and with views of work being done in other parts of the building. Two groups share a foreman and production engineer, and a sauna, changing rooms, showers, bathrooms, and clothes closets. The basis of the Kalmar project is not the carrier or the building, it is the group. The carrier and building are just the means of making work conditions productive, pleasant, and practical. About five hundred production workers, organized into about twenty-five groups, are involved in the production of each car. Members of these groups are experts in areas like steering and controls, electric systems, instrumentation, finish, and interiors. According to Kalmar management, when a team has its own area on the shop floor the sense of membership in the team seems to grow.

Each team at Kalmar organizes itself without any prompting from management. Each foreman acts as teacher/consultant and works with two teams. Groups have flexibility in choosing how they work, and most of the members have learned more than one job, which allows rotation of jobs. Generally each team divides itself into two or three subgroups to carry out team jobs. Each group does its own inspection, and there are computer-based television terminals that flash on the screen if there is a recurring problem. The only contact with management is daily delivery of a certain number of finished doors, installed brake systems, or interiors. If team members finish their assigned production early they are permitted to rest or have a cup of coffee or a cigarette.

The work-group approach has obvious benefits in terms of quality and cost for the company and better work and interrelationships for the workers. Productivity is as good as in other more conventional Volvo assembly line plants (Torslanda), and turnover and absenteeism are 5 percent lower than in other plants. Groups may have an effect beyond the drop in absenteeism that naturally occurs when the work becomes more interesting. For example, one member of a group was absent one morning. Another member phoned him at home and asked, "Why aren't you here?" He came in to work that afternoon.

Fundamental to Volvo's effort to make work more meaningful is the perception that an employee's influence in the work situation should be commensurate with his or her capabilities. So far, Volvo's experience has been encouraging. Employees have been more willing to accept responsibility, permitting management to take more risks and make more changes. Although Volvo was developed by utilizing capital, technology, and equipment resources, the company's future success will depend primarily on another key resource—its people.

While the emphasis on working groups was repopularized as a result of Volvo's famous Kalmar project, the work-team approach did not gain immediate widespread acceptance abroad or in the United States. However, as more and more companies recognize the importance of satisfying both human and economic goals, much of what was learned at Kalmar is being put into practice elsewhere.

For example, Shaklee Corporation of San Francisco adopted the self-managed work-team approach when it opened its Norman, Oklahoma, plant in 1979 to produce vitamins and other pills. More than 190 of the plant's 230 employees were organized into 13 teams, with 3 to 15 members per team. Teams were permitted to set their own production schedules based upon management's volume goals. They decide the hours they will work, select new team members from an approved personnel pool, and even initiate discharges if appropriate (3 people have been dismissed since the plant opened).

Salaries at the Norman plant are averaging $300 per week. Employees receive pay increases partly by demonstrating improved proficiency in a new skill over a six-month period—a provision adopted to encourage employees to develop new skills, making them more interchangeable.

Employees at Shaklee are pleased with the new team approach. They indicate more of a feeling of job ownership. Other results of the self-managed work-team approach are also impressive. The Norman plant produces eighty-eight units per man hour, compared with thirty units per man hour at an older Shaklee plant. Statistics suggest that Shaklee's Norman plant is producing the same volume as at an older plant, at 40 percent of the labor cost; one-third of the production increase can be attributed to better equipment, two-thirds to the self-managed work-team approach.

This case is adapted from Pehr G. Gyllenhammar, *People at Work* (Reading, Massachusetts: Addison-Wesley Publishing Company, 1977), pp. 52–65 and "The New Industrial Relations: The New Approach Is Already at Work," *Business Week*, May 11, 1981, p. 96.

Discussion Issues:

1. Categorize by type the groups identified in the case.
2. Would you expect individual work groups at Volvo's Kalmar plant and Shaklee's Norman plant to be highly cohesive? Explain.
3. Using information from the case, cite examples of group norms being used to influence behavior.
4. Explain the significance of the hexagonal shape of the Kalmar building.
5. Do you expect the trend of utilizing the work team and other more participative modes of management to continue in the future? Explain.

Controlling is the fourth and last major management function that must be performed for organizations to have long-run success. Sections 2 through 4 have dealt, respectively, with determining how the organization will get where it wants to go, establishing working relationships between resources that will help the organization to get there, and guiding the activities of organization members toward goal accomplishment. Section 5 points out that in addition to planning, organizing, and influencing, managers must control, or modify, existing organizational variables to ensure organizational success.

Chapter 16, "Controlling," defines the control function as making something happen the way it was planned to happen and defines controlling as the process that must be carried out to control. Controlling is presented in this chapter as a subsystem of the overall management system and as entailing three main steps: (1) measuring performance, (2) comparing performance to standards, and (3) taking corrective action. The three major types of control—precontrol, concurrent control, and feedback control—are discussed. The job of a controller also is covered in detail. The major topics that conclude this chapter are the importance of power to managers attempting to control, the potential barriers to successful controlling, and how to make controlling successful.

Chapter 17, "Control Tools," defines a control tool as a specific procedure or technique that furnishes pertinent organizational information in such a way that managers are aided in developing and implementing appropriate organizational control strategy. The first control tool discussed, management by exception, is described as a technique that allows only significant deviations between planned and actual performance to be brought to management's attention. Break-even analysis, another control tool presented in this chapter, is described as the process of generating information that summarizes various levels of profit or loss associated with various levels of production. Another control tool, ratio analysis, is presented as the process of summarizing the financial position of an organization. The last two control tools elaborated on in this chapter, budgets and human asset accounting, deal, respectively, with organizational financial plans and human resource issues.

Chapter 18, the last chapter in this section, discusses information as it relates to the control function. Information is defined as conclusions derived from data analysis. The value of this information is discussed in terms of its appropriateness, quality, timeliness, and quantity. This chapter also describes how managers can use computers as electronic tools for generating and analyzing organizational information. Materials requirements planning is presented as an area in which computer assistance can be valuable to a manager. The last major topic covered in this chapter is the management information system (MIS). An MIS is defined as an organizational network established to provide managers with information that will assist them in decision making. Planning, designing, implementing, and improving an MIS are discussed in detail.

Section 5
Controlling

Student Learning Objectives

From studying this chapter I will attempt to acquire:

1. A definition of control
2. A thorough understanding of the controlling subsystem
3. An appreciation for various kinds of control and how each kind can be used advantageously by managers
4. Insights on the relationship between power and control
5. Knowledge of the various potential barriers that must be overcome for successful control
6. An understanding of steps that can be taken to increase the quality of a controlling subsystem

Chapter Outline

Exhibit 16: Edward Acker Takes Corrective Action at Pan Am

Principles of Controlling

Introductory Case 16
Hospital Services, Inc.

In the 1960s considerable interest was generated in hospital care. The aged and the poor were heavily subsidized by government programs aimed, among other things, at helping those in need to get adequate hospital care. During the same time, the cost of hospital services doubled, and still there were not enough beds for patients. Federal and state governments saw the need to distinguish between the types of care that were most suitable. It was clear that not everyone needed the full-service care of general hospitals. The law contemplated that once patients were discharged from such a facility, they would be sent for a limited time to a convalescent hospital, where the service level and costs were much lower. And, theoretically, having completed the allowed time, or as much of it as was needed, in this institution, patients would be returned to their homes, where they could receive needed services.

Jules McDonald was among several people who had the idea of building or buying a chain of convalescent hospitals to serve the growing need for beds. He thought that a chain probably could achieve some economies of operation that a single hospital would not find possible. He intended to broaden his business by purchasing land, securing a mortgage to take care of the hospitals, and selling the whole package to investors. He would place his own optical stores and drugstores within each hospital, have his own wholesalers in drugs and hospital equipment, and create his own construction companies.

McDonald needed money to do these things. He knew that the stocks of convalescent hospital chains were being traded in multiples from 60 to 200 times earnings, and so he determined to tap the investment market for capital. He got together a few scattered assets, packaged them attractively, and took his business public. It could not be said that he could show any earnings, but he stressed his prospective earnings per share. Amazingly, the idea sold, and he raised about $15 million.

With cash in the bank and an attractive vision in his head, McDonald was ready to go with his Hospital Services, Inc. Plush offices came first. Then a group of lawyers and tax accountants was added. A salesman sold him a computer. Convalescent hospitals were purchased at high prices; land was bought across the country, and construction was begun; and acquisitions were eagerly sought. McDonald did not do this all by himself. He was specially gifted in his public relations, government relations, and negotiations skills and tended to specialize in them. Managers were hired to take care of construction, hospital management, and finance.

As the months passed, the cash raised from the public issue was fast used. On paper, the cash flow from operations should have been adequate, but it did not actually materialize. No one, it seemed, was able to get a reading on hospital finances. In some cases, there were no profits; in other cases, the individual institution kept its own cash balance; and in others, there was a heavy drain of funds to cover expenses. The government did not help, either. Its agencies were new at this activity; interpretations were being made in the law so frequently that no one knew what practice to follow.

Throughout this period of operation there was no slowdown in activity. McDonald was in his element, but his controller failed to warn him of imminent bankruptcy. There did come a day when he ran out of money. This occurred at a time when bankers were tightening up credit, and the stock market was falling fast.

As he looked over his wreck, he inquired, "What control system should I have had?"

From ESSENTIALS OF MANAGEMENT by Harold Koontz. Copyright © 1978 by McGraw-Hill Book Company. Used with permission of McGraw-Hill Book Co.

Discussion Issues

1. What do you think McDonald means by a "control" system?
2. Do you think that McDonald could have controlled Hospital Services by himself? Explain.
3. List several areas of Hospital Services that McDonald's controlling activities should have emphasized.

What's Ahead

Perhaps the most significant managerial weakness of Jules McDonald, the president in the introductory case, was his failure to design and implement an effective control system for Hospital Sevices, Inc. The material in this chapter would help a manager such as McDonald to overcome this weakness. The chapter emphasizes four main topics: (1) fundamentals of controlling, (2) the controller and control, (3) power and control, and (4) performing the control function.

Prospective managers need a working knowledge of the essentials of the controlling function.[1] To this end, the following sections discuss (1) a definition of control, (2) a definition of controlling, and (3) the various types of control that can be used in organizations.

Fundamentals of Controlling

Defining Control

Stated simply, **control** is making something happen the way it was planned to happen.[2] As implied in this definition, planning and control are virtually inseparable.[3] In fact, planning and control are so inseparable that they have been called the Siamese twins of management.[4] The following statement by Robert L. Dewelt describes this relationship between planning and control:

> The importance of the planning process is quite obvious. Unless we have a soundly charted course of action, we will never quite know what actions are necessary to meet our objectives. We need a map to identify the timing and scope of all intended actions. This map is provided through the planning process.
>
> But simply making a map is not enough. If we don't follow it or if we make a wrong turn along the way, chances are we will never achieve the desired results. A plan is only as good as our ability to make it happen. We must develop methods of measurement and control to signal when deviations from the plan are occurring so that corrective action can be taken.[5]

Making Things Happen as Planned

Obviously, for control activities to exist within an organization, some activity or a process must be taking place within that organization. Figure 16.1 shows a newsletter sent to General Tire employees by the corporate personnel office of the General Tire Company. Although the newsletter is essentially a lighthearted discussion of Murphy's Law, it does make the serious point that managers should continually control or check to make sure that organizational activities and processes are going as planned.

Murphy's Law

Defining Controlling

Controlling is nothing more than the process managers go through to control. According to Mockler, controlling can be defined as:

> A systematic effort by business management to compare performance to predetermined standards, plans, or objectives to determine whether performance is in line with these standards and presumably to take any remedial action required to see that human and other corporate resources are being used in the most effective and efficient way possible in achieving corporate objectives.[6]

Control and Controlling

Figure 16.1 Newsletter emphasizing the importance of managerial control.

MANAGEMENT IN GENERAL
A Newsletter for Management from Corporate Personnel-Akron

April 1976

MALICE IN BLUNDERLAND

Thomas L. Martin wrote a book published in 1973 called
<u>Malice in Blunderland</u>. If you haven't read it, you might
want to obtain it from your local library or the Corporate
Research Library. The following are some excerpts:

"MURPHY'S LAWS"

First Law: If something can go wrong, it will.
Second Law: When left to themselves, things always go from bad to worse.
Third Law: Nature always sides with the hidden flaw.

"REVISION OF MURPHY'S FIRST LAW"

If anything can go wrong (with a mechanical system),
it will, and generally at the moment the system becomes
indispensable.

"COROLLARIES TO MURPHY'S FIRST LAW"

It is impossible to make anything foolproof because fools
are so ingenious.

Any wire or tube cut to length will be too short.

Interchangeable parts won't.

Identical units tested under identical conditions will not
perform identically in the field.

After any machine or unit has been completely assembled,
extra components will be found on the bench.

Components that must not and cannot be assembled improperly,
will be.

All constants are variables.

In any given computation, the figure that is most obviously
correct will be the source of the error.

The book goes on and on with other laws as well. The thought hit us that
you might have your own contributions. So, if you have corollaries to
"Murphy's First Law," send them to us and we will publish them in a later
issue of Management in General.

From Thomas L. Martin, *"Malice in Blunderland"* (New York: McGraw-Hill, 1973). Used with permission.
Permission for newsletter format granted by the General Tire and Rubber Company, Akron, Ohio.

Figure 16.2 Relationship between overall management system and controlling subsystem.

Overall Management System

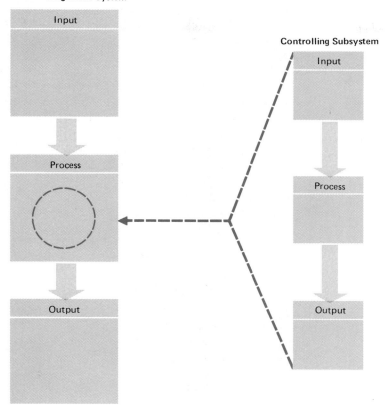

The relationship that generally exists between a supervisor and production workers illustrates how the control process works in organizations. Production workers generally have goals for levels of production they must achieve per day and week. At the end of each working day the number of units produced by each worker is recorded so that weekly production levels can be determined. If these weekly totals are significantly below the goal levels of production, the supervisor must take action to ensure that actual production levels are equivalent to planned production levels. If production goals are met, the supervisor probably should allow work to continue as it has taken place in the past.

The following section discusses the controlling subsystem and provides more details about the control process itself.

According to the preceding information in this chapter, for Jules McDonald, the president in the introductory case, to evaluate his control efforts at Hospital Services, he should have a clear understanding of control. Control within McDonald's organization simply would have entailed making things happen at Hospital Services the way they were planned to happen. In essence, McDonald's control would have had to be closely related to his planning activities.

Going one step further, controlling at Hospital Services would have been nothing more than the steps or process that McDonald would have had to go through to control. In general, this process would include a predetermination of plans, standards, and objectives at Hospital Services so that action could be taken to eliminate organizational characteristics that caused deviation from these factors.

Back to the Case

Figure 16.3 The controlling subsystem.

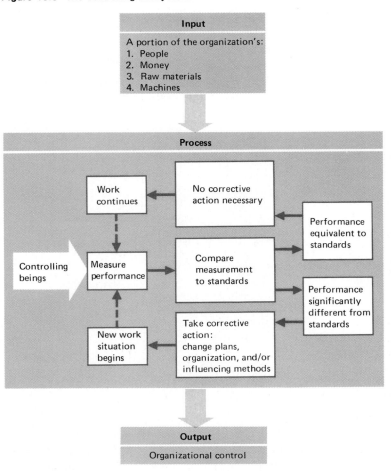

The Controlling Subsystem

The approach taken in this text is to view controlling, one of the four major managerial functions, as an organizational subsystem. As with the planning, organizing, and influencing subsystems described previously, the controlling subsystem can be viewed as part of the process of the overall management system. Figure 16.2 shows this relationship between the overall management system and the controlling subsystem.

The purpose of any management subsystem is to help managers to enhance the success of the overall management system. In more specific terms, the purpose of the controlling subsystem is to help managers to enhance the success of the overall management system through effective controlling. Figure 16.3 shows the specific ingredients of the controlling subsystem.

The Controlling Process

Steps in Controlling

As the process segment of figure 16.3 implies, the three main steps to the controlling process are: (1) measuring performance, (2) comparing measured performance to standards, and (3) taking corrective action. Each of these steps is described further in the following sections.

Measuring Performance

Before managers can determine what must be done to make an organization more effective and efficient, they must measure current organizational performance. Before such a measurement can be taken, some unit of measure that gauges the performance must be established and the quantity of this unit generated by the item whose performance is being measured must be observed.

Unit of Measure, Quantity of the Unit in Performance

For example, if a manager wanted to measure the performance of five janitors, the manager would first have to establish units of measure that represented janitorial performance. Such units of measure could be the number of floors swept, the number of windows washed, and/or the number of light bulbs changed. After these units of measures for janitorial performance had been designated, the manager would then have to determine the number of each of these units associated with the janitors. This process of determining the units of measure and the number of units per janitor would furnish the manager with a measure of janitorial performance.

Managers also must keep in mind that a wide range of organizational activities can be measured as part of the control process. As examples of the production process, the amounts and types of inventory kept on hand are commonly measured to control inventory, and the quality of goods and services being produced is commonly measured to control product quality. In addition, however, such performance measurements can relate to various effects of production. An example of such a production effect would be the degree to which a particular manufacturing process pollutes the atmosphere. As one might suspect, the relative degree of difficulty in measuring various types of organizational performance primarily is determined by the activity being measured. For example, the relative degree of difficulty in measuring the performance of a ditch-digger would differ greatly from the relative degree of difficulty of measuring the performance of a student enrolled in a college-level management course.[7]

Range of Controlling

Quality Control, Inventory Control

Comparing Measured Performance to Standards

Once managers have taken a measure of organizational performance, they should take the next step in controlling and compare this measure against some standard. A **standard** is the level of activity established to serve as a model for evaluating organizational performance. In essence, standards are the "yardsticks" that determine if organizational performance is adequate or inadequate.[8] General Electric is a practical illustration of the various types of standards that can exist in an organization. This company set performance standards for itself in each of the following eight general areas:

Yardsticks of Performance

Areas in Which Standards Can Be Made

1. *Profitability standards*   In general, these standards indicate how much money General Electric would like to make as profit over a given time period—that is, return on its investment.

2. *Market position standards*   These standards indicate the share of total sales of a particular market that General Electric would like to have relative to its competitors.

3. *Productivity standards*   How much various segments of the organization should produce is the focus of these standards.

4. *Product leadership standards*   General Electric would like to assume one of the lead positions in product innovation in its field. Product leadership standards indicate what must be done to attain such a position.

5. *Personnel development standards*   Standards in this area indicate the type of training programs to which General Electric personnel should be exposed to develop appropriately.

6. *Employee attitudes standards*   These standards indicate the types of attitudes that General Electric management should strive to develop in its employees.

7. *Public responsibility standards* General Electric recognizes its responsibility to make a contribution to the society of which it is a part. Standards in this area outline the level and types of such contributions that should be made.

8. *Standards reflecting relative balance between short- and long-range goals* General Electric recognizes that short-range goals exist to enhance the probability that long-range goals will be attained. These standards express the relative emphasis that should be placed on attaining various short- and long-range goals.[9]

A more specific example of standards established to help judge performance can be seen in the case of American Airlines.[10] This company set the following standards for appropriate performance of airport ticket offices: (1) at least 95 percent of the flight arrival times posted should be accurate in that actual arrival times do not deviate fifteen minutes from posted times, and (2) at least 85 percent of the customers coming to the airport ticket counter do not wait more than five minutes to be serviced. Many other standards for an airport ticket office could be set in addition to these two examples. As a general guideline, successful managers pinpoint all important areas of organizational performance and establish corresponding standards in each area.

Back to the Case

McDonald should have viewed his controlling activities at Hospital Services as a subsystem of the organization's overall management system. As such, to achieve organizational control, the controlling subsystem would have required a portion of the people, money, raw materials, and machines available at Hospital Services.

The process portion of the controlling subsystem at Hospital Services should have involved McDonald taking three steps: (1) measuring the performance levels of various productive units, (2) comparing these performance levels to predetermined performance standards for these units, and (3) taking any corrective action necessary to make the planned performance levels at Hospital Services consistent with actual performance levels. Areas in which McDonald probably should have developed standards at Hospital Services include desired profitability of various hospitals, production levels needed to achieve this profit level, and training necessary to equip employees to reach desired production levels.

Taking Corrective Action

Action to Bring Performance Up to Standard

Once managers have measured actual performance and compared this performance with established performance standards, they should take corrective action if necessary. **Corrective action** is managerial activity aimed at bringing organizational performance up to the level of performance standards. In other words, corrective action focuses on correcting the mistakes in the organization that have the net result of hindering organizational performance. Before taking any corrective action, however, managers should make sure that standards being used were properly established and that measurements of organizational performance are valid and reliable. Exhibit 16 gives some examples of the kinds of corrective action that C. Edward Acker plans to take at Pan American Airlines.

All organizations make mistakes simply by virtue of the human nature of people that run them. Managers, therefore, should encourage and reward suggestions to correct these mistakes rather than view suggestions as "boat-rocking," as in the case of the manager in the cartoon. The following sections discuss (1) symptoms and problems and (2) various types of corrective action.

"Don't rock the boat, Fennerman!"

Drawing by Mulligan; © 1975 The New Yorker Magazine, Inc.

Symptoms and Problems   At first glance, it seems fairly simple to state that managers should take corrective action to eliminate organizational problems. In practice, however, it may be extremely difficult to pinpoint the problem causing some undesirable organizational effect. For example, a performance measurement may indicate that a certain worker is not adequately passing on critical information to fellow workers. Once the manager is satisfied that the related communication standards are appropriate and that the performance measurement information is valid and reliable, he or she then must take some corrective action to eliminate the problem causing this substandard performance.

A good question related to this example, however, is: What exactly is causing the substandard communication performance? Is the problem that the individual is not communicating because he or she doesn't want to communicate? Or, is this individual not communicating adequately because the job being performed makes communication difficult? Another possible explanation is that this individual doesn't have the training needed to enable him or her to communicate in an appropriate manner. The manager must determine whether this lack of communication on the part of this individual is a **problem** in itself or a **symptom** of such possible problems as inappropriate job design or a cumbersome organizational structure.

Symptoms Are Signs That Problems Exist

Types of Corrective Action   Once the control system has been evaluated as operating appropriately, necessary corrective action can focus on one or more of three primary areas. As figure 16.3 implies, these areas relate to the major management functions of planning, organizing, and influencing. Correspondingly, corrective action can include such activities as modifying past plans to make them more suitable for future organizational endeavors, making an existing organizational structure more suitable for existing plans and objectives, or restructuring an incentive program to make sure that high producers are given higher rewards than low producers. In addition, since planning, organizing, and influencing are so closely related, there is a good chance that corrective action taken in one area probably will necessitate some corresponding change in one or both of the other two areas.

Corrective Action Focusing on Planning, Organizing, and Influencing

Exhibit 16

C. Edward Acker Takes Corrective Action at Pan Am

C. Edward Acker (Photo: Murray Sill)

When C. Edward Acker took over as chairman of Air Florida four years ago, it was a tiny intrastate airline with a fleet largely of propeller-driven aircraft. The 6-foot-4 Texan swiftly built Air Florida into one of the hottest pieces of airline property in the country. He turned a 1977 loss of $2.6 million into a 1980 profit of $5.7 million. Air Florida now flies a fleet of modern 737s, DC-10s and DC-9s on lucrative routes in the United States, the Caribbean, Latin America and Europe—and the brash upstart is giving competitors like Pan Am, Eastern and Braniff fits. Last week Acker stunned a meeting of New York security analysts by announcing that he was quitting Air Florida to take another job. "I talked to Cunard Lines and told them I was interested in a job as captain of the Titanic," Acker quipped. "They informed me that I was 50 years too late. Not having that challenge available, I decided to try to find one comparable to that. And so I am accepting the chairmanship of a company called Pan American World Airways."

Acker will need more than a sense of humor in his new job. His predecessor, William T. Seawell, stepped aside after failing to staunch the decade-long hemorrhage of red ink at the once proud airline. Pan Am lost $218 million in the first six months of this year [1981], and in the wake of the air-traffic controllers' strike, the carrier's operating problems are likely to continue at least for the rest of the year. Desperate for cash, the beleaguered airline earlier this year sold its headquarters skyscraper in Manhattan for $400 million and then last month sold its most profitable enterprise, the Intercontinental Hotel chain, to raise another $500 million.

At Air Florida, Acker—a former investment banker and president of Braniff Airlines—aggressively cut costs and insisted that the nonunion carrier offer only one low fare on its routes rather than the proliferation of discount fares offered by other airlines. He was also known for razzle-dazzle marketing promotions such as "Free Rides for a Kiss," a fill-the-planes scheme that gave customers a free trip if they kissed an airline employee.

Nose Dive: But Pan Am's problems run too deep to be solved by marketing gimmickry alone. Acker says he will slash unprofitable routes and continue the airline's efforts to persuade its unions to take pay cuts and boost productivity. He is especially eager to get the carrier's pilots to agree to a new contract similar to one just signed at United Airlines—resulting in productivity gains that United says will save it $75 million in the next 26 months. Acker indicated that he may be taking a pay cut of his own to accept the Pan Am challenge. He says his Air Florida income this year would have been about $500,000, but that he wants his remuneration from Pan Am to be based on his performance in the months ahead. If he can finally pull the old airline out of its nose dive, hardly any salary would seem too high.

If McDonald had determined that corrective action was necessary at Hospital Services, he would have had to be certain that the action was aimed at organizational problems rather than at symptoms of problems. Whereas Hospital Services resources used to eliminate symptoms would have been wasted, such resources used to eliminate organizational problems would have been well spent. Once Hospital Services' problems were solved through corrective action, related symptoms eventually would have disappeared.

McDonald's corrective action at Hospital Services inevitably would have focused on past planning, organizing, and/or influencing efforts. In addition, as McDonald made changes in one of these areas, he probably would have found that some corresponding changes in another area were needed. McDonald also should have kept in mind that corrective action could be very narrow in scope and relate perhaps only to a specific job, or very broad in scope and affect large segments of the company.

Types of Control

There are three types of management control: (1) precontrol, (2) concurrent control, and (3) feedback control. Each type primarily is determined by the time period in which the control is emphasized in relation to the work being performed.

Precontrol

Controlling Before People Work

Control that takes place before work is performed is called **precontrol** or feed-forward control.[11] Precontrol eliminates significant deviations in desired work results before they occur. In this regard, management creates policies, procedures, and rules aimed at eliminating behavior that will cause future undesirable work results. For example, the manager of a small record shop may find that a major factor in developing return customers is salespeople discussing various records with customers. This manager might use precontrol by establishing a rule that salespeople cannot talk to each other while a customer is in the store. This rule would be precontrol because it is aimed at eliminating anticipated problems with salespeople before those salespeople actually are faced with a customer. Precontrol focuses on eliminating predicted problems.

Concurrent Control

Controlling While People Work

Control that takes place as work is being performed is called **concurrent control.** Concurrent control relates not only to human performance but also to such areas as equipment performance or department appearance. For example, most grocery stores have rigid rules about the amount of stock that should be placed on the selling floor. In general, these stores desire generous amounts of all products on the shelves, with no "stock holes" or empty spaces. A concurrent control aimed at ensuring that shelves are stocked as planned could be a stock manager making periodic visual checks throughout a work period to evaluate the status of the sales shelves and, correspondingly, the performance of the stock crew.

Feedback Control

Controlling After People Work

Control that concentrates on past organizational performance is called **feedback control.** When exercising this type of control, managers actually are attempting to take corrective action within the organization by looking at organizational history over a specified time period. This history can concentrate on only one factor, such as inventory levels, or on the relationships among many factors, such as net income before taxes, sales volume, and marketing costs.

Figure 16.4 is an example of a report, developed for an oil company, that can serve as the basis for feedback control. This particular report contains graphs that show various trends over a number of years as well as handwritten notes that highlight various major trends. Management would use this report to compare actual organizational performance with planned organizational performance and then to take whatever corrective action is necessary to make actual and planned performance more equivalent. Of course, the structure of such reports varies from organization to organization, depending on the various types and forms of information needed to present an overview of specific activities that take place within that organization.

The Controller and Control

Organization charts developed for medium- and large-sized companies typically contain a position called controller. The following sections explain more about controllers and their relationship to the control function by discussing (1) the job of the controller and (2) how much control is needed within an organization.

The Job of the Controller

From the preceding discussion, it is clear that managers have the responsibility to compare planned and actual performance and to take corrective action when necessary. In smaller organizations, managers may be completely responsible for gathering information about various aspects of the organization and developing necessary reports based on this information. In medium- or large-sized companies, however, an individual called the **controller** usually exists.[12] The controller's basic responsibility is assisting line managers with the controlling function by gathering appropriate information and generating necessary reports that reflect this information.[13] The information with which the controller usually works generally reflects the following various financial dimensions of the organization: (1) profits, (2) revenues, (3) costs, (4) investments, and (5) discretionary expenses.[14]

Helping the Manager Control

A sample job description of a controller is shown in figure 16.5. As can be seen from the figure, the controller is responsible for generating appropriate information on which a manager can base the exercising of control. Since the controller generally is not directly responsible for taking corrective action within the organization and typically advises a manager of what corrective action should be taken, the controller position is primarily a staff position.

The Controller: A Staff Person

How Much Control Is Needed?

As with all organizational endeavors, control activities should be pursued if expected benefits of performing such activities are greater than the costs of performing them.[15] The process of comparing the cost of any organizational activity with the expected

Cost-Benefit Analysis

Figure 16.4 Example of report that can serve as basis for feedback control.

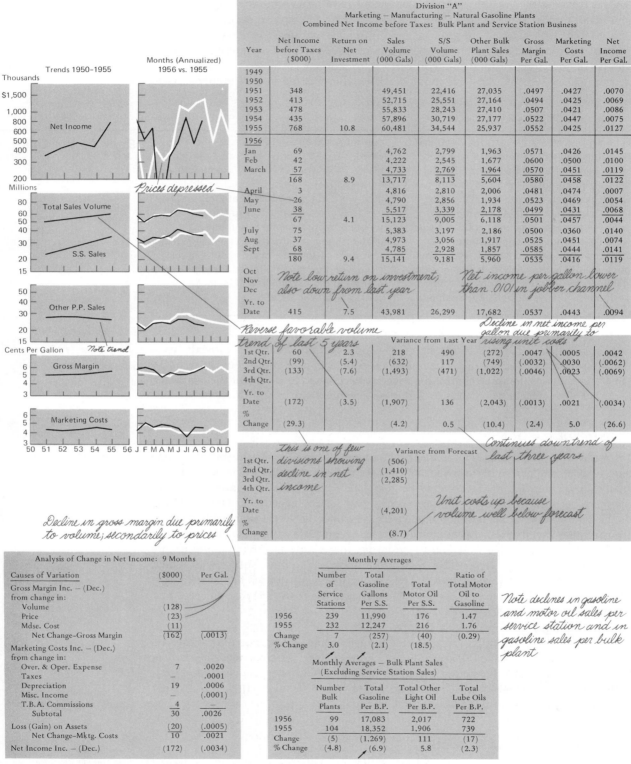

Figure 16.5 Sample job description for a controller in a large company.

Functions of the Controller in a Large Company

Objectives

The Controller (or Comptroller) of Accounts is responsible for the effective financial and cost controls of the company's activities.

Functions

1. Prescription of principles and methods to govern accounting controls throughout the enterprise
2. Provision of adequate protection against loss of the company's money and property
3. Prescription of principles of accounting determining cost of product, and normal volume of production in order to compute costs and install appropriate systems
4. Verification of the propriety of expenditures
5. Providing comparison of capital expenditures and appropriations
6. Preparation of the accounts of the corporation
7. Determination of income and expenditure allocation among plants and departments
8. Proposals regarding the nature of the corporation's financial statements
9. Preparation of the financial statements
10. Preparation of analyses assisting others to improve the earnings of the enterprise
11. Observation of the manner of performing accounting responsibilities

Relationships

The Controller of Accounts reports to the Vice-president for Finance.

benefit of performing the activity is called **cost benefit analysis.** In general, managers and controllers should collaborate to determine exactly how much controlling activity is justified within a given situation.

Figure 16.6 shows controlling activity over an extended period of time. According to this figure, controlling costs increase steadily as more and more controlling activities are performed. In addition, since the controlling function begins with the incurrence of related "start up" costs, controlling costs usually will be greater than increased income generated from increased controlling. As controlling starts to correct major organizational errors, however, increased income from increased controlling eventually will equal controlling costs (point X_1 on the graph) and ultimately surpass by a large margin controlling costs.

As more and more controlling activity is added beyond X_1, however, controlling costs and increased income from increased controlling eventually will be equal again (point X_2 on graph). As more controlling activity is added beyond X_2, controlling costs again surpass increased income from increased controlling. The main reason why this last development takes place is that major organizational problems probably have been detected much earlier, and corrective measures taken now primarily are aimed at smaller and more insignificant problems.

The following information about Franklin M. Jarman, a past chief executive officer of Genesco, Inc., makes the point very emphatically that a manager can exercise too much control. In 1973, Jarman fought his father, W. Maxey, for control of Genesco, a $1 billion retailing and apparel conglomerate. Jarman won. One of his first moves was to initiate a system of financial controls. These controls saved the company from ruin in 1973 when it lost $52 million. However, they ultimately may have been responsible for Jarman's downfall four years later.

According to people within Genesco, Jarman became obsessed with controls. Red tape and paperwork caused many delays and paralyzed operations. Management was centralized to the point of frustrating company executives. In its 1975 annual report,

Figure 16.6 Value of additional controlling.

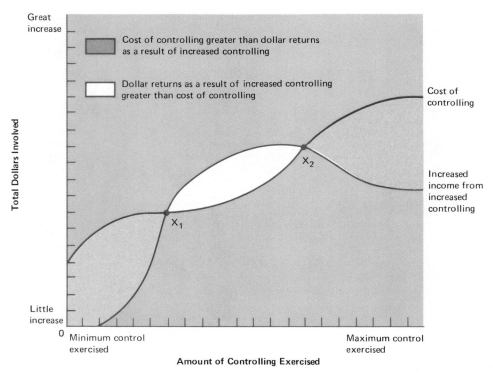

Genesco announced that in 1976 it would spend $8 million to open 63 stores and renovate 124 others. According to insiders, Jarman required so much analysis for these projects that decisions were postponed. Six months into fiscal year 1976, little of the projected work had been completed.

Because most of Genesco's business is in the fast-moving areas of apparel and retailing, delays and indecision can be very damaging. As a result, in January 1977 two dozen Genesco executives participated in a "palace revolt" that relieved Jarman of his responsibilities.[16]

Back to the Case

The introductory case ends with the statement that McDonald's controller "failed to warn him of imminent bankruptcy." The basic job of McDonald's controller at Hospital Services was to gather information and to compile reports based on this information that McDonald could use to take corrective action. The controller was not to take any corrective action at Hospital Services, but simply should have advised McDonald as to what corrective action should be taken. The root of the problem, however, was with McDonald. He failed to control the controller.

To have operated properly, McDonald should have determined, with or without the advice of his controller, exactly how much control was necessary at Hospital Services. In general, McDonald should have continued to increase controlling as long as the benefits from these control activities exceeded their cost. McDonald also should have kept in mind that, as in the case of Genesco, too much control could cause too much paperwork at Hospital Services and virtually bring decision making to a halt.

To control successfully, managers must understand not only the control process itself but also how organization members relate to the control process. Up to this point this chapter has emphasized nonhuman variables of controlling. This section, however, focuses on power, perhaps the most important human-related variable in the control process. The following sections discuss power by (1) presenting a definition of power, (2) elaborating on the total power of managers, and (3) listing steps managers can take to increase their power over other organization members.

A Definition of Power

Perhaps the two most often confused terms in management are power and authority. Authority was defined in chapter 9 as the right to command or give orders. The extent to which an individual is able to influence others so that they respond to orders issued to them is called **power.** The greater this ability to influence others, the more power an individual is said to have.

Obviously, power and control are closely related. To illustrate, after a manager compares actual performance with planned performance and determines that corrective action is necessary, orders usually are given to implement this action. Although these orders are issued on the manager's allotted organizational authority, they may or may not be followed precisely, depending on how much power the manager has over those individuals to whom the orders are issued.

Total Power of a Manager

The **total power** managers possess is made up of two different kinds of power: position power and personal power.[17] **Position power** is power derived from the organizational position a manager holds. In general, moves from lower-level management to upper-level management accrue more position power for a manager. **Personal power** is power derived from a manager's human relationships with others.

Steps for Increasing Total Power

Managers can increase their total power by increasing their position power and/or their personal power. Although position power generally can be increased simply by achieving a higher organizational position, managers may have little personal control over moving upward in an organization. On the other hand, managers generally have substantial personal control over the amount of personal power they hold over other organization members. The following statement by John P. Kotter stresses the importance of developing personal power:

> To be able to plan, organize, budget, staff, control, and evaluate, managers need some control over the many people on whom they are dependent. Trying to control others solely by directing them and on the basis of the power associated with one's position simply will not work—first, because managers are always dependent on some people over whom they have no formal authority, and second, because virtually no one in modern organizations will passively accept and completely obey a constant stream of orders from someone just because he or she is the "boss."[18]

What are the steps managers can take to increase personal power? In this regard, managers can attempt to develop:[19]

1. *A sense of obligation in other organization members directed toward himself or herself* If successful in developing this sense of obligation, other organization members will feel that they should rightly allow the manager to influence them within certain limits. The basic strategy generally suggested to create this sense of obligation is to do personal favors for people.

2. *A belief in other organization members that he or she possesses a high level of expertise within the organization*   In general, the manager's personal power increases as organization members' perception of his or her level of expertise increases. To increase this perceived level of expertise, the manager must strive to quietly make significant achievement visible to others and to rely heavily on a successful track record and respected professional reputation.

3. *A sense of identification that other organization members have with him or her*   The manager can strive to develop this identification by behaving in ways that other organization members respect and espousing goals, values, and ideals commonly held by other organization members. The following description clearly illustrates how a certain sales manager took steps to build the degree to which his subordinates identified with him:

> One vice-president of sales in a moderate-sized manufacturing company was reputed to be so much in control of his sales force that he could get them to respond to new and different marketing programs in a third of the time taken by the company's best competitors. His power over his employees was based primarily on their strong identification with him and what he stood for. Emigrating to the United States at age seventeen, this person worked his way up "from nothing." When made a sales manager in 1965, he began recruiting other young immigrants and sons of immigrants from his former county. When made vice-president of sales in 1970, he continued to do so. In 1975, 85 percent of his sales force was made up of people whom he hired directly or who were hired by others he brought in.[20]

4. *The perception in other organization members that they are dependent upon him or her as a manager*   Perhaps the main strategy the manager should adopt in this regard is a clear demonstration of the amount of authority he or she possesses over organizational resources. Action taken in this regard should emphasize not only influence over resources necessary for organization members to do their jobs but also influence over resources organization members personally receive in such forms as salaries and bonuses. This strategy is aptly reflected in the following managerial version of the Golden Rule: "He who has the gold makes the rules."

Back to the Case

For McDonald to have been successful in controlling at Hospital Services, he would have had to have been aware of not only the intricacies of the control process itself but also of how to deal with people as they relate to the control process. With regard to people and control, McDonald would certainly have had to consider the amount of power he held over organization members—his ability to encourage them to follow orders. Most of these orders, as discussed in this section, would have related to implementing corrective action that McDonald had deemed advisable for Hospital Services.

The total amount of power that McDonald possessed came from the position he held and his personal relationships with other organization members. Since McDonald was president of Hospital Services, he already possessed more position power than anyone else in the organization. Therefore, to increase his total power, McDonald would have had to emphasize developing his personal power. He could have attempted to do this by developing a sense of obligation in other organization members toward himself, the belief in other organization members that he had a high level of task-related expertise, a sense of identification that other organization members had with him, and the perception in organization members that they were dependent on him as a manager.

Controlling can be an extremely detailed and intricate process. The process typically becomes more detailed and intricate as the size of the organization increases. The following two sections furnish valuable guidelines for successfully executing this potentially complicated controlling function. These sections discuss (1) potential barriers to successful controlling and (2) making controlling successful.

Potential Barriers to Successful Controlling

Managers should take steps to avoid the following potential barriers to successful controlling:

1. *Control activities can create an undesirable overemphasis on short-run production as opposed to long-run production*   As an example, in striving to meet planned weekly production quotas, a manager might "push" machines in a particular area and not allow these machines to stop running to be serviced properly. This kind of management behavior would ensure that planned performance and actual performance are equivalent in the short run but may deteriorate the machines to the point that long-run production quotas are impossible to meet.[21]

2. *Control activities can increase employee frustration with their jobs and thereby reduce morale*   This reaction tends to occur primarily when management has a tendency to exert too much control. Employees get frustrated because they perceive management as being too rigid in its thinking and not allowing the freedom necessary to do a good job.[22] Another feeling that employees may have from overcontrol is that control activities are merely a tactic to pressure workers to higher production.

3. *Control activities can encourage the falsification of reports*   The following excerpt clearly makes this point:

> Not long ago, the Boy Scouts of America revealed the membership figures coming from the field had been falsified. In response to the pressures of a national membership drive, people within the organization had vastly overstated the number of new boy scouts. To their chagrin, the leaders found something that other managers have also discovered: organizational control systems often produce unintended consequences. The drive to increase membership had motivated people to increase the number of new members reported, but it had not motivated them to increase the number of boy scouts actually enrolled.[23]

Employees may perceive management as basing corrective action solely on department records with no regard to extenuating circumstances related to the records. If this is the case, pressure probably will be created to falsify reports so that corrective action regarding their organizational unit will not be too drastic. Various falsifications and related reasons why reports might be falsified include: (1) actual production may be overstated to look good to management, or (2) actual production may be understated to create the impression that planned production is too high and thereby trick management into thinking that a lighter workload is justified.

4. *Control activities can cause the perspective of organization members to be too narrow for the good of the organization*   Although controls can be designed to focus on relatively narrow aspects of an organization, managers must keep in mind that any corrective action should be considered not only in relation to the specific activity being controlled but also in relation to all other organizational units.

For example, a manager may determine that actual and planned production are not equivalent in a specific organizational unit because of various periods when a low inventory of needed parts causes some production workers to pursue other work activities instead of producing a product. Although the corrective action to be taken in this situation would seem to be simply raising the level of parts inventory kept on hand, this probably would be a very narrow perspective of the problem. The manager should seek to answer questions such as the following before any corrective action is taken: Is there enough money on hand to raise current inventory levels? Are there sufficient personnel presently in the purchasing department to effect a necessary increase? Who will do the work the production workers presently are doing when they run out of parts?

Controlling Is a Means, Not an End

5. *Control activities can be perceived as the goals of the control process rather than the means by which corrective action is taken* Managers must keep in mind that information should be gathered, and reports should be designed to facilitate the taking of corrective action within the organization. In fact, these activities only can be justified within the organization if they yield some organizational benefit that extends beyond the cost of performing them.

Making Controlling Successful

In addition to avoiding the potential barriers to successful controlling mentioned in the previous section, managers can perform certain activities to make their control process more effective. In this regard, managers should make sure that:

Controlling Should Suit the Situation

1. *Various facets of the control process are appropriate for the specific organizational activity being focused on[24]* As an example, standards and measurements concerning a line worker's productivity are much different than standards and measurements concerning a company vice-president's productivity. Controlling ingredients related to the productivity of these individuals, therefore, must be different if the control process is to be applied successfully.

Use Control to Achieve Many Ends

2. *Control activities are used to achieve many different kinds of goals* According to Jerome, control can be used for such purposes as standardizing performance, protecting organizational assets from theft and waste, and standardizing product quality.[25] Managers should keep in mind that the control process can be applied to many different facets of organizational life and that for the organization to receive maximum benefit from controlling, each of these facets should be emphasized.

Act Upon Information Quickly

3. *Information used as the basis for taking corrective action is timely[26]* Some time necessarily elapses as managers gather control-related information, develop necessary reports based on this information, decide what corrective action should be taken, and actually take the corrective action. Information should be gathered and acted on as promptly as possible to ensure that the situation, as depicted by this information, has not changed and that the organizational advantage of corrective action will in fact materialize.

Make Controlling Understood

4. *The mechanics of the control process are understandable to all individuals who are in any way involved with implementing the process[27]* Managers should take steps to ensure that people know exactly what information is necessary for a particular control process, how that information is to be gathered and used to compile various reports, what the purposes of various reports actually are, and what corrective actions are appropriate given various possible types of reports. The lesson here is simple: for control to be successful, all individuals involved in controlling must have a working knowledge of how the control process operates.

In addition to understanding the intricacies of control and how people fit into the control process, McDonald should have been aware of the potential barriers to successful controlling and the action he could have taken to increase the probability that his controlling activities would be successful.

To overcome the potential control-related barriers at Hospital Services, McDonald should have balanced his emphasis on short-run versus long-run objectives; minimized the negative influence controlling might have had on the morale of Hospital Services organization members; eliminated forces that might have led to the falsification of control-related reports; implemented a control

perspective that would have appropriately combined narrow and broad organizational focuses; and stressed controlling as a means rather than an end.

With regard to the action that could have been taken to increase the probability of effective controlling activities, McDonald should have made sure that various facets of his controlling subsystem were appropriate for Hospital Services activities, that components of the controlling subsystem were flexible and suited to many purposes, that corrective action was based on only timely information, and that the controlling subsystem was understood by all organization members involved in its operation.

Summary

The following points are stressed within this chapter:

1. Controlling and planning are closely related management functions.

2. The controlling function can be viewed as a management subsystem of the process of the overall management system. The process section of this subsystem has three main steps: (1) measuring performance, (2) comparing measured performance to standards, and (3) taking necessary corrective action.

3. To take corrective action, managers must be able to differentiate between a symptom and a problem. Once certain of the existence of a particular problem, managers generally solve this problem through modifications of activities that reflect planning, organizing, and/or influencing. This, of course, assumes that the controlling subsystem is valid and reliable.

4. Managers probably should use some combination of precontrol, concurrent control, and feedback control within a particular organization. This combination focuses on emphasizing the quality of work before it is performed, while it is being performed, and after it has been performed.

5. Some organizations have controllers—individuals responsible for assisting managers in gathering control-related information and compiling related reports. The responsibility for actually taking corrective action based on these reports, however, belongs to managers and not controllers.

6. Additional control activities should be included within a controlling subsystem only if the benefit the organization receives as a result of performing the control activities is greater than the cost of performing them.

7. A manager's power is of great assistance in influencing individuals to follow orders aimed at implementing corrective action. Since managers may have little control over the amount of position power they possess, they should try to increase their personal power to enhance the probability that proper corrective action will be taken.

8. When performing controlling activities, managers must take care not only to avoid major potential barriers to successful controlling but also to take definite action that generally ensures that controlling will be successful.

Issues for Review and Discussion

1. What is control?
2. Explain the relationship between planning and control.
3. What is controlling?
4. What is the relationship between the controlling subsystem and the overall management system?
5. Draw and explain the controlling subsystem.
6. List and discuss the three main steps of the controlling process.
7. Define the term *standards*.
8. What is the difference between a symptom and a problem? Why is it important to differentiate between a symptom and a problem when controlling?
9. What types of corrective action can managers take?
10. List and define the three basic types of control that can be used in organizations.
11. What is the relationship between controlling and the controller?
12. What basis do managers use to determine how much control is needed in an organization?
13. What is the difference between power and authority? Describe the role of power within the control process.
14. What determines how much power a manager possesses?
15. How can the amount of personal power a manager possesses be increased?
16. Describe several potential barriers to successful controlling.
17. What steps can managers take to ensure that control activities are successful?

Sources of Additional Information

Blau, P. *Exchange and Power in Social Life*. New York: John Wiley & Sons, 1964.

Burack, Elmer H., and Calero, Thomas M. "Seven Perils of the Family Firm." *Nation's Business* 69, no. 1 (January 1981): 62–64.

Dale, Ernest. *Management Theory and Practice*. New York: McGraw-Hill, 1978.

Drake, Rodman L., and Caudill, Lee M. "Management of the Large Multinational: Trends and Future Challenges." *Business Horizons* 24, no. 3 (May/June 1981): 83–91.

Duncan, A. J. *Quality Control and Industrial Statistics*. Homewood, Ill: Richard D. Irwin, 1965.

Emery, J. C. *Organizational Planning and Control Systems: Theory and Technology*. New York: Macmillan, 1969.

Hammer, W. Clay, and Organ, Dennis W. *Organizational Behavior, An Applied Psychological Approach*. Dallas: Business Publications, 1978.

Hogan, Peter. "Using the Behavioural Sciences to Measure Management Performance." *Personnel Management* 13, no. 2 (February 1981): 36–39.

Jerome, W., III. *Executive Control: The Catalyst*. New York: John Wiley & Sons, 1961.

Lawler, Edward E., III, and Rhode, John Grant. *Information and Control in Organizations*. Santa Monica, Calif.: Goodyear Publishing, 1976.

Mockler, Robert J. *The Management Control Process*. New York: Appleton-Century-Crofts, 1971.

Moravec, Milan. "Performance Appraisal: A Human Resource Management System with Productivity Payoffs." *Management Review* 70, no. 6 (June 1981): 51–54.

Newman, W. H. *Constructive Control*. Englewood Cliffs, N.J.: Prentice-Hall, 1975.

Rose, T. G., and Farr, D. E. *Higher Management Control*. New York: McGraw-Hill, 1957.

Shanklin, William L. "Strategic Business Planning: Yesterday, Today, and Tomorrow." *Business Horizons* 22 (October 1979): 7–14.

Tannenbaum, A. *Control in Organizations*. New York: McGraw-Hill, 1968.

1. Donald W. Murr, Harry B. Bracey, Jr., and William K. Hill, "How to Improve Your Organization's Management Controls," *Management Review,* October 1980, pp. 56–63.

2. Alan Thompson, "How to Share Control," *Management Today,* September 1976, p. 71.

3. An example of how a control system can be used with a formal planning model can be found in P. S. Raine, R. B. Flavell, and G. R. Salkin, "A Likelihood Control System for Use with Formal Planning Models," *Journal of Business Finance & Accounting,* Summer 1981, pp. 249–66.

4. Donald C. Mosley and Paul H. Pietri, *Management: The Art of Working With and Through People* (Encino, Calif.: Dickenson Publishing, 1975), pp. 29–43.

5. Robert L. Dewelt, "Control: Key to Making Financial Strategy Work," *Management Review,* March 1977, p. 18.

6. Robert J. Mockler, ed., *Readings in Management Control* (New York: Appleton-Century-Crofts, 1970), p. 14.

7. Insights concerning how such measurements can influence employee performance can be found in Mark K. Hirst, "Accounting Information and the Evaluation of Subordinate Performance: A Situational Approach," *The Accounting Review* 56, no. 4 (October 1981): 771–84.

8. Norton M. Bedford, "Managerial Control," in *Contemporary Management: Issues and Viewpoints,* ed. Joseph W. McGuire (Englewood Cliffs, N.J.: Prentice-Hall, 1974), pp. 507–14.

9. Robert W. Lewis, "Measuring, Reporting, and Appraising Results of Operations with Reference to Goals, Plans, and Budgets," in *Planning, Managing, and Measuring the Business: A Case Study of Management Planning and Control at General Electric Company* (New York: Controllership Foundation, 1955).

10. M. Miller, *Objectives and Standards: An Approach to Planning and Control* (New York: American Management Association, 1956), pp. 77–78.

11. H. Koontz and R. W. Bradspies, "Managing Through Feedforward Control," *Business Horizons* 15, no. 3 (June 1972): 25–36.

12. This position is also called comptroller.

13. David Anderson and Leon Schmidt, *Practical Controllership* (Homewood, Ill.: Richard D. Irwin, 1961).

14. Richard F. Vancil, "What kind of Management Control Do You Need?" *Harvard Business Review,* March-April 1973, pp. 75–86.

15. For other ways in which cost-benefit analysis can be used by managers, see T. J. Webb, "Cost Benefit Analysis," *Management Services,* April 1976, pp. 4–6.

16. Adapted from "What Undid Jarman: Paperwork Paralysis," *Business Week,* 24 January 1977, p. 67.

17. Amitai Etzioni, *A Comparative Analysis of Complex Organizations* (New York: Free Press, 1961), pp. 4–6.

18. John P. Kotter, "Power, Dependence, and Effective Management," *Harvard Business Review,* July-August 1977, p. 128.

19. Kotter, "Power, Dependence, and Effective Management," pp. 135–36.

20. Kotter, "Power, Dependence, and Effective Management," p. 131.

21. For several other examples that illustrate this potential barrier, see Frank J. Jasinski, "Use and Misuse of Efficiency Controls," *Harvard Business Review,* July-August 1956, pp. 105–12.

22. Arnold F. Emch, "Control Means Action," *Harvard Business Review,* July-August 1954, pp. 92–98.

23. Cortlandt Cammann and David A. Nadler, "Fit Control Systems to Your Managerial Style," *Harvard Business Review,* January-February 1976, p. 65.

24. Peter F. Drucker, *Management: Tasks, Responsibilities, Practices* (New York: Harper & Row, 1974).

25. W. Jerome III, *Executive Control: The Catalyst* (New York: John Wiley & Sons, 1961), pp. 31–34.

26. John Richard Curley, "A Tool for Management Control," *Harvard Business Review* (March 1951): 45–59.

27. C. Jackson Grayson, Jr., "Management Science and Business Practice," *Harvard Business Review,* July-August 1973, pp. 41–48.

Concluding Case 16
"Sneak Attacks" at Wendy's

(Photo: © 1982 Rose Stork)

After a Saturday shopping trip to suburban Columbus, Ohio, Ronald Fay, president of Wendy's International Inc., took his family to lunch at his "favorite restaurant." When they arrived they found a growing line of customers. After a few minutes of standing in line, Fay apologized to his family and then struck out to determine the cause of the slow-moving queue. When he finally cornered the startled restaurant manager in the rear office, the manager asked Fay what assistance could be given. He quickly replied, "You can get your butt up front and get those lines moving." The Fay family was lunching in no time.

The manager was shaken somewhat by the incident, but remains employed—something that cannot be said of another surprised victim of a "sneak attack." When Fay paid an unexpected visit to the director of Wendy's restaurants in the Memphis area, he was somewhat puzzled by the reluctance of the area director to tour the sixteen restaurants of the area with him. However, the cause of the manager's apprehension was quickly discovered when Fay was treated to soggy french fries and cold buns and he saw littered parking lots at the first three restaurants visited. Restaurants in the Memphis area have since made great strides forward under new management.

Other "sneak attack" converts include Eugene Ferkauf, the flamboyant founder of Korvettes, Incorporated and Charles Luce, chairman of New York's Consolidated Edison Company. In the 1960s, Mr. Ferkauf did not have a secretary, an office, or even a desk; he spent all of his time in Korvette stores across the country. Ferkauf recalls discovering in a Brooklyn stockroom a bundle of boy's shirts that were receiving no better treatment than the garbage that had accumulated over the work day. Ferkauf called the store manager aside, pulled a twenty-dollar bill from his own pocket and, as he tore the bill into tiny pieces, said "Merchandise is money." While today his methods have mellowed somewhat, Ferkauf still argues that it is necessary to have someone look down from the mountain into the valley to get an overall perspective.

In New York, a lanky sixty-three-year-old, wearing a meter reader's cap, spends his Sundays inconspicuously peddling around the city on his three-speed bicycle. Employees of Consolidated Edison Company now know that the utility's chairman, Charles Luce, can turn up almost anywhere on his thirty-to-forty-mile trips to inspect work crews. Luce can frequently be seen slipping past security barricades in Queens or peeking into open manholes in Brooklyn. While most employees that have had contact with Luce on his weekend excursions see him as a person that is kind of nutty but friendly, others have had the misfortune of seeing the sterner side of the man. For example, on one trip into Manhattan, Luce discovered a Con Ed cable truck left running and unattended. Luce climbed into the driver's seat and waited. When the driver returned he got a lecture from the boss and was later suspended for a day. While sometimes upset by what he finds, Luce says that he never takes on-the-spot action but waits until Monday to tell managers of discovered transgressions. Disciplinary decisions are left to the managers.

The wait-to-correct tactics used by Luce are not followed by all managers that favor the "sneak attack" approach. Consider the New Jersey supermarket cashier whose customer politely pointed out that the cashier had neglected to ring up a jar of jelly. "Just take it," the cashier said to the customer, who happened to be the company's president. The cashier was promptly fired.

Of the different ways captains of industry choose to review their corporate troops, the "sneak attack" may well be the most controversial. For some employees, it may also be the most costly.

This case is adapted from Jeffrey H. Birnbaum, "To Check on Ranks, A Few Top Officials Favor Sneak Attacks," *Wall Street Journal* (Eastern ed.) Used with permission.

Discussion Issues

1. Explain how the action taken by each manager is a control action.
2. Are these actions examples of precontrol, concurrent control, or feedback control? Explain.
3. Evaluate the effectiveness of control action taken by each manager in the case. Do you see any problems when approaching control from these perspectives?

Student Learning Objectives

From studying this chapter I will attempt to acquire:

1. Insights on how to use management by exception as a control tool
2. An understanding of how managers can use break-even analysis to guide an organization
3. Knowledge of various ratios managers can use to assess organizational performance
4. An appreciation for the importance of using budgets within an organization
5. An understanding of which control tools managers should use most often

Chapter Outline

Control Tools

Introductory Case 17
A Lack of Control

Laura Sprell is thirty-seven years old and recently purchased an operating bowling alley called Bowl-O-Rama. In deciding to buy this business, Sprell reasoned that although the automatic pinsetting and scoring equipment at Bowl-O-Rama soon would have to be replaced, the bowling lanes were in good condition, and the volume of business the company was doing seemed desirable. In addition, Sprell felt sure that the overall financial position of Bowl-O-Rama could be improved with modifications to the internal operations of the bowling alley lounge, billiards room, and pinball machine room.

Twenty-one people are employed at Bowl-O-Rama, twelve full-time and nine part-time. As did the previous owner, Sprell decided to function as the company's operations manager. In essence, Sprell took over as the top manager at the bowling alley.

As you might suspect, Laura Sprell spent most of her first day of work at Bowl-O-Rama trying to get acquainted with her new employees. One of Sprell's most significant conversations during this day was with Jim Powell, the assistant manager of the bowling alley. In speaking with Powell, Sprell was not at all surprised to learn that he thought that Bowl-O-Rama was basically a sound company. She was surprised to learn from this conversation, however, that neither Powell nor the previous owner spent significant amounts of time trying to control bowling alley activities.

As a result of this conversation, Sprell decided to spend her evenings for the next two weeks in the city library attempting to discover specific control tools she could use at Bowl-O-Rama. She was confident that the lack of control shown by the previous owner was a definite weakness and that an effective control program at Bowl-O-Rama probably would enable her to improve organization performance even more than she had anticipated originally.

Discussion Issues

1. Do you agree that the deemphasis of control by the previous owner of Bowl-O-Rama was a managerial weakness? Why?
2. What do you think Laura Sprell means by ''control tools''?
3. Will Sprell be able to make significant improvements in the operations of Bowl-O-Rama? Why?

What's Ahead

Laura Sprell, the new owner of the bowling alley discussed in the introductory case, feels quite confident that she can improve the operation of Bowl-O-Rama. In addition, Sprell feels that implementation of practical control tools within her organization is the key to this improvement. This chapter is intended to provide a manager like Laura Sprell with information on control tools she could use.

As discussed in the last chapter, controlling is the process of making something happen the way it was planned to happen. This chapter describes various control tools managers can adopt to assist in controlling and also explains how these tools can be used within an organization. The chapter, therefore, is divided into two main sections: (1) describing control tools and (2) using control tools.

A **control tool** is a specific procedure or technique that presents pertinent organizational information in such a way that managers are aided in developing and implementing appropriate organizational control strategy. Control tools help managers to pinpoint the organizational strengths and weaknesses on which useful control strategy must focus.

Describing Control Tools

What Is a Control Tool?

The best known and most commonly used of these control tools are (1) management by exception, (2) break-even analysis, (3) ratio analysis, (4) budgets, and (5) human asset accounting. Each of these tools is described more fully in the following sections.

Management by Exception

Management by exception is a control technique that allows only significant deviations between planned and actual performance to be brought to the manager's attention.[1] Actually, management by exception is based on the exception principle, a management principle that appears very early in management literature.[2] The exception principle recommends that subordinates handle all routine organizational matters, while managers handle only nonroutine or exceptional organizational issues.

Exception Principle

Although these exceptional issues might be uncovered when managers themselves detect significant deviation between standards and actual performance, some managers establish special rules aimed at allowing exceptional issues to surface as a matter of normal operating procedure. Two examples of such rules are:

1. A department manager must immediately inform the plant manager if actual weekly labor costs exceed estimated weekly labor costs by more than 15 percent.
2. A department manager must immediately inform the plant manager if actual dollars spent plus estimated dollars to be spent on a special project exceed the funds approved for the project by more than 10 percent.[3]

These rules focus on the area of organizational expenditures. In reality, such rules can be established in virtually any organizational area.

If appropriately administered, management by exception yields the added advantage of ensuring the best use of a manager's time. Since management by exception brings only significant issues to the manager's attention, the possibility that the manager will spend valuable time working on relatively insignificant issues is automatically

Making Best Use of Time

eliminated. Of course, the significant issues brought to the manager's attention could be organizational strengths as well as organizational weaknesses. The manager should try to eliminate the weaknesses and reinforce the strengths.

Back to the Case

Laura Sprell, the new owner of Bowl-O-Rama in the introductory case, could use management by exception as one of her new control tools. The implementation of this particular control tool would allow Sprell's subordinates to handle all routine organizational matters and bring only exceptional organizational issues to her attention. In this regard, management by exception would help Sprell to manage her time most advantageously. Successful implementation of management by exception at Bowl-O-Rama probably would require the establishment of a certain number of new rules. One such rule might be that bowling alley attendants should

inform Sprell immediately if the number of games bowled in a particular week deviates by more than 20 percent from the budgeted number of games to be bowled.

The information Laura obtains by using the management by exception technique should serve as a basis for formulating and implementing appropriate control strategy. For example, Sprell might learn that the actual number of games bowled during a particular week is 25 percent below the budgeted games to be bowled. Sprell then would be faced with formulating and implementing control strategy aimed at increasing the number of games bowled per week.

Break-Even Analysis

Levels of Profit or Loss Associated with Levels of Production

Another control tool commonly used by managers is break-even analysis. **Break-even analysis** is the process of generating information that summarizes various levels of profit or loss associated with various levels of production. The following sections discuss (1) basic ingredients of break-even analysis, (2) types of break-even analysis available to managers, (3) the relationship between break-even analysis and controlling, and (4) limitations of break-even analysis.

Basic Ingredients of Break-Even Analysis

Break-even analysis typically includes reflection, discussion, reasoning, and decision making relative to seven major ingredients. Each of these seven ingredients and their corresponding definitions follow. Since the discussion on break-even analysis is built on these definitions, they should be mastered before reading any further.

1. *Fixed costs*   **Fixed costs** are expenses incurred by the organization regardless of the number of products produced. Examples of these costs would be real estate taxes, upkeep to the exterior of a business building, and interest expenses on money borrowed to finance the purchase of equipment.
2. *Variable costs*   Expenses that fluctuate with the number of products produced are called **variable costs.** Examples of variable costs include costs of packaging a product, materials needed to make the product, and costs associated with packing products to prepare them for shipping.

Total Costs = Fixed Costs + Variable Costs

3. *Totals costs*   **Total costs** are simply the sum of fixed costs and variable costs associated with production.
4. *Total revenue*   **Total revenue** is all sales dollars accumulated from selling manufactured products. Naturally, total revenue increases as more products are sold.

Profit = Total Revenue − Total Costs

5. *Profits*   **Profits** are defined as that amount of total revenue that exceeds the total costs of producing the products sold.

6. *Loss*   **Loss** is that amount of the total costs of producing a product that exceeds the total revenue gained from selling the product.

7. *Break-even point*   A **break-even point** is defined as that situation wherein the total revenue of an organization equals its total costs; the organization is generating only enough revenue to cover its costs. The company is neither gaining a profit nor incurring a loss.

Types of Break-Even Analysis

There are two somewhat different procedures for determining the same break-even point for an organization: (1) algebraic break-even analysis and (2) graphic break-even analysis. More information on each of these procedures is presented in the following two sections.[4]

Algebraic Break-Even Analysis

The following simple formula commonly is used to determine that level of production at which an organization breaks even:

$$BE = \frac{FC}{P - VC}$$

where—

BE = that level of production where the firm breaks even
FC = total fixed costs of production
 P = price at which each individual unit is sold to customers
VC = variable costs associated with each product manufactured and sold

Two sequential steps must be followed to use this formula to calculate a break-even point. First, the variable costs associated with producing each product must be subtracted from the price at which each product will sell. The purpose of this calculation is to determine how much of the selling price of each product sold can go toward covering total fixed costs incurred from producing all products. The second step is to divide the remainder calculated in step one into total fixed costs. The purpose of this calculation is to determine how many products must be produced and sold to cover fixed costs. This number of products is the break-even point for the organization.

How to Use the Break-Even Formula

The following example shows how algebraic break-even analysis can be used. A textbook publisher could face the fixed costs and variable costs per textbook presented in figure 17.1. The publisher wants to sell each textbook for twelve dollars. The break-even point for the publisher would be calculated from the formula as follows:

$$BE = \frac{\$88,800}{\$12-\$6}$$

$$BE = \frac{\$88,800}{\$6}$$

$$BE = 14,800 \text{ copies}$$

This calculation indicates that if expenses and selling price remain stable, the textbook publisher will incur a loss if book sales are fewer than 14,800 copies, break even if book sales equal 14,800 copies, and make a profit if book sales exceed 14,800 copies.

Graphic Break-Even Analysis

Graphic break-even analysis entails the construction of a graph that shows all critical elements within a break-even analysis. Figure 17.2 is a break-even graph for the textbook publisher mentioned in the last section.

Figure 17.1 Fixed costs and variable costs for textbook publisher.

Fixed Costs (Yearly Basis)		Variable Costs per Textbook Sold	
1. Real estate taxes on property	$ 1,000	1. Printing	$2.00
2. Interest on loan to purchase equipment	5,000	2. Artwork	1.00
3. Building maintenance	2,000	3. Sales commission	.50
4. Insurance	800	4. Author royalties	1.50
5. Salaried labor	80,000	5. Binding	1.00
Total fixed costs	$88,800	Total variable costs per textbook	6.00

Figure 17.2 Break-even analysis for textbook publisher.

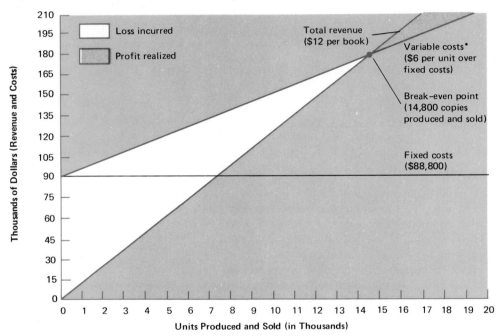

*Note that by drawing the variable costs line on top of the fixed costs line, variable costs have been added to fixed costs. Therefore, the variable costs line also represents total costs.

Using the Algebraic and Graphic Break-Even Methods

Both the algebraic and graphic methods of break-even analysis for the textbook publisher result in the same break-even point of 14,800 books produced and sold. However, the processes used to arrive at this break-even point are quite different.

When to Use the Algebraic Method

Depending on the situation managers face, they may want to use one break-even method rather than another. For example, if managers simply desire a quick yet accurate determination of a break-even point, the algebraic method generally suffices. On the other hand, if managers desire a more complete picture of the cumulative relationships between a break-even point, fixed costs, and escalating variable costs, the graphic break-even method probably is more useful. Managers in the textbook publishing company could quickly and easily see from figure 17.2 the cumulative relationships between fixed costs, escalating variable costs, and potential profit and loss associated with various levels of production.

Figure 17.3 Typical effects of increasing variable and fixed costs and decreasing selling price on the organizational break-even point.

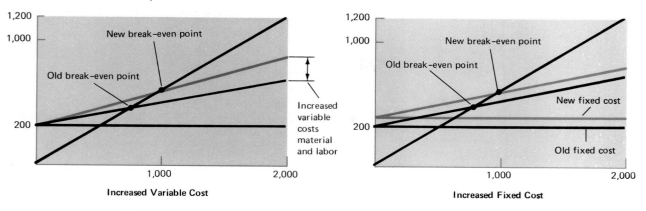

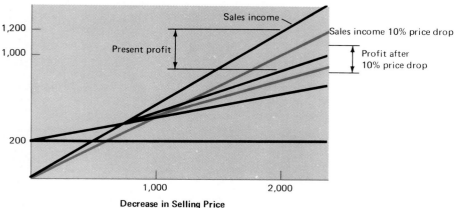

From MANAGEMENT CONTROL MODELS by Earl P. Strong and Robert D. Smith. Copyright © 1968 by Holt, Rinehart and Winston, Inc. Reprinted by permission of Holt, Rinehart and Winston.

Control and Break-Even Analysis

Break-even analysis is a useful control tool because it helps managers to understand the relationships between fixed costs, variable costs, total costs, and profit and loss within an organization. Once these relationships are understood, managers can take steps to modify one or more of these variables to reduce significant deviation between planned profit levels and actual profit levels.[5]

Profit Planning

Exhibit 17 tells how Connie Lane keeps close watch on cost factors in his bakery in order to reach desirable profit levels.

Figure 17.3 shows the results when an existing break-even situation is changed by causing (1) variable costs to increase, (2) fixed costs to increase, or (3) the selling price of a product to decrease.[6] The information shown in this figure indicates that increasing costs and/or decreasing selling prices have the overall effect of increasing the number of products an organization must produce and sell to break even. Conversely, managerial strategy for decreasing the number of products an organization must produce and sell to break even entails lowering or stabilizing fixed and variable costs, and/or increasing the selling price of each product. The exact control strategy, based on break-even analysis, a particular manager should develop and implement primarily is dictated by the unique organizational situation the manager faces.

Exhibit 17

Connie Lane's Cost Control System Helps a Bakery

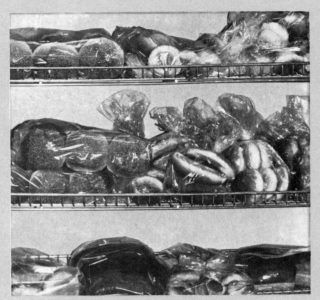

(Photo: © 1982 Rose Stork)

Though its name may suggest a contractor or an advertising agency, Campbell Taggart Inc. bakes bread. So much bread—sold mainly in Sunbelt states under the labels Manor, Colonial, Rainbo, and Kilpatrick's—that it is the country's second-largest producer after ITT Continental Baking, the Wonder bread company. But Campbell Taggart is no longer content to live by bread along. The Dallas-based company has been enriching its diet by acquiring related businesses with fatter profit margins and greater growth potential.

Four years ago, Campbell Taggart moved into the fast-growing Mexican-food field by buying El Chico, a full-service restaurant chain. Last April the company snared a slice of a $110-billion-a-year market by purchasing Los Angeles-based Larry's Food Products, which sells prepared entrées to such institutions as schools, hospitals, and company cafeterias. In August the company arranged a third nonbaking acquisition, Rod's Food Products, which sold about $35 million of refrigerated salad dressings, sandwich fillings, and dips to institutions and food brokers last year.

The Secret Is Cost Controls

Connie Lane is all business. He started at Campbell Taggart in 1947 as a cost-control analyst, figuring out ways to help subsidiary bakeries save on labor, production, and delivery expenses and thereby make more money. He's still doing the same thing, he says. Three and a half days a week he is out of town keeping a close watch on Campbell

Taggart's operations in 23 states. He visits plants, asking about production or labor problems, frequently pulling bread or a roll off the line to inspect or taste it. He whisks through supermarkets—as many as four an hour—checking displays on bread shelves.

Lane has eaten at every one of the 96 El Chico restaurants in 11 states, often making a quick count of the other diners and multiplying that number by $4.45, the amount of the average check. His universal greeting to his managers: "Making any money for us?" If the answer is affirmative, and it had better be, Lane responds, "Well, it's not enough."

Lane always knows exactly how well every bakery operation is doing, thanks to a cost-control system he developed in the early 1970s. "It's the best one I've ever seen," says veteran security analyst Leonard Teitelbaum of Merrill Lynch. A computer printout, which reaches Lane's desk by 10 A.M. Wednesday, shows the profit and loss of each Campbell Taggart bakery for the week that ended Tuesday night and compares that performance with the one the week before and the one a year earlier. The computer also analyzes the profitability of each of the 60 or so items in each bakery's line, and breaks out data like pounds produced per employee, waste per employee, and the number of stales—unsold bread that the bakery has to take back from supermarkets. If anything is out of line, Lane is on the phone to the local bakery president by Wednesday afternoon.

Potential Pitfalls of Break-Even Analysis

Break-even analysis, although generally considered to be a very useful managerial control tool,[7] has the following potential pitfalls:

Assistance in Making
Subjective Judgments

1. *Managers sometimes view break-even analysis as a mechanistic and objective means for making control decisions* This is simply not the case. As with all the control tools discussed in this chapter, break-even analysis only generates information managers can use for assistance in making primarily subjective control decisions. Break-even analysis *helps* managers to make control decisions but does not actually make those decisions.

Updating a Break-Even
Analysis

2. *Managers sometimes view the conditions reflected in a break-even analysis as lasting for long periods of time* Organizations continually are changing through the constant fluctuation of such factors as salary costs, product demand, and taxes. Managers should keep in mind that for a break-even analysis to remain useful, it should be updated continually in response to such changes.

Variable Costs Fluctuate

3. *Managers sometimes view variable costs as constant* In reality, however, variable costs tend to increase as production increases. Contributing to this increase are such factors as increased overtime salary expenses and a higher reject rate, which generally accompanies increased production levels. In most situations, as production levels increase or decrease, managers probably will see some corresponding fluctuation in related variable costs.[8]

Back to the Case

In addition to management by exception, Laura Sprell could use break-even analysis as one of her new control tools at Bowl-O-Rama. Break-even analysis would furnish Sprell with information on the various levels of profit or loss associated with various levels of activity at Bowl-O-Rama. To use break-even analysis, Sprell would need to determine total fixed costs necessary to operate Bowl-O-Rama, the price at which each unit of various goods or services were offered, and the variable costs associated with producing each of those units.

For example, if Sprell wanted to determine how many glasses of beer had to be sold in the bowling alley lounge for the lounge operation to break even, she could arrive at this break-even point algebraically by following three steps. First, she would have to total all fixed costs attributable to the lounge, such as lighting and some portion of the property taxes. Second, she would have to total all variable costs associated with selling each glass of beer and subtract this total from the price at which each glass of beer sells.

Variable costs would include such expenses as the cost of the beer itself and the cost of washing each glass used. Finally, Sprell would have to divide the answer calculated in step 2 into the answer derived in step 1. This figure would tell her how many glasses of beer she would have to sell to break even. Sprell also could arrive at this break-even point by constructing a graph that showed her fixed costs, variable costs, and selling price. The graph probably would provide her with a more overall view from which to formulate appropriate control strategy.

Regardless of whether she uses the algebraic method or the graphic method of break-even analysis, Sprell should (1) recognize that break-even analysis simply provides her with information from which she subjectively must develop appropriate control strategy, (2) be aware that break-even analysis must be repeated periodically to account for changing conditions, and (3) know that, in reality, variable costs at Bowl-O-Rama probably will fluctuate somewhat with different levels of activity.

Ratio Analysis

Ratios Are Relationships

The third major control tool to be covered in this chapter is ratio analysis.[9] A ratio is a relationship between two numbers that is calculated by dividing one number into the other. **Ratio analysis** is the process of generating information that summarizes the financial position of an organization by calculating ratios based on various financial measures that appear on the organization's balance sheet and income statement.[10] This section on ratio analysis discusses (1) various ratios available to managers and (2) using ratios to control organizations.

Kinds of Ratios

The ratios available to managers for controlling organizations typically are divided into four categories: (1) liquidity ratios, (2) leverage ratios, (3) activity ratios, and (4) profitability ratios. The following sections define each type and explain its purpose.

Liquidity Ratios

Meeting Financial Obligations:

Ratios that indicate an organization's ability to meet upcoming financial obligations are called **liquidity ratios.** The more an organization is able to meet these obligations, the more liquid it is said to be. As a general rule, organizations should be liquid enough to meet these obligations, yet not so liquid that too many financial resources are sitting idle in anticipation of meeting upcoming debts. The two main types of liquidity ratios are (1) the current ratio and (2) the quick ratio.

1. Can the organization meet current debts?

Current Ratio   The **current ratio** is calculated by dividing the dollar value of the organization's current assets by the dollar value of its current liabilities. The formula for the current ratio is as follows:

$$\text{Current Ratio} = \frac{\text{Current assets}}{\text{Current liabilities}}$$

Current assets typically include cash, accounts receivable, and inventory, while current liabilities generally include accounts payable, short-term notes payable, and any other accrued expenses. The current ratio indicates to managers the organization's ability to meet its financial obligations in the short run.

2. Can the organization meet current debts without inventory?

Quick Ratio   The **quick ratio,** sometimes called the acid-test ratio, is computed by subtracting inventory from current assets and then dividing the difference by current liabilities. The formula for the quick ratio is as follows:

$$\text{Quick Ratio} = \frac{\text{Current assets} - \text{Inventory}}{\text{Current liabilities}}$$

The quick ratio is the same as the current ratio except that it does not include inventory in current assets. Since inventory can be difficult to convert into money or securities, the quick ratio gives managers information on the organization's ability to meet its financial obligations with no reliance on inventory.

Leverage Ratios

Using Borrowed Funds:

Leverage ratios indicate the relationships between organizational funds supplied by the owners of an organization and organizational funds supplied by various creditors. The more organizational funds furnished by creditors, the more leverage an organization is said to be employing. As a general guideline, an organization should use leverage to the extent that borrowed funds can be used to generate additional profit without a significant amount of organizational ownership being established by creditors. Perhaps the two most commonly used leverage ratios are (1) the debt ratio and (2) the times interest earned ratio.

Debt Ratio The **debt ratio** is calculated by dividing total organizational debt by total organizational assets. The formula for the debt ratio is as follows:

$$\text{Debt Ratio} = \frac{\text{Total debts}}{\text{Total assets}}$$

In essence, this ratio gives the percentage of all organizational assets provided by organizational creditors. Whereas some managers strongly caution against using too much debt to finance an organization, Barclay Morley, Stauffer's chairman and chief executive, supports the theory that experiencing some debt is a critical ingredient of building a successful organization.[11]

Times Interest Earned Ratio The **times interest earned ratio** is calculated by dividing gross income, or earnings before interest and taxes, by the total amount of organizational interest charges incurred from borrowing needed resources. The formula for the times interest earned ratio is as follows:

$$\text{Times Interest Earned Ratio} = \frac{\text{Gross income}}{\text{Interest charges}}$$

This ratio indicates the organization's ability to pay interest expenses directly from gross income.

Activity Ratios

Activity ratios indicate how well an organization is selling its products in relation to its available resources. Obviously, management's goal is to maximize the amount of sales per dollar invested in organizational resources. Three main activity ratios are discussed: (1) inventory turnover, (2) fixed assets turnover, and (3) total assets turnover.

Inventory Turnover **Inventory turnover** is calculated by dividing organizational sales by the inventory. The formula for inventory turnover is as follows:

$$\text{Inventory Turnover} = \frac{\text{Sales}}{\text{Inventory}}$$

This ratio indicates whether an organization is maintaining an appropriate level of inventory in relation to its sales volume. In general, as sales volume increases or decreases, an organization's inventory level should fluctuate correspondingly.

Fixed Assets Turnover **Fixed assets turnover** is calculated by dividing fixed assets, or plant and equipment, into total sales. The formula for generating fixed assets turnover is as follows:

$$\text{Fixed Assets Turnover} = \frac{\text{Sales}}{\text{Fixed assets}}$$

This ratio indicates the appropriateness of the amount of funds invested in plant and equipment relative to the level of sales.

Total Assets Turnover **Total assets turnover** is calculated by dividing sales by total assets. The formula for determining this ratio is as follows:

$$\text{Total Assets Turnover} = \frac{\text{Sales}}{\text{Total assets}}$$

The focus of this ratio is on the appropriateness of the level of funds the organization has tied up in all assets relative to its rate of sales.

Profitability Ratios

Profitability ratios focus on assessing overall organizational profitability and improving it wherever possible. Major profitability ratios include (1) the profit to sales ratio and (2) the profit to total assets ratio.

Making a Profit

Profit to Sales Ratio   The **profit to sales ratio** is calculated by dividing the net profit of an organization by its total sales. The formula for this ratio is as follows:

1. Is the organization making enough profit per sales dollar?

$$\text{Profit to Sales Ratio} = \frac{\text{Net profit}}{\text{Sales}}$$

This ratio indicates whether or not the organization is making an adequate net profit in relation to the total dollars coming into the organization.

Profit to Total Assets Ratio   The **profit to total assets ratio** is calculated by dividing the net profit of an organization by its total assets. The formula for this ratio is as follows:

2. Is the organization making enough profit per dollar invested in total assets?

$$\text{Profit to Total Assets Ratio} = \frac{\text{Net Profit}}{\text{Total Assets}}$$

This ratio indicates whether or not the organization is realizing enough net profit in relation to the total dollars invested in assets.

Using Ratios to Control Organizations

Managers can use ratio analysis in three ways to control an organization.[12] First, managers should evaluate all ratios simultaneously. This strategy ensures that managers will develop and implement a control strategy appropriate for the organization as a whole rather than one that best suits only one phase or segment of the organization.

Review All Ratios at Once

Second, managers should compare computed values for ratios in a specific organization with the values of industry averages for those same ratios. (The values of industry averages for these ratios can be obtained from Dun and Bradstreet, Robert Morris Associates, a national association of bank loan officers, the Federal Trade Commission, and the Securities and Exchange Commission.) Managers can increase the probability of formulating and implementing appropriate control strategy by comparing their financial situation to those of competitors.

Compare Organizational Values to Industry Averages

Third, managers' use of ratios to control an organization also should involve trend analysis. Managers must remember that any set of ratio values is actually only a determination of relationships that exist in a specified period of time, perhaps a year. To use ratio analysis to its maximum advantage, values for ratios should be accumulated for a number of successive time periods to uncover specific trends within the organization. Once these trends are uncovered, managers can formulate and implement appropriate strategy for dealing with them.

Ratios and Financial Trends

In addition to management by exception and break-even analysis, Laura Sprell could use ratio analysis as one of her new control tools. Ratio analysis would indicate the financial position of Bowl-O-Rama by determining relationships between various financial factors on Bowl-O-Rama's balance sheet and income statement. More specifically, Sprell could use liquidity ratios to indicate Bowl-O-Rama's ability to pay its debts, leverage ratios to indicate the appropriateness of the amount of debt used to run Bowl-O-Rama, activity ratios to indicate the level of activity at Bowl-O-Rama relative to its resources, and profitability ratios to indicate the appropriateness of Bowl-O-Rama's level of profits.

Back to the Case

As with all control tools, Sprell must use these ratios as the basis for a more subjective development and implementation of appropriate control strategy. When using ratio analysis, Sprell should assess all ratio information for Bowl-O-Rama simultaneously; compare ratio values at Bowl-O-Rama to values of industry averages for those same ratios; and analyze ratio values for several successive time periods to identify and control any financial trends that might exist at Bowl-O-Rama.

Budgets

A budget is another useful managerial control tool. As described in chapter 6, a budget is a single-use financial plan that covers a specified length of time. The **budget** of an organization is its financial plan outlining how funds in a given period will be spent as well as how they will be obtained.

Tool for Planning and Controlling

In addition to being a financial plan, however, a budget is also a control tool.[13] As managers gather information on actual receipts and expenditures within an operating period, significant deviation from budgeted amounts may be uncovered. In such a case, managers can develop and implement a control strategy aimed at making actual performance more consistent with planned performance. This, of course, assumes that the plan contained in the budget is appropriate for the organization.

An illustration of how a budget can be used as an organizational plan as well as an organizational control tool is the following fictitious situation concerning a Father Walter James, rector and manager of St. Matthew's church. In response to organizational objectives, Father James developed a simple budget for St. Matthew's church (see figure 17.4). The budget is actually Father James's financial plan of how money will be spent to achieve organizational objectives.

In addition, however, Father James also can use this budget as a control tool. For example, as actual office supplies and expenses approach their maximum budgeted allowance of $2,250 during an operating period, Father James conceivably could take steps to minimize further expenditures in this area. On the other hand, after analyzing the entire situation carefully, Father James may decide to increase the budgeted amount for office supplies and expenses. Since the total amount of resources for this church or any other organization probably is fixed, an increase of the budgeted amount of one expense typically requires an equal decrease in the budgeted amount of another expense. For example, increasing the budgeted allowance of office supplies and expenses from $2,250 to $3,250 typically would require a $1,000 reduction in the budgeted amounts for other organizational expenses.

The following sections discuss (1) potential pitfalls of budgets and (2) people considerations in using budgets.

Potential Pitfalls of Budgets

To maximize the benefits of using budgets, managers must be able to avoid several potential pitfalls. These pitfalls include:

Emphasize Significant Expenses

1. *Placing too much emphasis on relatively insignificant organizational expenses* As a general guideline for preparing and implementing a budget, managers should allocate more time for dealing with significant organizational expenses than for relatively insignificant organizational expenses. As an example, the amount of time managers spend on developing and implementing a budget amount for labor costs typically should be much more than the amount of time managers spend on

Figure 17.4 Operating budget for St. Matthew's church.

St. Matthew's Operating Budget
Year 1983

Disbursements

Diocesan assessment	$17,220.00
Clergy salary	16,368.00
Secretary salary	7,200.00
Sexton	6,463.00
Organist/St. Matthew's choirmaster salary	4,576.00
Social security	2,000.00
Housing allowance	3,000.00
Auto lease	3,072.00
Auto gas allowance	1,100.00
Pastoral care	350.00
Pension premium	3,500.00
Utilities	7,920.00
Housekeeping	2,400.00
Repairs to property (bldg. fund)	5,000.00
Telephone	1,760.00
Office supplies & expenses	2,250.00
Postage	700.00
Bulletins & printing	1,500.00
Kitchen supplies & expense	3,000.00
Organ maintenance	200.00
T. H. Greater Fed. of Churches	100.00
Church school	2,500.00
Worship commission	
Planning commission	
Social concerns commission	
Youth commission	
Rector's funds (music, adult education, special programs)	4,500.00
Other expenses	3,200.00
Convention delegate expense	800.00
Insurance	5,500.00
Sexton's insurance	500.00
Clergy assistance	1,000.00
Altar supplies	2,000.00
Garden maintenance	500.00
Total Disbursements	$110,179.00

Receipts

For general purposes:		
Plate offerings	$ 501.47	
Pledge payments	74,761.11	
Parish organizations:		
Treasure House	1,320.00	
St. Thomas's Guild	2,019.32	
From diocese	325.00	
Other miscellaneous sources	828.59	
Investment income	16,645.00	$96,400.49
For special parish use:		
Communion alms	1,240.19	
Building fund (steeple repair)	1,050.00	
Designated gifts and memorials	1,239.25	
Miscellaneous sources	485.00	$ 4,014.44
For work outside parish		$ 152.55
Nonincome receipts:		
From endowment trust transfers		$13,552.75
Day school		16,918.28
Total Receipts		$131,038.51

developing and implementing a budget amount for office supplies. Whereas labor costs are generally a significant organizational cost and therefore should be scrutinized very closely, office supplies expenses are normally a relatively insignificant organizational cost and therefore should be given much less attention.

Justify Expenses Each Year

2. *Increasing budgeted expenses year after year without adequate information* It does not necessarily follow that items contained in last year's budget should be increased this year. Perhaps the most well-known method developed to overcome this potential pitfall is zero-base budgeting.[14] Zero-base budgeting is a planning and budgeting process that requires managers to justify their entire budget request in detail rather than simply to refer to budget amounts established in previous years.[15]

The Department of Agriculture's Office of Budget and Finance used the following instructions to implement its zero-base budgeting program:

A new concept has been adopted for the 1964 agency estimates; namely, that of zero-base budgeting. This means that all programs will be reviewed from the ground up and not merely in terms of changes proposed for the budget year. . . . The total work program of each agency must be subjected to an intensive review and evaluation. . . . Consideration must be given to the basic need for the work contemplated, the level at which the work should be carried out, the benefits to be received, and the costs to be incurred.

The fact that certain activities have been carried out for a number of years will not, per se, adequately justify their continuation. Nor will the fact that programs are prescribed by statutory law necessarily be a controlling consideration. Program goals based on statutes enacted to meet problems or needs that are today of lesser priority must be reevaluated in terms of present conditions.

It is implied in the zero-base budget approach that the need for programs and their recommended magnitude in the fiscal year 1964 be clearly and specifically demonstrated. . . . The justification should be prepared on the assumption that all information needed for making budget decisions should be included.[16]

Changing Budgets

3. *Ignoring the fact that budgets must be changed periodically* Managers should recognize that such factors as cost of materials, newly developed technology, and product demand constantly are changing and that budgets should be reviewed and modified periodically in response to these changes. A special type of budget called a variable budget is sometimes used to determine automatically such needed changes in budgets. Variable budgets outline various levels of resources to be allocated for each organizational activity, depending on the level of production within the organization. It follows, then, that a variable budget automatically indicates increases or decreases in the amount of resources allocated for various organizational activities, depending on whether production levels increase or decrease. Variable budgets also have been called flexible budgets.

People Considerations in Using Budgets

Budgets Can Cause People Problems

Many managers feel that although budgets are valuable planning and control tools, they can result in major human relations problems in an organization. For example, budgets have been shown to build pressures that unite workers against management, cause harmful conflict between management and factory workers, and create tensions that result in worker inefficiency and worker aggression against management.[17] Depending on the severity of such problems, budgets may result in more harm to the organization than good.

Training to Overcome People Problems

Several strategies have been suggested to minimize the human relations problems caused by budgets. The most often recommended of these strategies is the design and implementation of appropriate human relations training programs for finance personnel, accounting personnel, production supervisors, and all other key people involved in the formulation and use of budgets. These training programs should be designed to emphasize (1) both the advantages and disadvantages of applying pressure on people through budgets and (2) the possible results of using budgets to imply organization member success or failure.[18]

Back to the Case

In addition to management by exception, break-even analysis, and ratio analysis, Laura Sprell could use budgets to control activities at Bowl-O-Rama. The Bowl-O-Rama budget would be Sprell's financial plan indicating how much money would be spent on salaries, advertising, and so on, and also a source of information to help Sprell determine what type of control, if any, she should implement in her organization. For example, if 90 percent of the annual amount budgeted for advertising expenses at Bowl-O-Rama was spent after six months, Sprell would need to assess the situation carefully to determine what type of control, if any, would be necessary for the remainder of the year. Sprell might decide that advertising expenses should be increased to allow for the same level of advertising throughout the year. Naturally,

depending on the specific situation she faces, Sprell could make a number of different decisions about this budgeted allotment for advertising.

For Sprell to be successful in using budgets, she must focus on major Bowl-O-Rama expenses as opposed to minor expenses; attempt to rejustify budgeted expenses at Bowl-O-Rama each time the budget is revised; and change the amounts allocated to various budgeted expenses as conditions change and budget changes therefore become necessary. Sprell must also keep in mind that budgets can cause human relations problems and that training that focuses on how to minimize such problems should be provided for all people involved in formulating and using Bowl-O-Rama budgets.

Human Asset Accounting

The last major control tool to be covered in this chapter is human asset accounting. In general terms, **human asset accounting** is the process of establishing the dollar value of human resources within the organization. According to human asset accounting procedures, this dollar value generally is derived by adding two amounts: (1) the cost necessary to replace an individual and (2) the value of the individual's contribution to production.

Human Asset Value = Replacement Cost + Contribution to Production

Some disagreement exists on how the human asset accounting process should be implemented. Some managers believe that human asset accounting is mainly a subjective process and therefore should only be conducted on an informal basis. On the other hand, some managers maintain that the value of human resources can be measured objectively and that these values, once determined, should appear on organizational financial statements along with all other organizational assets.[19] Little disagreement exists, however, on the great potential value of human asset accounting as a managerial control tool. The following sections discuss (1) determining replacement costs of organization members, (2) determining the value of the contribution of organization members to the production process, and (3) controlling through human asset accounting.

Disagreement about Human Asset Accounting

Determining Replacement Costs of Organization Members

Perhaps the most obvious step in determining the value of an individual within an organization is to compute the individual's replacement cost. Replacement cost is the total dollars the organization would have to invest to fill a vacated position. Obviously, replacement costs for various jobs within any one organization can fluctuate greatly.

What Is Replacement Cost?

Figure 17.5 Major direct and indirect acquisition costs, learning costs, and separation costs that constitute total replacement cost.

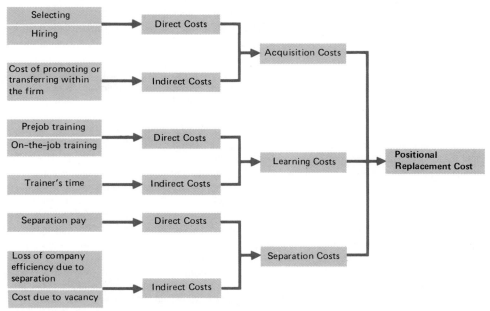

Eric G. Flamholtz, "Human Resource Accounting—Measuring Positional Replacement Costs," *Human Resource Management,* Spring 1973, Graduate School of Business Administration, University of Michigan, Ann Arbor, MI 48109.

Determining Replacement Costs

As figure 17.5 implies, replacement cost primarily consists of three main costs: (1) acquisition costs, (2) learning costs, and (3) separation costs. Acquisition costs are all expenses incurred to hire an employee. Learning costs are expenses incurred to adequately train an individual to perform a job. Separation costs are expenses incurred by the organization when the organization member's employment actually terminates. Severance pay would be an example of a separation cost.

Figure 17.5 also indicates that acquisition costs, learning costs, and separation costs can each be further subdivided into direct costs and indirect costs. Direct costs are those expenses that focus directly on the specific job an individual performs. Indirect costs are expenses that cannot be directly associated with the performance of a particular job but still are necessary to enable individuals to be productive in their jobs. Examples of direct and indirect replacement costs are shown in the figure.

Determining the Value of the Contribution of Organization Members to the Production Process

As mentioned earlier, simply determining the replacement cost of an organization member does not show the individual's total value to the organization. To this replacement cost must be added the value of the individual's contribution to the production process.[20] As with most of the management literature in this area, the following discussion focuses on determining the value of contributions managers make to the production process.

According to Rensis Likert, the contributions that various managers make to the production process can be assessed by evaluating the status of causal variables, intervening variables, and end-result variables associated with those managers.[21] Likert defines causal variables as independent variables that determine the course of developments within an organization as well as the results achieved by the organization.

Figure 17.6 Various relationships between causal variables, intervening variables, and end-result variables.

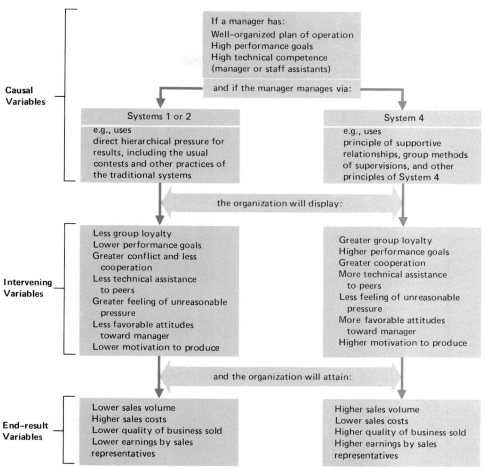

Rensis Likert, "New Patterns in Sales Management," in Martin R. Warshaw (ed.), *Changing Perspectives in Marketing Management,* Michigan Business Papers No. 37 (Ann Arbor, Mich.: Bureau of Business Research, Graduate School of Business Administration, The University of Michigan, 1962), p. 24. Copyright by the University of Michigan and reprinted by permission.

Likert defines intervening variables as factors that reflect the internal state or health of the organization. End-result variables are defined by Likert as dependent factors that reflect organizational productivity.

Figure 17.6 shows various types of Likert's causal variables, intervening variables, and end-result variables, and illustrates the relationships Likert claims exist between them. Systems 1, 2, and 4, as discussed in chapter 14, are Likert's major causal variables. Likert's work implies that as a manager uses a system 4 management style, advantageous intervening variables tend to develop, and correspondingly more desirable end-result variables tend to materialize. Hence, managers using a system 4 management style tend to have a more positive influence on production and therefore tend to be more valuable to the organization than managers who use some other system of management. It is obvious from this discussion that determining the precise value of the contribution an individual manager makes to the production process is a much more subjective process than determining the manager's replacement cost.

Determining Effects on Production

Controlling Through Human Asset Accounting

Once managers have determined and evaluated the value of human assets within the organization, they may need to take steps to make actual values more consistent with planned values. For example, in relation to replacement costs, a manager may find that selecting and hiring costs are too high for certain types of positions. In response to this observation, the manager can develop and implement some control strategy aimed at reducing these expenses.

Steps also can be taken to make the actual values of the contributions individual managers make to production more equivalent to the planned values of these contributions. This changing of the value of these contributions probably is best attained through the conscientious training of organization members.[22] Following Likert's concept, this training should focus on understanding the relationships between causal, intervening, and end-result variables and also should emphasize establishing desirable causal variables in everyday work situations.

Back to the Case

In addition to management by exception, break-even analysis, ratio analysis, and budgets, Laura Sprell could use human asset accounting as a control tool at Bowl-O-Rama. Human asset accounting would be a process Sprell would use to determine the value of each individual working at Bowl-O-Rama. The first major portion of this value would come from Sprell—determining the replacement cost of an individual working at Bowl-O-Rama. This replacement cost would be determined by adding both direct and indirect acquisition costs, learning costs, and separation costs associated with the individual.

The second major portion of the value of a human asset would be the individual's contribution to promoting productive activities at Bowl-O-Rama. Since managers and supervisors significantly affect the productivity at Bowl-O-Rama, it is especially important that Sprell determines the value of their contributions to the production process. Sprell can use the general guideline that as managers and supervisors possess more system 4 characteristics as opposed to system 1 characteristics, they make more positive contributions to the Bowl-O-Rama production process and are, therefore, of greater value to Bowl-O-Rama.

As with all control tools, human asset accounting simply provides Sprell with information about Bowl-O-Rama. Using this information, she will have to decide what type of control, if any, she must develop and implement. For example, if managers or supervisors at Bowl-O-Rama seem to be of relatively low value since they are more system 1 oriented than system 4, Sprell may decide to provide training for these individuals that emphasizes the benefits of system 4 management and the steps to be followed in implementing system 4 in everyday work situations.

Using Control Tools

Which control tool is best? The answer to this question is simply that no one control tool discussed in this chapter is necessarily better than any other. Each tool has a somewhat different purpose and has been shown over time to be useful to managers in achieving that purpose.

Management by exception, for example, brings only significant deviation from planned performance to the attention of managers. Break-even analysis is designed primarily for maintaining appropriate relationships among significant financial variables within the organization. Through break-even analysis, managers can develop and implement a control strategy that reflects the current situation with regard to fixed costs, variable costs, and the selling price of a product. Ratio analysis is designed to help managers evaluate the organization's ability to meet its debts, the extent to which debt is being used to finance the organization, the quality of organizational performance, and to evaluate earned profit levels within the organization. Budgets provide

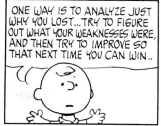

© 1973 United Feature Syndicate.

a financial plan for an organization as well as a basis for organizational control in relation to this plan. Human asset accounting determines the value of various organization members to the organization. Control that is based on human-asset accounting focuses on enhancing these values.[23]

Each of these control tools furnishes managers with somewhat different information about somewhat different but related organizational areas. If used specifically for their respective purposes, these tools are invaluable control instruments. As the cartoon implies, astute managers will use all of these tools, along with any others available to them, to obtain important information about the operation of the organization as a whole.[24] The more complete this information, the better equipped managers will be to decide on an appropriate control strategy for the overall organization.

Back to the Case

Laura Sprell should not stress one control tool too much over another at Bowl-O-Rama. Each control tool discussed in this chapter can provide Sprell with somewhat different but related information on the operations at Bowl-O-Rama. Ideally, Sprell should use several control tools to obtain an overall view of performance at Bowl-O-Rama. As she acquires this overall view, the probability increases that she will be better able to formulate and implement control strategy that will improve the overall operation of Bowl-O-Rama.

Summary

The following points are stressed within this chapter:

1. Management by exception is a control tool that brings only significant deviations between planned and actual performance to the attention of managers. Through management by exception, managers handle only major organizational issues.

2. Break-even analysis is a control tool that provides information that can help managers to project various levels of profit or loss associated with various levels of production. Break-even analysis can be either algebraic or graphic, but should not be viewed as a mechanistic or objective means for making managerial control decisions.

3. Ratio analysis is a control tool that assesses the financial position of the organization by evaluating relationships between various financial factors that appear on the organization's financial statements. These ratios furnish information that can be used to assess the organization's ability to meet financial obligations, the relative amounts of funds supplied by owners and creditors, the quality of activity within the organization, and the level of profitability achieved by the organization.

4. A budget is an organization's financial plan and also can be used as a control tool. Budgets should emphasize significant organizational expenses, be increased only after close scrutiny, and be revised periodically. To be used successfully, budgets should be designed and implemented only after considering the individuals who will be affected by them.

5. Human asset accounting is a control tool that provides managers with information on the value of human resources within the organization. This value is determined primarily by the replacement cost of an individual and the value of the individual's contribution to the production process. Once managers determine the actual value of human resources, appropriate strategy can be designed and implemented to make the actual values more equivalent to planned values.

6. Each control tool discussed in this chapter provides managers with somewhat different information about the organization. Successful managers normally evaluate all of this information, along with any other relevant information that can be gathered, to be better able to design and implement control strategy that best suits the organization as a whole.

Issues for Review and Discussion

1. Define management by exception and describe how it can help managers to use their time most advantageously.

2. List and define seven major ingredients of break-even analysis.

3. Write the formula for algebraic break-even analysis. Describe the steps necessary to use this formula and explain why these steps are taken.

4. When would managers probably use graphic break-even analysis rather than algebraic break-even analysis?

5. How can managers use break-even analysis as an aid in controlling an organization?

6. What potential pitfalls exist in using break-even analysis?

7. What is ratio analysis?

8. List and define the four basic types of ratios.

9. What is the difference between the current ratio and the quick ratio?

10. What information can the debt ratio and the times interest earned ratio give managers?

11. Explain the role of inventory turnover, fixed assets turnover, and total assets turnover in assessing organizational activity.

12. What can the profit to sales ratio and the profit to total assets ratio tell managers about organizational profitability?

13. What guidelines would you recommend to managers using ratio analysis to control an organization?

14. Define the term *budget*. How can managers use a budget to control an organization?

15. List three potential pitfalls managers must avoid when using budgets.

16. What is human asset accounting?

17. What are the two main variables needed to determine the organizational value of a human asset?

18. List and define the main expenses that comprise replacement cost.

19. How can the contributions managers make to the production process be assessed? Be sure to stress causal variables, intervening variables, and end-result variables.

20. How can managers use human asset accounting to control an organization?

21. Which control tool described in this chapter should managers emphasize most? Explain.

Bacon, J. *Managing the Budget Function.* New York: National Industrial Conference Board, 1970.

Beer, S. *Decision and Control.* New York: John Wiley & Sons, 1966.

Bowers, D. G., and Bowers, S. E. "Predicting Organizational Effectiveness with a Four-Factor Theory of Leadership." *Administrative Science Quarterly* 11, no. 2 (1966): 238–63.

Dubin, R. *Human Relations in Administration.* 4th ed. Englewood Cliffs, N.J.: Prentice-Hall, 1974.

Frankston, Fred M. "A Simplified Approach to Financial Planning." *Journal of Small Business Management,* January 1981, pp. 7–15.

Hennessy, J. H., Jr. *Financial Manager's Handbook.* Englewood Cliffs, N.J.: Prentice-Hall, 1977.

Hofstede, G. H. *The Game of Budget Control.* London: Tavistock Publications Limited, 1968.

Jerome, W. T. *Executive Control.* New York: John Wiley & Sons, 1961.

Kauffman, Mort. "An Administrator's Guide to Expense Account Management." *Administrative Management* 42, no. 7 (July 1981): 30–32, 39.

Likert, R. *New Patterns of Management.* New York: McGraw-Hill, 1961.

Mockler, R. J. *The Management Control Process.* New York: Appleton-Century-Crofts, 1972.

Murray, W. *Management Controls in Action.* Dublin: Irish National Productivity Committee, 1970.

Raiborn, Mitchell H., and Scurry, William C., Jr. "Equity to Debt Conversion—Promoting Investments in Small Business Firms." *Financial Executive,* September 1980, pp. 42–46, 48, 50.

Richman, Eugene, and Coleman, Denis. "Monte Carlo Simulation for Management." *California Management Review* 23, no. 3, Spring 1981, pp. 92–96.

Rowe, D. K. *Industrial Relations Management for Profit and Growth.* New York: American Management Association, 1971.

Tannenbaum, A. S. *Control in Organizations.* New York: McGraw-Hill, 1968.

Thornton, Billy M., and Preston, Paul. *Introduction to Management Science: Quantitative Approaches to Managerial Decisions.* Columbus, Ohio: Charles E. Merrill Publishing, 1977.

Vatter, W. J. *Operating Budgets.* Belmont, Calif.: Wadsworth Publishing, 1969.

Welsch, G. A. *Budgeting: Profit Planning and Control.* 3d ed. Englewood Cliffs, N.J.: Prentice-Hall, 1971.

Wilson, Richard M. S. *Cost Control Handbook.* New York: John Wiley & Sons, 1975.

Sources of Additional Information

1. Lester R. Bittle, *Management by Exception* (New York: McGraw-Hill, 1964).

2. Frederick W. Taylor, *Shop Management* (New York: Harper & Brothers, 1911), pp. 126–27.

3. These two rules are adapted from *Boardroom Reports* 5, no. 9 (15 May 1976):4.

4. For a clear discussion of more of the intricacies of break-even analysis, see Carl L. Moore and Robert K. Jaedicke, *Managerial Accounting* (Cincinnati: South-Western Publishing, 1967), pp. 427–46.

5. Robert J. Lambrix and Surendra S. Singhvi, "How to Set Volume-Sensitive ROI Targets," *Harvard Business Review,* March/April 1981, p. 174.

6. For graphs illustrating additional effects of fixed costs on break-even points, see R. Parker Eastwood, *Sales Control by Quantitative Methods* (New York: Columbia University Press, 1940), p. 74.

7. For information on the limitations of break-even analysis, see Donald L. Raun, "Limitations of Profit Graphs, Break-Even Analysis, and Budgets," *The Accounting Review* 39 (October 1964): 927–45.

8. Ted F. Anthony and Hugh J. Watson, "Probabilistic Break-Even Analysis," *Managerial Planning,* November/December 1976, pp. 12–19, 37.

9. This section is based primarily on J. Fred Weston and Eugene F. Brigham, *Essentials of Managerial Finance* (Hinsdale, Ill.: Dryden Press, 1977), pp. 35–61.

10. F. L. Patrone and Donald duBois, "Financial Ratio Analysis for the Small Business," *Journal of Small Business Management,* January 1981, p. 35.

11. "How Stauffer Outperforms the Industry," *Business Week,* 22 November 1976, pp. 129–30.

12. For an excellent discussion of ratio analysis in a small business, see Patrone and duBois, "Financial Ratio Analysis," pp. 35–40.

13. Robert L. Dewelt, "Control: Key to Making Financial Strategy Work," *Management Review,* March 1977, p. 20.

14. George S. Minmier, "Zero-Base Budgeting: A New Budgeting Technique for Discretionary Costs," *Mid-South Quarterly Business Review* 14, no. 3 (October 1976): 2–8.

15. Peter A. Phyrr, "Zero-Base Budgeting," *Harvard Business Review,* no. 6 (November/December 1970): 111–21.

Notes

16. Aaron Wildausky and Arthur Hammann, "Comprehensive Versus Incremental Budgeting in the Department of Agriculture," in *Planning Programming Budgeting: A Systems Approach to Management,* eds. Fremont J. Lyden and Ernest G. Miller (Chicago: Markham, 1968), pp. 143–44.

17. Chris Argyris, "Human Problems with Budgets," *Harvard Business Review* (January/February 1953), p. 108.

18. Argyris, "Human Problems with Budgets," p. 109.

19. R. Lee Brummet, William C. Pyle, and Eric G. Flamholtz, "Human Resource Accounting in Industry," *Personnel Administration* 32, no. 4 (1969): 34–36.

20. Rensis Likert, "Human Organizational Measurements: Key to Financial Success," *Michigan Business Review,* May 1971, pp. 1–5.

21. Rensis Likert, *The Human Organization* (New York: McGraw-Hill, 1967), pp. 29–77.

22. William G. Scott, "Executive Development as an Instrument of Higher Control," *Academy of Management Journal,* September 1963, pp. 191–203.

23. James A. Anderson, "Planning Control Systems to Include Human Factor," *Managerial Planning,* July/August 1976, pp. 30–35.

24. For information on audits as a control tool, see Ionnis Methodios, "Internal Controls and Audit," *Journal of Systems Management,* June 1976, pp. 6–14.

25. 1090 Report, Time Incorporated, p. 1.

26. Ibid., pp. 5–8.

27. Ibid., p. 7.

28. Ibid., p. 47.

29. Ibid., pp. 29–31

30. Ibid., p. 46.

31. "A March on Time," *Forbes,* 17 August 1981, pp. 21–22.

Concluding Case 17
Time Incorporated: Future Growth
Will Be In The Video Line

(Photo: David A. Corona)

Time was incorporated in New York in November of 1922. The two major activities of Time Incorporated are communications and forest products. The company's first magazine, *Time: The Weekly Newsmagazine,* began publication in March of 1923. Time has since become the largest publisher of "general circulation" magazines in the United States. The company's forest products business started in 1955 when it opened its integrated paper mill in Evadale, Texas. In 1973, it acquired Temple Industries, Inc., primarily a manufacturer of building materials. In November of 1978, Time acquired Inland Containers Corporation, which is engaged mainly in the manufacture of corrugated shipping containers and related products. The same year it acquired American Television and Communication Corporation (ATC), a cable television company.[25]

The principle lines of business of Time Incorporated are:

(1) *Publishing* Magazines that Time publishes are *Time, Sports Illustrated, Fortune, Money, People, Life,* and *Discover.* The company's book-publishing operation includes Time-Life Books, Book-of-the-Month Club, and Little, Brown & Company.[26]

(2) *Forest Products* Forest products include production of pulp, paper and paperboard, building materials, and containers and containerboard. Paper, pulp, and building materials are produced by Temple-Eastex Incorporated. The container and containerboard business is conducted by Inland Container Corporation. Both are wholly owned subsidiaries of Time Incorporated.[27]

(3) *Video* Video includes Home Box Office, a pay-television network; American Television and Communications, a cable television operation; Time-Life Films, a producer of motion pictures and television programming; and WOTV, a television station in Grand Rapids, Michigan.[28] Home Box Office, Inc., (HBO), a pay-television programming network service, includes motion pictures, special-interest programs, and sporting events. By the end of 1980, HBO had delivered programming to over six million pay-TV subscribers in more than twenty-five hundred cable television systems in all fifty states, Puerto Rico, and the United States Virgin Islands.

American Television and Communication Corporation (ATC) is a cable television company with approximately 1.3 million subscribers in 125 cable systems in 32 states; approximately 800,000 also subscribe to premium programming. ATC provides premium programming from HBO and other suppliers through its cable systems. Viewers pay a fee for this special program package.

Time-Life Films, Inc., is a producer of motion pictures and television programs for the following: worldwide theatrical and television distribution; United States commercial network television and syndicated television markets; the public television system; and the institutional and consumer markets.

WOTV, an NBC affiliate in Grand Rapids, Michigan, reaches approximately 543,400 households in the nation's 38th largest market.[29]

(4) *Other Activities* This line includes Selling Areas-Marketing, Inc. (SAMI), which markets computer-generated information on sales of food products; Pioneer Press, a publisher of suburban Chicago newspapers; *The Washington Star*,* a daily newspaper; Temple Associates, a contracting firm; and several real estate and land development activities.[30]

Case figure 1 shows the company's consolidated revenues and income before income taxes and extraordinary items attributable to each of these lines of business for the last five years. Data in case figure 1 suggests the increasing importance of the video line. In fact, cable TV is expected to be the largest profit earner for the company in 1981. For the first half of this year, the video line generated one-third of Time's operating profits. Time presently is investing hundreds of millions of dollars in cable. Its capital spending on the video group rose from 10 percent in 1978 to 51 percent in 1980 and is projected at 60 percent this year [1981]. Time, the nation's largest cable owner, has 55 percent of the pay-cable market. The company expects significant growth in this area during the next decade.[31]

Case figure 2 provides selected financial data from the 1980 Annual Report of Time Incorporated. Case figure 3 provides projected financial data for Time Incorporated and the industry for the years 1981 and 1982.

*The *Washington Star* discontinued publication early in 1982.

Discussion Issues

1. (a) Using the financial data in case figure 2, calculate the liquidity, leverage, activity, and profitability ratios for Time Incorporated for 1978 through 1980.
   (b) What can you say about the financial condition of the company from these calculations?
2. (a) Using the projected financial data in case figure 3, calculate the profitability ratios for Time Incorporated and the publishing industry.
   (b) What statements can you make when Time is compared to the figures for the publishing industry.
3. What additional information would you need to be able to make more robust statements about the future financial condition of Time Incorporated? Explain.

Case figure 17.1 Time Incorporated and Subsidiaries—lines of business.

Lines of Business
Time Incorporated and Subsidiaries

Years Ended December 31

	1980		1979		1978		1977		1976	
	(in millions)									
REVENUES										
Publishing:										
Magazines	$ 746.6	26%	$ 650.0	27%	$ 571.8	34%	$ 459.9	37%	$ 366.3	35%
Books (1)	499.0	17	425.0	17	340.9	21	258.2	21	227.6	22
Forest products:										
Pulp and paperboard	253.2	9	222.2	9	189.7	11	183.1	15	174.5	17
Building materials	192.7	7	208.6	8	225.9	14	176.8	14	132.4	13
Container and containerboard (2)	579.4	20	415.2	20	55.0	3	–		–	
Video (3)	427.9	15	299.3	12	116.9	8	78.8	6	54.7	5
Other activities (4)	174.0	6	173.8	7	157.4	9	93.0	7	82.7	8
Total revenues	$2,831.9	100%	$2,504.1	100%	$1,697.8	100%	$1,249.5	100%	$1,038.2	100%
INCOME BEFORE TAXES AND EXTRAORDINARY ITEM										
Publishing:										
Magazines	$ 56.5	25%	$ 70.3	30%	$ 66.2	31%	$ 53.3	33%	$ 37.0	34%
Books (1)	40.3	18	34.7	16	47.7	22	44.2	27	25.7	24
Forest products:										
Pulp and paperboard	38.0	17	37.4	16	26.4	12	22.7	14	36.8	34
Building materials	(3.8)	(2)	15.2	7	43.1	20	30.2	19	14.0	13
Container and containerboard (2) (5)	53.1	24	43.3	19	4.8	2	–		–	
Video (3)	72.5	33	68.5	29	24.9	12	6.1	4	(1.9)	(2)
Other activities (4)	1.3	1	3.4	1	11.2	5	15.3	9	12.2	11
Operating profit	257.9		274.8		224.3		171.8		123.8	
Interest expense	(46.6)	(21)	(35.0)	(15)	(12.5)	(6)	(10.4)	(6)	(10.8)	(10)
Corporate and other income and expense	(8.7)	(4)	(8.9)	(3)	5.3	3	.5	–	(3.6)	(4)
Unusual charge to income	–	–	–	–	(3.1)	(1)	–	–	–	–
Gain on sale of Paris building	20.1	9	–	–	–	–	–	–	–	–
Income before taxes and extraordinary item	$ 222.7	100%	$ 230.9	100%	$ 214.0	100%	$ 161.9	100%	$ 109.4	100%

(1) Publication of books, and recordings.
(2) Includes Inland activity from November 14, 1978, the date of its acquisition by the Company.
(3) Operation of cable–TV, pay–TV programming, TV broadcasting and film production and distribution. Includes ATC activity from November 14, 1978, the date of its acquisition by the Company.
(4) Marketing of information relating to the movement of supermarket products, newspaper publishing, and industrial contracting.
(5) Includes $21.2, $14.6 and $1.1 million of income from Georgia Kraft, a 50% owned affiliate of the Company, for 1980, 1979 and 1978 (from November 14, 1978, the date of its acquisition by the Company) respectively. The Georgia Kraft income amounts are deducted from manufacturing costs in the statement of income.

*From *1980 Form 10-K*, Time Incorporated, p. 2.

Case figure 17.2 Time Incorporated—selected financial data (in millions).

Time Incorporated — Selected Financial Data (in millions)			
	1980	1979	1978
Sales	$2,881.8	$2,504.1	$1,697.6
Operating income (gross income)	220.0	236.8	199.3
Interest expense	46.6	35.0	12.5
Net income	141.2	143.9	125.7
Inventories	262.8	250.2	196.8
Total current assets	864.9	794.1	650.2
Total current liabilities	431.0	396.0	379.3
Total fixed assets	1,127.0	971.9	**
Total assets	2,370.6	2,104.1	1,801.4
Total liabilities	1,243.4	1,078.3	**

*Not available in 1980 Annual Report.

Case figure 17.3 Projected financial data for Time Incorporated and the publishing industry for 1981 and 1982 (in millions).

Projected Financial Data for Time Incorporated and the Publishing Industry for 1981 and 1982 (in millions)*				
	1981		1982	
	Time Inc.	Industry	Time Inc.	Industry
Sales	$3,400	$13,300	$3,900	$15,275
Net profit	170	835	210	1,000
Total assets	1,350	5,150	1,465	5,800

*From *Value Line Investment Survey*, September 18, 1981, pp. 1784 and 1806.

Student Learning Objectives

From studying this chapter I will attempt to acquire:

1. An understanding of the relationship between data and information
2. Insights on the main factors that influence the value of information
3. Some potential steps for evaluating information
4. An appreciation for the role of computers in handling information
5. An understanding of the importance of a management information system (MIS) to an organization
6. A feasible strategy for establishing an MIS

Chapter Outline

Information

Introductory Case 18
A Question of Measurement

"Out of control? That's nonsense. Our organization has one of the most thorough control systems in the industry. I simply can't accept that statement." As Jack Wilkenson, president of Mega-Systems, Inc., made these comments, several members of the executive committee nodded in agreement. A smaller number showed no expression, while Natalie Greenberg, a new member of the executive committee, appeared unconvinced. Greenberg, a recently hired division manager, had drawn the heated remarks from the president by pointing out cost overruns on several recent projects. She had suggested that these overruns pointed to lack of effective controls in key parts of the organization.

"We're all aware of the overruns, Natalie," said Warren Turner, the controller, "But I don't think we should blame our reporting system. It's probably the most thorough series of checks and measurements we could devise at the present time. For example, our production supervisors alone receive at least fourteen monthly measures of their department's productivity. Everything from output per hour to equipment utilization reports is made available to them. Have you seen the stack of computer printouts they receive every month? They've got everything they need to control their operations if they will only study those reports carefully."

"And we enlarged and improved our overall reporting system two years ago," added Ed Simpson, director of information systems. "We brought in a management consulting group that worked with our system design staff to create a thorough and sophisticated management information system. Then we conducted a massive campaign to 'sell' the control tools to the managers who would be using them. We've literally left no stone unturned to develop a first-class control system. I'm very satisfied with its thoroughness."

"Without trying to appear cynical," said Greenberg, "I wonder if the system is too thorough."

"Natalie, I think you'd better explain your comment," said the president, looking quizzically at the new division manager.

From THE MANAGEMENT OF ORGANIZATIONS by Hicks and Gullett. Copyright © 1976 by McGraw-Hill, Inc. Used with permission of McGraw-Hill Book Company.

Discussion Issues

1. How does the series of "checks and measurements" mentioned by Turner fit into the control process of Mega-Systems, Inc.?
2. What do you think Greenberg meant by, "I wonder if the system is too thorough?"
3. How do managers determine if too many checks and measurements are being taken during the controlling process?

What's Ahead

The introductory case concludes with Natalie Greenberg, a recently hired division manager, implying that Mega-Systems, Inc. is not being controlled effectively due to the inadequacy of the control-related information that managers presently are receiving. This chapter presents material that Jack Wilkenson, president of Mega-Systems, should use in assessing the validity of Greenberg's implications as well as in evaluating the overall status of information within his organization.

This is the third and last chapter in the controlling section. Chapter 16 defined controlling as making things happen as planned. Of course, managers cannot make things happen as planned if they lack information on the manner in which various events occur within both the organization and the organizational environment. The purpose of this chapter is to discuss the fundamental principles of handling information within an organization. The two main sections of this chapter are (1) essentials of information and (2) the management information system (MIS).

Essentials of Information

The process of developing information begins with the gathering of some type of facts or statistics, called **data.** Once gathered, data typically are analyzed in some manner. Generally speaking, **information** can be defined as conclusions derived from data analysis. In management terms, information can be defined as conclusions derived from the analysis of data that relate to the operation of an organization.

Data vs. Information

The information managers receive heavily influences managerial decision making, which in turn determines what activities will be performed within the organization, which in turn dictates the eventual success or failure of the organization.[1] Some management writers consider information to be of such fundamental importance to the management process that they define management as the process of converting information into action through decision making.[2] The following sections discuss (1) several factors that influence the value of information, (2) how to evaluate information, and (3) computer assistance in using information.

The Importance of Information

Factors Influencing the Value of Information

Some information managers receive is more valuable than other information.[3] The value of information is defined in terms of how much benefit can accrue to the organization through the use of the information. The greater this benefit, the more valuable the information. In general, four primary factors determine the value of information: (1) information appropriateness, (2) information quality, (3) information timeliness, and (4) information quantity. Each of these factors is described in the sections that follow.

Benefit from Using Information

Information Appropriateness

Information appropriateness is defined in terms of how relevant the information is to the decision-making situation that faces the manager. Relatively appropriate information is quite relevant to the decision-making situation the manager faces. Conversely, relatively inappropriate information is quite irrelevant to the decision-making situation the manager faces. As a general rule, as the appropriateness of information increases, the value of that information increases.

Relevance to Decision Making

Figure 18.1 Characteristics of information appropriate for decisions related to operational control, management control, and strategic planning.

Characteristics of Information	Operational Control	Management Control	Strategic Planning
Source	Largely internal	→	External
Scope	Well defined, narrow	→	Very wide
Level of aggregation	Detailed	→	Aggregate
Time horizon	Historical	→	Future
Currency	Highly current	→	Quite old
Required accuracy	High	→	Low
Frequency of use	Very frequent	→	Infrequent

G. Anthony Gorry and Michael S. Scott Morton, "A Framework for Management Information Systems," SLOAN MANAGEMENT REVIEW, vol. 13, no. 1, Fall 1971, p. 59.

Figure 18.1 shows the characteristics of information appropriate for the following three main decision-making situations that commonly face managers in organizations: (1) operational control decisions, (2) management control decisions, and (3) strategic planning decisions.[4]

Operational control decisions relate to assuring that specific organizational tasks are carried out effectively and efficiently. Management control decisions relate to obtaining and effectively and efficiently using the organizational resources necessary to reach organizational objectives. Strategic planning decisions relate to determining organizational objectives and designating the corresponding action necessary to reach those objectives.

Appropriate Strategic Planning Information

As figure 18.1 shows, the characteristics of appropriate information change as managers shift from making operational control decisions to management control decisions to strategic planning decisions. Strategic planning decision makers need information that focuses on the relationship of the organization to its external environment, emphasizes the future, is very wide in scope, and is aggregate or presents a broad view of all information. Also, appropriate information for this type of decision is usually quite old and not completely accurate.

Appropriate Operational Control Information

Information appropriate for making operational control decisions has dramatically different characteristics than information appropriate for making strategic planning decisions. Operational control decision makers need information that focuses for the most part on the internal organizational environment, emphasizes the performance history of the organization, and is well defined, narrow in scope, and quite detailed. In addition, appropriate information for this type of decision is both highly current and highly accurate.

Appropriate Management Control Information

Information appropriate for making management control decisions generally has characteristics that fall somewhere between the extreme characteristics of appropriate operational control information and appropriate strategic planning information.

Information Quality

Representing Reality

The second primary factor that determines the value of information is **information quality.** The degree to which information represents reality is referred to as information quality. The more closely information represents reality, the higher the quality and the greater the value of the information. In general, the higher the quality of information available to managers, the better equipped managers are to make appropriate decisions and the greater the probability that the organization will be successful over the long run.

Information Timeliness

Information timeliness is the third primary factor that determines the value of information. The timeliness of information refers to the extent to which the receipt of information allows decisions to be made and resulting action to be taken so that the organization can gain some benefit from possessing the information. If information is received by managers at a point when it can be used to the advantage of the organization, the information is said to be timely. If, on the other hand, information is received when it cannot be used to the advantage of the organization, the information is said to be untimely.

Information in Time for Action

For example, the product of a particular company may be selling poorly primarily because its established market price is significantly higher than competitive products. This obviously would be important information for management to possess. If this information was received by management after the product had been discontinued, the information would be untimely. If, however, this information was received by management soon enough to adjust the selling price of the product and thereby significantly increase sales, the information would be timely.

Information Quantity

The fourth and final determinant of the value of information is called **information quantity.** Information quantity refers to the amount of decision-related information managers possess. Before making a decision, managers should assess the quantity of information they possess that relates to the decision being made. If this quantity is judged to be insufficient, more information should be gathered before the decision is made. If the amount of information is judged to be as complete as necessary, managers can feel justified in making the decision.

Amount of Information

Various factors can influence the value of information or the degree of benefit that can accrue to an organization through the use of information. To maximize the degree of this benefit, management should follow the general guideline of encouraging the generation, distribution, and use of organizational information that is appropriate, of high quality, timely, and of sufficient quantity. Following this guideline will not necessarily guarantee sound decisions, but it will ensure that important resources necessary to make such decisions are available.[5]

Back to the Case

The incident described in the introductory case focuses on the role of information in the control process. Information at Mega-Systems can be defined as conclusions derived from the analysis of data relating to the way in which Mega-Systems operates. Natalie Greenberg has implied in the introductory case that Mega-Systems managers currently are unable to make sound control decisions at Mega-Systems primarily because of the type of decision-related information they are receiving. The case ends with Jack Wilkenson, the president of Mega-Systems, attempting to evaluate the status of information at Mega-Systems.

If Wilkenson finds that the control-related information Mega-Systems managers are currently receiving is relatively valueless, he cannot fault his managers for making poor control decisions. Instead, to help his managers make better control decisions, he seriously should consider providing them with more valuable control-related information. Wilkenson might be able to increase the value of the information managers presently are receiving by forcing it to represent more closely activities as they actually occur at Mega-Systems; by making sure that such information is received by managers in sufficient quantity and in time to make controlling decisions; and by ensuring that such information is relevant to the control decisions of the various managers receiving the information.

Figure 18.2 Flowchart of main activities in evaluating information.

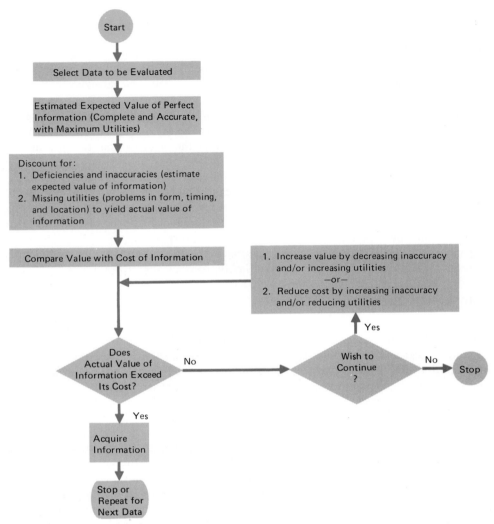

Roman R. Andrus, "Approaches to Information Evaluation," p. 44, *MSU Business Topics,* Summer 1971. Reprinted by permission of the publisher, Division of Research, Graduate School of Business Administration, Michigan State University.

Evaluating Information

Should Information
Be Gathered?

Since information is such an integral and important part of a manager's job, management periodically should spend some time evaluating organizational information. Evaluation of information is the process of determining whether or not the acquisition of specified information is justified. As with all evaluations of this type, the primary concern of management is to weigh the dollar value of benefit gained from using some quantity of information against the cost of generating that information.

Expected Value
of Information

The flowchart presented in figure 18.2 outlines the main steps managers should take to evaluate organizational information. This figure suggests that the first major

Figure 18.3 Characteristics that tend to limit the usefulness of information and how to eliminate them.

Characteristics That Tend to Limit the Usefulness of Information	Possible Actions to Eliminate These Characteristics*
Language and/or format not understood	Translate, revise, or change format
Volume excessive: Time required to examine information exceeds the intuitive estimate of the value of the contents	Condense
Received before need perceived	Store for possible future need
Received after needed	Insure against future occurrence
Inaccessible	Create access
Time or cost of access excessive	Relocate data, change access
No right of use, or closed communication channels due to conflicting subunit goals, authority relationships, and so forth	Relocate information; alter or open transmission channels; change relationships

*The organization will incur some additional cost by taking one or more of these actions.

Roman R. Andrus, "Approaches to Information Evaluation," p. 45, *MSU Business Topics*, Summer 1971. Reprinted by permission of the publisher, Division of Research, Graduate School of Business Administration, Michigan State University.

step in evaluating organizational information is determining the value of that information. According to the flowchart, managers should determine the value of organizational information by pinpointing the data to be analyzed and then determining the expected value or return to be received from obtaining perfect information based on this data. Next, this expected value should be reduced by the amount of benefit that will not be realized because of deficiencies and inaccuracies expected to appear in the information.

The second major step in evaluating organizational information is comparing the expected value of organizational information with the expected cost of obtaining that information. If the expected cost does not exceed the expected value, the information should be gathered. If, however, the expected cost of gathering information does exceed its expected value, managers either must increase its expected value or decrease its expected cost before the gathering of the information can be justified. If neither of these objectives are possible, management cannot justify gathering the information.

Expected Value of Information vs. Expected Cost

One generally accepted strategy managers can adopt to increase the expected value of information is to eliminate those characteristics of the information that tend to limit its usefulness. Figure 18.3 shows characteristics of information that tend to limit its usefulness and possible action that management can take to eliminate these characteristics.

Back to the Case

Jack Wilkenson's analysis of the status of organizational information at Mega-Systems definitely should include a determination of whether or not all the information furnished to Mega-Systems managers can be justified. To make this determination Wilkenson should compare the value of this information with its cost. If its value is greater than its cost, the present information received by managers can be justified. If its cost is greater than its value, however, the present process of furnishing information should be modified, and Greenberg's inference that managers are receiving too much control-related information would be valid. Wilkenson also should consider the possibility of increasing the value of organizational information by increasing its usefulness.

Figure 18.4 Computer operations that assist management in handling information.

Operation	How a Computer Can Aid Managers
Billing	Control of buying, inventory, selling; rapid paying cycle; improved cash position; data about customers, products, items, costs, prices, sales representatives, sales statistics
Accounts receivable	Shorten average collections of accounts receivables; highlight past due statements, improve cash flow, invoice summary
Sales analysis	Review sales volume on the basis of profit contributions as well as gross profit contribution; compute sales representatives' commission plans; pinpoint sales improvement for customers and sales representatives
Inventory	Provide control of inventory, generation of distribution-by-value report; i.e., quantity sold annual sales are accumulated and printed as percentage of total number of items and total annual sales; pinpoint marginal items; segment inventory; establish order quantities and order points; cycle reviewing of vendor lines
Payroll	Construct payroll accounting system; produce reports to management, employees, government agencies; reduce peak workloads, strengthen managerial control over human resources
Materials planning	Determine components requirements; plan inventory per item by time period; determine how change in order quantity or delivery will affect production schedule; consolidate requirements of multiple-use items; reduce materials planning costs
Purchasing	Provide performance figures by item, supplier, and buyer in terms of cost, quality, and delivery; achieve tangible savings by meeting discount dates through faster processing of invoices; simplify analysis of historical data; expedite purchase orders based on production shortages and late deliveries
Dispatching and shop-floor control	Reduce expediting costs because job status records are current; give early notification of exceptions requiring corrective action plus daily revisions of order priority by machine group
Capacity planning and operation scheduling	Make available labor requirements by time period in time to take corrective action; immediate information about effect of changes on work orders, simplified planning on availability of tools, realistic order release dates

Reprinted from IRON AGE, March 30, 1972.

Computer Assistance in Using Information

What Is a Computer?

Managers have an overwhelming amount of data to gather, analyze, and transform into information before making numerous decisions. Materials distributed by the Xerox corporation indicate that American businesses currently have more than 324 billion documents to generate annually, and this number is increasing by 72 billion each year.[6] A computer is a tool managers can use to assist in the complicated and time-consuming task of generating this information. A **computer** can be defined as an electronic tool capable of accepting data, interpreting data, performing ordered operations on data, and reporting on the outcome of these operations.

Value of a Computer

In general terms, Joseph D. Wessekamper, a director of the Haskins and Sells computer services department,* indicates that computers give managers the ability to store vast amounts of financial, inventory, and other data so that it is readily accessible for making day-to-day decisions.[7] Figure 18.4 complements Wessekamper's more general statement by listing several more specific operations computers can perform to assist management in handling information. In addition, as exhibit 18 implies, some

*The company has recently been renamed Deloitte Haskins and Sells.

Figure 18.5 Relationship among the five main functions of a computer.

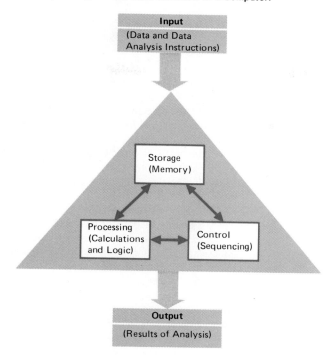

companies may be able to save on building costs and overhead costs by having employees work with computers in their homes. The following sections discuss (1) the main functions of a computer and (2) possible pitfalls in using a computer.

Main Functions of a Computer

A computer function is a computer activity that must be performed to generate organizational information. Computers perform five main functions: (1) the input function, (2) the storage function, (3) the control function, (4) the processing function, and (5) the output function. The relationships among these functions are shown in figure 18.5. The following paragraphs define each of these functions and also explain the relationships among them.

Computer Activities

Input Function

The **input function** consists of computer activities whereby the computer enters the data to be analyzed and the instructions to be followed to analyze that data appropriately. As figure 18.5 implies, the purpose of the input function is to provide data and instructions to be used in the performance of the storage, processing, control, and output functions.

Getting Material into the Computer

Storage Function

The **storage function** consists of computer activities involved with retaining the material entered into the computer during the performance of the input function. The storage unit, or "memory", of a computer is similar to the human memory in that various facts can be stored until they are needed for processing. In addition, facts can be stored, used in processing, and then restored as many times as necessary. As figure 18.5 implies, the performance of storage, processing, and control activities are dependent on one another and ultimately yield computer output. The following sections further describe the scope of this dependency.

Retaining Material Which Has Been Input

Exhibit 18

Terrence Howard Works from Home

Terrance Howard (Photo: J. Wilson, © 1981 *Newsweek*)

Gigi Howard, 10, was puzzled. For several hours each day, her father, Terrence, sat before a computer terminal in the Howard home in San Rafael, Calif. Gigi's young friends figured her dad had lost his job—a reasonable assumption since their fathers rushed to work each morning in three-piece suits while Howard lounged around the house in jogging shorts or other casual attire. "I think Gigi thought I was playing electronic blackjack all day long," said her father.

But Howard soon explained to his daughter that he had lost neither his job nor his mind. In fact, he is a pioneer in what some experts see as a new revolution in the American workplace. With the aid of computers and other sophisticated electronic gear, stockbroker Howard and hundreds of other workers are "telecommuters"—performing the jobs at home that they used to do at the office. Several large companies, including Control Data Corp., Continental Illinois National Bank and Arthur D. Little, Inc., a management-consultant firm, now offer a telecommuting option to some employees, and dozens of others are experimenting with the idea.

So far, telecommuting is limited mostly to jobs that can be performed efficiently without co-workers—for example, typists, brokers, computer programmers and statisticians. For them, working at home has obvious advantages. Terrence Howard, for instance, saves three hours a day in bumper-to-bumper commuting time. "It now takes me one minute to get to work," he says. Using the telephone and his computer he can contact customers, keep track of the market and place buy and sell orders from home as efficiently as he did at the office. He calculates that he saves about $500 a month on lunches, commuting and parking costs and the tax write-off he gets for using his home as an office.

Pat Kelly, a 43-year-old suburban-Chicago mother of three, takes dictation from Continental Illinois executives over a special telephone hookup, then types it back on her computer terminal. She corrects mistakes, then transmits the letter to the bank's electronic mail system. "There is nothing I dislike about this job," she says, "I like being here when my children come home from school and I don't miss the hustle and bustle of the city." Maxine Mesinger, a gossip columnist for The Houston Chronicle, sends in her column to the office each night on a home computer, and when she is out of town she transmits her copy on a portable "Silent 700" computer made by Texas Instruments. "I haven't been to work for twelve years," she says.

'Lonely': Telecommuting is not for everyone, of course. Sophie Wojcik, a word processor who was one of the first telecommuters at Continental Illinois, decided to return to the office after two years at home. "At first it was kind of nice," she recalls, "but after a while it got lonely. I missed talking to people at lunch and breaks and going out with the girls." And occasionally, crises at home can interfere: Terrence Howard once had to interrupt an important stock deal while he broke up a fight between the family cat and dog.

Managers also stress some obvious limitations. Ronald A. Manning is general manager of office technologies at Control Data, which employs a number of telecommuters itself and also markets a program for others, utilizing disabled persons. "Management today is not typically trained to handle the employee who is out of sight," he says. "The normal manager is comforted by the fact that he can see his employees, talk to them and see them working hard." There are other problems as well. Control Data's telecommuters, for example, can set their own hours. "What happens if an employee gets up at 3 a.m. and decides to do some work but trips over the cat on his way to the computer terminal?" Manning asks. "Should he be covered by workmen's compensation?"

But the pluses of telecommuting seem to outweigh the minuses. The limited evaluation of existing programs that Control Data has done indicates that 80 per cent of the managers favor the concept. In years to come, there is little doubt that more and more wives will discover they married their husbands not only for better or for worse—but for lunch as well.

TOM NICHOLSON with PAMELA ABRAMSON in San Francisco, DONNA FOOTE in Chicago and DIANE WEATHERS in Boston.

From: "Commuting By Computer," *Newsweek,* 4 May 1981, pp. 58, 61. Copyright 1981 by Newsweek, Inc. All Rights Reserved. Reprinted by Permission.

Processing Function

The **processing function** consists of the computer activities involved with performing both logic and calculation steps necessary to analyze data appropriately. Calculation activities include virtually any numerical analysis. Logic activities include such analysis as comparing one number to another to determine which is larger. Data, as well as directions for processing the data, are furnished by input and storage activities.

Control Function

Computer activities that dictate the order in which other computer functions are performed comprise the **control function.** Control activities indicate (1) when data should be retrieved after it has been stored, (2) when and how this data should be analyzed, (3) if and when the data should be stored after analysis has been performed, (4) if and when additional data should be retrieved, and (5) when output activities, as described in the next section, should begin and end.

Output Function

The **output function** is comprised of those activities that take the results of the input, storage, processing, and control functions and transmit them outside of the computer. These results can appear in such diversified forms as data on punched computer cards or words typed on paper tapes. Obviously, the form in which output should appear primarily is determined by how the output is to be used. Output that appears on punched computer cards, for example, can be used as input for another computer analysis but would be of little value for analysis by human beings.

Materials Requirements Planning: A Computer Application

The previous section depicts the computer as a sophisticated piece of equipment capable of performing the functions of input, storage, processing, control, and output. This section discusses **materials requirements planning (MRP)** as one area in which the use of computers continues to grow in order to increase the effectiveness and efficiency of the organizational production. The MRP process entails creating schedules that identify the specific parts and materials required to produce an item, the exact quantities of each needed to enhance the organizational production process, and the dates when orders for these quantities should be released to suppliers and be received for best timing within the production cycle.[8]

Figure 18.6 shows the main elements of a materials requirement planning system. As you can see from this figure, the computer is an important part of the MRP process. Input data for the computer comes from three main sources: (1) a master production schedule based on orders from consumers, sales forecasts, or product demand, and plant capacity; (2) a bill of material file that considers product design changes in determining the types and quantities of material needed within the production process; and (3) an inventory file that contains types and quantities of materials presently on

Figure 18.6 Basic elements of a material requirements planning (MRP) system.

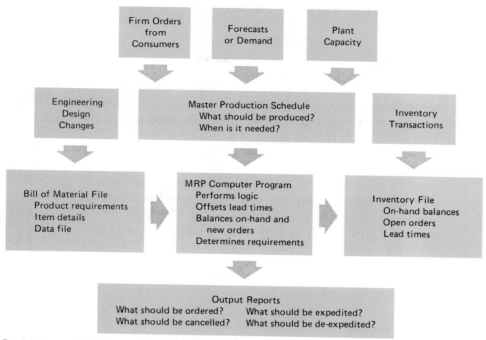

hand. The computer then performs the interdependent functions of storage, processing, and control in order to generate output reports. These reports indicate what materials should be ordered or cancelled as well as what materials should be expedited or de-expedited.

The usefulness of the computer in generating MRP information that is critical to maintaining production becomes greater as the MRP process becomes more involved due to the production of more complex products. In order to maintain this usefulness, however, managers must avoid the potential pitfall of inputting inaccurate data into the computer that results in invalid output reports and damaging managerial decisions based on these reports.[9] The following section discusses more potential pitfalls in using a computer.

Possible Problem with Computers and MRP

Possible Pitfalls in Using a Computer

The computer is a sophisticated management tool with the potential of making a significant contribution to organizational success. For this potential to materialize, however, the following possible pitfalls should be avoided:

1. *Thinking that a computer is capable of independently performing creative activities* A computer is only capable of following precise and detailed instructions provided by the computer user. The individual using the computer must tell the computer exactly what to do, how to do it, and when to do it. One computer expert describes his working with a computer as follows:

It's like talking to a moron. You have to tell it every little detail . . . When I was working my way through college, I used to work in a laundry. One of the boys . . . there had very low intelligence. I could say, "Jimmy, go over to the bench and pick

Computers Are Not Self-Directed

up that empty bucket and bring it to me." Jimmy would do it. But, if he found that the bucket was full of water instead of empty, he would become very confused. So I would have to tell him to take it to the sink and pour the water out. The trouble was that I had left out a step in his instructions, and he didn't have the ability to think what to do. It's the same with machines.[10]

Using Computers Is Expensive

2. *Spending too much money on computer assistance*[11]   In general, computers can be of great assistance to managers. The initial cost of purchasing a computer as well as updating it when necessary, however, can be very high.[12] Managers need to compare continually the benefit obtained from computer assistance with the cost of obtaining this assistance. A. R. Zipf makes the point (and the cartoon illustrates it) that this comparison can help managers to eliminate the seeming desire of many organization members to purchase computer time simply to "play with a new toy."[13]

People Determine the Worth of Computer Output

3. *Overestimating the value of computer output*   Some managers fall into the trap of assuming that they have "the answer" once they have received information generated by computer analysis. Managers must recognize that computer output is only as good as the quality of data and directions for analyzing that data that human beings have put into the computer. Inaccurate data or inappropriate computer instructions will yield useless computer output. A commonly used phrase to describe such an occurrence is "garbage in—garbage out."

Back to the Case

Part of Wilkenson's investigation of the status of information at Mega-Systems should include an analysis of the company's present computer assistance in handling information. Not only should the computer be storing and processing data related to performing the control function at Mega-Systems, but it also should be handling additional operations related to areas such as payroll, sales analysis, billing, and purchasing. To encourage wise use of Mega-Systems' computer, Wilkenson should tell organization members using the computer to keep in mind that a computer is not capable of performing creatively, that the benefits of using a computer should be greater than the costs of using it, and that computer output should be scrutinized carefully and not used as "the answer."

Management Information System (MIS)

In simple terms, a **management information system (MIS)** is a network established within an organization to provide managers with information that will assist them in decision making. The following more complete definition of an MIS has been developed by the Management Information System Committee of the Financial Executives Institute:

Getting Information Where Needed

An MIS is a system designed to provide selected decision-oriented information needed by management to plan, control, and evaluate the activities of the corporation. It is designed within a framework that emphasizes profit planning, performance planning, and control at all levels. It contemplates the ultimate integration of required business information subsystems, both financial and nonfinancial, within the company.[14]

The title of the specific organization member responsible for developing and maintaining an MIS varies from organization to organization. In smaller organizations a president or vice-president may possess this responsibility. In larger organizations, an individual with a title such as director of information systems may be solely responsible for appropriately managing an entire MIS department. The term *MIS manager* is used in the following sections to indicate that person within the organization who has the primary responsibility for managing the MIS. The term *MIS personnel* is used to designate those nonmanagement individuals within the organization who possess the primary responsibility of actually operating the MIS. Examples of these nonmanagement individuals could be computer operators and computer programmers.

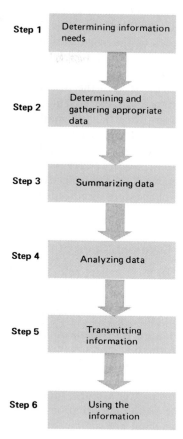

Step 1	Determining information needs
Step 2	Determining and gathering appropriate data
Step 3	Summarizing data
Step 4	Analyzing data
Step 5	Transmitting information
Step 6	Using the information

MIS managers must establish an effective MIS within their organizations. The following sections describe an MIS more fully and outline the steps managers take to establish an MIS.

Describing the MIS

The MIS is perhaps best described by summarizing the steps necessary to properly operate an MIS and by discussing the different kinds of information various managers need to make job-related decisions.

Operating the MIS

MIS personnel generally perform six sequential and distinct steps to properly operate an MIS.[15] The first of these steps is to determine what information is needed within the organization, when it will be needed, and in what form it will be needed. Since the basic purpose of the MIS is to assist management in making decisions, one way to begin determining management information needs is to analyze (1) decision areas in which management makes decisions, (2) specific decisions within these decision areas that management actually must make, and (3) alternatives that must be evaluated in order to make these specific decisions. As an example, figure 18.8 presents such an analysis for the manager making decisions related to production and operation management.

What Information Is Needed

The second major step in operating the MIS is pinpointing and collecting data that will yield needed organizational information. This step is just as important as determining the information needs of the organization. If data collected do not relate properly to information needs, it will be impossible to generate needed information.

After the information needs of the organization have been determined and appropriate data have been pinpointed and gathered, summarizing the data and analyzing the data are, respectively, the third and fourth steps MIS personnel generally should take to properly operate an MIS. It is in the performance of these steps that MIS personnel find computer assistance of great benefit.

The last two steps are transmitting the information generated by data analysis to appropriate managers and having managers actually use the information. The performance of these last two steps results in managerial decision making.

Although each of these six steps is necessary if an MIS is to run properly, the time spent on performing each step naturally will vary from organization to organization. Figure 18.7 summarizes each of the steps discussed and indicated the sequential order in which they generally are performed.

Different Managers Need Different Kinds of Information

For maximum benefit, an MIS must collect relevant data, transform that data into appropriate information, and transmit that information to appropriate managers. Appropriate information for one manager within an organization, however, may not be appropriate information for another. Robert G. Murdick suggests that the degree of appropriateness of MIS information for a manager depends on the activities for which the manager will use the information, the organizational objectives assigned to the manager, and the level of management at which the manager functions.[16] All of these factors, of course, are closely related.

Murdick's thoughts on this matter are best summarized in figure 18.9. As can be seen from this figure, since the overall job situations of top management, middle management, and first-line management are significantly different, the types of information these managers need to satisfactorily perform their jobs also are significantly different.

Back to the Case

Wilkenson's analysis of the status of information at Mega-Systems should include an assessment of the MIS within the organization. The MIS at Mega-Systems is the organizational network established to provide managers with information that helps them to make job-related decisions. In assessing the MIS, Wilkenson should check to see that activities performed by MIS personnel include determining information needs at Mega-Systems, determining and collecting appropriate Mega-Systems data, summarizing and analyzing these data, transmitting analyzed data to appropriate Mega-Systems managers, and having managers actually use received MIS information. Wilkenson also should check to see if information sent to managers through the MIS is appropriate for their respective levels within the organization.

Establishing an MIS

A discussion of management information systems would be incomplete without some mention of how to establish an MIS within an organization. The process of establishing an MIS can be broken down into four stages: (1) planning for the MIS, (2) designing the MIS, (3) implementing the MIS, and (4) improving the MIS. Each of these stages is discussed in the following sections.

Figure 18.8 Decision areas, decisions, and alternatives related to managing production and operation management.

Decision Area	Decision	Alternatives
Plant and equipment	Span of process	Make or buy
	Plant size	One big plant or several smaller ones
	Plant location	Locate near markets or locate near materials
	Investment decisions	Invest mainly in buildings or equipment or inventories or research
	Choice of equipment	General-purpose or special-purpose equipment
	Kind of tooling	Temporary, minimum tooling or "production tooling"
Production planning and control	Frequency of inventory taking	Few or many breaks in production for buffer stocks
	Inventory size	High inventory or a lower inventory
	Degree of inventory control	Control in great detail or in lesser detail
	What to control	Controls designed to minimize machine downtime or labor cost or time in process, or to maximize output of particular products or material usage
	Quality control	High reliability and quality or low costs
	Use of standards	Formal or informal or none at all
Labor and staffing	Job specialization	Highly specialized or not highly specialized
	Supervision	Technically trained first-line supervisors or nontechnically trained supervisors
	Wage system	Many job grades or few job grades; incentive wages or hourly wages
	Supervision	Close supervision or loose supervision
	Industrial engineers	Many or few such men
Product design/engineering	Size of product line	Many customer specials or few specials or none at all
	Design stability	Frozen design or many engineering change orders
	Technological risk	Use of new processes unproved by competitors or follow-the-leader policy
	Engineering	Complete packaged design or design-as-you-go approach
	Use of manufacturing engineering	Few or many manufacturing engineers
Organization and management	Kind of organization	Functional or product focus or geographical or other
	Executive use of time	High involvement in investment or production planning or cost control or quality control or other activities
	Degree of risk assumed	Decisions based on much or little information
	Use of staff	Large or small staff group
	Executive style	Much or little involvement in detail; authoritarian or nondirective style; much or little contact with organization

Figure 18.9 Appropriate MIS information under various sets of organizational circumstances.

Organizational Level	Type of Management	Manager's Organizational Objectives	Appropriate Information from MIS	How MIS Information Is Used
1. Top management	CEO, president, vice-president	Survival of the firm, profit growth, accumulation and efficient use of resources	Environmental data and trends, summary reports of operations, "exception reports" of problems, forecasts	Corporate objectives, policies, constraints, decisions on strategic plans, decisions on control of the total company
2. Middle management	Middle managers such as marketing, production, and financial	Allocation of resources to assigned tasks, establishment of plans to meet operating objectives, control of operations	Summaries and exception reports of operating results, corporate objectives, policies, constraints, decisions on strategic plans, relevant actions and decisions of other middle managers	Operating plans and policies, exception reports, operating summaries, control procedures, decisions on resource allocations, actions and decisions related to other middle managers
3. First-line management	First-line managers whose work is closely related	Production of goods to meet marketing needs, supplying budgets, estimates of resource requirements, movement and storage of materials	Summary reports of transactions, detailed reports of problems, operating plans and policies, control procedures, actions and decisions of related first-line managers	Exception reports, progress reports, resource requests, dispatch orders, cross-functional reports

Adapted from Robert G. Murdick, "MIS for MBO," *Journal of Systems Management*, March 1977, pp. 34–40. Used with permission of *Journal of Systems Management*, 24587 Bagley Road, Cleveland, Ohio 44138.

Planning for the MIS

Why Plan for an MIS?

Perhaps the most important stage of establishing an MIS is the planning stage. Commonly cited factors that make planning for the establishment of an MIS an absolute necessity are the typically long periods of time needed to acquire MIS-related data-processing equipment and to integrate it within the operation of the organization, the difficulty of hiring competent personnel to operate the equipment, and the major amounts of financial and managerial resources typically needed to operate an MIS.[17]

A Checklist for MIS Plans

These factors establish the need to plan for the establishment of an MIS within an organization. The specific form such plans take will vary from organization to organization. However, a checklist of topics that should be addressed in all such plans is presented in figure 18.10. In general, the more of the topics on this checklist that an MIS plan thoroughly addresses, the greater the probability the plan will be successful.

A sample plan for the establishment of an MIS at General Electric is shown in figure 18.11. This particular plan, of course, is abbreviated. Much more detailed outlines of each of the areas in this plan would be needed before it could be implemented. It is interesting to note that this plan includes a point (about a third of the way down the figure) at which management must decide if there is enough potential benefit to be gained from the existence of the MIS to continue the process of establishing it. This particular plan specifies that if management decides that there is not sufficient potential benefit to be gained by establishing the MIS, given its total costs, the project should be terminated.

Figure 18.10 Checklist for the contents of an MIS plan.

1. *Introduction*
   a. Summary of major goals, a statement of their consistency with corporate goals, and current state of planning vis-à-vis these goals
   b. Summary of aggregate cost and savings projections
   c. Summary of human resources requirements
   d. Major challenges and problems
   e. Criteria for assigning project priorities
2. *Project Identification*
   a. Maintenance projects, all projects proposed, and development projects
   b. Estimated completion times
   c. Human resources requirements, by time period and job category
   d. Computer capacity needed for system testing and implementation
   e. Economic justification by project — development costs, implementation costs, running costs, out-of-pocket savings, intangible savings
   f. Project control tools
   g. Tie-ins with other systems and master plans
3. *Hardware Projections (Derived from Projects)*
   a. Current applications — work loads and compilation and testing requirements
   b. New applications — work loads and reruns
   c. Survey of new hardware, with emphasis on design flexibility which will allow the company to take full advantage of new developments in hardware and in software
   d. Acquisition strategy, with timing contingencies
   e. Facilities requirements and growth, in hardware, tape storage, offices, and supplies
4. *Human Resources Projections (Derived from Projects)*
   a. Human resources needed by month for each category
      1. General — management, administrative, training, and planning personnel
      2. Developmental — application analysts, systems designers, methods and procedures personnel, operating system programmers, and other programmers
      3. Operational — machine operators, key punchers/verifiers, and input/output control clerks
   b. Salary levels, training needs, and estimated turnover
5. *Financial Projections by Time Period*
   a. Hardware rental, depreciation, maintenance, floor space, air conditioning, and electricity
   b. Human resources — training and fringe benefits
   c. Miscellaneous — building rental, outside service, telecommunications, and the like

Reprinted by permission of the *Harvard Business Review*, from "Problems in Planning the Information System," by F. Warren McFarlan (March–April 1971). Copyright © 1971 by the President and Fellows of Harvard College; all rights reserved.

Designing the MIS

Although data-processing equipment is normally an important ingredient of management information systems, the designing of an MIS should not begin with a comparative analysis of various types of such equipment available. Many MIS managers mistakenly think that data-processing equipment and an MIS are synonymous.

Stoller and Van Horn indicate that since the purpose of an MIS is to provide information that will assist managers in making better decisions, the designing of an MIS should begin with an analysis of the types of decisions managers actually make in a particular organization.[18] These authors suggest that designing an MIS should consist of four steps: (1) defining various decisions that must be made to run an organization, (2) determining the types of existing management policies that may influence the ways in which these decisions should be made, (3) pinpointing the types of data needed to make these decisions, and (4) establishing a mechanism for gathering and appropriately processing this data to obtain needed information.[19]

Designing an MIS Stresses Decision Making

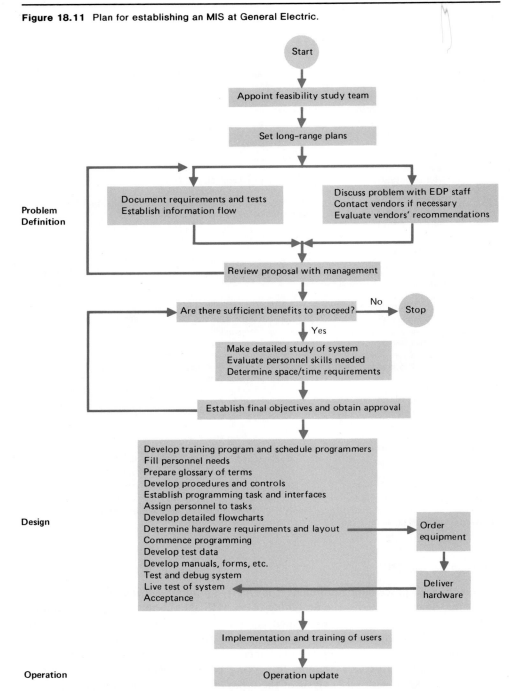

Figure 18.11 Plan for establishing an MIS at General Electric.

Start

Appoint feasibility study team

Set long-range plans

**Problem
Definition**

Document requirements and tests
Establish information flow

Discuss problem with EDP staff
Contact vendors if necessary
Evaluate vendors' recommendations

Review proposal with management

Are there sufficient benefits to proceed? — No → Stop

Yes

Make detailed study of system
Evaluate personnel skills needed
Determine space/time requirements

Establish final objectives and obtain approval

Design

Develop training program and schedule programmers
Fill personnel needs
Prepare glossary of terms
Develop procedures and controls
Establish programming task and interfaces
Assign personnel to tasks
Develop detailed flowcharts
Determine hardware requirements and layout
Commence programming
Develop test data
Develop manuals, forms, etc.
Test and debug system
Live test of system
Acceptance

Order equipment

Deliver hardware

Implementation and training of users

Operation

Operation update

From R. E. Breen et al., *Management Information Systems, A Subcommittee Report on Definitions* (Schenectady, N.Y.: General Electric Co., 1969), p. 21.

Implementing the MIS

Putting the MIS into Action

The third stage in the process of establishing an MIS within an organization is implementation, that is, putting the planned for and designed MIS into operation. In this stage the equipment is acquired and integrated into the organization. Designated data

Figure 18.12 Symptoms of an inadequate MIS.

Operational	Psychological	Report Content
Large physical inventory adjustments	Surprise at financial results	Excessive use of tabulations of figures
Capital expenditure overruns	Poor attitude of executives about usefulness of information	Multiple preparation and distribution of identical data
Inability of executives to explain changes from year to year in operating results	Lack of understanding of financial information on part of nonfinancial executives	Disagreeing information from different sources
Uncertain direction of company growth	Lack of concern for environmental changes	Lack of periodic comparative information and trends
Cost variances unexplainable	Executive homework reviewing reports considered excessive	Lateness of information
No order backlog awareness		Too little or excess detail
No internal discussion of reported data		Inaccurate information
Insufficient knowledge about competition		Lack of standards for comparison
Purchasing parts from outside vendors when internal capability and capacity to make is available		Lack of standards for comparison
Record of some "sour" investments in facilities, or in programs such as R&D and advertising		Failure to identify variances by cause and responsibility
		Inadequate externally generated information

Reprinted by permission of the Institute of Management Services from Bertram A. Colbert, "The Management Information System," *Management Services* 4, no. 5 (September–October 1967): 15–24.

is gathered, analyzed as planned, and distributed to appropriate managers within the organization. And line managers are making decisions based on the information they receive from the MIS.

Improving the MIS

Once the MIS is operating, MIS managers continually should strive to maximize its value. The following two sections provide insights on how MIS improvements might be made.

Making an MIS Better

Symptoms of an Inadequate MIS

To improve an MIS, MIS managers must first find symptoms or signs that the existing MIS is inadequate. A list of such symptoms, which has been developed by Bertram A. Colbert, a principal of Price Waterhouse & Company, is presented in figure 18.12.[20]

Colbert divides these symptoms into three types: (1) operational symptoms, (2) psychological symptoms, and (3) report content symptoms. Operational symptoms and psychological symptoms relate, respectively, to the operation of the organization and the functioning of organization members. Report content symptoms relate to the actual makeup of information generated by the MIS.

Signs That an MIS Should Be Improved

Although symptoms in figure 18.12 are clues that an MIS is inadequate, the symptoms themselves may not actually pinpoint MIS weaknesses. Therefore, after such symptoms are detected by MIS managers, the managers usually must gather additional information to determine what MIS weaknesses exist. Answering questions such as the following probably would be of some help to MIS managers in determining these weaknesses.[21]

1. Where and how do managers get information?
2. Can managers make better use of their contacts to get information?
3. In what areas is managers' knowledge weakest, and how can they be given information to minimize these weaknesses?
4. Do managers tend to act before receiving information?
5. Do managers wait so long for information that opportunities pass them by and the organization becomes bottlenecked?

Typical Improvements to an MIS

Inadequacies of management information systems vary from situation to situation, depending on such factors as the quality of an MIS plan, the appropriateness of an MIS design, and the type of individuals operating an MIS. However, several activities have the potential of improving the MIS of most organizations. These activities include:

Build Cooperation

1. *Building cooperation among MIS personnel and line managers*[22] Cooperation of this sort encourages line managers to give MIS personnel honest opinions of the quality of information being received. Through this type of interaction MIS designers and operators should be able to improve the effectiveness of an MIS.

Stress Decision Making

2. *Constantly stressing that MIS personnel should strive to accomplish the purpose of the MIS: providing managers with decision-related information* In this regard, it probably would be of great benefit to hold line managers responsible for continually educating MIS personnel on the types of decisions organization managers make and the corresponding steps taken to make these decisions. The better that MIS personnel understand the decision situations that face operating managers, the higher the probability that MIS information will be appropriate for decisions these managers must make.

Use Cost-Benefit Analysis

3. *Holding, wherever possible, both line managers and MIS personnel accountable for MIS activities on a cost-benefit basis*[23] This accountability reminds line managers and MIS personnel that the benefits the organization receives from MIS functions must exceed the costs. In effect, this accountability emphasis helps to increase the cost conscientiousness of both line managers and MIS personnel.

Consider People

4. *Operating an MIS in a "people conscientious" manner* An MIS, like the formal pyramidal organization, is based on the assumption that organizational affairs can and should be handled in a completely logical manner.[24] Logic, of course, is extremely important to the design and implementation of an MIS and never should be excluded from the MIS process. In addition, however, MIS activities also should include people considerations.[25] After all, even if MIS activities are well thought out and completely logical, an MIS can be ineffective simply because people do not use it as intended.

Resistance to Using an MIS

An example of a type of people problem related to the existence of an MIS can be found in a study conducted by Dickson and Simmons.[26] This study found several factors that can cause people to resist using an MIS. A summary of these factors according to working groups is presented in figure 18.13. This study implies that for managers to improve the effectiveness of an MIS, they may have to take steps to reduce such factors as threats to power and status that might be discouraging its use.

Figure 18.13 Causes for resistance to MIS working groups.

	Operating (Nonclerical)	Operating (Clerical)	Operating Management	Top Management
Threats to Economic Security		X	X	
Threats to Status or Power		X	X*	
Increased Job Complexity	X		X	X
Uncertainty or Unfamiliarity	X	X	X	X
Changed Interpersonal Relations or Work Patterns		X*	X	
Changed Superior–Subordinate Relationships		X*	X	
Increased Rigidity or Time Pressure	X	X	X	
Role Ambiguity		X	X*	X
Feelings of Insecurity		X	X*	X*

X = The reason is possibly the cause of resistance to MIS development.
X* = The reason has a strong possibility of being the cause of resistance.

Back to the Case

Mega-Systems presently has an MIS. Wilkenson, however, may be able to gain valuable insights on the status of information at Mega-Systems by evaluating the way in which the existing MIS was established. For example, Wilkenson should ask the following questions about the planning stage of Mega-Systems' MIS: (1) was appropriate data-processing equipment acquired and integrated? and (2) have appropriate personnel been acquired to operate the equipment? About the design and implementation stages of Mega-Systems' MIS, Wilkenson should seek answers to such questions as, (1) did the design of the present MIS begin with an analysis of managerial decision making? (2) does the present MIS exist as designed and implemented?

Wilkenson's assessment of the status of information at Mega-Systems also should include a determination of whether or not a conscientious effort to improve the organizational MIS is continually on the minds of MIS managers, other MIS personnel, and line managers. All such organization members should be aware of the symptoms that indicate that an MIS is inadequate and should attempt to pinpoint and eliminate corresponding MIS weaknesses once such symptoms are observed. Wilkenson also should consider the possibilities of improving his MIS by (1) building additional cooperation between MIS managers, MIS personnel, and line managers; (2) stressing that the purpose of the MIS is to provide managers with decision-related information; (3) using cost-benefit analysis to evaluate MIS activities; and (4) ensuring that the MIS operates in a people-conscientious manner.

The following points are stressed within this chapter:

Summary

1. Information can be defined as one or more conclusions drawn from data analysis.
2. The value of information is defined in terms of how much benefit can accrue to an organization through the use of the information. Information appropriateness, information quality, information timeliness, and information quantity are the main factors that determine the value of information.

3. Evaluation of information entails two major steps. First, the expected value of the information is determined. Second, the expected value of the information is compared with the expected cost of obtaining the information. Managers use this comparison to determine whether or not information should be obtained.

4. Computers perform input, storage, control, processing, and output functions in helping management to meet its information needs. Many managers have found great benefit in using a computer to solve problems related to materials requirements planning. For computers to be of maximum benefit to management, however, several potential pitfalls must be avoided.

5. An MIS is a network established primarily to furnish management with decision-related information that pertains to the operation of an organization. The proper operation of an MIS includes determining information needs, determining and collecting appropriate data, summarizing data, analyzing data, transmitting information, and using the information.

6. The steps necessary to establish an MIS within an organization include planning for the MIS, designing the MIS, implementing the MIS, and improving the MIS. The performance of each of these steps is critical in maintaining a useful MIS over the long run.

7. The quality of an MIS generally can be improved by building cooperation among MIS personnel and line managers, stressing decision-related information as the desired MIS output, employing a cost-benefit analysis of MIS activities whenever possible, and operating an MIS in a "people-conscientious" manner. The degree to which each of these activities improves an MIS, of course, depends on the specific organizational situation.

Issues for Review and Discussion

1. What is the difference between data and information?
2. List and define four major factors that influence the value of information.
3. What are operational control decisions and strategic planning decisions? What characterizes information appropriate for making each of these decisions?
4. Discuss the major activities involved in evaluating information.
5. What factors tend to limit the usefulness of information, and how can these factors be overcome?
6. Is a computer a flexible management tool? Explain.
7. How do the main functions of a computer relate to one another?
8. Summarize the major pitfalls managers must avoid when using a computer?
9. Explain how the computer can assist the manager in materials requirements planning.
10. Define an MIS and discuss its importance to management.
11. What steps must be performed to operate an MIS properly?
12. What major steps are involved in establishing an MIS?
13. Why is planning for an MIS such an important part of establishing an MIS?
14. Why does the designing of an MIS begin with analyzing managerial decision making?
15. How should managers use the symptoms of an inadequate MIS as listed in figure 18.12?
16. How could "building cooperation among MIS personnel and line managers" typically improve an MIS?
17. How can management use cost-benefit analysis to improve an MIS?
18. Describe five possible causes of resistance to using an MIS. What can managers do to ensure that these causes do not affect their organization's MIS?

Alexander, J. J. *Information Systems Analysis.* Palo Alto, Calif.: Science Research Associates, 1974.

Blumenthal, Sherman S. *Management Information Systems: A Framework for Planning and Development.* Englewood Cliffs, N.J.: Prentice-Hall, 1969.

Bocchino, William A. *Management Information Systems: Tools and Techniques.* Englewood Cliffs, N.J.: Prentice-Hall, 1972.

Boore, William F., and Murphy, G. *The Computer Sampler.* New York: McGraw-Hill, 1968.

Boutell, Wayne S. *Computer-Oriented Business Systems.* 2d ed. Englewood Cliffs, N.J.: Prentice-Hall, 1973.

Davis, Gordon B. *Management Information Systems: Conceptual Foundations, Structure, and Development.* New York: McGraw-Hill, 1974.

Greenwood, William T. *Decision Theory and Information Systems: An Introduction to Management Decision Making.* Cincinnati: South-Western Publishing, 1969.

Hodge, Bartow and Hodgson, Robert N. *Management and the Computer in Information and Control Systems.* New York: McGraw-Hill, 1969.

Kelly, Joseph F. *Computerized Management Information Systems.* New York: Macmillan, 1970.

Kindred, Alton R. *Data Systems and Management.* Englewood Cliffs, N.J.: Prentice-Hall, 1973.

Mockler, Robert J. *Information Systems for Management.* Columbus, Ohio: Charles E. Merrill Publishing, 1974.

Orlicky, Joseph A. *The Successful Computer System.* New York: McGraw-Hill, 1969.

Panko, Raymond R. "A Different Perspective On Office Systems." *Administrative Management* 42, no. 8 (August 1981): 30–32ff.

Reuter, Vincent G. "Utilization of Graphic Management Tools." *Arizona Business,* August/September 1978, pp. 10–19.

Sanders, Donald H. *Computers in Business.* 2d ed. New York: McGraw-Hill, 1972.

Staff. "The Spreading Danger of Computer Crime." *Business Week,* 20 April 1981, pp. 86–92.

Wagner, G. R. "Decision Support Systems: Computerized Mind Support for Executive Problems." *Managerial Planning* 30, no. 2 (September/October 1981): 3–8, 16.

Whisler, Thomas L. *Information Technology and Organizational Change.* Monterey, Calif.: Brooks/Cole Publishing, 1970.

Sources of Additional Information

1. Henry Mintzberg, "The Myths of MIS," *California Management Review,* Fall 1972, pp. 92–97.

2. Jay W. Forrester, "Managerial Decision Making," in *Management and the Computer of the Future,* ed. Martin Greenberger (Cambridge, Mass. and New York: MIT Press and John Wiley & Sons, 1962), p. 37.

3. The following discussion largely is based on Robert H. Gregory and Richard L. Van Horn, "Value and Cost of Information," in *Systems Analysis Techniques,* eds. J. Daniel Conger and Robert W. Knapp (New York: John Wiley & Sons, 1974), pp. 473–89.

4. G. Anthony Gorry and Michael S. Scott Morton, "A Framework for Management Information Systems," *Sloan Management Review* 13, no. 1 (Fall 1971): 55–70.

5. John T. Small and William B. Lee, "In Search of MIS," *MSU Business Topics,* Autumn 1975, pp. 47–55.

6. "A Wealth of Information Can Be Worthless," *Newsweek,* 7 August 1978, p. 28.

7. *H & S Reports: For the People of Haskins and Sells* 14, no. 4 (Autumn 1977): 28.

8. Richard B. Chase and Nicholas J. Aquilano, *Production and Operations Management: A Life Cycle Approach* (Homewood: Irwin Publishing Company, 1981), p. 516.

9. Robert W. Hall and Thomas E. Vollmann, "Planning Your Material Requirements," *Harvard Business Review,* September/October 1978, p. 107.

10. Robert Sanford, "Some Loose Talk about and with Computers," *Beehive* (United Aircraft Corporation), Fall 1960.

11. John Dearden and Richard L. Nolan, "How to Control the Computer Resource," *Harvard Business Review,* November/December 1973, pp. 68–78.

12. Martin D. J. Buss, "Penny-wise Approach to Data Processing," *Harvard Business Review,* July/August 1981, p. 111.

13. A. R. Zipf, "Retaining Mastery of the Computer," *Harvard Business Review,* September/October 1968, p. 70.

14. Robert W. Holmes, "Twelve Areas to Investigate for Better MIS," *Financial Executive,* July 1970, p. 24.

15. This section is based on Richard A. Johnson, R. Joseph Monsen, Henry P. Knowles, and Borge O. Saxberg, *Management, Systems, and Society: An Introduction* (Santa Monica, Calif.: Goodyear Publishing, 1976), pp. 113–20.

16. Robert G. Murdick, "MIS for MBO," *Journal of Systems Management,* March 1977, pp. 34–40.

17. F. Warren McFarlan, "Problems in Planning the Information System," *Harvard Business Review,* March/April 1971, p. 75.

18. David S. Stoller and Richard L. Van Horn, *Design of a Management Information System* (Santa Monica, Calif.: The Rand Corporation, 1958).

Notes

19. More detail on the design of an MIS can be found in Robert G. Murdick, "MIS Development Procedures," *Journal of Systems Management* 21, no. 12 (December 1970), pp. 22–26.

20. Bertram A. Colbert, "The Management Information System," *Management Services* 4, no. 5 (September/October 1967): 15–24.

21. Adapted from Henry Mintzberg, "The Manager's Job: Folklore and Fact," *Harvard Business Review,* July/August 1975, p. 58.

22. William R. King and David I. Cleland, "Manager-Analysts Teamwork in MIS," *Business Horizons* 14, no. 2 (April 1971): 59–68.

23. Regina Herzlinger, "Why Data Systems in Nonprofit Organizations Fail," *Harvard Business Review,* January/February 1977, pp. 81–86.

24. Chris Argyris, "Management Information Systems: The Challenge of Rationality and Emotionality," *Management Science,* February 1971, pp. 275–92.

25. Robert W. Holmes, "Developing Better Management Information Systems," *Financial Executive* 38, no. 7 (July 1970): 24–31.

26. G. W. Dickson and John K. Simmons, "The Behavioral Side of MIS," *Business Horizons,* August 1970, pp. 59, 71.

Concluding Case 18
Waterloo Revisited: John Deere's Computer-Controlled Tractor Works

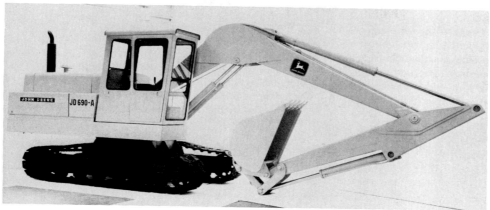

(Photo: Courtesy John Deere)

John Deere recently completed a new and innovative tractor factory in Waterloo, Iowa. The Waterloo John Deere Tractor Works consists of several facilities and includes approximately 16,000 employees. The new Tractor Works is the latest addition to the Waterloo factory and includes an office building, a Sound Gard body fabrication building, the tractor assembly building, a shipping facility, a receiving facility, an energy center, and a wheel manufacturing building.

The Waterloo Tractor Factory is a very innovative facility within the industry as it applies computer technology to the final assembly process. A computer network, which is part of a larger set of computer programs and applications, controls the entire Tractor Works Complex. Deere's investment in computer technology is for the purpose of increasing productivity in the design and manufacture of its products. This is done by a controlling computer network that interfaces with all of the assembly and inventory management functions.

The Tractor Works was designed and constructed around its computer control systems. Computers are used to control receiving and storage of materials, delivery of parts to the assembly lines through systems such as the interbuilding overhead conveyors, and the assembly operations. Computer control of these processes is not unique. However, the Tractor Works serves data processing and business management functions in addition to process control; therein lies the innovativeness of the system.

Ten minicomputers and a large centralized mainframe communicate with each other through a computerized network. Parts are requested from inventory, pulled out for delivery, and delivered. In the meantime, other computers are notified the parts are coming, replenishing inventory as required. Build orders are issued for sub-assemblies and

components. Assembly lines are integrated so that the appropriate part arrives at the proper time. Furthermore, the computers maintain accurate records of the entire process.

The parts system operates in the following manner. Parts to support sub-assembly and assembly lines enter the receiving building. The delivery of these purchased parts is made according to computer requests from the Sound Gard body, wheel manufacturing, and tractor assembly sections of the complex. As parts are received in each section, they are inspected, quantities are verified, and parts inventory records are updated. Finally, the parts are placed into a high-rise storage system by computer directed storage and retrieval cranes. The computer system is capable of monitoring the inventory placement in more than 16,000 storage locations.

Steel supplies for the forming of the bodies and appearance sheet metal are delivered to the Sound Gard body building. Sheet metal, press work, painting, and welding take place in this area. According to assembly requirements, steel supplies are pressed into the desired part forms. Finished press parts are placed in a high-rise storage retrieval system to supply the weld assembly lines as demanded. Manufacturing requirements are matched with raw materials orders by computers that communicate with computers at the welding and assembly stations.

The major chassis components (engines, transmissions, hydraulics, and four-wheel-drive front axles) are received at the tractor assembly building. They are manufactured in other Deere factories in the Waterloo area. Once received, they are placed in high-density rack storage under computer control and moved through the facility on a first-in, first-out basis. The computer maintains a two-day inventory to support factory build orders.

When assembly is initiated, computers start the retrieval of parts and components from storage, transfer them to the proper assembly point, and initiate inventory replacement requests. Computers continually communicate with each other to assure accurate inventories, rapid turnover of inventories, and finely meshed manufacturing schedules.

This case is adapted from "Computers Track Tractors as Deere Builds Them." *Data Management* 19, no. 11 (November 1981): 10–14. © Data Management Magazine. ALL RIGHTS RESERVED.

Discussion Issues

1. What operations is the computer system currently controlling?
2. What operations could be added to the computer's control?
3. During the assembly process that is initiated and controlled by the computer, what potential problems are found?
4. What is the primary function of the computer system?
5. How would the information John Deere uses for operational control differ from that needed for strategic planning? Explain.

Previous sections of this text have introduced the topic of management and presented detailed discussions of the four management functions: planning, organizing, influencing, and controlling. This last section furnishes a glimpse of what it will be like to manage in the future.

Chapter 19, "Social Responsibility," focuses on the responsibilities that managers of the future will have to society. Social responsibility is defined as the managerial obligation to take action that protects and improves the welfare of society as a whole along with organizational interests. Although there are arguments both for and against businesses meeting social responsibilities, it is hypothesized that managers of the future will spend more time dealing with social issues. Therefore, this chapter recommends that managers of the future strive to make organizations socially responsive and both effective and efficient in pursuing social responsibilities. The chapter concludes with the thoughts that managers of the future should plan, organize, influence, and control for social responsibility activities and that society should take positive steps to help businesses meet their social responsibilities.

Chapter 20, "Management Skills for the Future," discusses the skills that people of the future will need to be successful managers. The hypothesis is made that for individuals of the future to be successful as managers, they must possess the skills to apply both systems theory and functional theory to unique organizational situations. This chapter also predicts that the organizational situations of the future will be somewhat different in that the management systems will tend to be larger and more complicated and the work force will tend to be older and more deeply interested in such issues as quality of life and will contain more women managers. Energy, as known today, will be in short supply. The chapter concludes with a recommendation that training programs aimed at preparing managers for the future should stress that managers become future-oriented, approach the study of management as a profession, and bear in mind that the job of a manager is continually changing.

Section 6
Managing in the Future

Student Learning Objectives

From studying this chapter I will attempt to acquire:

1. An understanding of the term *social responsibility*

2. An appreciation for the arguments both for and against business assuming social responsibilities

3. Useful strategies for increasing the social responsiveness of an organization

4. Insights on the planning, organizing, influencing, and controlling of social responsibility activities

5. A practical plan for how society can help business to meet its social obligations

Chapter Outline

490

Social Responsibility

Introductory Case 19
Assisting the Handicapped

Nick Vicaro is president of Stylistics, a chain of thirty-six beauty shops spread out over Denver, Minneapolis, St. Louis, and New Orleans. Vicaro presently resides in Denver, the city in which company headquarters are located. By almost any criteria, Stylistics shops have been extremely successful over the past several years. In fact, Vicaro has just recently completed plans for opening seven new Stylistics shops in Baltimore in about six months.

It was Tuesday morning, and Vicaro had just arrived for work. Upon his arrival, his secretary handed him a special delivery envelope that had been delivered only twenty minutes earlier. Vicaro opened the envelope and began to read the following letter from a woman in St. Louis:

Mr. Nick Vicaro, President
Stylistics
1322 Manford Avenue
Denver, CO 80212

Dear Mr. Vicaro:

I have a special problem that I hope you can help me to solve. I live in the St. Louis area and hear nothing but fantastic comments about the beauticians you have in your shops in our city. I also hear very good things about how clean and well kept the shops themselves actually are.

My problem is that I am handicapped and am confined to a wheelchair. I can arrange transportation to and from any of your shops but cannot climb the several steps in front of each of them. From what I hear, it also would be difficult for me to have my hair washed in one of your basins, even if I could get into one of your shops. Friends also tell me that your shops are somewhat cramped and that there may be some areas where I would find it difficult to maneuver.

To solve my problem, I thought you might be able to install a ramp on the outside of your shops so that wheelchair customers like myself could enter your places of business. I also wonder if you can alter your equipment and facility somewhat so that individuals like myself can get hair washed and maneuver wheelchairs once within one of your establishments.

Thank you for your attention to this matter, and I hope you can make it easier for the handicapped to be your customers.

Sincerely yours,

Tiffany Ware

Tiffany Ware

When Vicaro had finished the letter, he was quite perplexed. All of Tiffany Ware's information about his beauty salons was accurate. He wondered, however, if he could or really should do anything about Tiffany Ware's problem.

Discussion Issues

1. Does Vicaro have a responsibility to make it possible for customers such as Ware to enter his beauty salons? Explain.
2. Assuming that Vicaro had such a responsibility, when would it be relatively easy for him to be committed to living up to it?
3. Assuming that Vicaro had such a responsibility, when would it be relatively difficult for him to be committed to living up to it?

What's Ahead

The introductory case ends with Nick Vicaro, the president of Stylistics, reflecting on a customer request to modify his beauty shops so that they are more easily accessible to the handicapped. This chapter presents material that a manager like Vicaro should understand to assess his social responsibility in this situation. Specifically, this chapter discusses (1) fundamentals of social responsibility, (2) social responsiveness, (3) social responsibility activities and management functions, and (4) how society can help business meet social obligations.

As the term *management,* the term *social responsibility* means different things to different people.[1] For purposes of this chapter **social responsibility** is defined as the managerial obligation to take action that protects and improves the welfare of society as a whole and also organizational interests.[2] The amount of attention given to the area of social responsibility by both management and society has increased in recent years and probably will continue to increase in the future.[3] The following sections present the fundamentals of social responsibility by discussing (1) the Davis model of social responsibility, (2) areas of social responsibility activity, and (3) varying opinions on social responsibility. Since the main thrust of recent social responsibility issues has focused primarily on business, this chapter focuses primarily on the social responsibility of business systems.

Fundamentals of Social Responsibility

Protect Interests of Society and Organization

The Davis Model of Social Responsibility

A generally accepted model of social responsibility was developed by Keith Davis.[4] Stated simply, Davis's model is a list of five propositions that describe why and how business should adhere to the obligation to take action that protects and improves the welfare of society and the organization. These propositions and corresponding explanations are:

Proposition 1: social responsibility arises from social power This proposition is built on the premise that business has a significant amount of influence or power over such critical social issues as minority employment and environmental pollution. In essence, the collective action of all business in the country mainly determines the proportion of minorities employed and the prevailing condition of the environment in which all citizens must live.

Building on this premise, Davis reasons that since business has this power over society, society can and must hold business responsible for social conditions that result from exercising this power.[5] Davis explains that society's legal system does not expect more of business than it does of each individual citizen exercising his or her own personal power.

Society Controls Business Power

Proposition 2: business shall operate as a two-way open system with open receipt of inputs from society and open disclosure of its operation to the public According to this proposition, business must be willing to listen to the representatives of society on what must be done to sustain or improve societal welfare. In turn, society must be willing

Society and Business Must Be Partners

to listen to the reports of business on what it is doing to meet its social responsibilities. Davis suggests that continuing, honest, and open communications between business and societal representatives must exist if the overall welfare of society is to be maintained or improved.

How Does Proposed Activity Affect Society?

Proposition 3: both social costs and benefits of an activity, product, or service shall be thoroughly calculated and considered to decide whether or not to proceed with it This proposition stresses that technical feasibility and economic profitability are not the only factors that should influence business decision making. Business also should consider both the long- and short-run societal consequences of all business activities before such activities are undertaken.

Society Must Ultimately Pay

Proposition 4: social costs related to each activity, product, or service shall be passed on to the consumer This proposition states that business cannot be expected to finance completely activities that may be economically disadvantageous but socially advantageous. The cost of maintaining socially desirable activities within business should be passed on to consumers through higher prices of the goods or services related to those socially desirable activities.

Help Others to Help Society

Proposition 5: business institutions, as citizens, have the responsibility to become involved in certain social problems that are outside of their normal areas of operation This last proposition makes the point that if a business possesses the expertise to solve a social problem with which it may not be directly associated, it should be held responsible for helping society to solve that problem. Davis reasons that since business eventually will share increased profit from a generally improved society, business should share in the responsibility of all citizenry to generally improve that society.

Back to the Case

Social responsibility is the obligation of a business manager to take action that protects and improves the welfare of society along with the interests of the organization. Nick Vicaro, the president of Stylistics beauty shops, presently is faced with an issue in the area of social responsibility. The material in this chapter up to this point implies that Vicaro should try to service Tiffany Ware while protecting and improving the interests of his company.

Following the logic of Davis's social responsibility model, Vicaro should attempt to service Ware because such an activity generally would help to improve society and thereby profit Vicaro as well as others. For example, with a new hairstyle from Stylistics, Ware might be able to get a job that would help her to make some additional contribution to society. Vicaro probably would profit from Ware's job as well because Ware would be able to return to the salon more often and might even recommend Stylistics to the people with whom she works.

The information presented thus far in this chapter also implies that Vicaro should decide what to do about Ware's situation by considering not only the technical feasibility and economic profitability of various actions, but also the possible effects of those actions on society as a whole. Of course, depending on what Vicaro actually does about this situation, the costs he would incur as a result of taking action would be passed on to his patrons. Obviously, he should not do so much that his prices are no longer competitive.

As a result of handling Ware's problem, Vicaro could acquire some expertise in the general area of assisting the handicapped. This expertise could benefit society if Vicaro shared it with businesspeople in other areas. For example, Vicaro might be able to help the president of another company make barber shops more accessible to handicapped customers.

Areas of Social Responsibility Activity

The areas in which business can become involved to protect and improve the welfare of society are numerous and diversified (see figure 19.1). Perhaps the most publicized of these areas are urban affairs, consumer affairs, and environmental affairs.[6]

Varying Opinions on Social Responsibility

Although numerous businesses are and will continue to perform social responsibility activities, much controversy persists about whether or not it is necessary or appropriate for them to do so. The following two sections present some of the arguments against and for businesses performing social responsibility activities.[7]

Arguments AGAINST Business Performing Social Responsibility Activities

The best-known argument against business performing social responsibility activities is advanced by Milton Friedman, one of America's most distinguished economists. Friedman argues that to make business managers simultaneously responsible to business owners for reaching profit objectives and to society for enhancing societal welfare represents a conflict of interest that has the potential to cause the demise of business as it is known today.[8] According to Friedman, this demise almost certainly will occur if business continually is forced to perform socially responsible behavior that is in direct conflict with private organizational objectives.[9]

Business Exists Mainly to Make Profits

Friedman also argues that to require business managers to pursue socially responsible objectives may in fact be unethical since it requires managers to spend money that really belongs to other individuals:

Social Responsibility and Ethics

> In a free enterprise, private property system, a corporate executive is an employee of the owners of the business. He has direct responsibility to his employers. That responsibility is to conduct the business in accordance with their desires, which generally will be to make as much money as possible while conforming to the basic rules of society, both those embodied in law and those embodied in ethical custom. . . . Insofar as his actions reduce returns to stockholders, he is spending their money. Insofar as his actions raise the price to customers, he is spending the customers' money.[10]

Arguments FOR Business Performing Social Responsibility Activities

The best-known argument supporting the performance of social responsibility activities by business was alluded to earlier in this chapter. This argument begins with the premise that business as a whole is a subset of society as a whole and exerts a significant impact on the way in which society exists. The argument continues that since business is such an influential member of society, it has the responsibility to help maintain and improve the overall welfare of society. After all, the argument goes, since society asks no more or no less of any of its members, why should business be exempt from such responsibility?

All Members of Society Must Maintain It

In addition, some make the argument that business should perform social responsibility activities because profitability and growth go hand in hand with responsible treatment of employees, customers, and the community. In essence, this argument implies that performing social responsibility activities is a means of earning greater organizational profit.[11]

Many more arguments for and against business performing social responsibility activities are presented in figure 19.2.

Figure 19.1 Major social responsibility areas in which business can become involved.

Categories of Social Responsibility Issues

Product Line

Internal standards for product
- Quality, e.g., does it last;
- Safety, e.g., can it harm users or children finding it?
- Disposal, e.g., is it biodegradable?
- Design, e.g., will its use or even "easy" misuse cause pain, injury, or death?

Average product life comparisons versus
- Competition
- Substitute products
- Internal standards or state-of-the-art regular built-in obsolescence

Product performance
- Efficacy, e.g., does it do what it is supposed to do?
- Guarantees/warranties, e.g., are guarantees sufficient, reasonable?
- Service policy
- Service availability
- Service pricing
- Utility

Packaging
- Environmental impact (degree of disposability; recycleability)
- Comparisons with competition (type and extent of packaging)

Marketing Practices

Sales practices
- Legal standards
- "Undue" pressure (a qualitative judgment)

Credit practices against legal standards

Accuracy of advertising claims—specific government complaints

Consumer complaints about marketing practices
- Clear explanation of credit terms
- Clear explanation of purchase price
- Complaint answering policy
  - Answered at all
  - Investigated carefully
  - Grievances redressed (and cost)
  - Remedial action to prevent future occurrences

Adequate consumer information on
- Product use, e.g., dosage, duration of use, etc.
- Product misuse

Fair pricing
- Between countries
- Between states
- Between locations

Packaging

Employee Education and Training

Policy on leaves of absence for
- Full-time schooling
- Courses given during working hours

Dollars spent on training
- Formal vocational training
- Training for disadvantaged worker
- OJT (very difficult to isolate)
- Tuition (job-related versus nonjob-related)
- Special upgrading and career development programs
- Compare versus competition

Special training program results (systematic evaluations)
- Number trained in each program per year
- Cost per trainee (less subsidy)
- Number or percent workers still with company

Plans for future programs

Career training and counseling

Failure rates

Extend personnel understanding
- Jobs
- Skills required later
- Incentive system now available
- Specific actions for promotion

Corporate Philanthropy

Contribution performance
- By category, for example:
  - Art
  - Education
  - Poverty
  - Health
  - Community development
  - Public service advertising
- Dollars (plus materials and work hours, if available)
  - As a percent of pretax earnings
  - Compared to competition

Selection criteria for contributions

Procedures for performance tracking of recipient institutions or groups

Programs for permitting and encouraging employee involvement in social projects
- On company time
- After hours only
- Use of company facilities and equipment
- Reimbursement of operating units for replaceable "lost" time
- Human resources support
  - Number of people
  - Work hours

Extent of employee involvement in philanthropy decision making

Environmental Control

Measurable pollution resulting from
- Acquisition of raw materials
- Production processes
- Products
- Transportation of intermediate and finished products

Violations of government (federal, state, and local) standards

Cost estimates to correct current deficiencies

Extent to which various plants exceed current legal standards, e.g., particulate matter discharged

Resources devoted to pollution control
- Capital expenditures (absolute and percent)
- R & D investments
- Personnel involved full time; part time
- Organizational "strength" of personnel involved

Competitive company performance, e.g., capital expenditures

Effort to monitor new standards as proposed

Programs to keep employees alert to spills and other pollution-related accidents

Procedures for evaluating environmental impact of new packages or products

External Relations

Community Development

Support of minority and community enterprises through
- Purchasing
- Subcontracting

Figure 19.1 (continued)

External Relations (continued)

Investment practices
- Ensuring equal opportunity before locating new facilities
- Identifying opportunities to serve community needs through business expansion (e.g., housing rehabilitation or teaching machines)
- Funds in minority banks

Government Relations

Specific input to public policy through research and analysis

Participation and development of business/government programs

Political contributions

Disclosure of Information/ Communications

Extent of public disclosure of performance by activity category

Measure of employee understanding of programs such as:
- Pay and benefits
- Equal opportunity policies and programs
- Position on major economic or political issues (as appropriate)

Relations/communications with constituencies such as stockholders, fund managers, major customers, and so on

International

Comparisons of policy and performance between countries and versus local standards

Employee Relations, Benefits, and Satisfaction with Work

Comparisons with competition (and/or national averages)
- Salary and wage levels
- Retirement plans
- Turnover and retention by level
- Profit sharing
- Day care and maternity
- Transportation
- Insurance, health programs, and other fringes
- Participation in ownership of business through stock purchases

Comparisons of operating units on promotions, terminations, hires against breakdowns of
- Age
- Sex
- Race
- Education level

Performance review system and procedures for communication with

employees whose performance is below average

Promotion policy—equitable and understood

Transfer policy

Termination policy (i.e., how early is "notice" given)

General working environment and conditions
- Physical surroundings
  - Heat
  - Ventilation
  - Space/person
  - Lighting
  - Air conditioning
  - Noise
- Leisure, recreation, cultural opportunities

Fringe benefits as a percent of salary for various salary levels

Evaluation of employee benefit preferences (questions can be posed as choices)

Evaluation of employee understanding of current fringe benefits

Union/industrial relations
- Grievances
- Strikes

Confidentiality and security of personnel data

Minority and Women Employment and Advancement

Current hiring policies in relation to the requirements of all affirmative action programs

Specific program of accountability for performance

Company versus local, industry, and national performance
- Number and percent minority and women employees hired by various job classifications over last five years
- Number and percent of new minority and women employees in last two to three years by job classification
- Minority and women and nonminority turnover
- Indictments for discriminatory hiring practices

Percent minority and women employment in major facilities relative to minority labor force available locally

Number of minority group and women members in positions of high responsibility

Promotion performance of minority groups and women

Specific hiring and job upgrading goals established for minority groups and women
- Basic personnel strategy
- Nature and cost of special recruiting efforts
- Risks taken in hiring minority groups and women

Programs to ease integration of minority groups and women into company operations, e.g., awareness efforts

Specialized minority and women career counseling

Special recruiting efforts for minority groups and women

Opportunities for the physically handicapped
- Specific programs
- Numbers employed

Employee Safety and Health

Work environment measures
- OSHA requirements (and extent of compliance)
- Other measures of working conditions

Safety performance
- Accident severity—work hours lost per million worked
- Accident frequency (number of lost time accidents per million hours)
- Disabling injuries
- Fatalities

Services provided (and cost of programs and human resources) for:
- Addictive treatment (alcohol, narcotics)
- Mental health

Spending for safety equipment
- Required by law/regulation
- Not required

Special safety programs (including safety instruction)

Comparisons of health and safety performance with competition and industry in general

Developments/innovations in health and safety

Employee health measures, e.g., sick days, examinations

Food facilities
- Cost/serving to employee; to company
- Nutritional evaluation

Figure 19.2 Major arguments for and against business performing social responsibility activities.

Major Arguments for Social Responsibility

1. It is in the best interest of the business to promote and improve the communities where it does business.
2. Social actions can be profitable.
3. It is the ethical thing to do.
4. It improves the public image of the firm.
5. It increases the viability of the business system. Business exists because it gives society benefits. Society can amend or take away its charter. This is the "iron law of responsibility".
6. It is necessary to avoid government regulation.
7. Sociocultural norms require it.
8. Laws cannot be passed for all circumstances. Thus, business must assume responsibility to maintain an orderly legal society.
9. It is in the stockholders' best interest. It will improve the price of stock in the long run because the stock market will view the company as less risky and open to public attack and therefore award it a higher price–earnings ratio.
10. Society should give business a chance to solve social problems that government has failed to solve.
11. Business, by some groups, is considered to be the institution with the financial and human resources to solve social problems.
12. Prevention of problems is better than cures — so let business solve problems before they become too great.

Major Arguments against Social Responsibility

1. It might be illegal.
2. Business plus government equals monolith.
3. Social actions cannot be measured.
4. It violates profit maximization.
5. Cost of social responsibility is too great and would increase prices too much.
6. Business lacks social skills to solve societal problems.
7. It would dilute business's primary purposes.
8. It would weaken U.S. balance of payments because price of goods will have to go up to pay for social programs.
9. Business already has too much power. Such involvement would make business too powerful.
10. Business lacks accountability to the public. Thus, the public would have no control over its social involvement.
11. Such business involvement lacks broad public support.

R. Joseph Mansen, Jr. "The Social Attitudes of Management" in Joseph W. McGuire, CONTEMPORARY MANAGEMENT, © 1974, p. 616. Reprinted by permission of Prentice-Hall, Inc., Englewood Cliffs, New Jersey.

Back to the Case

Figure 19.1 indicates that there probably are many other social responsibility areas in which Stylistics could become involved in addition to Ware's situation. Ware's situation, however, could be categorized under the heading of marketing practices, since Ware is suggesting that Stylistics's present method of marketing its services makes it extremely difficult for the handicapped to be consumers of those services.

Whatever Vicaro would do to ease Ware's problem probably would cost him money and, as a result, raise the cost of his services to his customers. While this action would cost him profits and perhaps seem unbusinesslike, performing such social responsibility activities could improve the Stylistics's public image and therefore seem very businesslike. Vicaro must decide to what degree, if at all, he will try to solve Ware's problem.

Conclusions about Business Performing Social Responsibility Activities

The preceding two sections presented several major arguments for and against businesses performing social responsibility activities. Regardless of which argument or combination of arguments particular managers might support, they generally should

Figure 19.3 Primary function of several federal agencies involved with social responsibility legislation.

Federal Agency	Primary Agency Activities
Equal Employment Opportunity Commission	Investigates and conciliates employment discrimination complaints that are based on race, sex, or creed
Office of Federal Contract Compliance Programs	Insures that employers holding federal contracts grant equal employment opportunity to people regardless of race or sex
Environmental Protection Agency	Formulates and enforces environmental standards in such areas as water, air, and noise pollution
Consumer Product Safety Commission	Strives to reduce consumer inquiries related to product design, labeling, etc.
Occupational Safety and Health Administration	Regulates safety and health conditions in nongovernmental work places
National Highway Traffic Safety Administration	Attempts to reduce traffic accidents through the regulation of transportation–related manufacturers and products
Mining Enforcement and Safety Administration	Attempts to improve safety conditions for mine workers by enforcing all mine safety and equipment standards

make a concentrated effort to (1) perform all legally required social responsibility activities, (2) consider the possibility of voluntarily performing social responsibility activities beyond those legally required, and (3) inform all relevant individuals of the extent to which their organization will become involved in performing social responsibility activities. The following sections further discuss each of these topics.

Performing Required Social Responsibility Activities

Federal legislation requires that businesses perform certain social responsibility activities. In fact, several government agencies have been established and are maintained to develop such business-related legislation and to make sure that such legislation is followed. Figure 19.3 lists several such federal agencies and their corresponding major functions. Examples of specific legislation that requires the performance of social responsibility activities include (1) The Equal Pay Act of 1963, (2) The Federal Water Pollution Control Act Amendments of 1972, (3) The Clear Air Act Amendments of 1977, (4) The Quiet Communications Act of 1978, and (5) The Highway Safety Act of 1978.

Laws Require Certain Social Activities

Voluntarily Performing Social Responsibility Activities

Adherence to legislated social responsibilities represents the minimum standards of social responsibility performance that business managers must achieve. Managers must ask themselves, however, how far beyond these minimum standards, if at all, they should attempt to go.

The process of determining how far to go is simple to describe, yet difficult and complicated to implement. The process simply entails managers (1) assessing both positive and negative outcomes of performing social responsibility activities over both the short and long runs and (2) then performing only those social responsibility activities that maximize management system success while making some desirable contribution to maintaining or improving the welfare of society.

How Much Is Enough?

Figure 19.4 Outcomes of social responsibility involvement expected by executives and the percent who expected them.

Positive Outcomes	Percent Expecting
Enhanced corporate reputation and goodwill	97.4
Strengthening of the social system in which the corporation functions	89.0
Strengthening of the economic system in which the corporation functions	74.3
Greater job satisfaction among all employees	72.3
Avoidance of government regulation	63.7
Greater job satisfaction among executives	62.8
Increased chances for survival of the firm	60.7
Ability to attract better managerial talent	55.5
Increased long-run profitability	52.9
Strengthening of the pluralistic nature of American society	40.3
Maintaining or gaining customers	38.2
Investors prefer socially responsible firms	36.6
Increased short-run profitability	15.2
Negative Outcomes	
Decreased short-run profitability	59.7
Conflict of economic or financial and social goals	53.9
Increased prices for consumers	41.4
Conflict in criteria for assessing managerial performance	27.2
Disaffection of stockholders	24.1
Decreased productivity	18.8
Decreased long-run profitability	13.1
Increased government regulation	11.0
Weakening of the economic system in which the corporation functions	7.9
Weakening of the social system in which the corporation functions	3.7

Rewards and Penalties of Social Activities

The results of a study conducted by Sandra L. Holmes can be of some help to managers attempting to assess the positive and negative outcomes of performing social responsibility activities.[12] Top executives in 560 of the major firms in such areas as commercial banking, life insurance, transportation, and utilities were asked to indicate the possible negative and positive outcomes their firms could expect to experience from performing social responsibility activities.

Figure 19.4 lists these positive and negative outcomes and indicates the percentage of executives questioned who expected to experience the outcomes. Although the information in this figure furnishes managers with several general insights on how involved their organization should become in social responsibility activities, it does not and cannot furnish them with a clear-cut answer to this question. Managers can determine the appropriate level of social responsibility involvement for a specific organization only by examining and reacting to specific factors related to that organization.

Communicating the Degree of Social Responsibility Involvement

Determining the extent to which a business should perform social responsibility activities beyond legal requirements is an extremely subjective process. Despite this subjectivity, however, managers of the future cannot afford to be without a well-defined opinion in this vital management area. Managers should determine their position on this matter, establish a personal code of ethics that relates to this position, inform all organization members of this position, and then consistently behave according to this position.[13] Taking these steps will ensure that managers behave consistently to support their position, that other organization members will be able to act consistently with this position, and that societal expectations of what a particular organization will achieve in this area will be realistic.

Informing Others

Back to the Case

Some social responsibility activities are legislated and therefore must be performed by business. Most of these legislated activities, however, are aimed at larger companies. There probably is no existing legislation that would require Vicaro to make Stylistics beauty shops more accessible to the handicapped.

Since Vicaro probably is not required by law to modify his shops for the benefit of the handicapped, whatever modification he might decide to make would be strictly voluntary. In making this decision Vicaro should (1) assess both positive and negative outcomes of modifying his shops over both the long and short runs and (2) then make those modifications, if any, that would maximize the success of Stylistics as well as make some desirable contribution to the welfare of the handicapped. Vicaro should let all organization members as well as Tiffany Ware know what he decides and, perhaps, his reasons for that decision.

The previous section discussed social responsibility as the business obligation to take action that protects and improves the welfare of society along with business's own interests. This section defines and discusses **social responsiveness** as the degree of effectiveness and efficiency an organization displays in pursuing its social responsibilities.[14] The greater the degree of effectiveness and efficiency an organization displays while pursuing its social responsibilities, the more socially responsive the organization is said to be.[15] Exhibit 19 presents some evidence supporting the notion that industry as a whole has probably become more socially responsive over the past few years. In addition, this trend is likely to continue in the future. The following two sections discuss (1) social responsiveness and decision making and (2) approaches to meeting social responsibilities.

Social Responsiveness

Effectiveness and Efficiency in Pursuing Social Responsibilities

Social Responsiveness and Decision Making

The highly socially responsive organization that is both effective and efficient meets its social responsibilities and does not waste organizational resources in the process. Deciding exactly which social responsibilities an organization should pursue and then how to accomplish appropriately activities necessary to meet those responsibilities are perhaps the two most critical decision-making aspects of maintaining a high level of social responsiveness within an organization.

Exhibit 19

Environmentalists in Industry

American Can's L. William Sessions (Photo: Patrick D. Pagnano)

Celanese's Leon Starr (Photo: Patrick D. Pagnano)

Chevron's Ivan Gilman (Photo: Lorraine Rourke)

In 1967, Frank K. Armour, a vice-president at Interlake Inc., a producer of steel and powdered metals in the Chicago suburb of Oak Brook, Ill., spent 95% of his time on engineering and research issues and the other 5% on environmental matters. Now those figures have been reversed. "We have found that environmental matters are no longer a secondary business function," he explains.

Armour, whose staff has grown to 40, says that his advice is now sought on all company activities that will affect the environment. He believes he is effective because he has a direct line to Interlake's chairman and chief executive officer, Reynold C. MacDonald. "I wouldn't be able to function if I didn't have the support," he says.

Armour's case is not unusual. Increasingly, corporations are upgrading the status and responsibilities of their environmental managers. Their staffs and budgets are being enlarged, and many are gaining more clout with top management. Atlantic Richfield Co.'s environmental staff, until this year tucked away in the public affairs office, is now headed by a vice-president who has direct access to President Thornton F. Bradshaw. Ivan H. Gilman, who is general manager of environmental affairs for Chevron U.S.A. Inc., also reports directly to the company president, Donald L. Bower, and describes his influence as "significant," adding: "Really, I'm envied by my colleagues."

Taking it seriously. The majority of corporate environmental officials are engineers by training and had technical responsibilities before being channeled into the environmental policy area. Armour, for instance, began as an engineer with Interlake 30 years ago. But more and more, companies are going outside to find qualified people. Patricia Rand, a senior science adviser at Arco, is a plant ecologist and has been a ranger-naturalist with the National Park Service and a professor at the University of Nebraska at Lincoln. Betsy Ancker-Johnson, General Motors Corp.'s vice-president for environmental affairs, was formerly Assistant Secretary for science and technology in the Commerce Dept.

Industry has upgraded them with staffs, budgets, and more independence

Although most corporate environmentalists profess a concern for clean air and water, few are apt to be regarded as true environmentalists, such as those who belong to organizations like the Sierra Club and the Environmental Defense Fund. Rather, these officials view environmental issues from the corporate perspective and, like top management, often argue that there must be a balance between environmental issues and business concerns. "We have a limited number of resources in this country," says Leon Starr, corporate director of environmental and health affairs for Celanese Corp. "A 2% to 3% difference [in emissions control] can be extremely expensive, with a limited return."

Still, there is evidence that many of these officials are serious about their role as the corporate environmental conscience. "We have to meet our perception of what the government will accept and what we as good citizens should do," explains L. William Sessions, vice-president for energy and environmental quality at American Can Co.

There are many reasons for top management's interest in having environmental experts, not the least of which is financial. These experts must study the complex rules issued by the Environmental Protection Agency (EPA) to determine what the company must do to comply. A company that fails to listen to its environmentalists, says Thomas R. Young, executive vice-president of Wyoming Fuel Co., "can end up with a cease-and-desist order against a multimillion-dollar operation."

Some are moneysavers. The environmental official must frequently throw a damper on management's enthusiasm for a new project by pointing out that the new installation will violate environmental laws. "All too often, we're waving the red flag," admits American Can's Sessions. He notes that some businessmen still do not understand that a company cannot build a plant in dirty-air areas without first meeting the EPA's rule to offset any pollution that will be created by a similar reduction in pollution at an existing facility, even one operated by another company. "It will take years for that to sink in," he says.

The environmentalist at 3M suggested a program that saved $20 million

In some cases, advice from the environmental expert not only has helped a company meet regulations but has saved money besides. An example is the "Pollution Prevention Pays," or 3P, program initiated at 3M Co. on the recommendation of Joseph T. Ling, vice-president for environmental engineering and pollution control. Ling says that the program aims to reduce pollution at the source by altering the manufacturing process instead of cleaning up at the end with expensive control equipment. In the U.S. alone, the program has saved the company $20 million since 1975.

There have even been instances when a company opted for a more expensive program than originally planned as a result of advice from its environmental representative. When Arco opened its Black Thunder coal

mine last year on 4,000 acres in Wyoming, it was faced with a federal requirement to devise a plan for restoring the land to its "previous productivity" after mining. But because the grassland's delicate ecology had been abused decades ago by farming attempts, its productivity was already low. "We could throw down a few handfuls of seeds and get it back to current productivity," says Arco's Rand.

Instead, pushed by Rand's department, Arco began testing various species of native prairie grass to come up with the best combination to restore the grassland to its original ecological balance. Getting this $75,000 test plot going was "a big selling job," says Rand. "We had to sell an environmental conscience to a coal operating group."

In the long run, though, maintains Interlake's Armour, it may be impossible to keep a company one step ahead of government regulations. "Down the road I won't have to demonstrate much ingenuity, because everything will be dictated by the bureaucracy," Armour asserts.

Winning respect. Despite their successes, corporate environmentalists worry about their credibility outside the company. "There is still some suspicion—perhaps stigma to some extent—to working for industry," says Matthew Gould, corporate director of energy and environment for Georgia-Pacific Corp. Some environmentalists, he says, cannot accept the fact that there might be "good guys" working for industry.

Some critics, in fact, regard the current efforts by companies to recognize the environment as window-dressing. "There is a great deal of lip service and hand-wringing, but top management does not give environmentalism the attention it deserves," says Charles O. Spielman Jr., division manager for mining and energy at Kellogg Corp., a Littleton (Colo.) consulting firm. Observers are quick to note, too, that environmentalism is seldom the corporate route to the top.

Yet some corporate environmentalists have won the respect of officials inside and outside the company. Chevron's President Bower says of the company's Gilman: "He's got great respect, not just from me and the rest of the company, but from the whole industry." Carl Pope, assistant conservation director of the Sierra Club, calls Gilman "articulate and reasonable" and notes that none of the environmental group's battles over the past few years has been with Chevron. "That may be an indication that Gilman is doing his job," he says.

Figure 19.5 Flowchart of social responsibility decision making that will generally enhance the social responsiveness of an organization.

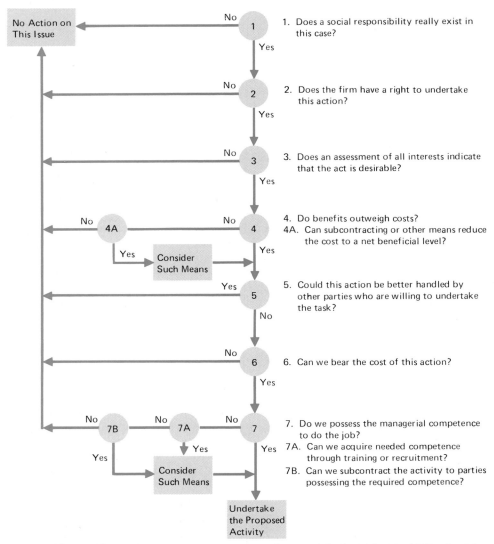

Ramon J. Aldag and Donald W. Jackson, Jr., "A Managerial Framework for Social Decision Making," p. 34, *MSU Business Topics*, Winter 1975. Reprinted by permission of the publisher, Division of Research, Graduate School of Business Administration, Michigan State University.

Socially Responsive
Decision Making

   Figure 19.5 is a flowchart that managers can use as a general guideline for making social responsibility decisions that enhance the social responsiveness of an organization. This figure implies that for managers to achieve and maintain a high level of social responsiveness within an organization, they must pursue only those social responsibilities that their organization actually possesses and has a right to undertake. Furthermore, once managers decide to meet a specific social responsibility, they must decide the best way in which activities related to meeting this obligation should be undertaken; that is, managers must decide if their organization should undertake the activities on its own or acquire the help of outside individuals with more expertise in the area.

Approaches to Meeting Social Responsibilities

The previous section discussed decision making as a major determinant of the level of social responsiveness an organization will achieve. This section discusses various managerial approaches to meeting social obligations as another determinant of the level of social responsiveness.

A study conducted by Harry A. Lipson provides many helpful hints on how to best approach the meeting of social responsibilities within an organization.[16] According to Lipson, a desirable and highly socially responsive approach to meeting social obligations (1) incorporates social goals into the annual planning process, (2) seeks comparative industry norms for social programs, (3) presents reports to organization members, the board of directors, and stockholders on social responsibility progress, (4) experiments with different approaches for measuring social performance, and (5) attempts to measure the cost of social programs as well as the return on social program investments.

Hints for Social Responsiveness

An article written by S. Prakash Sethi also contains numerous insights on the relationship between management approaches used to meet social obligations and the level of social responsiveness achieved by the organization.[17] In general, Sethi presents three main approaches to meeting social obligations: (1) the social obligation approach, (2) the social responsibility approach, and (3) the social responsiveness approach. Each of these approaches and the types of behavior typical of them on several different dimensions are presented in figure 19.6.

As figure 19.6 indicates, each of Sethi's three approaches contains behavior that reflects a somewhat different attitude with regard to business performing social responsibility activities. The **social obligation approach,** for example, reflects an attitude that considers business to have primarily economic purposes and confines social responsibility activity mainly to conformance to existing legislation. The **social responsibility approach,** however, is characterized by an attitude that sees business as having both economic and societal goals. The third approach, the **social responsiveness approach,** reflects an attitude that considers business as having both societal and economic goals as well as the obligation to anticipate upcoming social problems and to work actively toward preventing their appearance.

Disposition toward Social Responsibility

Reflection on Sethi's three approaches to meeting social responsibility generally leads to the conclusion that organizations characterized by attitudes and behaviors consistent with the social responsiveness approach generally are more socially responsive than organizations characterized by attitudes and behaviors consistent with either the social responsibility approach or the social obligation approach. Also, organizations characterized by the social responsibility approach generally achieve higher levels of social responsiveness than organizations characterized by the social obligation approach. The cartoon typifies behavior in an organization based on the social obligation approach.

Back to the Case

Vicaro should strive to maintain a relatively high level of social responsiveness when pursuing issues such as those in Tiffany Ware's situation. To do this, he should make decisions appropriate to his social responsibility area and also approach the meeting of those social responsibilities in an appropriate way.

In terms of decision making and the Tiffany Ware situation, Vicaro must first decide if Stylistics has a social responsibility to service customers such as Ware. Assuming that Vicaro decides that Stylistics has such a responsibility, he must then determine exactly how to accomplish the activities necessary to meet those responsibilities. For example, can the people presently employed by Stylistics install ramps in front of the beauty shops, or should Vicaro hire independent contractors to make the installations? Making decisions such as

Figure 19.6 Three approaches to social responsibility and types of behavior associated with each.

Dimensions of Behavior	Approach One: Social Obligations Proscriptive	Approach Two: Social Responsibility Prescriptive	Approach Three: Social Responsiveness Anticipatory and Preventive
Search for legitimacy	Confines legitimacy to legal and economic criteria only; does not violate laws; equates profitable operations with fulfilling social expectations	Accepts the reality of limited relevance of legal and market criteria of legitimacy in actual practice; willing to consider and accept broader extralegal and extramarket criteria for measuring corporate performance and social role	Accepts its role as defined by the social system and therefore subject to change; recognizes importance of profitable operations but includes other criteria
Ethical norms	Considers business value-neutral; managers expected to behave according to their own ethical standards	Defines norms in community-related terms, i.e., good corporate citizen; avoids taking moral stand on issues which may harm its economic interests or go against prevailing social norms (majority views)	Takes definite stand on issues of public concern; advocates institutional ethical norms even though they may be detrimental to its immediate economic interest or prevailing social norms
Social accountability for corporate actions	Construes narrowly as limited to stockholders; jealously guards its prerogatives against outsiders	Construes narrowly for legal purposes, but broadened to include groups affected by its actions; management more outward looking	Willing to account for its actions to other groups, even those not directly affected by its actions
Operating strategy	Exploitative and defensive adaptation; maximum externalization of costs	Reactive adaptation; where identifiable, internalizes previously external costs; maintains current standards of physical and social environment; compensates victims of pollution and other corporate related activities even in the absence of clearly established legal grounds; develops industry-wide standards	Proactive adaptation; takes lead in developing and adapting new technology for environmental protectors; evaluates side effects of corporate actions and eliminates them prior to the action's being taken; anticipates future social changes and develops internal structures to cope with them
Response to social pressures	Maintains low public profile, but if attacked, uses PR methods to upgrade its public image; denies any deficiencies; blames public dissatisfaction on ignorance or failure to understand corporate functions; discloses information only where legally required	Accepts responsibility for solving current problems; will admit deficiencies in former practices and attempt to persuade public that its current practices meet social norms; attitude toward critics conciliatory; freer information disclosures than approach one	Willingly discusses activities with outside groups; makes information freely available to public; accepts formal and informal inputs from outside groups in decision making; is willing to be publicly evaluated for its various activities
Activities pertaining to governmental actions	Strongly resists any regulation of its activities except when it needs help to protect its market position; avoids contact; resists any demands for information beyond that legally required	Preserves management discretion in corporate decisions, but cooperates with government in research to improve industry-wide standards; participates in political processes and encourages employees to do likewise	Openly communicates with government; assists in enforcing existing laws and developing evaluations of business practices; objects publicly to governmental activities that it feels are detrimental to the public's good
Legislative and political activities	Seeks to maintain status quo; actively opposes laws that would internalize any previously externalized costs; seeks to keep lobbying activities secret	Willing to work with outside groups for good environmental laws; concedes need for change in some status quo laws; less secrecy in lobbying than approach one	Avoid meddling in politics and does not pursue special-interest laws; assists legislative bodies in developing better laws where relevant; promotes honesty and openness in government and in its own lobbying activities
Philanthropy	Contributes only when direct benefit to it clearly shown; otherwise, views contributions as responsibility of individual employees	Contributes to noncontroversial and established causes; matches employee contributions	Activities of approach two, *plus* support and contributions to new, controversial groups whose needs it sees as unfulfilled and increasingly important

**"Here, I'm a rabid environmentalist.
At work, I'm a ruthless capitalist."**

© Charles G. Sauers, 1977. First published in the *Wall Street Journal.*

Back to the Case
continued

these appropriately will help Stylistics to meet social obligations both effectively and efficiently.

In terms of an approach to meeting social responsibilities that probably will increase Stylistics's social responsiveness, Vicaro should try to view his organization as having both societal and economic goals. In addition, he should attempt to anticipate the arrival of social problems, such as the one depicted by Ware's situation, and actively work to prevent their appearance.

This section discusses a social responsibility as a major organizational activity. As such, it should be subjected to the same management techniques used to perform other major organizational activities, such as production, personnel, finance, and marketing. Managers have known for some time that desirable results in these areas are not achieved if managers are not effective in planning, organizing, influencing, and controlling. Achieving social responsibility results is not any different.[18] The following sections discuss planning, organizing, influencing, and controlling social responsibility activities.

Social Responsibility Activity and Management Functions
A Major Area of Management Activity

Planning Social Responsibility Activities

Planning is defined in chapter 4 as the process of determining how the organization will achieve its objectives or get where it wants to go. Planning social responsibility activities, therefore, involves determining how the organization will achieve its social responsibility objectives or get where it wants to go in the area of social responsibility. The following sections discuss (1) how the planning of social responsibility activities is related to the overall planning process of the organization and (2) how to convert the social responsibility policy of the organization into action.

Reaching Social Responsibility Objectives

Figure 19.7 Integration of social responsibility activities and planning activities.

From Kenneth E. Newgren, "Social Forecasting: An Overview of Current Business Practices," in Archie B. Carroll, ed., *Managing Corporate Social Responsibility.* Copyright © 1977 by Little, Brown and Company (Inc.). Reprinted by permission.

The Overall Planning Process

Part of the Overall Planning Effort

The model shown in figure 19.7 depicts how social responsibility activities can be handled as part of the overall planning process of the organization. According to this figure, social trends should be forecast within the organizational environment along with the more typically performed economic, political, and technological trends forecasts. Examples of such social trends would be prevailing future societal attitudes toward water pollution or safe working conditions. In turn, each of these forecasts would influence the development of the strategic and tactical plans of the organization as well as corresponding activities undertaken.

Organizational Policies

A policy is a standing plan that furnishes broad guidelines for channeling management thinking in specific directions. Organizational policies should be established in the social responsibility area as well as in some of the more generally accepted areas, such as hirings, promotions, and absenteeism.

Effort by Top Management, Staff, and Division Management

To be effective, however, such social responsibility policies must be converted into appropriate action. Figure 19.8 presents a generally accepted outline of how this can be accomplished. According to the figure, conversion of social responsibility policy into action involves three distinct and generally sequential phases. Phase 1 consists of top management recognizing that its organization possesses some social obligation and, as a result, formulating and communicating some policy to all organization members about its acceptance of this obligation.

Phase 2 involves staff personnel as well as top management. In this phase, top management gathers information related to actually meeting the social obligation accepted in phase 1. Staff personnel generally are involved at this point to give advice on technical matters related to meeting the accepted social obligation.

Phase 3 involves division management in addition to organization personnel already involved from the first two phases. During this phase, top management strives to obtain the commitment of organization members to live up to the accepted social obligation and attempts to create realistic expectations about the effects of such a commitment on organizational productivity. Staff specialists encourage those responses within the organization that are necessary to meet the accepted social obligation properly. And division management commits resources and modifies existing procedures so that appropriate socially oriented behavior can and will be performed within the organization.

Figure 19.8 Conversion of social responsibility policy into action.

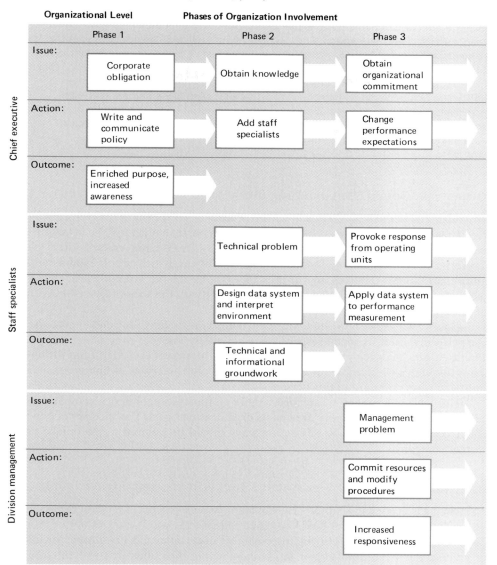

Organizational Level

Phases of Organization Involvement

Vicaro should know that pursuing social responsibility objectives probably will be a major management activity at Stylistics. As such, Vicaro should plan, organize, influence, and control Stylistics's social responsibility activities if the company is to be successful in reaching social responsibility objectives.

In terms of planning social responsibility activities, Vicaro should determine how Stylistics will achieve its social responsibility objectives. He can do this by incorporating social responsibility planning into his overall planning process at Stylistics. That is, Vicaro can make social trends forecasts along with his economic, political, and technological trends forecasts. In turn, these forecasts would influence the development of strategic plans, tactical plans, and ultimately, the action taken by Stylistics in the area of social responsibility.

Back to the Case

If Vicaro is to be successful in planning for social responsibility activities, he also must be able to turn Stylistics's social responsibility policy into action. For example, Vicaro may want to make Stylistics beauty shops more accessible to handicapped customers. To convert this policy into action, he should first communicate such a policy to all organization members. Next, he should obtain additional knowledge of exactly how

to make his shops more accessible and retain staff personnel who can help him with technical problems in this area. Lastly, Vicaro should make sure that all people at Stylistics are committed to meeting this social responsibility objective and that lower-level managers are allocating funds and establishing appropriate opportunities for organization members to fulfill this commitment.

Organizing Social Responsibility Activities

Social Responsibility Resources

Organizing is defined in chapter 8 as the process of establishing orderly uses for all resources within the organization. These uses, of course, emphasize the attainment of management system objectives and flow naturally from management system plans. Correspondingly, organizing for social responsibility activities entails establishing for all organizational resources logical uses that emphasize the attainment of social objectives of the organization and also are consistent with the social responsibility plans of the organization.

Figure 19.9 shows how Standard Oil Company of Indiana decided to organize for the performance of its social responsibility activities. The vice-president for Law and Public Affairs holds the primary responsibility in the area of societal affairs within this company and is responsible for overseeing the related activities of numerous individuals who report directly to this person.

This figure, of course, is intended only as an illustration of how a company might include its social responsibility area on its organization chart. The specifics of how any single company organizes in this area always should be tailored to the unique needs of that company.

Influencing Individuals Performing Social Responsibility Activities

Emphasis on People

Influencing is defined in chapter 12 as the management process of guiding the activities of organization members in directions that enhance the attainment of organizational objectives. As applied to the social responsibility area, influencing is simply the process of guiding the activities of organization members in directions that will enhance the attainment of the organization's social responsibility objectives. More specifically, to influence appropriately in this area, managers must lead, communicate, motivate, and work with groups in ways that result in the attainment of existing social responsibility objectives.

Controlling Social Responsibility Activities

Social Responsibility Activity: Going As Planned?

Controlling is the function managers perform to make things happen as they were planned to happen. To control, managers assess or measure what is occurring in the organization and, if necessary, change these occurrences in some way to make them conform to plans. Controlling in the area of social responsibility entails these same two major tasks. The following sections discuss (1) various areas in which social responsibility measurement takes place and (2) the social audit, a tool for determining and reporting progress in the attainment of social responsibility objectives.

Figure 19.9 How Standard Oil Company of Indiana includes the social responsibility area on its organization chart.

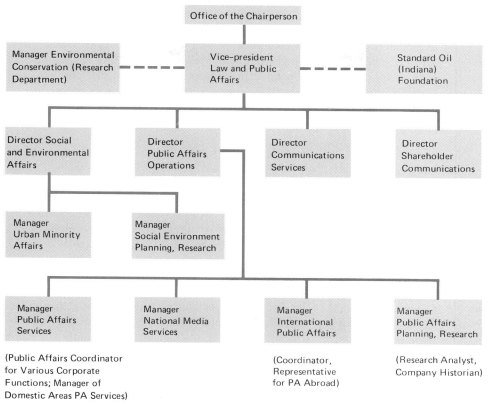

(Public Affairs Coordinator for Various Corporate Functions; Manager of Domestic Areas PA Services)

(Coordinator, Representative for PA Abroad)

(Research Analyst, Company Historian)

Areas of Measurement

To be consistent, measurements to gauge organizational progress in reaching its social responsibility objectives could be taken in any of the areas listed in figure 19.1. The specific areas in which individual companies actually take such measurements vary, of course, depending on the specific social responsibility objectives of those companies. All companies, however, probably should take such social responsibility measurements in at least the following four major areas:[19]

1. *The economic function area*   A measurement should be made of whether or not the organization is performing such activities as producing goods and services that people need, creating jobs for society, paying fair wages, and ensuring worker safety. This measurement gives some indication of the economic contribution the organization is making to society.

2. *The quality of life area*   In this area the measurement should focus on determining if the organization is improving or degrading the general quality of life in society. Such practices as producing high-quality goods, dealing fairly with employees and customers, and making an effort to preserve the natural environment all could be indicators that the organization is upholding or improving the general quality of life within society. As an example, some people believe that because cigarette companies produce goods that actually can harm the health of society overall, these companies are socially irresponsible.[20]

3. *The social investment area*   This area deals with the degree to which the organization is investing both money and manpower to solve community social problems. Here, the organization could be involved in assisting community organizations related to education, charities, and the arts.

4. *The problem-solving area*   Measurement in this area should focus on the degree to which the organization deals with social problems as opposed to symptoms of these problems. Such activities as participating in long-range community planning and conducting studies to pinpoint social problems generally could be considered dealing with social problems as opposed to symptoms of those social problems.

The Social Audit: A Progress Report

Monitoring, Measuring, Appraising

A **social audit** is the process of actually taking social responsibility measurements such as those discussed in the preceding section. The purpose of conducting a social audit is simply to provide managers with an assessment of organizational performance in the social responsibility area. The basic steps taken to conduct a social audit are monitoring, measuring, and appraising all aspects of an organization's social responsibility performance. The audit itself can be performed by organization personnel or by an outside consultant.[21]

No Standard Format

Figure 19.10 is a portion of a sample social audit prepared by Bernard Butcher, the executive vice-president for social policy at the Bank of America in San Francisco.[22] It should be noted that this figure does not illustrate any type of standard format used for writing up the results of a social audit. In fact, probably no two organizations conduct and present the results of a social audit in exactly the same way.[23]

Back to the Case

In addition to planning social responsibility activities at Stylistics, Vicaro also must organize, influence, and control them. To organize social responsibility activities, Vicaro must establish orderly use of all resources at Stylistics to carry out the company's social responsibility plans. Despite the relatively small size of his company, developing an organization chart that shows the social responsibility area at Stylistics along with corresponding job descriptions, responsibilities, and specifications for the positions on this chart might be appropriate steps for Vicaro to take.

To influence social responsibility activities, Vicaro must guide the activities of organization members in directions that will enhance the attainment of Stylistics's social responsibility objectives. He must lead, communicate, motivate, and work with groups in ways appropriate for meeting these objectives.

To control, Vicaro must make sure that social responsibility activities at Stylistics are happening as planned. If they are not, he should make changes to ensure that they will in the near future. One tool Vicaro can use to check Stylistics's progress in meeting social responsibilities is the social audit. With the audit he can check and assess management system performance in such areas as economic function, quality of life, social investment, and problem solving.

How Society Can Help Business Meet Social Obligations
Business Needs Help

Although the point previously was made that there must be an open and honest involvement of both business and society for business to meet desirable social obligations, the bulk of this chapter has focused on what business should do in the area of social responsibility. This section emphasizes action that society should take to help business accomplish its social responsibility objectives.

Figure 19.10 Portion of sample social audit report made by a practicing manager.

MNB Social Performance Report
Part 1—Mainstream Issues

Priority—Consumer Issues

Issue—Discrimination in Credit—Women

Potential	Growing public awareness of issue. Consumer Finance Commission Report should stimulate legislation within two years. Class actions a possibility.
Progress	New guidelines instituted for credit cards and small loans (under $5,000). Women's full income and employment now considered. No restrictions on married women obtaining credit in own name.
Problems	No change in real estate or larger personal loans because of Michigan's community property laws.
Position	Well ahead of competition. Better advertising of this fact would generate considerable new business.

Issue—Complaints and Errors

Potential	Errors prime reason for customers leaving bank. Five percent reduction in closed accounts would be equal to raising profits by $280,000. Quick handling of complaints could increase this to $400,000.
Progress	Instituted double-check system. Check-processing errors down 27 percent. Cost: $110,000. Instituted 800 line to handle complaints and questions. Good results. Cost for line, officer, and advertising: $90,000.
Problems	No progress in credit card billing errors.
Position	Reputation for personalized service improved. Closed accounts down 4.3 percent.

Priority—Employee Development

Issue—Affirmative Action

Potential	Close monitoring by government and others assured. Recent class actions indicate severe penalties for nonaction. Potential liability $1 million to 10 million. Upgrading large pool of underutilized talent in bank (especially women) could significantly increase productivity. Growing number of qualified minorities in Detroit.
Progress	Strong minority program instituted during year with goals, timetables, and enforcement mechanism. The record is good: *1968,* 18.3 percent of employees minority; *1970,* 20.5 percent; *1972,* 24.1 percent; *1975* goal is population parity (31.7 percent). Similar program for women (now 62 percent of labor force) will be ready in mid-1973.
Problems	Minorities and women still concentrated in lower rank:

Percent Bank Officers Who Are:	1968	1970	1972	1975 Goal
Minority	5.6%	6.1%	7.3%	12.0%
Women	18.2%	20.8%	23.3%	30.0%

	To reach 1975 goals, we must develop a better system of isolating promotables, training and placing them. Difficulty of attracting top minorities to banking. Some resentment from white males expected.
Position	This effort largely required. Other Detroit banks at essentially the same position. No competitive advantage or disadvantage.

Jerry McAfee (Photo: Gulf Oil Corporation)

Clarity

Attainability

Affordability

Future Orientation

Emphasis On Ends—Not Means

Jerry McAfee, chairman of the board and chief executive officer of Gulf Oil Corporation, indicates that while business has some responsibilities to society, society also has some responsibilities to business. McAfee implies that if society lives up to these responsibilities, it will assist business in living up to its responsibilities. In McAfee's own words, the responsibilities society has to business include:

1. *Setting rules that are clear and consistent*　This is one of the fundamental things that society, through government, ought to do. Although it may come as a surprise to some, it can be argued that industry actually needs an appropriate measure of regulation. By this is meant that the people of the nation, through their government, should set the bounds within which they want industry to operate.

　　But the rules have got to be clear. Society must spell out clearly what it is it wants the corporations to do. The rules can't be vague and imprecise. Making the rules straight and understandable is really what government is all about.

　　One businessman described his confusion when he read a section of a regulation that a federal regulatory representative had cited as the reason for a certain decision that had been made. "You're right," the official responded, "that's what the regulation says, but that's not what it means."

2. *Keeping the rules technically feasible*　Business cannot be expected to do the impossible. Yet the plain truth is that many of today's regulations are unworkable. Environmental standards have on occasion exceeded those of Mother Nature. For example, the Rio Blanco shale-oil development in Colorado was delayed by the fact that air-quality standards, as originally proposed, required a higher quality of air than existed in the natural setting.

3. *Making sure the rules are economically feasible*　Society cannot impose a rule that society is not prepared to pay for because, ultimately, it is the people who must pay, either through higher prices, higher taxes, or both. Furthermore, the costs involved include not only those funds constructively spent to solve problems, but also the increasingly substantial expenditures needed just to comply with the red-tape requirements. Although the total cost of government regulation of business is difficult to compute, it is enormous. To cite an example, the Commission on Federal Paperwork last year estimated the energy industry's annual cost of complying with federal energy-reporting requirements at possibly $335 million per year.

4. *Making the rules prospective, not retroactive*　Nowadays, there is an alarming, distressing trend toward retroactivity, toward trying to force retribution for the past. Certain patterns of taxation and some of the regulations and applications of the law are indications of this trend.

　　A case in point is the "Notices of Proposed Disallowance" issued by the Federal Energy Administration (now the Department of Energy) in 1977 against Gulf Oil for alleged overcharges on imported crude oil during the 1973–74 oil embargo. Gulf was struggling to supply the nation's energy needs and increasing imports with the government's support.

　　Gulf was doing its level best to follow the existing regulations on pricing imports. The charges against Gulf, as well as many other issues raised by the DOE, were the result of retroactive applications of vague, poorly written, and confusing regulations.

　　It is counterproductive to make today's rules apply retroactively to yesterday's ball game.

5. *Making the rules goal-setting, not procedure-prescribing*　The proper way for the people of the nation, through their government, to tell their industries how to operate is to set the atmosphere, but don't tell how to do it. Tell what you want made, but don't tell how to make it. Tell the destination we're seeking, but don't tell us how to get there. Leave it to the ingenuity of American industry to devise the best, the most economical, the most efficient way to get there, for industry's track record in this regard has been pretty good.[24]

As indicated earlier, there probably is no legislation that would require Vicaro to modify his beauty shops to make them more accessible to handicapped customers. Assuming that such legislation presently was being developed, however, there are certain steps legislators could take to help Vicaro meet social responsibilities in this area. For example, laws or rules established should be clear, consistent, and technically feasible. This would ensure that Vicaro would know what action is expected of him and that technology exists to help him to take this action.

Any rules established also should be economically feasible, emphasize the future, and allow flexibility. Vicaro should be able to follow the rules without going bankrupt and should not be penalized for what has happened in the past. Vicaro also should be given the flexibility to follow these rules to the best advantage of Stylistics. In other words, he should not be told to conform to the law by following specific steps.

The following points are stressed within this chapter:

Summary

1. Social responsibility is the managerial obligation to take action that protects and improves the welfare of society as a whole and also organizational interests. Basically, business is said to possess this responsibility because of its extreme power to influence societal conditions.

2. There are arguments both for and against business assuming social responsibilities. A minimum level of social responsibility assumption, however, is established by law. One question managers must ask themselves is how far beyond this minimum level, if at all, they wish to go in assuming social responsibilities.

3. Social responsiveness is the degree of effectiveness and efficiency an organization displays in pursuing its social responsibilities. The greater this degree of effectiveness and efficiency, the more socially responsive the organization is said to be.

4. There are two important strategies for increasing the level of social responsiveness achieved by an organization. First, management must decide to pursue social responsibilities they actually possess and decide how activities necessary to live up to these responsibilities will be best performed. Second, management must approach meeting social responsibilities with an appropriate attitude.

5. Meeting social responsibility represents a major area of management activity. As with any other major area of management activity, social responsibility activities will not be successful without adequate planning, organizing, influencing, and controlling on the part of management.

6. To determine the progress of an organization in meeting social responsibilities, measurements generally should be taken and assessed in the areas of economic function, quality of life, social investment, and problem solving. A social audit is the process of actually measuring and reporting organizational progress in these as well as other social responsibility areas.

7. In general, society establishes rules for its own welfare that business is required to follow. Society can help business to meet social responsibilities by setting rules that are clear and consistent; technically feasible; economically feasible; prospective, not retroactive; and goal setting, not procedure prescribing.

Issues for Review and Discussion

1. Define social responsibility.
2. Explain three of the major propositions in the Davis model of social responsibility.
3. Summarize Milton Friedman's arguments against business pursuing social responsibility objectives.
4. Summarize three arguments that support business pursuing social responsibility objectives.
5. What is meant by the phrase *performing required social responsibility activities*?
6. What is meant by the phrase *voluntarily performing social responsibility activities*?
7. List five positive and five negative outcomes a business could experience as a result of performing social responsibility activities.
8. What is the difference between social responsibility and social responsiveness?
9. Discuss the decision-making process that can help managers to increase the social responsiveness of a business.
10. In your own words, explain the main differences between each of Sethi's three main approaches to meeting social responsibilities.
11. Which of Sethi's approaches has the most potential for increasing the social responsiveness of a management system? Explain.
12. What is the overall relationship between the four main management functions and performing social responsibility activities?
13. What suggestions does this chapter make about planning social responsibility activities?
14. Describe the process of turning social responsibility policy into action.
15. How do organizing and influencing social responsibility activities relate to planning social responsibility activities?
16. List and define four main areas in which any management system can take measurements to control for social responsibility activities.
17. What is a social audit? How should the results of a social audit be used by management?
18. How can society help business to meet its social responsibilities?

Sources of Additional Information

Aaker, David A., and Day, George S. *Consumerism: Search for the Consumer Interest*. 2d. ed. Homewood, Ill: Richard D. Irwin, 1974.

Anshen, Melvin, ed. *Managing the Socially Responsible Corporation*. New York: Macmillan, 1974.

Baumhart, Raymond. *An Honest Profit: What Businessmen Say about Ethics in Business*. New York: Holt, Rinehart & Winston, 1968.

Bell, Daniel. *The Coming of Post-Industrial Society: A Venture in Social Forecasting*. New York: Basic Books, 1973.

Cannon, James S. *Environmental Steel: Pollution in the Iron and Steel Industry*. New York: Praeger Publishers, 1974.

Cavanagh, Gerald F. *American Business Values in Transition*. Englewood Cliffs, N.J.: Prentice-Hall, 1976.

Chatov, Robert. *Corporate Financial Reporting: Public or Private Control?* New York: Free Press, 1975.

Cowan, William M. "Office Accidents: Painful, Profitless—and Preventable." *Administrative Management* 42, no. 9 (September 1981): 68–70, 78.

Dales, J. H. *Pollution, Property, and Prices*. Toronto: University of Toronto Press, 1968.

Davis, Keith, and Blomstrom, Robert L. *Business and Society: Environment and Responsibility*. 3d ed. New York: McGraw-Hill, 1975.

Drucker, Peter F. *Technology, Management, and Society*. New York: Harper & Row, 1970.

Goldman, Marshall I., ed. *Controlling Pollution: The Economics of a Cleaner America*. Englewood Cliffs, N.J.: Prentice-Hall, 1967.

Harding, Charles F. "Why Administrative Offices Are Moving to Smaller Cities." *Administrative Management* 42, no. 9 (September 1981): 40–42, 66.

Hay, Robert D.; Gray, Edmund D.; and Gates, James E. *Business and Society*. Cincinnati: South-Western Publishing Co., 1976.

Kapp, K. William. *The Social Costs of Private Enterprise.* New York: Schocken Books, 1971.

McGuire, Joseph F. *Business and Society.* New York: McGraw-Hill, 1963.

Soothill, Keith. "The Extent of Risk in Employing Ex-Prisoners." *Personnel Management* 13, no. 4 (April 1981): 35–37, 43.

Steiner, George A. *Business and Society.* 2d ed. New York: Random House, 1975.

Stone, Christopher D. *Where the Law Ends: The Social Control of Corporate Behavior.* New York: Harper & Row, 1975.

Thomas, Dr. Edward (C.A.M.). "Conserving Energy—What's Being Done." *Management World* 10, no. 3 (March 1981): 14–17.

Walton, Clarence C. *Corporate Social Responsibilities.* Belmont, Calif.: Wadsworth Publishing, 1967.

Watson, John H., III. *20 Company-Sponsored Foundations: Programs and Policies.* New York: Conference Board, 1970.

Weidenbaum, Murray L. "The True Obligation of the Business Firm to Society." *Management Review* 70, no. 9 (September 1981): 21–22.

Woods, Barbara, ed. *Eco-Solutions.* Cambridge, Mass.: Schenkman Publishing, 1972.

Notes

1. D. Votaw and S. P. Sethi, *The Corporate Dilemma: Traditional Values Versus Contemporary Problems* (Englewood Cliffs, N.J.: Prentice-Hall, 1973), pp. 9–46, 167–91.

2. Keith Davis and Robert L. Blomstrom, *Business and Society: Environment and Responsibility,* 3d. ed. (New York: McGraw-Hill, 1975), p. 6.

3. Peter L. Berger, "New Attack on the Legitimacy of Business," *Harvard Business Review,* September/October 1981, pp. 82–89.

4. Keith Davis, "Five Propositions for Social Responsibility," *Business Horizons,* June 1975, pp. 19–24.

5. Stahrl W. Edmunds, "Unifying Concepts in Social Responsibility," *Academy of Management Review,* January 1977, pp. 38–45.

6. For a worthwhile study on these social responsibility areas, see Vernon M. Buehler and Y. K. Shetty, "Managerial Response to Social Responsibility Challenge," *Academy of Management Journal,* March 1976, pp. 66–78.

7. For a more detailed summary of the arguments for and against businesses pursuing social responsibility activities, see Keith Davis, "The Case For and Against Business Assumptions of Social Responsibilities," *Academy of Management Journal,* June 1973, pp. 312–22.

8. Milton Friedman, "The Social Responsibility of Business Is to Increase Profits," *The New York Times Magazine,* 13 September 1970, pp. 33, 122–26.

9. Neil M. Brown and Paul F. Haas, "Social Responsibility: The Uncertain Hypothesis," *MSU Business Topics,* Summer 1974, p. 48.

10. Milton Friedman, "Does Business Have Social Responsibility?" *Bank Administration,* April 1971, pp. 13–14.

11. Elizabeth Gatewood and Archie B. Carroll, "The Anatomy of Corporate Social Response: The Rely, Firestone 500, and Pinto Cases," *Business Horizons* 24, no. 5 (September/October 1981): 9–16.

12. Sandra L. Holmes, "Executive Perceptions of Corporate Social Responsibility," *Business Horizons,* June 1976, pp. 34–40.

13. William C. Gergold, "Corporate Responsibility and the Industrial Professional," *Industrial Management,* November/December 1976, pp. 5–8.

14. Frederick D. Sturdivant, *Business and Society: A Managerial Approach* (Homewood, Ill.: Richard D. Irwin, 1977), pp. 109–25.

15. For an interesting discussion of the comparative social responsiveness of Ford, Firestone, and Proctor & Gamble, see Gatewood and Carroll, "The Anatomy of Corporate Social Response," pp. 9–16.

16. Harry A. Lipson, "Do Corporate Executives Plan for Social Responsibility?" *Business and Society Review,* Winter 1974–75, pp. 80–81.

17. S. Prakash Sethi, "Dimensions of Corporate Social Performance: An Analytical Framework," *California Management Review,* Spring 1975, pp. 58–64.

18. Donald S. McNaughton, "Managing Social Responsiveness," *Business Horizons,* December 1976, pp. 19–24.

19. Frank H. Cassell, "The Social Cost of Doing Business," *MSU Business Topics,* Autumn 1974, pp. 19–26.

20. Donald W. Garner, "The Cigarette Industry's Escape from Liability," *Business and Society Review,* Spring 1980, no. 33, p. 22.

21. Archie B. Carroll and George W. Beiler, "Landmarks in the Evolution of the Social Audit," *Academy of Management Journal,* September 1975, pp. 589–99.

22. Bernard Butcher, "Anatomy of a Social Performance Report," *Business and Society Review,* Autumn 1973, pp. 26–32.

23. Raymond A. Bauer and Dan H. Fenn, Jr., "What Is a Corporate Social Audit?" *Harvard Business Review,* January/February 1973, pp. 37–48.

24. Adapted from Jerry McAfee, "How Society Can Help Business," *Newsweek,* 3 July 1978, p. 15. Copyright 1978, by Newsweek, Inc. All Rights Reserved. Reprinted by Permission.

Concluding Case 19
Heart Transplants at Massachusetts General Hospital?

(Photo: Michael Dispezio)

How much should society pay to prolong the life of a person who has an incurable disease? Should there be a top limit for spending to save a human life? While in the past, questions of this nature were of purely theoretical interest, today such questions have crossed the realm of theory and, in an era when society's agencies—the government or private insurance companies—pay most medical bills, are very pragmatic. Just how practical these questions are was revealed on 12 June 1979 when the government announced that, with few exceptions, Medicare will no longer pay for heart transplant operations. The average cost of such a procedure is around $100,000 and Health and Human Services Secretary Patricia Roberts Harris made it very clear that cost had played a major part in the decision.* While Mrs. Harris conceded that it was impossible to place a value on a human life, she argued that the cost must be determined; her concern, where should the limited funds be expended?

The act of denying Medicare payments for heart transplants may indicate that this country is finally learning, as the British did quite some time ago, that society cannot afford to "shell-out" for all the medical bills that would-be consumers of "free medical care" might generate. Britain's solution was to simply deny some procedures to particular classes of people; for example, kidney dialysis or transplants were denied to patients over sixty or sixty-five years of age, a policy that each year resulted in the death of one thousand or two thousand persons who might have otherwise lived longer.

The fact that only about fifty heart transplants are done each year in the United States and that the supply of hearts for such procedures is very limited, should not lead us to think that the issue being treated here has little significance in the national health picture. The fact is that the same kind of reasoning is going to be extended to other new and expensive types of treatments in the near future. For example, if interferon (an experimental drug recently utilized to treat cancer) proves to be a successful cancer

*Richard A. Schweiker replaced Patricia Harris as Secretary of Health and Human Services in 1981.

treatment, present estimates are that the per patient cost will be $30,000 to $50,000; the total interferon bill for the United States could be a staggering $20 billion annually to treat the estimated 750,000 Americans who develop cancer every year. This does not include the hundreds of thousands who develop skin cancer.

To further complicate the situation, even more horrendous costs could materialize if the artificial heart could be successfully placed into a patient's chest to replace the old defective natural heart, or, alternatively, if the immunologist comes up with a way to "turn-off" the body's rejection mechanism that threatens every transplant recipient. With such accomplishments, the demand for transplants could jump overnight, for it is the lack of available hearts and the problem of tissue rejection that are presently keeping the number of transplants low. In this event, experts estimate that the bills to the health care system will run into the two-digit billions annually! While some argue that increased activity will bring the costs down (as was the case with CAT scanners that have revolutionized medical diagnosis), the cost of such treatments remains staggering.

But it is not only the government that is pressured to assess the medical, social, economic, and ethical issues surrounding heart transplants and other costly medical treatments. In May of 1980, the *New England Journal of Medicine* ran an editorial titled: "Can We Afford to Treat Acute Leukemia?" The editorial answered the question in the affirmative, but it was very sensitive about the high cost and asked point blank: "Should these treatments be available to all or even most of the patients in our country, not to mention the world, who have this disease?" And in February of 1980 the trustees of Massachusetts General Hospital turned down a request from their surgeons to allow heart transplants to be performed there, a decision influenced largely by costs.

This case is adapted from Harry Schwartz, "How Much Is a Life' Worth?" *Wall Street Journal* (Eastern ed.) (15 September 1980). Used with permission.

Discussion Issues:

1. Is the hospital identified in this case acting in a socially responsible manner if, because of the costs involved, it refuses to perform a heart transplant to save a person who has a heart ailment?
2. Which proposition(s) of the Davis Model of Social Responsibility is the hospital violating by turning down the request for heart transplant surgery?
3. Is it right to deny medical treatment to certain sections of society? If it comes to it, what should the criterion be for determining who should receive life-saving medical treatments such as the heart transplant? Should it be age, academic achievement, professional or social contributions to society, or anything else?

Student Learning Objectives

From studying this chapter I will attempt to acquire:

1. An understanding of how systems skill relates to management in the future

2. An understanding of how functional skill relates to management in the future

3. An understanding of how situational analysis skill relates to management in the future

4. A better understanding of the labor force of the future

5. An appreciation for the impact of such factors as system size, energy, and technology on management in the future

6. A practical strategy for training managers for the future

Chapter Outline

Management Skills
for the Future

Introductory Case 20
What about Tomorrow?

Max Barton was feeling a real sense of accomplishment. He had worked at the Pleasant Ridge Candy Company as a department manager for twelve months and was just receiving a well-deserved compliment from his supervisor for a job well done. Barton's supervisor, Judy Shull, was telling Barton that his people had been very productive as a unit and that they seemed to identify very closely with company goals. In addition, Shull was telling Barton that the efficiency of his department was way above average. Barton could only surmise from Shull's statement that he was doing an overall excellent job as a department manager.

Shull's concluding statements, however, left Barton somewhat perplexed. Shull indicated that Barton certainly would seem to have a good future with the Pleasant Ridge Candy Company if he decided to remain. This, of course, pleased Barton. What puzzled Barton was that as Shull left, she turned around and advised him to prepare himself carefully for managing in the future. Barton had never really thought about consciously and systematically trying to prepare himself for a management position in the future. After giving some thought to this matter, however, Barton concluded that Shull was right. He was managing well today, but what about tomorrow?

Discussion Issues

1. What skills does Barton probably possess now that should still be valuable to him five or ten years from now?
2. Do you agree that Barton should be preparing himself for managing in the future? Why?
3. If you were Barton, what would you do to prepare yourself for managing in the future at the Pleasant Ridge Candy Company?

What's Ahead

The introductory case ends with Max Barton, a relatively new department manager at the Pleasant Ridge Candy Company, thinking about conscientiously and systematically preparing himself to be a good manager in the future. This chapter gives managers like Barton some insights on how such preparation can take place. More specifically, this chapter discusses various skills that managers of the future should possess and how a management system can train its present managers for the challenges they inevitably will face in the future.

Up to this point this text has recommended that to manage successfully, managers should apply both knowledge of systems theory and the four basic management functions to the unique management situations they face. However, will this recommendation change sometime in the future? The following sections attempt to answer this question by discussing (1) systems skill in the future, (2) functional skill in the future, and (3) situational analysis skill in the future.

Essential Skills for Future Managers

Systems, Functions, Situations

Systems Skill in the Future

Systems skill is the ability to view and manage a business or some other concern as a number of components that work together and function as a whole to achieve some objective. In essence, the systems approach to management is a way of analyzing and solving managerial problems.[1] Managers analyze problems and implement corresponding solutions only after examining those system parts related to the problem and evaluating the effect of a problem solution on the functioning of all other system parts.[2]

Seeing Parts as a Whole

What about the value of systems skill to managers in the future? Frank T. Curtin, vice-president of machine tools at Cincinnati Milacron, has seen the value of applying the systems approach to management problems in the past and indicates that the systems approach will be an extremely valuable tool for managers of the future.[3] According to Curtin, only after managers understand the "big picture," or see all parts of a company as a whole, will they be able to solve managerial problems appropriately. For the systems approach to management to become more useful to businesses in the future, however, Curtin suggests that more individuals be formally educated in the value of this approach and shown the steps that can be taken to implement it.

Frank T. Curin (Photo: Manufacturing Engineering)

Functional Skill in the Future

Functional skill is the ability to apply appropriately the concepts of planning, organizing, influencing, and controlling to the operation of a management system. The application of these four basic functions is of such vital concern to management that this text presents them as subsystems of the process of the overall management system. How these subsystems are related to the overall management system is shown in figure 20.1.

Applying Managerial Functions to Operation of Management System

What about the value of functional skill to managers in the future? The application of these four functions to managerial problems, of course, has long been suggested as sound management practice. In fact, the evolution of theory related to each of these functions has evolved over many decades as a result of insights contributed

Figure 20.1 Relationships among the four major functional subsystems and the overall management system.

Planning Subsystem

Input

A portion of the organization's:
1. People
2. Money
3. Raw materials
4. Machines

Process (Planning Process)

1. Stating organizational objectives
2. Listing alternative ways of reaching objectives
3. Developing premises upon which each alternative is based
4. Choosing best alternative for reaching objectives
5. Developing plans to pursue chosen alternative
6. Putting plans into action

Output

Organizational plans

Organizing Subsystem

Input

A portion of the organization's:
1. People
2. Money
3. Raw materials
4. Machines

Process (Organizing Process)

1. Reflecting on plans and objectives
2. Establishing major tasks
3. Dividing major tasks into subtasks
4. Allocating resources and directives for subtasks
5. Evaluating results of organizing strategy

Output

Organization

Overall Management System

Input

Resources

Process

Production process

Output

Finished goods or services

Influencing Subsystem

Input

A portion of the organization's:
1. People
2. Money
3. Raw materials
4. Machines

Process (Influencing Process)

Considering groups

Communicating

Leading

Motivating

Output

Appropriate organization member behavior

Controlling Subsystem

Input

A portion of the organization's:
1. People
2. Money
3. Raw materials
4. Machines

Process (Controlling Process)

Work continues

No corrective action necessary

Performance equivalent to standards

Controlling beings

Measure performance

Compare measurement to standards

Performance significantly different from standards

New work situation begins

Take corrective action: change plans, organization, and/or influencing methods

Output

Organizational control

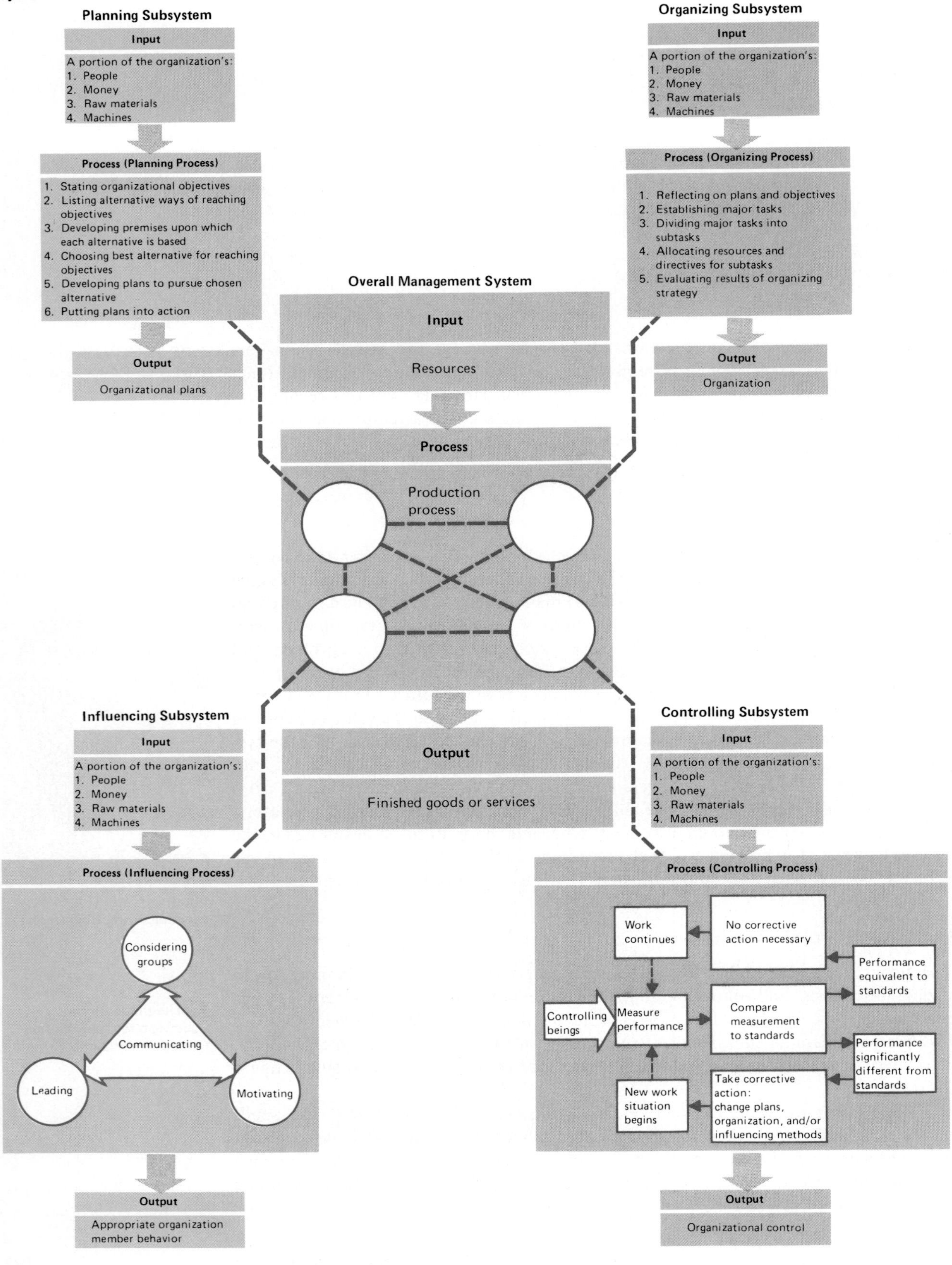

and accumulated by both management practitioners and management researchers. The probability is quite high, therefore, that functional skill will continue to be extremely valuable to managers of the future.

Valuable in the Future

Back to the Case

Max Barton probably has achieved his present level of managerial success primarily by using systems skill and functional skill. The application of systems and functional skills can be related directly to the fundamental aspects of Barton's job at Pleasant Ridge. Systems skill, for example, enables Barton to see and manage all parts of his department as a group of components that functions as a whole with other departments to help his company achieve its objectives. Functional skill, on the other hand, enables Barton to successfully plan, organize, influence, and control the various parts of his department to ensure that it will be coordinated with other departments and make a worthwhile contribution to the attainment of the company's objectives.

Because these skills are so entrenched in management theory, their use probably will be vital to Barton's management efforts in the future. Thus, developing his systems and functional skills is a sound strategy for Barton in preparing himself for a future management position at the Pleasant Ridge Candy Company.

Situational Analysis Skill in the Future

In addition to systems and functional skills, this text recommends that practicing managers possess situational analysis skill. **Situational analysis skill** is the ability to apply both systems theory and functional theory to the particular situations managers face. This skill emphasizes that managers must thoroughly understand their own unique management situation before they can use systems and functional skills to their best advantage. Obviously, the importance of situational analysis skill is supported by the thoughts and ideas of the contingency approach to management.

Importance Supported by Contingency Approach

Situational analysis skill probably will be extremely important to managers of the future. However, managers of the future almost certainly will face much different situational factors than either past or present managers.[4] Examples of these different situational factors for managers of the future include (1) the size of future management systems, (2) the characteristics of future management system members, (3) the amount of energy available to future management systems, and (4) the technology available to future management systems. The following sections discuss each of these future situational factors in more detail and offer possible strategies for dealing with them.

Valuable But Different

Size of Management Systems of the Future

Generally speaking, a tendency exists in American society for successful businesses and other types of concerns to grow larger over time. As this trend continues into the future, managers of the future, as a group, probably will be faced with managing larger systems than has any other generation of managers.[5] Also, since as management systems grow they tend to become more difficult to manage, managers of the future, as a group, probably also will be faced with the challenge of managing the most difficult-to-manage set of management systems that has ever existed. Specific characteristics of large management systems that tend to make the systems more difficult to manage include:

Large Systems Are Harder to Manage

1. *A diminishing ability of individuals within the system to comprehend the overall system* Obviously, the learning capacity of all human beings is limited. As a system increases in size, fewer and fewer individuals within

Limited Learning Capacity

that system are able to understand all system parts and the complicated relationships between those parts. Generating and disseminating information that adequately defines system parts and their corresponding relationships becomes both a formidable and important task for managers of large management systems.

Eliminating Decision-Making Input

2. *A diminishing level of participation in decision making* Overall, as management systems grow larger, managers tend to exclude the participation of other system members in decision making that takes place within that system. This tendency generally develops because as systems grow larger, managers typically feel that large-group involvement in decision making within that system becomes less and less feasible. As a general guideline, even as management systems grow larger, managers should continue to try to raise the quality of their decisions by allowing other system members to participate in the making of those decisions.[6]

Less Communication between Top and Other Levels

3. *A declining access of organization members to top decision makers within the system* As the number of system members increases, the proportion of those members who can communicate directly with upper management becomes smaller and smaller. If not overcome in some way—perhaps through special meetings of various kinds with system members—this characteristic of a large management system can put top management completely out of touch with its people.

4. *A growing involvement of experts in decision making within the system* As systems grow, they necessarily become more and more complex. As problem complexity related to those systems increases, managers tend to ask various kinds of experts for help in solving these problems. These experts only can be of help, however, if they can discuss specialized information in a way that can be understood and applied by managers. This can be, and often is, an extremely difficult challenge for experts to meet. Managers, however, must do everything possible to be sure that the experts they employ meet this challenge.

Hard-to-Understand Expert Advice

Costs of Running System Are High

5. *Increasing costs of coordination and control* As management systems grow larger, more and more authority must be delegated to various system levels and segments. To maintain coordination and control, however, managers must establish adequate communication between the various levels and segments, and establish effective plans to guide them. The cost of coordinating and controlling system segments never should exceed the contribution those segments can make to the system as a whole.

Rules Constrain People

6. *Increasing system rigidity* As systems gain in size, rules and regulations must be established so that new system segments operate in a predetermined and predictable fashion. Managers must recognize, however, that too many of such rules and regulations will create a rigid and inflexible system. Large systems should have enough regulations to ensure order but not so many that flexibility and creativity in solving unique management system problems becomes nonexistent.

System Weaknesses Go Undetected

7. *A growing deterioration of the overall system* The point was made earlier that as management systems grow larger, fewer and fewer system members are able to understand them fully. As a result of this lack of understanding, the deterioration of various segments of large management systems likely will take place, go unnoticed, and therefore, remain uncorrected. Managers of growing management systems must take steps to ensure that such deterioration is noticed and eliminated as soon as possible.

Since Max Barton is presently successful, he probably also possesses situational analysis skill in addition to his systems and functional skills discussed earlier. Situational analysis skill enables Barton to choose and apply those segments of both systems theory and functional theory that are best suited to the situation he presently faces in his department of the candy company.

In addition, as with the systems and functional skills mentioned earlier, situational analysis skill probably will be as valuable, if not more valuable, to Barton in his practice of management in the future as it is to his practice of management in the present. Thus, further development of his situational analysis skill is a sound strategy for Barton in preparing himself for a future management position at the Pleasant Ridge Candy Company.

Barton also should take into consideration, however, that the management situation he will face in the future probably will be much different from the management situation he presently faces. For example, if the Pleasant Ridge Candy Company is successful, his department, as well as other departments within the company, probably will grow over time and become more difficult to manage. As his department grows, Barton should be careful to instill an understanding within appropriate department members, as well as within himself, of all department parts and how they relate to one another and all other relevant company parts. In addition, Barton should attempt to involve others in departmental decision making, be accessible to departmental personnel, and establish appropriate amounts of rigidity within the department, even though these activities will become more difficult as the department grows.

Characteristics of Future Management System Members

The characteristics of further management system members is another significant situational factor that will face managers of the future. In this regard, the following sections discuss (1) union membership of professional workers in the future and (2) characteristics of the work force of the future.

Union Membership of Professional Workers in the Future

A significant number of management theorists predict that in the future an increasing number of professional workers will turn to unions. The traditional image of the union member as a factory employee fighting for better wages is likely to change in the future. Instead, an increasing number of engineers, professors, and doctors probably will join unions. This probably will be especially true for professionals employed by government agencies.[7] It appears that the needs of professionals who work within management systems simply are not being met by management.[8] Unless this trend is reversed, managers of the future probably can look forward to dealing with professional workers primarily through union representatives.

Professionals Turn to Unions

Characteristics of the Work Force of the Future

Insights on the future human resources of management systems can be obtained by studying the general makeup of the work force from which those resources will come. The next sections discuss the following characteristics of this work force of the future: (1) the average age of the work force, (2) the size of the work force, (3) the number of professional workers in the work force, (4) the jobs performed by the work force, (5) employment of the work force according to industry, (6) interest of the work force in the quality of work life, and (7) more women in management.

Average Age of Work Force   Overall, the work force of the future will have a much higher average age than the work force of today. In addition, these older workers will not be forced to retire because of age and generally will be sought by managers much

Older Workers

Figure 20.2 Projected percent change in employment from 1978–1990.

(In thousands)

Occupational Group	Employment			Openings		
	1978	Projected 1990	Percent change[1]	Total	Growth	Replacements[2]
White-collar workers	47,205	58,400	23.6	36,800	11,200	25,600
Professional and technical workers	14,245	16,900	18.3	8,300	2,600	5,700
Managers and administrators, except farm	10,105	12,200	20.8	7,100	2,100	5,000
Sales workers	5,951	7,600	27.7	4,800	1,700	3,100
Clerical workers	16,904	21,700	28.4	16,600	4,800	11,800
Blue-collar workers	31,531	36,600	16.1	16,200	5,100	11,100
Craft workers	12,386	14,900	20.0	7,000	2,500	4,500
Operatives, except transport	10,875	12,500	15.0	5,600	1,600	4,000
Transport operatives	3,541	4,100	16.2	1,700	600	1,100
Nonfarm laborers	4,729	5,100	8.1	2,000	400	1,600

[1] Calculated from unrounded figures.
[2] Due to deaths, retirements, and other separations from the labor force. Does not include transfers out of occupations.

From U.S. Department of Labor, 1980.

more intensely than their counterparts today.[9] As a result, managers of the future probably will have to deal with generally older workers who may have been employed within the management system for much longer periods of time.[10]

Size of Work Force   Work forces of the future probably will be smaller than at one time anticipated. As a result, managers of the future probably will have to face higher labor costs and more intense competition in hiring good employees than predicted earlier. The decreasing national population rate described in the following quote generally is cited as the basis for this prediction of a smaller work force in the future:

> So now it appears that the average American woman will bear only 2.1 children in her lifetime, instead of 3.1. If the trend continues, the United States population in the year 2000 will reach only 262 million instead of 340 million projected earlier. The increase is still large: the population today is only 214 million. But the lowered birthrate already means that more than 12 million Americans who had been expected to exist will not exist; the forecast ten years ago projected 226 million people in 1976.
> The number of Americans in the year 2000 could, in fact, be even lower than now foreseen. The smallest of three estimates recently made by the Commerce Department is only 245 million, and many economists and other analysts think this figure may turn out to be the most accurate.[11]

Number of Professional Workers in Work Force   Another characteristic of the work force of the future probably will be that the number of white-collar or professionally and technically trained workers in this work force will increase relative to the number of blue-collar or nonprofessional workers. This trend is illustrated in figure 20.2. This growth of professional and technical workers in the work force of the future implies that managers of the future probably will have to modify their strategies to suit generally more sophisticated workers.[12]

Jobs Performed by Work Force   A fourth characteristic of the work force of the future is that the future work force as a whole will be performing somewhat different jobs than the work force of today. In addition, the workforce of the future will want

Fewer Workers Than Once Expected

More Professionals

Fewer Kinds of Jobs

Figure 20.3 Employment growth by industry through 1990.

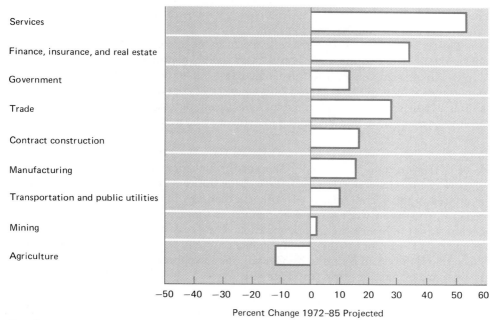

Percent Change 1972–85 Projected

From Bureau of Labor Statistics, 1980–1981.

to be responsible and efficient if it perceives its work as serving some meaningful purpose.[13] There probably will be primarily three types of jobs that human resources of the future will perform in management systems:

> There will be a few "workers"—probably a smaller part of the total labor force than today—who will be part of the in-line production, primarily doing tasks requiring relatively flexible eye-brain-hand coordination.
> There will be a substantial number of people whose task is to keep the system operating by preventative and remedial maintenance. Machines will play an increasing role, of course, in maintenance functions, but machine power will not likely develop as rapidly in this area as in-line activities. Moreover, the total amount of maintenance work—to be shared by people and machines—will increase. In the near future at least, this group can be expected to make up an increasing fraction of the total work force.
> There will be a substantial number of people at professional levels, responsible for the design of product, for the design of the productive process, and for general management.[14]

If, primarily, these three types of jobs materialize as predicted, managers of the future will be faced with a number of challenging problems. For example, if fewer employees work in production areas within management systems, difficulties regarding differences in the perceived level of importance of production work groups within the management system relative to the level of perceived importance of other work groups within the management system could develop. Other work groups within the management system might believe that since they are larger than the production work group, they are more important. Naturally, this type of situation easily could result in jealousy and a lack of cooperation between production and other work groups.

Another problem managers of the future will have to face will be to determine how to use their blue-collar employees as their blue-collar jobs begin to disappear.[15]

Employment of Work Force According to Industries   As figure 20.3 indicates, a greater percentage of the work force of the future will be employed within the service industry. The service industry is comprised of organizations that provide services, such

Service Industry Employs More People

as retailing, banking, insurance, and education. The service industry does not directly produce goods as do the manufacturing, farming, and construction industries. Although figure 20.3 projects only to 1990, many management theorists believe that this trend will continue well beyond this date.[16]

This information can be very valuable to managers of the future. Since service jobs probably will become more prevalent as society continues to grow, the ability to apply management concepts to this particular job situation will become increasingly important for managers to acquire. This analysis, of course, relates to all managers as a group. Individual managers in the manufacturing industry, for example, may never need to be concerned with managing individuals who perform service jobs.

Interested in Making Decisions about Work Situations

Interest of Work Force in Quality of Work Life A sixth characteristic of the work force of the future to be covered in this section is its degree of interest in the quality of its work life. Generally, the work force of the future probably will be more seriously interested in the overall quality of work life than any other work force that has preceded it. **Quality of work life** can be defined as the opportunity of workers to make decisions that influence their work situation. The greater the opportunity of workers to make such decisions within a management system, the higher the quality of work life within that system is said to be. Overall, the work force of the future probably will strive to make decisions that tend to create:

1. Jobs that are interesting, challenging, and responsible
2. Worker rewards through fair wages and recognition for their contribution
3. Work places that are clean, safe, quiet, and bright
4. Minimal but available supervision
5. Secure jobs that promote the development of friendly relationships with other system members
6. Organizations that provide for personal welfare and medical attention.[17]

Too Much Employee Control Is Dangerous

Managers of the future, as managers of both the present and the past, will have to emphasize the attainment of management system objectives. Unlike managers of the past, however, future managers may find that providing workers with a high quality of work life is an extremely important prerequisite for attaining these objectives.[18] The cartoon implies that managers of the future are somewhat limited, however, in the degree to which they can allow employees to make decisions relative to their work situation.

Women on the Move

More Women in Management This section discusses the chapter's seventh and last characteristic of the workforce of the future. As in the recent past, the future should contain a number of legal, educational, and social developments that will move a greater percentage of women into the mainstream of corporate management.[19] As an indication of this trend, not only is the percentage of women attending four-year colleges increasing faster then that of men, but a significant number of business schools are now offering courses aimed specifically at preparing women for management positions.[20]

A Complex Situation

Although at first glance, "more women in management" may seem to be a simple variable with which managers of the future must deal, when in reality, it is extremely complex. For example, based upon a study by Baron and Witte, several factors seem to increase the difficulty involved in men and women being able to work together productively.[21] These factors have been divided into four categories: (1) organizational problems and inequities; (2) personal characteristics of men and women; (3) men's perception of women; and (4) women's perception of men. Figure 20.4 shows specific factors contained in each of these categories.

Figure 20.4 Factors that seem to make it difficult for men and women to work together productively.

Organizational Problems and Inequities	Characteristics of Men and Women	Men's Perception of Women	Women's Perception of Men
Many women feel they are left out of the informal communication network.	Men seem to have difficulty understanding the subtle ways in which they discriminate or treat women.	Women are obsessed with terminology (a "he" rather than a "he/she" etc.).	Men treat women differently than men.
Women are seen by men as making advances because of government regulations and not ability.	Women compete and discriminate more against each other than do men.	Women use the idea of discrimination as a "crutch."	Men exhibit niceties, not acceptance.
Customers may have difficulty dealing with women.	Women appear to give their marriages and family roles greater importance relative to their jobs than men.	Women don't make a real commitment.	Men don't help women grow.
Women feel they are discriminated against for promotions.	Women behave with more emotion than men.	Women misconstrue being courteous as being patronizing.	Men don't relate to problems women have.
Women are seen as having more problems than men in relocating in another community.	Women are required to be more competent than men in comparable positions.	Women overreact.	Men either lack confidence in women's abilities or are afraid women are capable.
Men are seen by other men as having more long-term career goals than women.			

This figure is based upon Alma S. Baron and Robert L. White, "The New Work Dynamic: Men and Women in the Workforce," *Business Horizons,* August 1980, pp. 56–60. Adapted with permission.

Naturally, managers of the future must strive to minimize the effects of these factors if organizations are to maximize gains through men and women working together. Perhaps through special training programs, managers can help men and women better understand one another and, as a result, work more productively as a team.

Helping Men and Women Work Together

Back to the Case

One reason the management situation Barton will face in the future probably will be somewhat different is that people issues within his department and within his company as a whole probably will be somewhat different. For example, Barton likely will find that the professional people working in his department and other departments are represented by unions in the future, that the average age of his employees is much higher, and that very few people in his department actually retire because of age. In addition, Barton probably will find in the future that his company must compete with service industries to hire good people and that the people in his and other departments are more seriously interested in the quality of their work life.

Of course, Barton should not view any of these probable people issues as unmanageable in the future. Instead, he should see them as significant variables in the management situation that will face him and strive to apply those aspects of systems theory and functional theory that best help him to manage this situation.

Energy in the Future

The previous two major sections of this chapter discussed management system size and characteristics of system members as two major situational variables for managers of the future. Energy is a third such major variable. In the past, managers seem to

"I'm unwinding on company time because that's when I got wound up."

© 1976, Reprinted by permission of the *Wall Street Journal* and Bo Brown.

have operated under the assumption that an unlimited supply of energy could be obtained for such worthwhile and important purposes as powering equipment and providing adequate working light. Energy sources as known in the past, however, probably will become more and more scarce in the future. Although this scarcity is not expected to be crippling, the cost of energy available to management systems of the future probably will be very high. This prediction is based primarily on the premise that the oil supply in the world is expected to begin vanishing about 1990.[22]

Less Energy at Higher Cost

As new ways of using coal, solar, and nuclear energy are discovered, energy may again be readily available to managers of the more distant future. Managers of the more immediate future, however, probably will need to become involved in such activities as investing in reserve supplies of energy, finding or developing alternative sources of energy, and quickly cutting back production activities due to unexpected depletion of energy supplies.

Future energy shortages probably will force managers of the future to modify somewhat the way in which they operate their management systems. The most significant of these modifications typically will be forced on future managers who are directly responsible for management systems that exist primarily to supply energy products to consumers.

Technology in the Future

Technology is the fourth major situational factor that will face managers of the future. The future undoubtedly will contain numerous possible technological improvements that managers of the future must evaluate for use within the management system.[23] This evaluation, of course, necessarily must weigh the cost of using such technological improvements against the contribution they can make toward the attainment of management system objectives. In essence, managers of the future will be faced with the hard fact that sophisticated equipment is expensive to use and therefore must make a substantial contribution to the attainment of management system objectives. An example of technological improvement and the related situation the manager must face is the growth of word processing equipment discussed in exhibit 20.

Deciding about Using New Technology

Specific technological improvements available to managers of the future undoubtedly will be many and varied. The further sophistication of computers and calculators

Figure 20.5 Useful characteristics of managers of the past and future.

Skills Useful to Past Managers	Skills Useful to Future Managers
Familiar problem solver Intuitive problem solver Conservative risk taker Convergent diagnostician Lag controller	Novel problem solver Analytic problem solver Entrepreneurial risk taker Divergent diagnostician Lead controller

Adapted from H. Igor Ansoff, "Management in Transition," in Edward C. Bursk, ed., *Challenge to Leadership: Managing in a Changing World* (New York: The Free Press, 1973), p. 41. Copyright 1973 by the Conference Board, Inc. Used with permission.

for use in the area of information handling is likely. New and different means of distributing products to customers, as well as faster and safer means of human transportation, are expected. In addition, further developments in the area of communication will make it easier for people to share information more effectively and efficiently.[24]

Back to the Case

Barton may find that in the future, energy may be in shorter supply to his company. Given this fact, he may, for example, have to cut down on the work hours of the night shift to conserve the energy available to his department. Overall, however, Barton can take some consolation in the fact that managers responsible for companies that produce energy products for consumers probably will face many more ramifications of this future energy shortage than he will ever face in the candy industry.

Many technological improvements also probably will be available in the future to assist Barton and his people in the candy department. Barton must evaluate each of these improvements carefully and adopt only those whose benefits are more valuable than their cost.

Training Managers for the Future

Managers of tomorrow, if they are competent, certainly will be in high demand and of critical importance to the success of a management system. One strategy a company might adopt to ensure an adequate supply of future managers is to train its managers of today so that they are ready to cope with tomorrow's challenges. The following material discusses three main issues related to this training of managers for the future: (1) objectives in training managers for the future, (2) developing future-oriented managers, and (3) emphasizing professionalism and change.

Company Prepares its Own Managers

Objectives in Training Managers for the Future

To develop and maintain an effective and efficient program for training managers for the future, an appropriate set of objectives for such a program must be developed and pursued. These objectives should consider (1) skills that managers will need in the future, (2) decisions future managers will have to make, and (3) practices that managers of the future will follow. The following three sections discuss each of these three areas in detail.

Additional Skills for Future Managers

An earlier section of this chapter discussed three skills that inevitably will be helpful to managers of the future. These skills are systems skill, functional skill, and situational analysis skill. Figure 20.5 shows a set of characteristics of managers in the past, as well as an additional set of characteristics that probably will be needed by managers of the future.

Skills for the Future and Management Training

Exhibit 20

Jimmy Carter uses Word-Processing Equipment

A retired President working in his office in Plains, Ga., has focused attention on the new world of word processors—essentially high-priced electric typewriters with video display screens. But thousands of other Americans, mostly secretaries, are using them, too. Executives believe that the souped-up typewriters will bring about huge productivity increases in their offices, and they are wildly ordering the machines despite prices that average $12,000 per system.

Word-processor sales will jump at an annual rate of about 30 per cent over the next five years, says Charles I. Norris, of International Data Corp., a market-research company. The industry's volume, he predicts, will soar from last year's $2.1 billion to $7.3 billion in 1985. More than 100 companies hope to win pieces of the ever-expanding pie, including current leaders such as International Business Machines Corp., Wang Laboratories, Lanier, Exxon Office Systems, Xerox Corp. and Datapoint.

Newsrooms: There are two kinds of word processors: the "stand alone," consisting of a keyboard and from one to four display screens, and the "cluster," a series of terminals—found largely in newsrooms—on which the written story is fed into a central computer. Most of the current business is in stand-alone processors—and these machines initially seem enormously overpriced. A secretary, for example, types a letter on a keyboard and it is displayed on a screen. She can then correct spelling mistakes, add or delete words or move around whole blocks of type—all at the touch of a key. The machine then prints out the finished letter.

There are few savings in a single letter, but when a secretary has to type essentially the same letter several times, the efficiencies increase. With a word processor, she has to type the letter only once, then print as many copies as she wants. If slight changes have to be made on each copy, she can do it in a fraction of the time it takes to retype the entire letter. Legal secretaries, who have to type hundreds of pages of pleadings, find word processors particularly helpful. "A secretary's productivity can be increased 25 to 200 per cent with a word processor, depending on how much typing she does," says Dan McGlaughlin, vice president of IBM's office-products division.

The newest machines are even more versatile. IBM's new Displaywriter, for instance, will catch an operator's spelling mistakes. Equipped with a 50,000-word "dictionary" available in six languages, the machine checks copy for misspellings at the rate of ten seconds a page. Words that are misspelled, or not in the dictionary, are highlighted. Smallish Compucorp of Los Angeles upstaged giant IBM and produced an electronic dictionary of 1 million words that catches misspelled words—and corrects them.

The next breakthrough will occur when word processors are connected to data-processing systems, allowing companies to link work stations around the country in a single communications network. Instead of mailing many copies of the same memo, for example, a secretary will be able to send it instantly to its various destinations by telephone wire or satellite.

As the technology proliferates, so does the competition. And it's not necessarily the giant companies that win out. At least one major firm has failed to keep its products up to date. Exxon, which earlier set industry standards with its Vydec machine, has had such problems. Analysts say Exxon let short-term profit considerations interfere with its long-term goals and fell behind in developing new systems. The company has come out with a new Vydec unit, however, and says that its over-all sales were up 50 per cent last year.

Attack: Similarly, IBM, which at first dominated word processing, has lost its leading position to upstart Wang, which has grown into a $543 million-sales company. Wang is now attacking IBM's Displaywriter with a new word processor selling for just $7,500, and executive vice president John Cunningham predicts Wang's sales this year will exceed $1 billion. "Just because you're small doesn't mean that you're not going to succeed," says Leellen Spelman, a securities analyst with Martin Simpson & Co. "The companies that aren't innovative are the ones that will die." In other words, companies that promote productivity in the workplace will survive only if they themselves remain creative and ultra-efficient.

LEONARD GLYNN with MARC FRONS in New York, HOLLY MORRIS in Atlanta and DIANE WEATHERS in Boston

Figure 20.6 Decision making in the firm of today and the firm of the future.

Firm of Today	Firm of the Future
Content of Decisions	
Operating issues, corporate policies	Strategy formulation, design of systems for strategy implementation
Exploitation of firm's current position	Innovation in patterns of firm's products, markets, and technology
Economic, technological, national, intraindustry perspective	Economic, sociopolitical, technological, multinational, multiindustry perspective
Decision Process	
Emphasis on historical experience, judgment, past programs for solving similar problems	Emphasis on anticipation, rational analysis, pervasive use of specialist experts, techniques for coping with novel decision situations
Personnel-intensive process	Technology-intensive process
Information for Decisions	
Formal information systems for internal performance history	Formal systems for anticipatory, external-environment information
One-way, top down, flow of information	Interactive, two-way communication channels linking managers and other professionals with knowledge workers
Computer systems emphasizing volume and fast response information for general management	Computer systems emphasizing richness, flexibility, and accessibility of information for general management
Emphasis on periodic operations plans, capital, and operating expenditure budgets	Emphasis on continuous planning, covering operations, projects, systems resource development; control based on cost-benefits forecasts

An examination of figure 20.5 indicates that managers of the future probably will need somewhat different skills than their predecessors. Thus, objectives for training managers for the future should be established to develop managers who are novel problem solvers, analytical problem solvers, risk takers, diagnosticians, and lead controllers.

Decision Making for Future Managers

Objectives for training managers for the future also should take into consideration the decisions that managers of the future will have to make.

Figure 20.6 compares the characteristics of decisions, the decision process, and decision information as used in the company of today versus the company of the future. Since these two decision-making situations are dramatically different, objectives for training managers for the future should reflect these differences. For example, objectives for training managers for the future should emphasize the relationship between managerial decision making and such factors as strategy formulation, the use of expert specialists, and the use of computer systems to increase management system flexibility. Figure 20.6 indicates that objectives for training managers of today that relate to these same areas typically emphasize the relationship between managerial decision making and existing corporate policies, the use of personal judgment and operating history, and the use of computer systems to analyze large amounts of information quickly.

Decisions for the Future and Management Training

Figure 20.7 Past and future management practices.

Past	Future
Assumption that a business manager's sole responsibility is to optimize stockholder wealth	Profit still dominant but modified by the assumption that a business manager has other social responsibilities
Business performance measured only by economic standards	Application of both an economic and a social measure of performance
Emphasis on quantity of production	Emphasis on quantity and quality
Authoritarian management	Permissive/democratic management
Short-term intuitive planning	Long-range comprehensive structured planning
Entrepreneur	Renaissance manager
Control	Creativity
People subordinate	People dominant
Financial accounting	Human resources accounting
Caveat emptor ("let the buyer beware")	Ombudsman
Centralized decision making	Decentralized and small-group decision making
Concentration on internal functioning	Concentration on external ingredients for company success
Dominance of economic forecasts in decision making	Major use of social, technical, and political forecasts as well as economic forecasts
Business viewed as a single system	Business viewed as a system within a larger social system
Business ideology calls for aloofness from government	Business–government cooperation and convergence of planning
Business has little concern for social costs of production	Increasing concern for internalizing social costs of production

Courtesy of Dr. George Steiner.

Management Practices of the Future

Objectives for training managers for the future also should consider the management practices that future managers will be following. Naturally, such objectives should be aimed at training managers to carry out these future practices both effectively and efficiently. Figure 20.7 compares present and future management practices. According to this figure, training objectives for developing managers for the future should emphasize such factors as carrying out long-range comprehensive planning as opposed to short-term intuitive planning, meeting social responsibilities as opposed to meeting only profit responsibilities, and establishing a decentralized decision process within the management system as opposed to a primarily centralized decision process.

Practices for the Future and Management Training

Developing Future-Oriented Managers

In addition to developing and pursuing appropriate objectives, the process of training managers for the future should involve encouraging today's managers to be future oriented.[25] According to Nanus, **future-oriented managers** attempt to create their own future, whenever possible, and adapt to this future, when necessary, through a continuous process of research about the future, long-range planning, and setting objectives. Such managers make no important decisions without a systematic and thorough analysis of the future consequences of such decisions. Future-oriented managers see the future not as an *uncontrollable* development but as a factor that can be influenced significantly by present managerial behavior. Here, Nanus is suggesting that managers are best prepared for the future when they are shown how to participate in creating that future to the best advantage of the management system.

Creates Own Future

Emphasizing Professionalism and Change

Besides an appropriate set of objectives and a future orientation, the process of training managers for the future should emphasize both professionalism and change. The extremely complex nature of the future manager's job indicates that this job can best be learned by approaching its study as the learning of a profession. A **profession** is a vocation whose practice is based on an understanding of both a specific body of knowledge and the corresponding abilities necessary to apply this understanding to vital human problems. Additionally, professionalism stresses that knowledge related to a profession should be seen as constantly evolving and being modified as a result of insights derived from individuals actually practicing the profession.[26]

Professionalism necessarily involves changes. Managers trained for the future, therefore, should be warned of the inevitable changes that will occur over time. It is hoped that this warning of inevitable changes will help managers of the future to overcome "future shock" or the inability of an individual to adapt to changes.[27] Although some management theorists argue that such changes probably will be insignificant,[28] others would state strongly that these changes will be both extensive and significant.[29]

Back to the Case

The last section of this chapter described some of the main ingredients of the process a company like the Pleasant Ridge Candy Company could implement to prepare its managers for the challenges they inevitably will meet in the future. Even though this discussion focuses primarily on the process a company can implement, a manager like Max Barton can gain some understanding of what he as an individual can do to prepare himself for managing in the future. For example, Barton should attempt to train himself as a solver of novel or unique problems at the Pleasant Ridge Candy Company and focus on developing his talents as a thorough and complete analyzer of company problems.

Barton also should attempt to train himself to be able to make future managerial decisions successfully at the Pleasant Ridge Candy Company. In this regard, Barton should strive to develop such skills as (1) implementing a continuous planning program within his department to provide him with important decision-related information, (2) emphasizing the making of decisions that will encourage innovation within his department, and (3) anticipating the future as a rationale for making decisions as opposed to relying solely on departmental operating history.

Barton also should prepare himself to be able successfully to carry out management practices as they probably will exist in the future at the Pleasant Ridge Candy Company. In this regard, Barton should strive to develop the abilities to (1) apply both economic and social measures to evaluate the performance of his department, (2) emphasize both the quantity and quality of activities performed in his department, (3) maintain a long-range comprehensive planning program for his department, and (4) use social, technical, and political forecasts as well as economic forecasts as a basis for running his department.

Barton should know that studying and then practicing management is an extremely complex matter. However, since management can be defined as a profession, such complexity certainly should be expected. Also, the principles of management are continually evolving and being modified. As a result, Barton should expect that if he is to keep pace with the constantly changing management profession, he probably will have to manage somewhat differently in the future than he is today.

The following points are stressed within this chapter:

1. Managers of today should adapt systems theory and functional theory to management situations that face them. Systems skill, functional skill, and situational analysis skill will be as important, if not more important, to the practice of management in the future as it is to the practice of management today.

2. Management systems generally will be larger in the future than they are today. Larger systems often are more difficult to manage than smaller systems because they typically are difficult to understand, make participation in decision making difficult, cause difficulty in communication between upper and lower system levels, necessitate the understanding of expert advice, and are expensive to operate.

3. The work force of the future will have a higher average age, be smaller than once expected, contain more professionals, perform somewhat different jobs, be employed mostly in service industries, and be very interested in the quality of work life. There also will be more women managers in the workforce of the future.

4. The supply of energy available to managers in the more immediate future is expected to dwindle and become more costly. Managers of the more distant future, however, may find abundant alternative supplies of energy. Management systems directly involved in providing energy products to consumers will be most affected by the energy shortage of course.

5. Many different technological improvements will be available to managers of the future. These improvements, however, probably will be expensive to acquire and, therefore, must make a substantial contribution to goal attainment for such an acquisition to be justified.

6. Any company can ensure that its managers are ready for the future by training them today to meet the management challenges of the future. To do this successfully, however, an appropriate set of training objectives must be established, the concept of being future-oriented should be stressed, and approaching the study of management as the learning of a profession should be emphasized.

1. Define systems skill and describe its probable value to managers of the future.
2. What is functional skill? How valuable will this skill probably be to managers of the future?
3. What is the relationship between situational analysis skill, systems skill, and functional skill?
4. List and discuss four factors that can make large management systems difficult to manage.
5. If the predicted trend of more professional workers of the future joining unions actually materializes, how do you think it will affect the practices of management in the future?
6. State three probable characteristics of the work force of the future. Explain how each of your characteristics could affect the practice of management in the future.

7. What is meant by the phrase *quality of work life*?

8. Describe the types of decisions that employees of the future will attempt to make to increase the quality of their work life.

9. How will the predicted energy shortage, if it materializes, probably affect the practice of management in the future?

10. What is a major criteria that managers of the future should use to decide if a particular technological improvement will be employed within their management system?

11. Describe a strategy that can be adopted by a company to ensure that its managers will be able to face management challenges of the future.

12. Considering the decision-making situation that future managers will face, how should managers be trained for the future?

13. What is a "future-oriented" manager?

14. Management is a profession. Fully explain the implications of this statement.

Sources of Additional Information

Byars, Lloyd L., and Mescon, Michael H. *The Other Side of Profit.* Philadelphia: W. B. Saunders, 1975.

Elbing, Alvar O., and Elbing, C. J. *The Value Issue of Business.* New York: McGraw-Hill, 1967.

Farmer, Richard N. *Management in the Future.* Belmont, Calif.: Wadsworth Publishing, 1967.

Greenleaf, R. K. *The Servant as Leader.* Cambridge, Mass: Center for Applied Studies, 1973.

Herzberg, Frederick. *The Managerial Choice.* Homewood, Ill.: Dow Jones-Irwin, 1976.

Hummel, Ralph P. *The Bureaucratic Experience.* New York: St. Martin's Press, 1977.

A Look at Business in 1990. Washington: White House Conference, U.S. Government Printing Office, 1972.

Moffitt, D., ed. *America Tomorrow.* New York: American Management Association, 1977.

Newman, William H. *Managers for the Year 2000.* Englewood Cliffs, N.J.: Prentice-Hall, 1978.

Paluszek, V. L. *Business and Society: 1976–2000.* New York: American Management Association, 1976.

Preston, Lee E., and Post, James E. *Private Management and Public Policy.* Englewood Cliffs, N.J.: Prentice-Hall, 1975.

Sample, Robert L. "Coping with the 'Work-at-Home' Trend." *Administrative Management* 42, no. 8 (August 1981): 24–27.

Staff. "What's Ahead for In-House Training." *Administrative Management* 42, no. 7 (July 1981): 41–47.

Staff. "High Technology—Wave of the Future or a Market Flash in the Pan?" *Business Week,* 10 November 1980, pp. 86–98.

Sethi, S. Prakash. *Up Against The Corporate Wall: Modern Corporations and Social Issues of the Seventies.* 3d. ed. Englewood Cliffs, N.J.: Prentice-Hall, 1977.

Talpaert, Roger. "Looking into the Future: Management in the Twenty-First Century." *Management Review,* March 1981, pp. 21–25.

Zangwill, Willard I. *Success With People.* Homewood, Ill.: Dow Jones-Irwin, 1976.

Zoffer, H. J. "Restructuring Management Education." *Management Review* 70, No. 4 (April 1981): 37–41.

1. J. Buckley, "Goal-Process-System Interaction in Management: Correcting an Imbalance," *Business Horizons* 14 (1971): 81–92.

2. Paul Adler, Jr., "Toward a System of General Management Theory," *Southern Journal of Business*, July 1969.

3. "Stressing the System Approach," *Manufacturing Engineering*, August 1969, p. 75.

4. Richard Allen Stull, "A View of Management to 1980," *Business Horizons*, June 1974, pp. 5–12.

5. Duane S. Elgin and Robert A. Bushnell, "The Limits to Complexity: Are Bureaucracies Becoming Unmanageable?" *The Futurist*, December 1977, pp. 439–49.

6. Kenneth A. Kovach, Ben F. Sands, Jr., and William W. Brooks, "Management by Whom?—Trends in Participative Management," *S.A.M. Advanced Management Journal*, Winter 1981, pp. 4–14.

7. Thomas A. De Scisciolo, "Labor Relations—Friends and Future," Third National Capitol Conference, International Personnel Management Association, Washington, D.C., 28 May 1975.

8. Dennis Chamot, "Professional Employees Turn to Unions," *Harvard Business Review*, May/June 1976, pp. 119–28.

9. Patricia Skalka, "Farewell to the Youth Culture," *Ambassador*, April 1978, pp. 43–48.

10. Susan R. Rhodes, Michael Schuster, and Mildred Doering, "The Implications of an Aging Workforce," *Personnel Administrator*, October 1981, pp. 19–22.

11. Alfred L. Malabre, Jr., "The Future Revised—U.S. Unlikely to Be As Big—or As Rich—As Analysts Thought," *Wall Street Journal*, 15 March 1976, p. 1.

12. Peter F. Drucker, "Management's New Role," *Harvard Business Review*, November/December 1969, pp. 49–54.

13. Frederick Herzberg, "Herzberg on Motivation for the '80s'," *Industry Week*, October 1979, pp. 58–61.

14. Herbert A. Simon, "The Corporation: Will It Be Managed By Machines?" in *Management and Corporations—1985*, eds. Anshen and Bach (New York: McGraw-Hill, 1960), pp. 17–55.

15. Robert Schrank, "Horse-collar, Blue-collar Blues," *Harvard Business Review*, May/June 1981, p. 133.

16. Keith Davis, "Some Basic Trends Affecting Management in the 1980s," *Arizona Business*, November 1976, pp. 18–22.

17. Tom Lupton, "Efficiency and the Quality of Work Life," *Organizational Dynamics*, Autumn 1975, p. 68.

18. John F. Mee, "The Manager of the Future," *Business Horizons*, June 1973, pp. 5–14.

19. Linda Keller Brown, "Women and Business Management," *Signs: Journal of Women in Culture and Society* 5, no. 2 (1979): 266–88.

20. Rose K. Reha, "Preparing Women for Management Roles," *Business Horizons*, April 1979, pp. 68–71.

21. Alma S. Baron and Robert L. Witte, "The New Work Dynamic: Men and Women in the Workforce," *Business Horizons*, August 1980, pp. 56–60.

22. "The Future Revised: No Crippling Shortage of Energy Expected, But Cost Will Be High," *The Wall Street Journal*, 29 March 1976, pp. 1, 21.

23. Henry B. Schacht, "The Impact of Changes in the Seventies," *Business Horizons*, August 1970, pp. 29–34.

24. Douglas P. Brush, "Internal Communications and the New Technology," *Public Relations Journal*, February 1981, pp. 10–13.

25. Burt Nanus, "The Future-Oriented Corporation," *Business Horizons*, February 1975, pp. 5–12.

26. For more information on professionalism, see Kenneth R. Andrews, "Toward Professionalism in Business Management," *Harvard Business Review*, March/April 1969, pp. 49–60.

27. Alvin Toffler, *Future Shock* (New York: Random House, 1970), p. 4.

28. Charles Perrow, "Is Business Really Changing?" *Organization Dynamics* 3, no. 1 (Summer 1974).

29. Gordon H. Coperthwaite, "Management: Its Changing Patterns," *Management Controls*, December 1972, pp. 281–86.

Concluding Case 20
Industrial Capital Corporation: The New Venture Capitalists Are Women

BEAU PERE

THE STORY OF AN EXTRAORDINARY SEDUCTION...

"'Beau Pere' is a subversive fairy , tenderer and more intimate than Blier's earlier films. It's a comical movie, steeped in melancholy.
Blier is a true romantic— albeit a modernist one who mixes ragic passion with comic pratfalls. 's a wonderful cast. Ariel Besse is true child-woman...she seems to go through a thousand subtle hysical transformations. Dewaere is never shown such a wide range.
Blier has always been a clever, xtremely gifted filmmaker, but he goes deeper here than he ever has. 'Beau Pere' is his best movie."
—David Ansen, NEWSWEEK

"Audaciously funny...sexier and re passionate than any March romance si
—Carrie Rickey

Virginia L. Eng-Wong (Photo: Thom O'Connor)

The field of venture capitalism has received an influx of people over the last four years. Industry analyses estimate it includes currently 1,000 professionals, up from 850 in 1977. The demand for venture capitalists has increased due to a capital-gains tax reduction in 1978 and a loosening of the laws governing pension fund investments in 1979. These two factors have increased the amount of funds available for investment by venture capital firms from $3 billion during the period from 1970 to 1977 to $4.8 billion in early 1981. By the end of 1981, over $5 billion was expected to be available.

One of the unusual things about the increase in professionals in this field is that over one hundred of them are women. Women have entered a field in which millions of dollars are gambled on the success of faltering companies. Women venture capitalists are challenging the "old boy" network that has historically dominated the field.

The entrance of women into the field is of more importance than simply a breakthrough into a new field. Psychologists suggest it signifies an emergence from a fear that has lessened women's ultimate success in business. According to some psychologists, women have a gut fear of taking risks. This fear is attributed to their traditional upbringing that has stressed security. In venture capitalism, no such fear is possible as risking money on certain enterprises and winning is the goal of the game.

Most women did not come to venture capitalism through the traditional channels as the men did. They have come from very non-traditional areas, such as the culinary arts and psychology; many of the women have very unusual backgrounds.

Virginia Eng-Wong, a 41-year-old vice-president of Industrial Capital Corporation, comes from a diverse background. She received her bachelor's degree in Greek from Wellesley College and taught high school English in addition to Chinese cooking to housewives in Ann Arbor, Michigan. From there she entered the credit department training program at the Industrial National Bank of Rhode Island in Providence. After two years of experience there, she joined Industrial Capital Corporation, a small business investment company wholly owned by Industrial National and is now the vice-president of Industrial Capital.

Patricia M. Cloherty, 39, is one of the most experienced women in venture capitalism. Cloherty spent two years in Brazil with the Peace Corps and earned a master's degree in international development and comparative education from Columbia University. Afterwards she joined the New York City venture capital firm of Alan Patricof Associates Inc. in 1969 as a research associate. While at Patricof from 1969 through 1977, she took finance courses, served as interim president of Childcraft Education Corporation, an Edison (N.J.) toy distributor, and gained partnership status there. For two years of the Carter Administration, she was deputy administrator of the federal Small Business Administration. In 1979, she started a firm with her husband in New York City.

Most of the women are new in the field and must develop their own network of communication, without which they are ineffective. Entrepreneurs usually seek financial backing from more than one firm. Venture capitalists trade potential clients much like realtors share listings. Men already have an established communication network and send the deals to their friends. Women, being so new to the field, are still establishing their communication network.

Dealings with potential clients can pose problems for women. One woman reports that two management teams clearly stated they resented working with women. Another woman reports an unusual telephone conversation with a sixty-year-old businessman. During the conversation he kept stuttering and jumbling his words. Finally, the gentleman apologized and said he had never dealt with a woman before who knew anything about business.

According to Judith Bultman, an investment officer at Continental Illinois Venture Corporation, a woman has to be nonthreatening and at the same time very firm. She further suggests that if women are not into trail blazing, venture capitalism is a field to avoid.

Being an unknown entity also has some advantages. Many entrepreneurs are not used to dealing with businesswomen and many times let down their guard. They relax when talking to women and reveal information about the venture that should not have been discussed and consequently, the businesswoman does not invest in that venture.

The field of venture capitalism is gaining status among the business schools and is attracting students. It is now easier for women to enter the field because a few women have paved the way and won respect for their success. However, according to some women, the field is still relatively new for women and they are still on trial, and women entering venture capitalism must keep this in mind.

This case is adapted from "Women: The New Venture Capitalists," *Business Week*, November 2, 1981, pp. 100–102.

Discussion Issues

1. What organizational problems and inequities do you see facing women in the capital venture field?
2. How might these problems be corrected?
3. Will the skills being displayed by these female venture capitalists be in greater or lesser demand in the future? Explain.
4. What do you feel will be the greatest challenge to professional women in the future?

Appendix
Comprehensive Case
The Hancock Company

The Hancock Company is a chemical manufacturer making primarily drug chemicals such as vitamin preparations, sulfa drugs, antibiotics, hormones, and reagents. Its products are used by pharmaceutical and drug manufacturing concerns; veterinary products manufacturers; food and beverage manufacturing houses; educational, commercial, and industrial laboratories; industrial establishments; and ultimate consumers to whom they are dispensed by hospitals or physicians or on physician's prescription through retail drugstores.

Sales of the company have grown very rapidly, as shown by table A.

Company profits have grown with sales, and its ratio of net profits to sales is about average for the large firms in the pharmaceutical industry.

No small part of this great expansion of sales has been the fruit of the extensive program of research that the company began in the early thirties and has continued to the present time. This department contains units specializing in organic and biochemical research, microbiological research, and physical and inorganic chemical research, plus a development unit specializing in chemical technology and production.

Since new products are frequently introduced into the line and the methods of use of the company products are constantly changing, the relative importance of different product groups in the sales pattern is constantly shifting. From time to time, new products or modifications of old products are introduced that do not fit exactly into existing product groups but that in either their research, production, or sales characteristics overlap almost any product grouping that may be set up.

For example, table B shows the shifts in the percentage of total company sales volume experienced by a number of product groups, which for obvious reasons cannot be named specifically, during a period of twenty years.

These shifts in product line and sales volume naturally create planning and coordination problems, and this case is primarily concerned with the dynamic nature of the company's business. First, the general organization will be briefly described; then measures taken to date for guiding individual products will be explained.

General Organization

The general organization structure is indicated in figure A. Naturally, the size and range of activities of each section varies, as is indicated in the following discussion.

Production

Production is carried on in four plants, each of which has a manager, manufacturing manager, plant engineer, personnel manager, purchasing clerk, and financial services manager. Information about each plant is shown in Table C.

In the production division there is a central manufacturing planning department that (1) determines production requirements for all products and subdivisions consistent with production capacity, inventory levels, minimum costs, and related factors; (2) schedules all manufacturing, packaging, and quality testing operations; (3) establishes inventory levels for all goods and materials in accordance with established policies; (4) requisitions materials and containers; (5) maintains stock records for all types of goods and materials; and (6) collects and informs other divisions about production schedules, deliveries, inventories, batches, costs, charging rates, yields, raw material factors, and all other production matters.

Table A Growth of Company Sales.

Year	Sales	Year	Sales
25 years ago	$ 8,100,000	5 years ago	$ 81,100,000
20 years ago	8,370,000	3 years ago	93,200,000
15 years ago	15,660,000	2 years ago	108,500,000
10 years ago	37,350,000	Last year	111,700,000

Table B Shifts in Sales Volumes of Product Groups.

Product group	Percent of Total Company Sales Volume		
	25 years ago	15 years ago	5 years ago
A	11.3	10	5
B	9.6	8	5
C	7.7	2	—
D	7.3	5	1
E	7.0	12	0.5
F	6.9	3	2
G	3.9	4	3
H	3.9	2	0.3
I	3.8	4	1
J	—	15	27
K	—	7	6
L	—	—	15
M	—	—	12
N	—	—	9
Others	38.7	28	13.2

Table C Hancock Company Plants.

Plant	Location	Employees	Products
Main	Baltimore, Md.	4000	Antibiotics, vitamin preparations, hormones, general drugs
Seneca	Oswego, N.Y.	1200	Antibiotics, sulfa drugs, reagents, laboratory chemicals
Sawmill	Three Rivers, Mich.	1500	Vitamins, hormones, antibiotics, general chemicals
Beacon	Beacon, N.Y.	550	Specialty products for retail sale under Hancock label

Figure A Organization Chart—The Hancock Company.

Organization Chart — The Hancock Company

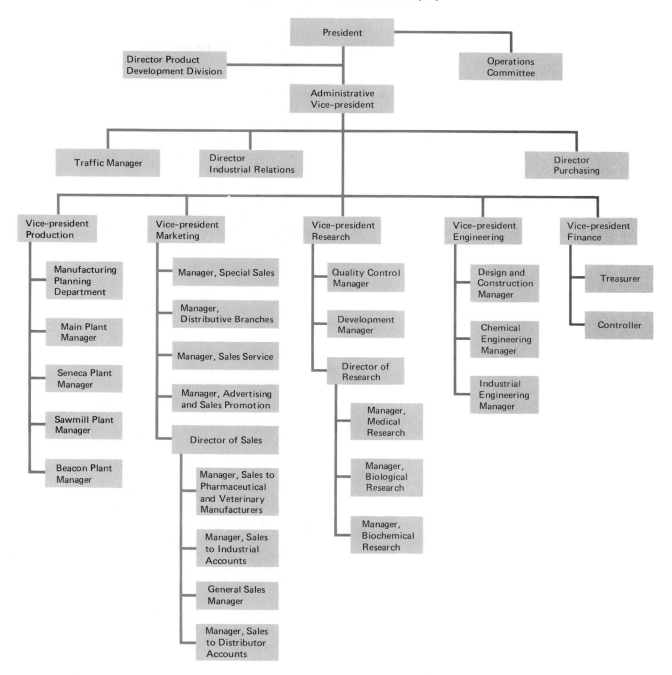

Marketing

The manager of special sales handles all sales to competing or complementary firms and to all other house accounts. The manager of distributive branches has charge of physical distribution of the products of the company through its four branch warehouses located at San Francisco, Chicago, St. Louis, and New York, and from the Baltimore plant. The manager of sales service handles complaints and adjustments and plans and supervises the handling of the paperwork order routine. All advertising and sales promotion work is directed by the manager of advertising and sales promotion.

The general sales manager directs the activities of the field sales force through twenty district sales managers, each of whom has under his supervision about ten sales representatives who call on wholesalers and pharmaceutical and veterinary manufacturers to make sales, on retailers to do missionary work, and on physicians and hospitals to do general promotional work. The manager of sales to pharmaceutical and veterinary manufacturers and the manager of sales to distributor accounts develop policies, prepare plans, and generally supervise contact with the groups of customers they serve, working through the general sales manager in so doing. Neither of them has any direct official authority over sales representatives. The manager of sales to industrial accounts directs a force of twenty-five sales representatives; they have no necessary contact with the district sales offices beyond occasionally calling on those offices for desk space and secretarial service.

Research

All medical, biological, and biochemical research either is done in the laboratories in Baltimore or is closely administered from there. The development section, which assists in the development and improvement of production processes and in the solution of production problems in the various plants, has representatives stationed in each of the several factories.

Also in the research division is the important quality control section, which is responsible for directing the establishment of quality standards and methods of testing. Purchased materials cannot be used in any plant until released by quality control; finished goods cannot be shipped until released by this section; and all wording on labels and advertising concerning quality must be approved.

Engineering

The engineering division is divided into three departments. The design and construction department has charge of planning, construction, and installation of new equipment and facilities, including buildings. The industrial engineering department devotes its efforts to setting standards through time and motion studies and statistical analysis. It also studies operating methods and develops and plans improvements in equipment. The chemical engineering department deals mainly with planning, development, and improvement of processes, including pilot plant operations on new products.

Records and Finance

The activities of the controller's division and the treasurer's division are centralized in Baltimore, where a fairly complete battery of IBM machines is maintained. Customer billing is done there, and branch plant and warehouse payrolls are handled there. These divisions perform the normal accounting, tax, and financial functions, but they do not take an active part in the interpretation of financial data in terms of management problems.

Traffic

The traffic department handles all traffic operating procedures, selection of carriers, tariff work, schedules, and requests for rate revisions. Branch plants and sales branches comply with traffic instructions issued at Baltimore.

Purchasing

The work of the purchasing division is somewhat more decentralized. The purchasing clerks in each plant are authorized to write purchase orders up to $500 for any one order. In all other cases they requisition the central purchasing division in Baltimore.

Industrial Relations

The industrial relations division develops and administers employee relations programs to maintain high quality personnel and desirable employee attitudes. These programs include personnel research, placement and education of employees, collective bargaining, wage and salary administration, employee services, security, health, and safety.

Special Arrangements for Products

The organization of The Hancock Company just described represents an expansion of the structure the company has had for many years. With the increase in dollar volume and number of products, however, a number of difficulties have arisen. To overcome these difficulties, a product development division has been set up. The history of this division illustrates the character of the internal strains facing the company.

Product Development

New products are typically discovered or at least developed in the research division. After a useful product has been found and the production processes have been worked out in the laboratory, it is then passed on to the engineering division for pilot-plant operation, planning of new equipment, and carrying through to the factory floor until the product is ready to be produced as a full-fledged member of the line.

Unfortunately, this arrangement for the technical aspects of new product work fails to solve all the problems connected with it. When a new article is ready for production and commercial use, it still has to be tested and released for distribution by the Food and Drug Administration and has to be worked into the sales line. If this work were left until the test-tube and pilot-plant stages were completed, the ultimate results from a profit standpoint might prove to be far from satisfactory. The commercial aspects of a new product need to be explored concurrently with its technical features. Stories are current in the industry of a firm that spent half a million dollars developing a new product only to find that its total possible sales were about $50,000 a year. The sales department was too heavily burdened with the day-to-day crises that attend the work of capturing and holding customers to do much with the task of exploring the market possibilities of a new product let alone that of appraising its probable effect on the cost and profit structure of the firm.

For many years top executives of The Hancock Company personally gave attention to this work, but as the company grew they had less and less time for it. After several makeshift arrangements, top management decided, five years ago, that a separate product development department was needed. Paul Stanton was appointed head of this new unit, and he set out to explore the areas within which his unit might operate to the profit of the company.

Stanton soon felt himself handicapped by what seemed to him a lack of product policy on the part of the company. For example, there seemed to be no clear-cut determination as to the extent to which the company should sell products, such as insecticides, that were somewhat outside the drug field. There also seemed to be some confusion whether the company should develop a line of products to be sold over the retail drug counter under the Hancock label.

During the next three years, Stanton attempted to build up the organization of the product development department and to expand its activities. (A statement of duties that Stanton prepared for inclusion in the company organization manual is given

Figure B Statement of Duties for Director of Product Development Department.

> **Director, Product Development Department**
>
> Reports to: the President.
> In carrying out his responsibilities he:
> 1. Correlates and directs all matters related to the establishment of new products by the company.
> 2. Surveys and analyzes the sales and market possibilities for present and new products in existing and new fields.
> 3. Determines sales potentials for products in development or suggested for development.
> 4. On the basis of market surveys and analyses, recommends development or production of new products.
> 5. Estimates actual sales of new products to guide the planning of necessary production and sales facilities.
> 6. Coordinates the company's efforts in developing new products, including the recommending of manufacturing capacity, sales programs, and distribution plans.
> 7. When necessary, carries out initial sales of new products prior to turning them over to the marketing division.
> 8. Studies and reports on the probable effects of the introduction of new products on the financial, cost, and profit structure of the company.

in figure B.) In the process of doing so he engendered antagonism among several of the operating divisions to such a point that neither he nor his assistants were able to obtain the cooperation that was so vitally necessary to the proper performance of the department's functions. For example, he urged that the product development department should employ a small force of specialty salespeople to conduct pilot marketing programs in the course of introducing new products to the market, and that most new products should not be turned over to the marketing division until the bugs had been worked out of the system of distributing them as well as producing them. This did not exactly endear his department to the members of the marketing division. Finally, Stanton made a connection elsewhere and left the company. His place was taken by John Boyle, a very able young man with excellent technical and business training, pleasing personality, and great vigor and drive, who previously had been an executive of a smaller company.

Marketing Research

About this same time, at the suggestion of the administrative vice-president, careful study was given to the establishment of a marketing research department. This step was finally decided upon when Boyle assumed direction of the product development department (now elevated in the organization hierarchy to the status of a "division") and the new department was made a part of the enlarged division. Since Boyle was not able immediately to dissipate the lack of sympathy between his division and the sales groups and since the tasks of sales analysis and making sales estimates still remained in the marketing division, the work of the marketing research department has been confined mainly to explorations of the market for new products and to economic studies for top management.

Product Managers

The large number of products made by the company and their diversified nature caused other complications. Each product, or at least each group of them, possessed problems of its own with respect to its improvement, the control of its quality, its production, and its marketing. For example, the problems involved in handling narcotics are especially unique in the rigid control required because of government regulations and the socially dangerous nature of the products themselves. Several years ago the management decided that these problems required special attention. A product manager was appointed to devote all her attention to the narcotics line. Later, other persons

Table D Product Development Division.

Product or Activity Group	Personnel	Salaries
General administration	1	$ 27,000
Miscellaneous products	1	18,000
Industrial products	1	15,000
Narcotics and vitamins	3	34,000
Veterinary products	1	16,000
Pharmaceutical products	2	31,000
Specialties	1	10,000
Antibiotics	2	26,000
Laboratory chemicals	1	15,000
Inorganic chemicals	1	15,000
Total	14	$207,000

were assigned to this type of work, each specializing in the problems of a separate group of products.

The responsibilities of a product manager are described in the organization manual of the company as follows:

Product managers are responsible for assisting general management and operating executives in improving the profit contribution of the products assigned to them. Acting in a staff capacity, they are responsible for continuous analysis, evaluation, and coordination of all company activities affecting these products, including sales, production, scientific, purchasing, engineering, financial, and related matters. Serving as a focal point in the company for information about their products, they make recommendations, after close collaboration with interested operating departments, on policies and programs designed to strengthen the departments' competitive position and increase their profits. They are responsible for assisting in the management of contracts affecting the products and for maintaining outside contacts and relationships as assigned.

The results are not always happy. The operating executives sometimes complain that the product managers get in their way. For example, a product manager often feels the need of visiting members of customer trades in order to get a more realistic idea of the market conditions for his or her products than can be obtained from a desk in Baltimore. This is resented by the marketing division executives who feel that relations with a customer are a delicate matter and should not be disturbed by other representatives of the company whose questions might raise embarrassing doubts in the minds of the customers visited.

Likewise the sales executives are sometimes embarrassed by the estimate of sales possibilities issued by product managers. In estimating the sales of a product, the latter usually deal in terms of sales potentials, the volume that Hancock would get if it got all the sales of the product. When the sales executives submit their estimates of what they actually expect to sell during a coming budgetary period, general management sometimes fails to distinguish between the differing bases upon which the estimates are made, to the chagrin of the marketing group.

Initially, the product managers were to focus on *existing* products, serving as staff directly to the operations committee, whereas the product development department was to concentrate on *new* products. However, the distinction between modification of existing products and new products was hard to draw in practice. Also, individuals who became familiar with a new product had a background that could be valuable in watching its market position, profits, changing costs, and other warnings of trouble ahead. For these reasons the product managers have been merged into the product development division. The personnel picture (excluding secretarial help) under the merged setup is shown in table D.

Typical of the problems that arise almost daily at the Hancock Company are the following:

Proposal A

At a recent meeting of the Pharmaceutical Manufacturers Association, Hancock's chief engineer picked up the information that Upjohn is about to patent a new process for the production of cortisone (used in the treatment of arthritis) that presumably will reduce the manufacturing costs to a tenth of present costs. Further, Upjohn is willing to license one or possibly two other manufacturers to use the new process. The license fee would be a flat sum to cover most of Upjohn's research cost on this project, plus a royalty on production of about 25 percent of the new manufacturing cost.

Hancock's process development section has also been seeking a way to reduce cortisone costs. The research person in charge of the project says they have several interesting possibilities, any one of which might "break" in a few months. Of course, the output of any new process would have to be subjected to clinical tests, pilot plant operation, and FDA approval.

Proposal B

An assistant to the manager of sales to pharmaceutical and veterinary manufacturers proposes that Hancock's product "L" be promoted to veterinary suppliers. "L" is a hormone product that under some circumstances aids human female fertility, and it has achieved a recognized position in the ethical drug field. Recently a veterinarian who works with fox farmers reported that "L" apparently had beneficial effects in breeding foxes. (Most foxes will breed only once in the spring of the year. If a female does not conceive, as often happens, she will have to be maintained for another year with no pups.)

The veterinary sales group in Hancock is always alert to possible animal use of drugs that have proven helpful to humans. The conversion of antibiotics to animal use, for example, has been a profitable development for Hancock. So, the manager of sales has forwarded the "L" proposal to the veterinary product manager in the product development division with a note: "This looks like a good prospect. Can manufacturing supply us with the large quantities needed for our market at reasonable prices?"

The veterinary product manager has, to date, made two telephone calls. The director of medical research said that the person who knew most about "L" was now deeply involved in "the new pill" project and should not be distracted because of the high priority potential of this project. The Sawmill plant manager, where "L" is now manufactured, said that any large increase in output would require new facilities; he further commented, "I'd prefer to keep veterinary production out of our plant. It upsets quality control. To get costs down you cut corners, and the employees are likely to carry this attitude over to other products."

This case was taken from William H. Newman and James P. Logan, *Strategy, Policy, and Central Management,* 7th ed. (Cincinnati, Ohio: South-Western Publishing Company, 1971), p. 452. The case was written primarily by Professor Ralph S. Alexander for The Executive Program in Business Administration, Graduate School of Business, Columbia University. Used with permission of South-Western Publishing Company and R. S. Alexander.

Glossary

This glossary contains important management terms and their definitions as used in this text. Since it is sometimes difficult to understand a term fully simply by reading its definition, page numbers after each definition indicate where a more complete discussion of the term can be found.

Accountability   The management philosophy that individuals are held liable or accountable for how well they use their authority and live up to their responsibility of performing predetermined activities (page 212)

Achievement motivation   Behavior that results from the need for achievement, the desire to do something better or more efficiently than it has ever been done before (page 348)

Activities   In the PERT network, activities are specified sets of behavior within a project (page 143)

Activity ratios   Ratios used during ratio analysis that indicate how well an organization is selling its products in relation to its available resources (page 440)

Adapting approach   An approach to planning that is based on the philosophy that effective planning concentrates on helping the organization to change or adapt to internal and/or external variables (page 90)

Affirmative action programs   In the area of equal employment opportunity, programs whose basic purpose is to eliminate barriers and increase opportunities for the purpose of increasing the utilization of underutilized and/or disadvantaged individuals (page 236)

Appropriate human resources   Those individuals within the organization who make a valuable contribution to management system goal attainment (page 229)

Assessment centers   Programs in which participants engage in and are evaluated on a number of individual and group exercises constructed to simulate important activities at the organizational levels to which these participants aspire (page 240)

Authority   The right to perform or command (page 205)

Behavioral approach to management   Managing approach that emphasizes increasing organizational success by focusing on human variables within the organization (page 35)

Behavior modification   A program that focuses on managing human activity by controlling the consequences of performing that activity (page 358)

Break-even analysis   A control tool based on the process of generating information that summarizes various levels of profit or loss associated with various levels of production (page 432)

Break-even point   That situation wherein the total revenue of an organization equals its total costs (page 433)

Budget   A control tool that outlines how funds in a given period will be spent as well as how they will be obtained (page 131, 442)

Bureaucracy   A management system with detailed procedures and rules, a clearly outlined organizational hierarchy, and mainly impersonal relationships between organization members (page 178)

Centralization   That situation in which a minimal number of job activities and a minimal amount of authority are delegated to subordinates (page 218)

Change agent   Anyone inside or outside the organization who tries to modify an existing organizational situation (page 262)

Changing   The second of Kurt Lewin's three related conditions or states that result in behavioral change; changing is the state in which individuals begin to experiment with performing new behaviors (page 278)

Changing an organization   The process of modifying an existing organization to increase organizational effectiveness (page 260)

Classical approach to management   Managing approach that emphasizes organizational efficiency to increase organizational success (page 29)

Classical organizing theory   The cumulative insights of early management writers on how organizational resources can best be used to enhance goal attainment (page 178)

Closed system   A system that is not influenced by and does not interact with its environment (page 39)

Combination approach   An approach to planning that emphasizes the advantages and deemphasizes the disadvantages of the high probability approach, the maximizing approach, and the adapting approach (page 91)

Command groups Formal groups that are outlined on the chain of command on an organization chart (page 374)

Commitment principle A management guideline that advises managers to commit funds for planning only if they can anticipate, in the foreseeable future, a return on planning expenses as a result of the long-range planning analysis (page 82)

Committee A task group that is charged with performing some type of specific activity (page 375)

Communication The process of sharing information with other individuals (page 242)

Communication effectiveness index Intended message reactions divided by the total number of transmitted messages (page 299)

Communication macrobarriers Those factors that hinder successful communication and that relate primarily to the communication environment and the larger world in which communication takes place (page 297)

Communication microbarriers Those factors that hinder successful communication and that relate primarily to such variables as the communication message, the source, and the destination (page 296)

Comparative management The study of the management process in different countries in order to examine the potential of management action under different environmental conditions (page 361)

Complete certainty condition The decision-making situation in which the decision maker knows exactly what the results of an implemented alternative will be (page 111)

Complete uncertainty condition The decision-making situation in which the decision maker has absolutely no idea what the results of an implemented alternative will be (page 112)

Computer An electronic tool capable of accepting data, interpreting data, performing ordered operations on data, and reporting on the outcome of these operations (page 466)

Conceptual skills The ability to see the organization as a whole (page 15)

Concurrent control Control that takes place as some unit of work is being performed (page 414)

Consensus Agreement on a decision by all individuals involved in making the decision (page 106)

Consideration behavior Leadership behavior that reflects friendship, mutual trust, respect, and warmth in the relationship between the leader and the followers (page 327)

Contingency approach to management Managing approach that emphasizes that what managers do in practice depends on a given set of circumstances—a situation (page 38)

Contingency theory of leadership A leadership concept that hypothesizes that in any given leadership situation, success is primarily determined by (1) the degree to which the task being performed by the followers is structured, (2) the degree of the position power possessed by the leader, and (3) the type of relationship that exists between leader and followers (page 333)

Control Making something happen the way it was planned to happen (page 405)

Control function Computer activities that dictate the order in which other computer functions are performed (page 470)

Controller A staff individual whose basic responsibility is assisting line managers with the controlling function by gathering appropriate information and generating necessary reports that reflect this information (page 415)

Controlling The process the manager goes through to control (page 405)

Control tool A specific procedure or technique that presents pertinent organizational information in such a way that a manager is aided in developing and implementing appropriate control strategy (page 431)

Coordination The orderly arrangement of group effort to provide unity of action in the pursuit of a common purpose (page 188)

Corrective action Managerial activity aimed at bringing organizational performance up to the level of performance standards (page 410)

Cost-benefit analysis The process of comparing the cost of some activity to the benefit or revenue that results from the activity in order to determine the total worth of the activity to the organization (page 417)

Critical path That sequence of events and activities within a Program Evaluation and Review Technique (PERT) network that requires the longest period of time to complete (page 143)

Current ratio A liquidity ratio that indicates the organization's ability to meet its financial obligations in the short run (page 439)

$$\text{Current Ratio} = \frac{\text{Current assets}}{\text{Current liabilities}}$$

Data Facts or statistics (page 461)

Debt ratio A leverage ratio that indicates the percentage of all organizational assets provided by organizational creditors (page 440)

$$\text{Debt Ratio} = \frac{\text{Total debts}}{\text{Total assets}}$$

Decentralization That situation in which a significant number of job activities and a maximum amount of authority are delegated to subordinates (page 218)

Decision A choice made between two or more available alternatives (page 101)

Decision-making process The steps a decision maker takes to make a decision (page 109)

Decision tree A graphic decision-making tool tyically used to evaluate decisions containing a series of steps (page 115)

Decoder/destination That person or people in the interpersonal communication situation with whom the source/encoder attempts to share information (page 295)

Delegation The process of assigning job activities and related authority to specific individuals within the organization (page 213)

Department A unique group of resources established by management to perform some organizational task (page 180)

Departmentalization The process of establishing departments within the management system (page 180)

Division of labor The assignment of various portions of a particular task among a number of organization members (page 185)

Downward organizational communication Communication that flows from any point on an organization chart downward to another point on the organization chart (page 305)

Equal Employment Opportunity Commission (EEOC) An agency established to enforce the laws that regulate recruiting and other managerial practices (page 236)

Esteem needs Maslow's fourth set of human needs; these needs include the human desire for self-respect and respect from others (page 347)

Expected value A measurement of the anticipated value of some event; determined by multiplying the income an event would produce by its probability of making that income (page 114)

External organizational diagnosis The process of examining all outside factors that relate to organizational effectiveness (page 264)

Extrinsic rewards Rewards that are extraneous to the task accomplished (page 345)

Events In the PERT network, events are the completions of major product tasks (page 143)

Feedback In the interpersonal communication situation, the decoder/destination's reaction to a message (page 299)

Feedback control Control that takes place after some unit of work has been performed (page 414)

Fixed assets turnover An activity ratio that indicates the appropriateness of the amount of funds invested in plant and equipment relative to the level of sales (page 440)

$$\text{Fixed Asset Turnover} = \frac{\text{Sales}}{\text{Fixed assets}}$$

Fixed costs Expenses incurred by an organization regardless of the number of products produced (page 432)

Fixed position layout A layout pattern that, because of the weight or bulk of the product being manufactured, has workers, tools, and materials rotating around a stationary product (page 133)

Flat organization chart An organization chart that is characterized by few levels and relatively large spans of management (page 192)

Flextime A program that allows workers to complete their jobs within a forty-hour workweek they schedule themselves (page 358)

Forecasting A planning tool used to predict future environmental happenings that will influence the operation of the organization (page 137)

Formal group A group that exists within an organization by virtue of management decree to perform tasks that enhance the attainment of organizational objectives (page 373)

Formal organizational communication Organizational communication that follows the lines of the organization chart (page 303)

Formal structure Relationships between organizational resources as outlined by management (page 180)

Friendship groups Informal groups that form in organizations because of the personal affiliation members have for one another (page 382)

Function A type of activity being performed (page 181)

Functional authority The right to give orders within a segment of the management system in which the right is normally nonexistent (page 211)

Functional similarity   A method for dividing job activities within the organization (page 202)

Functional skill   The ability to apply appropriately the concepts of planning, organizing, influencing, and controlling to the operation of a management system (page 523)

Future-oriented managers   Managers who attempt to create their own future, whenever possible, and adapt to this future, when necessary, through a continuous process of research about the future, long-range planning, and setting objectives (page 537)

Gangplank   A communication channel extending from one organizational division to another; this channel is not shown on the lines of communication outlined on an organization chart (page 192)

Gantt chart   A scheduling tool essentially comprised of a bar chart with time on the horizontal axis and the resource to be scheduled on the vertical axis (page 142)

General environment   The secondary organizational environment that contains such variables as social norms, economic conditions, and government regulations (page 266)

Geographic contiguity   The degree to which subordinates are physically separated (page 189)

Goal integration   Compatibility between individual and organizational objectives (page 56)

Graicunas's formula   A formula that makes the span of management point that as the number of a managers' subordinates increases arithmetically, the number of possible relationships between that manager and those subordinates increases geometrically (page 190)

Grapevine   A network for informal organizational communication (page 307)

Grid organization development (Grid OD)   A commonly used organization development technique based on a theoretical model called the managerial grid (page 275)

Group   Any number of people who (1) interact with one another, (2) are psychologically aware of one another, and (3) perceive themselves to be a group (page 373)

Group cohesiveness   The attraction group members feel for one another in terms of desires to remain a member of the group and resist leaving it (page 389)

Group norms   Appropriate or standard behavior that is required of informal group members (page 390)

Groupthink   The mode of thinking that people engage in when seeking agreement becomes so dominant in a group that it tends to override the realistic appraisal of alternative problem solutions (page 379)

Hierarchy of objectives   The entire set of overall and related subobjectives assigned to various segments of the organization (page 62)

High probability approach   An approach to planning that is based on the philosophy that there should be a high probability that the organization will be at least somewhat successful (page 89)

Human asset accounting   A control tool based on the process of establishing the dollar value of human resources within the organization (page 445)

Human resources inventory   An accumulation of information concerning the characteristics of organization members; this information focuses on the past performance of organization members as well as how they might be trained and best used in the future (page 233)

Human skills   The ability to build cooperation within people being led (page 15)

Hygiene (maintenance) factors   Items that influence the degree of job dissatisfaction (page 356)

Individual objectives   Personal goals that each organization member would like to reach as a result of his or her activity within the organization (page 58)

Influencing   The process of guiding the activities of organization members in appropriate directions (page 291)

Influencing subsystem   Subsystem of overall management system; input of this subsystem is comprised of a portion of the total resources of the overall management system, and output is appropriate organization member behavior; the process of the influencing subsystem involves the performance of four primary management activities: (1) leading, (2) motivating, (3) considering groups, and (4) communicating (page 291)

Informal groups   Groups that develop naturally in organizations as people interact (page 381)

Informal organizational communication   Organizational communication that does not follow the lines of the organization chart (page 307)

Informal structure   Patterns of relationships that develop because of the informal existence of organization members (page 180)

Information   Conclusions derived from data analysis (page 461)

Information appropriateness The degree to which information is relevant to the decision-making situation that faces the manager (page 461)

Information quality The degree to which information represents reality (page 462)

Information quantity The amount of decision-related information a manager possesses (page 463)

Information timeliness The extent to which the receipt of information allows decisions to be made and resulting action to be taken so that the organization can gain some benefit from possessing the information (page 463)

Input function Computer activities whereby the computer enters the data to be analyzed and the instructions to be followed to analyze that data appropriately (page 467)

Input planning Development of proposed action that will furnish sufficient and appropriate organizational resources for reaching established organizational objectives (page 131)

Interest groups Informal groups that gain and maintain membership primarily because of a special concern each member possesses about a specific issue (page 382)

Intermediate objectives Targets to be achieved within one to five years (page 60)

Internal organizational diagnosis The process of examining all factors within an organization that relate to the effectiveness of an organization (page 264)

International management Performing management activities across national borders (page 18)

Intrinsic rewards Rewards that come directly from performing a task (page 345)

Inventory turnover An activity ratio that indicates whether an organization is maintaining an appropriate level of inventory in relation to its sales volume (page 440)

$$\text{Inventory Turnover} = \frac{\text{Sales}}{\text{Inventory}}$$

Job analysis A technique commonly used to gain an understanding of what a task entails and the type of individual who should be hired to perform the task (page 230)

Job description Specific activities that must be performed to accomplish some task or job (page 201)

Job enlargement The process of adding to the number of operations an individual performs in a job (page 355)

Job enrichment The process of incorporating motivators into a job situation (page 356)

Job rotation The process of moving individuals from one job to another and not requiring individuals to perform only one job over the long run (page 355)

Job specifications Characteristics of the individual who should be hired to perform a specific task or job (page 230)

Jury of executive opinion method A method of predicting future sales levels primarily by asking appropriate managers to give their opinions on what will happen to sales in the future (page 138)

Lateral organizational communication Communication that flows from any point on an organization chart horizontally to another point on the organization chart (page 305)

Layout patterns The overall arrangement of machines, equipment, materials handling, aisles, service areas, storage areas, and work stations within a production facility (page 133)

Leader flexibility The ability of leaders to change their leadership styles (page 332)

Leadership The process of directing the behavior of others toward the accomplishment of objectives (page 319)

Leadership style A behavioral pattern a leader establishes while guiding organization members in appropriate directions (page 327)

Lecture A primarily one-way communication situation in which an instructor trains by orally presenting information to an individual or group (page 242)

Level dimension of plans The level of the organization at which the plan is aimed (page 126)

Leverage ratios Ratios used during ratio analysis that indicate the relationship between organizational funds supplied by the owners of an organization and organizational funds supplied by creditors (page 439)

Life cycle theory of leadership A leadership concept that hypothesizes that leadership styles should primarily reflect the maturity level of the followers (page 330)

Line authority The right to make decisions and to give orders concerning the production, sales, or finance-related behavior of subordinates (page 207)

Liquidity ratios Ratios used during ratio analysis that indicate an organization's ability to meet upcoming financial obligations (page 439)

Long-run objectives Targets to be achieved within five to seven years (page 60)

Loss   That amount of the total costs that exceeds total revenue (page 433)

Management   The process of reaching organizational goals by working with and through people and other organizational resources (page 9)

Management by exception   A control tool that allows only significant deviations between planned and actual performance to be brought to the manager's attention (page 431)

Management by objectives (MBO)   A management approach that uses organizational objectives as the primary means by which to manage organizations (page 66)

Management functions   Activities that make up the management process; major management functions are planning, organizing, influencing, and controlling (page 9)

Management information system (MIS)   A network established within an organization to provide managers with information that will assist them in decision making (page 472)

Management inventory card   A form used in compiling a human resources inventory; this form contains both an organizational history of an individual and an explanation of how the individual might be used in the future (page 233)

Management manpower replacement chart   A form used in compiling a human resources inventory; this form is people-oriented and presents a total composite view of those individuals that management considers significant to manpower planning (page 234)

Management responsibility guide   A tool that can be used to clarify the responsibilities of various managers within the organization (page 203)

Management science approach to management   Managing approach that emphasizes the use of the scientific method and quantitative techniques to increase organizational success (page 37)

Management system   An open system whose major parts are organizational input, organizational process, and organizational output (page 40)

Managerial effectiveness   The degree to which management attains organizational objectives (page 12)

Managerial efficiency   The degree to which organizational resources contribute to productivity (page 13)

Managerial grid   A theoretical model based on the premise that concern for people and concern for production are the two primary attitudes that influence management style (page 275)

Manpower planning   Input planning that involves obtaining the human resources necessary for the organization to achieve its objectives (page 136)

Materials requirements planning (MRP)   Creating schedules that identify the specific parts and materials required to produce an item; the exact quantities of each needed to enhance the organizational production process; and the dates when orders for these quantities should be released to suppliers and be received for best timing within the production cycle (page 470)

Matrix organization   A more traditional organizational structure that is modified primarily for the purpose of completing some type of special project (page 268)

Maturity   As used in the life cycle theory of leadership, an individual's ability to independently perform his or her job, to assume additional responsibility, and to desire success (page 330)

Maximizing approach   An approach to planning that is based on the philosophy that the organization should be as successful as possible (page 90)

Means-ends analysis   The process of outlining the means by which various objectives or "ends" within the organization can be achieved (page 65)

Message   Encoded information that the source-encoder intends to share with others (page 294)

Message interference   Stimuli that compete with the communication message for the attention of the destination (page 297)

Motion study   Finding the "one best way" to accomplish a task by analyzing the movements necessary to perform that task (page 31)

Motivating factors   Items that influence the degree of job satisfaction (page 356)

Motivation   An individual's inner state that causes him or her to behave in a way that ensures the accomplishment of some goal (page 343)

Motivation strength   An individual's degree of desire to perform a behavior (page 344)

Mulinational Corporation (MNC)   A company that has significant operations in more than one country (page 18)

Needs-goal model   A motivation model that hypothesizes that felt needs cause human behavior (page 343)

Negative norms   Informal group standards that limit organizational productivity (page 391)

Negative reinforcement   A reward that is the elimination of an undesirable consequence of behavior (page 358)

Nonprogrammed decisions Decisions that typically are "one-shot occurrences" and usually less structured (page 104)

Nonverbal communication The sharing of ideas without the use of words (page 302)

On-the-job training A training technique that blends job-related knowledge with experience in using that knowledge in the actual job circumstance (page 243)

Open system A system that is influenced by and is constantly interacting with its environment (page 39)

Operating environment A level of the environment that is of more immediate concern to managers and contains such factors as organization customers, suppliers, competitors, and investors (page 265)

Operational objectives Objectives that are stated in observable or measurable terms (page 64)

Operations management The process of managing production in organizations (page 12)

Organizational communication Interpersonal communication within organizations (page 303)

Organizational objectives Targets toward which the open management system is directed (page 53)

Organizational resources Assets available for activation during normal operations; main examples are human resources, monetary resources, raw materials resources, and capital resources (page 12)

Organization chart A graphic representation of organizational structure (page 179)

Organization development A process that emphasizes changing an organization by changing organization members and that bases these changes on an overview of structure, technology, and all other organizational ingredients (page 275)

Organizing The process of establishing orderly uses for all resources within the organization (page 175)

Output function Computer activities that take the results of input, storage, processing, and control functions and transmit them outside the computer (page 470)

Overlapping responsibility A situation in which more than one individual is responsible for the same activity (page 202)

People change A type of organizational change that emphasizes modifying the characteristic of human resources within the management system (page 274)

People factors Attitudes, leadership skills, communication skills, and all other characteristics of the human resources within the organization (page 263)

Perception An interpretation of a message as observed by an individual (page 298)

Performance appraisal The process of reviewing individuals' past productive activity to evaluate the contribution they have made towards attaining management system objectives (page 246)

Personal power Power derived from the human relationship that one has with another (page 419)

Physiological needs Maslow's first set of human needs; these needs relate to the normal functioning of the body and include desires for water, food, rest, sex, and air (page 346)

Plan Specific action proposed to help the organization achieve its objectives (page 125)

Planning The process of determining how the management system will achieve its objectives (page 77)

Planning tools Techniques managers can use to help develop plans (page 137)

Plant facilities planning Input planning that involves developing the type of work facility an organization will need to reach its objectives (page 131)

Policy A standing plan that furnishes broad guidelines for channeling management thinking in specified directions (page 127)

Porter-Lawler Model A motivation model that hypothesizes that felt needs cause human behavior, that motivation strength is determined primarily by the perceived value of the result of performing the behavior, and the perceived probability that the behavior performed will cause the result to materialize; three additional characteristics of this model are: (1) the total perceived value of a reward is determined by both intrinsic and extrinsic rewards received when behavior is performed, (2) effective task accomplishment is determined mainly by an individual's perception of what is required to perform the task and his or her ability to perform the task, and (3) the perceived fairness of rewards influences desire to perform behavior that results in those rewards (page 345)

Position power Power derived from the organizational position that one holds (page 419)

Position replacement form A form used in compiling a human resources inventory; this form summarizes information about organization members who could fill a position should it become open (page 234)

Positive norms Informal group standards that contribute to organizational productivity (page 391)

Positive reinforcement A reward that is a desirable consequence of behavior (page 358)

Power The extent to which an individual is able to influence others so that they respond to orders (page 419)

Precontrol Control that takes place before some unit of work is actually performed (page 414)

Premises Assumptions upon which alternative ways of accomplishing objectives are based (page 88)

Principle of supportive relationships A management guideline that indicates that all human interaction with an organization should build and maintain the sense of personal worth and the importance of those involved in the interaction (page 360)

Principle of the objective A management guideline that recommends that before managers initiate any action, organizational objectives should be clearly determined, understood, and stated (page 60)

Probability theory A decision-making tool used in risk situations—situations wherein the decision maker is not completely sure of the outcome of an implemented alternative (page 114)

Procedure A standing plan that outlines a series of related actions that must be taken to accomplish a particular task (page 128)

Processing function Computer activities involved with performing both logic and calculation steps necessary to analyze data appropriately (page 470)

Process layout A layout pattern based primarily on grouping together similar types of equipment (page 133)

Production The transformation of organizational resources into products (page 11)

Product layout A layout pattern based mostly on the progressive steps by which the product is made (page 133)

Product life cycle Five stages through which most new products and services will pass—introduction, growth, maturity, saturation, and decline and obsolescence (page 139)

Product-market mix objectives Objectives that outline which products and the relative number or mix of these products the organization will attempt to sell (page 61)

Product portfolio analysis The development of product-related strategy that is based primarily on market share of products and growth of the markets in which products are selling (page 85)

Profession A vocation the practice of which is based on an understanding of both a specific body of knowledge and the corresponding abilities necessary to apply this understanding to vital human problems (page 538)

Profit The amount of total revenue that exceeds the total cost (page 432)

Profitability ratios Ratios used during ratio analysis that indicate the ability of an organization to generate profits (page 441)

Profit to sales ratio A profitability ratio that indicates whether or not the organization is making an adequate net profit in relation to the total dollars coming into the organization (page 441)

$$\text{Profit to Sales Radio} = \frac{\text{Net profit}}{\text{Sales}}$$

Profit to total assets ratio A profitability ratio that indicates whether or not the organization is realizing enough net profit in relation to the total dollars invested in assets (pae 441)

$$\text{Profit to Total Assets Ratio} = \frac{\text{Net profit}}{\text{Total assets}}$$

Program A single-use plan designed to carry out a special project within an organization (page 128)

Program evaluation and review technique (PERT) A scheduling tool that is essentially a network of project activities showing estimates of time necessary to complete each activity and the sequential relationship between activities that must be followed to complete the project (page 143)

Programmed decisions Decisions that are routine and repetitive; the organization typically develops specific methods for handling programmed decisions (page 104)

Programmed learning A technique for instructing without the presence of a human instructor wherein small parts of information that necessitate related responses are presented to individual trainees (page 243)

Punishment The presentation of an undesirable behavioral consequence and/or the removal of a desirable behavioral consequence that decrease the likelihood of behavior continuing (page 359)

Quality circle Small groups of workers that meet regularly with management to discuss quality-related problems (page 382)

Quality of work life Opportunity of workers to make decisions that influence their work situation (page 530)

Quick ratio A liquidity ratio that indicates an organization's ability to meet its financial obligations with no reliance on inventory (page 439)

$$\text{Quick Ratio} = \frac{\text{Current assets} - \text{Inventory}}{\text{Current liabilities}}$$

Ratio analysis   A control tool based on the process of generating information that summarizes the financial position of an organization by calculating ratios based on various financial measures appearing on balance sheets and income statements (page 439)

Recruitment   The initial screening of the total supply of prospective human resources available to fill a position (page 230)

Refreezing   The third of Kurt Lewin's three related conditions or states that results in behavioral change; refreezing is the state in which individuals' experimentally performed behaviors actually become part of themselves (page 279)

Relevant alternatives   Alternatives that are considered feasible for implementation and also for solving an existing problem (page 108)

Repetitiveness dimension of plans   The extent to which plans are used again and again (page 125)

Responsibility   The obligation to perform assigned activity (page 201)

Responsibility gap   A situation in which certain organizational tasks are not included in the responsibility area of any individual organization member (page 202)

Risk condition   The decision-making situation in which the decision maker has only enough information to estimate how probable the outcome of implemented alternatives will be (page 112)

Rule   A standing plan that designates specific required action (page 128)

Sales force estimation method   A method of predicting future sales levels primarily by asking appropriate salespeople for their opinions of what will happen to sales in the future (page 139)

Scalar relationships   The chain of command positioning of individuals on an organization chart (page 192)

Scheduling   The process of formulating detailed listings of activities that must be accomplished to attain an objective (page 142)

Scientific management   Managing approach that emphasizes the "one best way" to perform a task (page 30)

Scientific method   A problem-solving method that entails the following sequential steps: (1) observing a system, (2) constructing a framework that is consistent with these observations and from which consequences of changing the system can be predicted, (3) predicting how various changes would influence the system, and (4) testing to see if these changes influence the system as intended (page 37)

Scope dimension of plans   The portion of the total management system at which the plan is aimed (page 126)

Scope of decisions   The proportion of the total management system that a particular decision will affect (page 105)

Security needs   Maslow's second set of human needs; these needs reflect the human desire to keep free from physical harm (page 347)

Selection   Choosing an individual to hire from all of those who have been recruited (page 238)

Self-actualization needs   Maslow's fifth set of human needs; these needs include the human desire to maximize potential (page 347)

Serial transmission   The passing of information from one individual through a series of individuals (page 305)

Short-run objectives   Targets to be achieved within one year or less (page 60)

Signal   A message that has been transmitted from one person to another (page 294)

Single-use plans   Plans that are used only once or several times because they focus on organizational situations that do not occur repeatedly (page 127)

Site selection   Determining where a plant facility should be located (page 132)

Situational analysis skill   The ability to apply both system theory and functional theory to the unique conditions of a particular organizational situation (page 525)

Situational approach to leadership   A relatively modern view of leadership that suggests that successful leadership requires a unique combination of leaders, followers, and leadership situations (page 321)

Social audit   The process of measuring the social responsibility activities of an organization (page 512)

Social needs   Maslow's third set of human needs; these needs include the human desire to belong, and the desire for friendship, companionship, and love (page 347)

Social obligation approach   An approach to meeting social obligations that reflects an attitude that considers business to have primarily economic purposes and confines social responsibility activity mainly to conformance to existing legislation (page 505)

Social responsibility   The managerial obligation to take action that protects and improves the welfare of society as a whole and also organizational interests (page 493)

Social responsibility approach An approach to meeting social obligations that is characterized by an attitude that considers business as having both societal and economic goals (page 505)

Social responsiveness The degree of effectiveness and efficiency an organization displays in pursuing its social responsibilities (page 501)

Social responsiveness approach An approach to meeting social obligations that reflects an attitude that considers business to have societal and economic goals as well as the obligation to anticipate upcoming social problems and to work actively toward preventing their appearance (page 505)

Sociogram A sociometric diagram that summarizes the personal feelings of organization members about with whom in the organization they would like to spend free time (page 383)

Sociometry An analytical tool that can be used to determine what informal groups exist in an organization and who constitute the membership of those groups (page 383)

Source/encoder That person in the interpersonal communication situation who originates and encodes information that he or she desires to share with others (page 294)

Span of management The number of individuals a manager supervises (page 189)

Staff authority The right to advise or assist those who possess line authority (page 208)

Standard The level of activity established to serve as a model for evaluating organizational performance (page 409)

Standing plans Plans that are used over and over because they focus on organizational situations that occur repeatedly (page 127)

Status The positioning of importance of a group member in relation to other group members (page 392)

Storage function Computer activities involved with retaining the material entered into the computer during the performance of the input function (page 467)

Strategic planning Long-range planning that focuses on the organization as a whole (page 82)

Strategy A broad and general plan developed to reach long-range organizational objectives (page 82)

Strategy management The process of ensuring that an organization possesses and benefits from the use of an appropriate organization strategy (page 82)

Structural change A type of organizational change that emphasizes modifying an existing organizational structure (page 267)

Structural factors Organizational controls, such as policies and procedures (page 263)

Structure Designated relationships among resources of the management system (page 179)

Structure behavior Leadership activity that (1) delineates the relationship between the leader and the leader's followers or (2) establishes well-defined procedures that the followers should adhere to in performing their jobs (page 326)

Suboptimization A condition wherein organizational subobjectives are conflicting or not directly aimed at accomplishing overall organizational objectives (page 62)

Subsystem A system created as part of the process of the overall mangement system (page 151)

Successful communication An interpersonal communication situation in which the information the source/encoder intends to share with the decoder/destination and the meaning the decoder/destination derives from the transmitted message are the same (page 295)

Symptom A sign that a problem exists (page 411)

System A number of interdependent parts functioning as a whole for some purpose (page 39)

Systems skill The ability to view and manage a business or some other concern as a number of components that work together and function as a whole to achieve some objective (page 523)

Tactical planning Short-range planning that emphasizes current operations of various parts of the organization (page 85)

Tall organization chart An organization chart that is characterized by many levels and relatively small spans of management (page 192)

Task groups Formal groups of organization members who interact with one another to accomplish mostly nonroutine organizational tasks; members of any one task group can and often do come from various levels and segments of an organization (page 375)

Technical skills The ability to apply specialized knowledge and expertise to work-related techniques and procedures (page 15)

Technological change A type of organizational change that emphasizes modifying the level of technology within the management system. (page 267)

Technological factors Any types of equipment or processes that assist organization members in the performance of their jobs (page 263)

Testing Examining human resources for qualities relevant to performing available jobs (page 238)

Theory X A set of essentially negative assumptions about the nature of people (page 350)

Theory Y A set of essentially positive assumptions about the nature of people (page 350)

Theory Z An effectiveness dimension that implies that managers who use either Theory X or Theory Y assumptions when dealing with people can be successful, depending on their situation (page 354)

Time dimension of plans The length of time period the plan covers (page 125)

Time series analysis method A method of predicting future sales levels by analyzing the historical relationship within an organization between sales and time (page 139)

Times interest earned ratio A leverage ratio that indicates the organization's ability to pay interest expenses directly from gross income (page 440)

$$\text{Times Interest Earned Ratio} = \frac{\text{Gross income}}{\text{Interest charge}}$$

Total assets turnover An activity ratio that indicates the appropriateness of the level of funds the organization has tied up in all assets relative to its rate of sales (page 440)

$$\text{Total Assets Turnover} = \frac{\text{Sales}}{\text{Total assets}}$$

Total costs The sum of fixed costs and variable costs associated with production (page 432)

Total power The entire amount of power an individual within an organization possesses; the total is mainly comprised of the amount of position power and the amount of personal power possessed by the individual (page 419)

Total revenue All sales dollars accumulated from selling goods or services that are produced (page 432)

Training The process of developing qualities in human resources that ultimately will enable them to be more productive and, thus, contribute more to organizational goal attainment (page 240)

Training need An information or skill area of an individual or group that requires further development to increase the organizational productivity of that individual or group (page 241)

Trait approach to leadership An outdated view of leadership that sees the personal characteristics of an individual as the main determinants of how successful the individual could be as a leader (page 319)

Triangular management Managing approach that emphasizes using information from the classical, behavioral, and management science schools of thought to manage the open management system (page 41)

Unfreezing The first of Kurt Lewin's three related conditions or states that result in behavioral change; unfreezing is a state in which individuals experience a need to learn new behaviors (page 278)

Unity of command A management principle that recommends that an individual have only one boss (page 192)

Universality of management The idea that the principles of management are universal or applicable to all types of organizations and organizational levels (page 19)

Unsuccessful communication An interpersonal communication situation in which the information the source/encoder intends to share with the decoder/destination and the meaning the decoder/destination derives from the transmitted message are different (page 295)

Upward organizational communication Communication that flows from any point on an organization chart upward to another point on the organization chart (page 305)

Variable costs Organizational expenses that fluctuate wtih the number of products produced (page 432)

Verbal communication The sharing of ideas through words (page 302)

Vroom expectancy model A motivation model that hypothesizes that felt needs cause human behavior and also that motivation strengths depends upon an individual's degree of desire to perform a behavior (page 344)

Work team A task group that recently has become more widely used in organizations to achieve greater organizational flexibility or to cope with rapid growth (page 380)

Name Index

Pabst Brewing Company, 147
Pacific Gas & Electric Company, 132, 134
Paluszek, V. L., 540
Pan American Airlines, 410, 412–13
Pancrazio, James J., 312
Pancrazio, Sally Bulkley, 312
Panko, Raymond R., 483
Parsons, Talcott, 196
Pathak, Dev S., 253
Patrone, F. L., 451
Patton, Arch, 253
Payne, B., 165
Peanuts, 176, 449
Perham, John, 253
Perrin, J. F. R., 166
Perrone, S. M., 118
Perrow, Charles, 196, 541
Peters, Thomas J., 336
Peterson, E., 195
Petitt, Gerald W., 338
Pfeiffer, Jane Cahill, 96
Pharmaceutical Manufacturers Association, 552
Phiffner, John M., 222
Phillips, B. J., 367
Phyrr, Peter A., 451
Pietri, Paul H., 313, 425
Pinsky, Sheldon, 253
Pioneer Press, 454
Pizza Theatre, Incorporated, 102–3
Plachy, Roger J., 336
Plowden, William, 315
Plowman, E. G., 195
Poelker, John S., 329
Poffenberger, William, 367
Pollock, Ted, 223
Pood, Elliott, 396
Pope, Carl, 503
Porter, Lyman W., 345, 366
Post, James E., 540
Postman, Leo, 311
Powell, Malcolm, 315
Preston, Lee E., 540
Preston, Paul, 313
Price Waterhouse & Company, 479
Prime Computer Corporation, 224
Proctor & Gamble, 167, 168
Pyle, William C., 452

Quaker Oats Company, 151
Quality Inns, 338–39
Quible, Dr. Zane K., 395
Quinn, James Brian, 166

Raia, A. P., 282
Raiborn, Mitchell H., 451
Raiffa, Howard, 118
Raine, P. S., 425
Rand Mines, Limited, 70
Rand, Patricia, 502

Ratcliffe, Thomas A., 166
Raun, Donald L., 451
RCA, 96–97
Ready, R. K., 22
Reagan, Ronald, 42, 135, 314
Reddin, W. J., 337, 354, 366
Reddin, William, 336
Redding, Charles W., 313
Redding, W. C., 311
Reha, Rose K., 541
Reiley, A. C., 34, 46
Reuter, Vincent G., 483
Reynolds, William H., 166
Rhenman, E., 222
Rhode, John Grant, 424
Rhodes, Susan K., 541
Rice, George H., Jr., 196
Richman, Eugene, 451
Rider, George A., 253
Ringbakk, Kjell A., 131, 146
Rizzo, John R., 69
Roach, John M., 196, 367
Robert Morris Associates, 441
Robinson, Richard D., 23
Rod's Food Products, 436
Roehl, William, 384
Roethlisberger, F. J., 22
Rogers, David, 45
Rohrer, John H., 396
Roney, C. W., 77, 95
Roos, Leslie L., Jr. 222
Rose, T. G., 424
Rosenzweig, James E., 23, 118, 125, 146
Rosholt, A. M., 70–71
Ross, Joel E., 165
Rouse, Mary Ruth, 17
Rowe, D. K., 451
Rubenstein, A. H., 195
Rutherford, Bill N., 248, 255

Sachtjen, Wiber M., 196
Said, Kamal E., 166
Salkin, G. R., 425
Sammons, Margaret, 311
Sample, Robert L., 540
Samsonite, 356
Sanborn, G. A., 311
Sanders, Donald H., 483
Sands, Ben F., Jr., 541
Sanford, Robert, 483
Sarnoff, Robert, 97
Sasser, W. Earl, Jr., 23
Saunders, W. B., 118
Sawyer, George C., 95, 165
Saxberg, Borge O., 483
Sayles, Leonard R., 22, 396
Scanlan, Burt K., 69, 196, 366
Schact, Henry B., 541
Schaffir, Walter B., 159, 166
Schein, Edgar H., 396
Schiavone Construction Company, 314

Schlaifer, Robert, 118
Schleh, Edward C., 69
Schlesinger, Leonard A., 283
Schlumberger Limited, 249
Schmidt, Leon, 425
Schmidt, Warren H., 321, 324, 326, 337
Schneider, Arnold E., 313
Schonberger, R. J., 146
Schramm, Wibur, 312
Schrank, Robert, 541
Schriesheim, Chester A., 395
Schweiker, Richard A., 518
Scientific Data Systems, 78, 80
Scott, Michael S., 483
Scott, William G., 196, 222, 395, 452
Scott Paper Company, 167–68, 358
Scurry, William C., Jr., 451
Sears, 119–20
Seashore, Stanley E., 396
Seashore, W. E., 395
Seawell, William T., 412
Securities and Exchange Commission, 441
Seiler, Robert E., 166
Selling Areas—Marketing, Incorporated, 454
Sessions, William, 503
Sethi, S. Prakash, 505, 517, 540
Shaklee Corporation, 399
Shanklin, William L., 424
Shapiro, Benson P., 223
Shapiro, Issac, 367
Shatshat, H. M., 311, 312
Shaw, Marvin E., 396
Sheane, Derek, 223
Shearson Hayden Stone Incorporated, 217
Shein, Edgar H., 283
Sheinberg, George C., 216
Sheldon, Oliver, 34, 46
Shell Oil Company, 85
Shelton, Oliver, 34
Sheppard, H., 366
Sherif, Muzafer, 396
Sherwin, Douglas S., 196
Sherwood, Frank P., 222
Shetty, Y. K., 183–84, 196, 517
Shin, Bong-Gon P., 311, 312
Shrode, William A., 222
Shull, F. A., Jr., 118
Shull, Fremont, 118
Shumacher, C. C., 46
Sibbins, Gerald J., 282
Sierra Club, 502, 503
Sikula, Andrew F., 253
Silvern Leonard, 253
Simmons, John K., 480, 484
Simon, Harold, 118
Simon, Herbert A., 69, 104, 118, 195, 541

Subject Index

Influencing Subsystem

Input

A portion of the organization's:
1. People
2. Money
3. Raw materials
4. Machines

**Process
(Influencing Process)**

Considering groups

Communicating

Leading

Motivating

Output

Appropriate organization member behavior